THE FOUR NATIONS

FRANK WELSH was born in Washington, County Durham, and educated at Gateshead and Blaydon Grammar Schools. He won a scholarship to Magdalene College, Cambridge, where he studied history. After a varied career in international business and banking, including service on the boards of nationalised industries and as a member of the Royal Commission on the National Health Service, he returned to historical studies. A Fellow of the Royal Historical Society, his books include *The Profit of the State*, *Uneasy City*, *Building the Trireme*, *A History of Hong Kong* and *A History of South Africa*. He lives in France and England.

D1343192

THE FOUR NATIONS

A History of
the United Kingdom

FRANK WELSH

HarperCollins*Publishers*

HarperCollins*Publishers*
77–85 Fulham Palace Road,
Hammersmith, London W6 8JB

The HarperCollins website address is
www.**fire**and**water**.co.uk

This paperback edition 2003
3 5 7 9 8 6 4 2

First published in Great Britain by
HarperCollins*Publishers* 2002

ISBN 0 00 653211 X

Set in PostScript Linotype Minion with Photina
and Bauer Bodoni display

Printed and bound in Great Britain by
Clays Ltd, St Ives plc

This book is for our European grandchildren,
Max, Anna, Ilya and Matilda,
in the hope that it will explain
something of their varied heritage

CONTENTS

CONTENTS

ILLUSTRATIONS

For three centuries Emperor Hadrian's wall marked the division between Latin Britannia and the Caledonian tribes. *(© Adrian Woolfitt/Corbis)*

Massive ruins of Roman Britannia impressed the invading Germanics, and served as a useful quarry; the stones of Virconium built the nearby Saxon church of Wroxeter. *(© British Tourist Authority)*

Pope Gregory's pun: 'Not Angles, but angels.' *(Author's collection)*

Pictish culture, exemplified on the Aberlemno stone, remains enigmatic. *(Historic Scotland)*

The early-fifth-century crosses of St Ninian's, Whithorn, mark the rapid decay of craftsmanship and the resilience of Christianity. *(Historic Scotland © Crown Copyright)*

Gosforth Cross, Cumbria. *(Dorothy Burrows)*

Ruthwell Cross, Dumfries. *(Historic Scotland © Crown Copyright)*

Irish crosses, impressively massive, contrast with the slender and sophisticated Anglian work. *(© Bord Fáilte Eireann – Irish Tourist Board)*

Such Celtic monasteries as Clonmacnoise were centres of learning, the arts, private devotion and communal worship; and tempting targets for Norse and Irish raiders. *(Imagefile, Dublin)*

Boyle Abbey, County Roscommon. *(© Bord Fáilte Eireann – Irish Tourist Board)*

The 'Declaration of Arbroath', an appeal to the Pope for support against England, was later appreciated as a nationalist manifesto. *(National Archives of Scotland – SP13/7)*

After the English defeat at Bannockburn, the national independence of Scotland was an established fact. *(Mary Evans Picture Library)*

Royal and Marcher castles such as Caerphilly stamped English authority on Wales in the thirteenth century, but did not quench Welsh ambitions for independence. *(© British Tourist Authority)*

Plas Mawr, Conwy. *(CADW: Welsh Historic Monuments Crown Copyright)*

Claypotts Castle, Angus. *(Historic Scotland © Crown Copyright)*

Hardwick Hall. *(© British Tourist Authority)*

Sir William Bruce's splendid work at Holyroodhouse marks the start of Scotland's golden age of Enlightenment – a full generation before the union with England. *(Historic Scotland © Crown Copyright)*

For over three hundred years the Stewart (Stuart) family ruled over Scotland, and, for most of the seventeenth century, over England as well. *(National Galleries of Scotland)*

Puritan leader Robert Rich, Earl of Warwick. *(Metropolitan Museum of Art, New York)*

Scottish hostility towards the English was matched by English derision of the Scots. A 1745 cartoon caricatures Scottish toilet training. *(© British Museum)*

Visceral English distrust of 'Popery' lead to the worst riots in modern history: Newgate prison stormed in 1780. *(Author's collection)*

Fifteen years after Newgate, Irish Catholics congratulate King George III following the annulment of the anti-Catholic Penal Laws. *(Author's collection)*

'Grattan's Parliament', in its magnificent chamber. *(Author's collection)*

Henry Joy McCracken. *(Ulster Museum)*

Michael Dwyer. *(National Gallery of Ireland)*

Theobald Wolfe Tone. *(Author's collection)*

Napper Tandy. *(Author's collection)*

The massacre of Protestants on Wexford Bridge. *(From* History of the Irish Rebellion in 1798, *by W.H. Maxwell, 1845)*

Daniel O'Connell, the 'Liberator'. *(Mary Evans Picture Library)*

'Miss Kennedy distributes clothing to the needy at Kilrush' (1849). *(Mary Evans Picture Library)*

'Varieties of Races in England and Wales' – a nineteenth-century ethnologist's view. *(Author's collection)*

Few of William Smith O'Brien's contemporaries could take his pretensions seriously. *(Author's collection)*

The American cartoonist Thomas Nast satirises Irish-American enthusiasm for giving cash, ostensibly for 'England's destruction'. *(Author's collection)*

'Waking the Home Rule Bill'. Gladstone, accompanied by his cabinet and the mournful Parnell. *(Author's collection)*

After Parnell's divorce, the Irish party disintegrated. *(Author's collection)*

Erskine Childers' yacht, with Mrs Childers and Mary Spring Rice as crew, bravely managed to bring 1500 obsolete rifles to arm Irish Nationalists.

The Protestant Ulster Volunteers chartered a steamer to import over twenty-four thousand modern rifles, with the encouragement of British Conservatives. *(The Illustrated London News Picture Library)*

Punch's cartoon of 12 April 1922. Four months later Michael Collins was killed by the IRA. *(Author's collection)*

Punch's view of Collins' death in August 1922. *(Author's collection)*

'Bloody Sunday', 30 January 1972, when British troops opened fire on a Londonderry civil rights demonstration, killing thirteen people. *(Belfast Telegraph)*

The new Scottish Parliament arises, much delayed and over budget. *(PA Photos)*

Although the Welsh Assembly made a workmanlike beginning, its future home is still the subject of acrimonious debate. The Assembly site, 2001. *(The Western Mail and South Wales Echo)*

MAPS

ACKNOWLEDGMENTS

This book is the result of countless journeys through the British Isles, and owes much to the helpful assistance of many people. The staff of Trinity College Dublin, the National Library of Ireland and the Public Records Office Northern Ireland (an admirable institution), the National Library of Wales in Aberystwyth (surely the most spectacular setting of any) and the Scottish Records Office were all assiduous. At the Royal Archives in Windsor Castle Sheila de Bellaigue, and her successor Pamela Clark, carefully produced some valuable items from the royal treasure; and the Cambridge University Library, which continues its generous policy of open stacks and lending, remains unequalled among university libraries.

Special thanks are due to Stephen Dawson, First Secretary of the Irish Embassy in London, and Dr Daniel Bradley of Trinity College Dublin, for a patient explanation of recent genetic research, which must lead to a demolition of hoary racial myths.

The staffs of the Scottish Parliament and Welsh Assembly were quite remarkably helpful, with Mrs Janice Pickwick of Cardiff being memorably energetic, and I am grateful to Rhodri Morgan for his eloquent advice. Scottish politicians, on the other hand, seemed a shy and retiring bunch, the Labour Party machine refusing all interviews, although the SNP were notably better, and Tam Dalyell, as always, clear and consistent in presenting the results of his long experience. Paul Bevan of the South-East Regional Authority provided much information on the work of his, and of the other, much-neglected bodies.

On the ground the various Tourist Offices performed admirably (it is surely an optimistic sign of the times that the British Tourist Centre in Lower Regent Street now also houses the Irish Tourist Board). As well as providing copious amounts of information and well-researched publications, Tourist Offices also provide that essential service, booking accommodation. Star among many of the bed-and-breakfast landladies encountered must be Lily Doyle of Skerries.

Individual thanks are due to Robert Maxtone Graham, Dick Brown, Chris Ennis, and Claire Gaskell, for her thoughtful gift of the Tom Merry cartoon. In particular I am, as often previously, grateful for the patient understanding of Richard Johnson and Robert Lacey of HarperCollins, and to Caroline Hotblack for her assiduity and skill in searching out illustrations. Valuable suggestions and emendations were made by Professor John Morrill and Gareth Jenkins, doctoral research student at UCL in Irish secretarian history. Without the encouragement and professionalism of Andrew Best, for many years a valued literary agent and for even longer a dear friend, no book of mine would ever have been published, and without Agnes' skill in deciphering my handwriting and industry in exploring museums, galleries and archives this particular volume would never have been written.

Finally I thank all those who have lent their personal support: Ken Borneo and Sheila and Clifton Ibbett and, last but not least, Monsieur Philippe Grollier, Mayor of Chatain, the Municipal Council and citizens of Chatain, who allow me to live and work in their tranquil commune.

FRANK WELSH
March 2002

INTRODUCTION

THIS BOOK does not set out to be a history of the British Isles in any comprehensive sense. That particular task, fascinating as it would be, has been prudently avoided by most historians: the most prominent recent effort, *The Isles* by Professor Norman Davies, only serves to illustrate the many pitfalls.[1] Apart from the complexity of the subject, involving as it must so many specialist (and often mutually contradictory) studies, there is its uncomfortable ambiguity. Inhabitants of other countries can define themselves as 'French', 'German' or even 'Italian' without great difficulty, but those of the British Isles may wish to be known as English, Scottish, Welsh, Irish or British, to say nothing of Jerseymen, Guernseymen or Manx. Sporting events illustrate both the distinctions and the confusions. The 'Six Nations' rugby union contest is between England, Scotland, Wales, Ireland, France and Italy. In it the Irish team is drawn from Northern Ireland and the Republic of Ireland, but in football (soccer) internationals each part of Ireland has its own team. Irish rugby players form a substantial minority of the British Lions team. English sportsmen are greeted with sustained (if exaggerated) ferocity in Scotland, resentful antipathy in Wales, but with polite warmth in Ireland (where the soccer hero of recent times was their English manager, Jack Charlton). The English cricket team comprises representatives of all four countries, and is presently captained by a player born in Madras, and it is a United Kingdom squad which takes part in the Olympic Games.

To the French 'English', '*Anglais*' and '*Britannique*' are practically synonymous; anything thought to be typically English, such as a sense of humour or Earl Grey tea, is likely to be described as '*très* British'. Such lack of discrimination will irritate, if not infuriate, any Scot or Welshman, who would never admit to being English; and quite rightly, for the three countries have very different histories and identities. 'British' on the other hand is vague, inchoate, almost a term of art, carrying with it echoes of a misty past. A British citizen's passport 'requests and requires' all others to assist the bearer in the name of 'Her Britannic Majesty'. A fine imperial flourish, that 'requires', but one that lacks resonance now that the British Empire has nervously retreated from its origins to become simply the 'Commonwealth of Nations'.

Yet the very vagueness of 'Britishness' is also its great merit. Without sacrificing their own national or regional identity any inhabitant of the UK can claim to be 'British', although such a claim is unlikely to be made with much enthusiasm outside Northern Ireland, where the majority still cling fiercely to their status as British – although most of their fellow Britons see Ulstermen as incontrovertibly Irish.

A semantic difficulty arises in referring to the British Isles, since 'British' in terms of citizenship does not include the Republic of Ireland (although that situation is hardly clear-cut, since Irish citizens have citizenship rights in Britain and vice versa), and some Irish people profess a strong dislike of all things British. Many historians have attempted to accommodate these sensibilities by terms such as 'these islands' or 'the Atlantic Archipelago'. In the interests of simplicity and acknowledging the much greater historical weight of Britain in terms of size, and of political and economic power, the well-understood term 'British Isles' is used here.

If 'British' is vague, the United Kingdom is at least a definable political entity, but one which carries little emotional charge. Men have not fought and died for the United Kingdom; when crowds at sporting events sing with passion 'Flower of Scotland', 'Land of my Fathers' or 'Land of Hope and Glory' they do not celebrate the United Kingdom. Whilst the Scottish saltire and the red dragon of Wales float unquestioned in their own countries, the Union flag is often seen more as an official badge, of doubtful vexillological authenticity, a fashion accessory or a mark of origin; the red cross of St George of England is relegated to church fêtes and football matches, often then as a demonstration of right-wing views with an undisguised racist edge.

Rather than attempting a comprehensive history, this book therefore focuses instead on the many attempts to construct an internal English empire, from King Aethelfrith of Northumbria to William Pitt, and on the resistance to such endeavours; more prosaically, on the develop-

THE BRITISH ISLES

ment of those communities which in 1801 became the United Kingdom of Great Britain and Ireland and how, very soon afterwards, they began to disintegrate. Inevitably therefore some aspects and periods are dealt with in much greater detail than others. The seventeenth century, which saw three successive Unions – of England and Scotland in 1603 and 1707, and that of all countries under Cromwell's Protectorate in the 1650s – is more closely examined; so too is the nineteenth-century impetus towards Irish Home Rule, and its subsequent messy compromises. The growth of a Scottish nation, and the dogged survival of a Welsh national consciousness, are treated at some length. Omitted, or only glanced at, are many constitutional developments peripheral to the main subject; there are few battles, other than those truly decisive, no analyses of social and economic trends except when these lead to some dramatic result – the Irish famine of the 1840s, a tragedy of fearful proportions and lasting effect, being the most significant. The most significant omission is probably any continuous treatment of specifically English history. Only when events in England interact critically with the other countries are they dealt with in any detail. Edward I's reign, for example, receives a good deal of attention as being a turning point in Scottish and Welsh affairs, together with the turbulent seventeenth century, but much else is unavoidably skimmed over.

History is very rarely as tidy as writers would have us believe it should be. Great social and economic movements may shape general trends, but can be abruptly diverted by inconvenient happenstance. Sheer force of circumstances – 'Events, dear boy, events,' as Prime Minister Harold Macmillan put it – can define one of several possible futures. To take two only: if Edward I's plan to unite England and Scotland through a diplomatic marriage in 1290 had not failed – and failed only through the unexpected death of his son's child-bride – the future relations of the two nations would certainly have been very different. So too may well have been the result of those long-drawn-out wars with France if England had not, at the same time, had to contend with Scottish hostility. Six centuries and more later, in the summer of 1914, Irish Home Rule was already law: had any of those events which led to the First World War not happened, or even been delayed, the new status would have been implemented, and all Ireland might still be part of the United Kingdom.

Navigating through the innumerable books and articles on aspects of British history brings its own peculiar difficulty in the sometimes startling prejudices of the writers. Traditionally these have been anglo-centric in the manner of Henry Thomas Buckle, whose *History of Civilisation in England* concerns itself at length with Scotland. More recently, especially among Irish writers, and even in some Welsh historians, these have been markedly anglophobic distortions. Some of the more egregious sillinesses are here exposed – the whole idea of eight hundred years of English oppression being one such simplistic fallacy underpinning them all.[2]

Nationalist sentiment also entails reluctance to acknowledge obvious facts. Scottish writers debate at length the merits and disadvantages of the Acts of Union of 1707, but neglect the enormous economic inequalities between the two nations. At that time the ratio of the two economies was forty to one, and Scottish GDP per capita was one-eighth that of England. Such an uneven balance made Scottish independence impossible and Union inevitable once England had decided to insist on it.

History can and should be read on the ground as well as in the study. The stones of the little Shropshire village of Wroxeter, for example, illustrate a thousand years of prosperity and decay, from Celtic village through legionary fortress to Romano-British town; its subsequent decline, the replacement of stone by timber structures; and its eventual desertion after the legions left, when the scattered stones were gathered to build the little Saxon church. On the other side of the country Dover Castle epitomises two millennia of English history, from the original Celtic hill-fort, through its occupation by the Roman Counts of the Saxon Shore, followed by eight hundred years as a bastion against the French, to its role as the furthest outpost of a beleaguered Britain in the Second World War. The Irish monasteries of Clonmacnoise and Boyle in the Shannon valley contrast the Celtic and Roman traditions of Christianity better than can any written descriptions. Those many grim castles, from Caerphilly to Beaumaris, demonstrate the determined effort King Edward deployed in order to quell Welsh resistance; and the bleak fortifications of Berwick how the Scots were able to limit English ambitions.[3]

The history of the 'furthest Britons', the description of one Roman poet, is that of a succession of immigrants, drifting westwards from mainland Europe, and more recently from more distant parts, to form a complex cultural nexus. The pattern in which immigrants distributed themselves has had lasting effects: political divisions still mark off the anglicised south and east of Wales from the Celtic north-west; the reluctance of Ireland to admit Jewish refugees has impoverished cultural life there.[4] Britain is only geographically insular: just as medieval Scotland began as a cultural province of England, its language, institutions and skills seeping in from the south, so England, for perhaps even longer, imported its culture from France (consider the number of Caxton's productions which were translations from the French).[5] It was only when the English resigned themselves to being able neither to subdue the Scots nor to control any part of France that British unity became possible.

The book is divided into twelve chapters, each covering, with some overlapping, a chronological period.

Chapters 1 to 4 are a much-reduced summary of the history of the constituent parts of the British Isles from the Roman occupation up to the Reformation. Going back two millennia is essential, since it was during the four centuries of Roman administration that the internal boundaries of the islands were defined. Give or take some parts of Northumberland, the borders of the Roman province of Britannia are those of England and Wales today; beyond Emperor Hadrian's great Wall the Caledonians were left to their own devices, and the smaller island of Hibernia remained untouched. Such an outcome was not inevitable. Northumbria between the Tees and Tweed might as well have become part of the Scottish as of the English realm; a more united Wales could have adopted, as did Scotland, the customs of the Anglo-French and either become absorbed into the English state or developed a degree of national independence; twelfth-century Ireland might have been subdued and integrated with the Angevin Empire. 1485, the traditional date with which modern English history is assumed to begin, does not serve badly as a marker for the other countries in the British Isles. By that time England and Scotland had both emerged as independent nation-states, among the first such in Europe, and with England clearly pre-eminent in the equation; Welsh independence was a lost, if not entirely a forgotten, cause; and Ireland was little more than a geographical entity, divided between a quasi-colonial region controlled by established Anglo-Irish magnates and with extensive regions still following traditional rulers and ancient customs.

Chapter 5 deals with the 'Tudor Revolution',[6] which drastically affected every kingdom, whilst that other great upheaval, the Reformation, took different forms in each country. On the eve of the first Union, achieved by James VI of Scotland succeeding to the English throne as James I in 1603, Scotland had become a radically Presbyterian country, while England had accepted a state Church which followed – with a fair amount of internal dissent – much of Catholic doctrine and practice. That same year brought the end of a brutal and protracted conquest of Ireland, which left English rule and Protestantism established, but with the majority of the population doggedly faithful to the Catholic Church.

Chapter 6 covers the period between the first and second Unions of England and Scotland, that of King James and the later attempt of the Cromwellian Commonwealth to unite all three countries in a British Republic. That first modern attempt at republican government was short-lived, and has been the subject of agitated propaganda. The facts of Henry Cromwell's liberal administration of Ireland, and of Lord Broghill's reform of Scottish justice, and of the New Model Army's proposals for a democratic and tolerant constitution, have been given a much-needed airing.

More a constitutional monarchy than a real republic, the Commonwealth brought the absolutist pretensions of British monarchs to a drastic finality. Chapter 7 deals with the evolution of the parliamentary system in the three kingdoms, and the events leading to the integration of England and Scotland in the third Union of 1707, itself the central fact in modern Scottish history. This section offers some new interpretations, inevitably controversial, since some Scottish historians are querulously resentful of English accounts of the event, whilst Irish history of the period is a metaphorical minefield. For two hundred years that island's history has been used – misused would be more accurate – as a political tool. Even today, when racism and nationalism are well understood as dangerous threats to civil society, Ireland is often indulgently regarded as a special case, where murder is accepted as a political statement. Serious historians in Ireland have disentangled fact from myth effectively, but their researches have not leached through into commonly accepted versions. This is especially true in the United States, where an effective Irish nationalist propaganda machine has manipulated public opinion for the past 150 years.[7]

Chapter 8 concentrates on the evolution of Irish claims to independence in the eighteenth century, culminating in the bloody rebellion of 1798 and the reluctant integration of Ireland into the United Kingdom by the 1800 Act of Union. The long-delayed removal of Catholic disabilities, which began in the 1760s, was not completed until 1829, with what was misleadingly called 'Catholic Emancipation'. An attempt is made to straighten out the long-successful political 'spin' put on that event.

Irish events also occupy much of Chapter 9, with the beginnings of the constitutional debates on Irish independence – 'Repeal' and 'Home Rule'. The British response to that overwhelming nineteenth-century tragedy, the Great Irish Famine, and its results in encouraging a resentful diaspora, lead into Chapter 10. William Gladstone is the central figure in this period, when the ultimate disintegration of the United Kingdom became inevitable, and the partition of Ireland was first discussed. Scottish and Welsh issues are also covered in this chapter, but Chapter 11 is devoted to the constitutional developments in Ireland, which resulted in the division of that island between a Southern republic and a North remaining insistently part of the United Kingdom.

Chapter 12 concludes the book with a review of national consciousness in Scotland and Wales and the efforts of British governments to limit their effects, culminating in the rush of legislation in 1998 which left Scotland and Wales with elected representative assemblies, London with a directly elected Mayor, Northern Ireland with a new constitution and England with very little indeed. The paradoxes and anomalies resulting from this brave, but essentially flawed, endeavour are exposed and some tentative conclusions reached.

The United Kingdom of Great Britain, Ireland, the Dominion of Wales and the Town of Berwick on Tweed (an official description of the mid-eighteenth century) has little of the permanent about it. Even after three centuries of Union Scotland remains a separate nation with its own institutions; Ireland as a whole made but a brief stay, between 1800 and 1922; and Berwick was quietly resumed into England in 1855. Underpinning these shifts, however, is a bedrock of stability. Political units may cohere or disintegrate, but, making due allowance for regional languages or culture, the striking fact is the persistence of a British (or archipelagic, to accommodate Irish sensibilities) identity. Similar values, methods of government, laws, games and a common literary tradition persist, and have had a long history.

As an example, take the library of Trinity College Dublin, through whose gates so many famous Irishmen – and women, since former President Mary Robinson is a graduate – have passed. Its greatest treasure is the magnificent Book of Kells, executed in Scotland at the end of the eighth century; many of the Book's artistic elements derive from the Lindisfarne Gospels, created a century earlier in Northumbria, in the reign of King Aldfrith, who studied in Ireland; the library's great collection was begun in 1602 by a gift of £1800 from the officers of Queen Elizabeth's army, well spent by one of Trinity's earliest scholars, James Ussher, whose family had been Irish since the days of Edward I; Ussher's own library, collected in conjunction with Thomas Bodley of Oxford, after an adventurous career which included being captured by Welsh robbers, was finally brought back to Trinity by funds raised for the purpose from the troopers of Cromwell's New Model Army. All of which indicates the complexity of the islands' history and the risk of hasty generalisations.[8]

Such an extended and involved unity survives political change. Symbols of monarchy were violently spurned by Irish republicans and equally violently flaunted by Irish Unionists; but Sinn Fein officials in Dublin still post their letters in pillarboxes bearing the royal initials, albeit painted green rather than red, and the Royal National Lifeboat Institution rescues sailors from the shore of Bantry Bay without an eyebrow being raised. Nor have we seen the last of border adjustments. Ireland will probably be united within a generation, not as the sectarian nationalist Gaelicised state dreamed of by Sinn Fein and de Valera, but as a prosperous little country with civil liberties guaranteed by a closer European Union.

Perhaps only the most optimistically deluded of Welsh nationalists can foresee a future Welsh state, but a core Welsh-speaking province of the four western counties might emerge. Drawing a bow even more wildly at a venture, it might be that if northern England's complaints are not adequately addressed its people will turn to Edinburgh rather than London, reinstating the ancient culture province of greater Northumbria; and indeed something of the sort can be seen emerging.

What is certain is that any moves towards increasing devolved authority, or to making devolution permanent, would involve consulting English voters. So far the English electorate has been generally sympathetic, but were Scotland, for example, to be perceived as receiving unfairly preferential treatment, such sympathy might evaporate. The current United Kingdom constitution is generally admitted to stand in need of radical reform, and the process, when attempted, is likely to be painful.

Finally, this book is inescapably anglocentric. England is so much the biggest of the Four Nations as to make this inevitable. Three out of four inhabitants of the British Isles are English; the English economy is the third largest in Europe; the intellectual powerhouse represented by the Universities of London, Oxford and Cambridge, and the financial expertise of London are unparalleled outside America. Any history that does not squarely acknowledge this fact within the context of the nations' history is certain to be partial.

CHAPTER 1

54 BC–AD 500

Fiercest and most distant of men

TAXES AND HOT BATHS, bishops and apricots, central heating and notebooks, tiles and coinage, surgery and rabbits, all came to Britain with the Romans. So too did the first administrative division of the two Atlantic islands, Britannia/Caledonia and Hibernia. It was a Roman general who decided that Caledonia, the northern part of his new province, was best left to its pugnacious inhabitants. The same officer, Gnaeus Julius Agricola, charged by Emperor Vespasian in AD 78 with suppressing any rebellious natives and implanting civilised Imperial rule, came to the sensible conclusion that the smaller island of Hibernia, dimly perceived across the Irish Sea, could safely be ignored. His policy was followed by successive rulers of Britannia for over a millennium. A generation or so later the Emperor Hadrian himself ordained the building of that great stone and earth fortification that slashed a near-hundred-mile divide between Roman order and Caledonian tribalism; and which, give or take Northumberland and a fraction of Cumberland, still marks the border between England and Scotland.

Geography was the weightiest factor in such decisions. A simple division between the two large islands was obvious (although the complexities that followed have still not resolved themselves), but where the northern boundaries of Britannia should be drawn has caused much subsequent argument and expense. That the line should be somewhere in the bleak fells lying between the wasp-waist of Caledonia, formed by the Firths of Clyde and Forth, and the inviting lowlands of the Tyne Valley was generally accepted, but its precise delineation took centuries.

The distinction between the desirable and accessible Lowlands, and the bleak and uninviting Highlands, has continued a strategic division.

One might choose to walk four hundred miles in very nearly a straight line from Cape Wrath to Stoke on Trent and only slip below five hundred feet on three occasions (two of these in fact where the Emperors Hadrian and Antoninus Pius chose to build their walls). Tracking this line to the east, the railway from Berwick on Tweed to London follows a plain broken by only a few hills around Durham: a Roman, or any succeeding army had therefore a quick route from north to south, but under the eyes of any dissidents in the Pennine hills that form the spine of England.

On the other side of the island the mountainous knob that occupies much of Wales, neatly isolated by the river valleys of Severn and Dee, together with the smaller peninsula over the Bristol Channel, formed by Dartmoor and Exmoor, were both brought within the Roman province. Well-engineered roads linked forts and towns, but the hill-people were left largely to their own devices. Distinctions between those parts of the island that were thoroughly Romanised, those left untouched, and those lurking warily on the borders, were to form the building blocks of subsequent political divisions.

First-century Lowlanders and Highlanders both, together with the Hibernians, shared a culture and a language (although with very considerable regional variations) with the inhabitants of Gaul, the great Continental province conquered by Julius Caesar more than a century before Agricola's arrival. All had, over several hundred years, developed as part of an extensive culture, that of the Celtic-speaking peoples.

They originated, considered Herodotus, from lands near the source of the river Istros – the Danube. Warlike and too much given to drink, reported Plato, traits to be expected of run-of-the-mill barbarians; useful mercenaries, however, according to Xenophon. Greek city-states had already found that the newcomers were capable of adapting to civilised practices, since as early as the fifth century BC they had settled in the Greek colony of Massilia (Marseille).[1]

They were the people variously referred to as Keltoi, Galli and Galati – the Celts, the first inhabitants of the British Isles whose history is anything but conjectural, but not by any means the first arrivals. Since the melting of the ice caps brought people to the previously uninhabitable parts of northern Europe successive waves of immigrants had brought with them new technologies of farming, pottery, stone- and metal-working, without ever completely displacing the original inhabitants. Extensive remains evidence the varied technical skills possessed by the Celts' precursors, including such magnificent works as the ritual complexes of Stonehenge and Avebury, but they left few other records. Some of their culture and even their language were passed on to the newcomers, explaining certain differences between the insular and Continental Celts; some of their centres, such as the hill of Tara in Ireland, continued in use into historic times; but the earliest recorded British history is that of the Celts.

By the time Plato wrote, in the early fourth century BC, Celtic communities could be found anywhere between present-day Turkey and County Cork, and the Celts were forcefully bringing themselves to the notice of the emergent Roman Republic. In 390 BC, led by one Brennus, a Celtic raid smashed through the Roman defences to sack Rome itself, forcing the Senate (warned by the Roman geese) to take refuge in the Capitol. Following this victory the Celtic tribes settled in northern Italy, in what became known as Cisalpine Gaul.

Over on the other side of the Mediterranean, Galatia, which covered an extensive part of Asia Minor, was the result of a successful Celtic invasion in the third century BC, which left a Celtic aristocracy, one of exceptional ferocity, ruling over the original Phrygian inhabitants. Gradually assimilating Asian Greek culture, the inhabitants, by the time the Apostle Paul wrote his chiding letter to the 'foolish Galatians', were hardly to be distinguished from any other Greek provincials of the Roman Empire.

Galati or Galli, the Celts were formidable. 'What shall we call a man who is excessively fearless,' Aristotle wondered, 'who fears nothing, neither earthquakes or wars, as they say of the Celts?'[2] 'Fiercest and most distant of men', as Catullus described the Britons newly encountered by his contemporary, Julius Caesar. To the Mediterranean world Celts were also frighteningly different. Long hair, often dyed, spiked with grease, moustaches and trousers, all most un-Roman, together with a swagger that remained unsubdued even in captivity, the disciplined resources of the Roman legions were needed to subdue them.[3] To the only conventionally pious Romans of the Empire, the Celtic religions were disturbingly inhumane. Nothing in classical, or even medieval, art can be compared in sheer horrific power with the Monster of Noves, squat, scaly, powerful, an arm protruding from its grim jaws, a human head grasped in each massive paw. The Celts' delight in headhunting and human sacrifices characterised the Druidic temples, with pillars ornamented by severed heads, surmounted by a monstrous stone bird.

It is likely that by about 600 BC a Celtic-speaking warrior elite had established itself in the British Isles, and that its culture and language had been adopted by the previous population. Two millennia of inter-breeding have ensured that few inhabitants of the islands (recent immi-grants excepted) do not have genes from all the races, but local differences persist. Recent research has confirmed the existence of what might be called a genetic gradient from east to west, with later strains more prominent in the east. The Picts, who populated most of Scot-land, may well have been descendants of the previous influx, and the people of the extreme west of Ireland still indicate pre-Celtic origins, but Celtic genes persist in all parts of the islands. (The idea of Celts, contrasted with Anglo-Saxons, each with vices and virtues depending on one's prejudices, a hobby-horse much ridden by nineteenth-century writers, although still prevalent is nothing more than a racist myth.)

At the time Rome first showed an interest, the British Isles possessed a more homogeneous culture (hardly a homogeneous *society*, since acrimonious disputes and open war were common) than it has at any subsequent time, and a culture that was shared, together with a similar language, with the societies across the English Channel. Roman writers described Celts as a collection of aristocratic societies, with knights (*'equites'*) often having numerous supporters, and labourers (*'plebs'*). All Gauls were much given to religion, represented by the third class, the druids, who studied for twenty years and 'have much knowledge of the stars and their motion, of the size of the world, of natural philosophy, and of the powers and spheres of action of immortal gods'. Druids had many methods of divination, one of which fascinated Roman observers. A suitable victim was stabbed 'in the region above the diaphragm, and when he has fallen they foretell the future from his fall, and from the convulsions of his limbs and moreover, from the spurting of his blood'.[4]

Thirty-three Celtic tribes were reported in Britannia, often having as their 'capital' a great earthworks such as that of Maiden Castle in

Dorset, or Uphall Camp in Essex, which would house a considerable population. Stanwick in Yorkshire, the tribal centre of the Brigantes, whose territory stretched right across northern Britannia, covered some 850 acres, enclosed by an earth rampart. The Brigantes' neighbours, the Parisi, the East Anglian Iceni and the Belgae, centred in Kent, were late arrivals, coming from Gaul not long before Caesar's first expedition of 55 BC.

Like so many subsequent migrations to the British Isles, that of the Gaulish Celts had its origin in Europe. When the migration of the Indo-European peoples began, those displaced by war or by natural expansion found their movement eastward eventually checked by the deserts of Central Asia, behind which lay the great Chinese Empire, or, at a later date, by the Mesopotamian kingdoms. Emigrations going west were eventually brought up by the Atlantic Ocean, by which time they had lost much of their original momentum. Neither the Romans nor the Anglo-Saxons ever got as far as Ireland, and the east and south coasts of England were always the most susceptible to Continental influence.

Another Indo-European stream both paralleled and succeeded that of the Celts. The Teutonic, or Germanic tribes made their way further to the north, and rather later, than the Celts. It was about 100 BC that the German invaders made their first impact on the Roman Republic. Two tribes, the Cimbri and the Teutones, poured through Gaul in 109 BC to threaten Italy, and were only halted after years of pillage and struggle. Many Gauls must then have considered Britain a safe refuge, and crossed the narrow seas in considerable numbers.

One of the groups leaving Gaul for Britain, the Bellovaci, were political refugees who had led a resistance to Rome in 57 BC, when the Republic was in a state of some turmoil. The Germanic invasions had been succeeded by civil wars, out of which one politician and warrior of genius had emerged. Julius Caesar's swift campaigns after 58 BC had swept through Gaul and brought that country up to the Channel coast under Roman control. Why he then decided to risk an expedition to Britain is not very clear: there may well have been good reasons for keeping safely away from the violent politics of Italy, and yet another Triumph celebrated in Rome would be convenient; young Napoleone Buonaparte tried a similar trick in Egypt two millennia

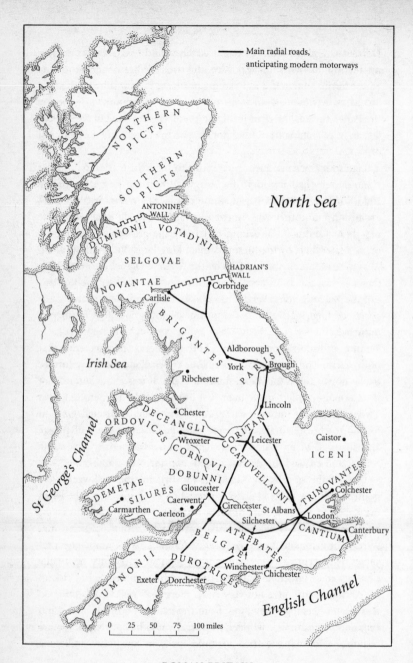

Main radial roads,
anticipating modern motorways

North Sea

NORTHERN
PICTS

SOUTHERN
PICTS

ANTONINE
WALL

DUMNONII   VOTADINI

SELGOVAE

HADRIAN'S
WALL

NOVANTAE   Corbridge
        Carlisle

B R I G A N T E S

Irish Sea

                        Aldborough
                        York   Brough
        Ribchester   P A R I S I I

        Chester
            DECEANGLI   Lincoln
ORDOVICES   C O R I T A N I
        Wroxeter
            CORNOVII   Leicester   Caistor

                CATUVELLAUNI   I C E N I
        DOBUNNI

DEMETAE   SILURES   Gloucester   TRINOVANTES
Carmarthen   Caerwent   Colchester
        Caerleon   Cirencester St Albans
                              Silchester   London
                    B E L G A E   Canterbury
                        ATREBATES   CANTIUM

St George's Channel

DUMNONII   DUROTRIGES   Winchester
                        Chichester
        Exeter   Dorchester

English Channel

0   25   50   75   100 miles

ROMAN BRITAIN

later. It was also possible that the Britons might rally to the support of their Gaulish cousins, rekindling the rebellion there. Sheer ignorance of the Straits of Dover and what might be expected on the other shore may have encouraged Caesar, and his first expedition in 55 BC was really little more than a reconnaissance in force. Landing on the shingle beach at Walmer, the Roman expedition was hard put to resist the British attacks and was obliged to retreat to Gaul in the face of typical Channel weather.

A much larger army and a much better-informed commander sailed the following year. The short campaign of 54 BC established that, given the relative ease with which some British chiefs could be persuaded to ally themselves with the invader, and the seeming impossibility of their ever forming a permanent combination among themselves, the subjection of the island would not be too difficult. But a crisis was brewing in Gaul, and Caesar once more disembarked his army without any permanent achievement, other than a few British captives and some splendid loot to adorn a Triumph. Besides, as one of his officers remarked, the weather was beastly and there was nothing of value to be had.

In the following century, before the next Roman effort, Caesar had replaced the Republic with an Empire, that was to continue in one form or another for 1500 years. Transalpine Gaul had become, with the establishment of the Empire in 27 BC, the Imperial Province of Gallia, and the British grown more familiar with Gallo-Roman habits; tribal rulers had their own coinage minted, some of which was widely circulated, and adopted Latinised names. They had not however been convinced of the necessity to unite their forces in a resistance to any invasion. Relations between the tribes has been well described as a 'kind of chronic riot',[5] as leaders found little difficulty in gaining support among their followers, always ready for at least the first fight, although thereafter pugnacity tended to wane. In spite of common language and customs, any sense of what might be described as 'nationality' took over a millennium to appear

With the next invasion in AD 43, organised by the prudent and intelligent Emperor Claudius, the recorded history of Britain really begins. Claudius, as a newly elected Emperor, badly needed a quick Triumph to establish his position, and a large extension of the Empire would very conveniently achieve that desirable end. The legions were not enthusiastic at being required to cross 'beyond the Ocean' – the boundaries of their known world. The expedition had to be carefully planned, with two separate landings at Richborough, a much better-protected haven than the open beach at Walmer, and the other on the south coast, near Chichester. Such a move, involving sea crossings of different lengths, needed excellent co-ordination and command, provided by two of Rome's most successful soldiers, Aulus Plautius and the future Emperor, Vespasian. The actual battles, although fiercely fought, proved the ineffectiveness of Celtic methods. Their handsome long swords and magnificent shields were of no avail against the tight Roman ranks, and the Britons were soon defeated. Most of the fighting was confined to Kent and Essex, and Claudius was able to make a glorious entrance into his chief opponent, Caractacus' capital, Camulodunum – Colchester – an immense enclosure which the Emperor made the site of his new province's first capital. A Triumph was duly proclaimed in Rome, two triumphal arches erected, and the Emperor's son, the ill-fated Britannicus, named after this latest addition to the Empire, the province of Britannia.

Smaller tribes who had been battered into submission by such expansionists as Caractacus welcomed the stability offered by Roman rule. Those first-century Britons, on the other hand, who had been successfully attacking the smaller tribes, were less pleased and looked for an opportunity to restore the satisfactory old free-for-all. Within twenty years of the Claudian invasion the Iceni of East Anglia revolted, led by their queen, Boudicca, for long better known as Boadicea. The historian Dio Cassius, writing more than a century after the event, imagined her as 'huge of frame, terrifying of aspect, and with a harsh voice. A great mass of red hair hung to her knees'[6] – a description which, however fanciful, has served as a model for subsequent genera-tions. It must have been a particularly foolish Roman official who chose to arrest and flog Boudicca, and to have her two daughters raped. His action caused an immediate revolt, in which the Iceni were joined by the neighbouring Trinovantes, and a general rebellion erupted. Two newly-built capitals, Camulodunum and Verulamium (St Albans), were destroyed, and Londinium, already an important centre of trade, was abandoned. Tacitus, a near-contemporary, wrote:

> The Britons took no prisoners, sold no captives as slaves and
> went in for none of the usual trading of war. They wasted no
> time in getting down to the bloody business of hanging, burn-
> ing and crucifying. It was as if they feared that retribution
> might catch up with them while their vengeance was only
> half-complete.[7]

It is an axiom of any Imperial policy that an example must be made
of rebellious subject-people. One Roman army was scattered before
Boudicca's rebellion was bloodily suppressed. Suetonius Paulinus
slaughtered the Britons, and not only those who had rebelled, but
many who had merely stayed neutral. This was effective, for Boudicca's
rebellion, only eighteen years after the occupation, was the last serious
revolt against Roman rule in southern Britannia for three centuries.
The numbers involved on both sides were enormous, very much greater
than those of any later clash between Celtic populations and invaders;
certainly the Roman army was twelve thousand strong, while estimates
of Boudicca's forces exceed a hundred thousand.

Another protracted campaign in AD 71–72 was needed before the
Brigantes were brought to heel, and the Roman occupation was
extended to the Tees. In the west the Silures of south-east Wales were
called to order less violently, transformed from a tribe to the 'Republic
Civitatis Silurum', and surrounded by new Roman posts, centred on
the huge legionary base Castra Legionis, Caerleon.

Where Rome fixed her borders depended upon competing demands
for resources. The Empire's frontiers stretched from the Persian Gulf,
the Red Sea, the Caspian and Black Seas to the mouth of the Rhine. For
much of their length boundaries were defined naturally by mountains,
deserts or rivers. It would have been in accordance with this practice
to extend Roman rule over the whole island of Britain, and in the first
century AD succeeding governors were not kept short of troops or of
the authority needed to achieve such an aim.

Much also depended upon the character of the men appointed.
Some, such as Frontinus, a very distinguished civilian (AD 73–78),
concerned themselves primarily with conciliation and development,
settling the Silures into the new town of Caerwent. Others, more
expansion-minded, threw themselves into pushing the boundaries
further out. Of these the most famous was Gnaeus Julius Agricola,

governor between AD 78 and 84. A 'thruster' who had previously served in Britain, Agricola's reputation was preserved for posterity by his son-in-law, Tacitus, whose panegyric biography is nevertheless also accurate reporting. In his first year Agricola, having 'nearly annihilated' the Ordovices in northern Wales, swept over to Anglesey to destroy the centre of the Druid cult, perceived as a hotbed of potential insurrection. With the Severn valley and the Dee estuary controlled, all Wales became formally part of the province, surrounded by Roman towns and fortresses, and linked by a system of roads. Legionary forts formed a chain from Caerleon north, through Glevum (Gloucester), Virconium (Wroxeter) and Deva (Chester). In the following year, with perhaps thirty thousand troops in two columns, Agricola moved north, building forts and leaving garrisons as he went, as far as the Firth of Clyde, which was eventually to mark the furthest limits of the province of Britannia.

Agricola was faced with the same problem that has confronted subsequent governments in the Atlantic islands, that of defining the units of administration and prescribing their borders. The most obvious solution was to bring all the island of Britannia under Roman rule, forcibly if necessary, and to allow the survivors to benefit from Roman civilisation; the same answer was eventually adopted by rulers of the newly united states of America when faced with not dissimilar difficulties.

The forty years that had elapsed since Claudius' invasion had produced only a limited knowledge of the northern part of the island, Caledonia. Even today little is known with any degree of certainty about the Picts, 'the painted people', as the Caledonians were nicknamed by the Roman soldiery, and their very brief records were absorbed into the later kingdom of Alba before any reliable chronicler described their habits. Like the other Celtic societies, theirs was an aristocratic culture, resting on a population probably composed largely of descendants of the previous inhabitants. Their highly individual stone carvings – the best collection is in the museum at Meigle, north of Dundee – the hundreds of stone 'brochs' and the well-preserved houses of Skara Brae and the cairn of Maes Howe on Orkney all suggest continuity with a pre-Celtic culture.[8]

Serious resistance to Agricola's advance was only encountered in

AD 83, and in AD 84 the main Caledonian army appeared under a chief named Calgacus – 'the Swordsman'. The result was the complete defeat of the Caledonians at the battle of Mons Graupius – probably Benna-chie, in Aberdeenshire – but not their obliteration. Most of the defeated combatants were able to escape; the Roman aggression was a minor incident in the long Pictish history, and the battle marked the furthest limits of Roman penetration. Roman commanders were constantly made aware that their forces were expensive, and the cost–benefit analysis indicated that nothing could be offered by the Caledonians to justify the expense of subduing them. Unless some easily defensible frontier could be found, the northerners would remain outside the Imperial frontiers.

As well as being pacified, Britannia had to be civilised. Just as nineteenth-century British officials saw to it that young Indians were properly instructed in cricket and the classics, Agricola saw it as his duty to educate the natives. Tacitus recorded, after the governor's first year of office:

> The following winter [AD 79] was spent in useful statecraft. To make a people which was scattered and barbarous, and therefore prone to warfare, grow accustomed to peace and quietness by way of their pleasures, Agricola used to persuade them by private exhortations and public assistance to build temples, forums, and houses, with praise for the eager and admonitions for the laggard.[9]

Ironically, and anticipating a strong current of twentieth-century thought, the historian continued, 'The next step was towards the attractions of our vices, lounging in the colonnades, baths and refined dinner-parties. They were too ignorant to see that what they call civilisation was really a form of slavery.'

Much was gained. Literacy in Latin introduced the British to classical culture and, later, to Christian teaching. Britons became members of an Empire in which all citizens had established rights, and the protection of an elaborate, written code of laws. Inter-tribal warfare was replaced by voluntary service with the Roman army, with twenty years in the legions bringing the rewards of citizenship and the grant of a parcel of land. There was no general disruption of existing ownership and the improvements in agriculture begun before the occupation continued. New crops, cherries, walnuts, carrots, turnips and leeks, made diet more varied: and, most importantly, the vine was grown. The new Roman towns, with their expanding populations, encouraged artisans and traders, and municipal institutions on the Roman model prompted self-government and respect for law.

The Romanised Britons did not, however, become first-class Romans; from being interesting barbarians they graduated to the status only of boring provincials, condescended to even by their fellow Celts in Gaul. Ausonius, poet, scholar and landowner, whose name is commemorated in a distinguished St Emilion vineyard, writing at a time when Britannia had undergone three centuries of Romanisation, sneered at the only recorded British poet of the time, one Sylvius Bonus:

> What Sylvius? Good?
> No Briton could
> Be – better he had
> Been Sylvius Bad![10]

At least the Gauls spoke Latin, or a corrupt form of it, as their common speech, whilst the Britons stuck to their old language. For them Latin remained the mark of an elite, desirable for polite conversation, and essential for advancement; there are parallels with the use of English in India, or French in Imperial Russia. Latin was the only written language, and was certainly commonly spoken in towns, as many graffiti attest, such as the aggrieved comment of a tilemaker, now in the London Museum: '*Austalis dibus xiii vagatur sib cotidim*' (Austalis has been wandering off on his own these last thirteen days).

To some extent this odd state of affairs – that by the end of the first century AD, Belgae living a few miles apart across the Straits of Dover were speaking two different languages, yet both writing in Latin – is explained by two factors. Nearly a century separated the conquest of Gaul from that of Britain. A hundred years of assimilation and centralisation had brought Gaul tightly under Imperial control before the Emperor Claudius began the subjugation of Britannia. Secondly, Gaul was both more accessible and a good deal richer and more attractive than Britannia. Imperial administration, and later the

Church, offered many career opportunities nearer the centre of power than were ever available in Britannia. Not only trade, but language follows the flag, and the attractions of Britannia never lured enough Latin-speakers to its shores to alter the spoken language. When Rome abandoned Britannia to its own devices after 410, Latin disappeared from general use, preserved only by the Christian priests, whereas in the Roman provinces of Gaul, Iberia, Lusitania (France, Spain and Portugal) and Italia itself, although equally subject to barbarian onslaughts, adapted forms of the language continued in use. The vernacular in Britannia which survived the occupation was Brittonic, known to linguists as 'P-Celtic', later developed into modern Welsh and Breton.[11]

In lowland Britain settled society developed without interruption. Agricola's successors chose not to exploit his defeat of the Caledonians. Border policy was to establish a permanent frontier, supplemented by an agreement with the neighbouring tribes beyond the pale to refrain from troublesome activities in return for a subsidy – very much as British India did with the tribes on the North-West Frontier. The Tyne was Britannia's equivalent of the Indus, marking the boundary of Imperial authority. Beyond those tributary societies, north of the Sea of Scotland – the near-conjunction of the Firths of Clyde and Forth in the marshy lowlands around Stirling – the country was left to the Picts.

The new frontier defences were to be in stone, replacing the former timber structures, and were perfected by the Emperor Hadrian, who visited Britannia in AD 122. Hadrian's Wall stretches seventy miles from Wallsend on the Tyne to Bowness on the Solway, and is continued by a chain of fortifications stretching down the coast to the – still very visible – post at Maryport. The Roman Wall was the Empire's most extensive fortification, much more complex than that single term implies. A continuous curtain wall, fronted by a defensive ditch, studded at regular intervals with small forts, and backed by an earthwork, the *vallum*, lined by a paved road, sheltered such considerable settlements as Corstopitum and Vindolanda, as well as many smaller communities. Hadrian's successor, Antoninus Pius, pushed the frontier through the demilitarised zone north of the Wall on to the Forth–Clyde line. His wall was less complex than that of Hadrian, a turf construction with wooden fortifications, and the Antonine strategy of forward defence was short-lived. Within little more than ten years the frontier contracted and Hadrian's Wall regained its status as defining the limits of Britannia. Backed by its excellent road system, and sufficiently garrisoned or guarded by the tribal allies to the north, the Wall constituted a major obstacle, for a strong force could be assembled at any point on its length in a matter of hours. When an extensive raid overran the Wall early in the 180s it was repressed, in the usual Imperial fashion, with efficient brutality. The lesson was fortified by Septimus Severus in 209 and 210, whose armies simply slaughtered everyone they came across in the course of suppressing another revolt.

It was behind the Wall that the province, protected from northern invasions, enjoyed comparative peace. Administratively divided into some sixteen '*civitates*' – areas reflecting the original tribal components, each with its own capital, and almost all south of the Wash/Mersey line – southern Britannia's population prospered, growing to a size not equalled until the Elizabethan age, probably between four and six million. The cities, some twenty in all, were self-governing municipalities, administered by '*decurions*', men of substance, given responsibility for water supply and sewerage, defences, theatres and circuses, the maintenance of temples and the regulation of marketplaces together with the administration of the neighbouring countryside. The experience that, over a period of four hundred years, this must have given to the provincials goes some way to explaining why, when the legions left and tax income dried up, British communities were able to keep functioning, and – some of them – to develop into new independent states.

Agricola had looked across the Irish Sea, considering the possibility of an invasion of that other island. It would only need, he calculated, a single legion to subdue those people, well known to be even more primitive than the Celts of Britannia. The fact that the endeavour was never made, and that Hibernia, like Caledonia, remained outside the Roman Empire, was to shape the future of the Britannic archipelago.

Although Hibernia remained free from Roman rule, its links with Britannia and the outside world were maintained. These were ancient connections indeed, going back some two thousand years or more. Prevailing westerly winds make for easy connections between the northern and southern shores of the English Channel and between western France and Ireland. An extensive network of sea-lanes united a 'culture province', already well-defined by Roman times, comprehending the littoral and hinterland of the Irish Sea. Movements of Celtic-speakers continued uninterrupted as immigrants crossed the sea to settle in the accessible areas on the opposite coasts. Speaking a similar language to that of the Britons, 'Q-Celtic' or Goidilic Celtic, the predecessor of modern Irish and Scots Gaelic, the newcomers were absorbed without too much trouble. The Lleyn peninsula in north Wales preserves in its name, analogous to that of Leinster in Ireland, a testimony to its Irish inhabitants. Unlike their kinsmen across the Irish Sea, the Hibernians who emigrated to Britannia had their memorials written in Latin, as well as being marked with the evolving Ogham script. One marks the resting place of *Quenvendani fili Barcuni* – 'Little Whitehead son of Doghead'.[12]

Barbarian concerns

However convenient, it is always misleading to divide history into 'periods', and to assume continuity throughout such a period. Subject to that warning, and more than most such divisions, that of the history of Roman Britannia is useful. Between AD 42 and about AD 410 Britannia was formally governed by Imperial representatives: the last two, Chrysanthus and Victorinus, the final early-fifth-century appointments, went on respectively to become a bishop in Constantinople and a country gentleman in Aquitaine, a fair indication of how widely and diversely Imperial posts were allocated. A parallel might be drawn with the career of Sir George Grey, who in the nineteenth century established Imperial rule in New Zealand, governed South Australia, served as High Commissioner in South Africa, and helped to found the Australian Labour Party. But between the time of Aulus Plautius and that of Chrysanthus much had changed.

Britannia, now the Diocese of the Britons, had been divided into four, or perhaps five, provinces. Each province was administered by a civilian, a '*Praeses*' responsible to a '*Vicarius*', probably based in London, who himself reported to the Prefect of the Gauls at Trier. Military authority was vested in the '*dux Britanniarum*', although the '*comes litoris Saxonici*', the Count of the Saxon Shore – the title indicates whence came the main threat – seems to have held an independent command. Bearing in mind that civilians were forbidden to carry arms, this division of powers was to have a decisive effect. Britannia as a whole, and its cities individually, were governed not by such tough fighting men as Agricola, but by prosperous landowners and ecclesiastics.

Defence had been less of a problem in Britannia than in Gallia. The Germanic tribes, who had been suppressed by Julius Caesar, and unified behind the Rhine, formed two confederations, the Alemanni ('allmen') and the Franci (the Franks – the freemen). In 260 the Rhine frontier collapsed and the Alemanni invaded Gaul, followed by the Franks, who set about constructing a state in the country which was eventually to bear their name. Britannia's defence against such raiders depended primarily on the maintenance of a fleet, working closely in co-operation with well-manned coastal forts, some of which survive almost intact – that of Porchester near Portsmouth being a fine example. In its day the '*Classis Britannicus*', the first British navy, was a formidably professional organisation. While Gallia was crumbling under Germanic attacks, Britannia remained peaceable for a century.

British society was forced into action by mounting external pressure, manifested in 367 by a concerted attack by the northern Caledonians, accompanied by an invasion of Gaul by the Germanic tribes, some of whom also looked in on Britannia. Order was restored by Count Theodosius, who was accompanied by his son, later Emperor Theodosius, but the firm Roman grasp had permanently slipped. The beginning of the end came as part of the confused affairs that culminated in the sack of Rome by Alaric's Visigoths in 410. Desperately looking for reinforcements to fight off the Visigothic assaults on the Danube frontiers, the Roman commander in the west, Flavius Stilicho, detached a legion from Britannia, 'the protector of the furthest Britons, who curbs the ferocious Scot'.[13] The 'furthest Britons' were worried and discontented at the rapid removal – the legion mentioned was only one of a number of such troop withdrawals – of protection for which they had dutifully paid taxes for four centuries.

Britannia's defences had been further weakened when one of the senior officers gathered enough support to have himself proclaimed as Emperor Constantine III in 407, and organised an invasion of Gaul, taking with him many of the remaining garrison. Other neighbouring barbarians seized the opportunity, and in 408 the Germanic tribes 'attacked everywhere with all their strength and brought the people of Britannia and some of the nations of Gaul to the point where they revolted from Roman rule and lived by themselves, no longer obeying Roman law. The Britons took up arms and, fighting for themselves, freed the cities from the barbarian pressure.'[14] In 410 the Emperor Honorius, struggling ineffectively for the survival of the Empire in the west, warned that Britannia would have to look to its own defences.

The departure or expulsion of the Roman officials must have been a low-key affair, for diplomatic relations continued for many years, but the leading British citizens and landowners were under no illusions: their defence had to be their own responsibility, and it was to be a responsibility seriously carried out. 'The capacity,' Peter Salway perceptively remarked, 'of bureaucracy to survive and the depth to which it was imbedded in Roman life'[15] invites the probability that Roman civil society survived at least for some time in Britannia as it did in Gaul. And there was by now the added bond of Christianity.

Christianity had spread to Britannia as it had done to all parts of the Empire. After the early persecutions Christianity was first tolerated, and then required. St Alban, killed in about 208, is the proto-martyr, whose shrine became a place of pilgrimage after Christianity was made the official religion of the Empire in 313. Britannia, or at least the southern half, had adopted the new religion with varying degrees of enthusiasm. Three British bishops and a priest attended the Council of Arles in 314, Christian inscriptions began to appear in domestic settings, and small churches were built, often on the sites of previous temples. As part of the Roman Church, still hanging on loyally in Gaul at a time when Italy itself was crumbling under barbarian attacks, British Christians received what assistance could be offered. Providing this support, Bishops Germanus and Lupus visited Britannia in 429.

The fifth and sixth centuries in Britain have long been known as the 'Dark Ages', for good reasons. The details of the career of Germanus – an impressive figure, Imperial Count and bishop both – and that of Lupus, are well documented,[16] but we do not even know the name of the British ruler who welcomed the Imperial and papal mission:

tradition, two centuries later, has him as 'Vortigern'. On his 429 mission Germanus not only preached to the people and to the notables, 'conspicuous for riches, brilliant in dress, and surrounded by a fawning multitude', but went on pilgrimage to the already famous shrine of St Alban and commanded an army in a successful battle against an invading force reported to comprise Picts allied with Saxons, the most prominent of the troublesome German tribes. In 447 Germanus was back again, probably in response to an appeal from the British to Aetius, the Roman general, conqueror of Attila the Hun, and then the effective ruler of the western provinces. On this visit, Vortigern having vanished from the scene, Germanus met one Elafius, *'regionis illius primus'*, a description which illustrates how the precisely-ranked Roman officials of a previous generation had disappeared, to be replaced by undifferentiated senior citizens.

The contrast between contemporary Gaul and Britannia is striking. Even fifty years earlier Britannia was comparatively tranquil until the troubles of the 360s, largely undisturbed by the waves of barbarians pouring into Gaul. Those Germans who had made their way across the North Sea had settled peaceably, often employed as auxiliary troops to defend the 'Saxon Shore' against their unauthorised kinsfolk. Traces of early Saxon settlements, such as that of the village overlooking Mucking Flats on the Thames estuary, were well-sited to guard against intruders seeking to make their way upstream towards Londinium. Those citizens of Britannia who had taken over the responsibilities of Victorinus and Chrysanthus certainly sought and obtained help from other Germans. By the time of his second visit, however, there was no question of Germanus leading another campaign, for the Romans were preoccupied with the Hunnish threat: and not only the Romans. In battles which culminated in the decisive engagement at Châlons-sur-Marne, Aetius could draw upon the Alans, Burgundians and Visigoths who had settled in Gaul: *his* barbarians were becoming absorbed into the Empire, decaying as it was, whilst the Saxons proved unreliable allies of Britannia, and from about 440 began to take over the province for themselves.

The end of Britannia

Some, at least, of the subsequent history of Britannia is explained by the nature of its barbarian invaders. Coming from beyond the borders of the Roman Empire, from the lowlands of Denmark and northern Germany, the first of the newcomers to take over large areas were untouched by any Roman influence, pagan 'rednecks' preserving their ancient culture of a heroic warrior aristocracy. Arriving as they did in small ships, a few at a time, creeping down the North Sea coast to cross at some point where tide and wind served, the Germanic invaders could not have been numerous. After any initial resistance was crushed the newcomers simply took over the existing infrastructure, livestock and tools, continuing to employ what was left of the locals. In all probability it was only the prominent or bolder Britons who fled or were killed; the peasantry were merely exchanging one set of masters for another. Exchanging also two languages for one, as the new Germanic tongue was adopted in place of both Latin and Brittonic.

Germanic penetration into other parts of Britannia was both slower and of a different character, infiltration rather than invasion. Along the southern coast the newcomers came from more Romanised backgrounds, with links to the consolidating Frankish state, which from 493 took control of northern Gaul. British resistance in the rest of the island depended upon local and geographical circumstances, but the general tendency was to abandon Roman methods and revert to old Celtic institutions. In this process the survival of the tribal areas, the *civitates*, was decisive. When allowed a breathing space from foreign intervention *civitates* were able to transmute into the beginnings of kingdoms, but central government disintegrated, and the Latin language vanished from common use. In Gaul some Roman social structures survived, exemplified by the history of the Apollinaris family. Emperor Constantine III's deputy in Rome in 409 was a Gaulish noble, Apollinaris; his grandson was the rather reluctant Bishop of Clermont, the poet Sidonius Apollinaris, who died about 480; and *his* son, also Apollinaris, succeeded him in the see. Such a family history is unrecorded in contemporary Britannia.

One, perhaps the most important, explanation of the different fates of Britannia and Gaul lies in the structure of the Church. In Gaul such bishops as Germanus and Lupus, Martin of Tours and Hilary of Poitiers, combined the functions of Christian leaders and Imperial representatives. Lupus was sent on what must have been one of the more difficult diplomatic missions known to history, that of negotiating with Attila: he survived. City life, which had all but disappeared in Britannia, continued in Gaul, where the ecclesiastical and civil administration enabled taxes to be collected and the mechanics of society kept in some sort of working order. In much of Britannia the Church dissolved before the pagan Saxons, the surviving clerics being driven off to the west and to Ireland and the structure of episcopal authority destroyed.

At some time about AD 500 some of the British united under a single leader, possibly the otherwise legendary Arthur. A decisive battle was won against the Saxons at a place known as Mons Badonicus, probably between 491 and 516 – the range being an indication of the uncertainty attaching to the whole period. It was a defeat serious enough to set many of the Saxon invaders thinking better of their enterprise and returning to their previous homes.[17]

Gildas, a shrill and furious British monk whose work is the most important source for the period, writing about 550, described the victory of Mons Badonicus as leading to a period of good order and tranquillity, during which 'rulers, public persons and private, bishops and clergy, each kept their proper station'. But Gildas was writing in the monastery he founded near Vannes, having like so many others of the British left to begin a new life in the new Britannia, Brittany, and taking their language with them. Again the contrast with the Continent is striking. Venantius Fortunatus, a younger Italian-born contemporary of Gildas, chaplain to St Radegunde's convent at Poitiers, left a number of poems, including the famous hymns 'Vexilla Regis Prodeunt' and 'Pange lingua, gloriosi, Proelium certaminis'.[18] Writing to the saint (formerly wife to the Frankish King Clothair) apologising for having drunk too much at dinner – 'it seemed the table swam in wine' – Fortunatus is seen settled in a society which has preserved Roman traditions and amenities even after three centuries of barbarian invasions and had begun to convert the barbarians. Things were sadly different in Britain.

If Arthur existed – and someone must have been responsible for the successful campaigns against Saxons and Irish attributed to him – he would have been a near contemporary of Clovis (c.450–511), the first of the Merovingian kings. Clovis, who succeeded in uniting much of Gaul, was able to make use of what remained of the Roman administration and assume not only the trappings of Imperial power, but the infrastructure of a chancery, a civil service and tax revenue. None of these were available to Arthur, who could have been nothing more, whatever the legends might say, than one of the British leaders who organised, for over a century, a determined resistance to the German invaders.

After 'Arthur', according to Gildas, five kingdoms ruled by 'wicked tyrants' persisted in Britannia. Vortipor (Gwrthefyr), 'tyrant' of the *civitas* Demetae, now become the realm of Dyfed (roughly Pembrokeshire), whose throne was 'stained from top to bottom with diverse murders and adulterers', and Maglocunus (Maelgwyn Fawr) of Gwynedd, 'first in evil, mightier than many both in power and malice', were the most prominent. Vortipor is commemorated by a memorial at Castell Dwyran which ranks him as a '*Protictoris*', confirming the survival of Latin as a language of prestige.[19] Similar memorials in Gwynedd describe one Cantiorix, cousin of Maglos, a '*magistratus*', as '*Venedotis Cives*' – a member of the *civitas* Venedotis.

Dumnonia – Cornwall, Devon and Somerset – was ruled by Constantinus, pilloried by Gildas as 'tyrant whelp of the filthy lioness'. Exactly which regions were controlled by the remaining tyrants, Aurelius Caninus and Cuneglasus (it is interesting to note both Latin and British names among the rulers), is unclear. Powys, the most exposed and most prosperous of the British states, extended well into the Midlands, and was ruled by the descendants of Vortigern, by then execrated for having invited in the pestilential Saxons.

Gildas was describing only those regions he knew, Wales and the west, and those 'tyrants' known to him were only the most prominent of the western British rulers. Many smaller states (or perhaps those whose rulers had not offended the indignant monk) existed east of the Severn, and to the north. Indicating their lower status, Gildas referred to their rulers as '*duces*' – generals – some among whom 'had left the broad way and found the narrow' and were exhorted to pray for, or punish, the tyrants. It does not seem that their prayers were effectual, for the splintered British states were even then being submerged by the incessant waves of Teutonic newcomers.

CHAPTER 2

AD 500–1066

The first English kingdom

THERE ARE SOME interesting modern parallels with the decline of the Roman Empire in the west. Beginning in 1947 Britain abandoned its control of the Indian sub-continent, leaving it divided into two large countries, India and Pakistan (since split once more between Pakistan and Bangladesh), and a number of smaller states, including Burma and the island of Ceylon. In the biggest of these states, India, the imperial structure of law and the constitution continued mostly intact; the imperial language remained an official language, the essential medium of communication among the educated classes of all ethnicities; and the borders remained on the whole stable. Ceylon – Sri Lanka – although ravaged by civil war, has retained the characteristics of a liberal democracy. Similarly, in Pakistan and Bangladesh, although more perilously, something of the old imperial systems has continued, while in Burma chaos has descended.

So it was with Rome. Roman law, the Latin language and the culture of the Roman Church remained pervasive in Gaul, Italy and Iberia, even though no centralised civil authority emerged in these countries for a considerable time. In contrast, over most of Britannia Latin perished, pagan barbarians overran the most populous areas, whilst elsewhere the people reverted to the native languages, laws and forms of control. Gradually and through many complex developments, Britannia moved back into the European system, and brought with it Hibernia. To a great extent the formation of the United Kingdom traces this movement.

Many Germanic customs were little different from those of the Celtic peoples who had not become affected by Roman rule – the passionate loyalty of warrior to lord is expressed as strongly in the Welsh bard Taliesin as in Anglo-Saxon poetry – but between the newcomers and those Britons who had, over three centuries, become accustomed to Roman institutions, there was a profound gap. Romanised Britons lived in well-established units, many of which survived the legions' departure. The regrettable absence of the soldiers involved the more welcome departure of the tax gatherers. With them went the whole machinery, buildings and all, of centralised authority. Towns rapidly decayed, a decay accelerated by Roman techniques of official building, all constructed in the Mediterranean style, with Roman-tiled low-pitched roofs, necessitating frequent repair in order to resist British weather (even today such 'Roman' roofs are only found well south of the Loire). Once the factories producing tiles had closed, repairs were impossible. The low-pitched roofs did not allow covering with thatch, the only available alternative; consequently the Roman works were abandoned, the stones being used for new construction. In spite of physical decay some *civitates*, the basic units of authority, remained, transmuting into minor kingdoms. As a symbol of this change their centres were often now not the Roman towns, but the original Celtic hill-forts and emergent Christian foundations.

The eighth-century historian Bede identified three peoples among the Germanic invaders – Angles, Saxons and Jutes. Whilst the Jutes showed signs of having been influenced by the Franks of Gaul, reasonably enough given the proximity of their own land of Kent, the similarities between the Germanic newcomers were more marked than any differences. All were pagans, valuing fidelity to their leaders above any other quality. Tacitus had noted that 'it is a lifelong infamy and reproach to survive the chief and withdraw from the battle'. Six hundred years later the finest Early English poem, 'The Wanderer', described the anguish of a warrior bereft of his lord, and therefore of his place in society, his very identity as a man, 'exiled from home and from my kinsmen, ever since the day when the dark earth closed over my generous lord, and I wandered away over the expanse of waters, destitute and distraught with the dangers of winter, looking in sorrow for the abode of a generous prince'.[1]

The successors of Gildas' five tyrants formed a continuing opposition to the German newcomers. Their independent British states included most of the former province of *Britannia Prima*, extending in an unbroken line from Devon to mountainous north Wales and Anglesey. There the old *civitas* of the Ordovices had become the realm of Gwynedd, which continued independent until the thirteenth century, when it was reconstituted as the Principality of Wales. More exposed, Powys was losing its midland territory to the Anglians, being forced back on the natural barrier of the River Severn. Outside the region known to Gildas other Christian British communities continued. Once away from the cantonments on and behind the Wall the upland tribes had remained at best quiescent under Roman rule. There integrated tribal societies, 'kingdoms' by courtesy, soon stabilised after the Roman withdrawal. In the southern hills and on the eastern coastal plain the realm of Elmet survived until the seventh century. Further north and west Rheged, modern Galloway and Cumbria, sheltered behind the protective barrier of the Pennines. Better attested than the rather shadowy Rheged, the realm of Strathclyde, centred on Dumbarton, maintained its independence until in the eleventh century it was absorbed into the emerging Kingdom of Scotland. Eastwards around the Firth of Forth, the Votadini, previously one of the buffer states funded by the Romans, had transmuted into 'a full-blooded barbarian Celtic aristocracy accoutered in Iron Age torques and engaged in the characteristic reckless bravery of their continental ancestors'.[2]

After the Anglian arrival some at least of the Votadini found their way to Wales, bringing with them the earliest poetry in Welsh, forming perhaps the oldest vernacular literature in modern Europe, the works of bards known as Taliesin and Aneirin.[3] Both deal with contemporary historic events, although Taliesin's verses are praise-poetry, whereas Aneirin's single epic recounts the defeat of his people, by then known as the Gododdin, at the hands of the Northumbrians at the battle of Catraeth – probably Catterick. Poetry and refugees alike found shelter in that last bastion of British culture, the diverse kingdoms of Wales, all that was left by the mid-eighth century of the old province of Britannia as the Teutonic incomers settled themselves in what became England.

Continuity with the Irish Sea culture was underlined by the migration, highly significant in future developments, of northern Hibernians to Dalriada, today's Argyll and its islands. At some time about

500 Fergus Mor, an Irish chieftain, moved with some of his people from the country around present-day Antrim across the North Channel, only twelve miles wide at its narrowest point. At that time the Irish were known in Latin as 'Scotti': Fergus' people therefore became 'Scotti Brittaniae'. All subsequent Scottish monarchs can claim descent from Fergus, but for many years Dalriada was little more than an Irish colony, and one divided between quarrelling clans.

To the original inhabitants of Britain the newcomers remained Saxons – 'Sassenachs' or 'Saesen' – but by the seventh century, and perhaps before, they were, following the celebrated pun of Pope Gregory, 'Non Anglii, sed angeli' – 'Not Angles but angels' – English. Yet just as today Yorkshiremen, for example, consider themselves as having an identifier other than that of mere English, so did the new 'English' think of themselves also as 'men of Bernicia', of the East or West Saxons, or of Kent. When Bede entitled his great work Historia ecclesiastica gentis Anglorum ('The Ecclesiastical History of the English People'), he conflated his own Anglians with Saxons and Jutes into a single people chosen by God to bring order to the island, but displayed all the characteristics of a patriotic Northumbrian. In some ways Bede himself can be taken as the first identifiable Englishman, attempting verse in his native language, writing scholarly books interspersed with little anecdotes, and closely observing the movements of the tides in order to prepare a scientific treatise.[4]

When the invaders developed from the original raiding parties into recognisable political entities these consisted of the kingdoms of Kent, of the South, East and West Saxons, of the East Anglians, the Mercians and the Northumbrians, each attempting, when occasion offered, to gain hegemony over the others and to extend their territories into the remaining British regions. It would be a mistake to see the struggle as a simple Saxon against Briton issue; when an opportunity occurred Saxon and British leaders could unite for their individual ends, pursuing them by diplomacy as well as war. Dynastic intermarriage was not unknown – Oswiu, King of Northumbria between 643 and 670, married successively an Irish girl, Fina, daughter of an Uí Néill chief; then Riemmelth, great-granddaughter of the British King Urien of Rheged; and finally Eanfled, his predecessor Edwin's daughter. Some Saxons, such as Cerdic, the founder of the Wessex dynasty, and Cadwalladon,

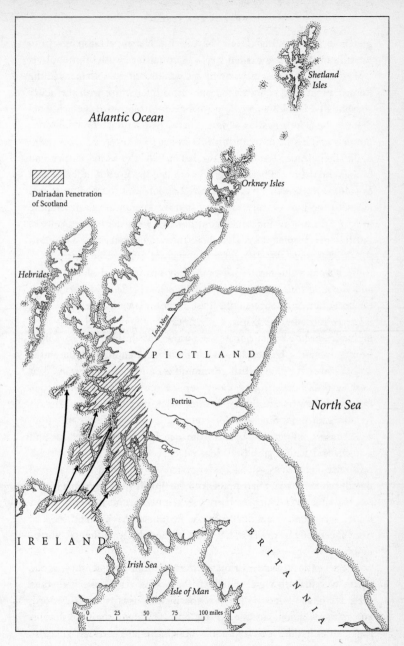

Shetland
Isles

Atlantic Ocean

Orkney Isles

Dalriadan Penetration
of Scotland

Hebrides

P I C T L A N D

Loch Ness

Fortriu

North Sea

Forth

Clyde

I R E L A N D

Irish Sea

Isle of Man

B R I T A N N I A

0   25   50   75   100 miles

DALRIADAN PENETRATION OF SCOTLAND

pretender to the same throne, have Celtic names, presumably from their mothers; on less exalted levels, intermarriage was commonplace.

The earliest of these new kingdoms was that of the Oiscingas in the Kentish peninsula, conveniently placed for intercourse with the newly consolidated Frankish state. Kentish expansion westwards was checked first by the South Saxons – never themselves serious contenders for power – and by the more formidable and aggressive West Saxons, who under their leader Ceawlin in the last half of the sixth century had brought all the south between the Severn and the Weald under control of some sort. North of the Thames, London and the Chilterns had fallen to the East Saxons, and an extensive kingdom was developing in East Anglia, a region which controlled very considerable resources. But the first Anglian kingdom whose ruler could make a real claim to the title of '*Bretwalda*', overlord of Britannia, lay further north.

Even before the famous, if doubtfully historic, arrival of Hengist and Horsa in fifth-century Kent, Anglians had settled in what became the Kingdom of Deira, in the East Riding of Yorkshire. They had been recruited by the British authorities to supplement the garrison, probably about AD 350, but it was another two hundred years before later immigrants had expanded their numbers enough to present a serious threat to the British communities. Deira, with its capital at York, and its northern neighbour Bernicia, centred on the great rock fortress of Bamburgh, then fused into what became the first English state to gain pre-eminence, Northumbria.

Bernicia's ruling family stem from one Eosa, who arrived around AD 500, and whose grandson, Ida, established himself in 547. British resistance kept Ida's successors confined in a limited area around Bamburgh until 592 when Aethelfrith (or Ethelfrith), who ruled until 616, was able to claim sovereignty over the two realms of Bernicia and Deira. An extensive area between the Pennines/Cheviots and the sea, from the Tweed to the Humber, then formed the Kingdom of Northumbria.

The seventh century is primarily the Northumbrian century, as the eighth was that of Mercia. Aethelfrith, 'a king very brave and most eager for glory' – less politely an unprincipled and ruthless warlord, known to his enemies as 'the Twister' – was the last of the Anglo-Saxon pagan kings in the grand tradition, whose brutal successes left a permanent mark on Britain. At some time about 600 a coalition of north British forces, from the Votadini-Gododdin in Lothian to the British of Cumbria, invaded Aethelfrith's country, only to be obliterated at Catraeth, the battle commemorated by the British bard Aneirin. Striking westwards, Aethelfrith led the Anglian forces against the Britons at Chester. That was little more than a raid – although one bitterly remembered by the Welsh, since the pagan Northumbrians slaughtered over a thousand rash monks in the course of their victory – and was not followed by Anglian settlement. A more permanent result was achieved at the battle of Degsastan (location unknown, but somewhere in northern Bernicia) in 603. This was in response to an invasion by the King of Dalriada, Aedan mac Gabran, described by the precise Bede as a 'king of the Irish living in Britain', the successor of that Fergus who had led the emigration from Ireland. Degsastan was a decisive victory of great significance; Bede commented: 'From that time no Irish king in Britain has dared to make war on the English race to this day.' While this was hardly true of Aedan's successors, henceforward the region between the Tyne and the Firth of Forth was, whoever might claim the lordship, to be Anglian and later English-speaking.

Aethelfrith's successor, Edwin (617–33), consolidated Northumbrian gains, controlling a region from Edinburgh to the Trent valley, and able to strike far west to invade Anglesey and Man. His reign marked a decisive change as the new religion was brought to Northumbria through the King's marriage to Aethelburh, the daughter of King Aethelbert and Bertha, the newly converted rulers of Kent, and through her mother a descendant of Clovis, the founder of the Frankish kingdom. With that alliance Edwin was able to crush the West Saxons, and to secure the allegiance of the East Angles, becoming the *Bretwalda*, who had a Roman standard carried before him on his journeys. 'It is related that there was so great a peace in Britain, wherever the domain of King Edwin reached that a woman with a newborn child could walk throughout the island from sea to sea and take no harm.'

It was probably in Edwin's time, and perhaps at Edwin's orders, that the great fiscal document of Saxon England, anticipating the Domesday Book by four centuries, was prepared. The 'Tribal Hideage' divides all England south of Northumbria, excluding those western areas still in

British control, into 'hides' – the nominal unit of a peasant holding, used as a basis for taxation. Nineteen separate kingships are noted, with the number of hides appertaining to each. Allowing for doubtless many arbitrary calculations, such a document implies a society more organised than any other in western Europe, and incomparably more developed than any other in the islands. In the absence of surveys, divisions were only nominal, and in fact a single peasant – a '*ceorl*' – could rarely have worked an area as extensive as the hide, which might extend to 120 acres, with his own family.

In some areas the Britons – the *Wealas* – would be in some form of servitude, and slavery was common. Not all *Wealas* were confined to the lower levels of Saxon society: some possessed as many as five hides, a holding important enough to confer what was then the thanely, later knightly, status.[5] All inhabitants were subject to the same laws, although very different values were placed on individuals when compensation was assessed. So widespread and detailed an administrative framework survived individual monarchs and dynasties and continued in one form or another in succeeding Saxon states.

Northumbria's military power subsequently declined as King Ecgfrith (670–85) attempted further conquests. An expedition against the Picts was repulsed at Dunnichen Moss in Forfar, and the first English invasion of Ireland in 684, although 'wretchedly devastating a harmless race that had always been most friendly to the English', was unsuccessful.[6] Although what had for a short time seemed to be a Northumbrian empire later disintegrated, what might be called a Greater Northumbrian culture region survived. Kings were succeeded by earls, but the region between the Tees and the Forth remained English-speaking and largely independent, while acknowledging whichever more powerful authority seemed prudent; and the great achievements of Northumbrian culture were only then beginning to unfold, as another clash was emerging, that of different interpretations of Christianity. King Edwin had been duly baptised in the new church of St Peter in his capital of York by Paulinus, the Kentish royal chaplain. An intimidating figure, formerly a monk in Rome, Paulinus represented the orthodox and increasingly powerful Church of Rome; but his was not the only brand of Christianity on offer.

Saints and scholars

After the collapse of Roman rule the Christian Church had maintained an existence within the British states, although the extent of these was shrinking under the pressure from the pagan newcomers. The tenacious British Church did not resemble the formal ecclesiastical structure of contemporary Gaul, where bishops had been regularly appointed to defined sees, with their headquarters alongside those of the royal counts, in cities which retained something of their previous integrity, and where Latin was the written language of civil and religious life. With the increasing pressure from pagan Saxons, Picts and other barbarians, Christianity became a distinction of the still literate and organised British communities but, isolated from Rome, took its own peculiar forms. Without a definite diocesan or parochial structure the centre of religious life in post-Roman Britain lay rather in the influential and proliferating monasteries. Again, these bore no resemblance to the tightly disciplined hierarchical communities even then (St Benedict composed his Rule in 515) being established on the Continent. The Celtic tradition stemmed originally from those collections of hermits who gathered together in the North African deserts, searching out solitude and tranquillity. Privacy for meditation, the essential factor, took priority over communal worship, and was ensured by each monk having his own cell or hut within a monastic enclosure.

Among the earliest of such foundations in Britain was that of St Ninian at Whithorn in Galloway, where the 'Candida Casa', the White House, was built in 397, to become the centre of zealous missionary work. 'Te Domine Laudamus', begins an inscription on the monument of Latinus and his daughter, erected at Whithorn probably during the lifetime of St Ninian, who died about 430, its bad Latin and crude lettering indicating graphically how quickly the classical traditions had decayed. On the mainland Ninian's mission expanded slowly, struggling north to reach Dumbarton, where Kentigern became the first Bishop of Strathclyde about AD 600, but moved swiftly across the sea to Ireland.[7]

Hibernia had remained largely untouched by the Roman occupation of Britannia; apart from evidence of a trading station on the south-east coast there is little evidence of Roman presence before the fourth century AD.[8] British bishops continued to have contact with Continental Christians – one *Britonensis ecclesiae episcopus* named Mahiloc attended the Council of Braga in Spain in 572 – but the Church in the Irish Sea province continued its primitive traditions. On the other hand there was extensive contact between the British and Irish, and in both directions, with quite substantial settlements being made. Dyfed had an Irish-speaking aristocracy by 400, and other colonies existed in north Wales and Dumnonia, whilst in Scotland Fergus Mor's immigration formed the Argyll settlement of Dalriada. None of this interaction had noticeable effect on Irish society, which remained that of the pagan heroic age, pastoral, illiterate and engaged in endemic warfare.

One of the first precise dates in Irish history is 431, when Pope Celestine I sent one Palladius 'to minister to the Irish who believe in Christ' – possibly those converted by St Ninian of Whithorn's disciples – but it is St Patrick who takes most of the credit. In Patrick's time – he probably died in 491 – Ireland was a region of fragmented statelets, perhaps as many as 150, geography always having militated against Irish unity.[9] The midland plain, some sixty miles wide, stretching from coast to coast, is drained by the Shannon running through it to form a complex of lake, swamp and river for over two hundred miles. To the north and south short rivers cut up the land into hilly blocks, high and bleak in the north and west. Warfare was endemic, often however of a symbolic, or even sporting nature. Fighters, and the bards who sang of their exploits, were highly regarded. All acknowledged customary 'Brehon' law, administered by hereditary jurists, which recognised different grades of 'kingship' ranging from the *ri tuaithe*, a local chieftain, to *ri ruirech*, 'king over kings', a provincial magnate who might also be *ri coicid*, 'king of a fifth' – one of the ancient five provinces, Ulster, Leinster, Munster, Connacht and Meath. From time to time a successful warlord might claim to be 'high king', but unlike the succession of English *Bretwaldas* the title was never accompanied by anything more than a temporary and restricted eminence.[10]

Even before Patrick, Latin learning had begun to influence Ireland, and, although Latin obituary inscriptions only date from 671, the spread of the language was certainly much speedier. Religious teaching was very much a two-way traffic, missionaries from Gaul making their way

EARLY IRELAND

to Ireland from the end of the fourth century, reinforced by Britons from the newly established church at Whithorn and from Wales, where St David and St Iltyd – born in Brittany – formed influential schools. Soon after the establishment of Christianity Irish missionaries carried the Word abroad in their turn. St Columba (Columcille) founded the monastery of Iona (Hy) in 563, in the developing Kingdom of Dalriada, whence the work of evangelising the Picts and Anglians began. Striking across Scotland through the Great Glen, Columba persuaded the formidable Pictish King Bridei to allow Christianity to be preached to his people. Their ultimate conversion was a slow process, merged as it was with an expansion of Dalriadan influence, ultimately consolidated only in 863, but by the time of Columba's death in 597 Celtic Christianity was firmly established in south-west Scotland and was extending into the Saxon regions. In the following century Ionan offshoots, an extensive chain of daughter '*paruchia*' – monasteries – had spread from Aberdour, through the Hebridean islands as far as Kells in Ireland, and to the northern parts of England.[11]

There followed, with striking rapidity, the golden age of Irish religious culture, with the production of such extraordinarily magnificent works as the Book of Kells, a masterpiece of European art, and the flow of Irish scholars all over western Europe, a movement which continued for centuries. Irish society, in spite of the political fragmentation, was homogeneous, with a common language, law and culture, but without any tradition of literacy, yet within a century religious and legal work of a high standard was being produced. By the mid-seventh century, before Bede was born, the Irish author of *De mirabilibus sacrae scripturae* ('The Wonders of Holy Writ') displayed an encyclopaedic knowledge both of the early fathers and more recent commentators. Cumine Ailbhe (Cuine, or Finn), Abbot of Hy, in his learned defence of the Roman system of calculating Easter, asserts not only patristic authority but claims knowledge of Greek, Hebrew and Egyptian calendars.

Extravagant claims have been made for the Ireland of Saints and Scholars, but culture in the early Middle Ages was anything but nationalistic. Aldfrith, King of Northumbria from 685, had been educated in Ireland, and was a famous writer of Irish verse; the Northumbrians instructed the uncultivated Franks of Charlemagne's court; but a generation later the Irish scholar John Scotus Erigena, joking with the Emperor Charles the Bald ('What difference is there between a Scot and a sot?' asked the Emperor at dinner. 'A table,' John replied), had gone far beyond the English in his knowledge of Greek.[12]

Scholarship and art were centred in the monasteries, almost small towns, set in large enclosures scattered with timber workshops and huts, often later with one of those astonishingly lofty round towers which have survived a thousand years of Irish weather. The churches were tiny, and only rarely of stone, the architectural glory of the monasteries being concentrated in the stone crosses, representations in stone of the scriptural stories. The enclosure at Monasterboice contains two massively impressive examples, together with a tower and two small (but not original) churches, but the best impression of a Celtic monastery is gained by visiting Clonmacnoise, on the shores of the Shannon, where the stonework of the eighth-century chapel and the definition of the encircling wall survive. Abbots, the rulers of these monasteries, were usually kin to lay magnates, 'urbane ecclesiastic aristocrats'. Bishops also existed, and in considerable numbers, since every petty king required a bishop of his own, but episcopal qualifications were modest; it was found necessary, for example, to insist that no candidate should have more than one wife. Both abbatial and episcopal offices were often hereditary.[13]

Different forms of ecclesiastical organisation and a more relaxed attitude towards clerical celibacy were not the only things that distinguished the Celtic Church from the rest of Christendom. A different method of calculating Easter, and the shape of the tonsure (a patch on the crown in Europe, and a total shave from above the ears in the Atlantic provinces), passed unnoticed in the general tumult of the fifth century, but the expansion of the Celtic Church and the arrival of Irish missionaries in Europe, strangely dressed, with darkened eyelids, compelled attention. When the two traditions competed for acceptance in a single state, a clash was inevitable.

During the sixth century Europe emerged from the tumult of the Dark Ages and assumed a recognisably medieval character. The Emperor Justinian (reigned 527–65), himself a Slav, provided stability and a new code of law in Italy; Clovis (481–511) founded the Frankish empire in Gaul, which evolved into what became the Holy Roman

Empire of Charlemagne. St Benedict (480–*c.*550) began to organise monasticism, and Pope Gregory the Great (590–604) established the see of Rome as the undoubted leader of Christianity in western Europe, leaving the east and Asia under separate rule.

From this base the work of reclaiming Britannia for the Christian empire could begin. In 597, only a few years after St Columba's foundation of Iona, Pope Gregory dispatched a rather reluctant monk, Augustine, with some companions to convert what seemed 'a barbarous, fierce and unbelieving nation whose language they did not even understand'.[14] They tried to turn back, but the Pope insisted. Landing in Kent, the apprehensive missionaries found an ally in Queen Bertha, Clovis of Gaul's great-granddaughter, already Christian. King Aethelbert succumbed to the missionaries' persuasion, and Augustine became the first Archbishop of Canterbury, with another see established in 604 at Rochester. A 'church of becoming splendour, dedicated to the blessed apostles Peter and Paul', the remains of which now form part of St Augustine's abbey in Canterbury, was begun in 598.[15]

When Bertha's daughter Aethelburh brought Christianity to Northumbria, that kingdom had already been influenced by the Celtic Church. Aidan (*obit.c.*651), 'a man of outstanding gentleness', sent from Iona to convert the Anglians, founded a monastery at Lindisfarne, the tidal island adjoining the Deiran stronghold of Bamburgh. From Lindisfarne, monks, assisted by the swords of the Northumbrians, converted Penda of the Mercians, Cynegils of Wessex and the East Saxons. By 660 all Saxons and Anglians except those of Sussex and the Isle of Wight were officially Christian, but of two different varieties, those following Rome and those adhering to the Celtic traditions. The great apostle of the north, St Cuthbert (*obit.* 687), one of the few English saints still to be remembered by the population – if only for his having given his name to 'cuddy ducks' (eider ducks) and 'cuddies' (donkeys) – combined Lindisfarne asceticism with obedience to Rome.

Faced with this division in his kingdom, King Oswy of Northumbria took the lead in establishing unity by summoning a synod at Whitby, where representatives of the two Churches met in 664. Since Church affairs were then, as ever, inextricably mixed with political factors, and given Oswy's authority as *Bretwalda*, the participants were also deciding whether England would acknowledge the authority of Rome, and thereby develop in a European rather than an Anglo-Celtic context.[16]

The conference was attended by the rising star of the Northumbrian Church, the aggressive Wilfred of Ripon; Bishop Agilbert of Paris, whose Latin pronunciation the English found ridiculously incomprehensible; and the influential St Cedd, apostle of the East Saxons. Not unexpectedly the conclave reached the conclusion that Oswy wanted. The English Church was to follow the Roman rule and customs, thereby pulling England into the mainstream of European life, and leaving the Celtic societies to follow their own tradition. One striking example of the divergence was shown at the synod itself, since its venue had been chosen by reason of the famous convent established there by St Hilda. A member of the royal family, Hilda played an active part in the proceedings. It would have been unthinkable for a woman to occupy such an influential position in any of the Celtic Churches, and the contrast between the powerful women figuring in English – rather less so in Scottish – history, and the absence of any in historic Ireland or Wales, is striking.[17] Queens Cartimandua and Boudicca; Hilda herself; Queen Bertha, whose influence converted Kent; Queen Emma, wife to two English kings in the eleventh century; Margaret of Scotland; the ferocious Empress Matilda and Eleanor of Aquitaine have no parallels in the Celtic states: indeed, with the notable exception of St Brigit, a very doubtfully historical character, it is difficult to identify any Irishwoman in a position of influence before the twentieth century.

Celtic virtues continued to be cherished after Whitby had settled the future of the English Church, but in Ireland the ecclesiastical structure slipped back into being little more than an adjunct to lay potentates, and social life relapsed into the old pattern of fragmented and discordant statelets. Northumbria, on the other hand, followed by the rest of the English states, together developed their links with Rome and Europe; the career of the York monk Alcuin at Charlemagne's court was paralleled by that of St Boniface of Crediton (680–755), who followed the Irish St Kilian (*obit.*689) in bringing Christianity to the pagan Germans.[18]

The limited success of Augustine and his followers was expanded and reinforced in 669 by the new Archbishop of Canterbury. A seemingly odd choice, Theodore of Tarsus was an elderly Levantine philosopher, who was only ordained at the age of sixty-six, and promoted from layman to archbishop within weeks. Theodore spoke no English, but was accompanied by the Northumbrian Benedict Biscop, a rich and learned man. After settling Theodore into Canterbury, Biscop returned to his native land to establish the twin monasteries of Jarrow and Monkwearmouth, a few miles apart in Durham. Built in the Roman style, adorned with sculpture and stained glass, their churches were the finest in Britain, matched only by Wilfred's new foundation of Hexham (the contrast between these Northumbrian and such Irish foundations as Monasterboice is a good illustration of the differences between the two traditions, as is that of the slender Anglian crosses with the more massive and cruder Celtic examples). Biscop brought a quantity of books which enabled his young pupil Bede to write his history, and to assist in founding the schools which, together with their offshoot at York became the chief centre of west European learning. Lindisfarne had already produced two surviving masterpieces, the Book of Durrow and the Lindisfarne Gospels, but from Jarrow came the Codex Amiatinus, the largest medieval work ever known, a complete bible in 2600 vellum sheets, weighing over seventy-five pounds: and it is only one of three produced in Jarrow.[20]

Although Northumbria remained for some time the cultural centre of England, political leadership passed south to Mercia with the advent of King Aethelbald in 716. Written charters, one significant identifier of an organised realm, began to appear in some quantity and evidenced the increasing use of written English. The first, from Wulfhere, is perhaps from 674; confirming a land sale, it has the boundaries of the estate, at Dilingtun, defined in English; later charters, as an 812 deed of gift to Christchurch, Canterbury, are entirely in English.[21] Aethelbald's successor, Offa, claimed to be 'King of the English' in his charters. The claim would not be recognised in Northumbria, nor in Wessex, although that kingdom acknowledged Mercia as in some way a protector. Offa corresponded with his contemporary Charlemagne on equal terms, being addressed by the first Holy Roman Emperor as his 'dearest brother' (the correspondence began with a complaint from the Franks about the quality of English woollens delivered to the Continent). Abandoning any attempt to extend into Northumbria, Aethelbald and Offa, who between them reigned for eighty years, suppressed East Anglian and Kentish independence, and defined a new border with

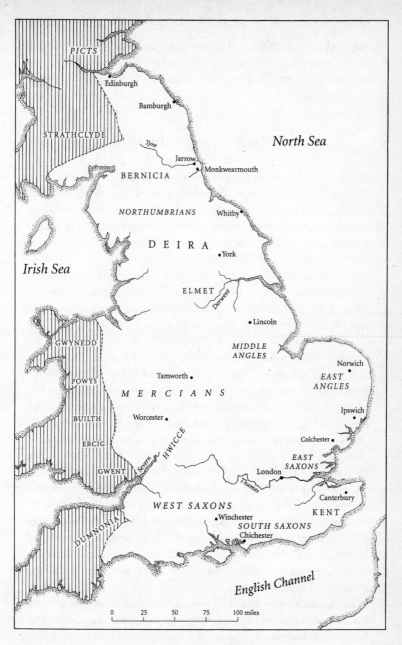

ENGLAND IN THE EIGHTH CENTURY

the Welsh states. Offa's Dyke, that great earthwork which stretches from north to south for 150 miles, was intended to serve not primarily as a defensive work but as a very visible boundary, which in great measure it still does.

Picts, Scots, Britons and Anglians

By the time hegemony of the English kingdoms had passed from Northumbria to Mercia all the territory of what is now England, with the exception of isolated pockets of Britons in the west, had come under Anglo/Saxon rule. To the north rapid changes characterised the area as Britons, Picts, Northumbrians and the intrusive Irish – all usually quarrelling among themselves – fought to establish competing territorial claims. On the east, although warfare continued, with temporary gains being made by one side or another, Lothian, the region south of the Forth, remained English-speaking, part of Greater Northumbria, facing the Pictish states on the northern bank.

Those extended at least over the whole of eastern Scotland north of the Forth, including Orkney and Shetland, with some Pictish sites scattered in the west, from the Hebrides down to Galloway. There seem to have been two major political units, in which a central power was exercised through regional officials, '*mormaers*', a term which continued well into the Middle Ages. Challenging Pictland in the west of Scotland were the Dalriadans, whose colony had formally divided from the Ulster mother community; by 700 the '*Scottii*' were distinct from the '*Hibernii*', and it becomes possible to speak of the 'Scots' as one of the peoples inhabiting Caledonia. They did not yet form a unified state, being subdivided into three, often hostile, clans. South of Dalriada, with its capital on the unassailable rock of Dumbarton, its boundaries stretching from Stirling to the Solway, the Kingdom of Strathclyde was precariously independent, but was confined by Northumbrian expansion, which had collapsed the neighbouring British Kingdom of Rheged.

By the mid-eighth century Pictland, now united by King Oengus, had emerged as the major power in Caledonia. Pictish forces, which had halted the northward advance of the Northumbrians in 685, crushed the

Dalriadan Scots in 741. Although a Pictish dynasty went on to rule Scotland north of the Clyde and Forth, these were not struggles between nation-states or even between mutually incompatible cultures: Northumbrian exiles found sanctuary in Pictland; Picts and Scots intermarried; joint rule of Picts and Scots by the same king was not unusual. The centre of government moved nearer to the geographical centre, Fortriu, modern Strathearn. Northumbrian pretensions at overlordship in Scotland had ended, but not Northumbrian power or influence. As in England, however, the anglicisation of Lothian did not represent the extermination of the Gael, but rather an integration of the two societies. The magnificent Anglian crosses in Bewcastle, Cumberland and Ruthwell, Dumfries, exemplify the spread of Northumbrian culture to the west and the fusion of the two traditions.

Strathclyde's rulers had been losing much of their independence before the last, Owain the Bald, disappeared some time after 1018. By then the original Brittonic-speakers had been to a great extent supplanted by the Northumbrians, followed by Norse Vikings coming first from Ireland and later from Scandinavia direct. Although the dominant language later became English, the inhabitants remain to this day ethnically distinctive, Scandinavian in appearance and with many Norse elements of speech. Coniston, in Cumberland, was founded in the reign of King Stephen; anywhere else in England, it would have been 'Kingston', derived from the Saxon rather than from the Norse root. South of Carlisle lakes are 'meres' or 'waters'; further north they become 'loughs' or 'lochs'. To the north of Cumbria, the population of Galloway was a mixture of the original Britons, Northumbrians, Picts and Norse – the Galwegians, the Gall-Gaidhil, or foreign Gauls, who gained a fearsome reputation for savagery.

It was the Viking raids that gave the Dalriadan Scots the opportunity to assert their strength. Some two hundred nautical miles – less than two days' fair sailing – separate Bergen in Norway from the Shetland Isles. Thence, for seven degrees of latitude, south to the Mull of Kintyre and the Isle of Man, enterprising Norse settlers took over the whole of the coastline, supplanting the Dalriadans from much of their territory, forcing them eastwards towards the Picts. In 839 a devastating battle with the Norsemen left the warriors of Fortriu slaughtered 'beyond counting'; among the dead were numbered Eoganan, King of Picts and Scots. One Kenneth, a shadowy figure who claimed to be the son of a possibly fictitious Alpin, had established himself as leader of the Dalriadans in the west and was now able to effect a permanent rule over both Picts and Scots. Given a common language, the union of the two peoples came more easily; from that time the Picts as a separate people disappear, their capital of Scone taken over as the centre of MacAlpin rule.[22]

With the integration of Picts and Scots under a recognised monarch the Kingdom of Scotland, or Alba, the Gaelic name for Scotland north of the Forth, can be said to begin. Although Kenneth MacAlpin (843–58) is nearly a contemporary with Alfred, the Scottish kingdom was in no respect comparable with the English. Such elementary indications of statehood as the minting of coinage, first issued in England during the eighth century, did not emerge in Scotland until the twelfth century. An episcopally controlled Church, which could ensure the supply of literate clerics to staff a chancery, did not develop until much later than in England; only in 1108 is the name of a bishop, one Turgot, linked with that of a diocese, St Andrews. Geographically too, the MacAlpin rule was limited: Moray, north of the river Dee, was the land of the Cenel Loairn whilst the Atlantic seaboard, with the offshore islands, continued Norse. Southwards, although in a negative fashion, MacAlpins benefited from Viking activities. At the time when the Wessex kings were fighting for survival against the Danes, Northumbria, from the Tees north, remained comparatively undisturbed. There the confrontations were between MacAlpin kings and Anglian earls, during which King Malcolm I was able to profit by obtaining Cumberland and Westmorland in 945.

Furor Normannorum

Those famous and infamous raiders and colonists, the Vikings, came from three nations, the Swedes, Danes and Norwegians. Their victims did not get the opportunity to decide which fierce intruder was about to slaughter them, and termed them all Vikings, 'Men of the North', praying fervently to be delivered 'ex furor Normannorum'. Of these the Swedes were by 800 the most solidly established, drawing great prestige from the famous pagan shrine at Upsala, and were turning their attention eastwards, where they penetrated the river systems to found the states of Kiev and Novgorod and to attack Byzantium. In contrast geographical factors militated against Norway being anything other than a scattered land of petty chiefs, from whom small colonies had already left to settle in the Northern Isles of Orkney and Shetland. It was these Norsemen who first swept down on the British Isles at the end of the eighth century.

Previous raiders, Saxons and Frisians, had been essentially coastal rather than blue-water sailors, but the Norsemen faced long voyages with equanimity, settling not only Iceland but Greenland, and making one expedition to North America. An unfortunate civilian, a Wessex reeve, was their first English victim, but subsequent, better-informed raids chose easier and more accessible targets. In 793 Cuthbert's Lindisfarne was sacked, followed within the next two years by Bede's Jarrow and Columba's Iona. Thereafter the raiders concentrated on the Irish Sea coasts, with the first raid recorded in 795. Again coastal monasteries were the preferred targets, followed by raids inland; Armagh was repeatedly sacked by 'great sea-cast floods of foreigners'.

Given the fragmented state of Ireland a concerted resistance was impossible, and the newcomers saw opportunities in allying themselves with one native faction against another, and carving out permanent settlements for themselves. Inevitably these were at convenient harbour locations: Dublin, which became the most flourishing slave market in the Isles, had a permanent Norse population by 841, followed by Wexford, Waterford, Cork and Limerick, each with a small hinterland.

Other Ostmen, as the Irish Vikings described themselves, settled in the Hebrides, Islay and Mull – the Sudreys, the Southern Isles (the name is commemorated in the title of the Bishop of Sodor and Man) – and in the Isle of Man itself. In this way a great curve of Norse settlements ran north from Dublin to the Orkneys, united rather than separated by the sea. From the kingdoms of Dublin and of Man to the Earldom of Orkney, dozens of independent states owed – when forced so to do – allegiance to kings of Norway or Alba and, less formally, to whoever was pre-eminent in Ireland.

Vikings operating from Denmark pursued very different policies from those of their Norwegian kin, restricting their operations south down the North Sea and the Straits of Dover, and coming in considerably larger numbers. Until 854 the Danes were held back by their own centralised monarchy, wary of Frankish power, but the collapse of the Danish royal house in that year and the decline of the Carolingian state allowed enterprising adventurers to set forth; and England became a prime destination.

Whereas previously, given internal cohesion and secure borders, it seemed that England might evolve as three, or perhaps four, independent states, this prospect dissolved under the pressure of the Danish attacks: unity was forced upon the English kingdoms by the Viking onslaught. In their day, Saxons had been violent enough, but the Vikings set new standards of horror. With their splendid ships they ravaged the coasts of western Europe, ascending the rivers to raid the inland cities. The frantic efforts of the established states could not evict them; at best they could be restrained, or diverted.

In Britain the resistance was headed by the Saxon Kingdom of Wessex. As early as 700 Wessex had extended its influence as far as St George's Channel, following Bishop Aldhelm's negotiations with Prince Geraint of Dumnonia. By 825 Egbert of Wessex, moving in the opposite direction, was able to annex all the land up to the Straits of Dover. For a time Mercia was subjected, and even Northumbria acknowledged Egbert's leadership. When the Viking attacks intensified from the 850s they were more than raids: large armies descended on Britain, capturing York in 867, East Anglia two years later, and preparing to assault Wessex in 870. King Aethelred, with his younger brother Alfred, had to resort to bribery to persuade the Danes to turn their attention to Mercia, which was duly conquered instead of Wessex. But in 878 Alfred defeated the Danes in a decisive battle, following which their leader, Guthrum, converted to Christianity (his followers were given no choice but to follow suit). Henceforward, Wessex, at least, with most of western Mercia – a line from London to Chester – was English, the rest of the country as far as the Tees, Danish: the Danelaw, acknowledging English sovereignty, but looking after their own affairs.

Conversion to Christianity did not necessarily entail the transformation of deceitful and aggressive leaders into virtuous adherents of the Faith; that may have sometimes happened, but the examples are unconvincing. What conversion did effect was the grouping of the

Danes within the ecclesiastical structure of western Europe. Bishops were restored, cathedrals repaired, rulers provided with trained clerical administrators who made both the collection of taxes and the conduct of diplomacy much more efficient. The contrast with Ireland is significant. There the Ostmen remained restricted to the ports, localised powers among many other native states; neither their language nor their customs were transmitted to the Irish, whereas the English Danes became an integral part of England, although retaining distinctive local characteristics. Linguistically, contemporary English and Danish were sufficiently close to be mutually comprehensible, and modern English includes many Norse elements: even the pronouns 'they' and 'their' are Scandinavian in origin; the Old English was '*hie*', '*him*' and '*hiera*'. Integration of Danes and English was rapid. When, in 918, the Dublin Ostmen invaded Northumbria to establish the Kingdom of York, Jorvik, Danes as well as English were displaced. When the York Vikings were eventually crushed, in 954, by English forces, the local Danes celebrated their English countrymen as liberators from their fellow Norse.

Even more than Offa had been, Alfred was a monarch in the accepted European style. The state was organised, charters granted, coins issued, laws applied and learning, which had been badly damaged with the destruction of the monasteries, revived. Alfred himself made translations into the vernacular from the most important Latin works – including Bede's history – and encouraged trade. For the first time since Roman rule collapsed recognisable towns appeared built to a regular plan.[23]

Backed by organisation of this quality, Alfred's successors (he died in 899 and was succeeded by Edward, the Elder, Athelstan and Edmund, who died in 946) were able to recover much of the Danelaw. By 937 Athelstan had regained the whole territory of England and had become the ruler of what was perhaps the largest and most prosperous country of western Europe, treating on equal terms even with Emperor Otto (the young Emperor asked to marry one of Athelstan's sisters: the English King sent him two to choose from). The royal council, the *Witan*, predecessor of the later privy council, formalised and recorded business. Previously existing local assemblies were replaced by an organisation of shires, with a shire reeve in charge. Shires were divided into 'hundreds', each with its own court and obligations, and sub-divided into groups of ten households. Coinage, of an unsurpassed quality for the time, was standardised, and the Church, on which government depended for the provision of officials, reformed and re-endowed. Buildings of considerable size (the cathedral at Winchester was 250 feet long) and of the finest quality – Brixworth in Northamptonshire is a prime example – were erected.[24]

No consistent attempt was made by tenth-century English kings, distracted as they were by problems with the Danes, to extend their own boundaries. Northumbria therefore remained semi-detached from the remainder of England. In a remarkable display of continuity the old royal house of Bernicia, founded in the sixth century, remained in control until the eve of the Norman conquest. Isolated as they were from the Saxon south by the Danish Kingdom of York, Northumbrian earls were left to fend for themselves. If, as happened in 937, a Scottish army with support from Vikings and from the remaining Britons could force its way south, King Athelstan could crush the intruders, but maintaining Northumbrian borders was not a priority of Wessex kings, and in 945 Edmund found it convenient to cede Cumberland and Westmorland to the Scottish King Malcolm in return for a vague pledge of loyalty.

On the north-eastern frontier Northumbrian influence was being extended even as Northumbrian territory was being lost. The tenth and eleventh centuries saw the beginning of the anglicisation of Scottish administration, as the Gaelic titles 'mormaer' and 'toisech' became replaced by 'earl' and 'thane', and the land became divided into 'shires' – which is not to suggest that the persons so designated were necessarily Anglo-Saxon, but thanages were established all over the east coast from Haddington to Dingwall, and English became the dominant language of that region.

Like Scotland, Wales was moving towards a political consolidation, as many of the smaller states were beginning to be absorbed into three major kingdoms of Gwynedd, Powys and Deheubarth.[25] Unity and nationhood should have been easier to attain in Wales than in Scotland, divided as that country was between Britons, Picts, Scots, Anglians and Norsemen. External boundaries had been defined by Wat's Dyke and Offa's Dyke – although definition did not necessarily

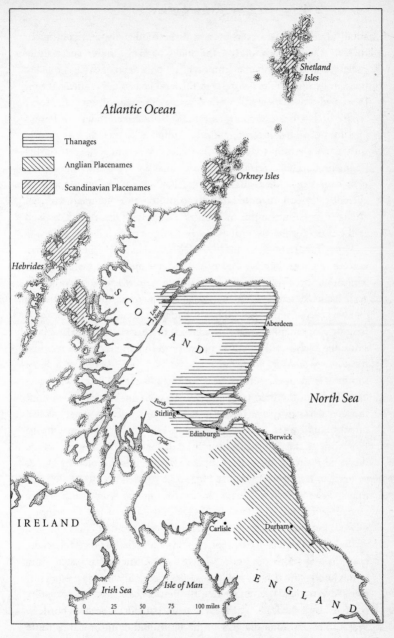

ANGLIAN AND SCANDINAVIAN SCOTLAND
IN THE ELEVENTH CENTURY

entail unquestioning acceptance, and the border disputes continued. In spite of these advantages, the states of Wales never successfully coalesced into more than a temporary unity, whereas Scotland quickly became a nation-state, before even England had so done. Viewed from the outside, Wales was still a kaleidoscope of dozens of small divisions, separated by the mountainous outcrops and river valleys. All were lordships of some sort, often at odds with neighbours, and frequently shifting allegiances as magnates flourished or declined. In spite of this fragmentation, the Welsh saw themselves as a distinct and remarkable people, the only descendants of the Britons still to maintain their ancient culture, transmitted directly from Roman Britannia. Until well after the first millennium they called themselves '*Brytaniaid*', as well as the later '*Cymry*'.

More important than any physical boundary, river or earthwork, was the linguistic barrier. Those who did not speak Welsh were aliens, while pure-bred Welshmen were 'innate gentlemen'. The long war against the Saesen had left the Welsh still intact in the heart of their country, even if some fringe districts had been nibbled away by Saxons, Irish or Norsemen. Even after the much more serious Norman incursions, the Welsh could recover, defeat powerful armies, and regain lost territory. Moreover, while no medieval Irish chief was ever able to summon enough support to speak for the 'mere Irish' ('mere', it might be noticed, in the then current sense of 'pure' or 'unmixed', without the later derogatory overtones) in negotiations with invaders,[26] Welsh princes could often agree treaties with English kings, from Offa to Edward I, as did Scottish monarchs. Not that the Welsh rulers made the same royal claims as the Scottish kings. It was accepted by Welsh princes, in theory at least, that English kings exercised some superior rights. Such acknowledgment, of course, did not carry with it any guarantee that the Welsh would not take advantage of any opportunity offered: but that was accepted by all parties.[27]

Wales benefited from the replacement of Mercia, its powerful neighbour, by Wessex as the leading English state. Mercia had eaten away at the border districts of Powys and Gwynedd, up the river valleys of Dee, Severn and Wye, and along the north coast, but Wessex, fully occupied with the Danes, had less time to spare for its western borders. Wales' most pressing dangers in the ninth and tenth centuries came

WALES IN THE TENTH CENTURY

from the Irish Viking raiders, who made Anglesey, prosperous and adjacent, their main target. Irish incursions, and sporadic attacks from the Mercians, encouraged Welsh leaders into an alliance with Alfred, the only ruler who had withstood the Danes.[28] Alfred's successors, including his militant daughter Aethelflaed, forcibly reminded the Welsh chiefs of the tribute that they considered was due. Asser, the Welsh Bishop of Sherborne who educated Alfred and wrote his biography, makes it clear that the south Wales regions '*pertinebant ad Alfred regem*'. Welsh princes were frequent attenders at the Wessex courts, witnessing charters in their capacity as *subreguli* – under-kinglets. Some notables like Edwin ap Einion or Gwgan mab Elstan took English names, and the English word for 'prince', '*aetheling*', in the sense of king's son, passed into Welsh as '*edling*'. Such submission was nothing more than prudent, but prudence did not commend itself to all, and the famous poem 'Armes Prydein' (*c*.930–40) is an agitated call to resist the 'dung gatherers of Thanet', and to reproach the Welsh collaborators.[29]

The rich lands of France, intersected by great rivers, were also a magnet for invaders, who sailed unhindered up the Seine, Loire, Charente and Garonne; as had been done in England, the French authorities had to compromise with the Danish raiders. Their most persistent adversary was one Rollo, a former ally of Alfred's opponent, Guthrum, who between 911 and 933 was granted the territory now known as Normandy, on condition that his people adopted Christianity and recognised the overlordship of the French King, Charles the Simple. In this way separate bands of Norse invaders were settled in eastern England and western France, each adopting the language and customs of their reluctant hosts. Not much of France was in fact left in the control of the French King. The great duchies of Aquitaine and Toulouse sealed off the country south of the Loire; in the west Brittany and Normandy and in the east Burgundy were effectively independent states.

The Kingdom of England held together better until the end of the millennium, fending off renewed Danish raids either by resistance or by payments of 'Danegeld'; but as Kipling pointed out, 'If ever you pay the Danegeld, you never get rid of the Dane.'[30] What the need for raising Danegeld did produce was an efficient tax system, which, although successful, did not make for popularity. Searching for allies, King Aethelred – the famous 'Unready' – looked over the Channel, where Rollo's 'Normans' were now developing their own vigorous society. Aethelred married the Duke of Normandy's daughter Emma in 1002, and with the marriage the ruling families of England and Normandy were fatefully united.

Horrified by the huge cost of buying off the Danes, Aethelred lived up to his nickname (in 'Aethelraed, Unraed', the original pun, '*unraed*' is literally 'without advice') by ordering the slaughter of all the Danes still living in England. This impossible command could never have been carried out, but there was a general massacre of the Danes in Oxford in 1002.

A credible excuse for a war of conquest was thereby handed to King Swein of Denmark. He was not immediately able to take advantage of it, but the raids continued with increased severity. England was thereby rapidly impoverished, its fighting forces damaged, and when Swein launched his decisive blow in 1013 resistance crumbled. Within weeks Swein was in control of England, and Aethelred a fugitive in Normandy. After fierce resistance by his son, Edmund 'Ironside', the conflict was terminated in 1016 by a treaty which stipulated that Swein's son Cnut – King Canute – should be accepted by the English as king after Edmund's death – which conveniently occurred within days.

England was now part of the Danish empire. Cnut left the administration of England divided among a new structure based on the old kingdoms of Northumbria, Wessex, Mercia and East Anglia, to be ruled by earls, of whom the most unscrupulous and violent was Godwin of Wessex. The Northumbrians remained loyal to their native dynasty, and after their Earl Uhtred had been murdered on Cnut's orders in 1016, his son Aldred continued to rule in Bernicia. When he too was assassinated in 1041 the Danish Earl Siward found it wise to marry Uhtred's daughter Elfleda. Uhtred had been able to annihilate a Scottish invasion in 1006 at Durham, but ten years later was defeated at Carham on the Tweed. For confrontation, Earl Siward substituted co-operation, taking his Northumbrian forces to enable King Malcolm to suppress Macbeth's revolt – and, as in Shakespeare's play, lost his eldest son in the battle.[31]

Cnut's reign provided a valuable breathing space, free from Scandinavian attacks, during which prosperity could be restored; some degree of continuity – and a further dynastic complexity – was ensured by the King's marriage to the widowed Queen Emma. During the eighteen years of his reign Cnut agreed that the by now largely Anglian Lothian should become part of Scotland, thus laying the foundation for the later Anglo/Norman character of the state. Cnut also continued the links with Continental Europe, making a pilgrimage to Rome and giving substantial donations to many churches, including the cathedral of Chartres.

Four years after Cnut's death in 1035, and the short reigns of his two sons, the throne of England reverted to the native dynasty of Wessex, the descendants of Alfred. Their last representative was Aethelred's younger son, Edward the Confessor (1042–66), a man too reasonable and too fair-minded to exert the hard rule necessary to control the unruly and independent earls. Edward's life until the age of twenty-five had been spent in the hospitable court of the Norman dukes: he spoke French, the first of the English kings to do so, imported Norman masons to begin his great abbey of Westminster, and a Norman clergyman to become Archbishop of Canterbury.

It was the death of Edward in 1066 that began the chain of events that made the year famous, the year in which English rulers laid their country open to complete domination by a much smaller power; indeed, it could be said that the English aristocracy committed collective suicide. After Earl Godwin's death in 1053 his sons Tostig and Harold became Earls of Northumbria and Wessex. Tostig made himself so unpopular in Northumbria as to provoke a rebellion. Harold attempted mediation, and agreed that his brother should be replaced by Morcar, younger brother of Edwin of Mercia. Tostig was furious, taking himself off to Norway, but while the Mercians were willing enough to defend their own territory against any external aggressions they felt no particular loyalty to Harold, either as Earl of Wessex or, as he became for a short time, King of England. Harold was unquestionably in a position of great strength, the most powerful man in the land, but one with little entitlement to the English throne. The clear and legal successor in the royal line of Wessex, when Edward the Confessor died childless, was Edmund Ironside's grandson Edgar

Atheling, Prince Edgar. Another contender was Duke William of Normandy, who argued, probably with some justification, both that Harold had promised to cede his claim on the throne to him, and that the dead King Edward, who had enjoyed the protection of Normandy during Cnut's reign, had also named him as his heir – which Edward's pro-Norman inclination also made likely. Since Edgar, who had been born in exile, was a child of about ten, the English *Witan* preferred Harold Godwinson as their new king. He was by some way the best choice they could have made, a brilliant leader capable of calm diplomacy, and a more experienced soldier than his Norman rival.

The Confessor died on 5 January 1066: Harold was elected, with the dying monarch's agreement, on the same day and crowned the next morning in Westminster Abbey. The following month he was in York, convincing the Northumbrians of the justice of his cause; in May Tostig, seeking revenge, unsuccessfully attempted an invasion; in September this attempt was repeated, now with the help of Harold of Norway, accompanied by a Scottish and Irish contingent. By the twentieth the invaders had forced York; on the twenty-fifth Harold was at York, and had scattered the invasion, at Stamford Bridge killing both Harold of Norway and Tostig. On 1 October news of Duke William's landing at Pevensey reached York; five days later Harold had hurried his men two hundred miles south to London, and on 14 October met the Norman invaders near Hastings. The outcome of the hard-fought battle is the best-known fact in English history; Harold's army had been badly depleted, having suffered many casualties in the fraternal battle with Tostig; the Mercian forces refused to join Harold, and there were many who regarded Edgar Atheling as the rightful king. So divided was the resistance to Duke William that after Harold's defeat and death at Hastings, serious fighting was minimal. At a conference at Berkhamsted Prince Edgar, Edwin and Morcar of Mercia personally swore fealty to the Duke, who was crowned on Christmas Day, to the general acclaim of the Londoners, shouting support in both English and in French.

The fateful year

1066 deserves its fame. Within a single generation the English were subdued, and England rigidly held under Norman control, with resistance entirely quelled. From an independent Anglo-Danish state, albeit one receptive to French influence, England had become a conquered province of a European power. The most threatening manifestation of resistance, that of the Anglo-Danes in Northumbria which erupted in 1069, defeating the first Norman army, was brutally suppressed in the 'harrying of the North'. The Normans' effect on the rest of Britain was however delayed. King William and his sons, who between them reigned from 1066 to 1135, had their attention constantly diverted from their new English kingdom to their old French duchy. Scotland was too far off and too poor to warrant undue interference. A more rewarding policy, and one that was to be a constant factor in the relationship between the two countries, was to establish a feudal superiority. Scotland was already a political entity, and could be encouraged to accept the same position with reference to England as Normandy did to the King of France, that of a feudal vassal.

Wales presented a different problem to the invaders. There was no ruler in an acknowledged position of power, but rather constantly shifting alliances of petty states. For a brief period the territory had been brought under the authority of the Gwynedd ruler, Gruffudd ap Llywelyn, described in the *Anglo-Saxon Chronicle* as 'King over the whole of Wales'. Gruffudd had expelled the Mercian Saxons from their intrusive settlements on the north coast, and raided as far as Hereford, where he burnt the cathedral in 1055, and killed the bishop and sheriff in battle during the following year. After his death in 1063, murdered by his own men during the course of a successful Saxon assault under the command of Harold Godwinson, Wales reverted to its customary state of 'family and inter-dynastic conflicts, raids, kidnappings and murders'.

Since even at the height of his power Gruffudd had accepted the status of *subregulus* to King Edward, the Saxon King's Norman successors naturally assumed similar authority, although enforcing this presumed right was postponed. A quick solution was needed to stabilise the situation, the simple answer being to provide a *cordon sanitaire* around Welsh boundaries, a solution which also had the merit of rewarding some of the adventurers who had accompanied William. Three new earls were created, in Chester, Hereford and Shrewsbury, and Pembroke, delegated to subdue as much Welsh territory as they could, their efforts being reinforced by an expedition led by William himself into south Wales in 1081. Subsequently Norman fortunes fluctuated, with rapid advances provoking vigorous Welsh reaction, but the general effect was to reduce the number of satellite states either by absorption into the Norman lordships, or into larger Welsh polities. By 1100 Wales was ringed around, from Chester to Pembroke, by Norman lordships, as it had been a millennium previously by Roman garrisons. Within these 'Marcher' earldoms authority was delegated entirely to the earls and their subordinates, who developed a system of law and courts that acted independently of royal authority. The subsequent history of Wales is as much concerned with the imposition of centralised authority on Marcher lords as upon Welsh princelings.[32]

The Norman Conquest was therefore geographically limited. Although Scotland never succumbed to them, or any other invaders, Norman influence there became quickly important, as early as 1067, when Edgar Atheling's sister, Margaret, married Malcolm III 'Canmore'. In Wales, although Normans quickly overran the west and south, the date of Wales' incorporation in the English state is more than two centuries later. Pedantically speaking, Ireland was never subject to a Norman conquest; it was the following dynasty, the Angevins, who began the painful process which was to lead to eventual subjection of Ireland – and that date is a matter of some debate.

But in England the change was immediate. The English became, as later did the Irish, a repressed majority in what had been their own country, subject to foreign rulers, speaking a strange tongue, and enforcing new laws. Inside a generation the English aristocracy had been supplanted by the newcomers, who married only within their own society; within two even many of the townspeople themselves were French-speaking.

It was however a time of rapid development all over Europe, which would have affected English life whether or not the Conquest had taken place. Within a few years of Hastings other Normans had driven the Byzantines from Italy, and founded new kingdoms both there and in Sicily. Parallel with this expansion came the revived power of the papacy, which had for the two previous centuries become a discredited and weakened institution. Only after 1047, when the German emperors hit upon a series of worthy nominees, were respectable Popes appointed and reform made possible. Gregory VII (1073–85) initiated the restored papacy, asserting his influence to the extent of forcing the Emperor to his knees in the snow at Canossa, and claiming – for the first time in a thousand years – supreme power over Christians in the west (including the title of Pope, previously accorded indiscriminately to all bishops). Calixtus II (1119–24) consolidated the supremacy of Rome, and from that time a resurgent papacy became inextricably enmeshed in European politics.[33]

Anglo-Saxon and Danish kings had made pilgrimages to Rome, archbishops had been regularly installed, and papal arbitration sought, but there were few reasons, other than dynastic relations and the protection of trade, for England to be involved with the Continental powers. Whilst English kings did not therefore intermeddle overmuch with countries outside the British Isles, the Dukes of Normandy were in permanent opposition to their feudal overlord, the King of France, and inevitably enmeshed with foreign disputes. For at least four centuries after the Conquest England was therefore caught up, often to its disadvantage, in Continental struggles.

After the triumph of Canossa the Holy See played a much more important part in English politics. The monastic orders of Citeaux, Cluny and Grandmont spread with great rapidity, and the beginnings of a new philosophy and respect for learning were discernible. Neither British kingdom could have avoided the consequences of these developments, and indeed the new monasticism had already been established in England during the tenth century. Both countries, the conquered and the free, evolved similar institutions and progressed side by side – although often in violent disagreement. Much of English life continued little altered, especially in the regions south of the Humber. Such new laws as were introduced concerned mainly the administration of forests; for the rest Anglo-Saxon types of administration continued with changes of name rather than more fundamental alterations, as thanes became earls, reeves sheriffs, shires counties. The Anglo-Saxon researchers and scribes who prepared the Conqueror's Domesday Book worked in a tradition already four hundred years old in creating a new version of the Tribal Hideage, and the Bayeux Tapestry recording William's triumph was worked by English ladies. It was however the eventual emergence of the English language that signified the final digestion of Norman influence into the cultures of both England and Scotland.

CHAPTER 3

1066–1300

Family quarrels

SINCE IN TWENTY-FIRST-CENTURY EUROPE neither religious nor dynastic matters are considered important – and those who take religious matters seriously are often, not without reason, distrusted – it is a mistake to believe that these were not vital considerations in previous generations. The smallest theological, or even liturgical, differences could be hotly argued, and result in violent conflict. A weak or tyrannical king could bring misery to a nation, and a disputed royal succession might result, as it did in England after 1135, in a generation of anarchy. The family affairs of English, Norman and Scottish rulers therefore merit attention, and are rarely dull.

The death of William the Conqueror in 1087 left three sons with a claim to the succession. It was a complex inheritance. As King of England, duly acclaimed and crowned, William was himself an emperor responsible to no external power. As Duke of Normandy on the other hand, he owed allegiance to the King of France (not that the latter was usually in a position to insist on his feudal privileges). The Conqueror intended that his second son, William Rufus, should inherit the Kingdom of England, the eldest, Robert Curthose, should have the Duchy of Normandy, whilst the youngest, Henry, should content himself with a money payment.

Rufus and Henry were both unscrupulous and violent characters, though Henry was the abler of the two; Robert seems a more attractive personality, without the concentrated malevolence that made his father and siblings so formidable. Neither Robert nor Rufus was content with his inheritance, and a period of rebellion and civil war duly followed, ending with Rufus assassinated and young Henry crowned King of England (1100–35), planning to dispossess Robert from his Duchy of

Normandy. When this was achieved, at the battle of Tinchebrai in 1106, what has been called the English conquest of Normandy was completed; Robert was packed off on a crusade. In the remaining years of his reign, Henry I consolidated the English hold on Normandy against any French attempts to assert their rights, and secured his family's position by dynastic alliance.

Henry's active and wide-ranging sex-life had produced twenty-odd bastards, but only one surviving legitimate child, Matilda. As self-centred and aggressive as any male Norman, Matilda had been married off to the German Emperor Henry V, it being hoped thereby to encircle France with an Anglo–German alliance. Widowed in 1125, the Empress Matilda – she insisted on retaining the title – was then married to Count Geoffrey of Anjou, who controlled the lands south of Normandy. In spite of her advanced age, thirty at the time of the birth of her first child, Henry, in 1133, she went on to produce three boys, thus securing the succession.

But not an undisputed succession. When Henry I died in 1135 the heir was the two-year-old Prince Henry, opposed by an acceptable adult contender, the old King's nephew Count Stephen of Blois. From 1135, when Stephen assumed the crown, until 1153, when a settlement was finally reached allowing for the succession of Prince Henry, much of England was sporadically devastated. The prolonged period of anarchy also presented opportunities both to the Welsh and to England's northern neighbours, which they were quick to seize.

Like England, Scotland was becoming an Anglo-Norman kingdom, but with one very great difference: Scotland had been spared conquest and all that followed. After an inconclusive sortie King William contented himself with accepting some form of homage from the Scottish King Malcolm, and the new castle built on the Tyne by Robert Curthose in 1081 was intended to be an isolated outpost of English sovereignty.[1]

It was the old Saxon royal family, descendants of Alfred, who initiated the changes to Scottish society. In 1069 Margaret, sister of Prince Edgar and granddaughter of Edmund Ironside, married Malcolm III 'Canmore' of Scotland (1058–93). Queen, and later Saint, Margaret brought both Norman and English standards of comfort and civility to what was then deemed wild and barbarous country. Malcolm, who is the Malcolm who brings Shakespeare's Scotch play to a close, was a Celtic monarch of the old style, but one who accepted his wife's innovations. Queen Margaret's chapel in Edinburgh Castle is one of the few surviving examples of the new architecture brought to Scotland by her English followers. In liturgy and ecclesiastic law, relaxed Celtic practices were superseded by more rigid Roman standards. The Queen's influence continued under the reigns of her sons Edgar (1097–1107), Alexander (1107–24) and David (1124–53), who between them controlled Scotland for over fifty years. This long period of anglicisation, which included many ecclesiastic developments, such as the establishment of the new see of St Andrews (the building being supervised by masons brought north from Durham), reinforced the existing Northumbrian settlements. King David made a special effort to persuade his subjects to 'live in a more civilised style, dress with more elegance and eat with more refinement' by offering tax exemptions. The culture and language of the Scottish kingdom was henceforward primarily English, albeit an individual version with Gaelic undertones, although the Kingdom of Scotland was to be defiantly independent of England, and relations between the two countries frequently less than friendly.[2]

Anglo–Scottish borders remained in dispute. In the normal course of events Scotland, poorer and with fewer men to call to arms, could never make much headway against England; but when English attention was diverted by European wars, or by internal dissent, the opportunity to invade was tempting. The civil wars which followed Henry I's death presented too good an opportunity for the Scots to resist. King David erupted into northern England, ravaging the region in 1136–38 with a brutality that horrified that not very sensitive epoch. After his attack David was able to lay claim to England as far south as the Tees and the Ribble, the whole of the former Bernicia. It could not last, and a reckoning was sought. The battle of the Standard, which took place in August 1138 near Northallerton, was the culmination of a holy war, led by Archbishop Thurstan of York, which smashed the Scottish army – actually composed of Scots, English, Galwegians, Norsemen and Germans – and encouraged King David to concentrate on securing his position in Scotland.[3]

It was in this period that Norman adventurers took the lead in Scotland. The de Bruis (who became Bruces), FitzAlans (who became

Stewarts), Morvilles, Comyns and other French families used their talents and influence to carve out extensive holdings, often straddling the borders, while Norman ecclesiastics administered the estates, churches and abbeys that David established, as far north as the Moray Firth. Unlike the situation in England, where within a generation after the Conquest almost all the English proprietors had been dispossessed, many of the Celtic lords continued undisturbed in Scotland. The Canmores were not only Anglo-Norman but Celtic kings, speaking Gaelic as well as French and English, uniting in themselves the Gael and the Gall – the Celts and the foreigners. The ancient symbols of Celtic kingship were retained, including until the thirteenth century the royal inauguration ceremony, in which the '*ollamh rig Alban*', the king's poet, presented the royal sceptre, and, for much longer, the royal harpist continued to play. Saxons, too, survived less molested in Scotland than in England: post-Conquest charters are sprinkled with English personal names – Ulfkil, Aethelstan and Alfric. English, or 'Scottis' as the variant on northern English became known, more rapidly supplanted French in both polite and legal intercourse than it did in England. The subjects of Scottish kings were rightly described as being '*Francis, Anglis et Scottis*', the last being the Gaelic-speaking Picts and Scots.[4]

David's enlarged kingdom could not survive the restoration of order in England, symbolised by the peaceful accession on King Stephen's death of Matilda's son as Henry II. King David's grandson, Malcolm, the Maiden (1153–65), was obliged to return the northern English counties, and sent forces to help the English against the Count of Toulouse. William the Lion (1165–1214), Malcolm's brother, tried to regain that lost territory forcefully in 1174 by invading England.

Captured at Alnwick and imprisoned at Falaise in Normandy, King William was obliged to submit. Scotland officially became a subject state: churchmen and barons, as well as the King, swore loyalty to the King of England 'against every man in respect of Scotland and in respect of all his other lands'.

Scotland was only a part of King Henry II's empire.[5] As well as the Kingdom of England and the Duchy of Normandy, Henry was also heir to his father Geoffrey, Count of Anjou, and took his family cognomen of Plantagenet. When in 1151 he married Eleanor (Alienor) of

Aquitaine, he therefore controlled an empire ranging from Scotland to the Pyrenees. During his long and by no means uneventful reign, the character of England changed. Before the Conquest it had been a prosperous Anglo-Danish state, with old-established links to the Continent, but closely tied to Scandinavia. As a unit of the Angevin Empire, England became an integral part of the wider European community. Whereas before there had been two languages, Anglo-Danish and Latin, now there were three: that fusion of Anglo-Saxon and Norse which was becoming recognisably English; French, or that rather peculiar variety imported by the Normans and rapidly anglicised, the tongue of the aristocracy and of love letters; and Latin, persisting, as it had been in the time of Bede, the language in which law, administration and serious discussion was conducted. The new Norman earls might talk to their wives in French, as the old Saxon *earldormen* had in English, but the important business of life was conducted by their chaplains and chancellors in Latin.

There is some evidence that, as might be expected, French-speaking barons learned enough English to make their demands known, as later a colonial settler would use the local African language. English thus became simplified, losing much of its previous grammatical structure, making the combination of Norse and Saxon easier, so that when it emerged as a literary language in the fourteenth century it was incomparably flexible, free of the artificial conventions which restricted other European languages.

But Latin took the strain of that dramatic eruption of learning and discussion that characterised the twelfth century. English scholars could study at the emergent schools of Oxford, but for advanced work were able to choose between the courses offered in philosophy at Paris or Laon and the medical schools of Bologna or Salerno. Little by way of scholarship had come from England during the previous 150 years of disruption, but now English philosophers were numbered among the most famous in Europe. Adelard of Bath and John of Salisbury were from Norman families, but others including Alfred the Englishman, one of the pioneers of rediscovered Aristotelianism, were clearly Saxon; distinctions of race and language were dissolved in the melting pot of Latin learning.

Henry II was a man of his times, well-educated, interested in the arts, a world removed from his rough illiterate forebears of the previous century (his grandfather, Henry I, was known as 'Beauclerc' on the strength of his rare ability to read and, after a fashion, to write). During his turbulent reign, in which the King had to take personal control of events as far distant as Scotland, Ireland and south-west France, his chancery continued to produce documentation, and his justiciars to oversee the administration, of the empire. One interesting sign of the new cohesion was that the most powerful of the King's chief officers, Walter of Coutances, was despite his appellation of English – in fact, given his birth in Cornwall, probably of British – descent. No one knew Richard of Ilchester's parentage, and Thomas Brown hardly sounds like a Norman aristocrat, yet both were numbered among Henry's most trusted advisers. It was no longer necessary to rely only on the Norman/ French to provide English leadership.

A better pattern of living

Given that Henry II was so fully occupied with the affairs of his great empire it is understandable that Ireland remained low on his list of priorities. In 1169, when the first tentative expedition to Ireland set out from Milford Haven, on the west coast of Wales, Ireland was little more than a geographical expression. Its inhabitants, although linked by a common language, religion and culture, were divided among dozens of independent chieftainships, with the only small towns those developed by the descendants of Norwegian Vikings. The idea of an Irish nation, enthusiastically propounded centuries later by nationalist historians, is, to say the least, questionable. Scotland, apart from the western and northern islands, occupied by other Norwegians, was by then an independent Anglo-Norman kingdom; England, which had achieved unity under the Anglo-Saxon kings over two hundred years before, was now, together with Wales, a constituent of the most power-ful state in Christendom, capable of summoning unmatched military strength.

There was considerable need for this. The Conquest, the suppression of the 1069 rebellion, devastating Scottish raids and the twenty years of anarchy had left much of England battered into insensibility. In

Wales the native principalities had continued to render the homage previously paid to Anglo-Saxon kings, a tribute confirmed in July 1163 at a meeting with the King and his heir at Woodstock, but conditions were never settled enough to give much hope that this would be maintained. Only months later Rhys ap Gruffudd – the Lord Rhys, Prince of Deheubarth – invaded Ceridigion. Henry's punitive expedition of 1165, supported with all the resources of the Angevin Empire, was a humiliating failure.[6] In north Wales Owain ap Gruffudd, Prince of Gwynedd, was able to take advantage of this by initiating a correspondence with Louis VII of France, in which he styled himself for the first time as '*Waliarum princeps*'. Lords of Gwynedd had been expanding from their centre in Anglesey since the early days of the remarkable Gruffudd ap Cynan, Owain's father, who by the time of his death in 1137 had survived for over sixty years, extending his territory into that of his neighbours, and avoiding conflict with the Normans. Owain's own rule – he died in 1170, thus giving an unparalleled near-century of continuity – established that the princes of Gwynedd were able to claim hegemony over all north Wales from Anglesey to the Dee, and considerable influence elsewhere, but the south remained to the same extent subject to the Lord Rhys. From the 1170s onwards relations between the Crown and Welsh princes were more clearly formalised. Owain's heirs were anxious to reach an accommodation, and the Lord Rhys acknowledged Henry as his feudal superior and in return – quite remarkably – was appointed as Justiciar, in effect viceroy in *Pura Wallia* – Welsh Wales beyond the Marches.

Further afield the newly established Kingdom of Jerusalem, held by Henry's Lusignan vassals, was the object of persistent Islamic resentment, ensuring a constant drain of resources into the Crusades. Henry was also faced with intermittent rebellions from his unruly sons, who could count upon support from at least some of his nominal subjects, bent on dividing the empire during his lifetime. The feud between the King and Archbishop Thomas à Becket was finally settled by Becket's murder in 1170, but this had the effect of embarrassing the King even further as St Thomas of Canterbury became an instant, and very popular, martyr.

Why, then, an expedition to Ireland? That island was only just recovering from the prolonged devastation of the Viking raids. Its

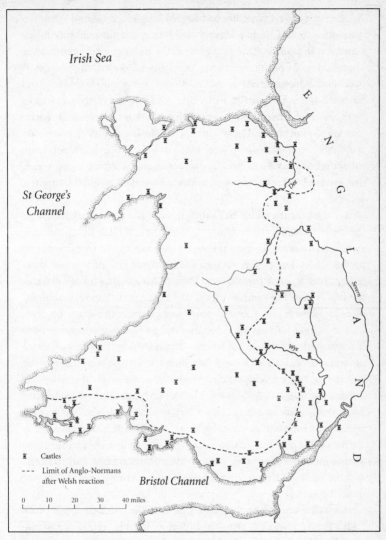

THE NORMANS IN WALES IN THE TWELFTH CENTURY

incoherent political structure had altered little in a thousand years. No contender to the High Kingship had succeeded in giving as much substance and permanence to the title as the Northumbrian and Wessex kings had made of the equivalent Anglo-Saxon 'Bretwalda'. The economic and cultural advances that had benefited Anglo-Saxon England bypassed Ireland. Nowhere in Ireland could be found such towns as York, Norwich or Ipswich, to say nothing of that international centre, London, or such churches as St Albans, Hexham or Winchester. To the lithocentric Normans, who left a trail of huge buildings from Edinburgh to Damascus, the tiny oratories and scattered monasteries, and even the tall round towers, of Ireland signified an almost barbaric society.[7]

But the century and a half since the death in 1014 of Brian Boru, the most successful of the aspirants to the title of High King, had seen significant changes. During the prolonged and vicious warfare of the previous two centuries monasteries had suffered at least as much from fellow Irish as from the Vikings. Phelim, King-bishop of Munster in the first half of the ninth century, was a singularly famous plunderer of other clerics, and Clonmacnoise was raided more often by Irish than by either Vikings or Angevins. As the Ostmen's enclaves were brought under Irish control warfare diminished and major provincial powers emerged. The Uí Néill, for long the foremost contenders for hegemony, had become dominant in Ulster, although the tribe was divided between hostile factions. The Dal Cais, who had evolved under Brian Boru to become the O'Brien dynasty, had established themselves as rulers of Munster, contending with the O'Connors of Connacht. A degree of stability was achieved as the larger units began to function as recognisable states, with written laws, officials, taxes and charters, and the status of minor kings changed to something resembling that of feudal vassals.

Ironically, since their forebears had done so much damage to the Irish Church, it was the Ostmen, with their links stretching across the Irish Sea to Britain, and further afield through the Viking diaspora, who started the slow process of bringing Ireland back into wider Western society. King Sihtric Silkbeard of Dublin (obit.1042), after a pilgrimage to Rome, founded a bishopric, with the first incumbent, Donatus, nominated by Canterbury. The Norman conquest of England strengthened these links, as that brisk Italian, Archbishop Lanfranc of Canterbury, imposed his authority on the Ostmen. The bishops-elect of Dublin, Waterford and Limerick, most of whom had previously been monks in England, were consecrated by Lanfranc's successors, who also despatched admonitions to the O'Brien kings of Munster, calling upon them to summon ecclesiastic councils to reform Church abuses. Apart from the usual complaints of simony and laymen holding ecclesiastical offices, two specific items worried Canterbury and Rome – the proliferation of bishops without diocesan responsibilities, and unsatisfactory marriage laws: 'It is said that men exchange their wives as freely and publicly as a man might change his horse.'[8]

Ecclesiastical councils were duly held, and both the old Irish and the new Canterbury bishops agreed to a reconstruction of the Irish Church, with four provinces, Armagh, Cashel, Dublin and Tuam, although it would be many years before the new structure became properly effective. More immediate results came with the reforms of St Malachy (1148), a close friend of Bernard of Clairvaux, who was also the Irish saint's biographer. By the mid-twelfth century the Irish Church began to conform to the habits of the Catholic world, and buildings recognisable to Norman eyes as proper churches, such as Mellifont or Boyle abbeys, were started. Nevertheless, the perpetual political divisions made it unlikely that a unified ecclesiastical system could be achieved; and the outsiders' perception of much of the country as 'almost beyond redemption and not a part of the truly Christian elite' was not without foundation.[9]

King Henry had previously, as something of an insurance policy, obtained from Pope Adrian IV (Nicholas Breakspear, the only English Pope) permission – indeed, a command – to take political control of Ireland and to pull the country into the body of the Roman Church. Having obtained this authority, the King set it to one side. Besieged as he was by other more pressing concerns, Henry would, left to himself, have been reluctant to assume even more expensive responsibilities by interfering with Ireland. Expensive they certainly would have been. Few rich abbeys remained to provide a quick return in the shape of loot, and only the Viking ports offered a potentially reliable tax base; all that Ireland could provide to warrant an expedition was land. And the acquisition of land involved more than a successful invasion

– the dispossession of those already holding it: nothing less than the consolidation of a conquest such as had been enforced by King Henry's great-grandfather in England and taken twenty bloody years in the enforcing.

Through a network of plots and enterprises embarked upon by minor characters Henry was however eventually inveigled into Ireland. This began, as have so many colonising enterprises, by answering an appeal from a native with a grievance. The native in question was Dermot Mac Murrough, King of Leinster, who had begun this particular feud by kidnapping Devorgil, wife of the one-eyed Tiernan O'Rourke of Meath. O'Rourke's retaliation was swift, and Dermot found himself deprived of most of his power. After some years of submission, with no prospect of any Irish support, Dermot decided to appeal to King Henry, and in 1166 made his way, via Bristol, to the King's court at Tours.

It was a bad time to gain attention from Henry. Occupied as he was with two existing wars against the Celts of Brittany and Owain Gwynedd of Wales, as well as expecting trouble from the young King William the Lion of Scotland, negotiating marriages with the Norman King of Sicily, the German Emperor and the King of Castile – all reflecting Henry's extensive responsibilities – Henry put off Dermot with good wishes. Accepting the proffered homage of feudal submission, and mollifying his new vassal with suitable gifts, the King authorised any of his subjects who had the time and inclination to help Dermot regain his lands – leaving it to Dermot to reward them suitably.

Little enthusiasm was evinced. Only Richard of Clare, Earl of Pembroke, nicknamed Strongbow, one of the three great Marcher lords, reacted, and that after an interval and at second hand. Strongbow's neighbour, the Lord Rhys, offered to liberate a troublesome captive of his, one Robert FitzStephen, a relative of the Earl's, on condition that Strongbow provided the resources for an expedition to Ireland. Off, therefore, in the spring of 1169, sailed Robert FitzStephen, with his half-brother Maurice FitzGerald and some four hundred soldiers, to regain Dermot's lands on behalf of the Earl of Pembroke.

The fate of this and subsequent expeditions is well recorded, primarily in the works of Gerald de Barri – Giraldus Cambrensis, Gerald the

For three centuries Emperor Hadrian's wall marked the division between Latin Britannia and the Caledonian tribes.

The massive ruins of Roman Britannia impressed the invading Germanics, and served as a useful quarry; the stones of Virconium built the nearby Saxon church of Wroxeter.

Pope Gregory's pun; 'Not Angles, but angels'.

Above right Pictish culture, exemplified on the Aberlemno stone, remains enigmatic.

Right The early-fifth century crosses of St Ninian's 'Whithorn' mark the rapid decay of craftsmanship and the resilience of Christianity.

Three centuries after St Ninian the now-Christian Anglians were producing elegant stone crosses in the same region. Gosforth, Cumbria (left) and Ruthwell, Dumfries (above).

Opposite Irish crosses, impressively massive, contrast with the slender and sophisticated Anglian work.

Such Celtic monasteries as Clonmacnoise were centres of learning, the arts, private devotion and communal worship; and tempting targets for Norse and Irish raiders.

Boyle Abbey, County Roscommon. Norman reformers and Angevin raiders brought a new style of monastic life, confined, regulated, disciplined and defensible.

The 'Declaration of Arbroath', an appeal to the Pope for support against England, was later appreciated as a nationalist manifesto.

After the English defeat at Bannockburn, the national independence of Scotland was an established fact.

Welshman – grandson of the Welsh princess Nest, one of the army of administrators needed to support Henry II's extensive empire.[10] Educated in Paris, he was employed constantly in both Wales and Ireland, writing four books of travel and history (the *Descriptio Kambriae* and *Itinerarium Kambriae* on Wales, and the *Topographia Hiberniae* and *Expugnatio Hibernica* on Ireland). Although Gerald was undoubtedly voluble and vain, always ready to neglect his narrative by swerving off at a tangent to recount some miraculous event, or to chastise one of his pet hates, his work is that of a trained scholar, based on personal observation and first-hand accounts. When supplemented by such other sources as the Norman-French *Song of Dermot the Earl* and the Gaelic Chronicles, Gerald's accounts give a vivid picture of the first Angevin attempts to secure a foothold in Ireland.

It is worth emphasising that these were Angevin, rather than English. Gerald writes that 'Men of three races formed the greater part of our garrison [in Ireland]; Normanni, Angli, nostri.'[11] It is understood that the first, 'who could not do without the wine on which they had been brought up', are those newly arrived from Normandy; the 'Angli' those from Norman families now permanently settled in England; and the 'men of our race' Gerald's own Norman-Welsh, and especially his own family, the Geraldines, who have been leaders of Ireland ever since – Garret FitzGerald was Taoiseach (Prime Minister) between 1981 and 1987.

Even a century after the Conquest the loyalty of the Anglo-Saxons could not be trusted too far: the militia were prepared to defend their homes against the Scots, but were rarely included in any overseas adventures. One can therefore search in vain for an Anglo-Saxon name in the annals of the first expeditions. The leaders of these were representatives of the same families that had conquered England the previous century and were even then consolidating their rule in Scotland, with the foot soldiers including formidable Welsh archers from Strongbow's lands – all contrary, as it turned out, to the desires of King Henry.

FitzStephen's expedition was only a limited success. His small force of armoured knights on powerful horses, interspersed with the bowmen, was irresistible in open battle, but much less effective in broken and wooded country against the lightly-armed Irish (the axe was their preferred weapon). Many of his men deserted to the opposition, but

Dermot at least was reinstated, although having to recognise his old enemy Tiernan O'Rourke as 'High King'. And Strongbow had been afforded a base for operations in Ireland, of which he took advantage the next summer. His price for helping Dermot had been marriage to the Irish chief's daughter, Eva, and succession to his lands, thereby giving the Anglo-French their first foothold in Ireland.

With a larger force Strongbow in person was more successful in the following year, capturing Dublin and Waterford, and consolidating the previous hold on Wexford – all taken from the Ostmen rather than from the Irish. Since Dermot obligingly died within a few months, Strongbow was left in actual possession of the towns and the largely theoretical rule over Leinster. This was altogether too much for King Henry, who had no desire to see one of his barons cutting out a new kingdom for himself. Profiting by a brief interlude of tranquillity in his Continental affairs the King determined (the decision was made, typically enough, at Argentan) to take Irish affairs in hand. After having accepted Strongbow's apologies for his premature enterprise, Henry embarked for Ireland with the most powerful army ever seen there, five hundred knights and some three thousand archers, conveyed together with all their equipment and provisions in four hundred ships. When he arrived, on 17 October 1171, it was too late in the year for campaigning, and indeed the King had no intention of serious fighting: his spectacular force was meant to impress.

And impress it did. Without a blow being struck almost all the Irish chiefs of the south and midlands made their submission. Only Rory O'Connor of Connacht, who claimed the High Kingship, remained for a time aloof, but eventually journeyed to England to settle with Henry at Windsor in 1175. Normans, Welsh and Irish celebrated Christmas together at Dublin, when the Irish guests 'greatly admired the sumptuous and plentiful fare . . . and most elegant service by the royal domestics . . . and even began to eat the flesh of the crane, which they had hitherto loathed'. But the royal feast was held in a temporary wattle-and-daub hall, there being no Dublin building suitable for such a party.[12]

Superior military technology enables invaders to effect speedy conquests, but does not guarantee permanent rule in the face of continued opposition. For this Romans, Normans and their British successors depended upon the acceptance of a system of law. When this had been successfully imposed, the survival of the conqueror's values could be ensured for a very long time indeed. The English-speaking world, including such countries where English is only one of the official languages, such as South Africa and India, still follows the legal principles of Magna Carta, reluctantly granted by Henry II's son John; Roman law, the basis of legal systems in the francophone and Hispanic worlds, has an even longer history. In Ireland Brehon law had been recognised since the beginnings of Celtic settlement, and had evolved into a sophisticated system suitable for a pastoral, hunter-gatherer society, although the urban settlements had developed their own mercantile laws. Land belonged to the community, and succession was within a kinship group – the system known as tanistry – rather than the Roman practice of primogeniture. Norman administrators, brought up on the Institutes of Justinian, appealing to copious written authorities (forgery of spurious documents was something of an industry in medieval Europe), had little sympathy for the usually orally-transmitted Irish law.[13] With the appointment of Hugh de Lacy as Justiciar – effectively viceroy – and the grant of a charter to Dublin the process of anglicising Ireland began.

After civil affairs came ecclesiastic. The Irish Church had long been a source of worry to Rome and Canterbury, given as the clerics were to concupiscence and subjection to the depredations of the lay power. Church worked closely with state in any medieval society, both exacting contributions in return for their services and maintaining the cohesion of society. If Ireland was to be brought under Norman discipline, the Irish Church must follow Roman orders. The Irish had however a strong sense of their past importance in Christian history, and remained proud of their traditions of sanctity. Those clerics who met at Cashel for the council in 1171–72 were divided between the pro-Normans, led by Christian O'Connor, Bishop of Lismore, trained in France, Papal Legate and fellow novice at Clairvaux of Pope Eugene, opposed by the traditionalists, headed by Archbishop Laurence O'Toole (Lorcan Ua Tuathail) of Dublin, canonised as St Lawrence in 1226.

Naturally enough, it was the Papal Legate's party that prevailed at Cashel, and the council accordingly issued decrees ensuring that in the Irish Church 'all matters relating to religion are to be conducted on the pattern of Holy Church, and according to the observances of the English Church'. It was, Giraldus smugly reflected, 'proper and most fitting that just as by God's grace Ireland has received her lord and king from England, so too she should receive a better pattern of living from that same quarter'. It is not perhaps too fanciful to see in the comfortably superior attitudes of the Anglo-Normans, condescending towards the Irish, a foretaste of those that characterised the English in their relations with their subject and allied communities in the later Empire, or indeed a reflection of the Romans' treatment of their imperial subordinates. When Giraldus describes Domnall of Limerick as 'a man, who, for an Irishman, was not devoid of good sense', one can detect the same smug note found in Tacitus' appreciation of the Caledonians, or in Kipling's tribute to Gunga Din.[14]

There was no time for King Henry to do more, since the rest of the Empire was demanding attention. Rome was investigating the death of Thomas à Becket, and demanding Henry's appearance before Papal emissaries. The King had therefore to leave Ireland on 17 April 1172, after only six months, in order to justify himself before the Pope's legates at Avranches, which he did satisfactorily. So satisfactorily in fact that, with typical Norman thoroughness, he felt able to ask Pope Alexander III to confirm his previous appointment as 'Lord of Ireland'. This the Pope obligingly did, adjuring all Irish princes and bishops to obey the King, and exhorting Henry to extirpate the 'abominable foulness of the Irish'. As a bonus, Henry considered that Ireland might make a suitable lordship for his youngest son, John, hitherto unprovided for, and accordingly in 1177 declared the ten-year-old to be King of Ireland, although in fact the royal title was never actually conferred and Ireland remained a 'lordship', attached to the English Crown. From that date, for many centuries, Ireland was to be an appendage, not wholly integrated into any British state, engaging the attention of British governments only when trouble there threatened or when no more pressing matters interfered. Sporadic efforts were made – King John, Richard II, Elizabeth, James, Cromwell (famously), William III, Pitt, Peel and Gladstone were only the more prominent of those who attempted, in their rather diverse ways, to complete the unfinished work.

Henry II died in 1189 a disappointed man, harassed by rebellious sons and a resurgent France. The King had provoked his own misfortunes by preferring the younger John to the elder son Richard, who joined forces with the King of France, the young Philip Augustus, in an attempt to assert his rights.[15] Richard was supported by his mother Eleanor, at least as effective an ally as the French King. Henry lost the subsequent dynastic conflict, and was forced to acknowledge Richard as heir and to swear obedience to the counsel and the will of the King of France; but the Plantagenet territories in France were preserved. Since Henry expired two days later the oath was inoperative, and Philip vitiated it further by then helping John to remove Richard (the sequence of events, which included the famous capture of Richard on his return from the Crusades, forms the background to the Robin Hood stories). When Richard was released – 'Look to yourself, the devil is loosed,' was the message rushed from King Philip to the wicked Prince John – the Plantagenet ascendancy was restored in full. Although Richard had been born in Oxford, almost all his adult life had been spent in Aquitaine, and as king he spent only six months of his ten-year reign in England. That country served only as affording the weighty title of kingship, and as a reservoir of troops and money. It did not do so for long, since the succession of Richard's brother John in 1199 brought with it a series of what contemporaries saw as unmitigated disasters.

Ever since the Conquest, now a century and a quarter in the past, the division of power and responsibility between England and the Continent had been a source of weakness, and as the Angevin Continental empire grew, the underlying strains developed. Richard's re-establishment of the family fortunes was only achieved at tremendous financial cost, and was to prove temporary. After Richard's death, killed in a banal skirmish, John proved no match for the diplomatic pressures of the French King. His barons in Normandy and Brittany saw that their future lay with France, and switched sides: by 1204 nothing remained of Rollo's Duchy of Normandy but the name of duke and the actual possession of the Channel Islands. Magnates with lands in both Normandy and Britain had to decide which to hold; those who sacrificed their Norman territories had their interests focused in England, and the King of England was free to settle accounts with his island neighbours.

In the generation since Henry II's landing, events in Ireland had been localised, depending on the relationships between Norman barons and Irish chiefs. Some were amiable: Hugh de Lacy the first viceroy married the 'High King's' daughter and William de Burgh the daughter of Donnell O'Brien, bringing most of Limerick and Tipperary into the Norman world and founding another great Irish family, the Burkes. Others were more aggressive. Hugh de Courcy was so successful in his conquest of Ulster that he had to be suppressed by a royal army. When a man of real ability and character, such as William Marshal, was in charge, stability and justice followed, but there was no effective central-ised machinery of administration within the Anglo-Norman territories until the arrival in 1210 of King John.

John had, as a young man, already visited Ireland once in 1185, when he succeeded only in alienating both Irish and Normans, but his second, nine-week stay imprinted royal rule on Ireland. Progress had already been made as English settlers flooded in: the first Irish coinage, bearing the harp insignia, was issued in 1207, and English laws extended. Former feudal 'liberties' had been replaced by shire courts and shrieval administration – Dublin in 1190, Limerick, Tipperary, Waterford and Cork by 1207, and John's arrival in person brought decisive change. Twenty Irish chiefs found it prudent to render homage, and both the O'Connor kings of Connacht and the O'Brien kings of Limerick joined the royal forces in suppressing too-powerful Norman barons. The baronial justiciars were replaced by trusted English church-men, and by 1217 a Treasurer, supported by a team of exchequer clerks, had begun to collect the royal revenues. The King's Council in Ireland, originally composed of feudal magnates, was reinforced by these royal officials who, together with local representatives, began to meet as a parliament. Dublin Castle, newly built in stone, and a network of smaller fortresses, including a royal castle constructed at the strategic ford on the Shannon at Athlone, the gateway to Connacht, symbolised the royal authority over nearly two-thirds of the island. In this region the population was able to enjoy a hitherto unknown tranquillity, largely free from raiding, and with oppression levied in an even-handed and understandable form. Although no Irish prince had ever exercised control over the whole island, the concept of a High King had long existed; just as Queen Victoria could be accepted as a successor to the Moghul emperors of India, and as a paramount chief by African monarchs, an English king, with the prestige of a crowned sovereign, authorised by the Vicar of Christ, could be fitted into Irish traditions. Irish chiefs and Norman barons alike were accustomed to accepting a superior authority which was expected to maintain order and administer impartial justice, and as intermarriage continued distinctions between natives and newcomers became increasingly blurred.

King John's operations in Scotland were similarly effective. Richard, a man of great charm – he became a close friend of his nominal enemy Saladin, even knighting the Saracen Prince's nephew – had forged a similar personal friendship with King William of Scotland. For a consideration – the substantial sum of ten thousand marks – the penalties imposed by King Henry at Falaise were lifted by the Quitclaim of Canterbury in 1189. Future historians, pressing the claims of one side or the other, either neglected this renunciation or exaggerated its importance; legalities, and their support by copious documentation, were of much importance, but the audit of war was the final arbiter. Scotland remained a dependent state, open to English threats and the extortion of sums that could be ill-afforded, and the good personal relations ended with Richard's death. Relations between the countries similarly soured. King John prepared for war, and Scotland was only saved from invasion by the payment of another large sum and a complete submission, in which both William and his son pledged absolute allegiance to the English Crown.[16]

An opportunity to improve Scottish status seemed to be offered when circumstances in Europe changed. King John had not given up hope of regaining his Norman territories. His mother's inheritance of Poitou and Aquitaine remained, albeit often restlessly, and in 1214 he made the region a base for an offensive against the King of France, in alliance with the Emperor. The battle of Bouvines (27 July), which should have been a certain French defeat, turned into a decisive French victory, and from that date the establishment of a real national sovereignty over a considerable part of France can be dated.

More trouble stemmed from the defeat. Some English barons, previously deprived of their Norman territories, had seen no reason why they should support the King abroad, and after his defeat were insistent on having their mutual responsibilities defined. This attempt at clarification led to the signing of Magna Carta on 19 June 1215, an event of much significance to later history, but with limited effect at the time. By September many barons were in open rebellion, appealing to the French and Scottish kings for help.

The powerful King William of Scotland died in 1214, succeeded by his sixteen-year-old son Alexander II. After an initial attack, repulsed in person by John 'driving the red fox cub back to his den', both Alexander and his successor Alexander III (1249–86) opted for maintaining good relations with England. A more precise delineation of the border was begun, and the local 'Laws of the Marches' which recognised the peculiar situation there were formalised. Unlike the Welsh Marches, the Anglo/Scottish border was henceforward an international boundary between sovereign nations, although one not finalised until late in the fifteenth century.

During the reigns of the two Alexanders royal power in Scotland was extended to include the previously near-independent west. Norse and Gaelic elements had merged in the Lordship of the Isles, founded by the adventurous Somerled a century previously, uniting the Sudreys with the western Scottish seaboard. Successive Kings of Scotland and Norway continued to dispute the territory, largely controlled by Somerled's descendants the MacDougalls and MacDonalds, until the Scottish victory in the battle of Largs in 1263. At the resultant Treaty of Perth in 1266, it was agreed that the western Highlands and islands should become part of Scotland. This was a reflection of the actual situation, by which the former Norse colonies had become linguistically and culturally predominantly Gaelic; although Orkney and Shetland remained Norse until 1472 with the bishopric subject to the jurisdiction of the Trondheim metropolitan. Norse in tradition too was the north-eastern mainland, where the foundation of the see of Elgin in 1224 and the creation of shrievalties marked the firm establishment of royal power.

It was indicative of the new unity of Gael and Gall in Scotland that the King's most active supporters included not only the Gaelic magnate Farquhar MacTaggart, who became the Earl of Ross, but the Norman Comyn Earls of Menteith and the de Moravia (originally Freskin, an example of linguistic upward mobility) Earls of Moray.[17] It was MacTaggart who suppressed revolts in both Moray and Galloway, thus

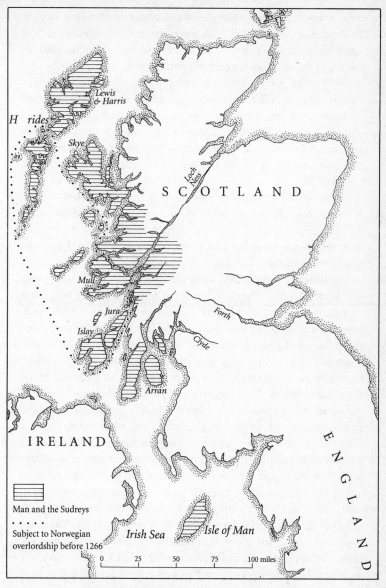

Man and the Sudreys

• • • • •
Subject to Norwegian
overlordship before 1266

0   25   50   75   100 miles

THE KINGDOM OF MAN AND THE ISLES
IN THE THIRTEENTH CENTURY

completing the extension of royal jurisdiction over the whole of what is now Scotland. Jurisdiction, however, was not the same as effective authority. In a situation not unlike that of contemporary Ireland, control could only be exercised through the great families, Celtic and Anglo-Norman; but whereas in Ireland the King was an almost permanent absentee, Scottish kings were constantly and intimately involved with political affairs. Disputes between Scottish magnates led to civil war and the weakening of central authority, causing following Scottish generations to look back on the reigns of the Alexanders as something of a golden age, and its end as a time when 'our gold was changyd into lede'.

In England Henry III succeeded his father John in 1216 at the age of nine, and was fortunate enough to have a reasonably quiet minority. A gifted man, but considerably less competent than either his brother Richard of Cornwall or his brother-in-law Simon de Montfort, Henry attempted to restore his grandfather's French empire. Failing miserably in this endeavour, the Treaty of Paris in 1259 left only Gascony still held by the English Crown. Even as the treaty was being negotiated an absurd adventure of the King's – an extremely expensive attempt to conquer Sicily as an inheritance for his second son Edmund – led to the English magnates taking over the government. Actual civil war broke out in 1264, with the opposition led by Simon de Montfort, ending the next year at the battle of Evesham with a royal victory. The King's eldest son, the Lord Edward, who succeeded as Edward I in 1272, continued the Angevin tradition of foreign adventures, only arriving in England two years later after preparing for a crusade, and after visiting his French territory. A very different character from his father, Edward 'Longshanks' was a hard, unyielding man of great energy and ability, but with a real respect for law and an insatiable appetite for argument, during whose reign English law and custom was organised and codified and royal administration enforced. In Scotland, Wales and Ireland, Edward's successes and failures shaped all future history. In Wales, the English conquest was complete and definitive; in Scotland equally a failure, in spite of brutal and vigorous efforts; in Ireland the situation remained fluid, leaving the island divided and restless.

Welshmen are Welshmen, and you need to understand them properly

After the battle of Bouvines England experienced eighty years free from foreign wars; even though serious and expensive civil conflict occurred, attention was turned inwards and to the realm's own neighbours. Following Magna Carta, subsequently confirmed and revised half a dozen times during the following fifty years, a series of laws circumscribed royal power. In 1258–59 the Provisions of Oxford and Westminster, followed by the Statute of Marlborough in 1267, and the Assizes of Clarendon and Northampton, all confirmed the superior authority of the law, and the burgeoning influence of what became Parliament. Hitherto a preserve of the baronial magnates, Parliaments were henceforward attended by the gentry, the knights of the shires, and tradesmen, the burgesses to whom both nobles and gentry were often indebted.

Reinforced as it had been by the civil war with de Montfort, the consciousness that the king had to operate with a framework of statutes differentiates Henry and Edward from their predecessors. With Edward, too, a consciousness of specific Englishness becomes apparent (the King himself may have spoken a little of the language, and royal proclamations were beginning to be made in English); one of the most outspoken objections to his father's rule had been the number of Frenchmen employed at court. This consciousness was to be strengthened by the royal attempts against the Scots and the Welsh.

It was under Edward that the borders of Roman Britannia, last effective eight hundred years before, were restored. Wales had survived the Norman Conquest remarkably intact. Certainly large areas of the most profitable land were occupied, and although some Welsh were displaced by English and Flemish incomers, life in occupied areas was reasonably stable and prosperous. Much of Wales remained unoccupied, controlled by Welsh-speaking rulers enforcing Welsh law and observing Welsh customs. The Welsh language survived and flourished, producing a vernacular literature of unparalleled richness for the time, although little was done in Latin that could bear comparison with that in twelfth-century England or France.[18]

Bishop Sulien, Bishop of St Davids in the eleventh century, who had previously studied in both Scotland and Ireland, together with his four sons – whose existence itself is an indication of relaxed Celtic standards – provided an exception. In a remarkable guide to Welsh feelings in the generation succeeding the Norman invasion Euan ap Sulien describes his father in classical hexameters as 'born of the famous race of Britons [which] once withstood the Roman army energetically, when Julius Caesar retreated, a fugitive'.[19] Euan describes his own background as: 'the land of Ceredig is certainly my homeland . . . once extremely rich, spiteful to enemies, kind to travellers, excelling all Britons in hospitality'. Another son, Rhigyfarth (Ricemarch), wrote lamenting the Norman invasion and went on to lament the failure of Welsh resistance:

> One vile Norman intimidates a hundred natives with his command, and terrifies [them] with his look. Alas the fall of the former [state], alas the profound grief: it is not possible to leave, nor even possible to stay. The people become debased, naked of limb; each man ploughs the earth, for with curved foot the nobleman as well as the poor man turns over the soil. Now the pomp of the mighty falls from the heights; each company is sad, the court is sad: there are continual sorrows and fears . . . No youth takes delight in pleasantries, there is no pleasure in hearing the poems of poets. But instead the broken spirit falls, weighed down by lethargy, and immersed in shadows, does not know that it is day . . . Serfdom is brought to the neck with a meat-hook, and learns that nothing can be had at will . . . You Wales, do not dare to carry the quiver of arrows on your shoulder, nor stretch the bow with tight bow-string, nor gird your loins with broadsword, nor raise the shield on your left shoulder. Nor does the lance vibrate in the open fist.

It is interesting to compare Rhigyfarth's sad complaint with Giraldus' writings. Rhigyfarth died in 1099; his son, another Sulien, who devoted himself to making peace with the Normans, died in the same year (1146) that the cosmopolitan Cambro-Norman Giraldus was born.

In King Edward's day the Norman policy of surrounding *Pura Walia* with buffer lordships had survived two centuries. To English monarchs, preoccupied with Continental affairs, the Marcher Lords presented a potential threat greater than that of any Welsh unrest: civil war and organised pressure by over-mighty subjects had forced the hand of all the successors of the Conqueror. Welsh rebellions might be worrisome and expensive to suppress, but never threatened the dynasty, or the state's stability, as did the King's Anglo-French barons.

The Lord Rhys' power in Deheubarth had been underpinned by his relationship with Henry II, a relationship carefully cultivated by the Welsh prince, but one which ended with Henry's death. When Rhys himself died in 1197 his achievements disintegrated and Deheubarth was partitioned. Native Welsh hegemony passed to Gwynedd, a region well placed to defend itself from either Welsh opponents or royal forces. Rugged mountains and wide estuaries cut off the heartland – the rich cornfields of Anglesey and the fertile northern river valleys – from the rest of Wales.

After Owain Gwynedd's death in 1170 dynastic strife tore into his country.[20] Owain himself had murdered and mutilated rather more of his kinsfolk than was judged appropriate by his not-too-judgmental contemporaries, and the custom was continued, three of his sons being killed or maimed by their relatives. Only after 1194 when Owain's son Dafydd was defeated by his nephew, Llywellyn ap Iorwerth, was stability restored. Llywellyn, a remarkable man, appropriately later entitled 'the great', followed the Lord Rhys' example of allying himself with strong English governments, but taking advantage of every opportunity to consolidate and extend his own power over a great part of Wales. Formal treaties in 1201 and 1218 with the English Crown acknowledged Llywellyn to be 'Chief among Welsh Princes', and he himself claimed no greater status, never attempting to annex his major territorial conquests, regarding himself rather as head of a Welsh federation.

Llywellyn the Great's grandson, Llywellyn ap Gruffudd, succeeded in 1240.[21] Styling himself only 'Prince of Wales', the younger Llywellyn functioned almost as a king, issuing charters, corresponding with foreign rulers, including the Pope, while acknowledging – when so obliged – Henry III as his feudal superior. That necessity was deflected by the Prince's combination of astute diplomacy and brilliant leadership in war, which frustrated all Henry's attempts to assert his authority. By December 1262 the King was obliged to appeal to the Lord

Edward, then pleasuring himself in Gascony, warning him of impending Welsh troubles, and admonishing the errant son in true paternal style: 'This is no time for laziness and boyish wantonness ... I am getting old ...'.

Edward dutifully bestirred himself, but since shortly after his return the civil wars with Simon de Montfort broke out, any settlement with the Welsh was delayed until the Treaty of Montgomery was signed in 1267. In consideration of a large payment Llywellyn was acknowledged as Prince of Wales, with the right to exact homage from all Welsh lords – but always himself as a vassal of the King of England. The Wales of Llywellyn was an impermanent principality, 'never more than a loose confederation kept together by fear, success, and the force of his personality'.[22] It excluded the whole of the south-west coast from Cardigan to the Severn, as well as the Marcher lordships, but within that area Llywellyn was acknowledged by all other Welsh rulers. But as so often family disputes broke the painfully settled agreements, when Llywellyn's brother Dafydd conspired with the Lord of Powys Wenwynwyn (southern Powys) to displace the Prince. The plot was discovered, Dafydd fled to London, while Gruffudd of Powys began a series of raids into Wales, from the shelter of Shrewsbury in English territory.

Whether Dafydd's presence in England was a cause or an excuse, Llywellyn refused to come to London in order to pay due homage to King Edward I on his access to the throne. His disobedience proved an error that perhaps sealed the destiny of Wales, as in the next five years Llywellyn 'fumbled his way to disaster'. By that time Edward had, since his first appointment in 1254 as Lord of Ireland, Gascony and the great castles of Bristol and Chester, acquired considerable experience of Welsh affairs, but perhaps little understanding of the Welsh people. To him Llywellyn was nothing more nor less than one of the 'greater of the other magnates of our kingdom', owing homage and obedience, whilst remaining free to administer justice within his own territories, according to traditional practice. Edward, who was always keenly attached to legality, especially when it suited him, behaved with unusual patience. The King 'so far demeaned our royal dignity' as to receive Llywellyn not in London, but Shrewsbury and Chester, on 'the confines of our land', but in spite of protracted negotiations Llywellyn did not show up. A final attempt at mediation failed, and after more than a year, in November 1276, Edward was ready for action. His campaign was short, sharp and entirely effective. Within a few months in the spring and summer of 1277 the royal army had dissolved Welsh resistance: Gascon crossbowmen and chargers were brought by sea, engineers built new roads, and the largest army since Roman times (half of whom were themselves Welsh), made success inevitable. Llywellyn was forced to terms in the Treaty of Conway. He retained his title, albeit with a much reduced jurisdiction, due homage was sworn, and the Prince was married, under Edward's patronage, to Eleanor de Montfort. Edward once his point had been gained was magnanimous, and Llywellyn went out of his way to fulfil his side of the bargain. Peaceable relations seemed a real possibility, but the appearance was deceptive.

Llywellyn's brother Dafydd, once again, began the next uprising in March 1282. When Llywellyn himself joined in Edward was furious, determined to 'put down the malice of the Welsh'. After taking charge in person the King quickly and brutally suppressed the rebellion, and this time there was no compromise. Llywellyn was killed in a scuffle by one of his own men, while Dafydd perished painfully and ignominiously on the scaffold.

1282 was not the last rebellion in Wales, but after Edward's vigorous programme of consolidation all Wales was reduced to the status of an English dominion. The most visible signs of Edward's policy, expressed in the statute issued from Rhuddlan, are such great castles as those of Conway and Caernarvon. Such magnificent fortifications, unsurpassed anywhere in Europe, served as anchors to walled towns of considerable size, in which the inhabitants could rest secure against future surprise attacks; and such burghers were almost all English. Privileged and prosperous beyond the hopes of any Welshmen, the townspeople had always been resented, and their new status could only exacerbate Welsh grudges. Edward's reconstruction reached every part of Welsh society. West Wales, from Anglesey to Carmarthen, was reorganised into shires on the English pattern. The old states of trans-Conway Gwynedd, Ceredigion and Deheubarth became the new shires of Anglesey, Merioneth, Caernarvon, Carmarthen, Cardigan and Flint, administered by royal sheriffs. The rulers of the remainder of Wales and the Marches, whether Welsh or English, were left with substantial local powers, but held as vassals to the English King. It was a situation not unlike that of the Indian raj, divided into British India, run efficiently by the British Crown, and the 'Native States', in which the hereditary rulers were left to their own devices, but under Imperial supervision.

Were Llywellyn's revolts demonstrations of what might be called Welsh nationalism? He was certainly widely supported at all levels of society. Many members of the princely families of Deheubarth and Powys joined with Gwynedd, and Llywellyn's supporters wrote of '*nostra nacio*', but other Welsh magnates allied themselves with King Edward, and the population of south-west and south-east Wales contributed handsomely to the royal forces. Although there was widespread support for 'our rights and laws', no Welsh prince ever managed to mobilise the population in a united resistance, as the Scots had succeeded in doing. Princely dynasties were often split between themselves – Powys permanently after 1160 – and it was common for the boundaries of states to change with the fortunes of succeeding generations. Leaders might acknowledge the pre-eminence of another, but would join in, or refrain from, warfare only as their own interests and sentiments dictated. Edward's future policies, however, did much to increase resentment, and a consequent sentiment of separateness, among all Welsh people.

Edwardian rule was efficient. Criminal law was also brought into line with that of England, but much else that was traditionally Welsh survived. Welsh law, which had emerged from a tribal society, in which women could not inherit, causing the property to revert to the chief, was in many respects inappropriate for a cash-based, contract-respecting society; the tribal division between land belonging to free subjects and that held in villeinage added to the complications. Nevertheless much customary civil law remained, essentially that of Hwyl Dda, administered in the old '*commote*', renamed 'hundred' in the English style, by Welsh officials. The Parliaments of 1322 and 1327 included some Welsh representation, and Welshmen began to take their place among the more senior officials, but the most important posts were occupied by Anglo-Normans – and, increasingly, by those bearing recognisably English names. The justiciars, who acted as quasi-viceroys, included such non-English names as that of Otto of Granson and Robert Tybetot, but also that of John Havering. Such men acted almost as a proto-colonial civil service, moving easily between administrative posts in Wales or Gascony, and indeed much of Edwardian Welsh policy foreshadowed much later colonial practices. One such was the systematic recruitment of Welsh soldiery, who speedily became a very important constituent of English armies. Attitudes typical of much later colonisation also emerged in official attitudes. 'Welshmen are Welshmen, and you need to understand them properly,' agreed English officials: a cleric, arrested simply 'because he is a Welshman', had to be released by royal order.[23] The townsmen, who had seen their neighbours slaughtered in the rebellions, remained angrily resentful, refusing any assimilation with the Welsh. Among the Welsh hostility simmered.

Edward I himself was convinced of the need for reconciliation. In one of the more successful recorded public relations coups, in 1301 the King had his young son, Edward, who fortunately had been born in Caernarvon in 1284, formally installed as 'Prince of Wales', declaring him the legitimate successor of the princes of Gwynedd in what was now the Principality of Wales.[24] The plan was immediately effective, and the young Prince, known as 'Edward of Caernarvon', enjoyed wide-ranging popularity among the Welsh. His eventual deposition, forced by his wife in favour of their son, who became Edward III in 1327, occasioned much resentment in Wales, which included a plot to rescue the imprisoned King. In later years the title of Prince of Wales was often bestowed on the monarch's eldest son, but only rarely was much Welsh enthusiasm generated.

It was some measure of Edward I's success that Wales became the supplier of men to the Plantagenet empire, as Gascony was of money. Welsh infantry formed a major part of English armies in Scotch and French wars, as well as in the suppression of Welsh revolts. In 1297 a force of 'bare-legged' Welshmen, 'great drinkers', accompanied the English army to Flanders, where they 'endamaged the Flemings very much'. In the following year ten thousand Welsh infantry were at the battle of Falkirk. Edward II's ineffectual expedition to Scotland in 1322 included at least 6500 Welshmen, led by Sir Gruffydd Llwyd and comprising half the infantry contingent. In the French wars more than three thousand Welsh archers, clad in green and white, perhaps the first example of a national uniform, helped the English to victory at Crécy.[25] Welsh squires, increasingly prosperous in the later years of the century, assumed the leadership in place of the hereditary lineages (although the squires themselves could usually prove princely descent). Welsh produce and trade were safeguarded by the same measures that applied to England, in effect making the principality part of an extensive free-trade zone which included Ireland and Gascony. Plantagenet power was able to exact much greater benefits from other trading partners, such as Flanders, than even a united Wales, or contemporary Scotland, would have been able to do. But Welsh soldiers were bows and swords for hire, having no permanent allegiance to their employers, and towns, the main beneficiaries from trade protection, were populated, as a matter of policy, by non-Welsh.

Welsh literature continued to flourish. That astonishing poet Dafydd ap Gwilym, probably the greatest lyric talent in Europe, anticipating and surpassing Charles d'Orléans and François Villon, with a sense of fun that matched Chaucer's, inhabited a country integrated not only into English, but European society. The poems have to be read in Welsh to appreciate their technical excellence, but translations give a flavour of the poet's genius. His subjects include, in one vein, such comic interludes as falling over the furniture in trying to get to a servant girl's bed, or seeking refuge from an angry husband in a goose-shed; or, in lyric contrast, anticipating Shelley in an ode to the skylark:

> Upwards you fly, with Cai's own attribute,
> and upwards as you go you sing each song
> a splendid charm near to the rampart of the stars,
> a long-revolving journey to the heights.
> Your feat [is now] accomplished, you have climbed high enough,
> you have indeed attained to your reward.[26]

CHAPTER 4

1300–1540

The wars of independence

ONLY TWO REIGNS span the thirteenth century from 1216 to 1307, those of King Henry III and his son Edward I. In this period the future of the constituent parts of what became the United Kingdom were settled. Edward I's conquest of Wales brought about the virtual incorporation of the principality into the English state, although leaving the Marcher lordships much of their traditional independence. The contrast with his ferocious, protracted and ultimately unsuccessful attempt to subdue Scotland, which ensured the survival of that country as an independent kingdom, is striking. Ireland, on the other hand, was governed as a royal domain with a viceroy, known as either a Justiciar or Lord Deputy, a council and, at the end of the century, a parliament; but only part of the country was under English control. Irish princes still supervised the administration of their own laws and settled arguments among themselves in the ancient fashion; and during the fourteenth century were able to extend their power and territories.

Relations between Scotland and England in the thirteenth century have been well described as a 'wary friendship, ruffled by occasional tiffs'.[1] Whatever the merits of the argument that Scottish rulers owed a duty of fealty to Kings of England, as the latter had been insisting since the tenth century, the attitude of the Scottish Council of Regency – the Guardians – to Edward I was at least an acknowledgment that some such sort of obligation existed. The Guardians, originally appointed to run Scotland during the minority of Alexander III, were elected by an assembly, met for the purpose at Scone. Comprising two bishops, two magnates and two barons, the Guardians represented Scotland north and south of the Forth, and the constituent parts of political society.

When the last Canmore King, Alexander III, died in 1286, almost the first action of the Guardians was to approach King Edward for advice, and from that advice came the first agreement on the unification of the two kingdoms. The Treaty of Birgham (1290), which foresaw the marriage of Alexander's heiress, Margaret, 'the Maid of Norway', and Edward's son, the four-year-old Edward of Caernarvon, was a carefully negotiated text. The Scots had insisted – and their conditions were accepted by Edward – on maintaining their own Church, parliament and legal system. A formal acknowledgment of Scotland's equal status as a sovereign kingdom was obtained, and in all the Guardians' terms were very much the same as those that emerged in the first 'Union of the Crowns' after 1603. 'The rights, liberties and customs of Scotland' were guaranteed, but it was accepted that the King would be expected to hold court for most of the time in England. This prospect was wrecked with the premature death of little Margaret, and King Edward was then called upon to adjudicate a disputed succession. No fewer than thirteen claimants, the 'Competitors', came forward, of whom only four had any serious case to advance.

Having been handed by the Guardians the role of arbiter, King Edward abandoned the admission of Scottish independence and took full advantage of his power to insist on his status as overlord. The adjudication was to be settled by a majority vote of 104 'auditors', forty of whom represented each of the surviving Competitors, now reduced to two. These were Robert Bruce – de Bruis – and John Balliol – de Baillieu – both Anglo-Norman incomers. Edward nominated the balance of the auditors, who could, of course, prove decisive. In fact this did not prove necessary, since Balliol gained the verdict, with no fewer than twenty-nine of Bruce's auditors voting for him. This conclusion was accepted as a correct indication of the real wishes of the Scottish people as well as prudent obedience to King Edward's clear preference: and there was little dissension shown during the short reign of King John of Scotland, who duly paid homage to Edward as overlord.

The outcome would probably have been the same had Bruce been chosen. Edward was a passionate adherent to the rule of law as governing relations between overlord and vassal. His possessions in France were held as a vassal of the French King, and Edward spent a good deal of his own time arguing out points in the Parlement of Paris and the French court. John Balliol was expected to do no less, but upon shakier legal grounds. Edward insisted that English law should take precedence in cases between the kingdoms, claiming that the Treaty of Birgham's terms had been modified by the homage given by King John. Just as Llywellyn had done, John found this incompatible with his dignity, an affront to the Scottish people. He was 'King of the realm, and dare not make answer in anything touching his kingdom, without the advice of the people of his realm' – by which was meant, of course, not the generality of people, many of whom lived in semi-slavery, but the nobility, gentry and Church. The actual *casus belli* was Edward's call to Scotland in June 1294 to provide assistance in his war against France. Not only was this refused, but King John began negotiations with the King of France. Since France asked that the alliance should be confirmed by representatives of the towns, the arrangement was meant to be something more than one of the shifting, evanescent deals brokered between kings and magnates. The start of the 'Auld Alliance' may be dated from October 1295, when the first Franco–Scottish agreement was made.

To Edward this was the grossest treachery, and his response was the brutally effective police action of an enraged potentate. An English army – although many, possibly most, of the infantry were Welsh archers – rapidly swept north, assaulted Berwick, where Edward ordered the massacre of all male creatures, down to dogs and cats, including the respectable guild of Flemish merchants, and went on to take the other great castles and force King John to ask for peace. There followed the famous episode when John earned the nickname of 'Toom Tabard' (empty surcoat), by being formally stripped of his royal regalia in an act of ritual humiliation, a gesture which had the effect of uniting Scotland and initiating what, much later, became known as the War of Independence.

The initial spontaneous uprising against the English occupation on behalf of King John, led by Sir William Wallace and another laird, Andrew Murray of Bothwell, was followed by a successful guerrilla campaign and an unexpected victory over an English army in the pitched battle of Stirling Bridge in 1297. The Scottish triumph was brief. Within a year the battle of Falkirk crushed Scots resistance, but underlined the inherent contradictions of Edward's policy. There was no hope of incorporating Scotland into the English realm as Wales had already been incorporated. Unlike Wales, Scotland had experienced centuries of national identity that went much further than the local loyalties reinforced by racial antipathy that was the main source of any Welsh resistance. More substantially, Scotland, or at least a large part of it, was feudal territory. A Scottish King, when he was in control – a far from inevitable state – could exercise the power of a feudal lord, paying off subordinate nobles by judicious rewards. No Welsh prince, unable – and indeed unwilling, so foreign it would be to Welsh law and custom – to dispose of the lands of other Welshmen, was ever in so commanding a position. Nor, given the humiliation inflicted on King John by King Edward, was there much scope for the reconciliation and future union between the two kingdoms envisaged by the Treaty of Birgham. Edward, who had abandoned his previous policy of strict legalism for that of brute force, entirely denied the independence of Scotland; it was, he insisted, like Ireland a 'terre', subject completely to English domination. Events proved this impossible, and its impossibility should have been obvious from the beginning. Wales, so much smaller, and lacking a unified kingship, had required a tremendous effort to subdue. Edward's campaigns there had cost at least £100,000, a huge sum for the day, and his castle-building programme nearly as much. Scotland would inevitably be an even more intimidating prospect.

Murray died at Stirling Bridge, and Wallace resigned his position as Sole Guardian – effectively viceroy on behalf of the exiled King John – but resistance continued under the leadership of Sir John Soules, with the support of only some of the Scots magnates. Robert Bruce, Earl of Carrick, the grandson of the original Competitor, had not given up hope of gaining the Crown, and speedily showed himself to be capable of both treachery and murder in its pursuit. Bruce began by assisting King Edward in his devastating campaign of 1304, which swept through Scotland, forcing even the formidable castle of Stirling. Almost all the Scots nobles decided to accept the rule of the apparently invincible Edward. The Parliament summoned by the English King to meet in Perth in 1305 was well attended, and submitted a plan for the government of Scotland as an English terre. That Ordinance was dramatically different from the agreement reached at Birgham only fifteen years before. As in Ireland, Scotland was to be ruled by a viceroy who, together with all his senior officials, was to be English, although assisted by a council of Scots ecclesiastics and barons. Scots and English were to be associated in revising and administering the laws, and ten Scots were to attend Westminster Parliaments. Foremost, it should be noted, among the royal councillors, and joint author of the recommendations, was Robert Bruce.

Consternation was therefore universal when in February 1306 Bruce, in a brawl in the Dumfries church of the Greyfriars, murdered his chief rival, John Comyn, head of another Anglo-Norman dynasty, who had proved himself a stauncher opponent of Edward than had the devious Bruce. Magnates were not above having inconvenient rivals finally disposed of, but to do it themselves, and in front of the high altar of a church, as did Bruce, was profoundly shocking, and led to Bruce's excommunication. But Bruce had read the mood of a section of the Scottish people correctly, and while posing as a supporter of Edward had been planning a *coup d'état*. It was successful insofar as within weeks Robert was crowned King of Scotland at Scone, but the popular support did not materialise. The Scottish Council, their forces led by Lord John of Argyll, defeated Bruce's army; by June his most prominent supporters had been captured, and Bruce himself was on the run. King Edward seemed to have been almost deranged by what he saw as Bruce's gross treachery and took the most brutal revenge. Much worse would doubtless have happened had Edward's own expedition to Scotland not been halted by the old King's death in July 1307.

An ambitious usurper and murderer did not present an attractive leader of a patriotic movement, and civil war between the partisans of Bruce and Balliol took the place of resistance to the English, wavering since the French had been forced into making peace in May 1303. The Auld Alliance was, from the start, shaky, and the French King did not concern himself with consulting his putative allies before deserting them.

Wallace, captured in the 1304 campaign – in which Bruce was supporting King Edward – was taken to London and after a show trial executed as a rebel. After Edward I's death in 1307 and the succession of his less effectual son as Edward II, Robert was able to concentrate on defeating the Balliol supporters in Scotland. A savage war of attrition was waged by the Bruce brothers, Robert and Edward, in which the Comyn country of Buchan was depopulated and Galloway, a nucleus of Balliol power, systematically devastated. That region had always been a thorn in the side of Scottish kings. A compound of Gaelic, Norse and Anglian traditions – the see of Whithorn remained attached to the province of York until the fourteenth century – the cession of Cumbria to Henry II in 1157 had encouraged Galwegian resistance to Scottish claims. Fergus 'King of Galloway' had established good relations with England, marrying his son Uhtred to the Cumbrian noble Waltheof's daughter – the Northumbrian names are striking – guaranteeing support for his claim to independence. Until the 1230s this was maintained by Uhtred's successors, culminating in the famous Devorguilla, Fergus' great-granddaughter, who married King John Balliol's father and founded Balliol College in Oxford.[2]

By 1313 Robert was accepted, even if sometimes unwillingly, as King by much of Scotland, and had expelled the garrisons from most of the Scottish castles that were still held by the English. It was in an attempt to relieve Stirling, one of the few remaining English strongholds, that a considerable English army (composed, again, largely of Welsh), led by Edward II in person, was soundly defeated. The battle of Bannockburn in 1314 was an unexpected and humiliating defeat for the English, and an inspiring victory for the Scots, but it was decisive only as part of a relentlessly protracted struggle.

Diplomacy played as important a part as combat, as both sides jostled for position at the papal court. The papacy's initial support for Scotland waned, and the English Lincoln Parliament of 1301 formally declared that no King of England would admit any outside power to interfere with his temporal rights, an action of considerable importance in constitutional history. Even more significant in the history of Scotland was the uncompromising response to the Lincoln Declaration: 'The kingdom of Scotland belongs to us *pleno jure . . .*' In spite of the advocacy of Master Baldred Bisset, on behalf of the Scots, the stronger power prevailed at Rome; it was difficult for any pope to support a King of Bruce's reputation, but the diplomatic discussion eventually led, in 1320, to the famous 'Letter from the Barons of Scotland to Pope John XXII', better known as the Declaration of Arbroath. Intended to persuade the Pope that Robert Bruce, excommunicated and a murderer, was not as black as he appeared, and owing much to Master Bisset, the major part of the letter was the – completely fictitious – rehearsal of the antiquity of the Scottish throne, tracing its origins back to Pharaoh's daughter Scotia. But the document went further, concluding, in sonorous Latin, with the stirring declaration that 'so long as an hundred remain alive we are minded never a whit to bow before English dominion. It is not for glory, riches or honour that we fight: it is for liberty alone, the liberty which no good man relinquishes but with his life.' The Declaration was, it is true, to be taken with several pinches of salt. The most famous passage is cribbed, almost word for word, from Sallust's history of the Catiline conspiracy – '. . . we seek neither dominion nor wealth . . . but freedom, which no honest man gives up but with his life' – but a good quotation is not to be sneezed at. And freedom in the early fourteenth century was a limited commodity: a great number of Scots were still in a state of servitude, in which some were to continue till the end of the eighteenth century. An extract from a single document, subsequently disregarded, does not prove that in 1320 all Scotland was united by a unanimous nationalism, and although at the time the Declaration was a damp squib, and remained forgotten for centuries, yet with hindsight it breathes a spirit of national identity that no other country in Europe at that time had developed; certainly not Ireland, Wales, or even England could demonstrate as much unity of purpose.

After Bannockburn the war dragged on for another fourteen years. An attempt to strike at England through an invasion of Ireland, led by Robert's brother Edward, devastated that country for three years, but eventually led to a Scots retreat. Formal peace was eventually agreed at the Treaty of Northampton in 1329. Scotland paid reparations, but had its independence 'separate in all things from the kingdom of England' confirmed. But the mutual irritation and the discontent of Balliol's dispossessed supporters ensured future strife. A second civil war, with the English again supporting the Balliols, erupted. Like all following Anglo–Scottish clashes, it was futile. Neither side had clear war aims. Scotland's independence had been acknowledged, but it never took too long before an attack was launched on England – an attack always impossible of success. For their part, English rulers could have no real hope of anything better than a reasonably co-operative Scotland, but found it difficult to resist retaliation – and sometimes succeeding in getting the retaliation in first.

After Edward III succeeded his father in 1327 the attention of England was diverted by the beginning of another interminable conflict, the Hundred Years War against France in which the Plantagenets attempted to re-establish the Angevin position. From Edward III's first expedition, when Welsh and English archers proved themselves masters of any battlefield, in 1332, which culminated in the battle of Crécy, to the last hopeless fight at Castillon in 1447, when the old Earl of Shrewsbury charged the French guns, the military energy of the kingdom was diverted over the Channel. Scotland was the object of only intermittent concern.[3]

When English policy was driven to consider Scotland it was usually in the context of France and the revived alliance between the two countries, which usually however contained more of a threat than the reality of any practical assistance. On the contrary, the opportunities that seemed to be offered by the absence of the English forces in France resulted in disaster for the Scots. Defeats in 1332 and 1333 were crowned by the particularly destructive battle of Neville's Cross, in 1346, which resulted in the capture and eleven-year imprisonment of King David II (1327–71). David was the last of the brief Bruce dynasty and was succeeded by Robert Stewart (Robert II, 1371–90), nephew of *the* Robert Bruce and the first ruler of a family the last of whose monarchs, Queen Anne, finally superintended the union of England and Scotland.

For a century after Robert Stewart's accession English and Scottish clashes were limited to the occasional raid or retaliatory expedition. For many years life continued uncomfortably primitive, as Aeneas Sylvius Piccolomini, later Pope Pius II, reported in the 1430s. He liked the oysters, found the women 'fair, charming and easily won', and noted that 'there is nothing the Scotch like better than to hear abuse of the English', but only when he made his way back as far as Newcastle did he find 'a familiar world and a habitable country', distinct from 'rude and uncultivated' Scotland.[4] The Western Isles, under the Mac-Donald Lords of the Isles, retained a high degree of independence, and the territorial magnates exercised great power, especially during the long periods when the monarch was captive, invalid or infant. Beyond the Highland line, Gaelic-speaking chiefs pursued their own courses. Only in the central and eastern Lowlands did an organised feudal society develop, the Border nobles remaining as independent as the Highland chiefs.

In spite of permanent internal dissension Scotland began that construction of a modern state apparatus that had started in England six centuries previously, and had resulted in its becoming the most tightly organised state in Europe. Comparisons between the two countries are often therefore misleading; one has only to recall that during King Cnut's reign some forty million coins were issued, a century before the first Scottish coinage appeared (and that was minted in Durham). The gap between the limited resources of Scotland and the much greater power that English rulers could deploy was growing. English magnates could, and did, exercise great influence – Warwick earned his title of the 'kingmaker' – but, once 'made', the monarch had at his disposal formidable resources. Scotland during the fourteenth century had seen a virtual usurpation of royal jurisdiction by the great families. Such nobles as the Douglases made agreements with other barons to settle disputes between themselves, disregarding royal laws; the King could exercise justice, or go to war, only if he could persuade a sufficient number of his barons to follow him. In England, the restriction on royal ambitions was beginning to be the ability, or the willingness, of Parliament to provide cash.

Scottish national institutions were, however, developing. James I (1406–37), released from a long semi-imprisonment in England in 1424, attempted a reconstruction of the Scottish Parliament along English lines. It went only so far: barons, bishops and burghers, as they had done since 1326, still assembled as a single body, and an attempt to provide for the office of Speaker, and to introduce county representation, was not successful, but much new legislation was enacted. Twenty-seven Acts provided a new framework of law, reinforced royal influence and introduced systematic taxation. Earlier Scottish Parliaments had been informal affairs, with all gentry having a right – legally an obligation – to attend. Such unwieldy gatherings were phased out, replaced by Parliaments convened with proper notice, with decisions taken at other times by a convention of the estates, later developed into that useful body known as the Lords of the Articles, which became an instrument for securing royal control by preparing all legislation before its submission to the Scottish Parliament.

In one respect Scotland moved ahead of England, the fifteenth century seeing the establishment of no fewer than three universities – St Andrews, Glasgow and Aberdeen. It was some time before these became comparable with Oxford, or even Cambridge, but the difference with Ireland was marked, official interest in education there being minimal.

From Parliament too sprang the courts of law, the Session of certain 'discreet' parliamentarians sitting with the Chancellor in Edinburgh, now the accepted capital. Parliaments could provide the machinery for levying taxation, and Scotland was developing a money economy, although rents in kind were common for a long time to come: as late as the sixteenth century the Scottish King could keep ten thousand sheep on his own account. Cash was becoming increasingly necessary as new luxuries and technologies had to be paid for. Of these artillery was the most important, the *Ultima Ratio Regis* – the King's final argument. Only the monarch could afford the cost of sufficient quantities of this devastating new weapon, and with it in royal hands, no rebellious magnate could feel safe in his own stronghold.

Cash was, however, difficult to come by. From 1387 the Scots pound, which had enjoyed parity with sterling, began the downwards slide that left it worth only one-twelfth of an English pound. Scots foreign earnings stemmed from exports to England, chiefly cattle on the hoof, and from sales of wool, hides and fish to the Low Countries through the Scots 'staple' – essentially a free port – settled at Veere, in Walcheren. Piracy being rife, such exports were liable to interruption, but one vital Scottish export, one that has quite literally changed world history, continued unimpeded; and that was men. Bred in conditions where survival often depended on strength, activity and aggression, Scots fighting men were welcomed in foreign armies in the fifteenth century, especially in that of France, where they formed the senior company of the Royal Guards from that time until the Revolution. In later years a brief survey of Scottish names among American presidents from James Monroe and Andrew Jackson onwards is enough to indicate the strength of the Scots diaspora.[5]

England was during the fifteenth century too embroiled, first with the French wars and then with its own internal quarrels, to intervene overmuch in Scotland. Apart from occasional disturbances – Berwick changed hands twice in the period – Anglo–Scottish warfare was limited to the endemic fighting on the Borders; but there was violence enough in the Scottish royal house. James I was murdered, killed in his own privy; James II (1437–60) killed the Earl of Douglas with his own hand and was himself killed by an exploding cannon; James III (1460–88) was assassinated in the course of a rebellion on behalf of his son James IV (1488–1513), who was to die at Flodden. Yet through the series of bloody struggles with the great nobles, central control, exercised by an alliance of King and Parliament, was slowly strengthened.

Owain Glyn Dwr

Wales had accepted the Edwardian assertion of authority sullenly, although for the most part quietly. Constitutional remedies for complaints were sought; as in Ireland petitions from individuals or communities to be allowed to adopt English law were frequent, and often successful. Discrimination was most bitterly resented in the towns, where charter privileges were reserved for English-speakers, who complained bitterly about Welsh 'malevolence' and 'enmity': but the letter of the law was widely evaded. By 1330 more than half the burgesses of Aberystwyth and Beaumaris were Welshmen. Intermarriages were not uncommon, and both Welsh and English names were used: Iowerth ap Morgan ap Iowerth Foel of Chirkland's son was better known as Morgan Yonge.[6]

The discontent and restlessness that sprang up in Wales during the disruption of civil society following the disastrous plague, the Black Death, was paralleled in England and elsewhere. Welsh risings were trivial in comparison with the English Peasants' Revolt against the poll tax – 'the evil subsidy' – in 1381. Not only farmers and labourers, but townsmen and artisans, from Essex and Kent ransacked London, where they broke open the prisons, burned the Savoy Palace and even captured the Tower, where the Archbishop of Canterbury and the Royal Treasurer were murdered. Short-lived, but viciously fierce revolts afflicted a great swathe of south-east England, with St Albans, Bury St Edmunds and Cambridge suffering greatly.

Welsh resentment, however subdued, was still dangerous. The English rebels protested their loyalty, and were quickly contented with promises of reform and actual reforms; but in Wales racial animosities were able to transform social tension into a national movement. Even such devoted servants of the Crown as Sir Gruffudd Llwyd could lament to Edward Bruce the way in which both Welsh and Scots had suffered at English hands. Sorrow at the days of glory now past was a common subject even of bards and historians like Geoffrey of Monmouth, and prophecies of a new Arthur who would liberate the enslaved Britons were widely circulated. One such potential liberator, Owain Lawgoch, a great-nephew of Llywellyn the Last, proclaimed his ambitions to invade, assisted by a company of young Welsh and French – *moult beauls hommes*, according to Christine de Pisan, the French poet, who had an eye for a handsome man. In 1378 Owain succeeded, with French assistance, in mounting a formidable invasion fleet, which however got no further than Guernsey, Owain himself being murdered by an English agent.[7]

Another Owain had been linked in praise poems with the expected liberator: this was the Welsh squire Owain Glyn Dwr, the 'Owen Glendower' who features prominently in Shakespeare's *Henry IV*.[8] Owain remains, in spite of many contemporary records, a mysterious figure, given to mystical visions, capable of stimulating ardent loyalty, a man of education and social standing. The proximate cause of his insurrection, which began in 1400, is uncertain, but it followed on a general unease that affected both England and Wales. After King Edward III's death in 1377 the child King Richard II had developed into an unrealistically ambitious and unscrupulous ruler, but one who commanded considerable support in both Ireland and Wales. His attempts to act as an absolute monarch eventually provoked a successful rebellion, resulting in his deposition by the Duke of Lancaster's dispossessed son, Henry Bolingbroke, in 1399. When the new King Henry IV had Richard secretly murdered indignation was widespread. Since the Conquest the royal inheritance had passed in a legitimate, if not always orderly, fashion, and for over five centuries Welsh princes had derived an important measure of authority from their recognition by the English Crown. It now seemed to many that the old order had perished.[9]

Owain Glyn Dwr's 'extraordinary, even bizarre' act of proclaiming himself Prince of Wales in September 1400 therefore took place in a new context. Previous Welsh rebellions had been those of powerful princes asserting some degree of authority against the English Crown; Owain's was that of a country gentleman against the whole principle of English rule, amounting to a declaration of Welsh independence. Once begun his rising was not limited to Wales but attracted support beyond Welsh borders. Owain had grand ideas of his own standing, seeking assistance from his 'lord and cousin', the King of Scotland, claiming that a prophecy had declared that Wales would be delivered from the 'tyranny and bondage of the Saxons' by the 'aid and succour' of the Scottish King.[10]

A more realistic threat lay in the English allies Owain was able to attach to his cause. Chief among these was the powerful Percy family of Northumberland, who had played a major part in securing Boling-broke's succession and had subsequently not obtained what they considered was their fair share of the proceeds. Harry Percy, the famous 'Hotspur', was defeated and killed at Shrewsbury by the royal army before he was able to join forces with Owain, but his father continued to seek help from other discontented northerners, including the Arch-bishop of York. Political weight was added when Owain was able to recruit the assistance of the powerful Mortimer family. Young Edmund Mortimer had as good a legal claim to the throne as Henry IV, and the 'Tripartite Indenture' drawn up between Owain, Mortimer and the Earl of Northumberland in 1405 therefore constituted a serious challenge to royal authority. Providing as it did for a Wales which extended to the Trent, the foundation of two new universities, and a Welsh Church independent of Canterbury, the Indenture was a fantasy that could never have been realised; but with Wales in an uproar, the north always willing to follow a Percy, and the French King Charles VI hovering ready to take advantage of any opportunity, English alarm was justified.

When French assistance materialised in August 1405 with the arrival of an expeditionary force at Milford Haven the potential threat was much increased. Glyn Dwr, however, by far the most experienced and

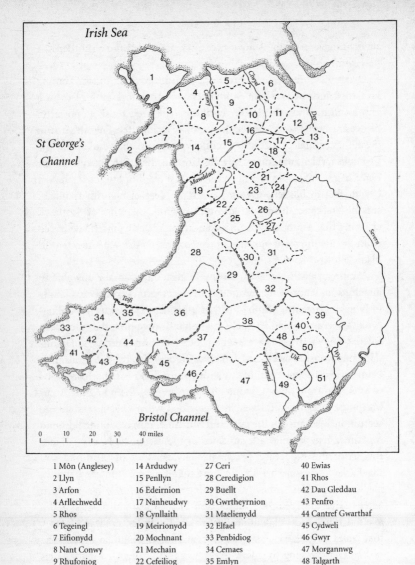

Irish Sea

St George's
Channel

St George's Channel

Bristol Channel

1 Môn (Anglesey)	14 Ardudwy	27 Ceri	40 Ewias
2 Llyn	15 Penllyn	28 Ceredigion	41 Rhos
3 Arfon	16 Edeirnion	29 Buellt	42 Dau Gleddau
4 Arllechwedd	17 Nanheudwy	30 Gwrtheyrnion	43 Penfro
5 Rhos	18 Cynllaith	31 Maelienydd	44 Cantref Gwarthaf
6 Tegeingl	19 Meirionydd	32 Elfael	45 Cydweli
7 Eifionydd	20 Mochnant	33 Penbidiog	46 Gwyr
8 Nant Conwy	21 Mechain	34 Cemaes	47 Morgannwg
9 Rhufoniog	22 Cefeiliog	35 Emlyn	48 Talgarth
10 Dyffryn Clwyd	23 Caereinion	36 Cantref Mawr	49 Gwynllwg
11 Ial	24 Gorddwr	37 Cantref Bychan	50 Gwent Uwchcoed
12 Maelor (Bromfield)	25 Arwystli	38 Brycheiniog	51 Gwent Iscoed
13 Maelor Saesneg	26 Cedewain	39 Ergyng (Archenfield)	

MEDIEVAL WALES

able commander in the Welsh forces, remained within Wales, and the royal armies slowly gained the upper hand. Earl Percy's renewed northern army was beaten, the French force did little of importance beyond ravaging south-west Wales, and the revolt petered out by the summer of 1409 without any large-scale military activity. There was little need for revengeful punishment: negotiations were frequent between the royal officials and those of Owain's supporters who had not been 'exhausted, frightened and demoralised by eight years of turmoil and violence'.[11]

The slow dissolution of Owain's revolt left English opinion decidedly anti-Welsh. The campaigns had been expensive and proved, were proof needed, the perfidy of the Welsh. Harshly punitive measures were taken by English Parliaments between 1401 and 1410: Welshmen were forbidden to carry arms, to infiltrate Welsh towns, which were to be purely English in future, to own a fortified house, or even to pay minstrels and poets, those carriers of sedition. Welshmen had been 'reeling like drunken Crows', the poet Iolo Goch lamented to Owain, but many quickly made their peace with King Henry. Maredudd ab Owain of Cardigan and Gruffudd Don, prominent rebels, fought alongside the loyalist Dafydd Gam in King Henry V's army at Agincourt. Undisturbed by the Wars of the Roses – no major battles took place in Wales – the economy recovered. Better posts in the Church and state were held by Welshmen; the discrimination built into the penal legislation fell into disuse, and was finally ended at the end of the century when those villeins still held in a form of servitude were emancipated.

'Ireland is separate from the realm of England'

Irish rulers, Gaelic or Norman, acknowledged the feudal superiority of the English King, but did not allow this to interfere too much with the violent assertion of their own interests against those of their neighbours. As in Wales, the Anglo-Norman invasion of Ireland brought only limited territorial gains, concentrated in the east, from Carrickfergus to Cork together with patches of land around the west-coast ports. Within this settled area the country was transformed. New techniques of agriculture were introduced, more land brought under the plough, new crafts and market towns were established and an export trade expanded. Canon law was enforced in the Church, and castles and monasteries – these in the approved Roman style – were founded. Outside this area of English control the quality of government is indicated by an admiring obituary of Cathal O'Connor, who died in 1224, described as 'the King most feared and dreaded ... who most blinded, killed and mutilated rebellious and disaffected subjects: the King who best established peace and tranquillity of all the kings of Ireland'.[12]

This division between an orderly English periphery and a less-developed Celtic hinterland was common to both Ireland and Wales, but the two countries were not alike. Sheer distance accounted for some of the differences. Isolated by the Irish Sea and the whole width of England from London, Ireland was too far distant to arouse great interest. Nor did any concentration of native Irish power succeed as well as had the princes of Dyfed or of Gwynedd; there was no Irish equivalent of the Lord Rhys or of Llywellyn the Great. But whereas Wales sent members to the Westminster Parliament, Ireland, or at least that part of it under English rule, developed its own parliamentary institutions. These followed the English pattern, the King's Council comprising the Anglo-Norman magnates, Parliament itself consisting of representatives of the gentry and burgesses. Its meetings were irregular, called whenever the viceroy – Lord Deputy or Justiciar – wished, and wherever was found convenient. Theoretically forty-two members were summoned to Parliaments, but in practice no representatives from Ulster or Connacht turned up; only Dublin, Kildare, Louth and Meath returned members with any regularity.

One attempt, in 1258, was made at achieving unity among the remaining Irish chieftains, that of Brian O'Neill of Tir Owen and Aed O'Connor of Connacht, who between them controlled most of north-west Ireland. No English intervention was needed, since the rising ended in defeat by the local Crown forces at Downpatrick. By contrast with the more sustained, fierce and much more threatening Welsh insurrections this was comparatively minor, and Edward I never found it necessary to come to Ireland in person. Legally minded as he was, the King nevertheless listened sympathetically to peaceable Irish pleas. One of the most pressing of these came in 1277 when the Arch-bishop of Ossory demonstrated his sincerity by raising ten thousand marks in an attempt to persuade King Edward to extend English common law to all his Irish subjects. The King was sympathetic, but the Irish Parliament, representing as it did only settler interests, refused. English governments, striving to assimilate Ireland to English norms without realising the very different conditions in the two countries, have continued ever since to make similar mistakes.[13]

The 'middle nation', as the Anglo-Irish called themselves, asserted not their independence, but their distinctiveness, in 1324. They were then in a strong position to do so since, without English help and after a protracted and bloody campaign, they had six years previously expelled a Scottish invasion led by Edward Bruce, the ambitious brother of King Robert I of Scotland. When Edward III's government sent over some trusted administrators to Ireland they were received with hostility. Richard Ledred, Bishop of Ossory, was violently denounced as 'this foreigner who comes from England' and defames the reputation of 'this land'; the accuser was no Gaelic patriot but the English-speaking colonist Arnold Power.[14]

A generation later the Black Death struck Ireland, particularly affect-ing centres of population and therefore of trade and prosperity. The 'land of peace' shrank progressively, as ruined and impoverished tradesmen and citizens returned to England. Control in the Irish-speaking provinces returned to the old dynasties and was accompanied by something of a revival of Gaelic culture. After the murder of the Anglo-Norman Earl of Ulster and Connacht in 1333 the whole north slipped out of English control. Art MacMurrough Cavanagh felt able to style himself 'King of Leinster'; the senior O'Neills claimed to be 'Princes, and Governors of the Irish in Ulster', and it was possible to rejoice on the inauguration of Niall Mor Ó Neill of Tir Owen in 1364 that:

> Ireland is a woman risen again
> Free from the horrors of reproach.[15]

Stretching across southern Ireland were the lands of the dominant Anglo-Norman families, the Butler Earls of Ormond, and the Fitz-Gerald Earls of Kildare, and of Desmond. Whereas in Wales the Anglo-Norman Marcher earls, fortified by their proximity to England, remained culturally distinct from the Welsh princes, their Irish kins-men were becoming increasingly Hibernicised. Ancient Norman families such as the de Burghs transmuted into Irish Burkes, just as in Scotland the de Bruis had become Bruces. Gerald FitzGerald, the third Earl of Desmond, was said to be able to instruct all the English and many of the Irish in knowledge of the Irish language, poetry and history. In at least one respect the Gaels were adopting foreign methods. The first wave of Anglo-Norman invaders were able to vanquish much greater numbers of relatively ill-disciplined and unprotected Irish fighters, but the nature of warfare changed with the recruitment of mercenaries – kerns, lightly armed Irish irregulars, adept at guerrilla warfare, and galloglasses, 'foreign warriors', Scots heavy infantry. Apart from sieges, where only a royal army could deploy the necessary special-ised equipment, warfare tended to be evenly balanced – and therefore both more destructive and protracted.

One of the rare English interventions occurred between 1361 and 1366, when Lionel, Duke of Clarence, a younger son of Edward III, came to Dublin. Clarence's stay in Ireland marked the beginning of an unusually sustained royal interest in that country, followed as it was by expeditions of his nephew King Richard II in 1394–95 and 1399. Duke Lionel began by calling a Parliament at Kilkenny, in response to an appeal from the Irish Council for 'succour and remedy' from their troubles, to be provided by 'a good and sufficient captain, stuffed and enforced by men and treasure'. The Statutes authorised by the Kilkenny Parliament in 1366 attempted to restrict the colonists to the settled areas, the 'obedient shires'. There they were to remain, having no intercourse with the 'Wild Irish' beyond or to imitate their seductive but disreputable ways. They must have respectable English surnames, speak English, dress properly, practise archery and not the native sport of hurling (although football was equally condemned; sport at that time had not become racist, as nineteenth-century Gaelic revivalists succeeded in making it), and on no account entertain Irish minstrels or storytellers.

London responded to the appeal of the Kilkenny Parliament, sending more than £90,000 over the following twenty-five years; at a time when the total annual income of the Irish exchequer was £2000, this was a substantial sum. Even weightier was the effort expended by Richard II, who arrived in 1394 with the largest army ever to be seen in Ireland, funded by money granted by Parliament and by loans raised from English magnates. Richard was always capable of grand plans, and offered full legal status as subjects of the Crown to all Irish chiefs. The response was gratifying. The heads of the most powerful tribes – the O'Neills, O'Briens, O'Connors and MacCarthys – personally offered submission to the King; even the recalcitrant Art MacMurrough Cavanagh submitted, and was knighted by Richard. There was an aura of 'the divinity that doth hedge a King' about Richard, King of England, Lord of Ireland, Duke of Normandy and of Aquitaine. No English King had visited Ireland since John, the better part of two centuries previously, and it is a measure of their neglect of that dominion that the next English King to come to Ireland was James II, three hundred years later (and since he had been deposed, it might be more accurate to date the next visit from a reigning monarch as that made by George IV in 1821). The effect of King Richard's visit was only temporary. The powerful personal influence exercised by a King evaporated soon after his departure, and unless the same scale of effort as had been expended on subduing Wales was applied to Ireland, there could be little hope of effecting stability there.[16]

After Richard II's visit, Ireland was again left to itself, with the result that the powers of the magnates, English and Irish, grew at the expense of central government. Clarence's Kilkenny Parliament had attempted to clarify a division between the 'Wild Irish enemies' and the peaceable settlers of both tongues. At that time and for many years subsequently there were at least three points of view in addition to that of the English government. The settlers of the 'middle kingdom', after the manner of later colonials, felt neglected, over-taxed and unprotected. For their part the magnates and chiefs, both Anglo-Norman and Irish, strove to get the better of their neighbours when and where they could, by force or diplomacy. And the great majority of the population, Irish or English, the farmers, labourers and artisans, only hoped to be allowed to keep a reasonable proportion of their earnings and to survive with their families intact. They stood a much better chance of this in either the 'obedient shires' or in those more distant regions where border struggles were rarer than in the turbulent marches.

In 1415 Henry V's famous and unexpected success at the battle of

Agincourt once again distracted English attention to the old dream of French conquest, which progressively weakened the ability to intervene in Ireland. Thomas Butler, Prior of Kilmainham, had been able in 1419 to bring a mixed force of Gael and Gall – all described as Irishmen ('Erenchaig') – to help the King in France, but by 1436 the Irish Council reported that the 'King's land in Ireland is well nigh destroyed, and inhabited only with his enemies and rebels'.[17] Only the eastern settlements, in particular those around Dublin, protected after 1450 by a fortified earthwork, the Dublin Pale, provided a secure environment in which commerce could flourish. Outside – 'beyond the Pale' – Gaelic Ireland remained an economy of subsistence agriculture and payment in kind. Royal authority was usually delegated to the Earls of Kildare as successive Lords Deputy, whose efforts to repel Irish incursions were hampered by their continuous feud with the rival family of the Butlers.

The despairing efforts to hold on to some of the French conquests finally collapsed in 1457, leaving only Calais in English hands; two years later the first battles of what was to prove thirty years of civil tumult, the Wars of the Roses, were fought. King Henry VI, never an effective monarch, was sliding through illness to terminal incapacity and final assassination, leaving the realm intermittently in charge of his cousin, Richard Duke of York. While keeping out of harm's way in Ireland, in February 1460, Duke Richard called a Parliament at Drogheda which declared what amounted to independence, not from the English Crown, but from the English Parliament. The Drogheda assembly declared that 'the land of Ireland is and at all times hath been corporate of itself by the ancient laws and customs used of the same', and that 'Ireland is nevertheless separate from the realm of England and from all laws and statutes thereof', unless these had also been authorised by the Irish Parliament. There was no question of impugning royal authority – citizens of the middle kingdom were painfully aware of their ultimate reliance on English power – but the first claim to Irish parliamentary independence had been made.[18]

Tudors and Stuarts

1485 is one of those key dates which divide 'periods' of English history. Whether or not it signals the start of Modern History has been a favourite examination question for many years. What unquestionably did occur was the death in battle of King Richard III, the able and unscrupulous son of the Duke of York, and the succession of the Earl of Richmond as Henry VII. Claiming the throne on doubtfully legitimate grounds (his mother was a descendant of the Plantagenet Duke of Lancaster, his paternal grandfather one Owain Tudur, whose family had been a power in Anglesey for many years, and who succeeded in marrying Henry V's widow), the new King consolidated his usurpation by disposing of his rivals. The Earl of Warwick was executed in 1499 and the Duke of Suffolk consigned to the Tower; the peerage was slashed as more than a hundred other members of noble families, accused of treason, were disposed of and their estates confiscated. Dynastically Henry united the rival families of York and Lancaster by marrying Edward IV's daughter Elizabeth, who became the mother of the future Henry VIII and of a daughter, Margaret. 'An unknown Welshman (whose father I never knew, nor him personally saw)' had been King Richard's opinion of the usurper, but Richard was dead, and the support of the Welsh for a dynasty undoubtedly stemming from an ancient princely family was to prove valuable.

The Tudors could bring no added dynastic authority to Ireland as they were able to do in Wales. The Earl of Kildare had lent his support to the first rebellion against King Henry, that of the pretender Lambert Simnel in 1489, and, more discreetly, to that of Perkin Warbeck in 1494. Both risings were suppressed, and one of Henry's trustworthy aides, Sir Edward Poynings, was sent to replace Kildare. His mission, in 1494, was primarily to secure English government in the Pale by curbing the pretensions of the Irish Parliament, and by reversing the 1460 declaration of modified independence. A nervous Parliament was therefore persuaded to pass an Act – 'Poynings' Law' – drastically limiting its own powers. The Act declared that future assemblies could only be called by the King in council and after having submitted a list of the measures which it was intended to take; in reverse, all English laws must apply to Ireland. The Dublin Pale had to be made secure, both by the digging of a boundary ditch and the requirement that every man within it should have suitable arms. Within that region royal authority was continuously exercised, and in the other settled areas some efforts were made to enforce English law, but with a force of only one thousand men Poynings, although an experienced soldier, could not be expected to make any inroads into the Gaelic-speaking areas. More as a matter of form then, Ulster and Connacht were declared to be royal property. Any assertion of these rights would have been too expensive for Henry, who allowed Kildare to return to Dublin as the least unacceptable of the alternatives.

Between the Pale and the Gaelic-speaking hinterland a sharp contrast could be drawn. North of the River Boyne Ulster was still bush country, where power remained in the hands of the old Gaelic families, the O'Neills and the O'Donnells, with their allied supporters, and where the royal castle of Carrickfergus formed almost the only reliable outpost of the Lordship. Elsewhere a high degree of linguistic – hardly racial, since the Anglo-Norman families were, after three centuries, well inter-mingled – separation existed. Bishoprics were divided among English- and Gaelic-speakers, the English naturally having the richer dioceses. *Inter Hibernicos* the Church retained some of the 'unabashed forms of a pre-Hildebrandine indigenous order', serenely unaffected by the twelfth-century reformations. Priestly celibacy was a lost cause: Cathal MacManners, Archdeacon of Clogher, compiler of the *Annals of Ulster*, said to be 'a gem of purity and a turtle dove of chastity', boasted of his horde of children. Hereditary bishops were not unknown – Bishop Turlough O'Brien of Killaloe's son Matthew became Bishop of Kilmac-duagh, and his son in turn succeeded to his grandfather's diocese; the Bishop of Clonmacnoise and his son, the Archdeacon, were killed in a battle with discontented family members; Abbot Kavanagh of Leighlin had his Bishop murdered and was flayed alive by the Earl of Kildare for the crime.[19]

Efficient Church government is however not necessarily synony-mous with the Christian life and pastoral care, and spiritual life among the Irish flourished in spite of the clergy's failings. The most striking indication of devotional literature is the surviving body of popular religious verse in Irish. Not, it is said, in the best of classical Irish, in translation the poetry is quite remarkably fresh and powerful. From a hymn to the Virgin Mary:

> Oh master-stroke of women; O chart of the sea-path home;
> O fair-tressed sinless lady, O branch over wood, O bright sun.
> O spring unfailing, peace-bond of the six hosts, before whom
> war recoils; O subduer of God's wrath.
> O help of the living world, let me not cause thy poverty to
> have been in vain, O ivy bearing fresh wine, O guardian of
> God's child.[20]

Outside the settled areas tribal warfare continued rife. Even more civilised Irish chiefs, such as Manus O'Donnell of Tyrone, as literate and sophisticated as any English counterpart, who gained the name of 'the Magnificent' by his appearance in 'a coat of crimson velvet with aglets of gold, 20 or 30 pair, over that a great double cloak of right crimson satin, girded with black velvet . . . and a bonnet with a feather, set full of aglets of gold', gained power by ejecting his father and retained it by fighting with his son.[21] European visitors were all struck by the primitive conditions under which even the Irish magnates lived. Viscount Ramon de Perellos, a Spanish nobleman, visiting in 1397, was entertained by O'Neill of Tir Owen in a fashion 'which to us seems very strange for someone of his status. His table was of rushes spread out on the ground while nearby they placed delicate grass for him to wipe his mouth.' His lords wore 'neither hose nor shoes, nor do they wear breeches, and they wear their spurs on their bare heels. The King was dressed like that on Christmas Day.' The Queen went barefoot, and her handmaidens were dressed 'with their shameful parts showing'. But like so many later visitors, Perellos, while deploring Irish backwardness, found the people 'among the most beautiful that I have seen anywhere in the world'. Such families as the FitzGeralds or Butlers may have adopted slightly less relaxed habits, but were quite as energetic in waging internecine warfare as their Gaelic counterparts. Until a decisively superior English force was deployed the only prudent course for any government was to revert to reliance on the Earls of Kildare as viceroys.

'The best businessman ever to sit upon an English throne',[22] one who personally checked every page of the accounts submitted to him,

Henry VII was in many ways the opposite of his Scottish contemporary. James IV enjoyed with panache all the delights and splendour available to an extravagant Renaissance prince, his court a glittering array of the finest poets and musicians, assembled in his new palaces of Stirling and Falkland. Among them were such talented lyricists as William Dunbar, without question the best poet writing in English (or Scots) of his day. Henry, by contrast, was immensely careful over details and strained to avoid all unnecessary expenditure. No great palaces were built in his reign, and although anxious – with some reason – for his own soul, Henry undertook the construction of the magnificent chapels of Westminster and King's College, Cambridge, the expense of these fell largely upon his successor. The 'unknown Welshman' ruled in a new and personal way, selecting his advisers and ministers from 'new men', professionals of modest origin, who fulfilled their tasks with a ruthless mastery of detail that was to become a hallmark of Tudor rule. Henry VII's councillors, Morton, Empson and Dudley, were the forerunners of Wolsey and Cromwell in his son's time, and of the Cecils, father and son, during the reign of Elizabeth. The Court of Star Chamber, essentially the executive committee of the Privy Council, and the regional royal Courts of the North and of the Marches, provided speedy, if often ruthless decisions.

In his protracted efforts to restore the fabric of government Henry VII took care to avoid foreign conflicts. A brief clash with France in 1492 was concluded, much to Henry's financial advantage, without a serious battle. Since France's capacity to interfere with England could best, as proved in the next three centuries, be effected through Scotland or Ireland, it became a particular aim of Henry VII's policy to establish good relations with Scotland. Truces were renewed, at Henry's instigation, in 1488, 1491 and 1492, but James IV was ambitious for martial glory in a way that Henry was not; ambitious, but unsuccessful. His first attempt against England, in 1496, in breach of the current truce, ended in a rapid retreat. Henry took advantage of the threat to increase English taxes, which caused widespread discontent. In Cornwall, where the old language and traditions were still jealously guarded, miners objected to being made to pay for 'a small commotion made of the Scots which was assuaged and ended in a moment',[23] and rebelled. Unlike any attempt ever made from Wales or Scotland, the Cornishmen got to the very gates of London before they were stopped at Deptford.

In 1497 James made another attempt on England. A short raid, easily repelled, was followed by a new truce intended to last for the lifetime of both kings (July 1499). In 1502 a Treaty of Perpetual Peace was negotiated in London, which provided for the marriage between James and Henry's daughter Margaret, which duly took place in 1503, 'the marriage of the Thristle and the Rose'. Although little thought was then given to union of the two countries the marriage was one of prime significance, since any child born of it would be in direct line of succession to the throne of England should Henry VII's sons produce no heirs: and exactly one hundred years after the wedding of King James and Queen Margaret their great-grandson succeeded to the English Crown as James VI of Scotland and I of England. With this alliance, and the treaty in place, future relations between the two countries looked promising. Scotland had altered since Aeneas Sylvius' visit the previous century, and the English wedding guests were surprised by the sophisticated comforts they found at the royal court. During Henry's lifetime cordial relations continued, and one of Henry VIII's first acts on his succession in 1509 was to renew both the treaty with Scotland and that with France. But while Henry VII was prudence personified, little swayed by personal feelings, with small appetite for show or glory, his son, entering upon a rich heritage amassed by the father, was as extravagant and aggressive as James of Scotland. A clash was highly likely.

It was in fact Henry's ambitions in Europe that sparked off the conflict. Pope Julius II (1503–13), a warlord rather than a spiritual leader, persuaded Henry to join a 'Holy League' against France and accordingly in 1512 Henry began a war with that country. Louis XII of France (1498–1515) therefore claimed Scotland as an ally. While Henry was pursuing a successful, although extremely expensive, campaign in northern France, James launched an invasion of England, ostensibly in support of the French King.

The resulting battle of Flodden, in August 1513, in which King James lost his life, as did nine earls, the Archbishop of St Andrews and many other magnates and ecclesiastics, was shattering. It was the culmination of a hopeless undertaking. Warfare over the centuries had shown that Scottish invasions of England could not achieve more than a temporary success, and almost always ended in a crushing defeat. That of Flodden, inflicted by a second-division English force while the main royal army was engaged in France, was devastating. James IV's defeat on land was matched by the failure of his maritime hopes. In what was a *folie de grandeur* he had ordered the construction of a navy, of which the most important unit was the great ship *Michael*, the most powerful man-of-war ever built, carrying twenty-four iron cannon and three huge bronze 'basilisks' mounted fore and aft; but Scotland had not enough sailors to crew her ships, no workshops to cast the guns, no facilities for providing ammunition and essential equipment – the compass had to be bought in Middlesbrough – or for repairing the ships, which had eventually, after being the subject of vast expense, to be handed over to France. Misled by the fiction of the 'Auld Alliance' successive generations of Scots failed to realise that prudent French policies saw in Scotland only an opportunity to annoy England, to distract attention from the conflict between the two larger countries, and had no intention of providing serious support for action within Britain.

John, Duke of Albany, next heir to the throne after the infant son of James IV, revived the Auld Alliance to the point that a French army actually arrived in Scotland. Apart from emptying the citizens of Edinburgh's larders it did nothing, but James V (1513–42), when he came of age, was willing to renew the ancient struggle, in which, as many of the Scots magnates now well understood, there was never any hope that their country might achieve a permanent success. At the battle of Solway Moss on 24 November 1542 the Scottish army, although outnumbering the English by more than three to one, either surrendered or ran; James joined the general retreat, and died shortly after.

The final debacle reinforced the lesson of Flodden: the Auld Alliance was a dangerous deceit, and the possibility of an independent foreign policy for Scotland dim. Apart from the gross imbalance of power – the wealth of England was perhaps thirty times as great as that of Scotland – the non-existence of a Scottish navy (James' was the last attempt to provide one) meant that a blockade could isolate Scotland. Bannockburn had established Scotland's domestic independence, but its very existence as an international power was becoming clearly questionable. Once again an infant was heir to the Scottish throne – Mary, only a few days old, the daughter of James and the French Princess Mary of Guise; and Mary would have a claim to the English throne if her great-uncle Henry VIII could not produce heirs.

At the time of James V's death King Henry had three children, Mary, Elizabeth and Edward, which made the prospects of the little Scots Mary succeeding to the English throne doubtful. One obvious solution was to marry her to the future Edward VI, only six years older, a proposal which was actually agreed at the Treaty of Greenwich in 1543. That this did not occur was due partly to Henry's attempt to force its acceptance upon recalcitrant Scots. The 'Rough Wooing' of 1544–45 was a ruthless attack which brought about wholesale devastation. It failed totally, since those Scots who were beginning to advocate a union of the two countries were alienated. The subsequent clumsy diplomacy of Protector Somerset, acting on behalf of the young King Edward VI, resulted in the battle of Pinkie, yet another bloody Scottish defeat and, like its predecessors, one that profited England not at all. Had the marriage project been successful, the two countries would have been united by coming under a joint monarchy, much as had been envisaged by the projected marriage of Edward II and the Maid of Norway; but such a solution, even in the 1540s, would have been premature. Written probably by Robert Wedderburn, a Dundee priest, the *Complaynt of Scotland* compared the two nations (to the considerable disadvantage of the English). It was, Wedderburn contended, 'impossible that English and Scottish remain in gude accord under ane prince ... be raisoun of the grit difference that is betwist their naturis and conditiouns'. If not perhaps impossible, the next 450 years have proved it tolerably difficult; and as Wedderburn was writing, another factor had arisen to alter the established relations between England, Scotland and France.[24]

CHAPTER 5

1540–1603

The Elizabethan settlement

THE CATHOLIC CHURCH had been greatly weakened during the Great Schism of the fourteenth century, when two popes – and even, for some time, three – contended for authority. Attempts at reform in the two councils of Constance and Basle between 1414 and 1420 had not been followed through, and a succession of really deplorable Popes, who between them committed every sin in the calendar, from Paul II in 1464 to Leo X in 1513, had brought the papacy into near-universal disrepute. Drastic reform was inevitable, and was signalled in 1509 by the humanist scholar Erasmus' *Praise of Folly*, and eight years later by the German monk Martin Luther's attack on the Church's corruption in his Ninety-Five Theses, nailed to the Wittenberg church door.

The two men's careers symbolised different possibilities. The Church might be reformed from within, as Erasmus advocated, and as had been attempted a century before, but it was not until 1559, with the election of Pope Pius IV, that internal reform was seriously implemented. By that time breakaway Protestant Churches had been established all over northern Europe. Principally divided between followers of Luther and those of the French theologian Jean Calvin, all differed from the Roman Church in repudiating the authority of the Pope, and in some doctrinal matters, the central controversy relating to the nature of the Eucharist. In Church discipline Protestants asserted the primacy of Biblical texts and of the individual conscience, and claimed the right to participate in Church government. Once the legitimacy of central authority had been denied in this way, a plethora of religious choices was on offer. The fact that England and Scotland chose different forms of the Reformed religion, each with remarkable unanimity, while Ireland remained largely true to the Roman Church, did much to decide future history.

England slipped gradually into Protestantism, over half a century, beginning with the marital and economic difficulties of King Henry VIII. The King's first marriage, with the Spanish Princess Catherine of Aragon, produced only one surviving child, Princess Mary, born in 1516. Henry urgently required a male heir to secure the succession, and had selected a young woman, Anne Boleyn, as his next wife. In order to obtain a divorce the King needed papal consent, which was not forthcoming. Henry's answer was therefore to deny all papal authority.

In doing so he precipitated a confrontation which still exists today. Without any doctrinal or liturgical changes to complicate matters Henry simply took over the function of the Pope as the 'only Supreme Head on Earth of the Church of England'. It was not the first time that an English King had fallen out with the Holy See. Edward III had severely restricted papal power by the Statutes of Provisors (1351) and Praemunire (1353). Henry claimed a not dissimilar right 'to keep [the realm] from the annoyance as well of the see of Rome as from the authority of other foreign potentates'. Between 1532 and 1536 the English Parliament passed a series of Acts – Annates, Appeals, Supremacy, Succession, Treasons, and an Act against the Pope's authority – which left the King established as Supreme Head of the Church of England, and made it treason to deny, or even to wish to deny this. Under this draconian statute Sir Thomas More and Cardinal Fisher were decapitated, and six staunch London Carthusian monks suffered the more horrible penalty for treason of hanging, drawing and quartering. The King himself remained, in his own opinion, devoted to the Catholic faith and a staunch opponent of Protestantism, valuing the title of 'Defender of the Faith' bestowed on him by the Pope for his anti-Lutheran tract, and proving his continued fidelity by burning the occasional heretic.

Given the King's continued doctrinal orthodoxy serious negotiations between England and Rome might have led to a reconciliation. It was not the first time that a King had been excommunicated, as Henry was in 1538, and the popes could hardly claim the moral high ground: Paul III (1534–49) was an affectionate father to his four children; his successor Julius III preferred boys. Although not a first-class European power England could be a vital makeweight whose adherence to either France or Spain could tip the balance between those contenders for hegemony; and either could exert great influence on papal decisions. But doctrinal changes were to become irresistible.

His religious convictions did not prevent the Defender of the Faith from the destruction of all the monastic institutions, and the distribution of their property, at market prices, to his supporters, thus ensuring that a substantial part of political society would be reluctant to see any return to the old order: the process, it might be added, continued even under his daughter the Catholic Queen Mary. Some of the proceeds were usefully employed in the foundation of new dioceses, but the end result was a permanent weakening of Crown finances. The cash soon disappeared, and so did the easily taxable wealth of the clergy. Henry VII had been able to raise £100,000 at a stroke, in addition to regular income, from that source. His granddaughter, Elizabeth, would remain permanently harassed by want of ready money.

Henry VIII died in 1547, leaving three children. In addition to the Princess Mary, a daughter by Anne Boleyn, Princess Elizabeth, had been born in 1533, and the long-awaited son, Edward, was born to Henry's third wife, Jane Seymour, in 1537. When the precocious nine-year-old Prince succeeded as Edward VI the country, under the guidance of the 'Protector', the unsteady Duke of Somerset, took a clearly Protestant direction. 'Images, which be things not necessary' were smashed, murals were mutilated and painted over, and more treasures of medieval art were destroyed. In an attempt to define doctrine Archbishop Cranmer of Canterbury published two English prayerbooks (1549 and 1552). These closely followed the medieval English rites, simplified, and with alterations in the most important section, that of the Eucharist. Cranmer was concerned to repudiate what the Articles of Religion of the new Anglican Church described as 'the blasphemous fables and dangerous deceits of the Roman Mass' – the insistence that the bread and wine were literally 'transubstantiated' into Christ's flesh and blood. Both prayerbooks were written in Cranmer's magnificent prose, resounding and dramatic yet capable of great sensitivity, most of which survived subsequent changes. Together with the English translation of the Bible, begun two centuries earlier by John Wyclif and continued by William Tyndale, Cranmer's liturgy is the first manifestation of that unparalleled literary explosion which over the next two centuries did so much to create a specifically English sense of national identity. What had been lost when works of art had been destroyed was replaced by words and phrases which fired the imaginations of all who heard them.

The Earl of Warwick (later the Duke of Northumberland), who had overthrown the Somerset administration (and had Somerset himself executed), terminated the unsuccessful and expensive foreign adventures begun by Henry VIII. Of the former English empire in France only Calais remained, and that for a very short time. Faced with the prospect of the chronically ill young King being succeeded by his half-sister Mary, like her mother a devoted Catholic, Northumberland planned a *coup d'état* to divert the succession to his own daughter-in-law, Lady Jane Grey. The plot failed, Lady Jane and Northumberland were executed, and on Edward's death Mary Tudor became Queen of England in July 1553.

Queen Mary's – Bloody Mary's – short reign (she died in November 1558) marked a turning point in English history. In 1554 she married the equally fervent Catholic, Philip, King of Spain from 1556. The inevitable war with France led to the final loss of Calais (January 1558); the attempt to bring England back to the True Faith, signalled by burning those who disagreed – including the venerable Archbishop Cranmer – roused so much opposition as to practically ensure that England remained Protestant.

On the Queen's death, still childless, the accepted heir was Mary's half-sister, Elizabeth, daughter of King Henry and Anne Boleyn. Only twenty-five at the time, Elizabeth had endured a precarious childhood, stigmatised as a bastard by Mary, imprisoned in the Tower of London, in imminent danger of execution, and only at the last moment recognised as Mary's heir. She came to the throne already wary of commitment, determined to avoid religious controversy or foreign entanglements prejudicing the uncertain stability of her reign.

The official religion of the country having veered towards Protestantism under Edward VI and backed to Catholicism with Mary, young Queen Elizabeth committed it to a middle course. Henry VIII's reformation had been political and social, rather than theological. The Peace of Augsburg in 1555, which patched up the wars of religion in Germany, had concluded that the ruler of each state should decide whether his subjects should be Catholic or Protestant. Those subjects who disagreed could go elsewhere. It is the nature of such a Church that it must have a single, unified system of belief that commands obedience, a requirement which, given the ebullience of the new thought, was made difficult to the point of impossibility. Once released from the rigid bounds of accepted orthodoxy, new interpretations burgeoned. The Swiss Reformer Ulrich Zwingli had already contradicted some of the most central Lutheran propositions; Calvin was only the most important of the second generation of Protestant theologians; the letters are full of the arguments between Henry Bullinger, Peter Martyr and such 'obstinate and insolent revilers' as Stancaranus. When the theories of later writers, the Dutchman Arminius being the most influential, and such native thinkers as Richard Hooker are added, many possible theoretical structures were subjected to heated debate.

Left to herself Elizabeth would have continued the religious policy of her father, a Catholic Church without the Pope, with vestments and ceremonies intact and priests continuing celibate. 'As to ceremonies and maskings, there is a little too much foolery. That little silver cross, of ill-omened origin, still maintains its place in the Queen's chapel,' complained the reforming Bishop Jewel of Salisbury.[1] The Queen however clung to one insistent personal belief, that the Catholic doctrine of the Mass was indeed a 'blasphemous fable', and, like her father, insisted on rejecting papal authority: as a result the existing bishops – with only one exception, old Bishop Kitchen of Llandaff – together with a substantial minority of the nobles, refused to support their new monarch. But the House of Commons, meeting on 24 January 1559, sided with the Queen, and in this they reflected the sentiments of most of their constituents.

The Bill creating Elizabeth Supreme Governor (not Head, as Henry VIII had been) of the Church of England was easily passed, and a new middle-of-the-road prayerbook issued. In London the new arrangements were enthusiastically welcomed, and in the rest of the country given at least a tacit acceptance. No severe penalties were enacted on those who refused to accept the Act of Uniformity. Loss of office, and in rare cases imprisonment, rather than hanging, drawing and quartering, were at that time the limits of martyrdom exacted from the most intransigent Catholics. Damage to Church property was more severe as 'the dumb remnants of idolatry'[2] were pillaged and destroyed by urban mobs in what was described as 'an insensate furor of vandalism', during which many more magnificent pieces of medieval art were lost. Coming on top of the pillage of the monasteries, the sack of many parish churches added to the ruin of England's medieval heritage.

With the doctrinal changes confirmed by Elizabeth the relations of the English Church with Rome changed fundamentally. A state-established Church is potentially a dangerous institution. If obedience to the state is taken to demand adherence to the state Church, those subjects not sharing the same faith are relegated, in a greater or lesser degree, to an inferior status. The new Church of England attempted to make its formularies so loose, and became so flexible in its practices, as to keep most of the English within its boundaries but *in extremis*, and when under threat the Church could, and did, invoke state power in support of its own officially-approved views.

Popular feeling against any return to Rome was reinforced by the publication in 1563 of John Fox's *Book of Martyrs*, one of the most influential propaganda works ever written. Like the best propaganda, it was based on factual, although selective, evidence. If Fox's reports of Protestant suffering at the hands of Catholics were frequently exaggerated, his readers needed little reminder of such incidents as that which had occurred in Guernsey in 1556, when a young woman charged with heresy and burned at the stake gave birth in the heat of the fire. The bailiff – a Jerseyman – caught the living child and threw it back into the blaze. When those responsible were charged with murder in 1562, the prosecution was cut short by Elizabeth, who pardoned the bailiff; there were to be no retroactive persecutions, even in the most blatant cases.[3]

As had her father – and she was always conscious that she was the daughter of an unusually formidable ruler – Elizabeth sought out and employed talented middle-class officials. Francis Walsingham, a Cambridge lawyer, ran her efficient secret service; the Cecils – father William, Lord Burleigh and son Robert, Lord Salisbury – acted as political managers throughout her reign; and such men did not have to fear, as did Henry's ministers, the axe as a consequence of royal displeasure. Forcefully opposing the royal will, however, could be fatal.

Domestic calm was shattered in 1569. The Duke of Norfolk, the only duke left in England after the previous Tudor cull, had ambitions to be married to Queen Mary of Scotland. He entered into a loose and ill-defined conspiracy to overthrow Cecil and his colleagues, and replace them with a council of pro-Catholics. The Duke's support came from the north of England, where the Earls of Northumberland and Westmorland were ready to go further, and replace Elizabeth with Henry VIII's great-niece, Queen Mary of Scotland. When Cecil discovered the plot Norfolk lost his nerve, but the two earls, backed by many thousands of experienced fighting men, stormed into action, entering Durham Cathedral, setting fire to the prayerbook and English Bible and celebrating, for the first time in ten years, the Roman Mass. Sympathy in the north was sufficient to make resistance apathetic: the serviceable Earl of Sussex, with ten years of Irish fighting behind him, was sent to quell the revolt, and reported, 'the gentry brought as few men as possible while the infantry grumbled about the weather and spoke in an unintelligible local accent' (a protective device still not unknown on Tyneside). The rebels got as far south as Selby before retreating. There was only one battle, near Carlisle in February 1570, before the rebellion collapsed, and the north was again subjected to a deliberate campaign of punitive destruction and executions.[4]

The rebellion was a signal for another, more permanent move against Elizabeth. After an initial, unsuccessful venture in aid of French Protestants the Queen had made many concessions and compromises in order to avoid becoming officially involved in any Continental quarrels. In so doing the co-operation of the papacy was invaluable, and this had for some time been forthcoming.

Paul IV (1555–59), a ferocious old reactionary who established the Index of forbidden books and the Roman ghetto, had been replaced by Pius IV (1559–65), more conciliatory, who made an earnest effort at reconciliation with the Protestant states, but with the election of Pius V (1566–72), formerly Grand Inquisitor, an ardent counter-Reformation policy began. On 25 February 1570, rather too late to benefit the northern earls, but stimulated by the hope generated by their rebellion, Pius issued a Bull excommunicating not only Elizabeth but any Catholics who continued to recognise her as their sovereign. The Bull *Regnans in Excelsis* was accompanied by a letter to the earls which exactly foreshadowed the *fatwa* issued in 1989 by Ayatollah Khomeini against the novelist Salman Rushdie.

> Should they lose their lives in His service, it was better for them to pass at once into Paradise by a glorious death, than to be the mean slaves of a licentious woman, and to lose their immortal souls.[5]

The effects of the Pope's *fatwa* were mixed. Internationally it received only lip service. Neither France nor Spain, the only possible wielders of a papal sword, were inclined to take action against a potential ally. For her part Queen Elizabeth continued the policy of avoiding conflicts, going so far as to gloss over the massacres of French Protestants on St Bartholomew's Day in 1572. But in England the effect on Catholics was devastating. The choice of obedience to the Pope could be taken to mean nothing less than treason to the state.[6] Radical Protestants seized the opportunity to advance their own cause. Fox's book, reissued in 1570, was ordered to be placed in every cathedral, in all colleges and on every man-of-war. In 1571 Parliament declared it treasonable to publish any papal bulls, and only the Queen's opposition prevented further penalties being levied on Catholics; but the execution of young missionary priests began. Persecution was accelerated when ten years later another Act made it simple treason to convert or be converted to Rome. The idea was imprinted in the popular mind that professing Catholics were incapable of loyalty, and had, by choosing fidelity to Rome rather than Westminster, relegated themselves to the rank of second-class citizens, surviving only conditionally and under constant scrutiny. It was to be a long-lived conviction, reinforced by stories of the horrors of the Spanish Inquisition and the persecution of heretics, and, periodically, by the actions of some English Catholics. More than two centuries later George IV was still insisting that to allow equal status to Catholics would be to violate his coronation oath.

Catholics were not the only ones to suffer for their beliefs. At the opposite religious extreme, the radical Protestants, becoming known as Puritans, were not encouraged. Archbishop Grindal of Canterbury was dismissed for undue Puritan sympathies in 1577; his replacement, John Whitgift, began an active campaign of repression. Himself sympathetic to Calvinist theology, Whitgift proved an implacable opponent of free speech, imposing vigorous controls on the press, breach of which could lose offenders their ears, hands, or sometimes their lives. The Welshman John Penry, one of the authors of the Martin MarPrelate pamphlets, was hanged, drawn and quartered in 1593.[7]

Reformation in Wales and Ireland

WALES[8]

Henry VII's Welsh ancestry assured him of the warmest support in Wales from the moment of his landing in Pembroke, which he later cemented by such gestures as incorporating the Welsh red dragon in his arms and coinage and christening his eldest son Arthur, who died in his father's lifetime, after the legendary British hero. It was therefore entirely possible for Welsh political society to perceive Henry VII, and even his successor Henry VIII, who had little time to spare for Wales, as overthrowing the Saxon yoke and establishing what has been described as 'Home Rule' for Wales.

What might have been expected to arouse Welsh resentment, the brusque incorporation of Wales within the English state, met with little resistance. The process began in 1536, with an Act providing for justices of the peace to be appointed in the existing counties, creating the new shires of Monmouth, Brecknock, Radnor, Montgomery and Denbigh, and sweeping away the Marcher Lordships. Such Welsh traditional law as remained was to be replaced by English Common Law, and all the Welsh were to enjoy the same freedoms as the English, including the right to send members to Parliament, and the perhaps less attractive privilege of paying taxes.[9]

The new masters were, however, to be Welsh. The law was to be administered in the first instance by justices drawn from the ranks of the Welsh gentry, who eagerly competed for the post. Justices were to become more influential as English administrative systems evolved, 'the beasts of burden on whose broad shoulders the government continually devolved new tasks'. Of these tasks the administration of the Elizabethan poor laws with their responsibility to discourage vagabonds (by drilling their ears, whipping them or sending them to row in the galleys) and to provide relief for honest paupers gave the magistrates much power, and entailed great responsibility.

Since Edward I's establishment of royal administration Wales had been gradually conforming to the English model, which was itself evolving in that period. Welshmen had been attending the universities and Inns of Court, and taking their places in the lay and ecclesiastical administration. Sir Edward Carne of Glamorgan was sent to Rome as an ambassador by both Henry VIII and Queen Mary; William Thomas, author of a famous defence of Henry's policies and of the first Italian grammar, became political mentor to King Edward VI. 'The number of Welsh students entering Oxford and Cambridge and the Inns of Court grew prodigiously between 1540 and 1640, and especially during the latter half of the period.' Oxford was more popular, especially after the foundation of Jesus College, still famous for its Welsh alumni, in 1571 by Dr Hugh Price (or Apryce). For the better part of a century before 1657 all Jesus' principals were Welsh, and mostly related to each other. When Queen Elizabeth visited Oxford in 1566 three of the four distinguished scholars who debated before her were Welsh. Even in the less favoured university two Welsh clerics, John Hughes and Robert Evans, were instrumental in founding Magdalene College, of which house Evans became the first Master while William Glynn, Bishop of Bangor, was President of Queens' College and Regius Professor of Divinity.[10] Welsh émigrés almost flocked to London, probably representing 1 per cent of the total population. It was perhaps optimistic to believe that the Tudor monarchs had a 'great care and natural love and affection . . . unto their subjects of Wales above all others', but Welshmen did well at Henry VIII's court. In a sample of 661 Welsh migrants in the first half of the sixteenth century no fewer than 169 held court appointments.[11]

Welshmen also prospered in trade: the Myddelton brothers became prosperous London citizens, famous for providing fresh water to the capital, brought from Hertfordshire in a conduit nearly thirty miles long, the first such enterprise since the Romans left. No fewer than eleven street names around the still-existent terminal in Islington commemorate the arrival of the Myddeltons' 'New River'. In Bristol the Lloyd family were setting up the iron foundry that in due course provided the funds to found the eponymous bank; further afield Sir

Richard Clough became one of Amsterdam's most influential burghers, and was instrumental in founding the London Royal Exchange. John Dee, Queen Elizabeth's 'Intelligencer', was perhaps the most eclectically learned man of his times, astronomer, astrologer, mathematician, classicist, navigator, alchemist and stage manager.

Wales, according to Ben Jonson, 'had long been a very garden and seed plot of honest minds and men. Whence hath the crown . . . better servitors more liberal of their lives and fortunes.' Much of the country had made an impressive recovery from the Glyn Dwr Rebellion. Sir Rhys ap Thomas' magnificent Carew Castle, scene of a splendid tournament in 1506, Sir Rice Mansel's Oxwich Castle and Margam Abbey, together with the Herbert family's Raglan, testify to the prosperity of Welshmen enjoying royal favour. The magnificent Plas Mawr in Conway town, probably the finest surviving Elizabethan townhouse in Britain, demonstrates a mercantile richness paralleling anything in comparable or even much bigger British towns. It is probably, however, the Myddeltons' purchase of Chirk Castle that best exemplified what ambitious and talented Welshmen could achieve. Originally built about 1300 for Glyn Dwr's ally the Marcher Lord Roger Mortimer, Chirk changed hands on numerous occasions before being purchased by Thomas Myddelton in 1595; and the subsequent transformation of the medieval fortress into a splendid house has all been Myddelton work for four centuries.

Such prosperity was not universal: the mountain districts remained impoverished, poorly served by scattered parishes staffed by wretchedly-paid priests, but such was also the state of affairs in upland England, and it was from the poorest and most conservative areas that the most serious English anti-Protestant dissent arose. Wales, however, took both the Reformation and Counter-Reformation quietly. Partly as a consequence of the lack of universities or other intellectual centres, Wales had been less influenced both by the late-medieval mysticism that flourished in the Low Countries and in England, and by Wycliff's proto-Protestant doctrines.[12] Henry VIII's anti-papal enactments caused some resentment – spies reported that one William ap Llywellyn threatened to 'souse the King about the ears till he had made his head soft enough' – but most accepted the royal supremacy without demur.[13] Similarly the dissolution of the monasteries occasioned little fuss.

Irish Sea

St George's
Channel

ANGLESEY
Conwy
Flint
Bangor
Denbigh
Chester
Caernarvon
DENBIGH
FLINT

CAERNARVON

MERIONETH

Dyfi

MONTGOMERY
SHROPSHIRE
Montgomery

Severn

CARDIGAN
RADNOR
WORCESTER

HEREFORD
Cardigan
Teifi
Wye

St Davids
BRECKNOCK
PEMBROKE
CARMARTHEN
Brecon

Haverfordwest
Carmarthen
Towy
Monmouth
Raglan
GLOUCESTER

Pembroke
MONMOUTH

GLAMORGAN

Swansea
Taff

Bristol Channel
Cardiff

• • • Welsh Heartland

- - - - Marcher Lands

0   10   20   30   40 miles

WALES IN THE SIXTEENTH CENTURY

Abbots were pensioned off (and their pensions faithfully paid), and some were promoted, Abbot Lewis of Cymer becoming, for example, Bishop of Shrewsbury. Monastic lands were sold for the most part to Welsh gentry, which strengthened the position of that already powerful class.

Some indignation was aroused by the doctrinal changes made by Edward VI. Protestantism was an alien English faith, and the married clergy 'conceited goats', but there was no such general uprising as that of the Pilgrimage of Grace in England. Although Wales slipped quietly into Edwardian Protestantism, 'easily digesting' the new religion, Queen Mary's succession was greeted with some relief. While most had found, and continued to find, it easier to follow whatever the Church by law established chose to preach, the imposition of a rite in another foreign language was unpopular. But the bards over-egged the pudding when Mary was acclaimed as the 'genial Queen from the heart of Gwynedd with her fortunate face', and Elizabeth's accession was as warmly welcomed in Wales as elsewhere.[14]

Alongside the justice, the Welsh parson became much like his English counterpart, armed with a new vernacular order of service and Bible. This was largely due to Richard Davies, the energetic Bishop at St Davids from 1561, and his colleague William Salesbury, who had published the first Welsh dictionary. Between them, with Salesbury doing most of the work, they prepared a translation of the New Testament, which together with a Welsh prayerbook was commanded to be used in every parish church in Wales, thus ensuring that Welsh remained the language of the population at large and was not supplanted by English, a factor of great future importance. By 1588 the whole Bible had been translated by Richard Morgan. All three men were thoroughly Welsh, well versed in Welsh literature, and their work might be said to have generated a new language, at once literary and popular, in much the same way as Luther's writings formed the foundation for modern German. Had the Reformation been expressed solely in English, its acceptance by Welsh-speakers would surely have been reluctant. One foreign language, Latin, would have been replaced by another, English. As the Catholic Counter-Reformers well understood, a vernacular Bible in the hands of a literate and thoughtful population was the Protestants' most devastating weapon.

On the other side of the religious divide, Welsh exiles were prominent in Counter-Reformation activities, the most prominent being Owen Lewis, a former Fellow of New College Oxford, Bishop of Bassano, and a founder of the English College at Rome, which he hoped would become 'a house of studies . . . for exiles who awaited abroad the inevitable return of England to Rome'. One returning seminary priest was executed, but the results of proselytisation were disappointing, partly because so few Welsh-speakers were despatched from the seminaries. Bishop Davies was able to report that there were no 'recusants' in his diocese, and in 1603 only 803 were admitted to exist in the whole of Wales, contrasted with 212,450 conformists. However grudging some of this conformity may have been, Wales emerged from the Reformation as fully Protestant as did Scotland.

IRELAND

Henry VII had accepted that Ireland could be ruled economically only with the assistance of the Geraldines, and for the thirty-eight years after Poynings' recall the Kildare FitzGeralds ruled Ireland, mounting successful expeditions against the 'Wild Irish', quarrelling with their great rivals the Butlers and occasionally being called to account by London, but always returning to rule in Dublin. The Earl of Surrey, a useful soldier, was sent to knock heads together in 1520, but was denied the 'great puissance of men' that he accurately judged necessary.[15] It was a policy of indirect rule, which was later adopted by Lord Lugard in Nigeria: tribal native rulers employed to act as agents of imperial governments. Ireland was however too near England, and too strategically important, for this to be permanent. The system unravelled in 1533 when, following a complaint by the Butlers, the ninth Earl of Kildare was placed under arrest in London. His son, Thomas Lord Offaly, 'Silken Thomas' – twenty years old and a 'hasty hotspur' – rose in rebellion, at first successfully. The citizens of Dublin held out, and when Thomas' own citadel of Maynooth had been stormed and its garrison slaughtered, the young Earl (his father had died of natural causes) surrendered to the English commander Lord Leonard Grey, on a promise that his life would be spared. Grey reneged on his promise, and not only Silken Thomas, but five of his uncles were executed as traitors. Other rebels were comparatively mildly treated by contemporary standards – seventy-five executions in 1533, a modest total by comparison with the bloodbath which followed the German peasant revolt of 1525.

Sporadic repression was no permanent solution, and from 1541 a different method was tried, one which formalised the actual situation. Royal supremacy would be asserted by elevating Ireland from the status of a lordship to that of a kingdom, co-equal with England. As a royal dominion, all land would be transferred to the Crown, which would thereafter re-grant the properties to their existing owners, to be held in perpetuity and to descend in an orderly manner as prescribed by English law. In a similar orderly and legal manner, if their owners rebelled, their lands would be taken back by the Crown – a valuable royal weapon indeed. The Gaelic chiefs would surrender their tribal status and traditional titles in return for recognised places under the Crown. In this way, as Thomas Cusack, Speaker of the Irish Parliament explained, the Irish would be 'accepted as subjects, where before they were taken as Irish enemies', and could be expected 'to continue then in peace and obedience'.[16]

Not a new device, nor especially English: King James II of Scotland had done the same in attempting to subdue the Douglas Earl (he later made sure of the job by killing the Earl himself). Nevertheless, under the new deputy Sir Anthony St Leger, who arrived in July 1540, all the major Irish lords, Gaelic and Anglo-Norman, accepted, agreed in principle, and considerable optimism prevailed. A Parliament met in June 1541, which passed an Act declaring Henry to be 'King of Ireland'. Having formally become a kingdom, parallel to that of England, the Irish could then be admitted on equal terms to all English rights and privileges, as the Welsh had been. In Dublin the new status was received with public rejoicing, and a general amnesty proclaimed, with bonfires and free wine flowing in the streets.

In London the reception was not so enthusiastic. Henry had not realised the full consequences of the new policy, and especially the financial effects of the obligations he had assumed. Not only was there an annual deficit – some £2000 – but the general acceptance of the new policy of 'surrender and re-grant' meant that there were no rebels whose land might be confiscated for the profit of the King. The Dublin government was angrily chided, but the King reluctantly agreed. 'The greatest lord of the savages who all his life had made war on the English', Conn Bachac O'Neill, would become the Earl not of Ulster, since that was properly a royal inheritance, but of Tyrone. Similarly the O'Brien and the O'Burke became Earls of Thomond and of Clanrickard, and lesser chiefs were accorded more junior titles. Under St Leger's prudent government negotiation began to be substituted for battle as a solution to disputes among the magnates, enabling the English garrison to be reduced to a scarcely more than nominal five hundred. For the first time too, Irish soldiers were recruited for campaigns in France and Scotland. 'The most wild and savage sort ... whose absence should rather do good than hurt', they made themselves unpopular with the French by decapitating their prisoners. One immediate benefit was that the most powerful of the Gaelic nobles signed up to the new religious order. Conn Bachac agreed to 'entirely renounce obedience to the Roman Pontiff and his usurped authority' and undertook to ensure that all his subjects did likewise. Typical of many, Earl Conn, the most powerful Irish chief, was illiterate, and had to make his mark on the declaration of renunciation.

It might have been one of Ireland's tragedies that St Leger's system was never given the essential royal support and was only implemented in part. Attacked by jealous and disappearing colleagues, his ability won him re-appointment under Edward VI, and again, in very different circumstances, in the reign of Queen Mary. St Leger's original assessment was cold but hardly inaccurate: 'unless it [the country] be peopled with others than be there already and also certain fortresses there builded and warded, if it be gotten one day, it is lost the next'. By a quirk of fortune it was during St Leger's last administration, under Queen Mary, that the 'peopling' of the island with newcomers was launched: and that experiment put paid to hopes for a peaceful settlement in Ireland, especially since a new dimension was being added to the problem.

Queen Elizabeth's first Irish Parliament (11 January–1 February 1560) was less enthusiastic for Protestantism than its English counterpart and was quickly dissolved, but all Irish bishops took the oath of allegiance to the new order, a very much better record than in England; but that was as far as they went.[17] The new prayerbook remained unused, and

Mass continued to be celebrated except in the dioceses of Dublin, Armagh and Meath. Even in Meath more than a hundred parishes were served only 'by a few Irish rogues having little Latin, less civility and learning'.[18] For ten years however there was no violent objection and it seemed that Ireland, like Wales, would accept the new dispensation.

The survival of Catholicism in Ireland could hardly be attributed to any remarkable qualities of the pre-Reformation Church, or any entrenched loyalty to the papacy. On the contrary, Irish ecclesiastical life in the later fifteenth century was often corrupt, ineffective and miserable. Only in the towns did conditions approximate to those found elsewhere in Europe, with lay confraternities, spiritual guilds, mystery plays and pageants supplementing the work of a reasonably well-educated clergy. The Youghal monastic library, for example, contained 130 books, considerably more than that of the Earl of Kildare.

The island was, as Perellos and other visitors proved, not entirely isolated from Europe, but contacts were usually made through the ports, in 'English' territory. Some chiefs, as Manus O'Donnell, had their own contacts with Europe, but there was nothing approaching the permanent intercourse across the narrow seas that characterised English relations with the Continent. Ideas generated by visitors such as Erasmus, who settled in Cambridge, or Cornelio Vitelli in Oxford, and adopted by William Grocyn and John Colet, simply did not penetrate to Ireland. Here the contrast with Scotland was marked. In that country humanists such as Hector Boece of Aberdeen and Bishop Gavin Douglas were close friends of Erasmus and Polydore Virgil. An Edinburgh Royal College of Surgeons, founded in 1505, became a centre for Renaissance medical studies. In Ireland the new learning had made little progress. The Youghal library contained some printed treatises, but the only identifiable near-contemporary work is that of a predictably orthodox Italian. There was no tradition of philosophical discussion, nor educated and earnest churchmen to dispute questions, although, as a bonus, there were no martyrs in Ireland under Henry, Edward or Mary.

The Reformation came hiccuping into Ireland: first the rejection of the papacy, with little more pressure than that of a royal growl, a threat of a look 'with our princely eye at his ingratitude' should anyone dissent. What should have been the decisive second stage, Edwardian Protestantism, was haltingly introduced, so that on Mary's accession there was little reform to undo. Married bishops were expelled, but there was no repetition in Ireland of the sustained persecution of Protestants that marked Mary's reign in England. One opportunity not let slip by Mary's government was that offered by Sir Edward Bellingham, Lord Deputy in 1548–49, during one of the intermissions in St Leger's government. Bellingham, an experienced soldier, crushed a Leinster revolt and dispossessed its leaders, whose lands were then offered to potential colonists. The districts previously and subsequently known as Leix and Offaly were then shired as King's County and Queen's County, and the towns of Maryborough and Philipstown established, but the young Duke of Suffolk, Mary's Lord Deputy, found it was all that he could do to control the constant warfare that still characterised much of Ireland outside the Pale. Little progress was made towards implementing the colonisations before Mary's death in November 1558.

Queen Elizabeth's position, throughout her reign, was analogous to that of the chairman of a large company faced with formidable competitors, and chronically underfunded. Parliament, representing the shareholders in a general meeting, had to be bullied and cajoled into providing funds, and in this they were no more discriminating than their commercial counterparts. Departmental heads had to be chosen from a small group either of nobles who enjoyed royal favour, or less decorative men of proven ability: once away from head office, with communications difficult, they were difficult to control and their reports to base often misunderstood or discounted. The chairman and chief executive served for life and had access to brilliant consultants, of whom Burleigh was the most prominent. Add to that the customers – the public who could only exercise power indirectly and intermittently, but whose consent was essential – and the analogy is complete. Given too that in 1559 England had no standing army in existence comparable with those of the great Continental forces, being very much a second-rate power, the temptation to leave the Irish, Gaels and Galls alike to their own fate was considerable. Revenue had dried up entirely, and no Irish faction exercised any influence at court. Only the necessity expressed more than a century before

to keepen Yreland that it be not loste
For it is a boterasse and a poste
Undre England and Wales is another,
God forbede but eche were othere brothere,
Of one ligeaunce dewe unto the kynge[19]

acted in the contrary direction.

Even so, considering the other imperative demands on English resources – the unsteady religious settlement, the dynastic threat posed by Mary Queen of Scots, and a renewal of hostilities with France – Ireland would have been a low priority had it not been for an immediate threat that demanded countering.

Ulster had been for centuries O'Neill lands, tribal territory in which the only royal outpost was often the single castle of Carrickfergus, garrisoned in 1556 only by 'twelve tormentarii, called harquebusiers', five archers and two bombardiers.[20] O'Neill hegemony was enforced among its neighbours, especially the O'Donnells of Tyrconnel and the Scottish MacDonnells settled in Antrim. One picturesque ruffian, Shane O'Neill, had murdered his way to the Earldom of Tyrone in succession to Earl Conn Bachac. Five years of Shane's violence against his neighbours was only ended in 1567 after Earl Hugh O'Donnell had joined with the English forces under Sir Henry Sidney. Further south in Munster, the FitzGerald Earl of Desmond proved how little separated the Gaelic tribal chieftain from the descendants of the Anglo-Normans. Sidney, examining the complaints of Desmond's depredations, reported that he had never seen a more desolate land, strewn with the 'bones and skulls of dead subjects, who partly by murder, partly by famine, have died in the fields'.[21] His recommendations on the action to be taken were plain and sensible. All the old tribal and palatine jurisdictions must be abolished and replaced by presidency courts on the Welsh model, all remaining land should be transferred to the Crown and re-granted as necessary, and English colonists should be brought in to strengthen the loyal population. 'Civility', which included the adoption of English dress and manners and conformity to English law, was to be enforced on all Irish. It is interesting to note that adherence to Protestant creeds was rarely mentioned.

At that time there was a prospect of success. Sidney's campaigns against Shane and Desmond had been well supported, and the resulting confiscations offered the possibility of new land grants. In Connacht a careful examination of the existing landholdings resulted in a distribution of Crown tenures and the extinction of feudal tenures, carried through without objection. Sidney was a prudent and sensible governor, but the colonisations – 'plantations' was the current term – were carried through by inexperienced and avaricious men, poorly planned and foully executed. The shires of King's County and Queen's County, established under Queen Mary, had not been notably successful, but the new enterprises were outstanding failures. Sir Thomas Smith, Provost of Eton and Vice Chancellor of Cambridge, attempted simply to take over some lands in the Ards peninsula and to people them with English. 'No Irishman, born of Irish race and brought up Irish, shall purchase land, bear office or be chosen of any jury,' nor 'wear English apparel or weapon upon pain of death'. So mad an enterprise, in the land owned by Sir Brian O'Neill, knighted for his co-operation against Shane, was deservedly short-lived, but was supported even by Lord Burleigh, who invested £333.6s.8d. of his own money. Ignorance of Irish conditions was so widespread in England that the elementary precaution of killing the fowl before attempting to pluck it was neglected. The attitudes of these 'New English' resembled those of Victorian English colonists surprised and offended when their gifts of nineteenth-century civilisation and order were rejected by African chiefs preferring to follow the venerable traditions of their people.

'Plantation' was a popular theme. At the same time that English investors were planning an invasion of part of the Queen's Irish territories, others were preparing expeditions to the New World. Humphrey Gilbert obtained permission from the Queen in 1578 to 'plant' America. That expedition to Newfoundland failed, but subsequent endeavours succeeded in dispossessing the Indians. In 1573 the first Earl of Essex obtained the same permission to annex most of Antrim – not the possession of some unknown tribe four thousand miles across the Atlantic, but the lands of other British subjects within sight of Britain itself. Essex behaved towards the Irish as the Spanish conquistadors did to the Aztecs, with gross cruelty and treachery, and did it with the full support of his Queen and the body politic, who paid the costs of the expedition. The unfortunate Sir Brian O'Neill accepted Essex's invitation to Belfast Castle, in which after three nights spent pleasantly and cheerfully, Essex's men murdered all O'Neill's family, carrying off Sir Brian and Lady O'Neill to Dublin where they were hanged, drawn and quartered. 'Such,' the annalist grimly remarked, 'was the end of their feast.' Acting under Essex's orders Captain John Norris stormed the stronghold of the MacDonnells on Rathlin Island and massacred the entire population; he and Essex were both congratulated by the Queen. In spite of seeing his family killed, Sorley Boy, the MacDonnell chief, was able to fight on, and ultimately, at the age of eighty, made his peace with the Queen.[22]

Henry VIII had, somewhat reluctantly, attempted a reasonable settlement in Ireland; under his daughter Elizabeth, who has been accorded a much better historical press, justice was trampled underfoot. Such atrocities as those of Essex, and their complacent reception in England, were enough to make the acceptance of English rule near impossible. Even worse, these attempted 'plantations' were unsuccessful, and the land remained in the hands of its previous owners. Only a co-ordinated effort with the full resources of the Crown behind it had any prospect of success, and such an effort Elizabeth was in no position to make. Permanently short of money, with no tradition of military service – seafaring was another matter – apart from that on the northern borders, Elizabethan armies were amateurish affairs, usually badly led and poorly supplied (soldiers had to pay for their own ammunition, which hardly made for proficiency in musketry).

Shane O'Neill's revolt, beginning as it did with a tribal quarrel between O'Neills and O'Donnells, had been a classic Irish brawl of the type that had been endemic for a thousand years. It was rendered more damaging by the fact that both sides were better armed and equipped, with cannon and small arms, cavalry and fortresses, than had hitherto been usual. Another novel feature was that Shane appealed, unavailingly, for help to the Scottish King, to the Pope and to both France and Spain. Thereafter such attempts to recruit foreign aid became more significant, but in the generation after Shane's death Ulster continued preoccupied with internal dispute. Sir Turlough O'Neill and Hugh O'Neill, Earl of Tyrone, quarrelled incessantly with each other and with the O'Donnells, altercations which culminated in murders and sanguinary battles. From time to time all participants might be called to order by the Lord Deputy, when their unconvincing promises to reform would be accepted.

Further south it was the Earl of Desmond's uncle, James Fitzmaurice FitzGerald, who took the first steps to convert the ancient feud between the Butlers and FitzGeralds to something approaching a full-scale war. James Fitzmaurice, a man with vision, sent Maurice Macginn, Archbishop of Cashel, on an embassy to Spain and Rome in 1569. He met with nothing but uncertain sympathy, since the Spanish priority was to discourage any English intervention on behalf of the Protestant Dutch, in revolt against their Spanish overlords. Only ten years later, after another rebellion had ended with James Fitzmaurice swearing loyalty to Queen Elizabeth, did the Archbishop's continued endeavours meet with any response. By then Pope Pius had been succeeded by Gregory XIII, fanatically opposed to Protestantism. King Philip of Spain not having responded to Gregory's exhortations to dispossess the heretic Queen, the Pope acted on his own, despatching an expedition to Ireland. It landed in July 1579, and consisted of Fitzmaurice, Dr Nicholas Sanders, acting as Papal Legate, and some two dozen Spanish and Italian soldiers, carrying a banner blessed by Gregory himself.[23] A holy war was proclaimed against 'Elizabeth, a woman that is hated of all Christian princes for the great injuries which she has done them hated of her own subjects as well for compelling them to forswear the Christian faith . . .' When the rising was joined by the Earl of Desmond it constituted a serious threat to English rule and was met with unusual determination, exacerbated by the fact that Spain had eventually succumbed to Irish pleas. An entirely inadequate and unofficial force, mainly of Italians, landed to take up a defensive position on the Dingle peninsula in the Fort del Oro. They were there for only a few weeks before surrendering to a new Lord Deputy, Arthur, Lord Grey de Wilton. All the garrison, some six hundred, including the women and children, was massacred. It was a form of atrocity not unknown to the period, the Spaniards themselves having slaughtered the inhabitants of Haarlem a few years before, but it is still chilling to realise that the Queen criticised Lord Grey for sparing the lives of the senior officers of 'so wicked an enterprise'. Grey himself claimed that since the invaders had not come under Spanish royal orders, but at the behest of a 'detestable shaveling . . . the right Antichriste', they were not entitled to military privileges. To discourage further such enterprises a great part of Munster was systematically laid waste, causing a famine in which thirty thousand died, 'creeping forth upon their hands, for their legs could not bear them' to eat the dead animals, and even human corpses.[24]

So drastic a series of atrocities worried even Lord Burleigh, who compared them with the much-condemned Spanish activities in the Low Countries: 'as things be altered it is no marvel the people have rebellions here, for the Flemings had not so much cause to rebel by the oppression of the Spaniards, as is reported to the Irish people'. Excusing himself, the Irish Treasurer, Sir Henry Wallop, explained in June 1582 that the Irish 'much hate our nation, partly through the general mislike or disdain one nation has to be governed by another; partly that we are contrary to them in religion; and lastly, they seek to have the government among themselves'.

As the repression succeeded, the leaders of the rising become its victims; FitzGerald was killed by a cousin, the Earl of Desmond slain by Owen O'Moriarty, revenging previous injuries. Any surviving rebels were amnestied, or arrested, and the Desmond lands forfeited to the Crown, thereby freeing, it was thought, some half a million acres for English settlement. Permission was therefore given to that remarkable soldier, explorer and poet Sir Walter Raleigh to populate Munster with twenty thousand skilled and industrious colonists. More promising than Essex's attempt at conquest, the Munster policy might have worked, but it was not given the chance. Elizabeth's policy of avoiding European conflicts had at last come to an end, and England was forced into a confrontation with Spain. During the 1579 uprising King Philip had clearly disclaimed any intention of intervention, even though the rebels were openly proclaiming their intention to overthrow the Queen and establish a Catholic ruler, but after the defeat in 1588 of the great 'Enterprise of England', the Armada, Spain and England were in a permanent state of war.

When, therefore, Hugh O'Neill of Tyrone, freed from his old enemy Sir Turlough by the latter's death in 1595, began his careful preparations for a revolt which would finally 'assert Catholic liberty and free the country from the rod of tyrannical evil', he believed that he could count on support from Spain. His rising, in which he was joined by the O'Donnell Earl of Tyrconnel, dragged on for seven years, with one successful battle and numerous truces and broken agreements. The second Earl of Essex, Queen Elizabeth's young favourite, proved notably incompetent, but the promised reinforcements from Spain did not arrive until it was too late, in September 1601. By that time the English forces were commanded by Charles Blount, Lord Mountjoy, one of the ablest generals of his day. When the Spanish force eventually landed at Kinsale Mountjoy was able to defeat both them and the Ulster rebels, on Christmas Eve. Being an official force, the Spaniards were allowed to depart with their arms, and at English expense. Their commander, Don Pedro Aguila, left with the comment that 'This land seems destined specially for the princes of Hell.'[25]

The fate of the Irish was less pleasant. Once again submission was forced by a scorched-earth policy; once again cannibalism was rife: in Newry women were killing and eating children; in Dungannon children roasted the body of their dead mother: 'no spectacle was more frequent than to see multitudes of these poor people dead with their mouths all coloured green by eating Nettles, Docks and all things they could rend above ground'. It could be claimed that peace in the new kingdom of Ireland had been restored, but it was a peace that Calgacus had accused the Romans of enforcing: 'They make a desert, and call it peace.'[26]

The history of Elizabethan Ireland is however not one of unadulterated misery and persecution. The English policy, projected in the 'Device for the better government of Ireland', described an ambitious project for establishing a learned and God-fearing society, in which new hospitals, grammar schools and a university were to be founded, and laws enforced that 'no honest man lose life or lands without fair trial'. Ireland was to be brought, as the current phrase had it, to a state of 'civility', of reasonable and orderly conduct; or at least as much of it as was available in the rowdy society of Elizabethan England. New arrivals, such as Richard Boyle, who came to Dublin in 1585, founded dynasties which brought great distinction to Irish society. Trinity College, later one of the world's most famous universities, was founded in 1591. Ireland, or at least Protestant Ireland, began to be brought back into the intellectual mainstream of Europe.

The story of the 'flight of the Earls' in 1607 has assumed a central part in Irish history, as the last of the great Gaelic chiefs, O'Donnell of Tyrconnel and O'Neill of Tyrone, sailed sadly from their ancestral shores for permanent exile. It was indeed a symbolic occasion, the end of the great Gaelic dynasties that had ruled in Ireland for perhaps two thousand years, and the beginning of the end of a widespread Gaelic culture. It became the task of four dedicated Franciscan scholars, the 'Four Masters', to research and collate the history of that era. Robbed of a romantic overview the facts, as so often, are disappointingly less attractive. Tens of thousands of, mostly poor, Irish had died either in the Earls' 'cause' or as a result of it, but the leaders themselves surrendered, having been promised that their lives would be spared, and were not only pardoned but restored to their previous estates. In London they were well received by the new King, James I, and the two earls thereafter returned to Ireland ostensibly as loyal peers of the realm.[27]

History has, however, a way of repeating itself, and the same conflict that had arisen in Wales after Edward I's settlement appeared in Ireland. Territorial lords, accustomed to ruling in a traditional tribal manner, found it impossible to accept their new status as subject to common law. Tyrconnel was the first to decide to go, reluctantly accompanied by Tyrone. The causes of the flight in September 1607 have been much disputed, but it is likely that Tyrone, although he may have been pushed into the timing of this move, saw it as a logical strategy to gain Spanish support for a joint continuation of the dispute with England; but by placing such reliance on Spain, the earls became pawns in a diplomatic game, and were doomed to disappointment. Spain would act only when it suited Spanish interests, and then only with great caution, and Ireland was a very low priority. Remaining in Ireland, reliant on English good faith, would doubtless have been risky, but risking all on the expectation of Spanish support proved a great error.

The monstrous regiment of women[28]

The confused and violent nature of Scottish politics in the sixteenth century made the Reformation settlement there initially rapid, but ultimately quite as protracted as that of England. There were enough similarities between the two countries to ensure that Scotland would emerge as a Protestant country. English-speaking Scotland, that is all the country except the Highlands and Islands, had developed a culture of its own with universities at St Andrews, Glasgow and Aberdeen. Their graduates had also studied abroad, and brought back with them a full complement of the new philosophical ideas that proliferated in the fifteenth century.

Hector Boece, the first Provost of Aberdeen University, in a part of the country 'inhabited by a rude illiterate and savage people', was a friend of Erasmus, and author of an influential, if imaginative, history of Scotland. Bishop William Elphinstone of Aberdeen (1483–1510), founder of the university, a distinguished canon lawyer and diplomatist, was an effective administrator and reformer. John Mair, or Major, who like Boece studied in Paris, was the foremost Aristotelian of his time, and also published a history of Scotland. Although admitting ecclesiastical abuses, he remained a supporter of Roman authority, a position which was not adopted by many of his students at Glasgow and later at St Andrews, who included John Knox and George Buchanan. Patrick Hamilton, another of Major's students, also deviated from his doctrines, and in 1529 was burnt as a heretic.

Official Scotland showed little sympathy for the new religion. In the confused state of political faction-fighting that marked the minority of James V, the most consistently powerful man in the kingdom was James Beaton (or Bethune), Archbishop of Glasgow and of St Andrews, the persecutor of Patrick Hamilton. After James personally assumed power in 1528 – he had to escape from imprisonment to do it – he was able to take advantage of the papacy's conflict with Henry VIII to extract more money from the Scottish clergy. Unlike his English cousin, James did not find it necessary to dissolve the monasteries: he merely filched their income. Some of the richer benefices were taken by the royal family, James being a prolific supplier of bastard sons who were granted remunerative Church positions as infants. Quentin Kennedy, a Catholic reformer, protested that it was commonplace to see 'ane bairn and ane babe, to quhame scarcelie wold thou give ane fair appil to kepe, get perchance fyve thousand soules to gyde'.[29] It was true that both convents and bishoprics were wealthy enough, since they in their turn had appropriated the lion's share of parochial income, leaving perhaps only one-quarter to pay the wretched curates, who had to extort enough to live on from their often miserably poor parishioners. The effect of both persecution and the impoverishment of the Church was exactly the opposite to that which Beaton or the King intended: priests became more discontented, ineffective and unpopular, and the people more inclined to listen to the new doctrines.[30]

James had died three weeks after the battle of Solway Moss, leaving his newly-born daughter Mary in the care of the Queen Mother, Mary of Guise, but with James Hamilton, Earl of Arran, acting as Regent with the old Archbishop Beaton's successor and nephew, Cardinal David Beaton, as Chancellor and Papal Legate. Arran had begun by demonstrating reformist sympathies, and authorised the publication of a vernacular Bible, but the younger Beaton won that argument. The Cardinal had political as well as theological reasons for attempting to extirpate the Scottish Protestants, since they were, with some reason, suspected of being a fifth column promoting English interests; but his murder in May 1546 was a purely Scottish affair, carried out in revenge for the burning of a popular reformer, George Wishart.

After the murder the conspirators took over the Cardinal's castle of St Andrews, where they were joined by a friend of Wishart's, John Knox. For more than a year theological debates ensued, until the castle was besieged by a French naval force, and in due course the reformers surrendered. Knox was sent with the other prisoners for a short time to work in the galleys, and on his release was welcomed in Edward VI's England. After refusing an offer of the see of Rochester – not because of an objection to episcopacy as such – Knox moved to Geneva in January 1554. There, and during a stay in Frankfurt as pastor to the refugee English congregation, his theological views developed. Although the man who brought Calvinism to Scotland, and having met Jean Calvin and many other prominent Protestants, Knox was less a theologian than a passionate politician. Calvin, over such matters as the trial of Michael Servetus, went through a good deal of heart-searching and self-examination, neither of which activities was in any way typical of John Knox, rarely given to self-doubt. The pre-eminent part played by Knox in the Scottish Reformation differentiates that movement from its parallel in England. No single reformer emerged with the authority enjoyed by Knox, perhaps because few Englishmen possessed the same dogmatic certainty that distinguished him (and not a few of his countrymen).

It was not until 1559 that the Reformation in Scotland came to life, a generation after that in England. As part of the second wave of Protestantism it was more radical than that of the more conservative Lutherans who had inspired the first English reformers. Calvinists believed in predestination – that the final destiny of all creatures was ordained from the beginning, and known to God. Such a doctrine was easily corrupted into the idea that individuals could themselves share this knowledge, and that there was therefore an identifiable body of the 'elect'. To oppose the elect was impiously to challenge the Divine Will; and the elect were conveniently identified with the new Scottish Church. In Scotland the Reformation was a popular movement, erupting quickly and spontaneously, in contrast to that in England which had to be force-fed by the Marian persecutions and the fear of foreign intervention. Moreover, by 1560 Queen Elizabeth was beginning to exert her own authority over the English Church, whilst royal authority in Scotland was at a low ebb. A cynical Englishman commented that the Scots 'have not suffered above two kings to die in their beds these last two hundred years' (although it might be pointed out that three English queens had lost their heads within twenty years of each other).

The outbreak of 1559 was triggered by political events. As long ago as 1548 the little Queen Mary had been betrothed to the Dauphin François, eldest son of King Henri II of France, and ten years later the young couple were married. A key provision of the marriage settlement was that the Dauphin would succeed to the throne of Scotland should his wife die first. The idea of a French Catholic becoming King of Scotland horrified Protestants, whilst all Scottish patriots feared the annexation of their country to France, as had happened only a few years previously to the ancient Duchy of Brittany. In such a tense climate the condemnation for heresy of a Protestant-inclined priest, Walter Mylne, was the spark that ignited popular indignation.[31] Although over eighty, Mylne was burned at St Andrews on 28 April. The next month Perth's convents were sacked and Knox returned from Geneva; by July the Protestant Lords of the Congregation, representing all sections of Scottish society, had purged St Andrews and Dundee; in September Edinburgh was in tumult. Mary of Guise was deposed as Regent, and a provisional government established. Unexpectedly, Henri was killed in a tournament, the Dauphin succeeding as François II, upon which young Mary quickly advertised her claims to be Queen of England and Ireland as well as of Scotland and France. In so doing she virtually signed her own death warrant, since the enmity of Elizabeth was instantly aroused, and the loyalty of many of Mary's own subjects impaired.

The French connection established by James V's widow, Mary of Guise, as Queen Regent, and reinforced by young Mary's marriage to François, had been strengthened by a large French force being stationed in Scotland, garrisoning Leith and controlling access to the capital. Such an army, representing so fiercely anti-Protestant a government as that of France (in June 1559 the royal Edict of Ecouen had authorised the rigid suppression of heresy, and in March 1560 hundreds of Protestants were executed in Amboise, some in the presence of François and Mary), threatened both the Scottish Protestants and England. Queen Elizabeth's decision to send a force to oust the French was therefore welcomed by many in Scotland. After some hard fighting a treaty was signed at Edinburgh by English and French commissioners and the Protestant Lords of the Congregation in July 1560. The Scottish 'Reformation' Parliament ignored Queen Mary's orders to avoid religious debate, and issued a series of anti-Roman Acts.

The Treaty of Edinburgh marked the beginning of the end of the 'Auld Alliance'.[32] England and Scotland were now, if not entirely united by religion, at least sharing a common enemy, the Catholic European powers. Even so modest a degree of unity encouraged both sides to substitute a wary amity for ancient hostility. In December of that year King François, still only eighteen, died, leaving the widowed Mary as Queen of Scots and next in line to Elizabeth for the English succession. On Mary's return to Scotland in August 1561 the question of her remarriage became a pressing diplomatic issue, solved in 1565 by a wedding with her cousin Henry Stewart, Lord Darnley. If Elizabeth did not produce an heir then any children of Mary's would inherit the throne of England, and in June 1566 a son, Charles James, was born to Queen Mary; seven months later Darnley was murdered.

For eighteen years thereafter, until James – the Charles was soon dropped – came of age, Scotland was in turmoil. Queen Mary was deposed and the thirteen-month-old James crowned as King James VI in July 1567. Between that date and 1585, when James assumed personal rule, Scottish government was at best confused, at worst anarchic. The 'creeping' Parliament of Edinburgh sat, with the King's supporters in the Canongate fired on by the Queen's in the castle; Regent Moray was murdered in 1570; his successor, Lennox, Darnley's father, lasted for just over a year before being killed in turn. Regent Mar also held office for a year, before he died. Lord Morton, regent from 1572 to 1578, was executed in 1582 – and his accuser, Lord Arran, murdered in 1595: the career prospects for Scottish regents were poor.

After losing the battle of Langside in 1568 the 'monstrous regiment of women' ended in Scotland and Queen Mary was forced to seek refuge in England. She was an unwelcome and dangerous guest, representing an attractive tool in the hands of those who wanted to overthrow Elizabeth. By 1584 it was clear that Elizabeth, fifty-one and still unmarried, would never produce an heir, and the Catholic powers were menacing. In July the Dutch Prince William of Orange was assassinated: Spain was planning the 'Enterprise of England' which culminated in the Spanish Armada four years later. King James' support and a defensive alliance with Scotland were therefore prudently and economically secured by an annual payment of £4000. When another plot to release Mary – quite possibly encouraged by Sir Francis Walsingham – was discovered, the unfortunate Queen was, after much hesitation on Elizabeth's part, executed in February 1587.

When James was able to take the reins of power in Scotland at the age of nineteen it was too late to impose a final shape on the Church settlement, which by then had become more complex.[33] Andrew Melville, more radical even than Knox, had influenced the Church in a severely Presbyterian direction, whilst James remained a supporter of episcopacy. Presbyterian theory required that each parish should be governed by a council of elders and the minister jointly, with parishes grouped into presbyteries who would elect the supreme governing body, the General Assembly of the Kirk. In such a Church bishops had no place, and were usually regarded with suspicion as essentially Romish. A compromise was reached only in 1592, when administrative episcopalian functions were transferred to the presbyteries, but bishops allowed to continue in office. Thereafter, especially when the pill was later sweetened by financial help, extreme Presbyterianism declined. Melville was exiled, and it was another century before the Scottish Church assumed a settled identity. The General Assembly of the Kirk, representing some six hundred parishes grouped into fifty presbyteries, was allowed to meet only when the King so wished it; and that was rarely.

An English nation?

In his play *Henry V*, written probably in 1600, Shakespeare introduces three characters intended to represent the Welsh, the Scots and the Irish officers. Fluellen, the Welshman, is the most important, valued by the King: 'Though it appear a little out of fashion, There is much care and valour in this Welshman,' while the Irish Captain Macmorris is resentful and gloomy: 'What ish my nation? . . . Who talks of my nation?' Scottish Captain Jamy contents himself with stirring up trouble between the others. Presumably by that time English audiences could recognise such characterisations and find them appropriate. It would have been much more difficult to create a typical English character, for an English sense of nationality was only then emerging.

Since the Norman Conquest England had never been seriously threatened by invasion. Scottish raids, although frequent, had never presented any danger to the realm's security. It was the English who in France, Wales, Scotland and Ireland had been the aggressors. Unsuccessful in Scotland and France, English invasions had stimulated resistance and national pride in both countries, whilst their failures had diverted English ambitions into other channels. At the start of the seventeenth century Ireland was the target for English expansionists, but the first expeditions to India and America were already being prepared. By the time of Shakespeare's death, in 1616, English trading stations had been established in India, the Muscovy Company had begun explorations of northern Canada, a colony had been established in Bermuda and the Virginian settlement had survived its initial misfortunes.

The sixteenth century had been a period of confusingly rapid change. A man born in 1540 who died in 1610 would have been christened in a Catholic Latin service, and buried according to a Protestant English rite. His country would have been transformed from being little more than a cultural province of France into the birthplace of the world's greatest literature. By the end of that century England would have become a European power, with colonies and trade protected by an unsurpassed naval strength. Before an unequivocal sense of Englishness had developed England itself was being extended far from the island; the empire that developed was to be 'British'.

It might be, of course, that even in that day Englishmen regarded Englishness as being the natural state of humanity, the norm from which all other nationalities were aberrations. The possibility is indicated in *Henry V* by the innominate Boy, who follows the King's rallying call 'God for Harry! England and Saint George!' with the timeless complaint of English soldiery: 'Would I were in an alehouse in London! I would give all my fame for a pot of ale, and safety.'

CHAPTER 6

1603–1660

The royal Crowns united

KING JAMES VI OF SCOTLAND and I of England has been saddled with a worse reputation than he deserves ever since Henri IV of France, that master of the epigram, called him 'the wisest fool in Christendom'. His early years were fraught with danger as his unattractive small person (odd, since both his parents were unusually tall and handsome) became a counter in power struggles between violent Scottish magnates. Even when James was able to assume personal rule, royal authority was always limited by the military strength that could be exerted by quite modest lairds in the most settled regions; as late as 1592 Alexander Forrester of Stirling was able to defy royal commands with a thousand armed men – and the Highlands, of course, together with much of the Borders, remained often 'clannit' and anarchic.[1]

James' position was the more exposed since he was, since the death of his mother, heir to the kingdom of England, a much grander prospect than the succession of the Scottish Crown. Queen Elizabeth refused to commit herself publicly, but it was a well-understood thing. When Queen Mary was executed, James, in spite of the fury of many Scots, contented himself with a dignified protest. Dignity in the written word came easily to him, even if in person and in speech it eluded him; he was known as a poor horseman and the sight of a sharp blade could bring about a fainting fit. Intellectually, however, James was a worthy successor to Queen Elizabeth, who, although unparalleled in pithy comments in several languages, was no great author. James, on the contrary, was a prolix writer with a lively style, expressed in his volumes condemning witches and tobacco smoking, and *Basilikon Doron*, his book of advice to his sons.

During his rule in Scotland James was on the whole an enlightened reformer. Parliamentary business was facilitated by his steering committee, the Lords of the Articles, responsible for introducing legislation; and since the Lords were selected as reliable associates of the King, Parliament became more responsive to royal direction. Scotland's fourth university was founded at Edinburgh in 1582; that city was now the centre of government, the law and the Church, and soon became the foremost seat of learning, all operating within a few yards of that Royal Mile which ran from the royal castle to the royal palace of Holyrood. Progress in rationalising Scottish law had been made by the establishment of a supreme civil court, the Court of Session, modelled after the Parlement of Paris, in 1532. Under James the foundation of the Society of Writers to the Signet and the Faculty of Advocates ensured that Scottish lawyers were properly qualified. Local justice however remained a muddle of diverse jurisdictions. Apart from the undefined but extensive powers of the Kirk sessions the barony courts acted independently of formal codes. These manorial tribunals adjudicated local disputes and issued innumerable regulations, fining miscreants for being sick on someone else's floor or putting Sabbath-breakers in the stocks, even in 1623 hanging a cattle-thief.

The whole of Elizabeth's reign had been harassed by the problem of succession, and it was to general relief that James was able to ascend the English throne in March 1603 without opposition.[2] The initial moderate enthusiasm was somewhat qualified when the King began to put his own absolutist ideas into practice. His Scottish experiences, beginning with a period of near-anarchy – which included being kidnapped and imprisoned for a year in 1582–83 – had convinced him that strong royal rule was essential. The King came to England brimming with grandiose ideals. In his own person he represented the union of the two kingdoms, or so he considered, but much greater projects were possible. Could not true unity and perpetual peace be brought to Europe by an ecumenical council, under the aegis of the Pope? If so, James declared that 'he could not act more nobly than to be the first to offer complete obedience to Council's decrees'. The proposal attracted some polite noises, but little support.[3]

King James of Scotland had become an experienced professional ruler; but he found himself uncertain on the larger English stage. Neither he nor his successor Charles I had undergone the painful learning process that Queen Elizabeth had endured, that of appreciating that an English Parliament must be cajoled, mollified, bullied and persuaded into supporting what Queen and Council wanted and providing the funds to do it. It was by royal decree and not by Act of either Parliament that the 'Kingdom of Greater Britain' was created. The King himself adopted the new style of King of Great Britain and designed a new flag, the 'Great Union', incorporating the St Andrew's saltire and the St George's cross. Parliament and the people remained suspicious.

The King had good reason for haste. Whilst he had been admitted to the succession of both Crowns without trouble, this was no guarantee that his heirs would be able to do likewise. In spite of his emotional homosexuality, which was to manifest itself more clearly later in his life, James had done his dynastic duty, producing two boys, Henry (named after his forebear Henry VII, with Queen Elizabeth acting as godmother) and Charles, and one girl, Elizabeth, from whom the present royal house is descended. If James could establish himself as King of Great Britain, rather than of England and Scotland separately, the danger of a split and disputed succession would be much reduced. It might also – and this was to become a major factor in James' policy – be able to bring the untidy kingdom of Ireland into the same unified state. James intended that the union should be formal and permanent, an 'incorporating union' rather than a mere federation, and introduced a Bill to Parliament, 'The Instrument of Union', which would have provided not only for free trade, but for a common nationality between the countries. This was too much for the English House of Commons, who politely rejected the King's ideas.

Much continued to separate the two countries, especially in the sensitive matter of religion. James, temperamentally supportive of episcopalianism, attempted to bring the countries nearer together. At the Westminster Conference of 1604 Presbyterian and Anglican divines discussed their respective ideas, but failed to agree. Law was another bone of contention. What, demanded English parliamentarians, many of whom were lawyers, would be the law of Great Britain, if the King's ideas were adopted? Wide divergences existed between Scottish and English law: the multiplicity of private and ecclesiastical jurisdictions that continued in the Scottish system were anathema to English lawyers.

King James was sympathetic to endeavours to amend Scottish law, realising that his 'feckless, arrogant' nobles attempted 'to thrall the meaner sort' and that the greatest obstacle to good government was the continuation of hereditary sheriffdoms. When, however, a remedy was attempted to bring the systems closer together, as it was in 1609, with the appointments of JPs in Scotland on the English model, it failed. Justices' powers were restricted: they might not, for example, deal with offences committed by 'landit gentlemen' with incomes of more than a thousand marks – about £70 sterling. Only when pressure was exerted from England, as it was in 1654 and 1662, was any progress made in reducing the privileges of feudal courts.

Conceptual as well as practical differences emerged. James, a descendant of Henry VII and all those English kings before him, saw himself as 'away taking of that partition wall which already, by God's providence, in my blood is rent asunder', and knew himself to be a reasonable man capable of compromise even with recalcitrant English parliamentary lawyers. For their part these tactfully acknowledged that 'God in his great mercy hath given us a wise King and religious,' but added that He 'also sometimes permit hypocrites and tyrants' to rule. The King was displeased at this breach of etiquette: 'I wish you had kept better form. I like form as much as matter. It shows respect, and I expect it, being a King well born (suppose I say it) as any of my progenitors' – two sentences which aptly illustrate the tolerance of King James at that stage of his reign, and present the monarch in a sympathetic light: old Queen Elizabeth would have been blisteringly direct.[4]

Scotland was no more enthusiastic than England for greater unity. If there were to be no commercial advantages, there seemed to be no others on offer. Scotland had nothing to fear from foreign aggression – except from England – thereby negating the advantage of a political union. Indeed, by making it impossible to continue the Auld Alliance, even that dubious source of strength had to be forgone; and it was clear that once James had tasted the social comforts of St James' and Hampton Court palaces he would be unlikely to spend much time in his native country (and in his twenty-two-year tenure of the English throne he paid only one visit to Scotland).

The Stuarts' absence from their native country was likely to be permanent. 'No prince born in Scotland will ever rule that country after his Majesty's son,' complained one Scot. 'Our kings will be Englishmen,' he continued, not so accurately, since many of them have been German or Dutch, 'London will be the ... capital of the whole island. Thence for the most part will be the laws that govern us, proceed, and to London we must look for direction.'[5] With some reluctance, the English Parliament agreed some concessions in the cause of unity: Scots born after the union were to be treated as English, hostile laws were repealed, the perennially lawless Borders converted into the 'Middle Shires'. But closer union was shelved *sine die*.

James vaunted that he was able to rule Scotland from London: 'Here I sit and govern it with my pen, I write and it is done.' His boast at the time was largely true. Reinforced by the authority he had gained in Scotland during his successful rule the Scottish Privy Council clearly understood their master's wishes, and faithfully implemented decisions. Episcopacy was gently restored, the Highlands and Islands 'brought into civility' by delegating power to the reliable Clan Campbell. That tenacious tradition of outlawry, exemplified by the Border 'riding families', was finally stopped up. Armstrongs and Elliots, always the worst offenders, were hanged in batches, and the Grahams exiled over the water to Roscommon; most of that clan did not stay, and slipped back to their homelands, sometimes thinly disguised under the name of Mahargs.

Neither achievement was permanent, for the underlying problems of the Scottish economy remained. Support from the landed classes was maintained only by an impossibly complex and grossly unfair system of taxation. Inflation eroded living standards, which in Scotland had fallen throughout the century. Every attempt to turn back the clock in Church affairs stiffened the resolve of those dedicated to Presbyterianism; and by now they were in a substantial majority. Nevertheless Alexander Hay, Lord Binning, was in the right when he contrasted the previous state of Scotland, a time when 'treasons, murthours, burningis, thiftis, reiffis, hearschippis, hoching of oxen, breaking of milnes, destroying of growand cornis, and barbarities of all sortes' were widespread, with the situation in 1617, when all such wickedness had been 'so repressed, puneissed, and aboleissed by your majesties wisdome, caire, power, and expensis, as no nation on earth could now compaire with our prosperities'.[6] The final clause was perhaps straining the truth.

When James died in 1625 it was after an unprecedentedly long and tranquil reign in Scotland. As James I of England he had at least survived, and kept the limited union that had been achieved intact. He had ruled according to the laws of England and not offended the prejudices of his southern subjects irredeemably, but had done nothing to bolster the Crown's prestige: anniversaries of Elizabeth's succession were celebrated with somewhat insulting enthusiasm. His reign's most significant achievement, one not much noticed at the time, was the beginning of England's overseas empire. In a small way, and trailing behind the Dutch, the Honourable East India Company made its first voyage to the East, a venture which eventually led to the nineteenth-century Indian Empire. In the Caribbean, St Kitts, followed three years later by Barbados and Nevis, together with Bermuda, and the new colonies of Virginia and New England, marked the start of English-speaking America. Nova Scotia, the single Scottish venture, was less successful, Scotland being too economically restricted to afford diversification into colonial ventures – as was very painfully proved to be true even eighty years later.

Loose and absolved from all rules of government

'Charles, *be* King,' was James' advice to his son, and it was faithfully followed. The young King, who succeeded his father in 1625, had to face down much powerful opposition from his English Parliament during the first years of his reign. By 1630 he had asserted his authority, and the next eight years saw a series of royal advances which left the parliamentary opposition baffled and Charles I well-established and solvent. The King was able to raise money for the expenses of government and for such projects as naval building without having to rely upon an unco-operative Parliament. In Scotland, however, where his father had boasted that he was able to rule from London with his pen, Charles got off to a poor start.[7]

At the very beginning of his reign Charles made himself unpopular with the Scots gentry and nobles by revoking all Crown land grants made in that country since 1540. This was not in itself an unexpected action for a new sovereign, intended as it was to begin a money-raising negotiation with the grantees, but it was unprecedented for a revocation to go so far into the past. Much worried uncertainty was generated, weakening support for the King among those who might otherwise have been his natural allies. Charles paid little attention to any advice coming from his Council in Edinburgh, whose President, the Earl of Menteith, was a minor figure of inconsiderable importance.

Only in 1633 did Charles make his way north for his coronation as King of Scotland, and what he found there was distasteful. The new Parliament house, begun the previous year, was not complete. There was little of the dignified ceremony of his London court, and his piety was offended by 'irregular services . . . held in mean churches by ministers who prayed and exhorted their flocks at enormous length'. This was not the King's conception of how religion should be ordered in his realms, which was guided by the ideals of William Laud, appointed Archbishop of Canterbury in the same year. Laud's predecessor, George Abbot, was a conciliator, and had been able to convince the Scots to accept a form of continued episcopacy rather than the Presbyterian government demanded by most of the ministers. Laud, a bitter foe of Abbot's for thirty years, was a man of very different opinions, and implacable in refusing to believe that he might be mistaken. Now in a position to do so, Archbishop Laud pursued the logic of an established Church, backed by the state power, to its fullest extent, demanding that the smallest details of worship must be regulated, and ecclesiastic regulations enforced, if necessary by severe punishment.

This did not go down well in England, where there was some sympathy for Calvinist principles, especially among the London townspeople, and a very general dislike of being told what to do by clergymen. In Scotland it was a fatal miscalculation. At a single stroke almost the whole of Scotland was alienated by the imposition of new ecclesiastical laws and a new prayerbook, which had a strong Laudian flavour. An occasion of particular offence was the omission, in the communion service, of the phrase 'Do this in remembrance of Me,' which transformed the celebration into something very like the sacrifice of the Mass. When, in July 1637, a service according to the new liturgy was attempted to be held in St Giles' Cathedral at Edinburgh, a riot ensued. Amid howls of rage a stool was thrown at the priest, and a 'she-zealot' shouted, 'The Mass is entered upon us.' The worried and moderate Dr Robert Baillie wrote, 'there was in our land ever such ane appearence of a sturr . . . I think our people possessed of a bloody devill'.[8]

Such insults to Scottish sensibilities were doubly resented because they were seen as English intrusions. James had been essentially a Scottish King, transplanted to England, retaining an informed and active interest in his native country. Charles, in contrast, was an English King, with an English court, and enjoyed little of his father's prestige in Scotland. In default of a negotiated compromise, the King decided on the arbitrement of war, but without an effective army this was unlikely to be successful. Charles' efforts to rule without a Parliament in England had worked only as long as the expense of maintaining an army was avoided. The Scots, on the other hand, had always relied on unpaid local levies to provide the backbone of their forces, and had a reservoir of trained talent among those Scots who had learned their trade in the Continental religious wars. These, which began in 1618 with a Protestant revolt in Bohemia, had spread all over Europe, and were to continue for thirty years, driving ever deeper the divide between Catholic and Protestant.[9]

Edinburgh, always a centre of extreme Presbyterianism, took the initiative in opposing the King. An assembly of gentry, burgesses, ministers and nobles gathered there united in what became nearly a revolutionary opposition. Their manifesto, issued in February 1638, was that seminal document, the National Covenant. The King was assured that 'we have no intention nor desire to attempt any thing that may turn to . . . the diminution of the King's greatness and authority', but the 'Covenanters'' demands were unequivocal. There must be both a free Parliament and a General Assembly of the Kirk, adherence to 'God's Word and the Christian Religion' (which was left in some respects undefined, to be taken as each man might wish). The Covenanters ended by undertaking 'to resist all those contrary errors and corruptions . . . all the days of our life'. Within weeks this Covenant was read in churches throughout Scotland and enthusiastically subscribed to, except in the loyally episcopalian north-east. In June the first General Assembly in twenty years met, packed with militant

Covenanters. Royal government dissolved and the King's representative, the unhappy Marquis of Hamilton, walked out in despair, groaning, 'Next Hell I hate this place.'[10]

The Covenanters were however reluctant to fight against their own Scottish King, to whom they professed continued loyalty. An intimidating Scottish army of some thirty thousand was gathered, under the leadership of Alexander Leslie, who had won an immense reputation in the European wars. Their opponents, a mixture of feudal cavalry and reluctant conscripts, were the incompetent best the King had managed to put together. The 'First Bishops' War' was therefore an undramatic conflict, limited to a few skirmishes before the two armies, glowering at each other outside Berwick, reached a treaty in June 1639 by which the King assured the Scots that the General Assembly should have full authority to determine Church matters. The reasons for objection seem today scarcely a cause for war. The strongest complaints were against moving the communion table from the body of the church to the east end, which was believed to be Romanist; such is ecclesiastical modishness that today all churches have moved the table back to its former position (and indeed the Protestant reformers' pivotal demand, that both bread and wine be offered to the laity, is now, together with clerical celibacy, quietly being conceded by the Vatican). But not only were such matters then of great importance, but the whole authority of the monarch was threatened by the successful Scottish defiance.

Charles, encouraged by Laud, determined to try again. The English Parliament was not minded to grant the funds essential for a new campaign since the King paid no attention to their long-delayed grievances. At this point Thomas Wentworth, Earl of Strafford, the King's viceroy in Ireland, took a hand. Wentworth's advice to Charles was vehement: 'Go on with a vigorous war, as you first designed, loose and absolved from all rules of government . . . you have an army in Ireland you may employ here to reduce this kingdom.' Whether or not 'this kingdom' meant Scotland or England was the subject of much later argument, but Wentworth was unquestionably given a commission with wide powers. Appointed 'Captain General over the army in Ireland, and of such in England as the King . . . shall add', he was ordered '. . . to resist all invasions and seditious attempts in England, Ireland and Wales, and to be led into Scotland there to invade, kill and slay'.

The Scots struck first, before Wentworth could move. General Leslie led a strong force over the border to smash a detachment of the royal army at Newburn and to take, without resistance, the vital port of Newcastle on 30 August 1640. As long as 'the lads about Newcastle sit still', the initiative in all things now lay with the Scots. Within weeks the war was over, all the 'killing and slaying', such as it was, having been done by the Scots. A truce was signed at Ripon in October, forcing the King into a second surrender. By acting 'loose and absolved from all rules of government' Charles eventually cost both Wentworth and himself their heads.

Very much unlike previous Scottish wars, the Scots victory in 1640 aroused little resentment in England. In London, the centre of parliamentary strength and Puritan opinion, it was said: 'We must stand or fall together ... we are Brethren.' At Ripon the King had agreed to pay £850 a day to the Scots until a formal peace treaty was signed; until then the lads would sit still. Scottish Commissioners were sent to London to negotiate – or, as they believed, to demand – terms of a treaty which in some respects was an attempt at closer confederal union, one in which separate parliaments would co-ordinate their activities and jointly agree on such matters as defence and foreign policy, as well as committing both kingdoms to radical Protestantism.

King Charles was faced with the unwelcome task of summoning a Parliament, and in November 1640 what proved to be the 'Long Parliament' assembled. The Scots negotiators arrived in high fettle; the military victory, in what had been little more than a skirmish, was nothing beside the immense political triumph. Scotland's own reformed Church, with the spirited backing of so many of its people, had forced a radical change of royal policy in that country. Imbued with a new sense of national self-confidence, it seemed quite likely that the Scots could also impose their will, and their Church, upon England. The English parliamentarians made polite noises, and agreed to appoint representatives to settle a treaty, but were in reality taken aback by Scottish presumption. The fact that a Scottish army was quartered in Newcastle was annoying, but in the English Parliament's view did not permit a smaller, and very much poorer, nation to dictate terms in London.

Parliament granted Charles enough money to pay off the Scots, but an additional price was exacted. Six months later, Wentworth, pursued by vengeful Scots and abandoned by the King, was executed on Tower Hill. There had been no such judicial murders (not counting a couple of heretics burnt by James) since that of Sir Walter Raleigh twenty-three years previously, and Wentworth's death was a harbinger of more such violence ahead. Archbishop Laud, and finally the King himself, were to follow him to the scaffold.

After Wentworth's execution events moved quickly. King Charles travelled to Scotland, in an attempt to seduce the Scots with honours – Leslie was made Earl of Leven – with promises to adhere to the Covenant, and by attendance at tedious Presbyterian services. Deceived by the loyalty shown to his person, as the latest representative of a Scots dynasty now 350 years old, attempting to follow Scots jokes and enjoying rounds of golf on the Leith links, Charles returned to London in November 1641 persuaded that he could rely on a Scots army to suppress English opposition. His optimism was reinforced by the news from Ireland.

Colonies nearer home

Unlike almost all other countries, England has no national festival, no Quatorze Juillet, no Independence Day. Such critical events as the battle of Trafalgar are recalled only among seafarers; the nation's saint and William Shakespeare share the same anniversary, but few remember when it falls. Other than 11 November – no day of celebration, but one of mourning and regret – the only date that resounds among the majority of citizens is 5 November. Guy Fawkes is one of the very few non-royal figures whose historical role the man in the street can describe. Even after four centuries 'Gunpowder, Treason and Plot' retains something of its significance.

At the time – which was 1605 – that conspiracy among Roman Catholics to destroy the whole government machinery at a single blow, by blowing up Westminster Hall, had a decisive effect upon public opinion. Papists, already targeted as suspect traitors after the Papal Bull of 1585, were ineradicably, for many years to come, regarded with nervous suspicion by most of their fellow citizens in England; and conversely, as religious persecution increased in Ireland, most Irishmen, remaining Catholics, saw their Church as a symbol of resistance to English oppression, and the papacy as a powerful potential ally.

Scotland and Ireland developed national identities in opposition to English power. The English faced no such permanent threat. French, Spanish, Dutch, French again, and Germans have featured successively, and sometimes simultaneously, as *the* national enemy, but only France seems to have permanently retained something of this position. The great opponent was not a foreign power, but what was seen as a foreign ideology, embodied in the Church of Rome. English Catholics became a small, loyal and quiescent minority, but for three centuries after Elizabeth's accession opposition to Catholicism and the papacy was near-unanimous and persistent among the English.

Another date, not now remembered, but of much greater historical significance, was 14 May 1607, when Captain Christopher Newport landed his hopeful colonists at what became Jamestown, Virginia, to found 'London's Plantation in the Southern Part of Virginia'. (Northern Virginia, by some truly horrible navigation, was to become better known as New England, when William Brewster and his company landed at Cape Cod instead of the mouth of the Hudson.) Plantations had been attempted in Ireland with small success, but after what seemed to be the final defeat of the old Gaelic chiefs, prospects seemed brighter. The high risks involved in both the Atlantic passage and the stabilising of settlements in hostile country could be avoided by colonising Ireland, much nearer and, it was erroneously believed, very much safer.

King James was suspicious of Ireland and the Irish. As King of Scotland he had experienced the annoyance of Irish MacDonnells' and Scottish Macdonalds' lawless ways. On acceding to the throne of England Ireland became his own problem, to which two different solutions offered themselves. He might pursue Elizabeth's policy of crushing revolt, which Mountjoy had so successfully concluded, and bringing Ireland under full English control, as King Edward had with Wales. Alternatively he might conciliate the Irish notables, confirm their status, and rely on them to control the people within and without the Pale, which the initial reaction of the Ulster Earls seemed to indicate was a clear possibility. When this hope was disappointed James chose instead to populate as much of Ireland as possible with decent biddable Scots.[11]

As well as symbolising the end of the venerable Gaelic tribal order, the flight of the earls left vast tracts of Ulster which could be sequestrated as Crown land. At first somewhat reluctant to assert his claim, for fear of offending Spain, with which country a peaceful settlement had just been (1604) negotiated, James proceeded delicately. One of his most reliable servants, James Hamilton, was in 1605 allocated a huge tract of land in Clandeboye (he later became Viscount Clandeboye), formerly the O'Neills' Antrim lands, which he shared with Conn MacNeill O'Neill and two fellow Scots, the Montgomery brothers. It was made a condition of the grant that the lands were developed and settled by reliably industrious immigrants; and reliability was assumed to be synonymous with Protestantism. Other Irish landowners, the O'Haras, MacQuillans, MacCartans and Magennises, also obtained substantial grants to seal their loyalty to the Crown. Of these the largest went to Sir Randal MacDonnell, who became the Earl of Antrim, now one of the oldest Irish titles.

Although the Antrim lands were described as 'now more wasted than America [when the Spaniards landed there] . . . with few miserable huts . . . ruined roofless churches', the Lowland Scots imported as settlers very soon had things put to rights, mills and harbours built, and the land brought back into cultivation. A school was built at Newtonards, and with a master teaching Greek and facilities for football and 'goff', it was all very much a transplanted Lowland Scotland.[12]

The benefits of having reliable Protestant settlers were underlined when in 1608 Sir Cahir O'Doherty of Inishowen, who had been regarded as a supporter of the Crown, quarrelled with the Governor of Derry and sacked the town. After his rebellion had been crushed the great expanse of Inishowen was also sequestered by the Crown. With the lands of the latest rebels added to the still unallocated estates of the earls, virtually all the north-east of Ireland was available for settlement. Lying only twelve miles off the Scottish coast, with a foothold already established by the 1605 plantation, this was too great an opportunity to be missed. In 1610 a prospectus was published defining the conditions under which almost all Tyrconnel, Coleraine, Tyrone,

Armagh, Fermanagh and Cavan was to be made available. 'Under-takers', who had to be Protestants, were required to warrant that they would plant ten families of English or 'inland' Scots on every thousand acres; 'servitors' – those who had served the Crown in some senior capacity – were offered similar grants on favourable conditions.

Sir Arthur Chichester, the experienced Lord Deputy, was concerned that not enough land had been given either to the 'deserving Irish' or to the servitors, likely to be the most trustworthy of settlers. Such a neglect would mean both that lasting resentment would be generated among the Irish, and that the means of resisting rebellion, when that resentment burst out, would be lacking. A perilous division developed between the 'man on the spot', experienced in Irish affairs, and the governments in London and in Edinburgh, who saw Ireland as a means of solving their own problems. In particular, there was no clear understanding as to whether Ireland should be treated as a separate country, with a balance struck between the interests of 'Old English' (descendants of earlier settlers), native Irish and the new settlers, rep-resented as they were by their own parliament, or whether it could be treated as a conquered country, to be dealt with as the victors pleased. But Ireland had not been conquered, and it was to be a risky business skinning the wolf before the animal was dead.

One other opportunity had been presented by O'Doherty's destruc-tion of Derry. It was decided to grant to the Corporation of London, a body undoubtedly having the financial strength to develop a colony of their own, a huge tract, together with the towns of Derry – to be known henceforth as 'Londonderry' – and Coleraine. The development was to be entrusted, as had that of Virginia, to a commercial company, the Honourable Irish Society. The Society had in fact, in spite of its wealthy backers, been asked to bite off more than it could comfortably chew. It was thought, the area being wide, unsurveyed and even unexplored by non-Irish, that the grants had been of some forty thou-sand acres: in fact they were ten times more extensive, and contained a large native population, essential to any development. In contrast to the successful Antrim plantation, that of Derry was disappointingly slow to develop.[13]

The confusion of policies was exacerbated in 1630 when Charles I began his attempt to govern without parliamentary support, an attempt which necessitated squeezing every alternative source of finance to the limit. His chosen instrument for squeezing Ireland was the Earl of Strafford. Autocratic and ruthless, Wentworth had no respect for such niceties as the law. His policy of 'Thorough and Thorough' began by calling an Irish Parliament, which he had been able to ensure would be submissive. This assembly of trustworthy episcopalians might well have proved valuable allies of the King, but before it had a chance to do anything beyond granting the vital funds, Charles insisted on its dissolution. Parliaments, insisted the King, like cats, 'ever grow curst with age'. Outside Parliament, arbitrary action, threats of execution and actual imprisonment extorted huge sums – £40,000 from the Earl of Cork and £70,000 from the Corporation of London for their failure to live up to expectations in their development of the Derry plantation. The new Ulster settlers, who should have been the most reliable of the Crown's supporters, were antagonised by being forced to take the 'Black Oath' of absolute loyalty to the King and to renounce any covenant: one family was fined £13,000 and condemned to life imprisonment for refusing to take this – entirely illegal – oath.

When Wentworth finally left Ireland in 1640, to help his master with the troublesome Scots, he reported the Irish 'as fully satisfied and as well affected to his Majesty's person and service as can possibly be wished for' – an impossibly vain boast, when in reality all sections of the Irish population were seething with resentment. The uprising that burst out on 23 October 1641 in Ulster (see pp. 167–8 below) among 'the O's and Mac's', as Wentworth had contemptuously termed the Irish, marked the beginning of the Irish part of the Wars of the Three Kingdoms. It was both a civil war and a war of independence, not from the English Crown, but for the assertion of Irish rights combined with a defence of the King of all three countries. Both the King and his enemies misunderstood its nature: Charles had been in correspondence with Sir Phelim O'Neill, a leader of the rebellion whom the King hoped might bring an Irish army to his aid in his fight with the Scots and the English parliamentarians; the parliamentarians feared exactly the same outcome; neither side realised that the Irish rebellion was also a desperate revolt against continued oppression, and not one subject to any person's control.

In London John Pym had emerged as the undisputed leader of the

House of Commons, employing every stratagem to force through the adoption of his 'Grand Remonstrance', a manifesto recapitulating all the errors and misdeeds of the King over the past fifteen years, and demanding a radical assertion of ultimate parliamentary sovereignty. Buoyed up with hopes of support from his other kingdoms, Charles returned from Scotland determined to crush Pym's 'juggling junto'. He arrived in London on 25 November 1641, two days after the Remonstrance had finally been approved by Parliament. It was a disturbed Christmas, as the London mob made its opinions felt. On 3 January 1642 the King struck his first blow, accusing Pym and four other members of high treason. The House of Commons refused to surrender them to the arresting officers, and the following day the King himself marched down, with some two hundred guards, to seize the five members. Pym, who was hoping for exactly some such misjudged initiative, left with the others at the last moment. Looking round the House, Charles commented, 'All my birds have flown,' and a week later he, with his family, fled a now violently hostile London. Although the fighting did not start until July, the next stage of the War of the Three Kingdoms was now inevitable.

The King's head

The first reaction of the Scottish leaders to the outbreak of war in England was to stay neutral, thereby disappointing Charles and depriving him of that assistance upon which he had confidently counted. If the Scots had rallied round their King the English Civil War might have been won within months, but the parliamentary forces were able to prevent the King's army from seizing London, which would probably have meant a royal victory. Guided by the Kirk, and still flushed with their success in the previous round of negotiations with the English Parliament, Scotland preferred instead to see what improved offers might be made. The new discussions resulted in the Solemn League and Covenant (not to be confused with the purely Scottish National Covenant), agreed between English and Scottish parliaments in 1643. Intended by the Scots to carry forward the federal union of all three countries, it was in many ways a meaningless document, since it purported to make the English Church Presbyterian, which would have been anathema to the very great majority of the English; and the Irish were not consulted. Presbyterianism entailed recognition of the Kirk sessions and presbyteries as legal courts, and its establishment in England would have meant setting up some ten thousand of these, which would monitor all aspects of civil life. Not only fornication and drunkenness were to be banned – there was a fair measure of agreement on that – but such reprobate activities as gazing out of the windows on Sunday were to be repressed with the force of law. If Englishmen were united about one thing it was the supremacy of the common law and an absolute rejection of other feudal or ecclesiastic jurisdictions. The Scots may not have converted England, but they received formal agreement, plus the solid gratification of £30,000 a month. A Scots army, twenty thousand strong, under Leslie, now Earl of Leven, accordingly joined the parliamentary troops in January 1644. Six months later the joint armies defeated the royalists at Marston Moor.

After that battle the Scots army did little to help in the English Civil War. The decisive battle of Naseby was won by Oliver Cromwell's New Model Army in 1645, by which time Leven had withdrawn to the Borders, since Scotland was having its own civil war between royal and parliamentary forces. The Marquis of Montrose, who had commanded the Scottish forces against the King in 1639, had declared for Charles, and had been joined by an Irish contingent led by Alastair MacDonald. A savagely brilliant campaign, accompanied by many atrocities, was waged by Montrose in the Highlands before being crushed in September 1645. By the autumn of 1645 both the English and Scottish civil wars had been decided in favour of the parliamentary parties; but the future was far from settled. The Scottish Commissioners in England, originally instructed to reach a definitive agreement with the English Parliament in 1640, were still debating indecisively at Westminster, and pockets of royal resistance held out doggedly. At one of these, the besieged town of Newark, King Charles surrendered in May 1646, but to the Scottish rather than the English parliamentary army. He was despatched thence, once again to Newcastle, there to be argued into Presbyterian correctness by the Covenanting minister Alexander Henderson. The minister died in the attempt, and Charles continued to give only evasive responses to Scottish peace proposals; meanwhile the Scottish army was not being paid.[14]

That vital point was settled in January 1647. £200,000 was handed over to the Scots, who left King Charles in Newcastle, a package to be collected as convenient. A flurry of negotiations followed between the King, the Scottish and English parliaments and, rapidly becoming the most important, the English army, now firmly under Oliver Cromwell's control. That Huntingdonshire squire had proved himself not only a brilliant cavalry general but an inspired selector of able subordinates. The New Model Army had developed its own command structure, the Army Council, which saw little merit in the Solemn League and Covenant. Its most influential members, and the majority of the rank and file, were Independents, who abjured both presbyters and bishops, maintaining the right of each congregation to choose its own ministers. The 'Heads of the Proposals' advanced by the Army Council in August 1647 reflected Cromwell's own principle of tolerance, for 'union and right understanding between the godly people – Scots, English, Jews, Gentiles, Presbyterians, Independents, Anabaptists and all'. It was a remarkable document, anticipating almost every constitutional advance that was to take place over the next two hundred years: regular parliaments, the sovereignty of the Crown in Parliament, with ministers jointly appointed, fair representation and, almost incredibly, a prohibition on all interference with any form of Protestant worship; even bishops were to be tolerated.[15]

King Charles was perhaps hardly serious in any of these negotiations, remaining convinced of the eventual triumph of his own cause, which he believed to be divinely justified. On 11 November 1647 he escaped from his house arrest to Carisbrooke Castle, and on 26 December signed a secret treaty with the Scots, the 'Engagement', by which it was agreed that the English Church should become, at least for a limited time, Presbyterian. It was in effect an attempt to renegotiate the Union of the Crowns, since in addition to the religious clauses there was to be 'a complete union of the kingdoms' in which 'all liberties, privileges, concerning commerce, traffic, and manufactures . . . should be common . . .' One third of the court and officers of the Crown were to be Scots, and the King and his heir, the eighteen-year-old Prince Charles, should promise regular visits to Scotland. The

English army's olive branch had been rejected in favour of the Engagement with the Scots, and another war was inevitable. Co-ordinated royalist risings broke out in the spring in Kent and Wales, and once more a Scottish army crossed the border. The result was decisive defeat for the Scots at Cromwell's hands in a running battle near Preston, with more than ten thousand casualties.

Scotland was now divided between those who had risked backing the King, the 'Engagers', and the 'Protectors', the more extreme Presbyterians, who now enjoyed a brief period of control during which all positions of power, including even junior ranks in the army, were purged – and witches, those seeds of evil, were persecuted with renewed vigour. They showed what bigoted fundamentalists could do, with 'daylie hanging, skurging, nailling of lugges . . . and boring of tongues', without great effect, since 'for adulterie, fornicatioun, incest, bigamie, and uther uncleanes and filthynes, it did never abound moir nor at this tyme'.[16]

In England the army was indignant. Preston had been a hard-fought battle, extending over three days, which the English force had been obliged to fight with their numbers much reduced by parliamentary economies. When war had become inevitable the Army Council had resolved, if they survived, 'it was our duty to call Charles Stuart, that man of blood, to an account for the blood he had shed'. After the victory, finding the Presbyterian majority in Parliament still unresponsive, the army acted. Colonel Thomas Pride marched his men into the House and expelled all members known to be opposed to the army's demands. Fewer than eighty members, all reliable Independents, were left in the 'Rump' Parliament, which therefore possessed a badly impaired authority.

The purged Parliament acceded to the army's demands, and King Charles was duly tried, found guilty and executed on 30 January 1649. Inconvenient monarchs such as Edward II and Richard II had been quietly murdered, but a public trial and execution on parliamentary orders was totally unprecedented. Reactions to the King's death differed in the three kingdoms. English opinion was shocked, but generally acquiescent, whereas in Scotland indignation was widespread. A Scottish King had been murdered on the orders of an unrepresentative English Parliament, at the insistence of an army which had so signally defeated a Scottish army the previous year. Within six days the young Prince of Wales was proclaimed as Charles II by the Scottish Parliament; within two months the English Parliament had abolished the monarchy and proclaimed a republic, the Commonwealth of England. Any thought of union between the two countries seemed impossible.

Abroad, although there was general horror and indignation – the execution of a King seemed an ominous portent of a world sliding into anarchy – there was no possibility of, or much enthusiasm for, immediate armed intervention. It was in Ireland that the immediate danger lay, and thither Cromwell took the by now invincible English army. By May 1650 that problem was settled for a generation by a combination of ruthless force followed by imposed settlements, leaving Cromwell free to deal with the other British kingdom, and King Charles II with no alternative than to try his luck in Scotland.

From his refuge in Jersey, Charles had already commissioned the Marquis of Montrose to act as his Scottish viceroy. Montrose's previous campaign had been only partly on behalf of the King, but also against the Campbells, much hated by most of the other Highland clans, and whose chief, the Marquis of Argyll, was the head of the Scottish Covenanting government. In 1650, with no external support and having caused much resentment by his army's brutal sack of Aberdeen, Montrose had little chance of repeating his previous success. His failure was made inevitable when Charles agreed to the Covenanters' conditions for accepting him as King. Religious fanatics are often poor judges of the possible, and the Covenanters' demands were thoroughly unrealistic, amounting to the King's undertaking to accept Presbyterianism in Scotland and to impose it in England; but a Scottish army was essential to any hope of his success. Montrose, abandoned by Charles, was defeated and captured. On 21 May the King's viceroy in Scotland was executed by Argyll's government, and in June the new King of Scotland landed in Cromarty to be welcomed by the same government.[17]

Young Charles had a miserable time in Scotland, being lectured at great length by Presbyterian ministers ('No religion for gentlemen,' he later commented). 'He wrought himself into as great a deportment as he could,' Bishop Burnet recalled. 'He heard many prayers and sermons, some of a great length . . . on one fast day there were six sermons

... I was there myself and not a little weary of so tedious a service.' More seriously, the King was made to condemn his father for marrying into 'an idolatrous family' and for causing 'all the bloodshed in the late wars'. Royal prospects were shadowed after Cromwell again destroyed a Scottish army at Dunbar (3 September 1650), but during the winter lull Charles II was crowned King of Scotland at Scone, as his forebears had been for more than three centuries. His subjects were little more enthusiastic for their King than the King for them; the coronation on 1 January 1651 was preceded by a fast to repent the sins of the royal family, and the sermon weightily questioned the sincerity of the young monarch's seeming godliness.

At the head of a Covenanting army, Charles now led the penultimate Scottish invasion of England, in August 1651, only to be annihilated at Worcester by Cromwell's army; two thousand Scots were killed and more than ten thousand taken prisoner at a cost of only two hundred English lives. Worcester marked a turning point. Scottish armies had fought both alongside and against English forces since 1639, and had suffered heavy casualties. Exhaustion had, for the moment, quenched the fires of independence. In Scotland Cromwell's able general, George Monck, quickly subdued any remaining resistance. Stirling's surrender was followed by that of Aberdeen and St Andrews; only Dundee held out, before being stormed and pillaged, and the last royalist force surrendered in October 1651.

Peace brought with it the problem of the English army's future. After the King's execution the work of government had devolved on an inexperienced Parliament. Ruling by a series of committees, this had been reasonably successful; some ideological attempts to abolish vice by law, always a temptation to British administrations, proved as unpopular and ineffective as might have been expected, but one serious Act of future importance had been passed. This was the Navigation Act of 1651, the first of a series which aimed at making all seaborne commerce a near-monopoly of English shippers and traders. As England's colonial and trading empire expanded – Jamaica was added in 1655 – the protection afforded by the Act was increasingly valuable, and under the Commonwealth was extended to Scotland and Ireland. But the Rump Parliament was the army's creation, and in the background, yet very much the indispensable man, commonly shown almost royal respect, was the army's Captain-General, Oliver Cromwell. For the better part of two years after Worcester, Cromwell, the more radical army officers and what was left of Parliament endeavoured to reach an accommodation until, having finally lost patience, Cromwell marched his musketeers into Westminster Hall. On 15 December 1653 the Captain-General assumed power as Lord Protector of the Commonwealth, and for the next five years the three kingdoms had a leader of unmatched strength and ability.

An ill-favoured massacre

Meanwhile in Ireland the incompetent conspirators who planned the Ulster revolt of October 1641 were hard-up young men of no great weight. Rory O'More was the central figure, supported by Sir Phelim O'Neill, 'a light, desperate young gentleman', and Lord Maguire, 'a dissipated young man . . . overwhelmed with debt'. On 22 October the Catholic Irish gentry of Ulster seized the forts at Dungannon and Lurgan, declaring that their action was 'in no ways intended against our Sovereine Lord and King, nor the hurt of any of his subjects, either of the English or Scottish nation, but only for the defence and liberty of ourselves and the Irish natives of this kingdom'. The plan had been for a *coup d'état* in Dublin, the failure of which jeopardised the whole scheme, but the timing was apt, taking advantage of the growing tension in England and Scotland.[18]

The army raised by Wentworth in Ireland, intended for his invasion of Scotland, had been forced to disband, leaving a reservoir of hungry and discontented troops. A firm resistance could not be looked for from the Ulster settlers, many of whom had fled back to Britain from Wentworth's persecution, 'reviled, threatened, imprisoned'. Within a week most of Ulster was in the rebels' hands, but slipping from its original leaders' control. Sir Phelim and his brother Turlough began by insisting that no Scottish settlers be harmed since Scotland was at that time siding with King Charles, acknowledged as King of Ireland by the rebels. The gentry, however, could not control the savage resentment of the 'lewd people', and the original intentions of the conspirators were buried under an avalanche of suppressed anger and accumulated hatred. What followed lost nothing in the subsequent telling, for the rebels' atrocities offered much too attractive propaganda for the Protestant cause. The massacres themselves have been dismissed by some writers, confined to inverted commas, but they were real enough. It was Turlough O'Neill himself who first used the word (on 22 November 1641) regretting 'that ill-favoured massaker neere Augher, of those that were first takin to mercie'.[19] That incident cost the lives of some four hundred Scots, and in all perhaps ten times as many people, all Protestants, perished, for the most part by hardship rather than by actual murder, in the first months of the rising. Such tragedies were hardly unknown in Ireland, for the Elizabethan wars had seen many worse horrors, but the 1641 rebellion was the first time in Irish history that a major part of the community had been attacked, killed and exiled, not for any defiance of laws, however unjust, or for simple loot and dispossession, but specifically because they professed the wrong religion. The rebellion became, like the Gunpowder Plot, a symbol of Catholic, and specifically Irish Catholic, violence; the consequences were to be terrible.

Only some five hundred regular troops remained in Ireland, and the immediate defence was the responsibility of the local militias. In Munster the Governor, Sir William St Leger, and his deputy Murrough O'Brien, Earl of Inchiquin, a direct descendant of Brian Boru himself – and a Protestant – were given time to organise. Outsiders took a part when Robert Munro led a Scottish army to Ulster in April 1642, slaughtering every Irish man or woman they came across. A few months later the Lord Deputy, James Butler, Earl of Ormond, brought a small contingent into action against the rebels, but neither side had enough strength to inflict a decisive defeat. In September 1643 a truce was agreed between the rebels and the Crown forces. For his part Munro, acting under parliamentary orders, continued to fight, and from 1644 was faced with both rebel and royalist armies.

Whatever had been the initial causes of the rebellion it was by now a religious war, with Protestant Scots, Old English, and such Irish Protestants as Inchiquin, fighting against the confederate Catholics, better known as the Confederation of Kilkenny, an alliance of Old English and Irish Catholics. The religious nature of the war was emphasised by the arrival, in October 1645, of a senior papal emissary, Cardinal Giovanni Rinuccini, a single-minded enthusiast, devoted to pushing forward the Counter-Reformation, supported by such local enthusiasts as the fighting Bishop Heber MacMahon. A more effective reinforcement for the rebel cause was provided by Owen Roe O'Neill, a nephew of Earl Hugh, who had spent thirty years in the Spanish service against the French. Marshalling an unruly and poorly armed Irish army was a much more difficult task than leading the disciplined Spanish *tercios*, but Owen Roe fought a brilliant campaign. He was well supported by his talented nephews Hugh, who later outfought Cromwell himself, and Daniel, 'Infallible Subtle', a skilled diplomatist. The confederate victory over the Scottish army of General Munro, a veteran commander in the Thirty Years War, in 1646 was a particular triumph of Irish arms.

The defeat of the English royalists after the decisive battle of Naseby in June 1645 left Parliament nominally in charge of Ireland, but still relying on the Scots and such royalists as Inchiquin and Ormond to suppress the rebellion. Inchiquin accepted a parliamentary commission as President of Munster, and this descendant of the High King ordered 'All the Irish' to be expelled from the strategic parts of Youghal, and in 1647 stormed the rock of Cashel, killing some three thousand, including thirty priests. A little later he changed sides, declaring for the King, and placed himself under the Lord Deputy's orders. Ormond, driven by the intransigent Catholic Confederates, who refused to countenance any negotiations, appealed to the English Parliament for help. Cromwell wished to co-operate but Parliament thought differently, and the force despatched to Ireland was too small to bring the war to an end.

From London the perspective was impossibly confused. John Milton was requested to investigate 'The Complication of interest . . . among the several designers against the peace of the Commonwealth' in Ireland.[20] The complex series of events that followed indicated how far Ireland was from developing anything resembling national unity. At one extreme was Rinuccini and his supporters, mainly Irish bishops, insisting on a return to the pre-Henrician Church, whilst the lay leaders continued suspicious of the Old English, whom they believed anxious to do a deal with their English royalist cousins. When Rinuccini exploded his final weapon, papal excommunication for any who disagreed with the Confederation, the split became permanent. The dissident Confederates immediately concluded a deal with Ormond and the Cardinal left in a huff. In Ulster another local faction, the Presbyterian settlers, sympathetic to their Scottish brethren, pursued their own agenda. A final decision to the conflict, which by then had drawn on for eight years, had to await the arrival in August 1649 of Oliver Cromwell, with twelve thousand soldiers of the New Model army.

The details of Cromwell's Irish campaign have become a powerful ingredient of Irish mythology: the 'Curse of Cromwell' is taken to have blighted the future of that land. As so often the facts are disappointingly different. Cromwell saw himself as 'an honest constable' charged with settling parish disturbances; a description which those who aroused his wrath might consider understated, but even his Irish enemies paid tribute to the Protector's 'powerful majestie to command, and an awful countenance to execute'. Certainly the campaign began bloodily enough, with the storm of Drogheda ending with the deaths not only of the garrison but of hundreds of civilians; but it was conducted according to the rules of warfare, which recognised that a city taken by storm was a very dangerous place in which to be caught. Cromwell, together with most of his contemporaries, was inflamed by the reports of the 1641 massacres, and determined both to punish those who could be held responsible and to prevent a repetition. Calls for extirpation of the Protestants had been made in 1645 by Cornelius O'Malley, and although his tract had been suppressed by the Kilkenny Confederation, its 'calls for genocide against the Protestants' were politically embarrassing.[21] Also in the forefront of all Protestant minds was the horror experienced in Magdeburg during the religious wars in Germany eleven years previously, when some twenty-four thousand of its citizens were slaughtered by the Catholic soldiery after a siege. Cromwell's reports after the killing at Drogheda, in which he deplored 'the effusion of blood' and hoped that it would prevent future slaughter, were in a very different tone from those of Queen Elizabeth in which she reprimanded Lord Grey for sparing the lives of the Spanish officers after the surrender of Fort del Oro. Even so, the unsparing ferocity with which Catholic priests were killed horrified contemporaries, the more as coming from Cromwell's troops, with their reputation for discipline.

After Drogheda and the equally violent sack of Wexford resistance crumbled and towns surrendered, as Cromwell had hoped.[22] At Kilkenny the garrison were allowed to march out not only unharmed, but with drums beating and colours flying. The New Model Army, well provisioned, usually paid, and kept under discipline (plunderers were hanged), did far less damage to Ireland and its people than had any previous force; and it succeeded in bringing an end to the fighting. When captured, Catholic priests, who were by law liable to the death penalty, were now reprieved. Cromwell made his own attitude clear in a ferocious 'Declaration' of 14 January 1651, in answer to the Convention of Clonmacnoise in which the Irish Catholic clergy had 'proclaimed a kind of holy war against the English'. Although the priestly convention was 'a covenant with death and hell', Cromwell did not intend to persecute the Catholic laity. 'What thoughts they have in matters of religion in their own breasts I cannot reach; but think it my duty, if they walk honestly and peaceable not to cause them in the least to suffer for the same.'[23]

Propaganda aside, it was the nature of the settlement rather than the conduct of the campaign that was of greater real importance. Cromwell left Ireland in May 1650, called away to deal with the new war in Scotland, leaving mopping-up operations to continue for the next two years. In Ulster these were of a different character to those in the south, for Cromwell's commanders were fighting not only against royalists and Confederates, but against the Scottish settlers who had for the most part declared for the King. The killing was eventually brought to an end, with amnesty being given to all those Irish rebels who had not been convicted of murder; in all some two hundred or so perished in that fashion. The new West Indian colonies formed a convenient dumping ground for some thousands more of the defeated, shipped out as indentured servants; some survived and even prospered.

In August 1652 the parliamentary commissioners in Ireland were presented with two Acts of the English Parliament – in the drafting of which they had no hand – proposing a final solution to the Irish problem. This was to move all Irish landowners from their existing estates into the west, the province of Connacht and the county of Clare, leaving the rest of the country to be resettled by parliamentary soldiers, who would accept land in lieu of cash for their arrears of pay, and to reimburse those individuals who had financed the repression since 1641. At bottom a device for paying off the army in default of the necessary cash, in many ways the legislation foreshadowed that of the Nationalist government of South Africa in the 1960s. An inconvenient section of the population was to be forbidden to hold land except in the less desirable part of the country, although they would be free to work for wages for the dominant minority. There was also, as in Africa, a distinctly racist flavour to the proposals, for the Irish were seen even by their Spanish allies as simple 'savages', and by the more moderate of the English as interesting curiosities with habits and clothing of a vanished era, or simply as 'barbarous wretches'. For their part the Irish poets tellingly characterised the English invaders as 'fluffy Saxons', 'the crafty thieving false set of Calvin', 'fat-rumped jeerers . . . with shaven jaws and English and braggart accent'.

There were, however, some important differences between Cromwellian Ireland and apartheid South Africa. All inhabitants of Ireland were subject to the same laws, laws certainly designed to benefit English rather than Irish, but executed with some degree of impartiality. David O'Dowd (Daibhi O Dubhda) of Castleconner, County Sligo had all his lands confiscated but was confident that his appeal against the sentence would succeed; it did, and David was allotted an estate in his family's Mayo territories. His wife's dowry, in 1656, suggests that not all Irish Catholic gentry had been impoverished: 'Forty great cows, to be milch cows next year, 15 heifers to two years, 15 yearling heifers, 100 sheep, one horse and a plough'.[24]

The projected transplantations were only partly effected, and many of the Irish landlords contrived to stay where they were. One such was Richard Power, later Earl of Tyrone, not only allowed to remain in possession of his extensive Waterford estate but given a cash allowance by the Cromwellian Colonel Richard Lawrence, since Power 'hath demeaned himself inoffensively that ever I heard, having killed tories and expressed much forewardness therein'.[25] In Antrim, Dublin and Carlow, some of the more prosperous regions, the proportion of Irish Catholic landowning gentry remained substantial. Although the Acts provided for drastic penalties for those exempted from the general pardon, these were rarely invoked, the preferred alternative being the offer of exile – with the likelihood of being forced into it as an encouragement. Permission was also given to foreign powers to recruit soldiers from among the population, diminishing further the numbers of potential malcontents. Daniel O'Neill was allowed to raise five thousand Irish for the Spanish army, and his brother Hugh, who fighting alongside their uncle Owen Roe had managed to outwit even Cromwell himself, was, after an initial imprisonment, permitted to go free.

The modernisation and reorganisation attempted by the Commonwealth in all three kingdoms benefited Ireland less than England, or even Scotland. Security, and not reform, was the prime concern of even so liberal an administrator as the Protector's son Henry, head of the Irish administration from 1655 to 1659.[26] Many bold ventures were however initiated. Trinity College was reformed, with chairs in mathematics and medicine; Robert Boyle developed his ideas for an 'Invisible University', which was later to become the Royal Society, and Henry Cromwell himself produced detailed proposals for a new Dublin University. William Hill, Fellow of Merton College, established a new grammar school, St Patrick's. Some of these projects took root and survived the Restoration; John Stearne was confirmed in his medical chair at Trinity, and his venture became the Royal College of Physicians of Ireland; and Henry Cromwell pushed through the purchase, funded by a voluntary collection from the army itself, officers and men, of Archbishop Ussher's library, 'that great Magazeen of Learning', which forms the nucleus of Trinity College's magnificent collection.[27] Other proposals fell by the wayside, but the cumulative effect of the decade of republican government in Ireland was to jump-start a new and radical intellectual life. Economically the major benefit was that of restored tranquillity, which would contribute to the vigorous expansion of eighteenth-century Ireland, and the establishment of a new prosperity. Communications were improved, and a postal service inaugurated, but the free passage of Irish produce continued to be inhibited by the objections of English agriculturalists. Nevertheless, conditions in the countryside visibly improved with 'manifestations of more modern methods in afforestation, hedges, new grasses and crops – clover, potatoes, turnips, and better horse breeding'.[28] The Navigation Act of 1651, which gave Ireland the same access to foreign trade as Britain and Scotland, was of only moderate utility, since Ireland lacked both shipping and industry.

It was ironic that the restoration of the monarchy in 1660 brought little relief to the Irish. Initially hopes were high among those who had campaigned so long and painfully for both the removal of discrimination and the return of their estates. They were to be comprehensively disappointed. Not only were there a substantial number of Presbyterians in the English Restoration Parliament, but the new Chancellor, Lord Hyde, was himself a formerly radical parliamentarian. In England a compromise was effected. Lands which had been confiscated were restored to their royalist owners, but when these had been purchased by third parties, they remained in the buyers' hands, thus leaving many faithful royalists impoverished. In Ireland the compromise was even more unsatisfactory to the dispossessed. The 1641 rebellion had been against the King, in spite of the rebels' protestations to the contrary, and there was therefore no question of compensating them for any losses they had incurred in that long-drawn-out episode. Those Catholic gentry who had survived the plantations and the wars lost whatever they had managed to retain. Investors who had been allotted land in recognition of their cash, or who had bought the army veterans' entitlements, were influential in both English and Irish Parliaments; both Colonel Lawrence and even Henry Cromwell were among those allowed to retain their Irish estates after the Restoration. This protection of existing grants left very little spare land available, and when account was taken of the large estates immediately given to Ormond and the King's brother, the Duke of York, complete confusion reigned. This was eventually settled in 1665 by the Irish Parliament's 'Act of Explanation' which shamelessly discriminated against all Catholics by decreeing that in disputes between Catholics and Protestants every ambiguity should be interpreted in favour of the Protestant party; decisions thereafter came quickly. William Petty, that informed observer, believed that in 1641 Protestants owned about one-third of the arable land, but after 1665 twice as much. The Cromwellian Settlement was left substantially intact, leaving the dispossessed resentful and betrayed.

Catholic hopes of royal intervention in religious affairs were also disappointed, since the penal laws dating from Elizabeth's time were not repealed, although they were applied with great laxity, enabling exiled bishops and priests to return and to begin the reconstruction of parish life. The Duke of Ormond, reinstated in Ireland as Viceroy, continued to prove himself humane and trustworthy. It was the turn of the Presbyterians in Ulster to be persecuted for their refusal to agree to compulsory Anglicanism, but after many ministers were ejected even this pressure was relaxed. One cruel irony was that it was under the Restoration, and not Cromwell's Commonwealth, that the most famous modern Irish martyr, Archbishop Oliver Plunket of Armagh, was judicially murdered. Plunket, a man of unblemished character, fell a victim to the English anti-Catholic hysteria of Titus Oates' 'Popish Plot' in 1681. After being judged innocent, as he undoubtedly was, by an Ulster Protestant jury, King Charles refused to alter the subsequent guilty verdict of an English court, and Plunket was accordingly hanged, drawn and quartered at Tyburn.

Economically, too, Ireland was no better off. As a member of the united Commonwealth the country had been part of the largest free-trade area then existing, but the Restoration brought a persistent attack on these privileges from English interests, which were able to impose a series of legal restrictions on Irish trade – on live cattle in 1666, subsequently also on mutton, butter and cheese, and on wool. In spite of, or perhaps in response to, such impositions Irish agriculture improved as the new settlers brought such initiatives as the establishment of sea fisheries, and manufactured woollen goods replaced fleeces. Most importantly, a generation of comparative peace enabled the whole population to recover from a decade of war.

The second attempt at Union[29]

After the victories of Dunbar and Worcester the English Parliament had to consider the future of Scotland. Should it simply be treated as a conquered province, with the whole region south of the Forth–Clyde line annexed, and the remainder perhaps being tossed to Charles I's youngest son, Henry, to rule as a puppet monarch? A parliamentary Bill to this effect was discussed in the autumn of 1651 but abandoned in favour of a complete integration into the 'Commonwealth of England, Scotland and Ireland'. Scotland was to be granted free trade, representation in the English Parliament and government by a separate Council of Scotland – conditions not at all unlike, and in some respects more favourable to Scotland than, those later agreed in 1707. The offer document, the 'Tender of Union', was difficult to reject, and with a little firm persuasion was accepted by twenty-nine of the Scottish shires and forty-six of the fifty-eight burghs. Security was initially assured by Monck's construction and garrisoning of a series of forts before a civilian government, the Council of Scotland, was established in September 1655.

The new Council was a credible national institution, its most prominent members having won considerable reputations in their own right as opponents of the English. Two Berwickshire lairds, John Swinton, the Quaker, and Sir William Lockhart were especially active. Roger Boyle, Lord Broghill, later the Earl of Orrery, President of the Council was said to enjoy widespread popularity. Broghill's career was typical of those confused times, demonstrating how difficult generalisations can be. Another of the fourteen children of the remarkable Richard Boyle, first Earl of Cork, Roger had served the King in Ireland, and after the execution of Charles I had instigated a royalist plot for the restoration of Charles II. He was therefore taken aback when Cromwell called personally at his London home to tell him that the full details of his plot were known, but that such was Cromwell's confidence in him that he offered the surprised conspirator a general's commission. Boyle agreed, and after a successful period in Ireland was appointed to head the Scottish Council, during which time he 'gained more on the affections of the people than all the English that ever were among us'.

Similarly, the career of Sir William Lockhart illustrates the flexibility of Cromwell's choices, and suggests some reasons for the relative success of the 'usurpation' in Scotland. Knighted by Charles I for his services in the first Civil War, Lockhart's obvious ability and his previous experiences in the French army influenced Cromwell to offer him the post of Ambassador at Paris, where he concluded a treaty with Cardinal Mazarin and Louis XIV. In the war with Spain that resulted Lockhart was given command of the English expeditionary force: indeed it could well be described as the first truly *British* army, composed as it was of troops from the Commonwealth, with a Welsh second-in-command and soldiers drawn from all three kingdoms. This army, made up of men who only a few years previously had been fighting against each other, took the leading part in the Spanish defeat in Flanders in 1658; by an ironical twist the enemy forces included two thousand Irish, Scots and English led by the King's brother, the Duke of York; and the Commonwealth corps was under the overall command of the French Marshal Turenne. To complete the story Lockhart was again appointed to the Paris Embassy after the Restoration.

Republican principles naturally demanded the end of Scottish feudal privileges, and a vigorous start was made on replacing manorial courts by a regular bench of JPs. The new Commissioners for the Administration of Justice, who took up office in May 1652, became accepted by Scots. As the diarist John Nicoll put it, 'And to speik treuth, the Englisches wer moir indulgent and mercifull to the Scottis, nor wes the Scottis to thair awin cuntriemen and nychtbouris, as wes too evident, and thair justice exceidit the Scottis in mony thinges.'[30] One of the great blots of Scots justice, the witch persecutions, was, if not removed, much amended. The Commissioners confirmed that

> there are very few if any of those men usually called witches and that the torments they were put to by the witch finders and the Malice of their neighbours together with the partiallitye or ignorance of the former Judges in Scotland (and I feare England too), hath taken away the lives not onely of many even persons but Good and pretious Christians too, by condemning them to the severest punishments of the fire.[31]

Many of the Commonwealth's innovations scarcely touched Scotland: the beneficial effect of the return of the Jews, after 350 years of exile, was limited for many years to London; and the toleration extended to all Protestant sects did not appeal to the more militant Presbyterians, who looked on the niggling restrictions on personal behaviour which so irritated most English as no more than proper. (Cromwell's daughter Mary was married in Hampton Court, by an Anglican priest, according to the prayerbook service; the wedding was followed by a masque – a proto-opera – in which the Lord Protector himself took part. The whole would have seemed a monstrous depravity to Scottish Presbyterians.)

Public expenditure on such projects as education in the newly-calmed Highlands and the funding of universities was weighed against the much greater sums taken in taxation, enforced by what many Scots could only regard as an army of occupation. What should have been the greatest advantage to Scotland of the first union, the free access to English markets and the protection of the English Navigation Acts, was vitiated since Scots foreign trade to any except the traditional markets of the Baltic and the Low Countries was minimal, and the main exports to England were cattle on the hoof. Similar theoretical benefits such as the ability of Scots to take up trades in England banned to 'aliens' were limited by the number of Scots willing, or able, to move south. The largest market, that of the now well-organised supplies to the army and navy, was well served by English contractors, and on such a scale as to make Scottish competition difficult.

It should have been something of an encouragement to see Scottish members sitting in a Westminster Parliament. For the first time thirty members from both Scotland and Ireland were included in the Commonwealth Parliaments. Most were biddable officials who sometimes acted as a bloc, to the irritation of English members; one indignant English MP, John Hobart, compared the Scots and Irish to 'the Pigg that . . . crowded the children from the fire'. Crowding was easier since Scottish and Irish members tended to spend all the sessions in London, while many English MPs were absent in their constituencies. But when all was said and done the Protectorate was very much a personal government, and to many Scots the victor of Preston, Dunbar and Worcester was a national enemy. To them this first 'incorporating' union was very much 'as when the poor bird is embodied in the hawk that hath eaten it up'.

CHAPTER 7

1660–1750

Restoration

THE WIDESPREAD RELIEF at the accession of Charles II in 1660
was not merely that of an oppressed nation rejoicing at having been
freed from a repressive Puritan regime. No doubt plum puddings,
playhouses and games on Sundays were welcome, but the Commonwealth had brought well-understood benefits. Ireland and Scotland
were under control, and the united Commonwealth had made its
power felt abroad so effectively that no external threat existed; at
home most people benefited from an unaccustomed level of religious
toleration. It was rather the peaceful nature of the Restoration that
caused the relief, since a non-violent transition was by no means
inevitable, and the memories of ten years of warfare and destruction
were fresh. Oliver's elder son, Richard, had succeeded to the Protec-
torship after his father's death in September 1658, but 'Tumbledown
Dick' had few of the necessary talents, and resigned within a few
months, leaving the whole constitutional future uncertain.

Whilst it is true that the civilian population had not been directly
involved in most of the fighting, and that the atrocities common in
Ireland, and even in Scotland, had been rare in England, so extended
a period of conflict was inevitably damaging. Apart from taking men
out of productive employment the direct effects of scores of thousands
of horse, foot and guns scrambling around the countryside disrupted
normal life, and although the parliamentary armies were usually properly supplied from the near-inexhaustible sources of London, those of
the King had often to live off the country. Escaping a repetition of
these experiences was the fundamental cause of that great exhalation
of relief that accompanied King Charles' return, described by John
Evelyn as he stood in the Strand on 29 May 1660: 'All this was done

without one drop of blood being shed, and that by the very army which rebelled against him ... such a restoration was never mentioned in any history ... nor so joyful a day or so bright ever seen in this nation.' It was indeed George Monck, Cromwell's general and admiral, who had quelled the flickerings of republican revolt, and accepted the King's requests for help in obtaining his restoration. Monck suggested that the King issue a manifesto, the Declaration of Breda, offering free and general pardon, confirmation of all sales of land made in the interregnum, liberty of conscience and, not least, the settlement of the army's pay claims. A peaceful transition was thereafter expected and achieved, and Charles returned at the invitation of Parliament, and committed to observing parliamentary independence.

For the most part the royal conditions were faithfully observed, although the first Restoration Parliament of 1661 was much less tolerant than the King would have wished. Having himself had his fill of religious discussion during those tedious Scottish sermons ten years before, Charles was in favour of allowing Protestant dissenters and Roman Catholics the freedom to worship as they wished. Not so his Parliament, which insisted that conformity to the state Church must be enforced. A series of Acts bolstered the position of the Church of England: the Corporation Act of 1661 restricted membership of town governments to Anglicans, the Five Miles Act of 1665 forbade any 'Conventicle' to be built or its minister to live within five miles of the nearest town, and public opinion was stifled by a severe censorship. Many Anglican clerics refused to subscribe to the new Church order, and some 20 per cent lost their livings, thereby giving Dissent a powerful boost. In the other direction, any movement towards relaxing pressure on Roman Catholics was abruptly halted by the hysteria accompanying the 'Popish Plot' which led to Plunket's martyrdom. In 1672 the Test Act required that any aspirant to civil or public office whatsoever take communion according to the Anglican rite and subscribe to a solemn oath that Roman Catholics would find impossible.

Abroad, King Charles himself continued Cromwell's policy of alliance with France, but to the extent of taking large sums secretly from his cousin Louis XIV in return for promises of political support – promises which Louis complained were frequently unfulfilled. At that time Louis was aggressively attempting to extend French borders, his most formidable opponent in the north being the Dutch United Provinces. Two expensive wars with Holland were fought by England in obedience to this policy, bringing only one moderate advantage, that of the cession of Nieuw Amsterdam, under English rule renamed New York and New Jersey.

As Charles grew older without having produced any legitimate children, it was apparent that his successor must be his brother, the Duke of York. James Stuart was a man of personal integrity, industrious and of proven competence. As Lord High Admiral he displayed courage at sea and gave solid support to the admirable Sam Pepys, his senior civil servant; and when sent out of harm's way to take charge in Scotland, between 1679 and 1682, had won grudging respect.

But James made no secret of his Catholicism, and the prospect of a Roman Catholic sovereign was one that was hard for English public opinion to accept. One of the conditions Louis XIV made for his investment in King Charles was that, at some convenient time, the King would publicly accept Catholicism; slippery to the end, Charles did so only on his death bed. The religion of the head of state had been made a matter of public policy, and the cry for a Protestant succession grew even louder. In 1683 the ineffective Rye House plot to murder the royal brothers was easily suppressed, but the Duke of York succeeded as James II of England and VII of Scotland with only restrained goodwill, and much relief that, again, there had been no blood shed. James' accession in February 1685 still left the eventual succession to the throne undecided. He was fifty-two, and his second wife, Mary of Modena, thirty-eight. In spite of many pregnancies no children had been produced, and James' heirs remained his two daughters by his first marriage, the Princesses Mary and Anne, both Protestants and both married to reliable Protestant princes, respectively to Prince William of Orange and Prince George of Denmark, who both also had the advantage of being descended from James I and VI. As long as no more royal children were forthcoming, which seemed unlikely, there was much to be said for putting up with James' Roman tendencies, while trusting that on his death Protestantism would be reasserted.

In 1685 the wild attempt of Monmouth, one of Charles' illegitimate sons, to dispute the succession was quickly crushed, but the vindictive conduct of the brutal Judge Jeffreys in the aftermath aggravated the popular concern about what was appearing to become an authoritarian government – and one increasingly controlled by Catholics, frequently opportunistic converts. When in the same year Louis announced the revocation of the Edict of Nantes, the Act that had guaranteed tolerance for French Protestants for nearly a century, it appeared that the writing was on the wall. Royal pressure to insert James' supporters into positions of power increased. Jeffreys was promoted to become Lord Chancellor and Catholics were forced on reluctant colleges – Magdalen College Oxford had twenty-five of her fellows dismissed for resistance, but the Master of University College, Obadiah Walker, prudently converted. In June 1688 the King had seven bishops sent to the Tower for refusal to obey one of his ecclesiastical orders. Two days afterwards the Queen gave birth to a son, who would, in the natural order of things, be expected to become James III. The Protestant Succession was in imminent danger, and attention focused on the alternative successors, Princess Mary and her husband, William of Orange, Statholder of Holland and leader of the Dutch forces in their fight for independence against French aggression.

Glorious Bloodless Revolution?

The Glorious Bloodless Revolution – a description which hardly bears close examination – began as nothing more than a *coup d'état* arranged by a handful of discontented English magnates. The 'Immortal Seven' who invited Prince William's intervention on 30 June 1688 claimed to speak on behalf of 'nineteen parts of twenty of the people throughout the kingdom who are desirous of a change'. This was probably not true even in England, and certainly not of Scotland. There was even doubt as to whether William should specifically make a claim to be King of that country. The Declaration of Rights in which William fulfilled his promises to his backers declared William and Mary to be 'King and Queen of England, France and Ireland, and the Dominions thereto belonging' – including, presumably, Scotland. The Declaration was drafted by English politicians, relied on English precedents and referred only to English issues, but has become a central document of the British constitution, guaranteeing the legislative supremacy of Parliament, free elections and the vital parliamentary monopoly of taxation. Reflecting the imperative of the time the succession to the throne was specifically (as it still is) barred to Catholics or to anyone married to a Catholic. Further restrictions on Catholics were embodied in two other Acts, the 'penal laws', which ordained that only Protestants should bear arms 'appropriate to their rank and station', own a horse worth more than £5 (and therefore of any use in war), hold office under the Crown or live in London or Westminster. Later measures restricted rights to own land and imposed harsh penalties on the celebration of the Mass. In Britain, where Catholics were a tiny minority, and the measures rarely enforced, the penal laws were of little significance; in Ireland they were potentially onerous indeed.

The dynastic irregularity of Prince William's succession was clear enough: the newborn son ought to have inherited; but Mary was at least the eldest child of King James II, and her husband his nephew. William's personal qualities were considerable – steadfast, sensible and tolerant, a man of the eighteenth century with little of the ideological lumber that previous British monarchs carried with them. But he was a man with a mission, the defence of his native country of Holland. For more than a century the Dutch had been forced to fight for their survival, first against the Spanish, followed by the English. They were now confronted by the formidable France of Louis XIV, unquestionably the greatest power in Europe. William did his duty by his British and Irish subjects, but his priority was always the successful prosecution of the French wars.

No blows were struck against William on behalf of James since, after some of his most senior officers deserted, James retreated. On the morning of 18 December he left his palace; in the evening Prince William arrived. No military action was attempted, although when a Dutch regiment replaced the Coldstream Guards at St James' Palace many soldiers were disgusted, especially among the Scots. Hundreds deserted, and when ordered to Europe the Royal Scots, the 'First of Foot', mutinied and had to be suppressed by a Dutch commander.[1]

The joint rule of King William and Queen Mary was accepted in England, but in Scotland the issue remained open. There the English invitation to Dutch William was viewed with mixed feelings. Militant

Covenanters were jubilant, but to many others James was still a Stuart, the latest monarch of a dynasty that had endured for more than three hundred years, a period that had seen no fewer than five families seated on the English throne. When the news of William's arrival with a substantial Dutch army reached James, he appealed, as his father had done before, to the Scots for help, which was rapidly given, the Privy Council sending all the regular troops south to Salisbury ready to fight the invaders. The Edinburgh mob took advantage of the upset to riot, sacking Holyrood Abbey and desecrating the Stuart tombs, but their action demonstrated the mob's propensity to take advantage of any excuse for a spot of enjoyable mayhem, and did not necessarily reflect general attitudes.

These had become more polarised since the Restoration, when the return of the Stuart dynasty had been greeted with widespread enthusiasm. In 1660 wine had flowed from the conduits, and a firework display showing Cromwell chased by the devil marked the dissolution of the first incorporating Union with England. To the Covenanters Charles II was, or at least could seem to be, if enough effort was made, one of them; Scottish churchmen had long ago ceased to feel any solidarity with the English Puritans, whose armies had so often trounced those of Scotland; conservative Scottish royalists, Episcopalian or Presbyterian, considered that they had been at best slighted, and at worst oppressed, by Monck and Broghill. The Commonwealth Union had aimed at replacing Scots law and practice with those of England, and relaxing the hold of Presbyterianism; but both law and Kirk were dear to Scottish hearts. The restoration of a Stuart monarch offered positions of power – which was equivalent to wealth – and restitution for those Scots whose property had been confiscated. All hoped for great things, the re-establishment of Scottish independence and institutions, and for increasing prosperity. All, to greater or lesser degree, were to be disappointed.

Once returned, King Charles showed only a moderate interest in either his Scottish or Irish kingdoms, and moved as little from London as possible. He had seen quite enough of the country to last him for a very long time, and during his reign rarely strayed north of Newmarket. Scottish affairs were left to John Maitland, Lord Lauderdale, a man of few scruples, loose habits, but very considerable ability, who contrived to hold the reins of power from 1662 to 1680 with only one interval.

As in England, a new Parliament was called in Scotland, and proved amazingly compliant, voting £40,000 sterling for the King's use. Considered a large sum in Scotland, and certainly a burden on the country's funds, the contrast with the sum provided by the English Parliament – £1.2 million – nevertheless represents a fair comparison of the wealth of the two countries.

Like a dog returning to its master the Scottish Parliament eagerly surrendered the small independence it had previously enjoyed, asking for the re-introduction of the Lords of the Articles, who had in the past so reliably drafted legislation to suit the monarch. Within six months nearly four hundred Acts were passed, giving the King almost absolute powers within Scotland. All laws that had been enacted since 1633 were repealed, so turning the clock back to well before the Covenant, and incidentally making the return to episcopacy inevitable. When the King's wishes were made known the Parliament readily agreed to accept the form of Church structure 'most suitable to monarchical government', code words for episcopacy, and a staggering blow to the hopes of the Presbyterians. Scotland was to find Stuart government a good deal more oppressive than that of Cromwell.

No parliament in touch with the national sentiment could so easily have agreed such a concession, and no king remembering the fate of his father should have encouraged it. The decision was even more strongly resisted on the ground in Scotland than it had been in England. Almost a third of Scottish ministers refused to accept the new order, contrasted with perhaps a fifth of the English, and the Scots dominies refused with passionate indignation. Rejection was concentrated in Galloway, where only three ministers retained their livings, and it was from that region the future militancy sprang. A cycle of rebellion and repression began in Dumfries in 1666. Unable to meet indoors, with preaching outside punishable by death, and the ministers hunted through the countryside, secret meetings in the secluded hills were attended by as many as eighteen thousand earnest Calvinists. Lauderdale, who had little patience with what he regarded as 'a drunken scuffle in the dark', attempted to quiet the dissidents by moderate toleration, not attempting to enforce the English liturgy nor limiting the powers of the Presbyterian Church government, but met with little success.

Resistance grew more dogged in the face of persecution. The murder of Archbishop Sharp of St Andrews in 1679 was a particularly shocking crime, in which the Archbishop was dragged from his carriage and cut to pieces in front of his daughter. A few weeks later the Dumfries men rose, led by Richard Cameron, only to be defeated by the Duke of Monmouth at Bothwell Bridge. Further government repression of the 'Cameronians' led to the 'killing time' in which dissidents were hunted down over the bleak fells of the western Borders. A comment by that perceptive historian Rosalind Mitchison sums up the difference between Commonwealth tolerance and Restoration violence:

> If we are to have a 'killing time' in Scottish history the name would much more appropriately belong to the period immediately after the Restoration, when the English and their courts were got rid of, and several hundred old and unpopular women were put into prison, tortured, tried, and condemned for witchcraft.[2]

James II's accession had provoked an ineffective rising in Scotland, and some increase in the persecution of the Covenanters, but was met with general acquiescence. As in England, ambitious politicians converted to Catholicism, and were duly rewarded. When Dutch William arrived in response to an English invitation Scots were taken by surprise, divided between 'Jacobites', mainly Episcopalians loyal to the dynasty, and Presbyterians ready to accept a Protestant King; prudent men left their options open. Within four months of King James' flight a well-planned rebellion broke out in Scotland led by John Graham of Claverhouse, 'Bonnie Dundee' or 'Bloody Clavers', the Cameronians' persecutor, who shattered a bigger government army at the battle of Killiecrankie. But the strategic Lowland centres displayed no loyalty to a Catholic King, and after Graham's death in battle the royalists were defeated, not by regular troops, but appropriately by a much smaller force of Cameronians. It was not until May 1690 that the menace of a Stuart success in Scotland could be written off – if only, as it proved, for the time being.

The Scottish Parliament took its time in accepting the new regime. William was offered the throne of Scotland subject to conditions, namely that episcopacy should be condemned and Presbyterianism established, and that taxation be levied only with the consent of Parliament. Most importantly, the Scots decided that King James had not abdicated but that he had been dismissed for failing to fulfil his royal duties. The implication expressed in this 'Claim of Right', that a monarch remained only as long as he retained the approval of Parliament, was a vital constitutional principle. Although William conditionally accepted the offer, he disagreed with its principles, and was much annoyed at the Scottish parliamentarians' persistence, telling Lord Halifax, 'the Scotchmen by their several stories distracted his mind more than anything'. In the following stalemate the King refused to ratify parliamentary legislation, and the Parliament refused to accept royal judicial nominations.

As a result of its persistence however, the Scottish Parliament secured for the first time some real powers. In addition to the supply vote, it had gained the power to initiate legislation: and the peculiar nature of the national Church was firmly settled. This Church of Scotland was to be solidly Presbyterian, the rights of laymen to nominate clergymen to parishes (a practice which has continued in England until very recently) was abolished, and a new General Assembly elected. As often happens, the previously persecuted willingly took on the role of persecutors, and summarily ejected any ministers who had accepted episcopal rule under Charles and James.

Settlement was eventually reached in June 1690, after the rebellion's defeat, and generally on Parliament's terms: but these terms limited the initiatives permitted to the Scottish Parliament. Ministers were to be appointed by the King, whose real and pressing interests lay always in the war with France, essential to the survival of Holland. Final victory in that struggle was only possible with the support of England, and it was securing this that occupied William's attention. The King disliked what he knew of Scotland, a difficult, disputatious and above all a poor country. It was England's wealth and military power that was essential to William. Neither Scotland nor Ireland could offer much except potential trouble. Relations between King William and his Scottish subjects were further worsened by his share in responsibility for the horrifying massacre of Glencoe. Although this was essentially an episode in tribal warfare between the Campbells and their rivals it appeared to have been done with royal assent, and horrified many.

James had been able to count on some support in Scotland, but his best hope was Ireland, and it was to Ireland that he went in person. No fanatic, and certainly no supporter of the papacy, the King was devout, confident that if the one true faith was given time and equal opportunity its manifest virtue would extinguish all Protestant sects. In England or Scotland the theory was manifestly optimistic, but in Ireland it corresponded closely to reality. The number of rapidly-converted Catholics who cast in their lot with James was encouraging, and there appeared no need for him to impose his faith, already supported by three-quarters of the population.

One major obstacle stood across the way – the determination of Prince William to prosecute his war with France. If James were to appeal successfully to King Louis for help in Ireland, then he automatically became a dangerous enemy of William's. Had he not done so, but relied upon Irish support, it is possible that William might have patched up some sort of compromise. An extension of the war with France was dangerous, and a friendly Ireland, which could supply many troops to help in a European war, would have been a welcome ally. Certainly when James arrived in Ireland in April 1689, compromise was in the air. The King, who was no admirer of the Irish, went out of his way to conciliate the Protestants, and refused to alter the position of the established episcopal Church of Ireland. But an appeal to France had already been made, and James was joined a month later by a French expedition; Ireland had become the theatre for an international conflict. The campaign lasted for over two years, and provided the foundation for some tenacious mythology. Ulster Protestants still celebrate the 105 days before July 1689 when the citizens of Londonderry were able to resist a besieging army in time to allow Williamite forces to arrive. It was indeed a heroic defence, with thousands perishing from wounds, illness or starvation; towards the end a dog's head fetched half a crown, and a rat a shilling. Then the battle of the Boyne followed, in which both kings commanded in person; the result is graphically commemorated on many Irish Protestant gable ends.

After his defeat at the Boyne in August 1690 James left, finally, for France and exile; the victorious William took ship back to England to resume his perennial conflict with the French.[3] The final battle, in July 1691, was fought at Aughrim, between a Jacobite force composed of

French, Spanish, English and Irish, commanded by a French general, the Marquis de St Ruth, famous for his brutality towards the Huguenots, and a Williamite army which included Danes, Russians, Germans, English, Irish and Scots, under the command of a Dutch general, Godert de Ginkel. Aughrim had not much to do with any conflict between the parties in Ireland; it was merely one incident in the great war that continued in Europe against the France of Louis XIV, and the French King's enemies rejoiced at this proxy defeat. One of the staunchest of these, it is entertaining to note, had been Pope Innocent XI, a consistent supporter of Protestant King William against the Catholic King James. Pope Innocent, appalled at the savagery of Louis' persecution of French Protestants, had gone so far as to excommunicate the French King, and had ordered the bells of Rome to be rung in celebration of King William's accession. In Ireland the port of Limerick still held out bravely, but surrendered on agreement of terms that formed the Treaty of Limerick. A subject of much later contention, the treaty was regarded at the time as far too lenient to the rebels. After a little tampering with the small print the Irish Parliament, hot for revenge and intent on establishing a permanent Protestant hegemony, disregarded the more favourable conditions, and embarked on an extended programme of suppressing the Catholic majority so rigidly as to obviate the possibility of any repeated rebellion; but Limerick and Aughrim were transposed into Irish Catholic mythology as the Boyne and Londonderry became Irish Protestant totems.

A Third World economy?

After Aughrim Ireland had a century of relative tranquillity, since it was from Scotland that the more serious challenges to the new order came. The reluctant accord reached in Scotland between King and Parliament was a settlement that concerned only the Lowlands, leaving the Highlands still largely supportive of the exiled King. Both Scotland and England agreed to differ on matters of religion, each with its own established state Church, but mutual irritation and antipathy remained.

However horrifying the Glencoe killings, the Highlands remained peripheral to the future of the new Scotland. Agriculture, manufacturing – still scattered and modest – and trade were all concentrated in the Lowlands, where the decade of the 1680s had seen some economic advances. Rapid expansion was only possible through increases in overseas trade, which had to face a wall of protective tariffs levied not only by England, but by the Scandinavian countries, Holland, France, Spain and Portugal. One remedy, it seemed, was the creation of a Scottish overseas empire, paralleling that of England, the profits of which could be funnelled as exclusively to Scotland as those of the East Indies were appropriated by Holland and England.

Such a happy outcome was meant to result from the 'Company of Scotland trading to Africa and the Indies', promoted by William Paterson, an ambitious and energetic entrepreneur. Paterson, born in Dumfriesshire, 'a man of no education, but great notions' according to Bishop Burnet, had made a fortune in London, trading with New England and the West Indies. A leader in the foundation of the Bank of England in 1694, he had already sought support for a trading company in Germany before deciding to float a joint Scottish–English company, with himself as chief executive. The company's title gave little indication of what became its principal activity, the establishment of a Scottish colony at Darien, on the Isthmus of Panama.[4]

Previous Scottish attempts at colonisation, in Nova Scotia, New Jersey and South Carolina, had met with limited success, and Paterson's proposals made no mention of a Panamanian venture. It was rather the establishment of a competitor to the rich and powerful English East India Company that attracted investors. No suggestion was made of specific colonial plans when Paterson's company applied to the Scottish Parliament for a charter which would grant it a perpetual monopoly of trade with Asia, Africa and America for a period of thirty-one years, the right to 'plant colonies' in any territory not occupied by a European power, and potentially valuable tax privileges.

The enterprise was badly timed, misjudged and unlucky. The initial authorisation given by the Scottish Parliament on 26 June 1695 – without King William's knowledge – confirmed the wide-ranging permissions sought. Of the twenty initial directors all but three were Scots, although seven of those lived in London and it was from London that the promoters sought funds. To the London market, the foundation of a Scottish chartered company, with its returns tax-free for twenty-one years, seemed to afford an opportunity of breaking the monopolies held by the Honourable East India Company and the Royal African Company, and the initial issue was enthusiastically subscribed.

But Sir Josiah Child, Chair (the title is not a modern fad) of the East India Company, had just spent the enormous sum of £170,000, allocated to 'Secret Services' in the firm's own books, on bribing ministers to secure a new charter for his company, and had no intention of seeing his money wasted. When East India stock collapsed from £91 in August to £50 in October, 'great complaints were made' and many ingenious objections advanced in the English Parliament. King William was in a quandary: his Scottish Parliament had acted 'as if there had been no king of Scotland', but if the Declaration of Rights meant anything at all it must be that the monarch could not suspend a law passed by either of his parliaments, and his two parliaments were now on a collision course. The King grumbled that he had been 'ill-served in Scotland', but hoped 'that some remedy may yet be found to meet the inconvenience that may arise from that Act', and dismissed the Scottish ministry.[5] Scotland was ablaze with indignation: 'a national fury seemed to have transported the whole kingdom', recorded Bishop Burnet.[6]

English investors took the hint, and withdrew; the whole sum needed for the adventure, estimated at £400,000, would have to be found in Scotland – and in cash, which amounted to a very considerable proportion of the money available in that country. It was the second such demand to be made on Scottish investors. In 1695 the Bank of Scotland had been founded with a capital of £1.2 million Scots – equivalent to perhaps £120,000 sterling – of which only one-tenth was initially called.[7] Even this comparatively modest sum was raised only with some difficulty over a period of two months (the year previously the new Bank of England had raised £1.2 million sterling, 60 per cent paid – i.e. £720,000, compared with the Bank of Scotland's £12,000 – in twelve days). Unlike the Company of Scotland, which attempted to muscle in on the bank's business, the Bank of Scotland was generally competently managed, but even so experienced a stormy initiation. The Company, now based in Edinburgh, opened its subscription book in February 1696, still with no concrete proposals for any colonial or even trading ventures. Nevertheless the whole amount was promised, and by a cross-section of the nation, incorrigible optimists, with uncritical enthusiasm, helped by the fact that only a first instalment would be payable immediately, many doubtless believing no more would ever be needed. Anne, Dowager Duchess of Hamilton pledged £3000, as did Paterson himself. Others, including Alexander Sheilds, the Cameronian minister, advanced substantial sums.

The new Company's first effort was an unpatriotic attempt to smash the Bank of Scotland, as part of Paterson's feud against the Honourable East India Company, by buying up as many of the Bank's notes as possible. It very nearly succeeded, but was foiled partly by the Company's incompetence when it was discovered that nearly half the enthusiastically subscribed funds had been embezzled. Only in July did Paterson present his plans for a Darien colony.[8] Weighty arguments were advanced against it, pointing out that the territory did not belong to some imaginary 'Emperor of Darien''s country as Paterson had been claiming, but to Spain, Britain's ally, and forecasting strong English objections. These were brushed aside, and although one successful voyage was eventually made to Africa, the new Company concentrated on the Darien project. From the beginning it was disastrous, and the disaster was inevitable. Paterson spoke glowingly of the golden prospects offered by a trading station which, linking by a short overland route the Atlantic and Pacific Oceans, could become 'the door of the seas, and the key of the universe [which] with anything of Reasonable management will of course enable its proprietors to give Laws to both oceans and to become "Arbitrators of the Commercial World"'. It was impossible nonsense. Any large commercial operation to be carried out in distant parts demanded the ability first to acquire, then to settle, defend and exploit, and finally to secure the return of the profits – in short, the existence of a navy; and Scotland not only had no navy, but no means of creating one. Previous Scots attempts at colonisation in North America had foundered for the same reason, the lack of a strong mother country. Only the Scots settlers in Northern Ireland had achieved stability, and the price of their success had been heavy, and enforced by an English army.

Scotland attempted to meet the deficiency of having no navy by buying two surplus English fifth- or sixth-raters, small ships of war suitable for suppressing piracy.[9] Scottish shipwrights were limited in their scope: the biggest vessels usually built in Scotland were small fishing boats; the lack of anything larger had led to the potentially profitable North Sea grounds being dominated by Dutch and Scandinavian fishermen, and an alarming increase in piracy. When it came to equipping ships purchased abroad, like the slaver financed by the Bank of Scotland's first Accountant, George Watson (who hoped to sell the slaves for £25 a head in Barbados; an enterprising fellow, he also profited by a second illegal venture exporting coins), almost all the fittings – guns, sails and ammunition – had to be bought in the Netherlands. So it was with the Company of Scotland's fleets, which sailed poorly-provisioned and without any protection.

Without a navy Scotland was in no condition to guarantee the essentials of success, and had to depend on the goodwill of the other nations. It was made clear that this would not be forthcoming from England, and since the proposed settlement was in territory claimed by Spain, and only a short sail from the powerful Spanish port of Cartagena, trouble was more than likely. Even had the project been handled with real ability it could never, under these conditions, have been successful, and it was instead plagued with both misfortune and incompetence. Paterson's purchasing agent made off with £25,000, of which Paterson himself had to refund £6000. He remained suspected of complicity in the fraud and had to finance his own passage to Darien, without official standing. Nevertheless, in July 1698 the first fleet of ships sailed from Leith, among scenes of jubilation, to plant the Scottish standard in New Caledonia in November. They had chosen one of the world's most unhealthy climates for their settlements of New Edinburgh and New St Andrews, with little prior investigation. None of the adventurers had been there before, and they relied on the descriptions furnished by an enterprising young buccaneer, Lionel Wafer; they had infringed the rights of Spain to that part of its extensive American empire; and they could look for no help from any British West Indian colonies. The Commodore of the Scottish fleet was the neurotic and self-important Captain Robert Pennecuik, whose most senior previous command had been that of an insignificant bomb-ketch. Robert and Thomas Drummond, soldier and sailor brothers, were brutally effective and usually at odds with everybody else. As the principal individual perpetrator of the Glencoe massacre, Thomas was renowned for his ruthless violence. By an incredibly feckless decision, command of the expedition was rotated weekly among its senior members, with predictably chaotic consequences.

The Company could indeed claim a royal charter from the King of Scotland, but the King of England had no obligation to get his subjects involved; and the charter was silent upon any expedition to Darien. And, to make matters worse for the unfortunate would-be colonists, as so often in British history events in Europe were exercising a decisive influence.

There alliances had dramatically shifted. By 1697 Louis XIV had decided that his war with Holland and England was not worth pursuing, and agreed to a negotiated peace. By the terms of the Treaty of Ryswyk, William was finally recognised by the French as King of Ireland, Scotland and England, and French assistance to James was officially ended. The two monarchs then proceeded to arrange European affairs to their joint satisfaction, the main object being to settle the situation in Spain, where the death of King Carlos II, without an heir, was thought imminent. Until this happened both France and Britain were obliged to maintain good relations with Spain, to avoid the still obstinately-alive Carlos from disturbing the arrangements.

William was also under pressure at home and personally distraught after the death of Queen Mary in December 1694 (the occasion of that great work of Henry Purcell's, *Funeral Music for Queen Mary*). In December 1697 the English Parliament, fretful at the expense of the war, insisted that the standing army be reduced and the Dutch troops dismissed, leaving the government scratching around for money. When, therefore, London financiers offered the munificent sum of £2 million in return for the charter of a second East India Company the opportunity was seized. The directors of the existing company, who had believed their previous bribes to have bought permanent support, were furious, but the two East India companies were left to fight it out, before ultimately merging.

At such a time the Scottish expedition to Darien could not have been welcome. Bishop Burnet reported: 'This was a very great difficulty on the King: he saw how much he was likely to be pressed on both hands and he apprehended what ill consequences were like to follow, on his declaring himself either way.' There was no doubt, as the English government acknowledged, that Darien had been Spanish territory for two hundred years: the fact, advanced by the Scots, that no settlements had been built was due to the other indisputable fact that the area was bereft of any products that might fetch a market and that it was riddled with fever, as might have been conjectured by its other name, the Mosquito Coast.

Secret orders were despatched by the English government to the English Caribbean colonies warning them not to send any help to the Scottish colonists, but the only assistance that would have been of any use was in evacuating the settlement. Illness, which had taken a heavy toll on the long passage out, quickly accounted for most of the newcomers. Paterson's wife and child died within days, and three-quarters of the others quickly followed. There was no trade to be done and no gold to be picked up (if there had been, one might assume that in the two centuries they had been in occupation the Spaniards would have found it).

The expedition dropped anchor in what was intended to be the colony of New Caledonia on 1 November 1698; within a month desertions had begun. By the following June it was admitted that the survivors would have to abandon the colony. It had not needed any Spanish action; disease and divided command combined with poor planning had been enough. With the Drummonds in charge, the remnant reached the new British port of New York. There Thomas prepared a relief ship which arrived in New Caledonia on 30 November. By that time a second fleet had arrived from Scotland. Scottish investors had perhaps been encouraged by the young musician John Clerk, whose cantata Leo Scotiae Irritatus urged Scots to 'fight off their enemies so that they might enjoy an idyll on "the sweet isle of Darien"'.[10] At any rate a supplementary fleet had been assembled, which reached the isthmus only to find the settlement abandoned. In spite of hanging a discontented carpenter the men were not encouraged to maintain a prolonged resistance. On 23 February 1700 Spanish ships put in to New Caledonia. Seeing no wish to incur unnecessary casualties – having been once worsted in an overland fight – they moved slowly, but by the end of March the exhausted garrison had surrendered and Mass was celebrated in the Presbyterian chapel. When the news arrived of the previous smart little skirmish 'the battle of Toubacanti' it was celebrated by a lively Jacobite riot in Edinburgh, but a week later the awful truth was known. The investors' money was irretrievably lost, and the debacle felt as a national humiliation.

England was unsympathetic. John Evelyn recorded 'A Scotch book about Darien was burnt by the hangman', on 14 January 1700, and that on 4 February Parliament voted that Scots settlement in Darien 'was prejudicial to our trade with Spain'. A motion was also passed that 'the exorbitant number of attorneys be lessened (now swarming, and evidently causing lawsuits and disturbance . . .'. Unfortunately, the proposal never became law.

Since the original £400,000 had never been called in its entirety – and some shifty investors never paid the subsequent calls – the total lost was £153,000 (a fact many historians have overlooked, seizing instead upon the higher figure); a sadly damaging sum, but not 'a mortal blow'. The Darien crash directly affected only the prosperous upper and middle classes, but it came on top of a famine which inflicted great suffering on the poor: actual starvation deaths in some Scottish districts exceeded proportionately those in the great Irish famine of 1845–48. God had to take responsibility for the hunger, but Darien was blamed on the hypocritical and deceitful English government.[11]

The Act of Union

Early in 1702 William had a fall while riding: on 8 March he died from the resulting pneumonia. Having had no children, the succession to the English throne devolved on his sister-in-law, Anne, the other daughter of James II. Queen Anne, who had little of the personal charm of Mary, had produced many children, all of whom died in infancy, the last in July 1700. The question of succession was therefore pressing once again, since in default of an heir the succession must devolve on one of the fifty-odd Stuart claimants. Jumping the gun, the English Parliament rushed to pass an Act which fixed the succession on the Protestant descendants of James's daughter, Elizabeth, 'Winter Queen' of Bohemia. These were members of the Electoral House of

Hanover, who had a convenient potential candidate in the Crown Prince, George, a stolid German. There were, of course, dozens of more legitimate candidates, but the Hanoverians were reliably Protestant, and, if suitably rewarded, thought to be biddable.[12]

But the Scottish Parliament had followed a different path in the 1689 settlement, and now claimed the right to decide for themselves who should become monarch of Scotland. Following the death of James II in 1701 one obvious choice was his son James Francis Edward Stuart, the Chevalier de St George, or the 'Old Pretender', then living at Louis XIV's expense. The Chevalier had many sympathisers in Scotland who would welcome a king of the old line, let the English do what they may, and the young James was a man of courage and integrity; if he had not remained as firmly Catholic as his father, a Scottish Parliament might well have decided in his favour.

That prospect was sufficiently unnerving to the English. A Stuart on the Scottish throne, or even a disputed succession, would inevitably lead to permanent trouble on the northern frontier, offering a dangerous opportunity to any foreign (for which read French) power. Queen Anne's first speech to Parliament therefore suggested, once again, the appointment of commissioners to discuss the formal Union of the two countries into a single political entity. Sound reasons could be advanced for a closer union. Economically, Scotland was little more than a minor appendage of the much larger English economy. When Union was finally negotiated in 1707 Scottish income from customs and excise stood at £63,500; that of England at £2,289,000. The single town of Newcastle upon Tyne enjoyed a revenue of over £10,000 per annum; the tax on beer levied in Yorkshire in 1689 was not much less than all the customs and excise for the whole of Scotland. The final accepted formula was that the ratio between English and Scottish tax bases was forty-two to one.

Compared to England Scotland was, in modern terms, a Third World economy. Roads were almost non-existent, and remained so for nearly a century. Wheeled vehicles were rare, even in towns: the first cart in Stirling appeared only in 1725. Moreover it was a Third World economy dependent on exports to England, of which the most important were the cattle driven down to fatten for slaughter on the more generous pastures of Yorkshire and the Eden valley, and even as far south as Norfolk. One estimate of Scotland's foreign trade made in 1704 showed exports and re-exports totalling £184,000, and imports of £356,000, consisting of such luxury wares as furniture, tobacco and wines – £60,000 on these three items alone – but also of such basic commodities as knives and tools, 'neeps and onions'; arms, ammunition and ships' stores amounting to £15,000; and salt, at £5000. Reducing somewhat the adverse balance was the income from such invisibles as remittances from foreign investments, smuggling and piracy.

After something of a post-1603 boom two bad periods had depressed the Scottish economy. For fifteen years after 1636 wars had dislocated society. Some improvement had begun under the Commonwealth with free trade between the countries initiated and the new linen industry beginning to develop. Cattle and sheep exports flourished, with probably a hundred thousand animals being driven south every year. Tenants were increasingly given formal, written leases long enough to encourage investment, and common land was brought into more productive use. These real, if modest advances had however been negated by unrelentingly poor harvests in the 1690s, probably as a consequence of climatic change. Trade was miserable. Exports of Scottish manufactures, which had been some £144,000 sterling between 1698 and 1700, slumped to £74,000 in 1701–03 and £54,000 in 1704–06, an amazingly low figure, less than the trade of the English port of Newcastle.[13] It was impossible for two such economically unequal states to co-exist in the same island without the weaker being permanently at the mercy of the stronger.

Although the hubris of 1641, when the Scots commissioners demanded that England accept the Scottish demands, had long since evaporated, the successful assertion of independence made by the Scottish Parliament and magnates in 1690 had bolstered national self-confidence. A very general proposal for Union was advanced in the same year, but William's government was much too occupied with the troubles in Ireland to spare time for what was bound to become a complex, lengthy negotiation. Commissions of both countries were appointed, and discussions ensued only to fizzle out ingloriously. In England there was little interest in the subject, and little interest indeed in anything concerning Scotland, but considerable anxiety to ensure a

Protestant succession to both kingdoms. Scots, on the other hand, were unhappy with the current situation. English difficulties presented an opportunity for a favourable renegotiation, but the Scottish commissioners overplayed their hand by insisting on the recognition of the Darien Company's rights, and the first negotiations collapsed in February 1703.

Each side then upped the stakes. The Scottish Parliament began with an Act of Security, demanding that no successor to the English Crown could be granted that of Scotland 'unless there be such conditions of Government settled and enacted as may secure the honour and sovereignty of this Crown and Kingdom, the freedom frequency and power of Parliaments, the religion liberty and trade of the Nation from English or any foreigne influence'. That Act was followed by an Act anent Peace and War, proclaiming Scotland's right to neutrality. The English Parliament countered with the Alien Act, which threatened that unless the Act of Security was repealed, and the earlier Hanoverian succession agreed, with a treaty under way by Christmas 1705, then Scots would be treated as foreigners, and Scottish exports to England banned.

Scottish crossness developed into anger when the Darien Company's last hope, the chartered ship *Annandale*, was illegally seized. In revenge an English ship, *Worcester*, was piratically taken while at anchor off Leith in August 1704 by Roderick Mackenzie. The original secretary of the Company and one of its few remaining employees, Mackenzie succeeded in persuading the directors, and through them the Scottish courts, that Captain Green of the *Worcester* had, in the course of his voyages, captured the Company's vessel the *Speedy Reserve* and murdered its crew.

This incredible fabrication was enough to get Green hanged, with two of his crew. 'What was left of the Company's honour and nobility died with these men on Leith Sands.'[14] The executions also purged much of the Scottish anger, and enabled negotiations on Union to begin, but much popular disgust, on both sides, still remained to be overcome. English public opinion was never overly impressed by Scots, seen generally as objects of derision, while the Scottish mobs had shown their hatred in a bloody fashion, baying for the blood of the unhappy Captain Green. Nevertheless most responsible opinion saw no alternative to a Union of the two countries; but Union of what sort was less an object of agreement. Andrew Fletcher of Saltoun, an eloquent and reflective Scottish patriot, pressed for a federal agreement, which would secure the increasingly vital economic concessions without sacrificing more Scottish sovereignty; but even Fletcher had previously considered 'we can never come to any true settlement but by uniting with England in parliaments' (January 1689).[15]

Since that date the Scottish economy had deteriorated so much, between poor harvests and the Darien disaster, as to make substantial and speedy assistance essential, and such assistance could come only from England. English anxiety to secure the settlement of the succession helped to ensure flexibility, whilst in Scotland Kirk and Parliament remained to be convinced. A swift assurance that the Church of Scotland would be unaffected, and the practised diplomacy of the Dukes of Hamilton and of Argyll, both well rewarded by the Crown, gave the negotiations a fair wind.

Beating the Christmas 1705 deadline, the Scottish Parliament agreed that once more commissioners should be appointed to negotiate a treaty, and that they should be appointed by the Queen.[16] That provision effectively sold the pass that Fletcher had hoped to defend, since the selected commissioners would be likely to agree with the English government. Union was to be no federation, but an 'incorporating' Union of parliaments, and negotiations were confined to deciding on the details. Scottish objections were vigorously expressed, and on diverse grounds. The Stirling Town Council feared 'ane insupportable burden of Taxationes ... which all Grants of freedome of Trade will never counterballance'; Lord Seafield was apprehensive that the projected Union would be 'contrarie to the Covenant' in that those abhorred bishops would sit in the House of Lords.

By the end of July 1706 the commissioners, English and Scottish, had agreed on the articles of Union; but these had to be ratified by the two parliaments, and both bodies were conscious that their constituents – using the word in its widest sense – were not happy with the whole idea. The key factors in securing the assent of the – very small – Scottish political nation were the assurance of independence for the Scottish Kirk, the continued use of Scots law, freedom of trade, and, perhaps most important, the re-financing the Scottish economy.

This was to be done by the English government supplying what was known as the 'Equivalent'. This sum of £398,085.10s. was to be applied in order:

a. to the losses which 'private persons' might sustain by the change of coinage;

b. to repay the capital of the Darien Company plus interest at 5 per cent, which amounted to £232,884;

c. to pay all other public debts, including arrears of pay and pensions.

On 1 May 1707 Great Britain was born, in fact as well as in theory, as the two kingdoms of England and Scotland each surrendered their sovereignty. That, at least, was the constitutional position, but since the English Parliament, reinforced by new Scots members, continued sitting in Westminster, proceeding according to its own ancient forms, it looked once more very much like Scotland's being swallowed by its bigger partner. As Chancellor Lord Seafield handed over the signed Scottish Act he said to the parliamentary clerk, 'Now that's ane end of ane old song'; but in fact the Edinburgh Parliament had only demonstrated much independence since its successful imposition of conditions on a resentful King William. Nor had the Scots Parliament ever possessed the prestige of the English body. Edinburgh Parliament House had become a useful spot for holding inferior courts and as premises for small traders; it was rather the General Assembly of the Kirk, and its constituents, that could claim to speak for the Scottish people. Parliament's authority as representing the country rested on so amazingly confined a base – fewer than five thousand men throughout the realm were entitled to vote – as to be untenable. But was the share of the reality a fair one? Under the new dispensation forty-five Scottish members were to join the existing 513 English and Welsh representatives, and sixteen peers elected to an Upper House of 190. If heads were to be counted, this was grossly unfair, since the population ratio was about one to five; but it was another two centuries before the idea that counting heads was accepted as the best decision-making device, and then only with many qualifications. Property, not people, was the basis of allocating political power in 1707, and on that standard the ratio of Crown revenues between the two countries, of about forty to one, indicated considerable generosity to Scotland. The sanctity of property reflected, in all probability, the foremost concerns of most people. The farmer's existence and the prosperity, such as it might be, of his workers depended on the security of his landholding, whether freehold or as a tenancy. The labourer's main property, his labour, needed to be protected by some codes of employment. The artisan relied upon the rules of his guild and his town's charter to ensure a free market. Elections formed no part of most people's existence: the selection of burgesses or parish elders was confined to a small number, and such elections were doubtless, as they often continue to be, largely fixed.

After the Act of Union much indignation was expressed at the supposed corruption involved. Robert Burns' memorable verse, nearly a century after the event, is the most famous:

> We were bought and sold for English gold!
> Such a parcel of rogues in a nation!

Burns' version of the Act of Union is however at least exaggerated. In fact, only a small proportion of the funds made available to Scotland were directed to the decision-makers. The accusation was first raised by George Lockhart, who had participated in the Union negotiations, referring to a sum of £20,000, most of which was ostensibly applied to payment of overdue salaries. Some, at least, of these payments were legitimate reimbursements of sums due, and even in an impoverished Scotland the rest can hardly have bought many votes. Besides, it would have been a very strange eighteenth-century arrangement that had not been lubricated by judicious rewards. It was not the availability of English gold, but an unhappy acknowledgment of Scottish lack of it that drove home the Union. As it turned out the total required to balance the books was greater than that of the Equivalent, and only the £30,000 owing to, among others, the Scots commissioners was reimbursed in full. An attempt was made to extinguish the balance by issuing 5 per cent government debentures, but the interest on these, which was to be secured on Scottish customs and excise receipts, was not paid when it fell due. Discontented debenture holders – one of the largest holdings was that of the irrepressible William Paterson –

complained bitterly. Backed by the powerful Argyll interests the creditors pressed successive governments into reluctant action. In 1724 an Act of Parliament created the Society of the Equivalent Company, with a capital of £248,550. The debenture holders then lobbied for conversion of their stock into the capital of a new Scots banking company, to compete with the existing Bank of Scotland. In 1727 the Royal Bank of Scotland duly received a charter and immediately began an attack on the Bank of Scotland.

Whatever disappointments the Act of Union brought to Scots, it proved in fact to be a great safeguard. Whereas the Commonwealth government had made strenuous efforts to modernise and reform, the new British state left Scotland for Scotsmen. Those national institutions that had survived – the Kirk, the law and the educational system – presented neither opportunities nor attractions to ambitious Englishmen. Irish and Welsh bishoprics and legal posts could be filled by English churchmen and lawyers, but the Scottish professions retained their own distinctive character and qualifications.

The first Jacobite reaction to the Union was not long delayed. After a brief interval the war with France had recommenced, and Louis XIV, who had been getting the worst of it, wanted a diversion. The Irish Colonel Nathaniel Hooke, sent as Louis' agent to Scotland, reported, quite inaccurately, 'the whole nation will arise upon the arrival of its king', and that the Earls of Errol and Panmure promised a force of twenty-five thousand foot and five thousand horse. Louis was enthusiastic and refused to listen to the sensible objections of the Comte de Forbin, the appointed commander. Forbin, an experienced fighter, previously among many other appointments an Admiral of the Siamese navy, was rightly reluctant, but sailed in March 1708. The expedition missed the Firth of Forth – not a difficult target – and retreated; none of the promised Scottish army appeared; it was to be the pattern of French expeditions against Britain. The British government had a nasty shock, but no drastic steps were taken against the Scots involved.[17]

The lack of interest exhibited in Scotland, and the relaxed reaction of the British government after its initial panic, indicate that the Union had been generally if reluctantly accepted. It was, after all, only the previous year that the countries had been united, and any widespread Scottish discontent had been offered a marvellous opportunity to manifest itself. The most usual reaction might well have been that described by Daniel Defoe: 'It lay between the English and the French: let them fight it out, there was nothing for the honest people, as they called themselves, to do.'[18]

The Chevalier de St George tried again in 1715, after Queen Anne's death brought, in accordance with the previous Act of Succession, the unknown and unpopular Prince George Lewis of Hanover to the British throne in August 1714 as King George I. At that time France was in no position to help, having recognised the validity of King George's claim by the previous year's Treaty of Utrecht. James Stuart was therefore dependent on his unreliable supporters in Britain.

There the atmosphere was more favourable than it had been seven years previously. The Act of Union had been tried, and in many respects found wanting. In English history the Act is an incident; in that of Scotland it is the central fact of modern times. Union with so much larger and more powerful a country changed the whole character of Scottish national life dramatically and permanently. At the time the changes did not seem for the better, and the 'singular insensitivity and clumsiness with which the English political establishment treated Scotland after 1707' irritated even co-operative Scots. Scottish legal rights had been infringed both by the imposition of the English treason law, and by the House of Lords being superimposed as a final court of appeal. The Kirk, that other pillar of Scottish nationalism, was made indignant by the Act of Toleration – never popular in the Kirk – and the Patronage Act, which reaffirmed the rights of laymen to appoint ministers, the source of much future trouble. Disgruntled Episco-palians, on the other hand, were often ardent Jacobites. By 1711 the shifty John Erskine, sixth Earl of Mar, the Scottish Secretary who had been well-rewarded for his support of Union, complained, 'What Scotsman will not be weary of the Union and do all he can to be quit of it?' His comment was validated two years later, when after an attempt was made to extend the expensive malt tax to Scotland, a proposal to dissolve the Union put to the House of Lords was defeated by only four votes – and those proxies.[19]

Much of the dissension stemmed from economic disappointments. The inequalities between the two countries, which had made Union imperative, were simply too great to make it trouble-free (the recent union between East and West Germany, where inequalities were much less marked than between Scotland and England in the early eighteenth century, has shown how stressful such an integration can be). Economically, the Union was revolutionary, moving into uncharted waters. All Europe at that time was divided into hundreds of states or provinces; even the great kingdom of France was divided by numerous internal customs barriers. Together, England and Scotland formed the largest free-trade area in the world, and adjustment to such an unprecedented situation would not come quickly. Only a generation after 1707 did the Scottish economy noticeably gather momentum. The initial douche of cold water should have been expected: free trade between an advanced and a developing economy made Scottish manufacturers uncompetitive; raw materials such as coal and salt were to be had cheaper in England, and it was only the beef trade that profited.[20]

There was too, for the more traditionally-minded, the fact that George Lewis was only so distantly a Stuart – four generations away from James I and VI – while 'James III and VIII' was indisputably the legitimate heir to the throne. A Scots Parliament had dismissed his father, so why should not Scotland decide to accept the son?

None of these arguments carried much force with England. The rebellion that began in Scotland in August 1715 was led by the incompetent Earl of Mar who had, unwisely, turned his coat. Some adventurous Northumberland gentry joined in, and a numerically formidable army was assembled. A half-hearted march south ended in defeat at Preston, and the Scottish Jacobites melted away after the drawn battle of Sherrifmuir. James arrived too late to inject any enthusiasm into the rebellion, and without any reinforcements or supplies. To the Scots who had taken part the British government was surprisingly lenient: there were no executions, and within two years a general pardon was issued. The Northumbrians fared worse: some of the leaders – the most famous of whom was the Earl of Derwentwater, an illegitimate grandson of Charles II – were executed, and many of the rank and file were either hanged or transported to America.

French policy now required the expulsion of the Jacobites from French territory; the Pretender found refuge in Rome, and some support in Spain. Somewhat surprisingly, an offer of help was made by the King of Sweden, but the next Jacobite raid – it was scarcely more than that, with fewer than four hundred Spanish troops – was a gesture from the King of Spain, made in 1719, from which James prudently absented himself. There was one set-piece battle, at the Pass of Glenshiel in Perthshire, after which the Spaniards surrendered and 'everybody else took the road he liked best'.

It was the end of Jacobitism as a political force in England. Other than the replacement of one monarch by a rather more sympathetic one, the Jacobites had no alternative policies capable of practical application, and offered nothing to make any upheaval acceptable. In Scotland, however, the old cause was not quite dead. The rising in 1745 by the 'Young Pretender', James II's grandson Prince Charles Edward, was intended to be accompanied by ten thousand French troops. None came, and the Prince was able to gather support only in the Highlands. His army's march on the English capital petered out at Derby, and the decisive defeat came on Culloden Moor in April 1746. That was not, as romantic nationalists would prefer it to be, a fight between English and Scots: both armies marched to the sound of the pipes, three regiments of the Hanoverian army were Scottish, and father and son could be found on opposing sides. Culloden did, however, mark the final pacification of the Highlands and the beginning of an integration of Gaelic and Sassenach Scottish culture.[21]

In the seventeenth century Scottish creative energies had largely been diverted into religious and political channels, but they diversified notably in the next century. The Act of Union perhaps secured a wider stage for the exercise of Scottish genius, but the remarkable achievements of eighteenth-century Scotland were native growths seeded in an old tradition. Such intellectual dynasties as that of the Gregorys, which practically monopolised the Edinburgh medical chair, passing as it did over more than a century from John to his great-grandson William, began with the brothers David and James, born in the reign of King Charles I; James followed his countryman Napier in developing mathematics, and designed the first reflecting telescope.

If there is one date when the Scottish Renaissance that transformed the whole of Scottish society within two generations could be said to have begun, it is 1720, with the foundation of the Honourable Society of Improvers in the Knowledge of Agriculture of Edinburgh. There had been modernising landlords previously – enclosing and rationalising holdings were encouraged by Parliamentary Acts between 1661 and 1695 – but it was such men as John Cockburn of Ormiston, MP, or George Dundas who imported English techniques of crop diversification and improvement that eventually brought a new prosperity to the backward Scottish farms. The pioneers were, to a considerable extent, pushing themselves forward as advanced thinkers and modernisers, always a dangerously uneconomic fashion, and it was not until towards the end of the century that the electrifying results were apparent. Throughout Scotland the medieval pattern was replaced, and tenants installed who were willing to get on 'with the job of adopting and altering English husbandry so that it fitted the Scottish situation'.

Rents from improved farms produced the most striking examples of post-Union Scottish prosperity. Beginning in the 1680s with the work of Sir William Bruce in the courtyard of Holyroodhouse and the central block of Hopetoun House, classical Scottish architecture set new standards of excellence. Colin Campbell, in his own work and in his publication *Vitruvius Britannicus*, disseminated the principles of the Classical Revival. It seemed that the ubiquitous Adam family could not put a foot wrong in any of their private or public works. They, and their followers through William Playfair down to Alexander 'Greek' Thomson, who died in 1875, transformed not only Edinburgh – still, in spite of subsequent barbarians an unequalled townscape – but much of London and country houses throughout Britain.

Edinburgh suffered not at all from the loss of its Parliament: the Kirk, government and the law, always a flourishing Scottish industry, remained as the centre of Scottish national life, together with the revived University of Edinburgh.[22] It was however an Irishman, teaching in Glasgow, who began the great tradition of the 'Enlightenment', that campaign of sustained rationality which transformed European thought in the eighteenth century and beyond. Francis Hutcheson, Professor of Philosophy from 1729 to his death in 1746, born in Saintfield, County Down, taught Adam Smith, and, before Jeremy Bentham (to whom the idea is generally attributed) was born advanced the idea that 'That act is best, which promises the greatest happiness of the greatest numbers' – which might be said to be the foundation of all subsequent political thought.

The most distinguished Scotsman of his day, and one of the key figures of the Enlightenment, never succeeded in being appointed to a University chair. David Hume (1711–76) drew his salary for some years as librarian to the Faculty of Advocates. One of the most telling pieces of evidence, both for the Scots sense of their own worth (but that hardly needs questioning) and for the great respect with which Scots intellectuals were regarded in England, is Hume's measured praise of the first volume of Gibbon's *Decline and Fall of the Roman Empire*:

> . . . Whether I consider the dignity of the style, the depth of your matter, or the extensiveness of your learning, I must regard the work as equally the object of esteem; and I own that, if I had not previously had the happiness of your personal acquaintance, such a performance from an Englishman in our age would have given me some surprise. You may smile at this sentiment, but as it seems to me that your countrymen, for almost a whole generation have given themselves up to barbarous and absurd faction, and have totally neglected all polite letters, I no longer expected any valuable production ever to come from them.

Gibbon's comment was that the letter 'overpaid the labour of ten years; but I have never presumed to accept a place in the triumvirate of British historians'.[23]

'Send us our boobies again'

The comparison with Ireland is revealing. After Aughrim, Gaelic Ireland was unequivocally a country conquered and occupied. For a century resistance was quelled; what organised opposition developed was led by the colonists themselves, and not the Gaelic population, but by that time many of the colonists had come to see themselves as Irishmen, and European society had changed out of all recognition. Constitutionally, the country now found itself in the same position as that of Scotland before the Union. From 1729, when the Irish Parliament was able to convene in its magnificent new home on Dublin's College Green, it appeared as a dignified and potent assembly, parallel to that of Westminster. It was in fact hesitant and riddled with contradictions. As was the British Parliament, that of Ireland was purely

Protestant, but whilst Britain was nine-tenths Protestant, Ireland was three-quarters Catholic; this represented much more than a religious distinction, but a cultural, social, and largely linguistic divide. The old Scottish Parliament, with its absurdly restricted franchise, was nevertheless sometimes capable of reflecting a true national view. That of Ireland, in which only a small minority – the Anglicans, of another minority, the Protestants – was represented, could never speak with authority. Moreover, Scotland was unquestionably a historic nation, while Ireland was little more than a geographical expression.

The persecution of the majority of Irishmen by this Irish Protestant 'Ascendancy' was considerably more repressive than any attempted by the English authorities. There had been restrictive laws against Catholics in England since 1606, and these were simply extended to Ireland by the Irish Parliament. While supplementary laws against 'the Further Growth of Popery' were reluctantly accepted by the Crown in 1704, the more extreme proposals were sometimes rejected. Roman Catholic priests were permitted to minister to their people on conditions; those who did not meet these conditions, the Irish Parliament suggested, should be branded on the cheek with a large 'P'. This was thought a little extreme by the Irish Privy Council, who suggested instead the milder deterrent of castration. It was to their considerable disappointment that King George's government refused their sanction to this measure, but as some compensation, a few years later Irish Catholics were deprived of the parliamentary franchise that a few of them had managed to retain and banned from the legal profession. Archbishop Hugh Boulter of Armagh, also a Fellow of Magdalen College Oxford, argued, and argued successfully, for these added restrictions to be imposed by the Irish Parliament. Other English officials were sometimes less harsh.

The third kingdom had been entrusted ever since the Angevin invasion to a viceroy, originally the Justiciar, subsequently, according mainly to his rank, denominated Lord Deputy or Lord Lieutenant. Viceroys were usually chosen by the British government as having some claim to office, or someone whose presence in England was inconvenient, but rarely for their likely contribution to the governance of Ireland. Although much depended on the Lord Lieutenant's character, his presence in Dublin Castle was intermittent, some incumbents never visiting Ireland at all. Continuous administration was provided by the committee of Lords Justices, usually including one of the archbishops, together with the Speaker of the House of Commons, invaluably faithful to 'the English interests', a fidelity duly repaid by rank and profits. Their work was not much incommoded by parliamentary interference: between 1726 and 1756 two Lords Justices, Richard West and Robert Jocelyn, continued in office; there was only one parliamentary election in the thirty-three years after the coronation of George II. Had there been more elections, their results were unlikely to have much changed the composition of the Irish House of Commons: of the 216 borough members (three hundred in all), 176 were reliably nominated by landlords, 123 of them by fifty-three peers.

The influence of any Irish institutions was increasingly repressed by the Westminster Parliament, which in 1720 passed the 'Declaratory Act' – reviled in Ireland as the 'Sixth of George I' – giving Westminster power to legislate 'to bind the kingdom and people of Ireland', and reserving decisions on all foreign affairs to London. This was followed in 1751 by the removal of any control over the country's finances, a power which had been delegated even to the American colonies. Some influential Irishmen resented what they saw as English oppression. Power to object had been confined by the suppression, almost the annihilation, of the old Gaelic aristocracy by the Dublin-based Protestant Ascendancy; and it was from that intellectual and political elite that Irish resistance grew. Dr William Molyneux's writings reflected similar opinions to those of the Scot Andrew Fletcher, and were even more influential. Molyneux's *The case of Ireland's being bound by Acts of Parliament in England*, published in 1698, argued from the same premises that the Americans were later to adopt: 'I take all power that is not with the consent of the subject to be arbitrary.' A muzzled and impotent Irish Parliament and an executive taking its orders from a London government in which Irishmen were not represented was just such an arbitrary power.[24] The book caused a tremendous shock, and was strongly condemned in Ireland as well as in England, but it came to be appreciated as an accurate and justified expression of Irish opinion, reinforced by the work of Molyneux's friend Jonathan Swift, dean of St Patrick's Cathedral.

In the economic as in the political sphere, Westminster power prevailed. English economic imperialism insisted on a total ban on the import of Irish woollen goods, an act that the agricultural reformer Arthur Young stigmatised as 'one of the most infamous statutes that ever disgraced a legislature'. Trade with the colonies, opened under the Commonwealth, had subsequently been jealously restricted. Only from 1748, after two severe famines, were the restrictions imposed on imports of food under Charles II removed, enabling the natural potential of rich Irish farmland to be realised.

When by some fortunate chance London sent a decent Lord Lieutenant to Ireland, something could be done. This happened between 1724 and 1730 when John, Lord Carteret was in office (Carteret's understanding of Irish aspirations might have been assisted by his family coming from Jersey; New Jersey is so named in their honour). It was in 1722 that the affair of 'Wood's ha'-pence' erupted. George I, to please his demanding and extremely ugly mistress the Duchess of Kendal, had caused one William Wood to be given the concession to introduce new copper money to Ireland (the Duchess made £10,000 on the deal). The outcry against Wood's coinage, which had less intrinsic value than that previously issued, was headed by that most brilliant of political pamphleteers Dean Jonathan Swift, who went well beyond attacking Wood, pillorying the whole corrupt business of raiding the Irish exchequer to provide lucrative posts for English supporters of the government.[25]

Carteret, who was more interested in the game of politics than in making money out of it, became a close friend of Swift's, and persuaded the British government to have Wood's concession revoked. Carteret was a match even for the Dean, who on one occasion, when the Lord Lieutenant had got the better of an exchange, snorted, 'What in God's name do you here? Get back to your own country, and send us our boobies again!'[26]

Boobies were not scarce. Swift listed some who had inherited or purchased their comfortable sinecures: 'Lord Palmerstown is First Remembrancer with near 2000£ a year, one Badington begged the Revision of Clerk of the Pells worth 2500£ a year. Mr Southwell is Secretary of State, and the Earl of Burlington Lord High Treasurer of Ireland, by Inheritance.'[27] By 1760 such individuals as the Princess of Hesse-Cassel and Prince Ferdinand drew very large salaries from the

Irish Treasury for doing precisely nothing, but the heaviest drains on Ireland's wealth were those extracted to finance the British army. Soldiers being unwelcome in England during times of peace, Ireland was used as a great barracks. Such exactions, coupled with the frequent contempt displayed for the Irish, Catholic and Protestant alike, by English officers, nurtured a very widespread resentment.

Not that the Irish themselves were slow to plunder the public purse. Castletown, that magnificent house at Celbridge, was built on the proceeds of William Connolly's political career as Speaker of the House of Commons and Commissioner of the Revenue (Connolly being the son of an innkeeper). Such houses as Castletown, or the spectacular Ardgillan Castle, near Skerries, built on fortunes extracted from Ireland, stand as permanent reminders of the successful exploitation of the Gaelic Irish; but these solid examples of conspicuous expenditure served at least to provide employment and develop Irish skills.

Dublin, which in 1690 was a shabby medieval town clustered around the castle, had within a hundred years become the second largest city in the British Empire, and probably the handsomest: the Customs House, the magnificent Parliament building, the Four Courts, Trinity College library, Leinster House, the splendid FitzGerald townhouse, the Kilmainham Royal Hospital, were all finer than most contemporary London buildings.

Edinburgh had flowered in similar fashion. Architecturally the New Town, and Robert Adam's work in the University and the Register Office, bear comparison with anything in Dublin and have survived better, since many of Dublin's best buildings were largely destroyed in the Civil War of 1922–23 and by crass development later. It is in the intellectual and cultural life that the most striking differences developed. Lords Lieutenant might differ in quality, but the existence of a viceregal court encouraged social life and public entertainments. Garrick and Foote played at Thomas Sheridan's theatre where Mrs Jordan's career began, Thomas Arne gave concerts, and the greatest musical event in eighteenth-century Britain, the first performance of Handel's *Messiah*, took place in the Dublin City Hall. In the countryside race meetings, hunts and the liveliest of fairs were the amusement of all classes and religions. The other side of the coin was the extraordinary level of socialised violence expressed in the duel. It was not uncommon

Left Royal and Marcher castles such as Caerphilly stamped English authority on Wales in the thirteenth century, but did not quench Welsh ambitions for independence.

Below Plas Mawr, Conwy. By the reign of Queen Elizabeth I prosperous Welsh burghers enjoyed domestic comforts equal to any in England.

Scottish domestic architecture (Claypotts Castle, Angus) remained uncompromisingly defensive and mediaeval at a time when English houses (like Hardwick Hall, below) reflected an expansive economy.

Sir William Bruce's splendid work at Holyroodhouse marks the start of Scotland's golden age of Enlightenment – a full generation before the union with England.

For over three hundred years (1371–1688) the Stewart (Stuart) family ruled over Scotland, and, for most of the seventeenth century, over England as well.

Sawney in the Boghouse

Above left The popular idea of 'Puritans' as dour kill-joys is contradicted in this portrait of Robert Rich, Earl of Warwick, a Puritan leader whose grandson married Oliver Cromwell's daughter, Frances.

Above Scottish hostility towards the English was matched by English derision of the Scots. This 1745 cartoon caricatures Scottish toilet training.

Left Visceral English distrust of 'Popery' led to the worst riots in modern British history: Newgate prison stormed in 1780.

Above Fifteen years after Newgate, Irish Catholics congratulate King George III following the annulment of the anti-Catholic Penal Laws.

Below 'Grattan's Parliament', in its magnificent chamber. Standing in the right foreground are Grattan and Flood; seated on the left is the other leading 'Patriot', Lord Charlemont. The assembly is being addressed by John Philpott Curran.

The 1798 rising in Ireland produced some real heroes, much vicious killing, and engendered many myths. Henry Joy McCracken (above left) and Michael Dwyer (above right) are numbered among the heroes. Theobald Wolfe Tone (above) was the inspirational leader, but Napper Tandy (left), a drunken buffoon, has gained an undeserved reputation.

The massacre of Protestants on Wexford Bridge is commemorated by a statue nearby –
dedicated to the killers.

for the most distinguished and solid citizens to have been 'out' and to have killed their man; even one Lord Lieutenant felt himself bound to accept the challenge of an angry Irish peer – and Lord Townshend shot his man, Lord Bellemont, although not fatally. Sir Jonah Barrington, in his memoirs, hardly exaggerated when stating that 'a duel was considered a necessary part of a young man's education'; certainly a man seen to have avoided a fight faced social scorn and exclusion. Richard Daley, manager of Dublin's Theatre Royal, fought nineteen duels in two years.[28]

Life was less fun in Edinburgh, if intellectually of higher quality. Bishop Berkeley was the most prominent Irish thinker of the time, but passed his days in the relative seclusion of the bishop's palace at Cloyne, and Trinity College was more distinguished for its lively social life than for its academic performance. In Edinburgh the ubiquitous influence of the Kirk still discouraged public manifestations of gaiety: theatrical performances were rare, confined to a few daring English players. The first theatre in Edinburgh, when built in the 1740s, had to be disguised as a concert hall; when one opened in Glasgow in 1764 it was burned down on its first night by an enraged and godly mob. Only by the closing years of the century did theatre-going become respectable, to the extent that when the famous actress Mrs Siddons appeared in 1784, the General Assembly of the Kirk amended its timetable so that the ministers might attend her performances. The cautious reserve of the Scottish audience in applauding only at the end of the performance was deplored by the great actress, who much preferred the Dubliners who would 'lavish applause' on any scene they particularly approved. Edinburgh conviviality flourished privately in the many and varied debating and conversation societies, ranging from informal tavern gatherings to such distinguished institutions as the Speculative Society, still flourishing today, which brought the liveliest minds among the Edinburgh young men together in amicable argument, without the public extravagance of Oxford debates.

An affectionate, tender-spirited people

There is said to be a Chinese curse: 'May you live in interesting times!' By this standard, the seventeenth and eighteenth centuries in Wales were tolerably blessed. No massacres or rebellions troubled Wales as they had both Ireland and Scotland between 1641 and 1746, and the War of the Three Kingdoms did not inflict permanent damage. The strong sense of loyalty that the Tudors had attracted was in some measure transferred to their successors, and sentiment was strongly royalist on the outbreak of the Civil War in spite of the influence of such gifted advocates as the Independent Vavasor Powell. One outstanding exception was Thomas Myddelton of Chirk, who beat a sizeable royal army at Montgomery in September 1644. No major battle took place on Welsh soil (there were two other small-scale parliamentary victories), and although the disruption caused by the fighting was distressing – Robert Vaughan of Hengwrt found 'each minute of every hour too long' – it was at least temporary. Since Wales was already incorporated into England the republican governments that ran Scotland under Monck and Broghill and Ireland under Henry Cromwell were not inflicted – or bestowed – upon it. James Berry, the clerk turned major general (Cromwell's promotions were as bold and successful as Napoleon's), proved a liberal administrator of those he termed the 'affectionate, tender-spirited people' who had 'suffered most'.[29]

The Restoration was greeted, as in England, with general relief, but many Welshmen found themselves fervently hoping for the return of more tolerant Cromwellian standards, under which George Fox was at liberty to propagate, very successfully, the new doctrines of the Society of Friends. A battery of legislation in the 1660s levied savage penalties – up to seven years' transportation – for those who worshipped without legal permission and banned all but members of the Church of England from any public office. Informers proliferated, and were rewarded by the magistrates. Once again, however, Wales was spared the worst: no persecutions paralleled the ferocity of those in Scotland.[30] Roman Catholics suffered more, in the brutal hysteria surrounding the 'Popish Plot' invented by Titus Oates, during which priests were hunted out of Cardiff and the Marches and subjected to the usual barbarous form of execution.

For both communities one remedy lay in emigration. Catholics could find a welcome in Maryland, and from 1682 hundreds of Welsh Quakers moved to Pennsylvania, to the counties of Haverford, Merion – most settlers came from Merioneth – and Radnor. England, however, remained both the easiest and the most rewarding destination for Welsh emigrants. Those who remained found that conditions improved after the Revolution of 1688, with the Toleration Act of the following year and, an important landmark, the abolition in 1695 of the Licensing Act, which had restricted the publication of books in England to London, Oxford and Cambridge. With this freedom the work of the translators was abundantly justified, as tens of thousands of Welsh Bibles and devotional books were published, together with translations of that most influential of spiritual manuals, John Bunyan's *Pilgrim's Progress*.

Whilst the survival of the Welsh language seemed assured the spread of English was unchecked. A linguistic division, still apparent today, was developing between the increasingly anglicised south and east and the conservative Welsh of the north and west, a boundary reinforced by a similar split between Dissenters and Anglicans. Methodism, the revival movement that began within the Church of England but developed into one of the largest Protestant communions, went further in dividing Wales. By 1780, of 428 Welsh Methodist societies, 346 were in the south-west counties, fifty-one in Montgomery and Radnor, but only thirty-one in the five counties of north Wales, where the established Church remained powerful. Since Welsh Methodism was, and remains, different in kind from Methodism elsewhere, an added dimension was given to Welshness. Unlike Dissenters, Methodists were not inclined to intellectual analysis or higher learning; their emphasis was on individual spiritual experience, reinforced by a 'class' system binding communities strongly together. But whereas Methodism outside Wales followed orthodox Anglican theology and – much simplified – liturgy, Wales was from the outset specifically Calvinist in doctrine, a difference to some extent reflected in social and political habits.

Whilst Dissenters did not often approve of what seemed an emotional, anti-intellectual movement, the energy of the Methodist evangelists was inexhaustible. Methodism preached a doctrine of sub-mission to the established authority, and enforced, under the firm leadership of Jabez Bunting, obedience to Church discipline. Revolu-tionary ideas could not flourish in a predominantly Methodist culture, which might well explain the calmness with which English workers and members of the lower-middle classes rode out nineteenth-century agitation. On the other hand, the tight Methodist class system and lay administration was a principal foundation for the later development of constitutional trades unions and friendly societies that was to result in the English Labour Party paying only the faintest lip service to Marxist ideology.

CHAPTER 8

1750–1830

Wild Geese

FACED WITH the drastic restrictions of the Cromwellian settlement, and the more ingenious persecutions envisaged by the Irish Parliament after 1690, hundreds of thousands of young Catholics left the island. Most went to Europe, where they were welcome recruits to Continental armies. France's Irish brigade was, with twenty thousand men, equivalent to an army corps. In one of the rare victories gained by the French over British troops, the battle of Fontenoy, the final charge led by the Irish regiments proved decisive. Daniel O'Connell 'the Liberator's' uncle, Count Daniel Charles, became a distinguished French general. Ricardo Wall rose to be chief minister of the Spanish King, and Bernardo O'Higgins the national hero of Chile. In the Imperial and Russian armies Irish generals abounded. More peacefully, the Irish at Bordeaux founded famous houses, including such châteaux as Dillon, Barton and Kirwan; on the quays of Tonnay-Charente it was brandy produced by such Irish distillers as Hennessy and Otard that was loaded on to smugglers' ships (Otard is said to have been started by relations of the Stuart kings). Anthony Vincent Walsh, a prominent St Malo slaver and privateer, brought the Young Pretender to Scotland in his own brig. This original exodus, of the 'Wild Geese', was maintained as a steady flow for the best part of a century. Barred from political life, from the legal profession, from tending their estates or even, except by special permission, from bearing arms, denied a university education, there was little to keep ambitious and talented Irish Catholics at home.

The consequences were varied and seriously damaging. No society could afford to lose so many of its able and energetic leaders, and it was many years before those Catholics who stayed at home produced men who could match the lost leaders of the Wild Geese. Irish political society in all respects remained solidly Protestant. Not, except in north-eastern Ulster, the doctrinaire Presbyterian Protestantism of Scotland, where on the very dawn of the Age of Enlightenment a young man could be hanged for blasphemy, but something nearer the easy-going Anglicanism of England – more tolerant in some respects, as with the dangers of Catholic rebellion receding the penal laws were applied only laxly. Those discriminatory laws that might have affected a Catholic family's prosperity were often ignored: only one instance is known of the provision that rents to Catholics must be maximised being enforced. Given the number of fox-hunting Irish Catholic squires and farmers, typified by another of Daniel O'Connell's uncles, Maurice 'Hunting Cap' O'Connell, the rules concerning the ownership of horses must only rarely have been observed. R.F. Foster in his *Modern Ireland* estimates that nine-tenths of the Catholic landowning class survived the Penal Laws during the first half of the century, before the moves to repeal the laws got under way.[1]

The mirror image of Ireland's solidly Protestant elite was that of its majority, politically and economically oppressed, deprived of its potential leaders by emigration and hampered by restrictions on land ownership. Economic improvement was a slow business, but with better trading conditions, improved techniques and more exports to hungry English cities, a class of 'strong farmers' emerged among the Irish Catholics. Between 1741 and 1822 Ireland enjoyed a period of unaccustomed prosperity, broken only by occasional poor harvests which, as in every other agricultural country of the time, brought subsistence crises and excess mortality. Between 1740 and 1770 Irish exports nearly doubled; static until 1780, between then and 1810 they again nearly doubled. Even if pastoral farming continued predominant, wheat exports increased twentyfold between 1772 and 1819. Domestic consumption was underpinned by increasing reliance on the potato as a staple food. It was an unequal and relative prosperity, differing greatly between the lowland agricultural regions and the bogs and mountains, where poor communications and the absence of markets preserved the medieval systems. Irish poverty horrified many visitors, who contrasted the striking decline between Dublin, 'more beautiful than London', and the 'well-cultivated appearance of the Pale countryside' with the wretched conditions in some other parts. After Athlone the country became 'another Siberia . . . nothing but large stones . . . and here and there a black mud cabin . . . some 6–8 feet high and 12 feet square . . . In a corner a bed of straw for humans, in another a sow with young, an ass, goats and such like, and in the third a table, chair and spinning wheel . . .'.[2] Such a diversity of livestock and possessions in isolated Dunamore denotes, however squalid, at least a degree of primitive comfort; many more penurious families must have existed.

In districts such as Wexford, where agriculture flourished, Catholic strong farmers could prosper. The Whittys of Duncormick kept Christmas in the old fashion, 'the house filled with friends, followers and neighbours, who ate brown barley bread, bacon and gritty, roast beef, boiled beef, ducks, chickens, pullets and turkeys', and the season being 'devoted to mumming, hurling, and dancing'. In the Walsh mountains of Kilkenny the Aylwards, a parsimonious peasant family who lived off potatoes and pigs' offal, had an income of over £600 a year, which would have kept even an English household in genteel comfort. Less prudent Catholic farmers also prospered, holding land on twenty-one to thirty-one-year leases, living in modern houses in some style, wearing 'round hats edged with gold, who hunt in the morning, get drunk in the evening, and fight the next morning'.[3]

The Catholic Church in Ireland, after the first flurry of Williamite repression, was certainly seriously disadvantaged, but hardly persecuted officially, as were the Protestants in contemporary France. Ireland has nothing comparable to the fate of the respectable bourgeois Jean Calas in Toulouse, who as late as 1762 was judicially murdered, in reality for being both Protestant and rich. By an Act of 1697 bishops were to be obliged to leave the country, but this prohibition was allowed to slide into oblivion; within half a century the Irish Catholic episcopacy had been brought up to strength.[4] Banished, too, were the regular clergy (members of religious orders); again, this was soon a dead letter, and by 1750 several hundred regulars were active. As early as the beginning of George I's reign, in spite of the 1709 Popery Act, diocesan clergy had been able to carry out their ministry in comparative freedom. With the waning of the Jacobite challenge, fear of insurrection decreased, and from 1745 onwards Catholic 'Mass houses' were officially authorised;

from 1767 prayers for the royal house were included in the Church ritual, and in 1774 an acceptable oath of allegiance to be taken by priests was devised. Sporadic attempts were made to enforce regulations (that old favourite, castration of unregistered priests, together with whipping of nuns, had two attempted introductions, in 1719 and 1721), but the greatest bar to the expansion of the Church was the lack of training facilities, all candidates for ordination being forced to obtain their education abroad. In spite of such difficulties many parish priests were often as well-educated as their Protestant counterparts, and accumulated respectable libraries. A major advance in this respect was made with the Catholic Relief Act, when a seminary was founded at Carlow, followed in 1795 by the national seminary, the Royal College at Maynooth, subsidised by the British government. From 1793 Catholics were also admitted to Trinity College, although only a few of the most liberal availed themselves of the opportunity.[5]

In spite of their improving fortunes it was still largely true that the Catholic Irish remained, on the whole, 'a defeated, depressed and leaderless people'. The old Gaelic culture and language was sliding into oblivion, becoming an agreeable occupation for scholarly gentlemen, with literacy usually confined to English. A French traveller in 1790 noted that while Irish was spoken throughout Kerry he saw no notices in that language. Some countrymen could still be found, alongside the improving strong farmers, continuing the old ways. James Cuffe, MP for County Mayo, recounted a night spent with a local chief near Lough Crib in 1750, with pipers, a bard, a great and whole sheep, boiled fish, a deal of punch and claret, and a singing girl with whom 'they were welcome to any liberties from the girdle upwards'.[6]

Banned from the professions, Catholics turned to trade, an activity scorned by Protestants with pretensions to gentility, and flourished thereby. Links with expatriate merchants were expanded, and Cork's favourable position as the nearest port to America assisted Ireland to attract a substantial share of the colonial trade. As early as 1708 Catholic Cork merchants insisted successfully on discriminatory practices being overturned. Even in Dublin, with its close English connections, as many as one-third of the burgesses were Catholic. Farmers as well as merchants and manufacturers profited during the endemic wars with France and their consequent demands for provisions – Irish beef supplied much of the Royal Navy's needs, and Irish linen sailcloth.

There was no dramatic confrontation between anglophobic Catholics and Ascendancy Protestants devoted to upholding British interests. In spite of doctrinal affinities and its integration into English society, the Ascendancy was by no means anglophile. Dean Swift, Dr William Molyneux and Dr Charles Lucas, in their different ways, produced reasoned and sometimes devastating criticisms of English policies – Swift's 'Modest Proposal' is a classic of savage satire. As had been proved four centuries previously, when Arnold Power denounced the Bishop of Ossory as an interfering Englishman, it did not take long to transform an English immigrant into an Irish patriot – no longer than it took the loyalist Washington family to become rebels against King George in the more distant American colonies. Bishop Evans of Meath complained in 1718 of the 'unaccountable aversion these people (tho lately come from England and Scotland) have to the English name'.[7]

Ireland already had a legislature, a judiciary and executive of its own, but all with crippling restrictions on their power. Parliament could only assemble when summoned; laws could be enacted only with the help of the English government; executive power was invested in the Viceroy, often resident in London; and judges could be dismissed at any time. The Declaratory Act of 1720 reinforced Poynings' Law by confirming Ireland's status as a dependent kingdom rather than an equal partner. The Irish legislature was, however, not without teeth, and, particularly after the accession of King George III in 1760, these were sometimes bared. It was a time of rising expectations, and the comparison with America did not escape contemporaries either in England or in Ireland.

George, Lord Townshend, appointed as Viceroy in August 1767, had first-hand experience of America, having fought as one of Wolfe's brigadiers at Quebec. His brother Charles, when Chancellor of the Exchequer, had infuriated the American colonists by his taxes, and George was aware of similar dangers in Ireland. When the new Viceroy was faced, soon after his arrival, with a polite refusal by the Irish Parliament to allow an increase in troop numbers being billeted in Ireland, and the defeat of an essential money Bill, it seemed that the Irish were likely enough to follow the American example. This was one of those occasions when Ireland forced itself upon the reluctant attention of a British government. Lord Shelburne, who had been a bitter critic of the government's unyielding policy towards the American colonists, pointed out that 'the American war had commenced upon less persecution than this country had given Ireland', and moved a vote of censure in the British Parliament on the government's neglect of Ireland (June and December 1779).[8]

Battle was joined on 12 October 1779, when, in reply to the Lord Lieutenant's request for more money, the Irish House of Commons retorted: 'It is not by temporary expedients, but by a free Trade alone, that this Nation is now to be saved from impending Ruin' – and backed up their defiance by flatly refusing, by 170 votes to forty-seven, to grant new taxes.[9]

The Triumvirate of 'Patriots' that inspired the Irish House of Commons to this resistance were James Caulfield, Earl of Charlemont, Henry Flood and Henry Grattan. Lord Charlemont's social prestige and charm combined well with Flood's robust oratory and Grattan's polished style in their campaign to establish the independence of the Irish Parliament as a separate institution not subordinate to that in Westminster. In so doing they had the very visible support of the Irish Volunteers, originally formed in Antrim as a response to a French landing at Carrickfergus in February 1760. On the outbreak of the American rebellion in 1775 Volunteer companies were again quickly mustered. Although middle-class Protestants, officered by the gentry both in Ulster and Dublin, formed the majority of Volunteers, Catholics were to be found, drawn from those prosperous farmers and townsmen who had flourished in spite of the Penal Laws. It began to look very much like a nation, or at least a political nation, in arms. When the Volunteers paraded, foot, horse and guns, in Dublin's College Green on 4 November 1779, the message passed by Parliament the previous month was powerfully reinforced. One placard read: 'A Short money bill: a free trade: or else.' Free trade, in so far as it related to opening up trade with British colonies, was quickly granted, and more concessions followed.

The Irish Parliament did not need too much encouragement, for while it was true that a good number of the members had been squared by the Dublin Castle officials to toe the government line, a majority, like most Irishmen, resented the subordinate status of their own legislature, dating back three hundred years to Poynings' Law. Grattan pulled no punches: in April 1780 he was able to claim 'as long as [England] exercises a power to bind this country, so long are the nations in a state of war . . . a country enlightened as Ireland, chartered as Ireland, armed as Ireland, and injured as Ireland, will be satisfied with nothing less than liberty'.[10]

Again, events in America were influential. Irishmen had been found on both sides in the long War of American Independence: Lord Rawdon's loyalist volunteers fought one of the most successful actions against the rebels, and staged the first New York St Patrick's Day parade. Their commander, later Marquis of Hastings, described the administration of Ireland as 'the most absurd, as well as the most disgusting tyranny', and went on to become one of the most advanced Governors General of India. Lord Cornwallis surrendered to the Americans at Yorktown in October 1781, and in March 1782 Lord North's government, having lost the war, resigned, to be replaced by a more amenable Whig coalition, with the radical Charles James Fox as leader of the British House of Commons. The new government acted quickly to assuage Irish discontent. In the two months of June and July 1782 the Declaratory Act of 1720 was repealed, Poynings' Law fundamentally amended, a Catholic Relief Act abolished the worst restrictions on the clergy, and the most annoying petty constraints on laymen were removed (the more serious restrictions on land ownership had been abolished in 1778). 'Grattan's Parliament', as it became known, fired by energetic Irish oratory, began to behave as a genuinely independent assembly.[11]

Important measures were also taken to bring Ireland into line with British practice by ending such instruments of arbitrary power as having the tenure of judges subject to government whim, and introducing, for the first time, the Habeas Corpus Act. The Irish legislature still had no control over the executive, appointed by the British government, but was more than a talking shop since British governments were not insensitive to Irish opinion, nor unreceptive to pressure for reforms; and such influential Irish members as Grattan and Flood also had seats at Westminster. There the most influential member, for over twenty years, was another Irishman, Edmund Burke, who could command the rapt attention of the House of Commons in support of Irish causes.

Limited reforms were, however, not enough for the Volunteers, now under the command of Lord Charlemont. A National Convention was held at Dungannon, in Ulster, in February 1782, which proposed resolutions claiming Irish rights to legislative and judicial independence. Since a 'convention' in British constitutional practice is understood to be an assembly of the Houses of Parliament called without royal assent, by choosing the term 'National Convention' for their Assembly, the Volunteers were hoisting a clear signal, reflected in their resolutions: 'In a free country the voice of the people must prevail.' Their demands for reform were undeniably justified. The Irish House of Commons was packed with nominees, both of government and of landlords: Jamestown in Leitrim, 'a wretched depopulated village'; Newtown-Limavady, a 'venal and rotten borough', under the control of Mr Dillon; or St Johnstown, 'a venal borough, at the absolute disposal of Lord Granard', were some of many identified by the Volunteers.[12] The Dungannon meeting was followed by a National Convention of Volunteer delegates, which in November 1783 assembled in Dublin's Rotunda to demand thorough reforms. The most sensitive of these was the demand that no MP should also hold an office of profit under the Crown. Not unnaturally, since so many of the members were drawing comfortable salaries for holding just such positions, the proposals did not secure the Irish government's assent. Searching for a further instrument of governmental pressure, the Most Illustrious Order of St Patrick was established, with magnificent regalia and fetching robes. Although intended to be an inexpensive measure of retaining support, the first installation was greeted with almost hysterical general enthusiasm as a symbol of Irish distinction, on a par with the English Garter and Scottish Thistle.[13]

In spite of their failure to secure reform of the Irish Parliament, the 'Patriots' were able to persuade the British government to agree to some significant advances. Some of the restrictions placed upon Irish trade, which had provoked the same sort of discontent as in the American colonies, were removed. The still entirely-Protestant Parliament was not unanimous on the subject of future Catholic relief, and the great advance came as a result of an approach directly to the King.

In January 1793 members of the Catholic Committee had personally presented a petition to King George III pleading that 'a century of uninterrupted loyalty, in which time five foreign wars and two domestic rebellions' (those of 1715 and 1745 – in Scotland, it should be noted), 'and given and being still ready to give, every pledge which can be devised, for their peaceable demeanour and unconditional submission to the laws', the Irish Catholics should be allowed to vote for Members of Parliament. This plea the King received sympathetically, and an Act to such effect was easily passed in the British Parliament.[14]

The Irish franchise was rather more democratic than that granted in England itself (voters were required to hold property to the value of £2 rather than £10 as in England, but property values were very different in the two countries). As in England, landlord influence and bribery combined with the still-restricted franchise to ensure that constituencies returned the members that their patrons required: it was common to speak of the ownership of parliamentary seats. Although Trinity College was now open to Catholics, the Test Acts still remained in force, by which sincere Catholics were excluded from taking seats in any Parliament, and from the most important public offices, but were allowed to accept military commissions of field rank and to occupy certain judicial positions. These included that of Chief Constable and the peculiarly Irish post of Assistant Barrister, with powers similar to that of an English Crown Court judge. Holders of either of these positions were capable of exercising great authority in the countryside, but it was some time before the Dublin Castle authorities could be forced into appointing Catholics.

By 1793 the potential consequences of unlimited obstruction to Irish and colonial aspirations were becoming painfully clear. Both language and the institutions of revolutionary change had become familiar. France had given the example of a National Convention, with delegates, resolutions and armed followers, which in September of that year abolished the monarchy, to be succeeded by Committees and Directories. The message to British governments was that the Irish Volunteers constituted a potentially dangerous revolutionary force; they were accordingly officially disbanded.

British liberals had greeted the French Revolution in July 1789 as the overturning of an oppressive government (and an upheaval severely damaging to the great rival). Wandering in France, dazed with excitement and love, the young Wordsworth caught the mood precisely:

> Bliss was it in that dawn to be alive,
> But to be young was very heaven!

Lord Fitzwilliam may not have rhapsodised so intensely, but when the Whig peer was appointed Viceroy in December 1792 it seemed as though a new era might have dawned in Ireland. Fitzwilliam's ideals were liberal enough, supporting as he did the removal of all remaining restrictions on Catholics, but his naïveté and incompetence led to his speedy dismissal the following February and to widespread disillusion and disappointment among Irish reformers. Access to the vote for small freeholders was hardly relevant to the mass of the population, and the limited devolution of parliamentary power seemed an inadequate recompense for so many unfulfilled hopes; to the more ardent reformers the alternative of revolution grew less alarming. Tom Paine, that extraordinary genius – corset-maker, privateer, American soldier, diplomatist, French deputy and master of English prose – had published the first part of his *Rights of Man* in March 1791. Its success was phenomenal, with sales, at sixpence a copy, reaching perhaps two hundred thousand, and its influence prodigious. Agitation for parliamentary reform took on a revolutionary tinge in all three kingdoms, and much to the alarm of the Tory government. Trees of liberty, planted in the market squares of even small Scottish burghs, seemed to be forerunners of the guillotine. Nowhere was enthusiasm for Paine's demands for democracy more marked than in Ireland, where the *Rights of Man* quickly went into seven editions. Even when Citoyen Député Paine, horrified by the Terror, risked his life by objecting to the execution of King Louis, many of his Irish followers continued their excited support of the Revolution.

William Pitt's government grew hysterically alarmed, and 'worked themselves up into such apprehensions' as to begin the imposition of a repressive system that was to continue for over thirty years, during which British liberties were severely restricted. Wordsworth again:

> Our shepherds [Pitt's ministers]
> Acted, or seemed at least to act, like men
> Thirsting to make the guardian crook of law
> A tool for murder.

Within weeks of King Louis' public decapitation in Paris in January 1793 the British government, siding with its European allies, was at war with the French Republic. What had previously been a constitutional reform movement in Britain and Ireland became potentially treasonable. The example of a country which was massacring so many of its citizens (Jean-Baptiste Carrier could not spare the time to guillotine his victims, preferring the more economic method of mass drownings) ceased to commend itself to liberals. Those who continued to support revolutionary principles became, by definition, more extreme, and any action they undertook in conjunction with the enemy was therefore treason.

Who dares to speak of '98?

> I met with Napper Tandy, and he took me by the hand,
> And he said 'How's poor old Ireland, and how does she
>   stand?'
> She's the most distressful country that ever yet was seen;
> They're hanging men and women there for wearing of the
>   green.

Unlike English history, that of Ireland is crammed with dates. In Ireland a reference to '41, '89, '98, '48, '67 or '16 is enough to call up a memorable occurrence; and of these 1798 is perhaps the most potent. The actors in that year's drama form the cast of what might be called the Irish Toy Theatre, after those Victorian nursery toys in which pasteboard characters (penny plain and tuppence coloured) could be made to perform on small wooden stages. Many melodramatic scripts are still performed, representing to enthusiasts a thousand years of an Irish struggle against oppression. All bear only a passing resemblance to the facts, but still serve to excuse violence which leads to real blood and corpses.[15]

So many mythological accretions have gathered around the rebellion of 1798 that some scraping clean is needed to arrive at the truth of the matter. To begin with at least three, only intermittently linked, spheres of action can be distinguished. First was that of the intellectuals and ideologues, for the most part Protestant Ulstermen, who burned with republican ambitions, kindled by American and French examples. Some were disabused by the example of the French Terror, which showed what republicanism might well involve. Others, with a command of strategy, and with ambitions to become omnipotent Directors of an Irish Republic, concentrated on obtaining French military support. Thirdly, a mass of resentful and violent poor peasants and some urban workers were avid for plunder and killing without clear aims, and were ready to fight bravely when vengeful authority pursued. Interspersed with these were a motley crew of drunkards, traitors, romantics longing for elaborate uniforms and the occasional straightforward hero.

The Irish Revolution might be said to have its beginning in the innocent days of revolutionary purity with the formation in October 1791 of the United Irishmen, initially as an offshoot of the Volunteer movement. Dr William Drennan of Belfast was their first chairman, and the initial meetings of the new society were held under the auspices of the Green Company of the Belfast Volunteers. Drennan had previously (1784) written an influential tract, 'Orellana; or An Irish Helot', advocating the unity of all Irishmen regardless of religion. He was powerfully seconded by the young Theobald Wolfe Tone, whose influential pamphlet 'An argument on behalf of the Catholics of Ireland' was published in September 1791; and Tone was one of those who had presented the Catholic Committee's petition to King George.[16]

It was natural enough that Ulster should become the first centre of Irish revolutionary politics. Dubliners had the excitement of Parliament to occupy their intellectual energies, and Dublin remained an Ascendancy city, susceptible to government control. Protestant Ulster, with traditions harking back to the Covenanters and embracing something of Cromwellian republicanism, was more receptive to radical arguments, and Belfast was becoming an industrial city with an educated middle class. Another Belfast founder of the United Irishmen, Samuel Neilson, launched their newspaper, the *Northern Star*, which also printed radical pamphlets and the famous *Collection of Original and Modern Patriotic Songs*, collected by the Reverend James Porter, a radical minister. Together with another of Porter's collections, *Paddy's Resource*, the United Irishmen's songs became immensely popular.[17]

Ulstermen had been initially romantic revolutionaries, proclaiming 'the heart which cannot participate in the Triumph, must either have been vitiated by illiberal politics, or be naturally depraved'. As late as July 1792 the Belfast Harp Festival, a Protestant celebration of Gaelic culture, celebrated Bastille Day; Presbyterians and Catholics were 'chequered at the head of the table'. The same day was celebrated less decorously by a dinner – half a guinea a head, with wines 'viz. Port, sherry, lisbon and claret ... the finest quality'. One participant recorded its progress: 'Everybody as happy as a King! . . . Huzza! God bless everybody! Stanislaus Augustus! George Washington! Beau jour! Who would have thought it this morning? Huzza! Generally drunk. Broke my glass thumping the table. Home, god knows how, or when. Huzza!'[18]

The first United Irishmen were far from united in being revolutionary fanatics. As late as 1795 Thomas Smyth, secretary of the Ballynahinch committee, drew up a list of demands which began:

WHAT EVILS WILL BE REMOVED AND WHAT
ADVANTAGES GAINED BY A REFORM IN PARLIAMENT

1st Tithes will be abolished and every man will pay his own clergy.

2nd Hearth money – that abominable badge of slavery and oppression to the poor – will cease.

3rd We will not thereafter be taxed to pay pensioners and sinecure placemen to vote against us. The consequence of this will be that tobacco for which we now pay 10d. per lb. will then be had for 4d. – Aye for 4d. – and every other article of imported goods cheap in proportion.

4th We shall have no excise laws: the merchant and shopkeeper will get leave to carry on his business quietly, without the intrusion of plundering revenue officers.

5th The expense and tediousness of the law will give place to prompt and equal justice – Gratis.

Hardly a revolutionary document, it would seem, rather one ready to attack privilege, without risking the safety of personal property; yet three years later Ballynahinch was to be the site of a pitched battle between government forces and the United Irishmen.[19]

When Britain entered the war with France lines of demarcation were drawn and a decision had to be made whether to carry on with activities which could well become treasonable. Some precedents existed for armed action in Ireland: Protestant and Catholic gangs had been fighting each other for some years, with the occasional murder of some innocents and a good deal of cattle-maiming, but eighteenth-century Ireland had been generally peaceful. Between 1760 and 1790 deaths resulting from agrarian disturbances did not exceed about fifty; compared, for example, with the thirty-five hanged in Sussex after the 'smuggling war' between 1748 and 1780, not to mention the over three hundred hanged or shot as a result of the anti-Catholic Gordon riots in London, or the slaughter after Culloden in 1746, violence in the Irish countryside was not excessive.

It might have been an incident in South Armagh on 28 January 1791, when a group of Roman Catholic roughs cut out the tongues and fingers of Mr Barkeley, the popular Forkhill schoolmaster and his wife, that marked a point of no return.[20] Such brutality was anathema to the United Irishmen's leaders, all middle-class Protestants, not dissimilar to those who had begun the revolutions in America or France. Henry Joy McCracken and Samuel Neilson were both prominent Ulster textile manufacturers; Thomas Russell had been a British Army officer who had seen service in India. Archibald Hamilton was English, adopting the surname Rowan when he inherited an Irish fortune; as a Member of Parliament one of his tasks became that of challenging any Irish MP who attacked the movement. Arthur O'Connor, 'eccentric, churlish, megalomaniac', became a Napoleonic general of brigade. Lord Edward Fitzgerald, a younger brother of the Duke of Leinster, was the most prominent, but without doubt the inspirational leader was Theobald Wolfe Tone, whose journals form one of the liveliest and most revealing personal documents of the period.

Few of these leaders saw much actual fighting; that was left to their unlucky followers. Some, like Hamilton-Rowan, were disgusted by what was actually happening in France and dropped out. When the conspiracy was uncovered – no Irish plot remained secret for long – most of the leaders, including O'Connor and Thomas Emmett, were rounded up, dismissed with a caution and exiled; Fitgerald was mortally wounded during his arrest. Among the few to take any part in action were the Ulstermen: McCracken who together with James Hope fought with gallantry in the battle of Antrim, and the young Scots draper William Monroe, who led the rebels at Ballynahinch. In June 1798 Wolfe Tone was captured by the Royal Navy after a stiff fight, but never had to come to blows with his fellow countrymen.[21]

Others were however ready for real action. It was also in Ulster that the two rival sectarian institutions were first formed, the Catholic Defenders and the Protestant 'Peep o' Day Boys', who became the Orangemen after 1795. Militant Catholics, the Defenders were ruthless, with a mixture of millenarianism and the savage revolutionary excitement of the Paris mob, leavened with the pleasurable ceremonies of a secret society, including salutes and a password, 'Elephesis'. Simplistic ideas of the French as a Catholic people burning to liberate their co-religionists in Ireland sat uncomfortably with the facts, and, given the unflinching opposition of Catholic clergy to civil disorder and revolutionary ideas, the Defenders received little support from that quarter. Orange Lodges, on the other hand, although discouraged by the authorities, developed a following among the respectable middle classes.

Armagh Defenders and Orangemen met in what was almost a pitched battle, the Battle of the Diamond in 1795, in which it was the Protestant faction who got the upper hand. In the aftermath thousands of Catholics were forced to flee from Armagh; the government seemed helpless to stop it. 'The Orange Boys has not left a papist family in all the lower part of the county [of Armagh] ... what the end of these things will be we know not.' Lord Gosford, the Armagh Governor, appealed to the magistrates on behalf of 'the wretched objects of this ruthless persecution', of whom 'a lawless banditti have constituted themselves the judges'. The appeal was answered only in part, and to many Catholics it appeared that the Defenders were indeed their only protectors. The leaders of the United Irishmen were readier to talk about armed insurrection than actually to take part in it, and the brutal potency of the Defenders made them admirable potential allies. When, between 1794 and 1796, a coalition of some sort was agreed between United Irishmen and Defenders, the combined organisations represented a real threat; and if French assistance could be provided the future of British rule in Ireland looked bleak.[22]

The Irish garrison was reduced as regular troops were drawn away into the war with France and the ancient system of raising local levies was implemented. A British militia had been formed on a territorial base since medieval times, and had kept pace with equipment and tactics, forming a reserve that could be sent on active service (although with Edward Gibbon as a colonel the effectiveness of some units would have been doubtful). Initially militia volunteers were to be supplemented by conscripts selected by ballot, but in Ireland violent protest resulted in the militia relying only on volunteers. Facing down objections from Irish officials, the British government insisted that Catholics must be free to volunteer, in order to 'connect all lovers of order and good government in a union of resisters to all the abettors of anarchy and misrule'. The militia force accordingly included many Catholics, especially in the south and west. Very quickly indeed, without any real training, the militia were called upon to prove their reliability, which they did outside Wexford in July 1793, when fifty militiamen drove off some two thousand armed Defenders; from then on the militia, Catholic and Protestant, were among the staunchest defenders of the regime. Civilians were also enrolled into a home-defence force of yeomanry which comprised both cavalry and infantry units. Since recruits had to be able to take unpaid time off from their work, most were, if not middle-class, closer to establishment values than were the ruck of farm labourers. By 1798 fifty thousand of this force, tolerably well armed but on the whole poorly disciplined, were ready for service. Another home-defence force was available in the 'Fencible' regiments, raised in Britain and despatched to Ireland. A high proportion of these were Scottish, and twenty-five Fencible regiments were employed in 1798. Powers to deploy these forces, entrusted to magistrates, were substantially increased by emergency legislation.[23]

British fears of French intervention were soundly based, and it was Wolfe Tone who eventually succeeded in organising this. Exiled to America as a result of his political activities, Tone made his way to France in 1795, with an introduction from James Monroe (later President of the USA).[24] In Paris he presented a painstaking and plausible assessment which persuaded the French government that an invasion would spark off an irresistible rebellion throughout Ireland. As a result of his efforts a well-equipped French expedition, accompanied by Tone, embarked on 16 December 1796. Commanded by Lazare Hoche, perhaps the finest soldier of his time, a general at the age of twenty-five, the most powerful force to threaten Britain since the Spanish Armada, with thirty-six ships, twelve thousand men, a field artillery park and forty thousand muskets, arrived off Bantry Bay five days later. It got no further; battered by gales – scarcely unusual at that time of year – the French admiral decided not to land, taking a frustrated Tone back to France. Had Hoche landed, Ireland would have been in very serious danger – a fraction of that number of French troops tore up the opposing Irish militia when it did succeed in disembarking two years later.

It had been a great escape, but 1797 was nevertheless a disastrous year: the first coalition patched together by Pitt against France had collapsed in 1795 and the French bloc which emerged victorious included Spain and Holland, together providing a powerful navy. French armies were overrunning Italy, while British forces were forced to evacuate the Netherlands; an expedition to Brittany had been foiled by Hoche's troops; eighty thousand men had been lost in the West Indian service; and that last defence of the realm, the Royal Navy, was threatened by mutiny in the Thames estuary, only thirty miles from the French coast. France, on the contrary, had survived the anarchical periods of their Revolution, with the Directory assuming a centralised control; and that enterprising young officer Napoleon Bonaparte had become one of the three Directors. In these circumstances a successful landing in Ireland might well be fatal, and a second expedition was even then being prepared. Lord Fitzwilliam's successor, Lord Camden, inexperienced and incompetent, allowed his frightened officials their heads. A rigorous suppression of any unconstitutional movements and a search for hidden weapons was begun. When these were not produced the yeomanry were deployed and brutally severe methods resorted to, suspects being mercilessly flogged and scalped with hot pitch. Respectable farmers and even Presbyterian ministers were hanged on the most dubious evidence.[25]

The fact that no French force had landed, and that so many weapons had been impounded, did not discourage the United Irishmen, who prepared elaborate plans for a rising. Any possibility of its success was forestalled by a government pounce on the Dublin leaders, almost all arrested on 13 March 1798, leaving only the rashly incompetent

Fitzgerald and the more practical but often intoxicated Neilson at liberty. After they too were arrested on 19 May the planned insurrection was leaderless. Nevertheless, the rebellion went ahead, starting on 24 May with a raid on the Munster mail coach, all of whose passengers were hacked to death. For the next three months widespread and savage killings by both rebels and government forces caused some thirty thousand deaths. Fighting fell into three main sectors. To the west of Dublin in Kildare, and to the south in Wexford the risings were dependent on the energy of local leaders, almost all Catholic. After the methodical degradation of the previous two centuries the recent savagery of the military had enraged many, and ignited the smouldering rural violence. Atrocities were frequent, the most memorable being the massacre of over a hundred Protestants, burned alive in a barn at Scullabogue (one two-year-old crawled out, only to be stabbed to death), and that of ninety-seven selected Protestants cut to pieces on the Wexford Bridge. Protestants were repeatedly singled out for death, giving the conflict the character of a religious war, although many of the government forces were themselves Catholics, thus absolutely negating the original intentions of the idealistic United Irishmen.

In the third sector, the Ulster counties of Down and Antrim, the character of the warfare differed. Here the rebels were largely Protestant and under McCracken's and Monroe's commands followed what might be called the rules of war. Their discipline did not benefit them much, for the repression was everywhere swift and ferocious. The wars of the previous century had been fought between armies who at least understood that rules applied, which is why the infraction of these excited so much indignation – the *jacquerie* of 1641, and Cromwell's actions at Drogheda and Wexford being examples. But both sides in the 1798 conflict acted as though no rules existed. Regular troops and militia were generally kept under better discipline, but Scots and English officers had nothing but contempt for the generality of the Irish yeomanry, who would not 'behave themselves with common decency and prudence' and 'committed the most unpardonable acts'. By the end of June both the Wexford and the Ulster rebellions had been suppressed, and the official punishments that followed were severe, if more measured. Between May and November 1798 336 death sentences were passed, some quarter of which were commuted.[26]

On 23 August, when the rebellion was effectively over, the French at last succeeded in making a landing. Just over a thousand soldiers landed in a remote part of Connacht, under the command of General Joseph Aimable Humbert. It was both far too little, too late, and in the wrong place, but the invasion caused a considerable flurry. Irish support was unreliable – Humbert had to shoot two mutinous officers – but so were the opposing Irish militia, who at the first battle threw down their arms and ran. At the next fight an overwhelming force of British regulars forced Humbert to surrender with few casualties. The French were treated with respect, but very many of the fleeing Irish were cut down by the cavalry pursuit.

On 16 September Napper Tandy himself, one of the original Volunteers, turned up in a French frigate, with the arms that Humbert would have found useful had he not already surrendered. Styling himself 'Commander of the Northern Army of Avengers', in the First Year of Irish Liberty, Tandy comforted his countrymen with the thought that if their friends were 'doomed to fall in this glorious struggle, let their deaths be useful to your cause, and their bodies serve as footsteps to the temple of Irish liberty'. His own contribution to the cause of liberating Ireland was to become insensibly drunk and to be carried back to the warship, pissing on the heads of his bearers.[27]

That debacle did not complete the story of unsuccessful French intervention in Ireland. Wolfe Tone, by far the most gifted of the United Irishmen, had persuaded the French Directory to fit out a ship of the line and eight frigates, with a brigade of infantry. On 12 October they were intercepted and defeated by a British squadron. Captured, tried and condemned, Tone committed suicide rather than face the gallows. Even had the French fleet made a landing the invasion could not have succeeded, since Lord Cornwallis was now firmly in charge and revolutionary enthusiasm extinct.

The insurrection was by no means a simple rebellion against British rule, but an altogether more complex phenomenon. In part it was a republican protest against an unrepresentative and oligarchic government (although the idea that by 1798 the French state still retained its republican purity was decidedly *naïf*). Like any strife in the preceding two centuries there was a strong element of religion. The Catholic hierarchy and most priests condemned the violence; most of the leaders were Protestants, but the *jacquerie* in the south-east was fiercely Catholic. Nor can the class antagonism be ignored. The Irish militia and yeomanry were drawn from a wide range of the more prosperous, and their bloody revenge was a frightened assertion of social power.

The proper distribution of loaves and fishes

In the British Parliament Fox and the liberal Whigs rallied to the defence of the Irish rebels. The Whig leader, Charles Grey, who thirty-four years later was to initiate the start of Britain's hesitant adoption of democracy, condemned 'that horrible system to which I for one shall for ever ascribe the present revolt', instancing 'the scourges and other tortures employed for the purpose of extorting confession'.[28] Such revelations were so likely to damage the government that the report of the debate, on 22 June, was suppressed. It was apparent that, after 1798, such views as Grattan's twenty years before 'that the country could be satisfied with nothing less than liberty' had radically altered. Protestant Irishmen could no longer convince themselves that the survival of their society was not now completely dependent upon England, and that to maintain it parliamentary independence had to be sacrificed. To Britain, now seriously concerned with the rising power of France, with its allies crumbling as Napoleon progressed on his way to dictatorial power, Ireland had to be made secure. After only seventeen years of something resembling an Irish national assembly, the Dublin Parliament had to be suppressed.[29]

The solution of integrating Ireland into Britain, as had been done at the start of the century with the Union between England and Scotland, was attractively obvious. After 1746 Scotland had settled peaceably into the Union, apart from some moderate unrest in the '90s, quickly suppressed by the ferocious judge Lord Branksome, and the more permanent indignation so tellingly expressed by Robert Burns in such verses as 'Scots wha hae for Wallace bled' – which was adopted by protesting English workers. The Union had at least created the conditions which transformed Scotland from its 'Third World' status into something comparable, and in many respects superior, to contemporary England. Henry Dundas, perhaps the most permanently influential politician in the kingdom, was making sure that Scots voters got more than their fair share of lucrative posts. Ireland, a much larger country, should benefit at least as much. As long ago as 1779 Dundas judged that 'A union would be the best if it can be accomplished,' but until that was possible the Irish Parliament 'must be managed by the proper distribution of loaves and fishes', an exercise in which Dundas was an acknowledged master.[30] Economically, the removal of all trade barriers should be an important benefit for Ireland, leading 'among the lower orders' to a 'change of manners, the result of habitual industry', and the country might also thereby lose 'an idle race of country gentlemen' and gain ports full 'with ships and commerce'. Politically, the prospect of even one hundred Westminster seats, a considerable underestimate if based – as nobody except a few enthusiastic democrats would have it – upon universal suffrage, but a fair assessment if property quali-fications were reckoned, should give a great, even perhaps decisive, influence on national policies. Until the Reform Act of 1832 changed the political landscape Irish constituencies, with Catholic voters increasingly numerous, were more representative of the people than the English, and much more than the rotten Scottish constituencies. From the British point of view the integration of Ireland promised the valuable bonus of diluting the proportion of Catholics in the popu-lation – three to one in Ireland, but three to fifteen in Great Britain.

It was the Irish Parliament that needed convincing. To be asked to lose that independence gained only seventeen years previously was a bitter pill to parliamentarians, and to the owners of the most amenable parliamentary seats. They at least could be satisfied by a substantial cash payment (generous, at £15,000 per borough, considering that the similar 1832 Act paid no compensation at all to dispossessed British patrons). Speaker Forster was allowed £5000 a year for life, Chancellor Clare £4000, parliamentary clerks between £2260 and £2700; even the fire-lighters were given pensions, R. Watham receiving six and a half guineas annually. Substantial sums were made available from the Secret Service account, which later had to be buried as effectively as possible; but the deed was done.[31]

Pitt had intended the Act of Union to be accompanied by further concessions to the Catholics, including that vital remaining ability to take a seat in the Westminster Parliament. There was no bar on a

Catholic standing for Parliament and being duly elected. The difficulty arose in the wording of the oath of loyalty all members were required to take, which included a declaration that 'the sacrifice of the Mass and the invocation of the Blessed Virgin Mary and other saints . . . are impious and idolatrous', an impossible blasphemy for a faithful Catholic. Any intention to abolish this absurd and offensive requirement would have exacerbated Protestant opposition, inflamed as it was by the atrocities of the rebellion (the more extensive, if less spectacular violence used in the suppression of the rising was ignored).

The young Ulsterman Lord Castlereagh and Lord Cornwallis, a sagacious and experienced soldier, who had supervised the ending of the rebellion, were given the task of managing the Act of Union. They went out of their way to avoid any specific commitments to the Catholics, and reported that this action was clearly understood by the Irish leaders; but equally clear was the British government's undertaking that such action would very quickly follow.

When the time came to present the result of their negotiations to the cabinet both Pitt and his two colleagues were surprised to find that many were implacably opposed. In particular the Chancellor, a devious Scot, Lord Loughborough, who had a malodorous reputation, used his influence with the unbalanced King George III to make absolute his opposition. Pitt, Castlereagh and Cornwallis resigned, together with their Under-Secretary, Edward Cooke, and Catholic Relief was abandoned for another generation. That lost generation was to spell the ultimate destruction of the Union. Only a minority of Irishmen could feel an unequivocal loyalty to the new Union flag that flew for the first time on 1 January 1801.

In its prime objective, that of safeguarding the vulnerable flank of Britain from its foreign enemies, the Union was successful: although the war dragged on over another fifteen years, the only Irish attempt at insurrection, Robert Emmett's unhappy excursion in 1803, dwindled into farce. Robert's brother Thomas had been one of the Directory of the United Irishmen, briefly imprisoned after '98. The prudent Thomas Emmett went on to make his fortune in America, but Robert attempted a Dublin coup, which failed in everything except in adding one more martyr to the cast of the Toy Theatre. All that occurred was a morning's riot on 23 July 1803, when dressed in a fine uniform of his own design, a green coat with gold epaulettes, white breeches and a feathered hat, Robert led a few hundred drunken Dubliners to murder a couple of victims before being arrested, tried and executed.[32]

The economic clauses of the Act of Union had been drafted by Lord Castlereagh in an attempt to treat Ireland generously. Whereas a comparison of populations would have allocated Ireland an inequitably high contribution to taxation, this was based instead on the revenue raised from taxes on consumption, which should have reflected actual prosperity. Nevertheless, Cormac Ó Gráda, the most authoritative Irish economic historian, estimates that 'Castlereagh's formula – unintentionally, it must be said – "over-taxed" Ireland at the outset,' but adds that, 'Contrary to traditional Irish nationalist claims, the economic impact of the Act of Union in the short run was minor.'[33] It is however incontrovertible that in the first half of the nineteenth century Irish industrial expansion was feeble, and entirely failed to match the astonishing English growth. Ireland remained a predominantly rural and agricultural economy, with industries allied to farming and food products. Of these the most obvious was the brewing trade, where the Guinness family's great Dublin porter brewery achieved worldwide fame. Other small manufacturing industries, sheltered by an initial protective tariff, began production which, in their own specialised fields, became internationally competitive: Wexford- and Dublin-made agricultural machinery was shipped not only to the colonies but to Continental Europe. Large-scale industry, however, when it later developed, was concentrated in a small area in the north-east.

Although Parliament left Dublin, much to the distress of tavern- and lodging-house-keepers, the Act of Union applied only to the legislature, and not to the executive. The Act had been an emergency measure, forced on the British government by the perils of war and insurrection; little attention was paid to the mechanics of government. Only after it had been passed – grudgingly in Dublin, even after all the bribery, by a majority of 158 to 115 – was it decided that, unlike Scotland, which had since 1707 been ruled from Westminster, the Irish administration should remain in Dublin Castle, under the nominal rule of the resident Lord Lieutenant. Except when the Lord Lieutenant was exceptionally well-placed politically, ultimate power lay with the Chief Secretary in London and the Under-Secretary in Dublin. Chief

Secretaries from time to time were bitten with the reform bug, but the other Irish officials could usually be relied upon to preserve the old Ascendancy.[34]

Those not blinded by prejudice, reinforced by fear of French principles acting on the Irish, were able to see the dangers. That admirable liberal cleric Sydney Smith wrote in the *Edinburgh Review* of July 1807 that 'the contemptible folly and bigotry of the English' made it appear 'quite impossible that so mean and so foolish a people can escape that destruction which is ready to burst upon us'. He was referring to the alarming success of Napoleon's empire, which was in due course averted; but in Ireland the folly and bigotry brought suffering and discredit in its wake.

Scotland has long groaned under the chains of England

When, on 15 July 1815, Napoleon Bonaparte, sometime Emperor of the French, left the bleak little Île d'Aix for permanent exile on even bleaker St Helena, it was obvious to Europe and the world that an era had ended. As to what the new age should bring with it, opinion was much divided. Some powerful interests sought a return to the *status quo ante bellum*, and were in a position to achieve at least the semblance of this. In France, Louis XVIII succeeded in restoring the superficial splendours of the Bourbon court; in Italy the conglomeration of feudal states reshaped by the French into republics was reassembled; the Holy Roman Empire, now reduced to the Hapsburg fief of Austria and its numerous Balkan and Italian colonies, emerged nervous but intact, united with the Tsar of Russia in a determination to preserve autocratic rule. But the men who put together a Europe shattered by more than twenty years of war, with all the victories, defeats, changing boundaries and shifting alliances that it had entailed, were well aware of the compromises that had been needed and knew that their achievement of a peace treaty to ensure the 'Concert of Europe' was susceptible to many internal threats. These duly materialised. Within fifteen years new revolutions were beginning to overturn the crasser attempts at reaction in France, Spain and many of the surviving satellites of the

Hapsburg Empire, and the next generation experienced generalised upheaval and irrevocable change.

One vital factor differentiated the United Kingdom from its victorious allies. Britain, which had begun the period of hostilities driven from most of its North American empire, ended it as the single world power, controlling some thirty colonies stretching from the Arctic provinces of Canada to the damp hills of Van Diemen's Land. The nuclei of three powerful countries – Canada, Australia and South Africa – were developing under British rule; British influence in the Indian sub-continent was unchallenged; and friendly relations were emerging with the independent United States of America. The whole worldwide system was knotted together by a great merchant fleet, its trade protected by the unparalleled forces of the Royal Navy. Within the United Kingdom the perspective shifted. England had long been the domestic economic giant, manipulating, sometimes ruthlessly, the smaller countries to suit English interests. It now became the leading partner in the power which controlled the British Empire – and it was a *British* Empire; no question of its ever being considered an *English* Empire. Scots, Irish and Welsh took their often profitable parts in imperial expansion as soldiers, merchants, administrators or simple emigrants. The process, however, entailed an uncomfortable gestation.

All three countries had contributed massively to the eventual victory over the French. At the decisive battle of Waterloo, Wellington, the commander, was Irish; his second in command, the Marquess of Anglesey, and the Divisional General Thomas Picton were both Welsh; and the great cavalry charge that shattered Ney's hitherto invincible squadrons was made by the Scots Greys. Splutterings of domestic discontent had been suppressed. Volunteer forces over half a million strong had been raised, armed, and trained against the threat of a French invasion, from all parts of the islands, and from all conditions of men. Yet with the impetus of self-defence removed, and the added strains of post-war economic depression, aggravated by the dumping of a million ex-servicemen on a shrinking labour market, British governments after 1815 seemed to have every reason for apprehension, and little idea of what should be done.

Irish farmers, who had benefited from high wartime prices, found that peace brought falling profits, and therefore increased pressure on landlords to improve productivity. As early as August 1815 agent James Brownrigg wrote to his employer, Lord Downshire, whose rents had shot up during the war, that 'The affairs of this estate are fast approaching a crisis . . . every investigation I make into the pecuniary resources of the tenantry confirms and extends my apprehensions of their inability to pay the rent laid on them.'[35] In this Ireland was not alone: in the rest of the United Kingdom the more modern techniques introduced by the 'Improvers' forced labourers out of work, causing widespread distress.

Wales experienced riots in Aberystwyth and a major strike among colliers and iron workers in 1816; Welsh bailiffs and constables were regularly attacked, ricks fired and animals maimed. Pressure on small farmers forced out of their unprofitable holdings was particularly bitter. In Montgomery and Carmarthen 'yeomen' formed by far the greatest proportion of the rioters, twice as many as labourers. In England a similar pattern emerged. The number of small farmers diminished, and forced sales were frequent. Many landlords proved sufficiently flexible (and rich enough) to cope with lean periods, reducing or remitting rents when necessary. Lord Sidmouth, political reactionary though he was, discounted rents by 15 per cent in 1818 and by 22 per cent five years later; by 1827 he was able to levy the full sums once more. Lord Pembroke reduced his Savernake rents permanently by 5 per cent in 1815 and 10 per cent in 1821. A general protection to cereal farmers was given from 1815 by the series of Corn Laws, which levied duties on imported grain, according to a sliding scale. And to some extent labourers were sheltered by poor-rate subsidies.[36]

Scotland had its parallel problems. Highland estates had always been extensive – many acres of upland grazing were needed for a single small cow – but they had given livelihood to communities of crofters, tenants of a cottage and garden, with grazing rights, who led a necessarily austere existence. They presented a tempting target for landlords committed to modernise their estates by deploying the latest technologies, including cottage industries, fisheries – and sheep. The easiest and most profitable solution was to replace the existing tenancies by sheep ranches, finding other work for the crofters if possible. Some landlords contrived to do this, but others either did not make any effort – Alastair Macdonnell of Glengarry being the most ruthless –

or, like the Duke of Sutherland who owned six hundred square miles of the north, abandoned earlier efforts to rehouse their evicted tenants. Although such evictions were only part – perhaps one-quarter – of the great emigration during which Highlanders sought a better life in the colonies or the south, they left a bitter aftermath.[37]

In Ireland other factors exacerbated the distress felt in all parts of Britain. In 1780 the Irish population numbered just over four million; by 1831 this had nearly doubled, to 7.77 million. Such an increase was not unlike that in the rest of the United Kingdom, but with the Irish population standing at over half of the English total (13.1 million), it represented dangerous rural overcrowding. While English poverty and misery was becoming increasingly centred on the great cities, mushrooming under industrialisation, Ireland was much less urbanised. At the turn of the century just over 7 per cent of the Irish lived in towns of over ten thousand; in England and Wales the comparable figure was over 20 per cent, and in Scotland 17 per cent. With a population of 186,000 in 1821 Dublin was second to London, although much smaller (over a million at that time, London's population had increased to near two million by 1841), but only Cork, with some hundred thousand inhabitants, could be ranked with the rapidly expanding British manufacturing cities. With so many Irish dependent on their potato crops, periods of agricultural distress were inevitably more fiercely concentrated on the rural poor; potential peril, too, lurked in the increasing reliance of rural Irish on their staple food, the potato.

Any generalisations about rural Ireland have to be qualified by the observation that regional differences were great. Wide variations in fertility, types of farming, local practices and the uneven rise in population – much higher in the west than in the east – led to great poverty and prosperity existing almost side by side. Ancient systems of landholding had been transmuted into more precise leases, much longer in Ireland than in England, but often subdivided into much smaller and dangerously short tenures. 'Conacre', the lease of a small plot for a period shorter than twelve months, enabled a labourer's family to supplement any cash income by growing potatoes – an acre, even on marginal land, providing subsistence for a family of six. If grazing could be found a cow would supply buttermilk for the family, and pigs could be fattened for sale. One dangerous difference between the systems in the two countries was that whereas in England improvements – drainage, fencing, new buildings – were done at the landlord's expense, in Ireland these were the responsibility of the tenant. The cost of such improvements should have either been taken into account by the landlord when calculating future rent, or repaid when the lease was terminated. Discontented tenants and decaying farms were often the result of their not so doing.

Fragmentation of holdings had broken relationships on many large Irish estates to such an extent that, even when landlords were not merely drawing rents and living comfortably in England, personal contact between the proprietors and the families who worked the fields was often minimal. With fewer social emollients to alleviate the perpetual irritation of religious differences, violence in the Irish countryside was proportionately more frequent and more savage than that in England. Secret societies proliferated, formed with the aim of combating the eviction of smallholders, increasing as landlords belatedly attempted to farm according to more efficient modern practices, and not to rely on the fragmented rentals. White and Black Feet, Terryalts, Molly Maguires, Threshers, Carders, Caravats, Shanavests, Rockites and Lady Clares and those generically known as 'Ribbonmen' shot enough of their perceived oppressors – landlords or those who took over evicted properties – and mutilated a sufficient number of their livestock to emphasise the seriousness of their plight.[38]

Although agrarian hardship in Ireland was shared with the rest of the United Kingdom, the divide in that country was much more than economic: it was squarely sectarian, for while it was true that not all landlords were Protestants, all small tenants and those cottiers forced out of their cabins were Catholics. In Ulster, where Protestants were in a majority, tenants had some protection through the ancient 'Ulster rights', approximating to the British system. Elsewhere, the land problem, which emphasised the religious divide, was to be central in any British government's Irish policies. In many parts of the country landlord and tenant lived, as one contemporary put it, 'in a constant state of mutual fear'.

Urban reactions in Scotland were not dissimilar to those in England. Thomas Hardy, the amiable London (although born in Scotland) bootmaker, founder of the London Corresponding Society, was tried for treason and acquitted; his Scottish counterpart, Thomas Muir, a Glasgow advocate, was found guilty of sedition and sentenced to fourteen years' transportation by the implacable Lord Braxfield. Robert Watt was less fortunate, having actually planned an insurrection, and was executed. A generation later Arthur Thistlewood and the Cato Street conspirators, who in 1820 planned to assassinate the entire cabinet, stole the thunder of James Wilson, Andrew Hardie and John Baird, leaders of a Scottish Radical rebellion which spluttered briefly into life the same year in Glasgow and Paisley. Few Englishmen remember Thistlewood, but Muir and his fellow sufferers are commemorated in an obelisk towering over Edinburgh from Calton Hill.[39]

Simple repression had its advocates, influential enough to secure a stream of reactionary legislation, but a generational change was in movement as younger men, from all political groupings, succeeded to positions of power. Middle-class Tories such as George Canning (born 1770), William Huskisson (born 1770) and Robert Peel (born 1788) were prepared to give serious consideration even to quite fundamental changes. Younger Whigs from ancient families, like John Russell (born 1792) and Charles Grey (born 1764), joined such ambitious newcomers as Henry Brougham (born 1778) in studying the new tools which economists and statisticians were making available to assist in the conduct of national affairs. 'Political arithmetic' was developing into statistics – Sir John Sinclair's *Statistical Account* of Scotland being a milestone; chairs of political economy were established at Hailebury, London and even Oxford, occupied by such famous thinkers as Malthus, M'Culloch and Nassau Senior. Surprisingly, the distinguished economists did not often share the same views, but a lust for hard information and for reliable method was evinced by the more earnest politicians. The age of the Blue Books, those massively earnest parliamentary reports, had begun; significantly, Russell, Brougham and Palmerston had chosen to study at the University of Edinburgh, rather than to follow the traditional paths to Oxford and Cambridge (although Palmerston subsequently progressed to St John's College, Cambridge).

It was easier for men of that generation than it had been for their elders to appreciate that they were living in an era of radical change, and that simple intransigence was no longer an option. (Poor Huskisson famously demonstrated his own problems of adjustment by getting himself killed by a railway locomotive in 1830.) For some years, however, it was the glorious opportunities to find more jobs for deserving applicants that were foremost in politicians' minds, and in the distribution of the lucrative posts Scots and Irish got their fair share, and often more. The long ministerial career of the Tory Dundases, uncle Henry and nephew Robert, in office with few intermissions between 1781 and 1830, ensured that Scots were well represented.[40] After the Whigs took over in that year Scottish influence was maintained by the succession of another Border family, the Elliot Earls of Minto, as dispensers of patronage, especially in the navy, and in imperial diplomacy. Within Europe, where posts were in the gift of the Foreign Office, Englishmen tended to garner the plum embassies, although Scots became ambassadors at Berlin and Vienna; but further afield, when governorships were assigned by the Colonial Office, Irish and Scots, perhaps less exigent and sharper in tooth, as well as more adaptable, did even better. Even without Dundas' influence, Scots succeeded independently. Sir John Moore's modernisation of the British infantry was the key to Wellington's successes; Admiral Duncan's victory at Camperdown established British naval supremacy beyond doubt. Of the seven plenipotentiaries despatched to negotiate with that most difficult of partners, the Chinese Empire, all except one (Lord Amherst, an immediate failure) were Irish or Scots: their most important interlocutor at the Imperial Court, the head of Maritime Customs, was the Irishman Sir Robert Hart.

India saw not only Scottish Governors-General and Viceroys, from Lord Minto onwards, but Commanders in Chief, and, in humbler circumstances, traders and bankers.[41] Scottish entrepreneurs took a hand in founding the National Bank of India, the Standard Bank, the Hongkong and Shanghai Bank; and such great enterprises as Jardine Matheson were founded by Scots. As the red areas on the world map expanded Scots, in particular, were well aware that the road to fame and fortune led through participation in a British Empire which, while not extinguishing other national or even regional characteristics, transcended them.

To the Irish, imperial prospects had been less attractive than to the Scots. Between 1815 and 1845, before the Great Famine's effects were felt, well over a million people left; by 1841 some 420,000 native-born Irish were living in Britain, and perhaps a similar number in North America. Others had left unwillingly as convicts to Australia, but in general, emigrants were more than usually enterprising, and prosperous enough to afford the passage. Contrary to the usual assumption that emigrants flourished more in the 'land of the free' than in British colonies, Canadian and Australian Irish were more successful, and that more quickly, than those who went to the United States. Both their enterprise and the success it brought are illustrated by the Australian figures, where, in spite of any 'convict heritage', by 1921 a higher proportion of employers (8.5 per cent) were Irish-born than those who had come from England (7.3 per cent) or Scotland (7.6 per cent).[42] Colonial societies were more open to merit than that of England, restricted by hardening social prejudices. By the 1850s both New South Wales and Victoria had Irish Catholic Attorney Generals – John Hubert Plunkett, highly respected and influential, and Edward Butler – whilst a little later Gavan Duffy, a former rebel, was a Prime Minister and James Pope-Hennessy had begun his not-very-successful career as colonial governor; even the indomitable Wicklow hero of '98, Michael Dwyer, had become Chief Constable of the Australian town of Liverpool.

Protestant Irishmen suffered no discrimination, and rose to high offices. Apart from the Irish-born Duke of Wellington, who complained that to be born in a stable doesn't make you a horse, the most admired soldier was Field Marshal Lord Gough of Limerick, whose fighting career spanned over half a century and more than half the world; Lord Macartney, who had to deal with the rulers of both Imperial Russia and of China, was from Belfast; Sir Richard Bourke, also of Limerick, shaped the futures of both the Cape and New South Wales; and the ranks of the British Army were disproportionately filled by Irishmen.

That many Irish should be discontented with the Union was natural enough, but there were signs of unhappiness even in newly prosperous Scotland. Thomas, Lord Daer, later fifth Earl of Selkirk, was a friend of Scott and Burns both, and a member of the Friends of the People. As a young man he wrote to his contemporary, Charles Grey:

Scotland has long groaned under the chains of England and knows that its connection there has been the cause of its greatest misfortunes. Perhaps you may shrug your shoulders at this and call it Scot's prejudice, but it is time at moments like these when much may depend on suiting measures to the humour of the people, that you Englishmen should see this rather as it is or at least be aware of how we Scotsmen see it. We have existed a conquered province these two centuries. We trace our bondage from the Union of the Crowns and find it little alleviated by the Union of the Kingdoms . . .

. . . We have suffered the misery which is perhaps inevitable to a lesser and remote country in a junction where the Governing powers are united but the Nations are not united. In short, thinking we have been the worse of every connection hitherto with you, the Friends of Liberty in Scotland have almost universally been enemies to Union with England. Such is the fact, whether the reasons be good or bad.[43]

But for this the Scots themselves were partly responsible. Scottish MPs rarely represented Scottish interests, being as they were thoroughly captured and corralled by Dundas, who by 1790 controlled thirty-four of the forty-one Scottish members. 'The Lord Advocate,' said one, 'should always be a tall man. We Scotch members always vote with him, and we need therefore to be able to see him in a division.'

It was Walter Scott who, almost single-handedly, reinvented Scotland. From Scott's works, in poetry and prose, stems that flood of tartanry that entranced Queen Victoria and millions of later visitors, even occasionally being adopted by resident Scots. From its inception with the elaborately arranged visit of George IV in 1822, his podgy frame adorned in the full panoply of what was presented as 'Highland Dress', complete with flesh-coloured tights, it was an almost entirely artificial cult. Scott's son-in-law John Lockhart, mildly disapproving, described Sir Walter as 'stage manager of the event'; more accurately, he was also director, song- and script-writer, and publicity agent. 'It was generally thought,' Lockhart reported, 'that the Highlanders their kilts and their bagpipes, were to occupy a great deal too much space . . . since they had always constituted a small, and almost always an unimportant part of the Scottish population.' However true this observation, the political sagacity behind this piece of historical propaganda was considerable. Memories of Highland raids, and of Culloden and its bloody sequelae, had withered; the depopulation of the Highlands, and the transformation of feudal clan chiefs into members of polite society, was near-complete; and Scottish regiments, Highland and Lowland, had fought with great distinction during the twenty-two years of war. King George's visit was intended to manifest the solidarity of Scots both with the Hanoverian dynasty and with each other; and it was a great success. The Scots Greys, the Dragoon Guards and the Midlothian Yeomanry escorted the King, and marshalled Celtic Club members, three clans of generic Highlanders, and such specified clansmen as 'Sir Euan McGregor and Tail of McGregor'.[44]

Sir Walter Scott was also responsible for the cleverest and most effective action in defining and advancing real Scottish interests. In February 1826, whilst still under the first shock of threatened bankruptcy, Scott found time to write the three 'Letters of Malachi Malagrowther', brisk political debate at its best, comparable with Swift's work a century earlier. The subject, that of restricting the issue of banknotes, was a typical example of English reformers seizing upon a remedy for specifically English problems and applying it without any consideration of its effects in Scotland. 'There has been in England,' Scott expostulated, 'a gradual and progressive system of assuming the management of affairs entirely and exclusively proper to Scotland, as if we were totally unworthy of having the management of our own concerns . . . Good Heaven, sir! To what are we fallen? – or rather, what are we esteemed by the English?'

To the Tory Scott the Union was sacred, even at 'the risk of becoming a subordinate species of Northumberland, as far as national consequence is concerned', and he gained his immediate point in persuading the Tory government of the day to drop their offensive project. 'God forbid,' he wrote, 'that Scotland should retrograde' towards the Irish situation, when 'Pat' was 'up with the pike and shilelah on any or no occasion'. By that date Ireland was in fact very near to gaining something like very belated justice in at least one respect, the need for which had been at last driven home to a British administration.

Unfinished business

King George IV had done his best to astonish his Irish subjects by a visit to Dublin in 1821 – made historic by his voyage in a steamship, if by nothing else – but without a Walter Scott, or a glamorous native garb (the saffron kilt being a later nationalist invention), Irish loyalties were not greatly stimulated. The time, it is fair to say, was hardly propitious, since the post-war United Kingdom was still faced with one important item of unfinished business before the serious task of reforming society could be tackled. The remaining restrictions on Catholics – principally the insistence on that preposterous oath before taking a parliamentary seat or holding the more senior Crown offices – should have been extinguished as part of the 1800 Union, but had been delayed by the dogged opposition of George III. In 1807, when pressed by Pitt's successor Lord Greville, King George was even more emphatic: he could not '*ever* agree to *any* concessions to the Catholics'.[45]

This failure defined the political agenda for the next century. British liberals – and some Tories – joined with the Irish Catholics to push the issue for nearly thirty years, during which time it became the single most important question in British domestic policies, paralleling that of the abolition of slavery in foreign affairs. Had the concession been made at the time of Union, quite different issues would have emerged, and Ireland would have been given a chance to co-operate in the institutions of the United Kingdom as an equal partner. The dangers of that delay appeared when the artificial stimulation of a world war subsided.

The story is told of an Indian army regiment which, troubled with a recalcitrant mule train, engaged a famous muleteer to advise. He had the regimental mules picketed, and walking down the line, hit each animal smartly across the head with a heavy stick. When asked the reason for such drastic action the expert replied, 'That was only to attract their attention.' Both British governments and public opinion, in the nineteenth century and later, have required similar treatment to persuade them to pay some attention to Ireland.

In so doing the Irish MPs were less effective than might be expected. There were, after all, one hundred of them in the House of Commons after the Act of Union, more than twice as many as the Scottish contingent, and elected by all qualified voters, including Roman Catholics since 1793. It nevertheless took nearly thirty years before a mechanism was agreed which would permit Catholics to take their seats in Parliament. The fundamental difficulty was that most of the British electorate remained strongly anti-Catholic, and were reinforced by many Protestant religious leaders and by the House of Lords. Rational MPs might pass Bills for Catholic Relief through the House of Commons, only to have them rejected in the other chamber. The eventual impetus that overcame such entrenched prejudice came from Daniel O'Connell, 'the Liberator', who threw his great influence and notable talents behind the cause of what Edmund Burke christened 'Catholic Emancipation', a resounding title for what boiled down to altering the oath elected MPs had to take before being allowed to sit in Parliament.[46]

O'Connell was one of the nineteenth century's most brilliant politicians, capable of splendid rhetoric, ruthlessly employed – and he was ruthless in other aspects, having killed one critic in a duel – but also a patient negotiator and careful organiser. He embodied the contradictions of Irish life, counting among his forebears Welsh Elizabethan immigrants. Educated in France during the Revolution, O'Connell returned to London determined to acquire 'those qualities which constitute the polite gentleman', and under the 1793 Relief Act he was one of the first Irish Roman Catholics to become a member of the Irish bar. Contemptuous of the United Irishmen as he was to be of their successors, Young Ireland, he believed 'the Irish are not yet sufficiently enlightened to bear the sun of freedom. Freedom would soon degenerate into licentiousness; they would rob, they would murder.' Previous advocates of greater Irish independence, whether such parliamentarians as Flood and Grattan or the revolutionaries of 1798, had been Protestants, typical idealists of the eighteenth-century Enlightenment. O'Connell, although he shared many of their liberal principles, was a faithful Catholic, and found ready to hand the great question of 'Catholic Emancipation', which he made his own.

From 1823 the Catholic Association, founded by O'Connell, mustered wide support; the 'Catholic Rent' of a penny a month produced amazing sums – £20,000 collected in the first nine months –

substantial enough to finance well-planned political pressure. O'Connell's natural constituents, the 'forty-shilling' freeholders enfranchised in 1785, were organised to such effect that at the 1826 general election four constituencies were able to return popular candidates in the face of the usual bribery and influence. The Association's work was orderly, legal and peaceful, but one effect was to be gravely harmful.

Catholic electors had demonstrated their power, and in doing so had perturbed many Protestants. Even though many counties in Ulster had Catholic majorities – Monaghan and Armagh were two of the counties to return Catholic Association candidates – Ulster was singled out for attack by some of the more militant Catholics. 'Honest' Jack Lawless, a journalist opponent of O'Connell's, 'a miserable maniac' according to the Liberator, had constructed a power base of his own, and advertised the 'invasion of Ulster'. On 17 September 1828 Lawless declared that he would lead fifty thousand followers in Ballybay, a predominantly Presbyterian Monaghan town. Such saner Catholics as Sir Thomas Wyse decried what they described as 'provocation' and an 'unwarranted intrusion on the territory of their enemies'. The implications are revealing. Wyse was no fanatic nationalist, but a member of the Old English gentry, a nephew-in-law of Napoleon, a graduate of Trinity College Dublin, later to become Secretary of the India Office and British Minister in Athens. Even so, he thought of Ulster Protestants as 'enemies'. Such attitudes were reciprocated by militant Ulster Protestants, eager to accept the designation of 'enemies' given them by their Catholic fellow citizens. Eight thousand 'Orangemen', the successors of the Peep o' Day Boys, assembled in Ballybay to resist the 'invasion'; a short fight ensued, leaving two Catholics dead, and cementing the fact of enmity in the minds of both communities. The Orange Order had been banned, but Lawless's foolish move (he beat a rapid retreat himself, mounted on a grey horse) inspired 'Brunswick' clubs, which initiated counter-demonstrations, armed parades with bands playing 'Kick the Pope' and 'Croppies Lie Down'. The separate modern identity of Northern Ireland might therefore be reckoned from the brawl at Ballybay. Protestant Ulster was feeling beleaguered, an entrenched and virulent sectarian hatred warping political judgment and too often destroying the work of the decent majority.[47]

A few weeks prior to Lawless' invasion O'Connell had experienced a great personal triumph in his election as Member for County Clare in 'a vast demonstration of populist organisation and clerical power'. It was only with difficulty that he had restrained the enthusiasm of his followers, who turned up at mass meetings in almost unbelievable numbers, certainly amounting to hundreds of thousands. His own triumphal processions were adorned with professions of loyalty to the Crown, but others were drilling menacingly. One alarmed landlord was struck by the discipline as 'some 2000 horsemen and an immense number of foot paraded 3 or 4 abreast in perfect order'. Not all meetings were peaceable. Quarrelsome factions with nothing to do with sectarian policies, animated only by local animosity – Four-year Olds and Three-year Olds, Blackhens and Magpies – fought out their often deadly feuds, and were only partly controlled by O'Connell's exhortations.[48]

An immediate and pressing problem faced the government, and especially the Home Secretary, Robert Peel. O'Connell had been elected as a Member of Parliament, but could not take his seat at Westminster without subscribing to that impossible oath, and Peel's fellow Conservatives, including the Prime Minister, the Duke of Wellington, were still opposed to any compromise. Progress in appointing Catholics to Irish posts had been disappointingly slow, blocked by Protestant bigots in the Irish administration. Some talented and industrious Catholics had made themselves indispensable – the barrister Anthony Blake was known as 'the backstairs Viceroy' on account of his influence in Dublin Castle – but more formal progress only began to be made in 1822 with the appointment of the Duke of Wellington's elder brother, Lord Wellesley, as Lord Lieutenant.[49] Explaining his actions in a stiff memorandum to his unsympathetic younger brother (Wellington was rigidly Protestant, and Wellesley had married a Catholic), the Lord Lieutenant wrote on his retirement in 1828 that his aim had been to 'correct the notion which has long unhappily prevailed in Ireland that there was one Law for the Rich and another for the Poor – one Law for the Protestant and another for the Catholic'. In pursuing this laudable aim, 'Lord Wellesley was not only permitted, but enjoined to admit Catholics to the enjoyment of a certain portion of the patronage of Government' by appointing them to 'such legal and other offices that by existing laws they were permitted to hold, but to which none had been appointed, although for many years they had been eligible by

Law to hold them'. The Lord Lieutenant had accordingly dismissed the worst of the bigots, and appointed some able Roman Catholics to judicial office, but had to work against 'the secret and unremitting opposition' of 'underlings in Office'.[50]

Wellesley's successor as Lord Lieutenant, Lord Anglesey, had no sympathy for 'O'Connell and his gang', but a few months in post convinced him of the urgent necessity for settling Catholic grievances. Nor had either Peel or the sternly pragmatic Duke of Wellington much sympathy for welcoming the likes of O'Connell into their gentlemen's club, but the writing was clear on the wall. George IV remained recalcitrant, 'manifesting much uneasiness and irritation' when the 'Catholic question' was raised, and complaining that 'his situation was dreadful' and that he was 'miserable and wretched'. The King's objections were reinforced by the Archbishop of Canterbury and the two senior bishops, London and Durham, but Peel was clear: 'I do not conceive it possible' that a government which could ignore such a parliamentary majority in favour of Catholic relief could function properly. The King's arm was duly twisted by Peel and the Duke, who obtained a very equivocal consent (hingeing upon what the confused King meant by 'go on'). In April 1829 what was nearly the last stage of Catholic emancipation was forced through.[51]

The 'Act for the Relief of His Majesty's Roman Catholic Subjects', popularly known as the Roman Catholic Relief Act and, in a masterpiece of misleading political 'spin', the Catholic Emancipation Act, burst upon the English Conservatives like a thunderclap. Its official title reveals the changed climate of opinion, since previous Acts had referred to 'Papists', or at best 'Persons professing the Roman Catholic religion'. Henceforward Catholics would be able to sit in the British Parliament and be eligible for all offices of state – except the viceroyship of Ireland and those concerned with religious affairs. Some disabilities remained in common with those attached to Protestant dissenters, including admission to the universities of Oxford and Cambridge. As well as putting the finishing touches on the previous Catholic Relief Acts, the new measure signalled a fundamental change in the constitutional balance of power. The monarch, the House of Lords and the bench of bishops had been forced to concede, and the decks were cleared for the House of Commons Whigs to begin the fight which concluded in the Reform Act of 1832, which in turn altered the political geography of Britain.

'Emancipation' had not been effected without cost, since the Irish electoral qualifications were simultaneously raised to the same level as that obtaining in England – the possession of real estate to the value £10 a year. Most of the 'forty-shilling freeholders' were thereby removed from the roll, and O'Connell's potential support accordingly weakened as Irish franchises plummeted from 216,000 to thirty-seven thousand. So severe a reduction of democratic rights undid many of the benefits of emancipation. The one hundred Irish members of the House of Commons were elected by a comparative handful of middle-class voters; and these were largely Protestant.

O'Connell's constitutional struggle had succeeded where the bloody rebellion of '98 had failed. The Irish electorate had become an integral part of the British system. A command of English, and the ability to manipulate the machinery of government at all levels, was essential for success. Irish parents demanded that their children learn English, to the extent that three-quarters of the post-Emancipation generation were unable to speak Irish. It was within the British parliamentary system and with the opportunities given by membership of the new local authorities, and with the debate conducted in English, that advances were seen to be made. 'Catholic Emancipation' had been a great victory, but O'Connell had to find a new target – a 'cry', in the jargon of the day. He chose to attempt a restoration of the Dublin Parliament by repealing the Act of Union: the cry was therefore to be 'Repeal'.

Exactly what would happen after 'Repeal' O'Connell was careful to leave vague; his position was well described as offering 'an invitation to treat', and he defined 'Repeal' in terms that he thought would suit his audience of the moment. Bearing in mind his personal piety and reverence for the Church it is likely that his letter to Archbishop Cullen of May 1842 was sincere: Repeal would be 'an event of the most magnificent importance to Catholicity, of an importance so great and valuable that I am prevented from presenting it in its true colours to the British people . . . It would mean nothing less than the disappearance of Protestantism from Ireland within ten years.' Such an internal contradiction made it impossible for O'Connell to clarify his policies and thereby to generate wider support.[52]

O'Connell's task ought to have become a great deal easier when, in November 1830, a new Whig-Liberal government headed by Earl Grey came to power. Grey had been consistently supportive of Catholic relief, going so far as to write (to Brougham) in December 1825, '. . . if I were an Irish Catholic I should consider myself as in a state of war with the English Government, and think only of the means of reducing to submission an enemy whom I could never hope to gain by conciliation', and had suffered thirty years of political isolation in consequence. He had also previously been solidly against the 1800 Union, and might have been expected to be equally in favour of Repeal – 'I feel as eager to defeat the Union as if I were myself an Irishman.' The votes of Irish Members had enabled him to carry through the 1832 Reform Bill (the second reading in the Commons was carried by just one vote in a tenuous majority that included fifty-eight Irish Members).

Lord Grey had, however, grown both older and less flexible. His reforms were intended to create, not a democratic Parliament, but one that reflected the realities of social and economic power, and acknowledged the pre-eminence of the middle classes. O'Connell's assistance was recognised, but not his methods of advancing his cause of Repeal: '. . . his measures to incite in the people of Ireland a spirit of the bitterest hostility, not only to the government, but to the people of England the Saxons, as he calls them, have always succeeded, as in a regular course, to his more moderate conduct in Parliament'.[53]

Grey accurately described O'Connell's style, but, as did many later English politicians, failed to distinguish between rhetoric and action, or to understand O'Connell's particular dilemma. Maintaining his power base against more radical agitators demanded the rhetoric: his power derived from the Irish masses, but he had to deploy it in the House of Commons. Palmerston, that experienced Irish landlord, got it right when he wrote (11 August 1828) to Laurence Sulivan that he thought the Catholic Association 'good patriots' whose '*measures* (I say nothing of their *speeches*) have been adopted to the attainment of a most legitimate object, with much temper and good judgement'.[54] It was a contradiction that remains: O'Connell's successors, from Parnell to the present day, have been obliged to present one face – of angry, usually anglophobic intransigence – to their Irish supporters while negotiating more reasonably with their opponents in Britain and

Ireland. This dilemma explains to some extent such recent gestures as those of Gerry Adams carrying the coffins of his murderous supporters while patiently negotiating peace terms with British and Irish governments. It was however becoming evident that O'Connell had assembled a parliamentary following which demanded attention. After a brief flurry of royal petulance had brought the Tories under Robert Peel back to power – and O'Connell could hope for nothing from the Tories – a general election in June 1835 found O'Connell with a reasonably reliable sixty-five Irish anti-Tory supporters. It was a remarkable achievement in only six years of parliamentary life.

At that time party discipline and structure did not exist in its later form. Whigs and Tories had not yet developed into Liberal and Conservative parties; the descriptions were those of social attitudes rather than policies. Both groups contained what might be anachronistically called extreme right-wing and moderate liberal elements, with even the odd progressive radical among the Whigs. Aristocratic Whigs wavered nervously in bringing themselves to support this disreputable Hibernian, but political realities prevailed. O'Connell and his supporters were accordingly invited to join the Whig caucus. Secret discussions produced an agreement – the Lichfield House compact – in which the O'Connellites agreed to support Whig reforms. The reformers' path was not easy: at each stage recalcitrant colleagues had to be coaxed into compliance, and the permanent Tory majority in the House of Lords continued implacably opposed to change of any sort.

Even before the Lichfield House pact some modest advances were made. A particular grievance had for long been the tithes levied on tenants to support the established Protestant Church of Ireland. All farms paid this tax and most farmers, being Catholics, regarded the Church of Ireland as a foreign heresy and a symbol of English repression. Tithes were collected at gunpoint by the military, even the Anglican parsons themselves joining in the 'quarrel between Catholic pauper and Protestant divine'. Analysed in some of the industrious Blue Books, some shocking examples were uncovered.[55] Such parishes as Modligo were identified, in which two clergymen were paid to serve the spiritual needs of exactly two Church of Ireland parishioners at an annual cost to the ratepayers – almost all Catholics – of £440; or Mahoonagh, with two parsons drawing £500 for the benefit of eight communicants. In neither of these parishes were there any resident clergymen at all – all the money went to absentees. One diocese, Emly, collected nearly £8000 a year to serve 1246 Church members, from a total population of 98,363.[56]

The Whig government's reform in 1832 helped only to a moderate degree – tithe payments were to be made by the landlord, rather than by the tenant – but many in England saw it as the thin end of the wedge, an infringement of the sacred rights of property. The commutation of Irish tithes was certainly an important stage in official recognition that Ireland was not Britain, and that different solutions were needed. Thereafter the concept of Ireland as being as much part of the United Kingdom as Wales or Scotland gradually frayed, to the extent that by the end of the century Irish legislation had become so distinct from that prevailing in Britain that devolution was very generally accepted as a logical progression – with the noisy and obstreperous exception of the Ulster Protestants.

Time was needed for these truths to become clear, as the first major legislation after the Reform Act proved. In 1835 a Royal Commission, which included the Catholic Archbishop of Dublin, Daniel Murray, considered the introduction of a new Poor Law for Ireland, to accompany similar measures in England and Scotland. The Commission, after careful study, recommended that a board should be established with compulsory powers to develop waste lands and improve the remainder. Labourers would have decent living accommodation and allotments provided, and agricultural improvements would be encouraged. Poor Law Commissioners would be empowered to levy rates to provide for the indigent, and emigration would be supported. Had these recommendations been implemented the subsequent history of Ireland might have been very different; but they were not. The Royal Commission's conclusions did not accord with accepted views in London. Ireland must follow British practice, surely the most carefully thought-out, supported by renowned economists, whose conclusions were recorded in many volumes of Blue Books.

Sir George Nicholls, formerly captain of an Indiaman, latterly banker and entrepreneur, who had made himself something of an authority on Poor Laws, was entrusted with designing an Irish scheme, which he did with great self-confidence, at least to his own satisfaction, although not to that of many critics offended by his 'hoity-toity notions'. Relief, Nicholls declared, was to be given – as in England – through a country-wide network of workhouses, where paupers were to be given as unappetising fare and uncomfortable accommodation as compatible with preserving life: 'A place of hardship, of coarse fare, of degradation and humility ... as repulsive as is consistent with humanity,' recommended the scholarly H.H. Milman, later Dean of St Paul's. The system was hated in England, satirised by Dickens in *Oliver Twist*, and remorselessly criticised by John Walter, proprietor of *The Times*, who eventually succeeded in July 1847 in having the Poor Law Commission suppressed.[57]

Unsuitable for England, the workhouse system implemented in 1838 was disastrous for Ireland. One vital difference was enough to stultify the administration of the Irish Poor Law. The new system was to be managed by local Boards of Guardians, controlling unions of parishes supervised by Poor Law Commissioners, with JPs as *ex-officio* members, the others being elected by ratepayers. Much therefore depended on the quality and generosity or otherwise of the Guardians and the ability of the ratepayers to fund the scheme. Whereas in England and Wales – in Scotland the system, although different, had similar characteristics – local administration, centred on the multifarious roles of the JP, had three hundred or more years of settling in, in Ireland local government had never developed to a similar extent. Conscientious magistrates existed, but the generally unsatisfactory nature of local administration was demonstrated when it was found necessary to insert a whole new layer of law officers – stipendiary or 'resident' magistrates. Given the scale of poverty in some rural areas, where the summer months were ones of at best scarcity, and at worst actual famine, heavy demands on the Poor Relief system were inevitable.[58]

Superimposing on this ramshackle and patchy structure the complex requirements of English laws, drafted by bureaucrats relying on the English system of administration, imposed a great strain on the edifice. 'Rancorous debates' between Catholic and Protestant Guardians marred Dublin meetings, as the new system 'settled like an invading army'. In many areas, however, the system worked well enough to begin with. William Thackeray came to the North Dublin workhouse in 1842 not prejudiced in favour of the 'huge gloomy edifice' capable of accommodating two thousand beggars, but found it 'a vast, orderly, and cleanly place, wherein the prisoners are better clothed, better fed, and better housed than they can hope to be when at liberty'. The four hundred or so 'old ladies [were] neat and nice, in white clothes and caps', but the novelist was not taken by the Friday dinner – rice pudding – or by the shallow graves; and his use of the word 'prisoners' is telling.[59]

On the eve of the Famine it seemed that provision was generally more than adequate; some workhouses were underused – the eight-hundred-place Strabane Union workhouse was two-thirds empty in 1844; North Dublin was half-empty in 1845–46. A thorough and expensive building programme had provided refuge for many of the neediest. Deaths from starvation were avoided, and it seemed that congratulations were in order. But disaster awaited.[60]

CHAPTER 9

1830–1860

Protestant ascendancy and Catholic degradation

FEW NINETEENTH-CENTURY British Prime Ministers had any direct experience of Ireland, and those who were most concerned with Irish affairs often had the least. Gladstone, who made Ireland the central point of his later policies, visited the island only once; Salisbury, rigidly opposing Gladstone's policies, similarly only paid a single visit, and that to ultra-Protestants in Ulster; neither Lord Aberdeen nor Disraeli crossed the Irish Sea. Lord Palmerston had estates in Sligo, upon which he spent considerable effort, but Palmerston was preoccupied with foreign affairs. Only Robert Peel had first-hand administrative experience of the country, as Chief Secretary from 1812 to 1816, exercising direct control from Dublin. To Lord John Russell must go at least the credit for having carried out some personal research. Lord John's father, the Duke of Bedford, had been Lord Lieutenant in 1806, when young John, then aged fourteen, had been able to see something of the country, if only from the windows of the viceregal lodge.[1]

By 1833, when he made his second visit to Ireland, Lord John had been a Member of Parliament for twenty years, a constant advocate of Catholic relief and one of the architects of the great Reform Act of 1832. His 1833 visit was a thoroughly organised research endeavour, during which he covered the country from Belfast to Cork, meeting priests, bankers, army officers, landlords and politicians (including O'Connell), and inspecting Maynooth College. He was not impressed, finding Ireland an occupied country, resembling 'nothing so much as Spain in 1810, in the occupation of the French', with the British cavalry officers pitying the peasantry, and disliking the gentry. Russell returned to England convinced that no real stability could be achieved in Ireland unless the Catholic Church, which was supported faithfully by the majority of the population, was enabled to become the motor of progress. As it was, the whole administration was based on 'nothing but Protestant ascendancy and Catholic degradation'. Such a system inevitably alienated the masses from any participation even in the informal structure of government, which in England, with a similarly restricted franchise, was frequently possible.

It was not long before Russell was able to put his experience to good use as Home Secretary in Lord Melbourne's 1835 Whig government. At that time the Irish executive was still almost pure Tory and Protestant; six years later, when the Whigs and their allies were defeated, probably a third of the newly appointed legal and administrative officers were liberal Catholics. Russell, with the support of the Catholic Archbishop Daniel Murray of Dublin and Thomas Drummond, the new Irish Under-Secretary, had been able to initiate a very different type of English rule. Drummond was a typical example of the dedicated professional reformer, a brilliant young engineer officer – at thirteen the youngest student ever to be admitted to Edinburgh University – he had already made himself famous by inventing limelight, used in theatre stage lighting, and went on to show what could be done with the wicked old problems of Ireland.[2]

By April 1840 Drummond was dead, worn out by incessant work, but while he lived it seemed that British rule in Ireland was beginning a new age, as O'Connell and the great landlord Duke of Leinster were persuaded to co-operate in reforms. The Whigs were sincerely concerned to improve Irish conditions to the extent that 'Repeal' would lose its attraction, and the new Irish Catholic MPs become reliable supporters of the Whig government. Much was done in a very short period: an effective police force 'composed chiefly of Catholic peasants' was organised, which in time became the Royal Irish Constabulary; the Orange Order was fragmented, and its processions banned; a professional magistracy was established as a check on biased JPs and the first Catholic Attorney-General appointed; Dublin Castle was thrown open to all comers, who were thus able to canvass Drummond personally. He left behind him a famous reprimand to the Irish landlords who had complained of rural violence: 'Property has its duties as well as its rights. To the neglect of those duties in times past is mainly to be ascribed that diseased state of society in which such crimes [shooting landlords] take their rise.'

Irish reform legislation proved more difficult than administrative improvements. The Municipal Corporations (Ireland) Bill, introduced in July 1835, which was to have been one of the first fruits of the Lichfield House arrangement, was welcomed by O'Connell as 'for the first time . . . identifying the people of Ireland with the British constitutions'. Certainly the measure was even more overdue in Ireland than in England; the Commissioners on Irish Municipalities reported that 'The greater number of the corporations may be generally described as consisting of self-elected irresponsible governing bodies.' Of course, they were also almost always Protestant. Only that of Tuam had a majority of Catholics; in Dublin they were specifically excluded. Yet such bodies exercised great power – they were responsible for the selection of local officers, judges, magistrates and police as well as the disposal of substantial funds. The Commissioners were unanimous: the failure of the corporations to provide an acceptable standard of administration had led to widespread distrust, and 'the early and effectual correction of the existing evils, and the prevention of future mischief, are anxiously desired, and essentially requisite'. It was not until 1841 that the Act was finally passed, by which time it had suffered many emendations by politicians of both parties anxious about the extension of even restricted self-government to Irishmen. Nevertheless the Act was a milestone in the development of democratic and responsible government in Ireland, establishing elected councils in the larger towns, with considerable executive authority. Even though the franchise was restricted to middle-class householders a Catholic majority was often obtained. O'Connell himself was elected Lord Mayor of Dublin in November 1841 – he much enjoyed the robes and being addressed as 'Your Lordship' – and piloted through a Repeal motion in the city council by forty-one votes to fifteen.[3]

In a pattern which was to be repeated in the next eighty years, Russell was shackled by the permanent Tory opposition in the House of Lords from any more decisive legislative advances, and when the Melbourne government fell in 1841, to be replaced by Sir Robert Peel's Tory administration, Lord John found himself once more in opposition.[4]

The defeat of the Whigs deprived O'Connell of his parliamentary influence, but at the same time freed him to develop an unrestricted campaign for Repeal in which his formidable talents for organisation and agitation produced rapid and dramatic results. A Repeal Association, founded in 1840, sucked in support, and not only from Ireland, for O'Connell was enthusiastically welcomed in all the great English cities. Mass meetings in Ireland again attracted huge numbers: one million were said to have gathered to hear the 'Liberator' on the Hill of Tara. 1843 was declared 'Repeal Year'; the highlight was to be a 'monster meeting' at Clontarf, which would elect an alternative Parliament. This the government determined to suppress, and O'Connell very wisely therefore cancelled the meeting. He was nevertheless given a short term in prison, which restored much of the reputation he had sacrificed among his more hot-headed followers by his continued prudence.

Under the leadership of Thomas Wyse and Smith O'Brien something very like an Irish parliamentary party had been gathered, which drafted a 'Solemn Remonstrance – a regular manifesto – and such as will *give unity of action and opinion* to our section at last'. A debate in the Commons on 4 July 1843 produced 164 votes for the establishment of a committee 'to consider the causes of the discontent . . . the redress of grievances and the establishment of a just and impartial government in that part of the United Kingdom'. The number of votes mustered was at least a sign of Irish and English liberal solidarity, but not enough to satisfy the discontented O'Brien.[5]

Dramatic mass meetings and solid municipal work were reinforced by a parallel movement, to result in what closely resembled a national – or more accurately a Catholic Irish – regeneration. Father Theobald Mathew's Temperance movement began in 1835, sweeping the country. Although without specific political aims, the rescue of thousands of Irishmen from alcohol dependence and their insertion into political life greatly strengthened nationalist organisations. But all these encouraging developments, which occurred in a very short space of time, were negated by the great catastrophe that was about to erupt.

The Great Hunger

The Famine of 1845–48 lies like a shadow across not only Irish, but British, American and even Australian history. Inevitably, it forms a major act in the 'Toy Theatre' production of Irish history, in which it appears as a monstrous plot hatched by the perpetually malevolent English.

Many parts of Ireland, even after a period of relative prosperity, remained impoverished and backward. In 1837, in one Donegal parish of nine thousand souls there was neither a pig, a clock, a pair of boots, fruit trees nor root crops other than potatoes. Between them the population could boast seven table forks, twenty shovels and a plough. Yet further off to the east in County Down, even at the height of the famines, a surveyor found any farm 'ready without preparation to produce a bit of cheese, with bread, butter and beer, for an unexpected guest'. Visitor after visitor reported harrowing tales of extended families sharing tiny earth-floored huts with the hens and, if they were better off than the Donegal population, a pig. Even after allowing for the facts that such shocking stories read better than any account of the modest comfort that could also be found, and that visitors most often came to Ireland in the summer months, the time of greatest rural privation before the harvest, one fact stood out. In the sixty years between 1740 and 1800 the population of Ireland had more than doubled, from between two and 2.4 million to five million; by 1845 it reached 8.5 million; and this phenomenal expansion was not accompanied by any significant new employment being offered in industry, or even in up-to-date farming. All was provided for by the ubiquitous potato. A diet based almost exclusively on potatoes and buttermilk was healthy enough, but demanded an enormous quantity of potatoes: two adults and two children would consume nearly twenty kilos a day. Reliance on potatoes was so widespread that alternative foods could only be procured, if at all, with great difficulty in the quantities needed.[6]

In spite of the increase in population and the monotonous diet the physical well-being of some Irishmen had improved to a level superior to many parts of contemporary England. Public health facilities, rudimentary and scattered though they were, rivalled the best in Europe.

County infirmaries and a network of more than six hundred dispensaries made health care available locally, whilst the larger towns had specialised hospitals. One signifier of better nourishment was that Irishmen were taller than their English counterparts. Arthur Young, that perceptive traveller, had put his finger on it when he wrote, 'a wholesome diet and plentiful inexpensive domestic fuel ... compensated for the tattered clothing and rudimentary housing of the Irish poor'. Peat and the potato contributed to make life tolerable for the rural poor, but the system that led to their availability lay at the heart of the disaster.[7]

Adapting a conservative farming society to change is never painless. In Scotland the clearances of smallholders in order to make space for sheep-runs and in England the enclosures of common land led to widespread distress and unrest, but in both countries social factors did something to alleviate the worst effects. Many Scottish agricultural tenants had strong rights to their land, as well as often a close connection with their landlords. The description 'tenant' was proudly engraved on large tombstones in prosperous kirkyards. English landlords found it not only profitable but fashionable to interest themselves in the best farming techniques; pictures of prize oxen as well as of favourite horses were cherished. Active landlords were not unknown in Ireland – Lord George Hill lived on his twenty-three-thousand-acre estate, learned fluent Irish, and reinvested all the estate's income – but making sense of a landholding system where a single half-acre could be claimed by twenty-six people, and rents could be as much as twenty years in arrears, could not be done without some pain. Cash rents were earned only with difficulty, the most remunerative method being that of seasonal emigration to England to work on the land, or to labour on the extensive canal and railway projects.[8]

When the potato blight, *phytophthora infestans*, struck in September 1845, the new Poor Law Boards were first in the firing line. Some coped better than others, but none had been in office long enough to develop crisis-management skills. In London the government quickly became concerned. Prime Minister Robert Peel had developed many of his views since his initial conservative stand. Facts had forced him to agree with Catholic Relief; experience had led – much to the horror of most English voters and of his brilliant young colleague William Ewart Gladstone – to his increasing the state funding of the Maynooth seminary. His government had been properly alarmed about the potential effects of the potato blight early enough. Peel was 'devoting every hour of his time' outside Parliament to 'watching changes and reading evidence of the heavy calamity' approaching. By 31 October he urged upon a reluctant cabinet the vital need to agree a temporary suspension of import duties on grain in order to provide alternative food supplies.

This was a subject of high political importance. Since 1838 the Anti-Corn Law League had been developing into what became the first national political pressure group that could equal the anti-slavery campaign in efficacy. Protective tariffs on grain had originally been introduced in 1804, and consolidated in 1815, in order to protect the incomes of landowners and farmers. The inevitable effect of these 'Corn Laws' was to increase both the price of bread, a vital constituent of the people's diet, and the profits of farmers. Manufacturers and workers joined with radicals to force the abolition of these restrictions, and Peel himself had, by 1845, been convinced of the inevitability of abolition. But his government was a coalition of liberal conservatives, prepared for reform, sitting uneasily with landowners who resisted what would be an attack on their incomes.

It was well appreciated that, once temporarily abolished, it would be a practical impossibility ever to restore the tariffs: the cabinet worried over the question for more than a month, but were inextricably divided, and no action was taken. Peel was forced to rely on other measures to counter the threatened famine, which were not ineffective. Loans were made to local authorities, and large quantities of American maize bought for subsidised distribution. Had the disease not continued these measures might have sufficed (although the maize was not popular), but the next year's blight brought total failure of the potato crop. Whilst previously there had been much privation, most people remained reasonably healthy until the summer of 1846, but by that time existing stocks of food had been consumed. Disease spread rapidly among a weakened population. Previously under-utilised workhouses were crammed to overflowing, and deaths in them, mainly from dysentery and typhus, which in 1845 had been fewer than six thousand, were sixty-six thousand two years later. Irish and British governments were faced with famine on an unprecedented scale, and proved incapable of finding adequate remedies.

Biting on the bullet, Peel forced through repeal of the Corn Laws, but in so doing split his party. By July 1846 a new Whig government was elected, headed by Lord John Russell. With the best of intentions, Russell too failed to alleviate the developing horrors in Ireland. Coming to power as he did on the back of the anti-Corn Law agitation Russell's government was dedicated to non-interference with market forces. Ireland must be assisted, but in accordance with the best and most modern economic practice.

Even more than the Tory reformers, Whig-Liberals were shackled to the Blue Books. To an extent unknown to free-marketeers in the twentieth century, their Victorian predecessors were devoted to private enterprise, and had a horror of state interference. When events forced Whigs to consider the smallest government intervention in the mechanics of the market they turned ashamedly apologetic; any such 'interposition of the state must be limited within so strict a boundary as not to go beyond the exact point necessary to accomplish its ends'. Faced with the ghastly reality of the Famine such apostles of free trade reacted with impassivity, believing that if market forces could not control Heaven's dictates it was 'impossible they can perform adequately . . . the duty of feeding the people'. That was Russell himself, abdicating ultimate responsibility for the greatest disaster of the century.[9]

Lord John was speaking against a background of considerable agitation in England itself. Even though no famine raged on an Irish scale, conditions in the workhouses were fiercely attacked. Those in the Andover 'spike' started a national scandal, but the ratepayers, who funded the Poor Law expenditure, watched anxiously over the rising costs. Underlying the British government's reluctance to spend even more – Russell believed the effort was costing £12 million a year – was a general disdain of Irish landlords and distrust of Irish labourers. The Irish poor, Russell complained, were 'incapable of the honest exertion, the prudence and the integrity' thought to be 'characteristic of the English worker'. Should '8,000,000 Irish . . . come crawling as beggars to the shores of England? Should not that people, or representatives of that people, indicate . . . some respect for themselves?'[10] Lying behind this intransigence was a dogmatic certainty that the inexorable laws of economics dictated that bitter medicines must be swallowed for the sake of ultimate prosperity. Very similar certainties were proclaimed in Britain during the 1980s, with consequences that were less fatal, but much resented; and behind both such hard-shelled ideologies lurked an unpalatable kernel of truth.

The first line of defence against hunger, that of relief administered through the Poor Law institutions, could not hold long. Well-run estates contrived to keep tenants and their dependants from utter misery, but the protracted distress was too much for many Poor Law Guardians to cope with. Writing from Swineford in County Mayo in January 1847 Sub-Inspector Hunt reported that the local Guardians were paying for food personally, but that money was almost useless: 'You would be horrified . . . starving men, women and children who daily and hourly swarm the town, soliciting with prayers and tears one meal of food.' But since the brand-new Poor Law organisation had been specifically designed to avoid what would have been the obvious solution – simply handing out food and money, as had been previously done in England – other remedies were sought.[11]

The starving Irish, it was decided, should be given the opportunity to regain their self-respect by engaging in a massive programme of public works, designed to improve the infrastructure and to provide a cash income for those employed upon them. This decision required a U-turn, since it was nothing less than adopting the remedies advocated by the Irish Commission on the Poor Law, which the government had so recently rejected. The government exerted great efforts in the new project: between September 1846 and March 1847 as many as 715,000 men were employed, supporting thereby some 3.5 million people, nearly half the Irish population. All reports were meticulously recorded and published in the Blue Books. Relief Commissioners attempting to superintend famine relief were overwhelmed by administrative red tape: 'vast numbers of forms and documents . . . upwards of 10,000 books, 80,000 sheets, three million card tickets', in all 'not less than fourteen tons of paper'. Many lives were doubtless saved, but given the uneven state of Irish local government uniformly effective implementation of such an undertaking was impossible. Moreover, many of the workers were so weak that they had to be paid for merely turning up; even so, the payments were too little to buy adequate food.[12]

Atlantic Ocean

Lough Foyle

LONDONDERRY

ANTRIM

Belfast Lough

DONEGAL

⌂ Omagh

TYRONE

Lough Neagh

Belfast

Strangford Lough

DOWN

Lough Erne

Sligo

FERMANAGH

ARMAGH

Shannon & Erne Junction

MONAGHAN

SLIGO

LEITRIM

CAVAN

LOUTH

MAYO

ROSCOMMON

LONGFORD

Lough Mask

Irish Sea

MEATH

R Boyne

Lough Corrib

GALWAY

Lough Ree

WESTMEATH

Galway

Ballinasloe

Galway Bay

KING'S COUNTY

Maynooth

Dublin

DUBLIN

Aran Is.

KILDARE

Lough Derg

QUEEN'S COUNTY

WICKLOW

CLARE

TIPPERARY

KILKENNY

CARLOW

Limerick

Kilkenny ⌂

LIMERICK

WEXFORD

Mouth of the Shannon

WATERFORD

Wexford Hbr

R Slaney

Dingle Bay

R Blackwater

Killarney

KERRY

CORK

Waterford Hbr

R Lee

Cork

Bantry Bay

Land Improvement	up to £500	Public Buildings	⌂
	up to £5,000	Coast Guard Stations	□
	up to £10,000	Piers and Harbours	▪
	over £10,000	Roads	
Drainage and Navigation		Fish Curing Stations	

0 10 20 30 40 miles

WORKS UNDERTAKEN TO ALLEVIATE

THE FAMINE IN IRELAND

Bombarded by agitated despatches from Lords Lieutenant Bessborough and his successor Lord Clarendon, who reported, 'The destitution and misery in some of the Western counties exceeds any thing that I could have believed,' and by the reactions of public horror to the graphic depictions of the *Illustrated London News* artists, the government was at last obliged to resort to direct methods of providing food. This was eventually done on a huge scale: by the summer of 1847 more than three million meals were being distributed daily. The remedy was immediately effective – even in such badly affected areas as Skibbereen 'the introduction of cooked food ... [was] universally productive of the best effects on the health and appearance of the people'. It was too late for many, as disease killed off far more than actual starvation. Nor were such measures carried through. In August 1847 the hard-pressed Commissioners were informed that the government had declared the Famine to be officially over. Despite bitter complaints that 'it becomes necessary, within a period of six weeks, to throw on their own resources three million of persons who had been provided with food', the government attempted to persist in its fiction.[13]

What was the death toll from the Famine is to some extent a matter of conjecture; but whatever the total it was staggeringly and tragically high. At least three-quarters of a million people died, one-tenth of the population, mostly from disease. But that was only part of the disaster. The whole pattern of rural life over much of the country was shattered. Before 1845 there were annually some 130,000 emigrants from Ireland, mainly to the United States; during and immediately after the Famine, 1.5 million left the country. The Westminster theorists, while regretting the suffering, congratulated themselves that the economists had been proved right: the population had grown beyond that which the land could support, and natural forces had done their beneficent work. Perhaps a more accurate reflection of upper-class English sentiment was that of Lord Lieutenant Clarendon, writing in March 1847 to the editor of the *Economist*, a supporter of non-interference: 'You lay down abstract principles and desire that men should be left to act upon them, which is quite right if ordinary men under ordinary circumstances were in question, but you have to deal with Irishmen ... It is a great misfortune for us to have such a people under our charge, but we cannot leave them entirely to their own devices at a moment when they are unusually incapacitated.'[14]

A comparison can be made with the simultaneous famine in Scotland. In many Highland and marginal regions reliance on the potato had been almost as great as in Ireland. Official remedies were applied in a similar way, but Scots landlords were generally more supportive than their Irish counterparts. One Scotswoman living in Ireland, Elizabeth Smith, describing the condition of Wicklow during the Famine, wrote: 'It is nonsense to talk of good landlords as the rule ... they are only the exception.' Her compatriots in Scotland did better: the Duke of Sutherland is said to have spent £78,000 on supporting his people; James Matheson, the Hong Kong and Canton opium smuggler, gave £40,000 to feed his tenants. One explanation for this might be that the long family connection between landowners and tenants had survived in Scotland, but during the two hundred years of British confiscation, plantation and rule had been shattered in Ireland.

Some Whigs believed they had done as much as could possibly be expected. In August 1847 Lord Palmerston, that experienced Irish landowner, complained to Russell that even after 'two or three million Irish have been saved from Famine and Pestilence by money, which if the Union had not existed, their own Parliament would have never been able to raise', the Repealers were still winning elections. In a conclusion that showed how an intimate knowledge of Ireland did not prevent total incomprehension, the annoyed peer stated: 'This is not natural.'[15]

It is difficult to resist the conclusion that Russell's government had reacted too slowly, and were too much wedded to modish economic theories, to control the Famine. More seriously, the decision to close food kitchens in 1847 was totally irresponsible. Left to themselves the Irish authorities were unable to meet the still-urgent demands, and it was not until 1850 that financial aid was resumed. The excess mortality in that period can, fairly and squarely, be laid at the door of Lord John Russell's government.

Expressions of exasperation and contempt for the Irish were probably little more than political verbiage, and did not affect the administration's increasingly desperate scrabbling to find additional relief measures which would not, as they firmly believed, risk fearful long-term economic consequences. In all some £10 million was spent on famine relief, in addition to generous individual charitable contributions, those of the Quakers being particularly notable. At a time when £1 million more or less was a matter of great import, leading to angry scenes in the cabinet, when annual deficits of £3.5 million caused acerbic criticism, and public finance was so confused as to necessitate four budgets in a single year, £10 million was a very considerable sum, which should rebut the charge of government apathy. Yet it is true that, a few years later, £60 million was spent on the Crimean war. Even today, however, resources devoted by rich countries to arms and warfare are enormously greater than those allotted to the relief of distress.

As for the accusation that the Irish Famine was a wicked English plot, that is of course quite absurd; but as in so many other things, the emotional myth remains much more powerful than the dull truth; and when all is said the suffering of the Irish people, and the loss to Ireland through death and emigration, had no European parallel in the nineteenth century.[16]

'Infant Ireland'

On 27 January 1848, Alexis de Tocqueville, one of the best-informed and clearest-sighted men of his times, asked the French Assembly: 'Can you at this very moment count upon tomorrow? Have you the smallest idea what a year, a month, even a day, may bring forth?' Received with amused condescension by the government, de Tocqueville was swiftly proved right. In less than a month the red flags were raised, the ministry had fallen, and King Louis Philippe abdicated. The subsequent two years saw not only France, but Italy, Germany, Poland, Austria, Hungary and Spain torn by revolutions, as new concepts of socialism reinforced the popular discontent stimulated by thirty years of repression. The British Isles survived the general upheaval with remarkably little trouble. London nervously awaited the delivery of a 'monster' petition from the Chartists, pressing for such shockingly radical reforms as universal (male) suffrage, but the apprehended demonstration was rained off. In Scotland 1848 saw the acquisition by

Queen Victoria of that unfortunate edifice, Balmoral, and the opening by her of the first Braemar Gathering, a milk-and-water version of the old Highland Games. In spite of Balmoral, Braemar and the cult of 'tartanry', the old Scotland seemed to be washed out by a tide of anglicisation. Henry Cockburn, distinguished liberal judge and diarist, writing in mid-century, lamented that

> the sphere of the Scotch language, and the course of Scotch feelings and ideas, is speedily and rapidly abridging, even in Scotland ... Scotch cannot be obliterated without our losing the means of enjoying some of the finest productions of genius, and of understanding the habits and characters of one of the most picturesque of European nations, and of losing an important key to the old literature, even of the south. Above all, we lose ourselves. Instead of being what we are, we become a poor part of England.[17]

One signifier of cultural difference is that of heroic status. In Scotland national icons are unequivocally Sassenach rather than Gaelic – Robert Bruce being the prime example, closely followed by David Livingstone, Walter Scott and Robert Burns, with William Wallace as a part-exception. Even Bonnie Prince Charlie, a doubtful hero figure, has no trace of the Celt, while his truly heroic followers are largely anonymous. In Ireland, in spite of spirited efforts to revive Gaelic history, Brian Boru is the only lay character from Celtic Ireland still to have some resonance; all the other historic figures accorded heroic status owe their reputations to having been defeated. If status is measured by statues, the trousered icons of O'Connell and Parnell are the true representations of Irish heroes. In Wales, by contrast, leaving aside the pre-Welsh and very doubtfully historic Arthur and his knights, actual and formidable heroes, all undeniably Celtic, proliferate. From the Lord Rhys through the Llywellyns to Owain Glyn Dwr, Welsh princes populate the pages of history.

The revolutionary tide of the 1840s produced only minor ripples in Ireland. The 'Young Ireland' movement was formed in opposition to O'Connell and in imitation of Giuseppe Mazzini's 'Giovene Italia', a driving force of Italian nationalism. There were however no Mazzinis, D'Azeglios or Garibaldis, no strategists, philosophers or soldiers in the

Irish version. Had Thomas Davis, co-founder of the Young Ireland newspaper, the *Nation*, not died prematurely the movement might have matured; instead it justified the gibe of 'Infant Ireland' and O'Connell's scathing remark of 'claptraps of juvenile orators'. Young Ireland was at the same time a continuation of O'Connell's campaign and a rejection of his legal and parliamentary methods, and his reliance on mobilising the Catholic vote. Its leaders were seen at their best in the attempt to create an Irish Confederation of all sections of the population, but it was too late to generate pan-Irish sentiment among the mass of Ulster Protestants. At their worst the Young Irelanders threatened the continuation of O'Connell's real achievements in securing reforms; like many of their successors, crying after the whole pig, they sacrificed the bacon.[18]

After the Liberator's death in May 1847 the Young Irelanders were lost lambs, with little unanimity. Where O'Connell had been a passionate advocate of liberty in all its guises, the dissident journalist John Mitchel had a much more selective approach, believing that slavery was the proper status for the blacks he despised and that O'Connell was a cowardly backslider who had sold out to the Whigs. William Smith O'Brien, an honest and agreeable gentleman, although with little sense of humour and absurdly vain, a member of the Westminster Parliament, was a most reluctant revolutionary. Sporting a uniform designed by Davis of a green coat with white lining and gilt buttons, green trousers and patent leather boots, white kid gloves and black satin cravats, the prosperous leaders could hardly be more out of touch with a people painfully emerging from the miseries of famine and disease. O'Connell could attract hundreds of thousands, but Young Ireland had hardly any political following. When a rebellion of sorts was attempted in July 1848 its final defeat (O'Brien was still recovering from being beaten by O'Connellites) took place in the Widow MacCormack's cabbage patch at the hands of a company of besieged policemen.

The rapid flight of the Young Irelanders and their subsequent short terms of comfortable imprisonment were in stark contrast to the heroism of Daniel Manin in Venice or of the Garibaldini in Rome. After some initial alarm (O'Brien formally being sentenced to death) a weary tolerance was shown by the British government; it was during their release on bail that the Young Ireland leaders went to Paris seeking help – unsuccessfully – from the new republican government. O'Brien, having retreated ('an O'Brien never turns his back on an enemy') and given his parole (after vowing not to), was released from his privileged exile in Tasmania before returning to end his days peacefully in Ireland. Mitchel joined the American Confederates in fighting – in print only – to preserve black slavery and degradation.[19]

A contributory reason for the collapse of the enterprise was the opposition of the Catholic hierarchy. Italian nationalists had reason to hope for better things when Cardinal Giovanni Maria Mastai-Ferretti was elected as Pope Pius IX in June 1846. The Cardinal had spent many years in Chile, and was known to cherish liberal ideals. Popularly known as 'Pio Nono', the new Pope drove immediately into action with his famous 'Amnesty' of 16 July 1846, pardoning all political offenders – liberals who had been imprisoned by his rigidly conservative predecessor Gregory XVI. Further reforms came slowly enough, but the Pope had done enough to frighten the Austrian rulers of northern Italy and the reactionary Bourbons of Naples. Popular protests were brutally suppressed, leading to real revolution. In February 1848 Pope Pius issued a letter concluding with the words 'God bless Italy', which became, although not at the Pope's volition, the revolutionary rallying cry. By April the liberal national revolutionary movement had swept through Continental Europe.

The papal tone changed radically as revolutions gained momentum. On 29 April Pio Nono issued another pronouncement, in effect withdrawing from the nationalist struggle. In France the socialist rising was brutally suppressed by the infamous General Cavaignac. 'The priests,' Lord Lieutenant Clarendon exulted, 'are now like Frankenstein. They recoil at the monster of their own creation.' All expressions of clerical support for Irish insurgency vanished before the bloody realities of nationalist revolt in Italy. It seemed that the Irish hierarchy could be enlisted to support Westminster's attempts to contain nationalism within constitutional backgrounds by a joint policy of prudent reform; but such hopes were to be evanescent.[20]

By that time the battle lines between fundamentalist believers and their rationalist critics, that still exist among such unsophisticated societies as those of Kansas and Iran, were being drawn. The conclusions of the Archbishop of Armagh, that the world was created in six days, beginning on 21 October 4004 BC, at nine in the morning, had been accepted since the seventeenth century. Quietly enough, so as not to disturb the believers, the geologists were proving the Archbishop mistaken. The self-taught William Smith had published his *Geological Atlas of Britain* in 1815; by 1863 Sir Charles Lyell, an Oxford-educated Scot, had published *The Antiquity of Man*. Charles Darwin noted that 'almost all scientists' admitted 'evolution under some form'.

It was singularly unfortunate for Ireland that the battle lines were drawn at this time. Both Russell and Clarendon were genuinely anxious to do whatever could be done to help Ireland. The future, Russell believed, depended upon a well-educated population capable of making its way in the modern world. At the primary level the best way to bring this about would be to subsidise the Catholic Church in the parishes, where he was fully aware that the priest was the central figure, and to provide more university education; in due course this should produce a parallel to the English system, where clergy and gentry worked together to keep the country tranquil. It seemed that a powerful section of the Church, led by the venerable Archbishop of Dublin, Daniel Murray, was willing to co-operate. The ignominious collapse of Smith O'Brien's revolt indicated that, in spite of the rhetoric, there was an acceptance that British rule was inevitable, and that constructive collaboration was the best option.

In 1850 Pope Pius dropped his bombshell, by announcing that a Catholic episcopate with territorial titles was to be established in England for the first time since the Reformation. The Irish Catholic Church had continuously exercised a parallel territorial jurisdiction with that of the Church of Ireland, and if the doctrine of the unity of the realm were taken seriously, its extension to England should have been no more than a formality; but the announcement was greeted with what today seems hysterical agitation. Certainly Cardinal Wiseman's announcement of the system was pompous and injudicious, guaranteed to upset those whom it did not amuse, but Russell's reaction was both exaggerated and untypical. He took the Pope's action as a personal affront, a demonstration of ingratitude for his own endeavours, which had won him only unpopularity in England. Not content with privately fuming, the Prime Minister sent a public letter to the Bishop of Durham in which he described the 'papal aggression' as 'insolent and insidious' and spoke of 'a nation which looks with contempt on the mummeries of superstition, and with scorn at the laborious endeavours which are now being made to confine the intellect and enslave the soul'. Although the desire 'to confine the intellect' was then the aim of most denominations, it bore heavily on those Catholics who refused to co-operate with Lord John's educational reforms, and the reference to superstitious mummeries was taken to apply to the Roman Church, causing great and justified offence.[21]

Russell's reward was instant popularity, and eventual disaster. A speedy Bill was introduced forbidding the assumption of territorial episcopal titles by Catholics, in Ireland as well as in England, and it was propelled through Parliament by massive majorities. A few years later the Act was quietly suspended, and the Cardinal Archbishop of Westminster allowed official recognition, but the Church's suspicion of British government was more permanent. However pressing the need for better education, the Irish hierarchy would accept public money only on its own, very restrictive, terms.

Welsh bards and Scotch dominees

Ireland's troubles during the nineteenth century were reflected only mildly in the other regions of the United Kingdom. All suffered from the strains caused by the Industrial Revolution and by agricultural developments. England, the most developed region, experienced the worst of these effects. The rapidly increasing population (doubling between 1801 and 1851) entailed, as in Ireland, drastic agricultural changes, although of a different order. Economic rural production demanded replacement of smallholdings by large fields: common lands were therefore enclosed and smallholders dispossessed, driving them and their families on the parish relief, fixed at the lowest possible scale. Arthur Young, enthusiastic advocate of reform, pictured the unhappy cottar reflecting outside an alehouse: 'If I am sober, shall I have land for a cow? If I am frugal, shall I have another half acre of potatoes? Bring me another pot!'

Desperate countrymen flocked to the rapidly expanding towns, where employment, of a sort, was becoming available. But such employment opportunities had their own costs, as independent hand-loom weavers were forced out of business by new textile-processing equipment. Machinery-breaking and rioting by the English equivalent of the Irish Ribbonmen, the 'Luddites' and the followers of 'Captain Swing', caused much alarm. Peaceful attempts to organise labour were suppressed – the example of the Tolpuddle Martyrs, which ended in the transportation of decent and respectable labourers, is typical. Justice was certainly linked to class interests: no working man sat on the bench, and the protection of property often took precedence over the rights of the individual. As Disraeli wrote, there were 'two nations' in England, but the oppressed nation only spasmodically sought relief in violence.[22]

Hardship – as in Ireland – was by no means universal. Tyneside, with its vigorous coal, chemical, shipbuilding and glass industries, was to the nineteenth century what the Ruhr and Texas were to the twentieth. Birmingham and the Black Country's engineering enterprises, upon which railways and all other manufacturing industries depended for their machine tools and instruments, thrived increasingly. British governments were quicker to respond to grievances erupting a few hours' travel away than to those in Ireland, rarely visited and comparatively inaccessible. If there was much hardship in nineteenth-century England, there was no general famine. Leaders and journalists might turn a blind eye to women and children working in underground collieries, might let epidemics go unchecked, but mass starvation was avoided.

As in the north of England, Wales developed coalfields and metallurgical industries, attracting workers and avoiding the distress that mechanisation had brought to English textile industries. Again, as in the north of England, Methodism caused a massive swing from the established Church, especially in the newly industrialised areas. But Welsh Methodism was individual and peculiar, renouncing the centralising practice and Anglican theology of English Methodism, adopting instead strict Calvinist theology and Presbyterian organisation. Popular songs are sensitive indications of attitudes: nineteenth-century northern English produced such rollicking songs as 'John Peel', 'Blaydon Races', 'Ilkley Moor' and 'Cushie Butterfield'; Wales confined itself to hymns and wonderful romantic melodies (which the Welsh sang better than did the Tynesiders).

Both societies attached signal importance to education and self-improvement, and were ready to insist on their rights; but while Tyneside keelmen and colliers could be unruly, violence in Wales was more protracted. In the coalfields and ironworks such gangs as the 'Scotch Cattle' reacted against the 'truck' system of payment in kind rather than cash, with intimidation, destruction of plant and one pitched battle with the Scots Greys (most of the soldiers in Wales at the time were Scottish). The 1831 riots in Merthyr were the most serious that had been seen anywhere in nineteenth-century Britain, with perhaps twenty fatalities, and one martyr for future hagiology, Richard Lewis (Dic Penderyn). Eight years later the Chartist attack on Newport left at least twenty dead. Merthyr and Newport experienced more armed risings, with thousands of participants, waving red flags, and at Newport dreaming of a republic. The 'Rebecca Riots' between 1839 and 1843 were well-disciplined attacks targeted at objects of popular loathing – tollgates, workhouses, 'monoglot English stewards, tithe receivers, builders of weirs, encroachers on the commons, greedy landowners and tenants who leased more than one farm'.[23]

The reactions of the British government to these disturbances were controlled: Dic Penderyn was the only one to suffer the death penalty as a result of either the Merthyr or Newport risings. After the Rebecca Riots, which had led to many assaults and at least one murder, no capital punishment was inflicted. Rather, in a typically earnest and sensible early-Victorian move, a commission of enquiry, headed by a Welsh landlord, T.F. Lewis, was appointed. Lewis held a series of open meetings and recommended reforms – which recommendations were adopted. Otherwise, he wrote, the people's 'only remedy was to take the law into their own hands'.

Although Welsh distaste for the Saxon never entirely abated, there was no such anglophobia that obtained in many parts of Ireland. The French invaders who landed in Pembrokeshire, led by the elderly Irish-American Colonel Tate in 1797, were not welcomed in Wales, but repelled with singular unanimity and effectiveness; it was indeed immigrant Irish who were more likely to be discriminated against in Wales than the English technicians who came to provide the skills needed by new industries.

For better and for worse, Wales had all the essentials for successful industries: abundant coal deposits of different characters, plentiful iron ore, copper and deposits of other ores, good harbours, an enterprising and industrious population, connections with the new technologies emerging in other parts of Britain, especially those nearby around Birmingham, and access to the greatest capital market in the world. Non-ferrous metal industries, processing zinc, lead and copper were centred around the northern coast; the great ironmaster John 'Mad Iron' Wilkinson's Bersham works produced guns and steam-engine parts; traditional industries such as stocking-knitting and woollen piece goods continued to flourish; fishing and boatbuilding, subsidised by state bounties, brought a new prosperity to the west.

It was however the south that saw the most dramatic changes. Swansea became, temporarily, and largely through its copper industry, the most populous town in Wales (with ten thousand inhabitants in 1801), although still only medium-sized by comparison with such English manufacturing towns as Birmingham, Manchester or Newcastle on Tyne). John Guest and Richard Crawshay established works in the valleys of Glamorgan and Monmouth that turned out iron at incomparably competitive rates and in huge quantities for the period. Between 1760, when John Guest set up at Dowlais, and 1851 the Welsh population had more than doubled to 1,163,000, and this expansion was consequent upon the growth of industry. From being almost entirely an agricultural economy, two-thirds of the population was now dependent upon industry. As in the rest of the United Kingdom, industrialisation was geographically limited, but in the much larger area of England the unbalancing effect of this was not as noticeable as in the smaller country.[24]

Together with Scotland and Ireland, Wales experienced a revived consciousness of traditions. The self-conscious 'tartanry' that has afforded innocent amusement to generations of non-Scots bypassed Wales, where the movement was more literary. The eisteddfod held at St Asaph in 1790, the first organised on a large scale for two centuries, was accompanied by completely spurious, very eighteenth-century rites, created for the 'gorsedd', the assembly of the bards which the antiquarian and poet Iolo Morganwg claimed to be the veritable ancient ceremonies of the Druids. Such entertaining extravagances – Iolo's gorsedd continues alongside the entirely respectable eisteddfod – were however nourished by a living language. Official and commercial forces were combining to encourage and even impose the use of English, but Welsh remained the first language of at least half the population, and Welsh book publication was supplemented by newspapers and journals to a far greater extent than was that in Irish or Scots Gaelic.[25]

Geography favoured Welsh integration with England. The rising industrial centres, north and south, were easily accessible to the Lancashire and Midlands conurbations, while communications with the interior of Wales were much more difficult (and so remain: it is quicker to get from Cardiff to London or Birmingham, by road or rail, than it is to reach Aberystwyth). Wales remained on the periphery of southern England, to a not dissimilar extent as did the English northern counties. With no universities outside Oxford, Cambridge and London, and Durham after 1838, Welshmen and northerners traditionally attended their accustomed Oxbridge colleges – Jesus for Welsh and Emmanuel for the northerners – and took advantage of the commercial opportunities of London, where such banks as Lloyds and Glyn Mills offered favourable openings.

Urbanisation and industrialisation produced new political theories – communism was founded on Friedrich Engels' Manchester experiences – and social organisations. Nonconformism provided experience of self-government and an existing affiliation to the Liberal reformers. Political power grew with successive extensions of the franchise. Although Wales was to become a future Liberal stronghold, returning only two Conservative members by 1880, the 1832 Act had little effect on the traditional hegemony of the gentry. Only after the 'Great Election' of 1868 was there any movement away from the traditional conservatism, and that rebellion was quickly punished by disappointed patrons. When the electors chose twenty-two Liberals and only eight Conservatives, George Douglas-Pennant, a disputatious reactionary, was one of those disappointed Conservatives, and at least twenty of his father's tenants were accordingly served notice to quit. By that time Wales had however become almost a one-party state, solidly Liberal at first, later to switch allegiance as unanimously to Labour.

In economic development and urbanisation Scotland followed a similar pattern to that of England, with at least equal originality. Scots were usually to be found in the advance guard of new industries –

cotton in the 1780s, iron in the 1820s, and at all times in shipbuilding. In the fifteen years after 1830 Scottish iron production increased tenfold. Shipbuilding, which was to become the driving force behind Glasgow's growth, began production of ocean-going iron ships in Robert Napier's Govan yard. Improved techniques of jute-spinning were beginning to give Dundee almost a monopoly of that valuable industry, a perquisite of Scotland's involvement in the East India trade. Dundee's expansion was part of the urbanisation of Scotland. By mid-century the four largest towns housed 20 per cent of the population – and Glasgow's population had soared from forty-three thousand in 1780 to over three hundred thousand. Industrial unrest in early-nineteenth-century Scotland was equal to that in England: the Peterloo massacre of 1819 was followed within months by the fracas at Bonnybridge, a more militant affair, which resulted in the executions of James Wilson and his comrades.[26]

Scots continued to command a near-monopoly of Scottish positions of influence, leaving no room for outsiders.[27] Concentrating as they did on domestic business, operating abroad only through correspondents (or having established their own foreign banks – Henry Hope's early-seventeenth-century Amsterdam establishment still survives in the dignified and respected house of Mees and Hope), Scottish banks lacked the international expertise of their English counterparts. This weakness may have contributed to the crisis of 1857 which 'came closer to pulling down the entire banking structure in Scotland than could be publicly admitted'. Invoking the shades of Malachi Malagrowther, Scottish bankers had resisted the extension of the 1844 English Banking Act to Scotland, and when a crisis struck in the aftermath of the Indian Mutiny, the Glasgow-based Western Bank failed. Glasgow blamed Edinburgh, but English opinion saw it as 'an attack upon our currency' brought about by incompetence and fraud. Similar suspicion was fuelled by the collapse in 1878 of the City of Glasgow Bank, following frauds for which the directors went to prison, and which bankrupted some 80 per cent of the shareholders. An effort made by the Disraeli administration to ban Scottish banks from England resulted in a compromise, which lasted for the next hundred years, ensuring that each country's banks would stay in their own backyards; but a further cause for some Scots resentment was established.[28] Scottish pride in the previous century's intellectual achievements had also been hurt by the movement of literary and academic distinction to London and the south. The two greatest Scottish scientists of the time, or indeed of any time, William Thomson, Lord Kelvin (actually born in Belfast) and James Clerk Maxwell, both came to Cambridge for their studies; by the end of the century it was only in medicine that the Scottish universities retained their pre-eminence. Thomas Carlyle, prototypically Scottish and the most influential mid-century literary figure, chose to live in Chelsea.[29]

It was in politics, however, that the most permanent divide, almost indeed a geological fissure, opened up between Scotland and England. The 1832 Reform Act made, for the first time, Scottish parliamentary representation more than a legal fiction. According to Francis Jeffrey, a well-informed witness, only four thousand Scots from a population of 2,370,000 were entitled to vote. After 1832 the number increased dramatically to some sixty-five thousand, still a modest proportion of the whole, but at last comparable to that of England. The new voters showed themselves to be solidly Liberal. In three general elections (1857, 1859 and 1865) no Conservative was elected for a Scottish burgh, although they did better in the counties. After the 1867 Reform Act the preponderance became massive. In 1868 Scottish voters returned fifty-two Liberals to eight Conservatives. Taken together with Wales, a heavy weight of Liberal votes was almost assured; if Irish MPs sided with them, the three countries could, and sometimes did, find their representatives able to override the Conservatives even when that party had a majority of English seats.

Quite as important as the change in political Scotland was that in the Scottish Kirk. On 18 May 1843 the retiring Moderator, David Welsh, read out a statement of protest before walking out of the General Assembly, followed by 123 other ministers. In essence it was the conclusion of an argument which had raged for a decade on the question of whether congregation or patron had the decisive voice in the appointment of parish ministers, but attached to the practical question were the obvious and inevitable social and political corollaries: the conflict was one between entrenched privilege and reform. Within a very short time Scottish Presbyterianism was almost equally divided between adherents of the Church of Scotland and the new Free Church of Scotland.

What seemed to be a purely domestic dispute had much wider implications. For two centuries the Kirk had been an integral part of social control through its parish courts, which explored the conduct of each member and decided who was able to communicate at the infrequent celebrations of the Eucharist (admission by ticket only). Education had been to a very great extent a Kirk matter. Within four years of Dr Welsh's walkout the Free Church had established schools for forty-four thousand children and built more than seven hundred churches as well as financing the salaries of all the ministers and teachers who had seceded. The fact that the Kirk's status was enshrined in the Act of Union entailed any alteration being a matter for the British Parliament, a body little interested in, and worse-informed about, Scottish affairs. The Duke of Argyll groaned that 'I have never yet met an Englishman who could understand, or even conceive, the idea of the relation between Church and state which was embodied in the constitution of Scotland. John Bull, with all his qualities, is a very parochial creature.' More radical Scots resented that such a purely Scottish affair could not be dealt with in Scotland. When one minister complained of this he was shocked by the response of his colleagues: 'I said, on the spur of the moment, that such injustice was enough to justify Scotland in demanding the repeal of the Union. With that, to my surprise . . . the meeting rose as one man, waving hats and handkerchiefs and cheering again and again.'[30]

Whilst the Free Church was by no means a working-class movement – one of its most influential members was the Reverend Dr Sir Henry Moncrieff – it was solidly Liberal. In the 1868 election for the Scottish Universities' parliamentary seats 607 of 640 Free Church ministers voted for that party. The mother Kirk, the Church of Scotland, was henceforward a purely Tory organisation – 1221 of its 1228 ministers voted Conservative. England was similarly moving from the established Church: the 1851 census showed that Protestant Dissenters comprised more than half the total population, with Catholics still in a small minority. Moral and political attitudes being very similar among Scottish Presbyterians, whatever their denomination, and English Dissenters, sectarian disputes did not stimulate Scottish nationalists – a very different situation to that obtaining in Ireland. And although the 'tartan and shamrock' romanticism flourished in both countries, that in Scotland was more solidly rooted in history. There was little likelihood that Lowlanders, very much in the majority, would want to parade about in unaccustomed kilts and sporrans, or would take an unduly sympathetic view of Highland grievances, even when these were very real: there were strong similarities between the not uncommon English view of the Irish as feckless and untrustworthy and the Scottish Lowlanders' conception of their northern neighbours.

The first sign of Scottish nationalist sentiment being translated into action began in 1853 with the establishment of the Association for the Vindication of Scottish Rights. Although the Association was headed by the arch-romantic Earl of Eglintoun, whose expensive and carefully stage-managed tournament was the talk of Britain in 1838, its stated aims were practical, and supported by a wide section of the community, including most town councils. They included petitions for more equitable representation in Parliament and a larger share of government expenditure. It was also essential that a Scottish Department headed by a Secretary of State should be established, instead of Scots interests being left as one of the many responsibilities of the Home Secretary, along with prisons and care of the insane. To some extent Henry Cockburn agreed. He lamented the sweeping away of 'every official thing connected with our ancient monarchy'. Anticipating Bagehot's distinction between the useful and the ornamental parts of the constitution he regretted that 'All the phylacteries of our royalty have been trimmed. We have lost nearly every paid office of dignity or show which had nothing but its antiquity and ancient Scotch nativity to defend it.' Above all Cockburn, like most Scots, resented 'the occasional disregard, if not contempt, by England, of things dear to us, merely because they are not English'. He wished the Association well, but found its rhetoric, of being 'degraded by intolerable wrongs, and talk of Bannock-Burn' folly.[31]

Neglect of Scottish measures was highlighted by the repeated failure to implement a national system of education, postponed for the sixth time in 1869. Lord Advocate Moncrieff, its sponsor, was, it is true, a young and lightweight politician, but it was painfully apparent that Scotland was in danger of being treated 'like an inconvenient West African Colony'. The Act finally reached the Statute Book in 1872, three years after its English counterpart. (It is a measure of change since then that the boot is now tightly on the other foot: Scotland has a more generous representation in the House of Commons and enjoys a considerably more generous proportion of public expenditure.)

CHAPTER 10

1860–1893

Bold Fenian men

IN THE FIRST HALF of the nineteenth century Britain had contrived to rule extensive regions of the world, from China to America, with tens of millions of inhabitants, and to exercise great influence on international events – the abolition of slavery, the encouragement of democratic rule and free trade, and the development of international law – as well as participating in the stately movement of great-power diplomacy. And, on the whole, to do so creditably: certainly the huge sub-continent of India had never been so peaceably and justly administered as during the British raj. Yet in the third kingdom, Ireland, the period had been one of turmoil, famine, repression and violence, as governments at Westminster, with the honourable exception of the Whigs after 1830, ignored or misunderstood Irish demands. After the Famine such attitudes were tempered by a worried search for solutions and some harrowing of English consciences (Scots and Welsh, with the resources of the Empire to develop and concerns of their own to be addressed, showed only a minor interest in their sister kingdom).

Obvious and important differences existed between the unity of England and Scotland and that of Britain and Ireland. The first was originally brought about by dynastic happenstance and sealed by economic necessity; it was one between two sovereign states each with a long history of nationhood, and had been tested by a long period of adjustment. Scottish complaints focused on unequal influence in the joint administration, and were at that time only remotely concerned with a dissolution of the Union. That cry of 'Repeal' that had been agitating Ireland for half a century was heard in Scotland only in moments of particular exasperation. Nor were there important differences in religion between the two nations. Gladstone might be able to convince himself that logic and the laws of God should ban all but members of the established Church of England from any formal participation in state affairs, but he convinced no one else, and even his eccentric opinions were changing. Queen Victoria scandalised her Prime Minister by attending Presbyterian services at Balmoral and even taking communion according to the Calvinist rite. But between Protestants of different denominations and Catholics there were few signs of reconciliation; indeed the Churches were more bitterly opposed than at any time since the Reformation, as the Vatican adopted more extreme positions as a defence against the modern threats of liberalism, Biblical scholarship (although that subject provoked horrified reactions among many Protestants) and democracy.

Irish opposition to its status as an integral part of the United Kingdom was based upon the definition of the inhabitants of Ireland as a nation, a doubtful reality. The truth was that they were splitting ever more sharply into two divided communities. One of Young Ireland's more laudable aims had been to make this idea of an Irish nation into a reality, to obtain a fusion of Protestant and Catholic into an Irish identity. The bathetic collapse of their enterprise signalled the hopelessness of the objective. After the death of Thomas Drummond and Thomas Davis, by some way the finest minds in Ireland, and the overwhelming tragedy of the Famine, Ireland was beyond dispute divided, and not only by religion. Taken province by province, Leinster, with its advanced agriculture and proximity to the capital, had escaped with least damage; Ulster had suffered only slightly more, and that in the border counties, Connacht and Munster between them suffering some 70 per cent of the deaths. As economic growth between North and South became more uneven, the divide deepened.

Belfast's development as an industrial city began almost as a joint satellite of Glasgow and Liverpool. William Gladstone's elder brother, Sir Thomas, established a modern ironworks, complete with forging and plate mills. The enterprise was initially not successful (Sir Thomas tended to be unlucky in such matters), and the equipment was used instead to begin a shipyard. Edward Harland of Govan and Gustav Wolff of Liverpool developed this, building iron hulls in Belfast but buying machinery from established Greenock works. Industrialisation and urbanisation were only beginning in Ulster, but their take-off was rapid. In 1850 there were only fifty-eight steam-powered looms in all Ireland; seventeen years later Ulster alone had over twelve thousand. Belfast's population, perhaps twenty thousand in 1800, was seventy-five thousand in 1841, still less than that of Cork, but Belfast was already, by 1835, Ireland's biggest port. Outside the *Kulturkreis* of Belfast, Glasgow and Liverpool, with its established links to both the London financial markets and the political establishment, and to north Germany through such families as the Jaffes and the Wolffs, development lagged and expansion slowed. In 1851 Dublin was still the second city of the Empire; ten years later it had been overtaken by Glasgow, and in another decade by Liverpool, Manchester and Birmingham as well.[1]

Although a majority of Ulster's population was Catholic, the Belfast area was dominated by Protestants: Belfast's corporation was as strongly Protestant as that of Dublin was Catholic. Belfast Catholics formed a substantial minority which, if not exactly oppressed, enjoyed few privileges; the city boasted sixty-six Protestant churches, while the Catholics had only seven. At a time when Catholics constituted nearly half the population, they numbered only 7.6 per cent of the magistracy and 15 per cent of the shipyard workers, but over 57 per cent of farm labourers. Economically, however, many of the Protestants were relegated to a level similar to that of the Catholics, competing for the unskilled jobs. Their only badge of distinction was that of their religion, and this they flaunted vigorously, encouraged by such magnates as Lord Roden, responsible for the fight between parading Orangemen and Catholic Ribbonmen at Dolly's Brae (the battle of Magheramayo, as the Blue Books had it) on 12 July 1849. Which side began the shooting was not clear, and the police and army did their best to control events, but at least thirty Ribbonmen were killed, and not a single Orangeman. Lord Roden was subsequently dismissed from his position as a magistrate, and the first Party Processions Act was passed at Westminster.[2]

If competition was the root cause of such outbreaks, they were exacerbated by the religious revival that characterised the second half of the nineteenth century. In Great Britain this was inextricably linked with politics, as indicated by Lord John Russell's trouble over the ecclesiastical titles. Archbishop Daniel Murray had been succeeded by Paul Cullen, Archbishop of Armagh and Dublin between 1850 and

1878. An intense supporter of the reactionary papacy, Cullen presided over the Synod of Thurles in 1850 at which it was agreed to insist that all education should become strictly denominational, and that Protestants marrying Catholics should guarantee that all children should be brought up in the True Faith – an unimproveable formula for future conflict. If Cullen's proposals had not been accompanied by a real religious revival they would have become a dead letter, but the enthusiasm that swept the Western world at mid-century stimulated fervour in Catholic and Protestant alike. New or revived cults of the Sacred Heart, the Immaculate Conception and the Assumption of the Virgin Mary, of St Thérèse of Lisieux and St Bernadette of Lourdes, were matched by such evangelical revivalists as the Americans Sankey and Moody, the British Charles Spurgeon and, on the wilder fringe, the Latter-Day Saints of Joseph Smith and Brigham Young. Separate faces of the same coin, both Catholic and Protestant revivals were sincerely fervent, moralistic, teetotal – or attempting so to become – and unquestionably convinced of the absolute rightness of their own particular brand of belief.

Irish Protestant triumphalism, fuelled by the clear evidence of British imperial power, turned increasingly nervous as Westminster governments moved nearer to acknowledging the Irish majority's demands. As frightened communities will, Ulster's Protestants became more aggressively assertive. In turn, the loud insistence of Orange supporters deterred Westminster from pushing through measures which would have both benefited the majority of the Irish people, and eased tension in the southern provinces. Prominent among the most pressing items were education and land tenure. As early as 1831, as one of the Whig government's first reforms, a National Board of Education had been established to fund non-denominational education; this was asking too much of intolerant zealots, and funding had instead to be allocated to schools, open to children of any denomination, but with religious instruction subject to parental wishes. In practice, most primary schools evolved into sectarian institutions. Teacher-training was provided at 'model schools', but after the Thurles Synod Catholic school managers were forbidden to appoint such trained teachers. The results were 'not far short of disastrous', with only 27 per cent of Catholic teachers (and 52 per cent of Protestants) having received any formal training; the effect of such sub-standard education on employment opportunities is obvious.

Sectarian interference affected higher education in a similar fashion. Peel's government had in 1845, just before the Famine struck, passed two important measures. As well as increasing the Maynooth seminary grant to £26,000, provision was made for three Queen's Colleges in Belfast, Cork and Galway. Once again, the Catholic hierarchy intervened to prevent attendance at the colleges. As late as 1869 Archbishop Cullen (now a Cardinal) was able to boast that only thirty-seven Catholic students were working for degrees. The only approved institution of tertiary education for Catholics was the struggling Catholic University, later University College Dublin.[3]

Well before the Famine so tragically proved the point, it had been clear that the Irish system of land tenure was potentially ruinous. In the aftermath of that terrible depopulation, a drastic reorganisation was inevitable. Tiny holdings offering only the most precarious support to single families must go; and further evictions were the consequence. In one of the ironies that stud Irish history, momentum was given to this consolidation by Sir William Gregory, MP, whose wife Augusta, Lady Gregory, was later to be an inspiration to so many nationalist writers. The 'Gregory Amendment' to the Poor Law Extension Act of 1847 made any tenant of a holding greater than a quarter of an acre ineligible for relief; the alternative to starvation for many was therefore the surrender of their plots of land.

No longer would the small Irish tenants be allowed to 'loiter about upon the land'. Holdings of less than five acres, uneconomical except for market gardening, dropped from 45 per cent of the total of Irish land to 15.5 per cent between 1831 and 1851. During the actual period of the Famine farms of over thirty acres rose from 17.3 to 26 per cent. Such holdings could however be much more labour-intensive than might be expected from comparable properties in England. One in Halverstown, Kildare, of four hundred acres, employed 110 men and women, who were given free accommodation and some food, but even on this well-run estate the cash wages were modest, the women being paid something over three shillings a week throughout the year. Such farms, on well-tended land, would be likely to survive, but the post-Famine norm was a movement away from arable farming to livestock rearing, which enhanced the tendency towards larger units employing less labour.[4]

After the trauma of the Famine, Ireland was appreciated as the United Kingdom's major domestic policy problem, and the most permanent. At the very onset of the blight, William Gladstone wrote to his wife on 12 October 1845: 'Ireland! That cloud in the West, that country of Storms . . . Ireland forces upon us these great social and religious questions'; but Gladstone was then in opposition. A few years later the party political structure had undergone a decisive change. Peel's abandonment of the Corn Laws had split the Tories, leading some of the more active reformers in that party to change sides. The old aristocratic Whigs were losing their hold on their party as middle-class voters exercised their new power. Whigs and Tories were in the process of transmuting into Liberals and Conservatives.

It was not until February 1852 that Gladstone found himself in office again, and that was in Lord Derby's Conservative government, which had little inclination to bother overmuch about Irish business. Russell's Whig-Liberals had been more active, and immediately after the horrors of the Famine began to recede well-meant legislation started to flow. The contemporary assumption, surely not too far from the truth, was that three major issues dominated the 'Irish Question'. The first of these was the unequal distribution of land, with extensive estates, often managed on behalf of absentee landlords, accompanied by great numbers of insecure tenants, or those who could not gain access to land by any means. Second came the privileges of the established Anglican Church of Ireland, which relegated the religion of the majority to subordinate status – particularly important since any government relied on the support of the Catholic hierarchy to maintain order. This co-operation was made more difficult by the existence of the third issue, that of constructing a modern educational system. Overarching and sometimes overwhelming all was the imperative of ensuring some control over the men of violence.

Post-Famine Whig attempts at reform began with the Encumbered Estates Act of 1849, which made it easier to sell off mortgaged land. The results were impressive: in eight years as much as a third of all Irish land changed hands, and of the eighty thousand buyers 90 per cent were Irish. It should therefore, as Act succeeded Act in forwarding this movement, have been impossible to blame the ills of Ireland on absentee – preferably English – landlords; but that did not stop the worn excuses emerging half a century later. The new owners proved no more considerate to their fellow-countrymen than had the absentees they often replaced: anxious to justify their expenditure, the incoming landlords ratcheted up the rate of evictions, many of which were faithfully recorded in both the British and the foreign press. Land policy was appreciated by successive governments as the most fundamental issue, and little progress was made on direct political advances, the most important being an adjustment to the franchise qualifications, which did little for the countrymen but brought many more town-dwellers on to the electoral roll.

After O'Connell's death and the Young Ireland debacle Irish parliamentary unity dissolved. A score or so of militant Liberal Members, the 'Irish Brigade', did well enough in the 1852 elections to provide the nucleus of what might possibly have become an independent party. Unable, however, to agree on tactics, the Irish Brigade floundered, its most prominent representatives bought off by government appointments. No successor to O'Connell, able as the Liberator had been to combine parliamentary organisation with a powerful and well-orchestrated agitation among the populace, appeared for another generation.

Extra-parliamentary pressure was patchy. After reaching a post-Famine peak in 1851, 'agrarian outrages' – a catch-all term including threatening letters and minor riots as well as violence against persons and property – dwindled for eighteen years. In the immediate pre-Famine years 'outrages' had totalled some 2100 annually (1820 in 1851), but between 1854 and 1878 they never exceeded four hundred; the threat of violence remained however a potent influence, and external pressures were mounting as a new movement developed within the Irish diaspora.[5] Contemporary anglophobic expatriates, and many later commentators, referred to the American Irish as though they were in some way united in their religion, depressed urban condition and hatred of 'English' rule. In fact many Americans of Irish extraction were both successful and Protestant, and little interested in Anglo–Irish feuds. Generals Grant, Sheridan, Sherman and 'Stonewall' Jackson had Irish roots; President Andrew Jackson was a devoted enemy of

Britain, but Sam Houston planned cordially with Captain Charles Elliot to preserve Texan independence.

The America-based anti-British campaign that was to flourish for a century and a half, and which has not yet entirely disappeared, began among the New York Irish displaced by famine reinforced, after 1848, by the unreconciled Young Irelanders. All of the rebels had been included in a general pardon issued in 1856, and many of the original principals had gone on to make Imperial careers; Gavan Duffy became Prime Minister of Victoria and a knight, an honour also bestowed on Thomas Davis' collaborator Samuel Ferguson, whilst John Blake Dillon, another of the 1848 activists, had been elected to the Westminster Parliament. Others, headed by James Stephens, Smith O'Brien's lieutenant, the inspiration behind the new organisation the Irish Republican Brotherhood, were irreconcilable but proved, on the whole, to be incompetent plotters. The name of 'Fenians', by which supporters of the American organisation were generally known, was taken from the medieval saga of Fionn MacCumhail, but such warlike endeavours as they mounted were generally inglorious. Anything but practical and without coherent policies, Fenianism relied on a hysterical view of Britain as a Satanic power, combined with a mystic interpretation of Irishness and a belief that an Irish republic was already 'virtually' established in Irish hearts.[6]

The American Civil War had provided many Irish volunteers with experience of war which they burned to use against England. On 31 May 1866 eight hundred 'bold Fenian men' set out to 'emancipate Ireland but also to annihilate England' by invading Canada. There they managed to kill twelve Canadian student volunteers before turning tail. Sixty Fenians were captured before the rest managed to escape, but victory was declared nevertheless: 'Irishmen, a glorious career has opened for you. The Green Flag waved once more in triumph over England's hated emblem.' When a year later the rising that was intended to inaugurate the Republic of Ireland in the Old Country, duly proclaimed on 4 March 1867, broke out, some policemen were captured, but at the only moderately serious skirmishes the rebels fled as soon as the first shots were fired. At Tallagt fourteen police repelled several hundred insurgents; at Drogheda forty police totally routed a thousand men. And at Ballyhurst, near Tipperary, the bold Fenians fled in panic, their American commander shouting, 'To the mountains! To the mountains!' Too late to be of any use, an American ship with five thousand modern rifles and three artillery pieces arrived; the crew were arrested without offering resistance.[7]

Open rebellion having again failed, the Fenians adopted a more effective tactic, which their successors, the various branches of the IRA, have used ever since – that of bringing urban terrorism to the mainland. The first episode was in part accidental, the shooting of a Manchester policeman in an attempt to rescue Fenian prisoners. Although not a deliberate murder, the utmost legal penalty was exacted and three men hanged. It would have been much wiser of the government to have commuted the sentences – all those involved in the rising itself were given at most short spells in prison – but shooting policemen has always been strongly discouraged. The 'Manchester Martyrs' were the first Irishmen to be executed for a crime with political overtones since the death of Robert Emmett, and their deaths caused widespread indignation in Ireland.

It was the second Fenian action that prompted Gladstone's change of heart, which was ultimately to lead to the separation of most of Ireland from the United Kingdom. On 11 December a bomb was exploded against the wall of Clerkenwell prison which killed twelve passers-by and maimed some thirty more.

'My mission is to pacify Ireland'

It would only be just to the memory of William Ewart Gladstone (and suitable retribution for a city that has demolished so many of its own great edifices and statuary) if a large statue of the statesman were to be erected in some prominent part of Dublin. For Gladstone, more than any other individual, was responsible for hammering the necessity to grant self-government to Ireland into the consciousness of the British public and, very nearly, on to the Statute Book.[8]

Gladstone's acknowledgment of the pressing need for a permanent adjustment in the constitutional position had begun as a direct result of the 1867 Fenian terrorism. In an article published that year in the October *Edinburgh Review* he had cogitated, 'What is our arrear in

Ireland? The pregnant word suggests a whole range of painful misgivings, and of a work which if much longer delayed threatens to become impracticable.' After the bomb explosion in Clerkenwell, Gladstone spoke out with great courage and foresight: 'We must not get on the high horse and say we will entertain no questions with regard to the measure of relief until what is called Fenianism is extinguished. No: when you attack social evils, don't attack them in their manifestations, but attack them in their roots and in their causes.' At that time Gladstone was in opposition, but by December 1868 the tables had been turned: he ousted his rival Disraeli, and formed his first government. When the news came Gladstone, who was engaged in his favourite exercise, felling trees on his Hawarden estate, 'looked up, and with deep earnestness in his voice and with great intensity in his face, exclaimed "My mission is to pacify Ireland."'

He was well aware of the obstacles. His radical views about attacking the roots of crime were not shared by most of his fellow countrymen (as his successor in office, Tony Blair, was to discover almost a century and a half later), and he could expect indignant opposition in England to any proposals which might satisfy Irish opinion. His own experience of Ireland was negligible, limited to the information contained in Blue Books; it was to be another ten years before he paid his first and only visit to the country. Nor was there any recognisable interlocutor among the Irish parliamentarians, who remained disorganised after O'Connell's death and the attempts at violence. Some improvement began in May 1870, when MP Isaac Butt founded the Home Government Association, later the Home Rule League. 'Home Rule' was a more constructive slogan than O'Connell's 'Repeal', but was equally capable of diverse interpretations. It could be forced into meaning either a devolved regional government, a kind of super-county-council, or full domestic independence, equivalent to 'responsible' colonial government, by which only defence and foreign policy were excluded from the colonial assemblies' powers. Butt's own suggestion, which he published in 1870, entailed a British federation, with Ireland having its own two-chamber Parliament responsible for all domestic affairs. He went to some pains to insist on the provisional nature of his suggestions; they were, in effect, as O'Connell's cry of 'Repeal' had been, a 'proposal to treat'.

It was indeed an Irish matter which had brought Gladstone to power, after he managed to introduce a Bill to disestablish the Irish Church, which succeeded in bringing down Disraeli's administration. A subsequent election, fought in November 1868 on a platform which specifically included Irish disestablishment, was a decisive victory for reform, with Liberals securing 382 seats and the Conservatives 276. Excluding the Irish votes on both sides, the Liberals had 317 seats and Conservatives 237. It was therefore a decisive mandate for radical changes in Ireland, and the only occasion in the nineteenth century when a majority of *English* votes, excluding those of the Scots, were cast in favour of Irish reforms, which were to begin with the removal of the Church of Ireland's official status.

The Church of Ireland had few friends. Lord Salisbury, the acerbic journalist becoming the rising star among the Conservatives, described it as combining 'in happy proportions, the lowest bigotry of the Scottish Free Church with the laxest view of clerical duty'. As Gladstone himself said, the Irish established Church was 'the token and symbol of ascendancy', and the significance of disestablishment for the future of the Union was well understood on all sides; Cardinal Cullen agreed that the Bill was 'very well adapted to promote the interests of Ireland', and would 'inaugurate an era of peace and prosperity'. Disestablishment brought with it the more painful consequence of disendowment, the confiscation of Church revenues. Tithes, that unpopular tax, had certainly been transferred from tenant to landlord, but the established Church retained a very large income indeed. After making reasonable provisions for both Catholics and Presbyterians, the Irish Church Bill, introduced in March 1869, allowed £6.7 million in compensation to the existing personnel and patrons, leaving nearly £9 million to be spent on Irish development projects. There was much Tory indignation at this 'great national sin', but the election had so clearly indicated the people's will that the House of Lords felt bound to allow the Bill's passage.[9] For the first time since the Reformation, all Churches in Ireland were placed on an equal basis, and what had been a bitterly resented discrimination ended. But other causes for Irish discontent were not so easily allayed.

Gladstone had much greater difficulties with his second Irish measure, the Land Act of 1870, which continued the programme of reform begun by the Encumbered Estates Act. Essentially, it put a restraining hand upon eviction, by requiring compensation for improvements effected by the tenant. Predictably, the Bill met with lively opposition and was much amended. Lord Salisbury was scathing: 'A paternal Parliament ... compensates the Irish to induce them not to shoot their landlords.' However emasculated, the Act established one great principle, that of compensation for non-renewal of a lease. The acceptance of this at once undermined the absolute rights of property, which had been for two centuries central to the British Constitution, and instituted a great difference between the Irish and British law; another sign that the character of the Union was being altered. Its importance was not so much that the new measure was instantly effective – indeed, it was probably irrelevant to the contemporary problems, and a second Act was needed eleven years later – but that, taken with the Church of Ireland's disestablishment, it signified the determination of Gladstone and his supporters to force through a radical redefinition of the relationship between Britain and Ireland.[10]

Altogether less successful was Gladstone's attempt to reform Irish university education. His Bill, introduced early in 1873, was a hodgepodge of incompatible ideas, designed to placate everyone and succeeding in arousing universal derision. The suggestion that university colleges would be banned from teaching philosophy or modern history tore the heart out of higher education, but the Catholic hierarchy, led by the ultramontane Cardinal Paul Cullen, now entrenched behind the anti-intellectual barriers raised by the 1870 Vatican Council, was staunch against any such dangerously stimulating teachings. In the House of Commons vote on 12 March, forty-three Liberals voted against their own government, an ominous sign of the resistance to Gladstone's measures from his own party.[11]

The Prime Minister's second difficulty, the lack of any organised Irish political party with whom negotiations might be held, began to move towards a solution. After the Electoral Reform Act of 1867 all male householders were given the vote, and in 1872 voting by secret ballot was initiated. At the election of January 1874 these modest steps towards democracy helped Isaac Butt's Home Rule candidates to win fifty-nine of the 105 Irish seats. The election however cost Gladstone his first period of government, for his reforms had so affronted many of his natural supporters in England that the Liberals slumped from 372 parliamentary seats to 244.

Between February 1874 and April 1880 the Conservative government was much concerned with foreign affairs, but paid little attention to Irish until these were forced upon them, and forced with increasing vigour after April 1875, when young Charles Stewart Parnell was elected to Westminster by the county of Meath. To all appearances Parnell was a typical Ascendancy figure, with generations of Protestant politicians in his ancestry. Great-grandfather Sir John had been Chancellor of the Irish Exchequer in the Grattan Parliament; grandfather William's work, *An Historical Apology for Irish Catholics*, had been eulogised by Sydney Smith: 'We are truly glad to agree so entirely with Mr Parnell . . . we admire his way of thinking; and most cordially recommend his work'; great-uncle Henry, member of both Grattan's and Westminster Parliaments between 1797 and 1842, had been a consistent advocate of Catholic emancipation and one of Lord Grey's ministers. A lieutenant in the militia at the age of twenty, undergraduate at Magdalene College, Cambridge, a useful cricketer and heir to a rich estate in Wicklow, Charles Stewart might have been expected to follow in these somewhat unadventurous liberal traditions; but there was a hard streak in the young man which responded to the changing conditions in Ireland. Temperamentally an heir to the duelling tradition of his country, Parnell's Cambridge career was terminated after his rustication for a brawl. His early interest in politics had been modest, but it was as natural a progression for him to take a seat in the House of Commons as it had been for him to become High Sheriff of his county. What was perhaps unusual was his decision to stand as a Home Rule candidate, although given the Parnell family tradition of support for Irish parliamentary independence and Catholic emancipation this was hardly surprising.[12]

It did not take long for the young Member to take the initiative. Butt's annual presentation of Home Rule Bills – which did not amount to much beyond a demand that the subject be investigated – were clearly never going to amount to anything in a House of Commons dominated by Conservatives. The Home Rule League was becoming increasingly agitated as its Fenian members, angry at the failure of parliamentary initiatives, pressed for more militancy. In the Irish

countryside the limitations of Gladstone's 1870 Land Act were demonstrated as evictions continued, exacerbated by a serious agricultural
depression, in which poor harvests were joined by increasing international competition. With improved mechanisation and cheaper rail
and sea transport, American wheat could be imported very much
cheaper than home-grown cereals could be sold. In Ireland poor harvests and diminishing yields caused the Registrar General to anticipate
an 'increase of poverty and distress' for 1880 following the worst year
in an unsettled decade. Wheat sales collapsed from £1,481,000 in 1871
to £899,000 in 1879; potatoes, still the staple food of many, slumped
from 2,794,000 tons with a value of £8,381,000 in 1871 to 1,114,000 tons,
representing £3,341,000, in 1879. The pig population, another index of
low-income well-being, declined from 1,621,423 to 1,012,000 during the
same period. Evictions followed a similar pattern. In the relatively
good years between 1874 and 1877 there had been no more than five
hundred; by 1880 there were over two thousand.[13]

Parnell's temperament, aggressive and supercilious, did not suit him
to be a follower of the amiable Butt, who was by then both in difficult
personal circumstances and a devoted follower of House of Commons
traditions. With the assistance of Joseph Biggar, MP for Cavan, Parnell,
brimming with generations of Ascendancy disdain for English habits
(probably increased by the anglophobia of his American mother and
his unsuccessful Cambridge career), put into effect an almost unprecedented display of obstructions and filibustering. It was not quite the
first attempt at legislation through disruption (Samuel Plimsoll, hammering through his controls of shipping, had resorted to some similarly
scandalous tactics in 1875), but the Irish Member's dogged determination was something alarmingly new. Supported by the hard core of
the Home Rule party Parnell succeeded in making parliamentary life
nearly impossible. The influx of Irish MPs, prepared to flout all conventions, evincing no interest in any subject other than Irish grievances,
was enough to bring the system to a halt. Even though Parnell rarely
commanded a majority even of Irish Members, the 'Parnellites' were
able to exercise disproportionate disruptive power.

Parliamentary pressure would have been less effective had not the
Irish Members also been able to rely upon threats of organised disorder
in the countryside. In a reflection of O'Connell's parallel policies of

synchronous constitutional effort combined with extra-parliamentary agitation, Parnell was able to deploy from October 1879 the National Land League of Ireland. This was the inspiration of Michael Davitt, the most admirable of Irish nationalists, whose love of Ireland was not tainted by the mechanical hatred of England displayed by many Fenians. Sentenced to fifteen years' penal servitude, of which he served seven, for collecting arms, Davitt's patriotic credentials were impeccable. Combining as it did so wide a spectrum of Irish nationalist opinion, the League was able to make its policy of rent-reduction and peasant ownership, highlighted by some well-publicised evictions, into a powerful weapon. As O'Connell had been, Parnell proved to be expert in combining adherence with the principle of 'moral', i.e. constitutional, pressure with 'physical' force – which was officially resistance to evictions except at the point of the bayonet, but which the Fenians, within and without the League, hoped might be simple terrorism. Sitting uncomfortably on the fence, Parnell contrived to give the impression to his Irish supporters of absolute commitment to independence at any price, while avoiding actually saying so; and when he was tempted into such indiscretion, wriggling out by often unconvincing and sometimes inaccurate denials.[14]

When the Liberals' turn came about again, in April 1880, Gladstone was able to form his second government. On paper the Liberal victory was absolute, with 349 seats against the Tories' 243 and the Home Rulers' sixty. The overall majority should have been impregnable, but Gladstone did not command a united party, certainly not on any questions appertaining to Ireland. British opinion was losing patience with Irish agitation, and the Prime Minister had only half an eye cocked upon Ireland. Foreign affairs, including dismantling Disraeli's European policies and the imminent dangers in South Africa, Afghanistan and Egypt, were pressing. Moreover Gladstone had chosen to take on the demanding post of Chancellor of the Exchequer as well as that of leading the government. And had he not, to his own satisfaction at least, set Ireland on the right road by his previous reforms? Only some fine tuning should be needed, and that, the always cheese-paring Chancellor insisted, at the most moderate expense.

As an experienced House of Commons man, Gladstone made one serious effort to effect a radical solution, by proposing a detailed system of 'devolution', a word that was to regain importance a century later. This might, he hoped, satisfy Irish demands and enable the business of government to continue, 'by devolving upon other bodies a portion of its [the House of Commons'] overwhelming tasks . . . of this devolution, part may be to subordinate and separate authorities'. Whilst this left the way open to much future action in the direction of regional assemblies, Gladstone did not develop the subject but went on to outline a system of 'Grand Committees'. These, he considered, 'may supply the means of partially meeting and satisfying, at least so far as it is legitimate . . . the call for what is styled (*in bonam partem*) "local government" and (*in malam*) "Home Rule"'. With a membership consisting of all parliamentary representatives of the region concerned – say, Ireland or Scotland – plus a limited number of those who expressed an interest and some government nominees, Grand Committees could, with many exclusions and limitations, act as a preparatory research and legislative body. One great merit would be that regional interests (Gladstone would not have admitted the idea of separate nations) could be adequately considered without derogating from the supreme authority of the Crown in Parliament, or involving demarcation disputes between different assemblies. This carefully-worked proposal was however so radical an innovation that the Liberal cabinet almost unanimously rejected it. Had it been accepted, much future trouble might have been saved.

Edging as he was towards an acceptance that, in order to satisfy Irish demands, a fundamental constitutional change would be needed, Gladstone concentrated on the immediately possible, a further programme of ameliorative measures.

The Kilmainham Treaty

It was the Compensation for Disturbance Bill which sparked off the greatest indignation. An attempt to answer the Land League's demand for a temporary limitation or suspension of rent, combined with a government-funded Land Purchase Scheme, the June 1880 Bill envisaged a twelve-month period of tenant protection. The principle that a tenant evicted after non-payment of rent could claim compensation from his landlord, although under tightly restricted conditions, did indeed constitute a radical diminution of landlords' rights. The law would so change the terms of previous contracts that if one party evaded its obligations 'the legislature would shield it from the consequences which in every civilized society result from a breach of contract'. Gladstone argued that the pressing need 'to keep the people from starvation' made it 'impossible to apply without qualification of some kind the ordinary rules of property'.

Such 'qualifications' had long since been imposed upon industrialists, subject to Factory Acts since 1833, passed with the consent of both parties; but landlords deployed much heavier muscle than factory owners. Trade brought only money, but the ownership of land conferred social prestige and political influence. Richard Cobden, John Bright (Chancellor of the Duchy of Lancaster) and the young Lord Mayor of Birmingham, Joseph Chamberlain (President of the Board of Trade), were the only tradespersons or industrialists to have gained political influence, whilst Gladstone's Liberal cabinet contained such territorial magnates and expectant heirs as the Duke of Argyll, Lord Lansdowne (who resigned on this issue), Lord Hartington, Lord Kimberley, Lord Ripon and Lord Spencer. Such great landowners were understandably perturbed at the thought that Irish solutions might be applied to Scotland or England. The Bill scraped through the House of Commons, with twenty Liberals joining the opposition and fifty abstaining, but was decisively rejected in the House of Lords by 282 votes to fifty-one.

The action of the peers – mostly Conservative – signalled the beginning of a determined resistance to constitutional reforms that was only to be overcome a generation later by the persistence of Asquith's Liberal government. Immediately after the Lords' rejection of the Compensation Bill Gladstone was left with little alternative other than to accompany a thorough revision of his former Land Act with 'Coercion' Bills, tough emergency legislation which might stabilise Irish unrest and comfort his restless right-wingers. In spite of Davitt's endeavours to rely upon the pressure of public opinion some Land Leaguers resorted to atrocious violence: in the first four months of 1881 there had been 1177 'outrages'; a year later the comparable figure was 1879.[15] The two Coercion Bills were strenuously opposed by Irish opinion and the Irish

Members, and by not a few of the English newspapers. Newcastle, Manchester and south Wales came out against coercion, while Birmingham, Liverpool and Scotland were all in favour; but without the carrot of coercion the House of Commons would never have passed the 1881 Land Act. As it was it took all Gladstone's parliamentary experience, fifty-five sittings, and the reluctant acquiescence of the House of Lords, purchased only at the cost of some damaging amendments, to pilot the Bill through the House.

The new Land Act did deliver most of the demands made by the Land League. Popularly known as the 'Three Fs' (Fair Rent, Fixity of Tenure and Free Sales), it laid the foundation for an Ireland of peasant proprietors supplanting a nation of landlords. Land ownership had, as the Conservatives had prophesied, been made so unattractive that a campaign developed to press for a state-funded scheme of land purchase. One unhappy landowner, Lord Kenmare, complained to the Queen's secretary Sir Henry Ponsonby on 10 April 1880: 'I cannot live or keep my family at my only home – I cannot sell my lands – I cannot borrow to help me [out] . . . I am marked out to receive no rent, while the Land Leaguer police are watching the Banks too closely to allow my tenants to pay in secret' – and added that several of them had been shot.[16] It would be reasonable to say that the Land Act killed the Land League, but it also marked the terminal decline of Ascendancy landlords, and with them the passing of an era: but Irish demands were merely diverted into other channels.

One of the casualties of the Land Bill had been Parnell himself, who had offered many hostages to fortune in the shape of inflammatory speeches. One in particular, in which he described Gladstone as the 'masquerading knight-errant, this pretending champion of the rights of every nation except the Irish nation', ensured that he would fall under the ban of the Emergency Acts. Accordingly on 13 October the Irish leader found himself incarcerated, not uncomfortably, in Kilmainham gaol.

It was a dire miscalculation on the government's part. Parnell himself predicted that he would be replaced by 'Captain Moonlight'. Certainly rural violence increased, and it was found advisable to reach an accommodation between the government and Parnell, resulting in the 'Kilmainham Treaty', by which Parnell undertook 'to co-operate cordially for the future with the Liberal party in forwarding Liberal principles and measures of general reform'. Parnell and many of his supporters were therefore released on 2 May: the Queen was scandalised, and took her Prime Minister severely to task, expressing herself *greatly surprised* to see *in* the newspapers that Mr Parnell has been *let out*'. Four days later a spectacular act of terrorism was perpetrated in Dublin.

Parnell's acquiescence in the government's conditions certainly stimulated some Fenians to revert to assassinations, but the murder on 6 May 1882 of Lord Frederick Cavendish, Gladstone's nephew-in-law, rocked both Britain and Ireland. Lord Frederick had just been appointed Chief Secretary for Ireland, and was killed together with his Under-Secretary while walking in Phoenix Park. It was a particularly brutal killing – both men were slashed to death with foot-long amputation knives – and Parnell was horrified. His mistress Katherine O'Shea recorded that on seeing the news he went rigid and 'crushed her hand, so hard that her rings cut into her fingers. His face was ashen.' He immediately offered his resignation to the Prime Minister, which was however refused, Gladstone stating that he was 'deeply sensible of the honourable motive by which it has been prompted'.[17]

The reaction both in Britain and Ireland was equally one of horror: Davitt and John Dillon published a 'Manifesto' protesting at a 'cowardly and unprovoked assassination' which had 'stained the name' of their country. Anti-Irish riots spread in England, and a new Coercion Bill was immediately introduced. But the shockwaves caused by atrocities are quickly dispersed, and Gladstone refused to be diverted from his mission, pressing ahead with another Bill to settle Irish rent arrears from the surplus revenues of the now disestablished Church of Ireland. In spite of Lord Salisbury's angry opposition the Bill was finally passed through the House of Lords. It was to be the last of Gladstone's reform efforts to be carried through in that reactionary assembly.

Isaac Butt's original proposals had left the nature of Home Rule open for discussion, which duly developed. It was Joseph Chamberlain, whose reputation had been forged in the municipal affairs of Birmingham, who made the next proposal, one for regional councils. Each historic Irish province could have its own council, responsible for education, Poor Law and public health, and the administration of the new Land Act, thus neatly disposing of the topics which had caused most heart-searching in Westminster. That suggestion was made on 7 April 1882. Two years later Chamberlain proposed a refinement, still along the lines of a municipalisation but on a much wider scale. There would be county boards, along English lines, which could also act as an electoral college for a Central Board, which would have all those earlier provincial powers, plus the ability to levy taxation for public purposes and – somewhat surprisingly – police powers. In spite of Gladstone's support, and that of the Irish hierarchy, the scheme failed to commend itself to the Liberal cabinet. In that body the division between the Whigs – essentially all those ministers sitting in the Lords – and the Radicals, Chamberlain and Charles Dilke, was deepening.[18]

On a different matter Chamberlain was triumphant. The Chamberlain of the early eighties was a radical capable of startling the country 'with a demagogic and class war note never heard before from a minister of the Crown'.[19] He now insisted that the franchise must be extended to include the urban working class, his own supporters, and forced his views on some reluctant colleagues. The Representation of the People Act, passed in December 1884, transformed the political landscape. Each constituency was to be, as far as possible, equal in number of votes – 'one vote, one value' – and some two million new voters were accorded the franchise; of these half a million were in Ireland, where the electorate more than trebled from 222,000 to 738,000. The first election to be held under the new franchise would therefore reflect the opinion of the nation much more accurately than had previous contests.[20]

But before this happened the Liberal government was defeated, on 8 June 1885, by a combination of Tory and Irish MPs, and accordingly resigned. For the next seven months Lord Salisbury was in charge, and the Liberals had to decide what strategy could be adopted in order to ensure that the decisive Irish MPs would remain faithful to the Kilmainham Treaty. Yet if Gladstone could not persuade his colleagues to pass the relatively uncontroversial Central Committee Bill, what hope was there for persuading them to back a much more radical Home Rule measure, which was the only thing that might satisfy the Parnellites?

Gladstone played his cards close to his chest, hoping that Lord

Salisbury might solve his problem for him through the intermediary of the newly appointed Conservative Lord Lieutenant, Lord Carnarvon. 'Twitters' Carnarvon, pleasant, intelligent, but lacking bottom, and given to resigning at awkward moments, had secret talks with Parnell and his lieutenant Justin McCarthy at which another idea was discussed. This was to allow Ireland self-government analogous to that of a large colony, such as Canada. Under such a constitution an Irish executive would be responsible to an elected assembly for all domestic affairs, leaving only foreign and international affairs, and any items which might oppress minorities (French in Canada, blacks in South Africa and Protestants in Ireland), to the Westminster Parliament.

Lord Salisbury however had not the smallest intention of allowing any such measure, his use of Carnarvon being merely a cynical move to ensure that Parnell would not support the Liberals at the forthcoming general election. At the election held in November 1885 Liberals gained 335 seats and the Tories 249, a majority of eighty-six – with Parnell commanding another eighty-six votes. Horrified at the prospect of Gladstone resuming office, Queen Victoria went to the very edge of constitutional propriety on 20 December in having her lady-in-waiting, the Marchioness of Ely, transmit a letter to two of the Liberal waverers, Forster and Goschen:

> Let me urge and implore you by *all* the sense of honour you
> so strongly possess, by your devotion and love for our own
> dear, great country, to do *all* you can to gather around you
> all the moderate Liberals, who indeed ought to be called 'Con-
> stitutionalists' to prevent Mr Gladstone's recklessly upsetting
> the government, without being able to form a government
> himself.[21]

As leader of the largest party in the House of Commons, Gladstone, despite the Queen's efforts, became Prime Minister for the third time on 3 February 1886. He had made his own position as clear as he ever did (always given to hiding behind smokescreens, he could become almost incomprehensible when it suited him) in an address to his own constituents on 17 September 1885:

> ... the wants of Ireland have to be considered as well as her
> grievances. Down to this hour Ireland has continued greatly

in arrear both of England and of Scotland, with respect to those powers of self-government which associate the people, in act and feeling, with the law, and which lie at the root, as I believe, of political stability, of the harmony of classes, and of national strength. This is a serious evil.[22]

Whatever his electors or colleagues might make of that, it was at least obvious that Mr Gladstone intended to do something significant about Ireland. Exactly what that would be was less clear; even, or especially, to Gladstone himself.

Parnell had provided his own ideas in a memorandum discussed with Gladstone by Mrs O'Shea – an example of that remarkable lady's personal influence. It had the merit of clarity and consistency, providing as it did for a single-chamber Parliament, with Protestant representation proportional to their numbers, to have 'powers to enact laws and make regulations for all the domestic and internal affairs of Ireland'. It would have revenue-raising and executive powers, together with control of the police, 'for the preservation of order and the enforcement of the law'. Subject to Crown approval the Irish Parliament would appoint judges and magistrates.

Parnell dismissed the problem of continued representation at Westminster, which 'might be retained or might be given up. If it be retained the Speaker might have power to decide what questions the Irish members might take part in as Imperial questions, if this limitation were thought desirable.'[23]

'I cannot allow it to be said that a Protestant minority in Ulster . . . is to rule the question at large for Ireland'

It has to be remembered that Gladstone's single visit to Ireland in November 1877 had been spent in friendly country houses, as was his custom in England. Not for the Prime Minister heart-to-heart meetings with Belfast businessmen; there was no token Irish meritocrat such as Bright or John Morley to highlight uncomfortable facts. In so far as

Gladstone ever met the 'people', who became in his mind the final court of appeal, it was when they were presented to him as an audience for one of his famous speeches. Entertained by the Dukes of Marlborough and of Leinster, Lords Fitzwilliam, Powerscourt, de Vesci, Meath and Annerley, he expected to have Irish affairs explained to him; coming from these sources such explanation would have been, to say the least, one-sided. Parnell was not much better. In spite of his raffish Cambridge career he was an Irish landowning gentleman, with the prejudices of his class.

Gladstone had therefore some excuse to be ignorant of the passion with which many in Ulster opposed the idea of Home Rule, but warnings came to him from his own supporters. Both James Bryce, the well-informed historian, and Oscar Browning, the famous Cambridge Liberal don, flashed red warning lights; the Liberal MP Colonel Salis-Schwabe suggested that a separate Belfast Assembly would 'make all the difference' to Ulster's acceptance of Home Rule. In his speech introducing the Bill Gladstone referred to the 'state of opinion in that wealthy, intelligent, and energetic portion of the Irish community which ... predominates in a certain portion of Ulster', but only to brush their views aside, and to treat the threats as 'momentary ebullitions'. Five-sixths of the lawfully chosen Irish representatives had voted for Home Rule, and 'I cannot allow it to be said that a Protestant minority in Ulster, or elsewhere, is to rule the question at large for Ireland.'[24]

The previous year's election had almost extinguished the Liberal Party in Ireland, where the struggle was now between Unionists and Nationalists. Lord Salisbury, of course, had never been in Ireland at all, and rarely evinced any interest in Irish affairs except when forced to do so. Speaking to a Conservative meeting on 15 May 1886 Salisbury comprehensively derided the idea of an Irish nation, and went on to deny any confidence in the Irish people:

> ... you would not confide free representative institutions to the Hottentots, for instance ... This which is called self-government, but which is really government by the majority, works admirably well when it is confided to the people who are of Teutonic race, but it does not work so well when people of other races are called upon to join in it.

Such racist nonsense came strangely from an experienced Foreign Minister who had to deal with such non-Teutons as the Italians, or the French, who might claim rather more success with their 'representative institutions' than could the British.[25]

One prominent Tory lost no time in exploiting Salisbury's claim that Ireland was 'two nations'. Lord Randolph Churchill had spent three years in Ireland between 1877 and 1880 as secretary to his father, the Duke of Marlborough, at that time Lord Lieutenant. While the Home Rule Bill was preparing, Churchill sped to Belfast to reassure Unionists that if the 'dark hour' of Home Rule dawned, there were those 'of position and influence in England who would be willing to cast in their lot with you'. Churchill's famous and prophetic phrase, first uttered at a meeting in Larne, was confirmed in a later letter: 'Ulster will fight, Ulster will be right.' Like many of Churchill's initiatives, his intervention in Ulster was purely cynical, since he made no secret of his contempt for the bourgeois of Belfast.[26]

The division was now sectarian. Some Catholics, including many in the hierarchy, remained suspicious of the Home Rulers. Although Protestants were still among the most prominent Home Rulers – Parnell himself being the obvious example – their numbers were quickly diminishing as attitudes hardened, whilst Ulster Unionists were solidly Protestant, often narrowly so. The riots that tore through Belfast that June may have been started by Catholic navvies expelling a Protestant, but it was Protestant mobs that looted the drink stores and fought the police. With considerable restraint, the police only resorted to firearms when all else failed; but when they did it was not only rioters that suffered. In all, probably fifty people were killed in the course of the worst violence seen in Ireland during the nineteenth century.[27]

With great skill and persistence Gladstone piloted his Bill through the Commons first reading, but fell at the second fence, albeit by a narrow margin, on 8 June. Conceding as it did self-government to an Irish Parliament, with certain matters excluded, including defence and foreign policy, the Bill would have satisfied all but the most intransigent Nationalists. There was however one obvious flaw, in that there was to be no Irish representation at Westminster. No Irish Assembly could have for long agreed to have no say in those 'reserved' subjects which had been withdrawn from their jurisdiction. Gladstone indicated his willingness to reconsider this, but was never given the chance, for the Bill fell at the second reading by 341 votes to 311. The Prime Minister had failed to hold his own party together. Liberals and Parnellites together had 421 votes and the Tories 249, which should have assured a large majority for the Bill, but this could not have been secured for such a radical measure. Devolution and provincial government perhaps might have been accepted, but an assembly with even limited executive control was too much for the Whigs to stomach. With good reason, opponents suspected that a new Irish Parliament would rapidly demand greater independence. Nor had the Ulster question been addressed, or the essential point of Westminster representation. Should this continue, an Irish Assembly would be restricted to essentially local-government status. If it was to end, an Irish government, elected by Irish voters, represented in Dublin by an Irish executive, would inevitably lead towards independence. One hundred and twenty years later the same unsolved dilemma remains.

As the vote had indicated, the Liberal Party divided. Gladstone's 'Liberal Unionist' opponents sided with the Conservatives, leaving Gladstone with a rump of the faithful. The defectors included some of the ablest men in the party – Lord Hartington, former leader during Gladstone's first retirement, G.J. Goschen, the eminent financial states-man, and most importantly Joseph Chamberlain, transformed over the Irish question from radical extremist to Tory fellow-traveller. That division was to keep the Liberal Party out of power, with one short interval, for nearly twenty years. When it revived, under Sir Henry Campbell-Bannerman, in 1906, it was a very different party.[28]

The new House of Commons elected in July 1886 was to be composed of 193 Gladstonians, seventy-six Liberal defectors, following Chamberlain to become Liberal-Unionists, 316 Conservatives, and a steady eighty-five Irish Nationalists. Over the next few years some dissidents returned to the Gladstonian fold, but most became more firmly entrenched with the Conservatives, who, after all, now had jobs and incomes to offer. Irish Nationalists were relegated, by the inexor-able force of parliamentary statistics, to impotence. Combined with their Liberal allies they could muster only 278 votes, fewer than even the Conservative Party on its own, without the Unionist defectors. Ireland had to accept what the Conservative government decided was good for it, which was an initial cold shower of restrictive laws, followed by conciliatory measures, 'killing home rule with kindness'. Arthur Balfour, Lord Salisbury's nephew, was given the opportunity to prove himself as Chief Secretary, which he did to Irish annoyance and Westminster's gratification. Once again, the appeal of extra-parliamentary agitation began to seem attractive, and although Parnell himself was at best lukewarm, John Dillon and William O'Brien designed a 'Plan of Campaign', essentially an organisation of tenants bargaining directly. Often successful, the movement was sometimes accompanied by violence and was regarded with suspicious disfavour by Parnell.

Balfour's brilliant mind was not unduly inhibited by any inconvenient attachment to principles, and his administration of Ireland was marked by more dirty tricks than most. The most notorious of his undercover schemes was one to destroy Parnell, which nearly worked. On 18 April 1887 *The Times* published a sensational and specially presented article on 'Parnellism and Crime', which purported to indicate that Parnell had himself known of the plan to assassinate Lord Frederick Cavendish. Only after a long trial was it proved that the evidence against him was forged, but in the course of the proceedings proof was given that many of his parliamentary colleagues had been involved in illegal operations.[29]

What brought an abrupt end to Parnell's career was an entirely personal matter. On 24 December 1889 his colleague Captain William O'Shea cited Parnell as co-respondent in his divorce plea. Parnell had, indeed, been living with Mrs O'Shea in conditions of some secrecy, and she had borne him three children. The intensity of this relationship and the need to conceal it had made Parnell even more secretive and unapproachable than usual. His roving life was well described as 'a fugitive and complicated affair', in which even his colleagues were sometimes unable to trace their leader. It was not the fact of his having a mistress that was damaging – Gladstone believed that it was no part of his duty as parliamentary leader to form a personal judgment on the moral conduct of any other politician; it was up to the Irish party to deal with their leader. But public opinion was not so tolerant. W.T. Stead, the influential journalist, warned Gladstone that after having tested many opinions, ranging from that of Cardinal Manning to Michael Davitt, Stead would 'most unwillingly' start a campaign against this 'convicted liar and thorough-faced scoundrel' unless Parnell resigned. Given Stead's brilliant record – his *Pall Mall Gazette* had proved its ability to shake governments and change laws – this was equivalent to a sentence of death on Parnell as a public figure.[30]

Inevitably, the Irish parliamentary party could not agree among themselves. The majority, under Justin McCarthy, rejected Parnell, leaving him with only twenty-nine supporters.[31] Parnell refused to resign, and attempted to rally support in Ireland. He failed lamentably, losing the last shreds of political credibility before dying in October 1891. Badly weakened, the Irish party had sacrificed much of the potential power which might have become a reality when the Liberals would be again able to form a government. This duly occurred in July 1892.

The election results gave Gladstone a working majority of forty, but conveyed no mandate to inaugurate Irish Home Rule. Excluding Irish Members, Unionists were in a majority of fifteen; any vote for Home Rule would be therefore against the expressed will of the rest of the United Kingdom. Liberals gathered less than half of the English vote, and not much more (53 per cent) in Scotland. With no fewer than seventy-one English MPs against Home Rule, Liberalism was beginning to be perceived as representing the concerns of the smaller countries rather than those of the English heartland. Ireland returned twenty-three Unionists, seventy-two anti-Parnell Nationalists, led first by Justin McCarthy, succeeded by John Dillon, and only nine who followed Parnell's successor, John Redmond. For the old Prime Minister, Ireland had become almost a monomania. Friends and enemies alike found the Grand Old Man 'half mad', riding pell-mell through all conventions of party management, refusing to discuss his ideas. His achievement in piloting the Bill through a querulous House of Commons was an outstanding parliamentary feat – and Gladstone was then eighty-four years old. The Bill survived its third reading by a vote of 301 to 267, only to be massively rejected – 419 votes to forty-one – by the House of Lords in September 1893.

In the course of the debate the Ulster Unionists had made their resistance plain. Applauded by twelve thousand delegates at an Ulster Unionist convention on 17 June 1892 Thomas Sinclair, Unionist MP, had declaimed:

> We are children of the Revolution of 1688, and cost what it
> may, we will have nothing to do with a Dublin Parliament
> (Loud cheers). If it be ever set up, we shall simply ignore its
> existence (Tremendous cheering).[32]

Colonel Edward Saunderson, Unionist MP for North Armagh,
replied to sceptics, 'before the army of Great Britain is employed to
shoot down the Irish loyalists you must have a British majority at your
back' – which majority was clearly lacking. In the Upper House former
Lord Lieutenant Lord Londonderry justified Unionists in shedding
blood 'to resist the disloyal Catholic yoke'. In early April Balfour, who
two years previously had been Irish Secretary and from whom better
things might have been expected, in an astonishingly irresponsible
outburst, told a Belfast march of eighty thousand loyalists that he
did 'not come here to preach any doctrines of passive obedience or
non-resistance . . . I do not think any rational or sober man will say
that what is justified against a tyrannical King may not under certain
circumstances be justifiable against a tyrannical majority.'

The other great unanswered question was that of Irish representation
at Westminster. Taking the objections to the first Bill into account,
the second had provided for eighty Irish MPs, a number reflecting the
current population, so much smaller a percentage of the UK total than
it had been in 1800. It was proposed that these should be banned
from voting on purely British domestic matters, but the difficulties
of this were so obvious that an amendment had to be passed by which
the rights of Irish Members were not to be restricted in any way.
This was not only illogical but very unpopular in England, although
Scotland and Wales felt, understandably, sympathetic to what might
be seen as a curtain-raiser for their own performance in the devolution
drama.

Bearing in mind the acknowledged lack of an electoral mandate for
Irish Home Rule the Bill was doomed to failure. Gladstone had not
however given up, and was willing to call a general election in order
to challenge the House of Lords; the controversy, he insisted, 'when
once raised, must go forward to an issue'. When he resigned in March
1894 it was however on a different issue, that of naval expenditure.
The Prime Minister, now old enough to be the grandfather of some
of his colleagues, was a revered figure, but one out of touch with their

ambitions and concerns. His successor, Lord Rosebery, speedily killed the prospect of further action on Home Rule until England was 'convinced of its justice and equity'. His lack of enthusiasm was by now shared by the British electorate. Much had been done for the Irish, and more urgent matters were pressing.

'Justice for Scotland means insulting neglect'

Home Rule for Ireland prompted a good deal of both 'me-too' and 'not-here-at-any-price' arguments in Scotland. These were encouraged by Gladstone, who had been persuaded by the young Lord Rosebery to stand, in December 1879, for the parliamentary constituency of Midlothian. Wisely keeping his definitions vague, Gladstone announced his sympathy for some form of devolution: 'I am friendly to local government. I am friendly to large local privileges ... I desire ... to see Parliament relieved of some portion of its duties.' And whatever arrangements were made, he would 'consent to give to Ireland no principle, nothing that is not upon equal Terms offered to Scotland and to the different portions of the United Kingdom'.[33]

This very sweeping commitment stood in little danger of ever being called upon. The pale shadow of Irish rural agitation that appeared in Scotland was, if not solved, at least sympathetically approached. Compulsory schooling after the 1870 Education Act (which permitted teaching in Gaelic) came expensive; Free Church ministers often encouraged radical views, which contributed to the single most striking demonstration of resistance to central government. Depopulation in the Highlands had increased as sheep-runs were displaced by deer forests. Crofters, the Scottish equivalent of Irish cottiers, demanded similar protection against eviction. In 1882 some Skye crofters refused to surrender their right to graze their beasts on the hill; the government despatched a gunboat, a ridiculous and infuriating measure. Rent refusal became common in what became known in newspaper headlines as the 'Crofters' War'. Following an anodyne Royal Commission report a Crofters' Holding Act of 1886 provided no radical solutions but at least recognised the Highlands as a distinct area, with a special land law and, as in Ireland, a Congested Districts Board to encourage development. But *ad hoc* Royal Commissions were no substitute for an institutional Scottish presence in the machinery of government.

As a first indication of his intentions Gladstone in 1881 offered Lord Rosebery the humble post of Under-Secretary at the Home Office with responsibility for Scottish affairs. This was much less than the influential, able and very rich young peer might expect, especially since Rosebery was temperamentally only semi-attached to political life, sensibly preferring racing or sailing, and apt to take off for foreign parts when discontented; but Rosebery stuck it for two years before resigning.[34] Had not Gladstone promised him as far back as 1871 that if Home Rule was established in Ireland, 'you will be just as well entitled to it in Scotland', and had thrown in Wales for good measure? Yet when the first Irish Home Rule Bill was introduced there was no suggestion that anything similar was proposed for Scotland. Rosebery expostulated: 'Justice for Ireland means everything is done for her even to the payment of her natives' debts. Justice for Scotland means insulting neglect. I leave for Scotland next week with the view of blowing up a prison or shooting a policeman.'[35] A Scottish Home Rule Association was accordingly formed in 1888 by Liberal MPs and sympathisers, who included the learned and immensely rich Marquis of Bute. A woolly and ineffective body, the SHRA managed in the 1890s to introduce a number of Home Rule Bills, none of which was taken at all seriously, although supported by a majority of Scottish MPs. At least Scots had the satisfaction of seeing Home Rule for Scotland adopted by the Liberal National Conference in 1888, tempered by the suggestion of a federal state with 'home rule legislatures in Scotland, England, Ireland and Wales'.[36]

As in the rest of the United Kingdom, the November 1885 elections, held on the new extended franchise, shifted the balance of power. Gladstone's preoccupation with Irish Home Rule had not gone down well in Scotland. Hardline Protestants were more common in the west of Scotland than anywhere in England: many were convinced that 'Home Rule' meant 'Rome Rule', and were attracted by the breakaway Liberal-Unionists. Although Liberalism remained influential, Gladstone's hitherto unquestionable supremacy in Scotland was never restored.

It was Salisbury who took the first tentative step to meeting Scottish objections by appointing the Duke of Richmond and Gordon as Scottish Secretary in August 1885, a choice whose essential frivolity was underlined by Lord Salisbury when he wrote to the Duke that he was 'pointed out by nature to be the man ... It really is a matter where the effluence of two dukedoms and the best Salmon river in Scotland will go a long way.' In one area, that of education, the new department began useful work, but it was many years before the post became anything much more than a convenient cabinet makeweight, a successor to that useful sinecure the Mastership of the Buckhounds. After Richmond there were seven appointments within seven years, and it was not until the appointment of John Sinclair in the 1906 Campbell-Bannerman government that the post began to enjoy some prestige and to exercise some power.

The creation of a separate Scottish Department did something to increase administrative effectiveness but nothing to meet the very valid criticism that not enough parliamentary time was devoted to Scottish affairs – a mere six hours annually. So meagre an allowance resulted either in Scottish Bills making an abnormally long passage through the legislative system – that on reform of lower court procedures took nine years to complete its journey – or having Scottish interests ignored. Arguments were also advanced that Scotland contributed more than its fair share to Imperial expenditure – an overpayment of £1.1 million was calculated – and received many fewer benefits. Why, for example, was there no naval dockyard in the country? And why were Scottish museums and scientific work so less well-funded than those in London (although that argument held good for all other regions in England and Wales)? Over all these practical objections was one of tone and attitude. Although the Empire, of which all were mightily proud, might be known to the world as the British Empire, the English kept appropriating the institution. Lord Salisbury was the worst offender (with so great a majority of Scottish seats Liberals were much less likely to ignore Scottish sensitivities), habitually using 'England' to signify 'Great Britain'. With Salisbury it was a matter of principle to insist that, just as 'mankind' embraces 'women', so must 'England' be taken to include 'Scotland'; but most certainly not Ireland. So majestic a misunderstanding, not to say falsification, of the facts of history and practice is breathtaking, but was carried further when in

1901 the new King took the title of Edward VII. The question had not been raised since 1707, since there had been no British or Scottish monarchs apart from the Georges and Victoria, and the coronation of William IV, who would have been William III of Scotland, passed unnoticed; but Edward VII should properly have been entitled Edward VII of England and I of Scotland. When his great-granddaughter Elizabeth succeeded in 1953 the omission was rectified, an indication of how far recognition of Scottish nationality had clarified.[37]

Although Scots were rightly indignant over such slights, there was little obvious desire for Scottish independence. Scots were staunch defenders of the integrity of the Empire, in which many had continued to do well, in spite of the examination system instituted after 1852, which favoured graduates from English universities (a facility in Greek verse, one of the more important requirements for success in public offices, not being much valued in Scotland). Nearly one-third of all colonial governors before the Second World War were Scots: Donald Currie of the Union Castle line and William Mackinnon of the British East African Company continued the tradition of the East India nabobs, and four of the seven Prime Ministers between 1868 and 1915 were (if one includes Gladstone) Scots. On the contrary, Scottish Home Rulers argued that Imperial unity was best served by domestic devolution. A Scottish Parliament, the Scottish Home Rule Association, formed in 1886, claimed, would 'maintain the integrity of the Empire'.[38]

More energy was injected into the Home Rule movement by the Young Scots Society, another Liberal group angered by the imperialism implicit in the Boer War; one of their meetings, addressed by the pro-Afrikaner Prime Minister of the Cape Colony, John X. Merriman, was disrupted by objectors. The Young Scots addressed themselves to pushing Scottish interests on to the Liberal agenda: 'New Scottish legislation is sorely needed on such subjects as education, land, liquor, Church and state, on which we have our own systems totally different from those of England. On these questions, Scottish opinion is far ahead of England.' One startling omission from this list, and an indicator of why Home Rule for Scotland was at the time an irrelevance, was any mention of an industrial and social programme. Verbiage about solidarity was proffered instead: 'A country resting on a starved and ignorant proletariat must inevitably confess its impotency and become a despotism ... it is among the elect of our working class and those in intimate relationship with them that we can still happily find the brawn and heart of our nation.' It was only from the existing leaders of the Liberals that social reforms would come, which could permanently affect all parts of the United Kingdom.[39]

Drink and divinity

Welsh interests had never been adequately represented at Westminster, it having been generally assumed, not altogether unreasonably, that what was suitable for England must necessarily apply to Wales. Scotland's individuality was more widely acknowledged: the Queen's infatuation with the Highlands, personified in her favourite John Brown, the novels of Sir Walter and the flow of Prime Ministers either being Scots themselves or representing Scottish constituencies, had ensured that Scotland remained prominent. Wales had few of these advantages: its own culture and traditions, protected by the inaccessibility of language, were never popularised as had been those of Scotland, and no writers sparked outsiders' imagination as did those of Scotland and Ireland. To mid-nineteenth-century England Wales was little more than an entertaining and accessible tourist destination.[40]

Wales, however, came in for some of Gladstone's attention; he was, after all, living on the fringes of the principality at Hawarden, and had married into a famous Welsh family. The Liberal Welsh MP for Montgomery, Stuart Rendel, a close friend of Gladstone's, energetically pushed Welsh interests within the Liberal Party. Rendel insisted that Welsh Liberals must safeguard their autonomy: 'Wales must not fall into the hands of the Central Association here in London ... We cannot allow our teeth to be drawn and our nails pared.' He got his chance to assert Welsh influence in 1888 when he became Chairman of the Welsh parliamentary party. Unlike the Irish equivalent, the Welsh caucus had no single driving aim. Its members were 'a scattered band, having no principles of cohesion', who differed on such important Welsh topics as disestablishment and devolution; one Bill introduced in 1891 failed partly because the sponsor, Alfred Thomas, was regarded by his colleagues as 'an aged pantaloon'. As Chairman, Rendel succeeded in establishing at least the idea that Welsh interests were specific, and should not automatically be judged at Westminster to be synonymous with those of England. One Welsh Member, Thomas Ellis, became Liberal Chief Whip at an early age, and quickly became recognised as a potential high-flyer. During Gladstone's visit to Wales in September 1892 the Prime Minister met another promising young Member when he was welcomed to Caernarvon by the constituency Liberal MP, David Lloyd George. Gladstone listened patiently to Lloyd George's speech, but would rather have explored the castle.[41]

Welsh Liberals agreed only reluctantly to fall in behind Gladstone on the Irish question, but, marshalled by Rendel, fall in they eventually did. Twenty-two Welsh Liberals voted for the 1886 Home Rule Bill, and seven against, but in the subsequent general election, in which the Gladstonian Liberals did so badly, with only 193 British seats, Wales remained loyal, with the breakaway Unionists scoring only one Welsh victory. Not that there was much pan-Celtic solidarity shown by Wales, although discontent with British governments certainly existed; whereas the violence of the Rebecca protests was matched by similar outbreaks in England, Welsh complaints inevitably had a racial tinge. Welsh protestors were not, as were the Chartists, or the demonstrators in Trafalgar Square on 'Bloody Sunday' in November 1887, angry with a government, but with an *English* government. In extreme cases, such as that of the irascible Reverend Michael Daniel Jones, the Patagonian pioneer, convinced that the Welsh were an oppressed nation, this was expressed in terms as anti-English as any that might be heard in Ireland.

Imperial appointments did not fall to Welshmen as frequently as to Scots, but there is not much evidence that they were sought. Welsh merchants and bankers – David Jones is still the great name in Australian shopkeeping – got their share of business, but opportunities at home were not scarce. If Scottish shipbuilders provided so great a proportion of the world's shipping – two-thirds of the British total between 1851 and 1870 – it was Welsh coal that fed the boilers, the bituminous steam coal from Glamorgan and the high-quality Swansea anthracite. Entrepreneurs like David Davies and D.A. Thomas (later Lord Rhondda) were able to make huge fortunes from coal and its associated industries; the Marquis of Bute amassed millions from his mineral resources and from Cardiff Docks; John Cory of Cardiff made enough from coalmining and distribution to give away £50,000 annually to charities. More modestly, the workers shared in Welsh prosperity: miners were the aristocrats of labour and, given the still powerful Welsh tradition of Nonconformist prudence, were able to raise families in moderate comfort.

But it was a fragile prosperity, unsupported by strong trades unions and reliant on traditions of local mutual assistance. Industrial discontent followed a similar pattern in both Wales and England, where conditions were very much the same, but with one important difference. Clashes between Tyneside miners or steelworkers were straightforward conflicts of interest between masters and men, whereas in Wales they could assume nationalistic overtones. The 'Red Dragon revolt' of Welsh steelworkers and miners in 1874 began as a simple internal disagreement, but was elevated by some into a struggle for 'the independence of Wales ... and the elevation of the Workers of Wales'.[42]

Prosperity was concentrated in south Wales, which became, in an odd inversion, a sort of Welsh Ulster. Nationalism flourished in north and central Wales, in a fashion that was not greatly appreciated in the industrialised south. Cymru Fydd – the Wales to Be – started life in London in 1886, and was given shape by Tom Ellis and the ardent nationalist Beriah Gwynfe Evans, with the enthusiastic support of the young David Lloyd George. Full of virtuous notions of a new nationhood 'in which the history, traditions, social culture, literature, and political institutions of [the] people would be organically linked' in a land of collective co-operation, Cymru Fydd was the voice of the north, and did not appeal to the majority of Welshmen. After an unedifying quarrel in January 1896 'the domination of Welsh ideas' from 'the isolated county of Caernarvon' was angrily rejected. Welsh nationalism may have been set back, but the demand for a greater say in the Welsh administration continued to be strong.[43]

To this demand at any rate Liberal governments felt obliged to pay some little attention. Their proposals for devolution amounted to little more than a Welsh Council to be formed by the local authorities and Welsh MPs, but even this modest suggestion perished of inanition. The Liberals' greatest achievement was the transformation of Welsh education. An investigation by Lord Aberdare reported in 1881 that only some 4500 children in Wales received any adequate secondary education, and that 'most Welsh children had no educational opportunity at all, above the most elementary level'. Educational reform was pushed through with astonishing celerity. Within three years of the Intermediate Education Act of 1889 there were ninety-five new 'county' schools in Wales, providing 'a network of opportunity and instruction superior to that of England'. Education became a passion for Welsh families, a means of liberation. By the 1950s the proportion of Welsh children in grammar schools was twice that in England; in Cardigan more than 60 per cent of students went on to higher education. From 1884 they had access to three university colleges at Cardiff, Bangor and Aberystwyth, all different in character but from 1893 united in the University of Wales. A century later the university had added schools of medicine and of science and technology at Cardiff, together with another large university college at Swansea and a little liberal arts college at Lampeter. The existence of a Welsh national university has constantly stimulated a sense of Welsh identity, but the constituent colleges both reflect and accentuate regional differences. Those at Cardiff and Swansea are mainstream institutions, part of the international university world, which the others are not. It is also interesting that both the President and the leader of Plaid Cymru, Gwynfor Evans and Dafydd Wigley, together with the first two Welsh Assembly First Secretaries, Alun Michael and Rhodri Morgan, went to English universities.[44]

What might have been a contentious issue, the poverty and insecurity of farming tenants, was defused by a Royal Commission appointed by Gladstone in 1892. It reported in 1896, to a Conservative government which disregarded its recommendations, but the members had done their duty by earnest prevarication, and problems of Welsh land tenure ceased to press. Another source of fretfulness, the anti-tithe movement, combined popular resentment of landlordism with Calvinist distaste for the established Church, but the 'Welsh Tithe War' was a restrained and even friendly confrontation, finally settled in 1891 by Lord Salisbury's adoption of the Gladstonian solution of passing responsibility from tenant to landlord. The religious issue that then remained to be settled was the future of the established Church in Wales, which became the 'central passion of the Welsh people'.[45]

At a distance the issue of Welsh disestablishment seems fragile enough. The Welsh dioceses of the Church of England had not served the people badly. Bishops were selected for their knowledge of Welsh, and parish clergy had been leaders in popular education and in maintaining Welsh traditions; but Welsh Nonconformists were vociferous and powerful. As in Ireland, although to a lesser degree, the Anglican Church in Wales represented an alien creed, supported by a minority of Welsh gentry. Its existence as an official, state-supported institution seemed to insist on English values in preference to those of Wales, and aroused extraordinary vehemence: 'Compromise was regarded as unthinkable, and vested with a biblical rhetoric that made it seem even sacrilegious.' In such an atmosphere any demands for devolution were swept aside.[46] The state-funded denominational schools were another constant source of irritation to Nonconformists, which delayed improvement in this sector for many years. Peculiarly Welsh, too, was the agitation for restrictive public-house licensing laws. In a society where one alcohol addict could force a family from reasonable affluence into misery, a fervent insistence on 'temperance' was eminently justified, and became along with disestablishment and Church schools a central factor in Welsh politics.

CHAPTER 11

1893–1950

The last of the Liberals

AFTER THE DEFEAT of Gladstone's second Irish Bill it was thirteen years before another Liberal government came to power. The United Kingdom had changed much during the period of Conservative rule between 1886 and 1892 and 1895 to 1906. Lord Salisbury's policy of 'killing Home Rule by kindness', by a 'grandfatherly government', intended to last for twenty years, had nearly run its course, and had seen considerable successes. Administered with a heavy dose of nepotism by the suave Arthur Balfour, Salisbury's nephew, from 1887, by Gerald Balfour, Arthur's brother, between 1895 and 1900, and thereafter by George Wyndham, previously Arthur's Private Secretary, 'kindness' was mixed with a stiff programme of repression which earned the Chief Secretary, on the whole unjustly, the appellation of 'Bloody Balfour'. The Land Acts of 1891, 1896 and 1903, taken together constituted a veritable Irish revolution, unparalleled in a non-communist society. Landlords were tendered offers that they could not refuse – to sell their estates to tenants and inevitably therefore also to speculators who bought from the tenants – and an element of compulsion was added in 1909 to sweep up those who had hung on to their lands. Massive state aid at low rates was given to buyers, and landlords were compensated out of public funds. By 1920, when the mechanics of a transfer of power to the anticipated Irish government began to be implemented, eleven million acres of Irish land had changed hands, at a cost of £84 million. Forcible evictions and rural violence were things of the past. Had, as the advocates of 'Repeal' demanded, Ireland become self-governing and had to rely on its own funds, so extensive a programme would have been nearly impossible.

In addition to this massive social movement the new Congested

Districts Board, financed originally from the proceeds of disestablishment, carried through an imaginative development programme. A modern system of local government with representative bodies elected on a democratic franchise – even including women – was introduced in 1898, when it quickly became dominated (Ulster always excepted) by Catholics and nationalists. A Royal Commission reported that Ireland had been over-taxed, a consistent Nationalist complaint, and remedies were proposed. Sir Horace Plunkett's agricultural co-operative movement developed into the Department of Agriculture and substantially improved a hitherto often backward industry. Compared to any other area of the United Kingdom, Ireland was receiving clearly favoured treatment – and that from a Conservative government.

When Balfour succeeded his uncle as Conservative Prime Minister in 1901 all looked set for a real prospect of reconciliation as grievances were settled and economic conditions improved. In 1904 the Irish Reform Association, formed by some of the largest remaining landlords, proposed a modified form of Home Rule. Official support to these suggestions was offered by the Irish Permanent Under-Secretary Sir Anthony MacDonnell, a Liberal by conviction and an advocate of Home Rule. This co-operation was a step too far, and when it was revealed in the House of Commons Wyndham was forced to resign; but that was in March 1905, and by then the Conservative government was crumbling.

The unprecedented expense of the Boer War (1899–1902) and its thoroughly unsatisfactory conduct, exacerbated by a particularly exciting scandal about Chinese workers in South African mines, featuring slavery, sodomy and flogging, had exhausted the public's patience with the Conservatives, but it was a serious split on trade policy – protection vs. free trade – that pushed Balfour to the point of resignation in December 1905.

The general election of January 1906 was one of the most dramatic in the century, equalled only by those of 1945 and 1997. A Conservative Party which had, since the defection to them of the Unionists, looked impregnable, crumbled at the polls. The new Liberal government could call on a solid majority of eighty-four seats over all comers, and a massive majority of Home Rule supporters – 377 Liberals, fifty-three from the new Labour Party, now a power in the land, and eighty-three

Irish Nationalists. The Irishmen were now for the most part united under the leadership of John Redmond, an experienced and honourable parliamentarian and, like Parnell, a substantial landowner. Once again, hopes for a parliamentary solution were revived. Without Parnell's leadership this had looked a lost cause, but from 1900 Redmond succeeded in harnessing the common Irish opposition to the South African war in the cause of unity. The parliamentary Nationalists, however, could not succeed in regaining that delicate balance between parliamentary pressure and outside agitation that had made O'Connell and Parnell so powerful. Redmond's policy of accepting British concessions as steps towards an ideal future, more especially in the Wyndham period, did not endear him to the more radical Irish, who wanted nothing less than independence, and who demanded it now.

Even with the return of the Liberals, little immediate action on Ireland was likely, apart from some modest devolution proposals. English electors were bored with what seemed to be perennial Irish grievances, increasingly apparently unfounded; Scottish and Welsh voters were developing their own programmes of devolution. Radical new social proposals were at the top of the new administration's agenda, pressed by the party's new men, David Lloyd George and Herbert Asquith; and the opposition of the House of Lords to any alteration in the constitutional status, which had so decisively crushed Gladstone's efforts, remained unshaken.

Sensing the mood of their constituents, Liberal candidates played down the Home Rule issue: more Liberal candidates (c.10 per cent) opposed Home Rule than specifically supported it (c.8 per cent), but even though Sir Henry Campbell-Bannerman's overall majority made him independent of the Irish party, the new Prime Minister never attempted to deny his own commitment. Both he and the Secretary for India, John Morley, had been in Gladstone's cabinet during the dramas of twenty years before, and intended to carry through his programme, but both were dependent on the acquiescence of their less enthusiastic colleagues. The first Liberal measure, tentatively presented to the Irish party for their consideration, represented very modest progress indeed – another part-elected Irish Council with limited powers. John Redmond found himself in a similar position to his predecessors: Home Rule – which was by now one of the few Irish issues left, after the reforms of the previous Conservative government, and those even then developing in the Liberal cabinet – could only be obtained by co-operation with the government, but the Irish electorate needed rhetoric, and Redmond was limited in that respect. A parliamentarian bred in the bone, Redmond had succeeded to what was almost a hereditary seat at the age of twenty-five, having already spent five years as his father's parliamentary aide. His speeches were thoughtful and convincing, but could never rouse a rabble.

Posterity, at least in Ireland – and posterity elsewhere is unanimously uninterested in the subject – has been scornful of Redmond, but in fact that brave and persistent statesman worked ceaselessly to persuade the Liberals, his only possible allies, to stick to their promises. In addition to the final achievement of Irish self-government, a great number of preliminary reforms which benefited the new state of Ireland are due to Redmond's patient negotiation.

Herbert Asquith, who succeeded as Prime Minister on Campbell-Bannerman's resignation in 1908, did not share that old Liberal's personal commitment to Gladstone's Home Rule, and had a difficult cabinet to keep in hand. The ornithologist Edward Grey's reserve, the ebullient and inconstant brilliance of Winston Churchill, the energy of that 'goat-footed Celtic Satyr' Lloyd George, and the unflinching Gladstonian morality of John Morley characterised a talented, but uncomfortably diverse team. In debate on 30 March 1908 Asquith announced that, after the failure to agree on the Irish 'Council' measure, as a step towards 'a larger measure of devolution', 'we have exhausted our powers with regard to the problem of Irish government'. A new general election would be needed before a specific mandate could be claimed for a more radical measure.[1]

Redmond could point to many important advances obtained by co-operation with the government: an Evicted Tenants Act provided financial compensation and resettlement, placing a full stop on an old grievance; a Town Tenants Act gave similar security; a Housing Bill led to the provision of thirty thousand new homes; and that old bone of contention, tertiary education was settled. The Irish Universities Bill, 'one of the greatest services to the Irish nation', provided for a triad consisting of a National University, essentially Catholic; Trinity College, old Ascendancy; and Queen's College Belfast, secular but with

Presbyterian overtones. All these excellent measures combined to defuse previous complaints, and even reversed them. Ireland was now well over-represented in Westminster on grounds of population, probably by thirty and perhaps by as many as forty seats; landowners, now most often middle-class and Catholic, were beginning to protest against coddling their tenants. Asquith's Old Age Pension Act benefited Ireland quite disproportionately. By 1910 some 45 per cent of eligible English and 54 per cent of Scottish over-seventies were receiving a pension, compared with an astonishing 98.6 per cent in Ireland. Pressing for even more concessions to that country was not going to be a popular cause in Britain. Another *casus belli* would be needed, and it was a dispute over Lloyd George's 1909 budget that gave Redmond the opportunity to draw the Liberals back to Home Rule.[2]

The new Chancellor's budget added children's allowances, a system of labour exchanges and a Development Commission to Asquith's previous social benefits, all expensive innovations and all to be paid for by increased taxation. Not only social expenditure, but the now urgent need, in view of increasing threats from Germany, to finance re-armament, especially the 'Dreadnought' building programme of modern capital ships, demanded extraordinary funding measures. Extra levies were put on drink and tobacco, death duties were raised, motor taxation initiated, and for the first time 'super-tax' was introduced on annual incomes over £3000. Amid a tremendous outcry from the opposition, the budget was passed by 379 votes to 149, only to be rejected in the Lords by a crushing 350 to seventy-five votes.

Asquith seized the opportunity to force that confrontation with the Upper House which Gladstone had wanted in 1893–94, and called a general election, held in January 1910. The results gave the Liberals 275 seats, Labour forty, Irish Nationalists remained steady at eighty-two – seventy of them still united under Redmond – and the Conservatives only 273. Of these the first three parties were united in wanting some form of Home Rule. If Liberals – and Labour Members would support them on this issue – chose to implement their undertakings to the Irish they could claim a specific electoral mandate, and had ample strength to exercise it in the Commons. The expected opposition from the House of Lords would be confronted with a determined government, fortified by popular support on the linked issues of social reform and Irish Home Rule.

The ultimate weapon in enforcing popular will was that which had been adopted in 1832 – prevailing on the monarch to create enough government peers to swamp the Tories in the House of Lords. Before King Edward was forced to decide – he had indicated that he would do so, but only after another general election had signified an unshaken mandate – he died on 6 May 1910.

Reasonable debate collapsed, to be succeeded by a shrill acerbity not seen for many years. Lloyd George was scathing about the rich, whose incomes would be – modestly – impaired in order to finance his social security measures; Leo Maxse denounced the 'Welsh Anglophobes' (Lloyd George) and 'Semi-Yankee adventurers' (Churchill) as 'cowards and tyrants' in his *National Review* editorials (May 1910). Very little of this fretfulness concerned Ireland directly. It was not the possible disintegration of the Union that so alarmed the Conservatives but the perceived attack on property, reinforced by deep unease at the prospect that their privileged existence was to be undermined by Radicals and by the threat of Bolshevism, somewhat indistinctly perceived in the rising strength of the Labour Party. The government needed Irish votes, and Redmond could demand his pound of flesh – an undertaking to implement an Irish Home Rule Bill.

The Lords soon showed their reactionary mettle by rejecting an excellent Education Bill which had been passed by a decisive majority in a House of Commons newly elected and beyond a doubt representing the popular will. After two false starts another Bill, although sponsored by the Archbishop of Canterbury himself, was similarly doomed. Four Land Reform Bills, which included an Irish Evicted Tenants measure, were either mutilated or rejected by an Upper House quite obviously determined to resist any reform. A Licensing Bill, supported by the Churches and many Conservative peers, and by the new King, George V, himself, was opposed by the brewers; it too, therefore, perished at the hands of the peers. This was one of the rare moments in modern British constitutional history when the monarch's role was pivotal. Only his agreement to coerce the Lords could break the deadlock, and this he was by no means obliged to give.

George V had been a career naval officer, and always carried something of the quarterdeck manner about him. During his naval service and after he had spent much time in the colonies, and had frequently visited Ireland; he had indeed a better knowledge of colonial affairs than any of his ministers. A conference between Liberals and the Unionists having failed to agree on a solution, the King agreed, as his father had done, to create enough peers.

Asquith, rather boldly – no previous government had won three elections running – decided to appeal once more to the electorate to clarify his mandate on Home Rule. As before, many Liberals hedged, only eighty-four of their successful 272 candidates and nine of the sixteen outgoing ministers mentioning Home Rule in their personal manifestos, but the Conservatives made up for this by making opposition to Home Rule their main issue. If a Liberal vote was not automatically one for Home Rule, then a vote for a Conservative was very definitely one against. The result, in January 1911, was still convincing enough – 271 Liberals and forty-two Labour Members facing 273 Conservatives and Unionists, with the Redmondites and allies at eighty-four.

The first business of the new government, in which the rising star Winston Churchill continued as Home Secretary and Lloyd George as Chancellor of the Exchequer, while Gladstonian traditions were represented by the veteran John Morley, who had been Irish Chief Secretary in 1886, was a Parliament Bill, to clip the powers of the second chamber – and thereby to procure the passage of the pending legislation, which would include a Home Rule Act. In spite of much hysterical opposition, Lord Salisbury's son, Lord Hugh Cecil, being the most violently vociferous, the Lords realised that King George would indeed support his ministers in creating a great number of new peers.[3] A list had already been prepared when in July 1911, with the utmost reluctance, the Upper House consented in the Parliament Act to their obstructive powers being reduced from veto to that of delay only. But a considerable delay: House of Commons Bills could be returned twice by the Lords, in separate sessions, thus giving a period of up to three years before their eventual enactment – and much could happen in that period. When the penultimate Home Rule Bill made its appearance in April 1912 it was therefore possible that it might not actually become law until the summer of 1914.

Whilst reflecting the changed circumstances, Asquith's proposals, shown to the Irish Members in 1912, were at the same time so similar to the 1886 measure that they might almost be called Gladstone's Final Home Rule Bill. As a piece of constitution-making it was however flawed, for, like Gladstone, Asquith was constrained by what he could persuade his party to accept. After the previous drastic split over Ireland, the Liberals had made a dramatic recovery, and Asquith could not risk a repetition of that disaster. Similarly Redmond had allies who needed to be satisfied: John Dillon, heir to the Parnellite tradition, son of the Young Irelander, and William O'Brien had half a dozen followers at Westminster challenging the leadership, while Tim Healy brilliantly followed his own individual line, at one time or another at odds with everybody else.

Continuity of Liberal policy notwithstanding, 1912 was not 1886 or 1893, and the new Bill reflected this. New constitutional models had become available, and the formal unity of neither the United Kingdom nor the British Empire needed to be regarded as sacrosanct. The self-governing colonies of Australia were now federated into a single Commonwealth, and a united South Africa had become an independent dominion in 1910, only eight years after the conclusion of that disastrous war. From its inception in 1906, the Liberal administration had South Africa very much in mind. Churchill, a key figure in the administration, had to be allowed a major share of the credit for the popular settlement made with the once-rebellious Boers in 1909. If such men as Generals Botha and Smuts, who had been fighting the Imperial Army doggedly for three bloody years, could be translated into staunch supporters of Empire, sitting in knee breeches on the steps of the throne, could not the same transformation be effected on the far less belligerent Irish? Ireland had been peaceful for twenty years, with the large-scale transfer of land from the great estates to individual farmers and the foundation of democratic local government, and even the demon of Ulster resistance appeared exorcised. Redmond, spoken of as the 'Irish Botha', would have agreed to powerful protection of minorities, just as the Liberals had insisted upon the retention of the black vote in South Africa very much against the wishes of the whites.[4]

Asquith's Bill left open the possibility of a federal option, proposing a system which could be applied to Scotland, and even to England and Wales. The Imperial Parliament would remain at Westminster, and the number of Irish MPs be reduced by nearly half, to forty-two.

An Irish Parliament would be responsible for all domestic matters – 'full self-government in regard to purely Irish affairs' – with rather more generous powers than those previously accorded. The radical reforms of Lloyd George and Asquith, pushed through against Conservative opposition, had transformed British society, and laid the foundations of the Welfare State. National Insurance, employment legislation and the introduction of old-age pensions had brought for the first time freedom from the worst poverty. By the automatic extension of these benefits to Ireland any taxation injustices were reversed, as Ireland became subsidised from central taxation. But what the Bill proposed was of much less importance than the unremitting hostility of Ulster Unionists.

Many practical grounds existed on which the Bill could be attacked. The financial arrangements were complex and obscure; the device of having a Lord Lieutenant who could continue in office after a change of government was fraught with difficulty; the proposed allocation of seats was weighted in favour of the rural areas; and the half-in half-out situation of the Irish Westminster MPs would perpetuate the problem that such a single-interest group could cause.

'There are things stronger than parliamentary majorities'

Few of these important points received much attention, although financial arrangements were indeed clarified and amended. Opposition to Home Rule had cohered around a single issue, advanced by a confident and able group led by the flamboyantly brilliant Irish lawyer Sir Edward Carson. They had a simple and powerful message, that which had been chosen a generation previously by Lord Randolph Churchill: the Protestant population of Ulster would never accept rule by a Dublin government with a Catholic majority. No time was lost in playing Lord Randolph's 'Orange card'.

In the debate on 15 April 1912 Carson pertinently asked, 'What argument is there that you can raise for giving Home Rule to Ireland that you do not equally raise for giving Home Rule to that Protestant minority in the north-east province?' Carson had also highlighted another point: in the province of Ulster, the religions were not unevenly balanced; only in the four counties of Antrim, Armagh, Londonderry and Down was there an indisputable Protestant majority. But exclusion of any part of Ireland was anathema to the Irish parliamentary party. 'Revolting, and hateful . . . unthinkable', insisted Redmond, who would 'resist most violently as far as it is within our power to do so' setting up 'permanent dividing lines between one creed and another and one race and another'. Redmond's definition of violence was strictly constitutional; but there were some in Ireland prepared for the ultimate in physical resistance.[5]

And not, at least in appearance, only in Ireland. The session ended with the Bill still extant, but having to await the end of the recess before progressing. On 27 July an open meeting at Blenheim Palace was addressed by Andrew Bonar Law, Edward Carson and F.E. Smith. Law, who had succeeded the ageing and ineffective Balfour as leader of the Conservatives the previous year, went far beyond what was constitutionally acceptable, to the verge of treason and past. He accused the government, which had demonstrated its mandate so convincingly in successive general elections, of being

> a revolutionary committee which has seized upon despotic power by fraud. In our opposition to them we shall not be guided by the considerations or bound by the restraints which would influence us in an ordinary Constitutional struggle. We shall take the means, whatever means seem to us most effective, to deprive them of the despotic power which they have usurped . . . there are things stronger than parliamentary majorities.

This may have sounded like irresponsible verbiage, but it was backed by aggressive action.[6] Even before the December 1910 election, which made the eventual passage of Home Rule almost inevitable, the Ulster Unionist Council, in which political Unionists co-operated with the Orange Order, issued tenders to foreign suppliers for the supply of twenty thousand rifles. Captain James Craig, a solid and effective member of the whiskey-distilling family and a Boer War veteran, proved outstanding, together with Edward Carson, both as organisers and as manipulators of Ulster opinion. From the beginning in September 1911, it was made publicly clear that armed resistance to Home

Rule was considered. 'We must be prepared on the morning Home Rule passes,' Carson thundered, 'to become responsible for the government of the Protestant Province of Ulster.' In September Carson produced a 'Solemn League and Covenant', designed to recall the seventeenth-century Scottish precedent much as his opponents had appealed to '41, '90, '98 and '48. It was in its own way as openly revolutionary a document as any Nationalist effusion.

> Being convinced in our consciences that Home Rule would be disastrous to the material well-being of Ulster as well as to the whole of Ireland, subversive of our civil and religious freedom, destructive of our citizenship and perilous to the unity of the Empire, we . . . do hereby pledge ourselves in solemn Covenant throughout this our time of threatened calamity to stand by one another in defending for ourselves and our children our cherished position of equal citizenship in the United Kingdom and in using all means which may be found necessary to defeat the present conspiracy to set up a Home Rule Parliament in Ireland.[7]

On the day the covenant was produced – 28 September 1912 – Belfast almost came to a stop. Nearly half a million men and women (more women than men) signed the document. Watching the proceedings, J.L. Garvin, editor of the pro-Unionist *Observer*, commented, 'No one for a moment could have mistaken the concentrated will and courage of those people.' By the following January an Ulster Volunteer Force was formed from among the signatories, the name chosen to reflect the original Volunteers of the 1770s. Under the command of General Sir George Richardson the UVF could muster well over a hundred thousand men, with machine-gun and signal corps, medical units and cavalry. As yet they were armed only in part, but over £1 million had been collected for the purchase of weapons.

Irish Nationalists were less united and organised than were Ulster Unionists. The majority of the parliamentary party, who understood the slow working of the political machinery and were able to monitor the Home Rule Bill's progress, relied upon its ultimate success. Sentiment in Ireland was less convinced. Much of the country was still adjusting to the near-revolutionary changes in social conditions that two decades of reforms had introduced, but a new intellectual wave was mounting. The nineteenth century had seen the formation of powerful central governments in most large European countries, and the creation of two new nation-states from the scattered parts of Italy and Germany. Smaller language groups protested against the imposition or adoption of metropolitan cultures within these centralised states: Catalans and Basques in Spain, Croats and Hungarians in the Austro-Hungarian Empire, Flemings in Belgium all insisted on their individual rights. Ancient tongues that were falling into desuetude were revived and attempts to preserve linguistic purity essayed: Frederic Mistral led the revival of Provençal in France; enthusiasts for Anglo-Saxon in England attempted to stop Latinisms; Germans insisted on 'Fernsprecher' rather than telephone. The revival of Gaelic in Ireland was therefore very much part of a wider movement. The spoken language at least was still well-used, but in danger of extinction. Enthusiasts such as Standish O'Grady were working to preserve and transmit Gaelic literature, at a time when writing in Irish had almost come to a halt. In Wales, by contrast, with a much smaller population, over eight thousand books were published during the nineteenth century in Welsh, new works were commissioned by British publishers, and some thirty Welsh periodicals commanded a wide readership.

However imperilled, Irish Gaelic had the potential to be more than an object of specialised interest; it could, with a lot of adjustment and optimism, be made to represent a tradition of nationality and the cornerstone of a potential nation-state. It was the Gaelic scholar and poet Dr Douglas Hyde, who in old age became the first President of independent Ireland, who gave the definitive expression of what was to become a pillar of the Irish state, a denunciation of 'anglicisation'. In his famous lecture to the Irish National Literary Society in November 1892, Dr Hyde blamed O'Connell for his failure '[to keep] alive racial customs, language and traditions'. Quite specifically, by Hyde's definition, 'Ireland' excluded that 'land planted with aliens', Protestant Ulster. The 'ancient Gaelic civilisation died with O'Connell' and the 'Celtic race' had lost 'all that they had – language, traditions, music, genius and ideas'. Given that at the time the Irishmen Sir Charles Villiers Stanford and Sir Arthur Sullivan were the only composers from the British Isles of any reputation, and that Oscar Wilde's first play had been performed earlier that year, this exemplified how even so cultivated and humorous a man as Hyde could be led astray by racist ideology. Irish 'genius and ideas' were in fact about to be manifested in an astonishingly concentrated outburst of literary activity.[8]

But it was to be a literature written in English. And what English! The ebullient creativity of modern Anglo-Irish literature, comprehending as it does George Moore, Wilde, Shaw, Yeats, Synge, O'Casey, Joyce, Elizabeth Bowen and Samuel Beckett (the list could go on for a great deal longer), remains unequalled. Only contemporary Russia could show a similar array of talent to that gathered at the Abbey Theatre in Dublin, founded by Annie Horniman, and under the patronage of Augusta, Lady Gregory, widow of Sir William of Poor Law notoriety, and Edward Martyn, a rich art-collector.

Paralleling the interest in European vernaculars was a new literary concern with the humbler sections of society. In their different ways and countries Emile Zola, Thomas Hardy and Giovanni Verga produced great works of gritty realism. Many Irish writers were taking a very different direction, harking back to a mythical past, both in the sense of reviving Gaelic myth and in an idealised view of the virtues of the Irish peasantry. When realism, even of the most delicate variety, as in Synge's *Playboy of the Western World*, crept in, it was vehemently denounced, leading to tumults in both Ireland and America. It is a reflection of the later stultifying aspects of Irish cultural nationalism that only Yeats and Synge pursued their careers in Ireland – and Yeats was semi-attached to his London flat, Oxford and America, eventually dying in the South of France, while Synge died before the cultural shabbiness that marked the first half-century of Irish independence became apparent. O'Casey was actually driven from the country, dropping as he did the earlier Gaelicisation of his name. George Russell (AE), who edited the *Irish Statesman*, the consistent voice of civilised sanity in the 1930s, died, disillusioned, in Bournemouth. Even the pioneer Standish O'Grady eventually went to live on the Isle of Wight.[9]

Dr Hyde himself had observed that 'it is the curious certainty that come what may many Irishmen will continue to resist English rule, even though it should be for their own good'. Illustrating this point, at a time when Ireland had been generously treated and past injustices rectified, a plethora of dissident organisations, all anti-Union, anti-English, anti-parliamentarian in some degree, bombinated in Dublin.

The Ancient Order of Hibernians, an unashamedly Catholic answer to the Orange Order, the Daughters of Ireland, National Council, the United Irish League, Dungannon Clubs, the Gaelic League, dedicated to de-anglicising the Irish and reviving the language, the Gaelic Athletic Association, Cumann na nGaedheal, the Oliver Bond Society, the Celtic Literary Society and James Connolly's Irish Citizen Army were widely separated and quite unco-ordinated. An effort, beginning in 1905, was made to bring some of these groups together in the shape of a new organisation.

Its name, Sinn Féin -'Ourselves', reflected the Italian Risorgimento motto '*Italia fara da se*' – 'Italy will do it alone'. Arthur Griffith was the creative spirit behind Sinn Féin, a silent, reserved man who had had experience of the world outside Ireland or America, the boundaries of most of his colleagues, having worked in South Africa. A printer and journalist with a realistic sense of the practical and possible, not a common quality among his colleagues, Griffith's greatest virtue was his unshakeable honesty. As represented by Griffith, Sinn Féin's ideal was an entirely independent Irish state, a prosperous, virile and independent nation; but, in the old tradition, Griffith was prepared to work towards it by using the instruments which lay to hand. These did not, at that time, include support for terrorism, but relied rather on developing the representative bodies that already existed in Ireland, especially the county councils. Sinn Féin placed little trust in the Irish parliamentary party, which was perceived as waiting to accept any crumbs of devolution graciously passed down to them (although with eighty-two MPs the parliamentary nationals seemed to represent the will of Ireland better than Sinn Féin, who when they did field a candidate lost by 1157 votes to 3103).

What was to become the stimulus for direct action came from the old Irish Republican Brotherhood, which had previously maintained only a shadowy existence. Assisted by an eclectic committee including John MacBride, who had fought for the Boers in 1900, the beautiful Maude Gonne, James Connolly, a militant labour organiser, and Edward Martyn, the new movement was encouraged by the wave of pro-Boer and anti-war emotion which swept not only Ireland but England as well. After a brief success the IRB declined into a collecting point for rebellious spirits discontented with the slow progress at Westminster. In what seemed a replay of 1798 a trio of young, well-educated Ulstermen, Bulmer Hobson, Denis McCullough and Professor Eoin MacNeill, began to take over the IRB leadership and started to introduce a more disciplined organisation, including a small 'Citizen Army' commanded by James Connolly.

So inchoate an assemblage of organisations was slow to counter the single-minded Ulster Unionist preparations. It was a group of London sympathisers who took the only effective action. Alice Stopford Green, widow of the historian J.H. Green, Mary Spring Rice, cousin of the British Ambassador to Washington, and Erskine Childers, Clerk to the House of Commons and author of the classic adventure story *The Riddle of the Sands*, arranged with Sir Roger Casement to obtain arms from Germany. Casement, an Irish-born Gaelic Leaguer, had distinguished himself in the Consular Service, especially for his exposure of the terrible conditions in the colonial Belgian Congo. He proved willing to go further than merely buying guns, not itself an illegal operation, and went on to establish close relations with the German military.

Realistically enough, neither Redmond's party nor his allies at Westminster took overmuch heed of such Dublin-based manifestations; it was to be in London that the future of Ireland would be decided. There, after fifty-two days of argument and deliberation, the third Home Rule Bill was passed with a convincing majority of 110 votes in the House of Commons. It was even more convincingly rejected in the Lords, on 30 January 1913, and the stately gavotte necessitated by the Parliament Act began. Once again the Bill was debated in the Commons; once again passed by almost exactly the same majority; and once again defeated in the Lords (on 15 July).

Arguments centred almost entirely on the question of Ulster. Exclusion of the Northern Protestants, in one form or another, was inevitable. Discussion centred on whether Ulster should be allowed to opt out for a limited period or permanently, and on what should be taken to constitute 'Ulster'. In the historic province of nine counties Home Rulers held a slender majority of Westminster seats – seventeen to sixteen – and Catholics outnumbered Protestants. Six counties only could be counted reliably Protestant: the four north-eastern counties were unequivocally so, while neighbouring Fermanagh and Tyrone had substantial Catholic minorities; and by 1913, while Catholic Unionists and Protestant Nationalists still existed, they were becoming endangered species: religion was now the defining factor in political allegiance.

By 1913 more pressing subjects than Ireland were being forced on the government's attention. Germany's aggression and rising power had forced Britain into expensive naval building; labour unrest was unprecedentedly militant, as were demands for women's suffrage. To many of the middle classes, brought up in the tranquil domesticity of late-nineteenth-century existence, revolution seemed imminent. Austen Chamberlain was told by a friend that 'he considered the situation so serious that he had been to a wholesale armourer's to buy five revolvers', only to find that the man was out of stock, having sold a hundred pistols since the day before.[10] Certainly political and social violence was spreading. In Liverpool troops killed two rioters, while in Llanelli seven died. Seen against this background the police baton charge during a Dublin tramway strike, which led to one fatality, in August 1913 assumes its proper proportion; but in Ireland the incident became part of Nationalist mythology, and led to the formation of Connolly's 'Citizen Army'.

Asquith, pressed by Churchill and the King, but with many waverers in his cabinet, continued negotiating with Redmond and the Unionists on the future of Ulster. Here Unionists found another weapon: what would be the attitude of the army should it be necessary to force a settlement on Ulster (there was no doubt about the military's willingness to squash troubles in the South)? Neither Law nor Carson had ever heard a shot fired in anger, which hardly excuses Law's appeal to the army on 28 November 1913 that they should refuse to obey orders. He went even further, advocating that the House of Lords refuse to pass the Army Act, which would have rendered the country defenceless – in April 1914!

In the Curragh 'mutiny' in March a majority of the Irish Cavalry Brigade officers declared that they would rather accept dismissal as an alternative to being ordered into action in the North. Grossly mishandled by the War Minister, Jack Seely, who had a rare talent for getting things wrong, the affair aroused widespread indignation in Britain.[11] Churchill, then in charge of the Admiralty, deciding that if the army was unwilling the navy would fill the breach, started to move the Battle Fleet to Ireland, for which he was violently attacked by the opposition as an 'egomaniac', the 'Belfast butcher', who planned a 'pogrom' of the Unionists. That it was the Ulstermen themselves who intended bloodshed was proved when on 24 April the steamer *Mountjoy II* landed 24,600 rifles and some three million rounds of ammunition at Larne. Efficiently distributed, with police and customs kept at arm's length, these enabled the Ulster Volunteers to muster the equivalent of perhaps thirty battalions of infantry. This enterprise was not only known to, but encouraged by, the official opposition. Austen Chamberlain, who had been a cabinet minister in 1902 and was to become Chancellor of the Exchequer and Foreign Secretary, recorded in his diary on 29 April:

> We were in some anxiety lest the attempt might result in bloodshed in spite of all precautions, but ... everything was carried through with a smoothness and a success, which reflects the highest credit on the brains of the Ulster movement.[12]

Nationalists could not hope to equal such organisation, or to command such funds, but they attempted to do so. On 26 July Erskine Childers' yacht the *Asgard*, crewed by Mrs Childers and Mary Spring Rice, landed 1500 obsolete rifles at Howth; a subsequent scuffle between troops (the King's Own Scottish Borderers) and an angry crowd developed into a tragedy when four people were killed by army fire (subsequently censured by a government inquiry). Ireland now contained two armed, and grossly unequal, camps.[13]

But it was neither in Belfast nor Dublin that decisions were taken. On 25 May 1914 the Irish Home Rule Bill, which provided for the Protestant Ulster counties to opt out for six years, passed its third reading. A final flurry in the House of Lords resulted in an undecided amendment as to whether the Ulster exception should not be permanent, but the deed was done. Over vociferous Conservative opposition, culminating in a mass walkout, the Home Rule Act became law. What O'Connell and Parnell had dreamed of was now reality, but with one significant reservation. Implementation of the new statute was to be delayed until that inconvenient interruption, the war declared on Germany on 4 August, should be terminated, an event expected to occur within a few months. Irishmen, North and South, flocked to join the colours, although the flocking was perhaps more enthusiastic in the six counties of Ulster. For the time being Ireland was united, and at one with the rest of the kingdom.

Some dissidents however remained. In May 1915, with the war going badly, Asquith's government had been replaced by a coalition cabinet in which Bonar Law and Edward Carson had places (Redmond was offered a seat, which he declined). Even though the composition of the House of Commons remained the same, and Lloyd George, Gladstone's successor as a proponent of Home Rule, became Prime Minister, it was surely possible that such a government would attempt to alter or even repeal the Home Rule Act. To extreme Nationalists the war represented an opportunity to use German power to defeat England. Roger Casement went over to the enemy – not that Sir Roger saw the German Empire in those terms – in order to form an Irish Brigade (the name was intended to have echoes of the 'Wild Geese' serving in foreign armies) from prisoners of war, very much as the Nazi Germans would recruit Belgians, Poles and other nationals to join the Waffen SS. Casement was less successful than Himmler was to be, persuading only some fifty Irish prisoners, the highest-ranking of whom was a corporal, to join this Brigade. In return Casement was promised a shipment of arms to effect a Nationalist uprising behind the lines.[14]

Gallant allies

The 1916 Easter Rising in Dublin was an extraordinary event. In the midst of the most devastating war the Western world had ever experienced, in which half a million Britons were engaged in a bitter struggle, after two years which had seen hundreds of thousands of casualties, two thousand or so men took up arms against their fellow citizens, appealing to the enemy for aid. It might have been construed as a noble if hopeless gesture, if one could have believed that Imperial Germany and Austria had right on their side, and that Great Britain and France were engaged in an unjust war of aggression; but that is a theory that precious few, then or now, would have cared to embrace.[15]

The fact therefore that the 'Easter Rebels' are still honoured in Ireland, celebrated in a garden of remembrance in the heart of Dublin, while the memory of those hundred thousand or so Irishmen who died in the Great War is slighted (precious few poppies are to be seen in Dublin on 11 November, and their memorial was until recently ignored and neglected), is, to the uninformed observer, at least curious.

The rebels themselves were an ill-assorted group. Those potential supporters whose judgment was clearer attempted to abort the Rising. Its leader, Patrick Pearse, was a sanctimonious schoolmaster with paedophiliac tendencies and an unpleasant yearning for 'blood sacrifices', since 'the old heart of the earth needed to be warmed by the red wine of the battlefield'. His followers included the cool and reserved Eamon de Valera, the bitter Marxist James Connolly, and the talented writer, admirer of Jane Austen, Thomas MacDonagh. After causing the deaths of about five hundred of their fellow citizens, civilians and soldiers alike, the surviving rebels surrendered, and fourteen of their leaders were executed.[16]

Some writers are still moved to the point of tears by their fate, while ignoring that of their victims; others see the episode as 'a hysterical evocation of Catholic-nationalist sentimentality, with macabre unwholesome and sectarian undertones', or 'a reaction almost Pavlovian in its dogmatism'.[17] The immediate public reaction was clear enough: the captured rebels were hissed and jeered at. But whatever view is taken of the episode the fact remains that the Rising formed a focal point for the generally unpleasant subsequent history of Ireland.

The one practical result of the Easter Rising was that after such a demonstration the Ulster Protestants would never accept any Irish administration which did not unequivocally exclude such men, unelected and unrepresentative even of those for whom they purported to speak, whose ideas were made plain in their Easter announcement of the Provisional Government of the Irish Republic:

> Having organized and trained her manhood through her secret revolutionary organization ... supported by her exiled children in America and by gallant allies in Europe, but relying first on her own strength, she strikes in full confidence of victory.

In the middle of the First World War the tribute to the rebels' 'gallant allies in Europe' would have been unforgivable to those whose relatives were engaged in that great conflict. Two months later the lesson was driven home when a new Allied offensive was launched on the Somme. On the first day the British Army suffered sixty thousand casualties, among whom were a great number of Irishmen, including many from the Ulster division. The day of the action was 1 July, an anniversary of the battle of the Boyne, and men went over the top wearing orange lilies; from six hundred of one battalion only sixty-four returned that night; their families, and those of the other Irish dead, could not but despise the 'Irish Republic'.[18]

Losses on such a scale could not be sustained by a volunteer army. Conscription had been introduced in January 1916 for British men, but not extended to Ireland. In an effort to make this extension possible, and to mollify Nationalist opinion, Lloyd George suggested the immediate implementation of the Home Rule Act, with all Irish seats in the House of Commons being retained. After much persuasion the Ulster Unionists agreed, guaranteed as they were the permanent exclusion of the six counties from the new Ireland, and Redmond was deceived by the Welsh wizard into agreement. Lloyd George's deal was also accepted by his colleagues in the cabinet, even including Bonar Law. It might have worked, but was not given the chance. Gladstone's former opponents the Whig grandees, led by Lord Lansdowne, who had resigned from Gladstone's administration as long ago as 1880 over the Compensation for Disturbance Bill, were adamantly opposed. Lansdowne insisted that there should be no amnesty for the interned Easter rebels, and that the wartime emergency legislation should continue.

A year later Lloyd George tried again, this time with the powerful assistance of Jan Christiaan Smuts. In his own person an example of a successful conflict resolution, Smuts, Cambridge graduate, Boer guerrilla, philosopher, subsequently in large measure responsible for both the League of Nations and the United Nations, proposed a repeat of the South African convention of British colonies and ex-Boer republics that had agreed the future constitution of South Africa. The Irish internees were accordingly released, and an uneasy peace prevailed. Unfortunately, whilst the South African conference had been attended by men of exceptional experience and integrity, the Irish convention was not. Chaired by the well-meaning but ineffective Sir Joseph Plunkett, with Redmond seeing his minimal support dissolving, the only party absolutely sure of itself and its constituents was Carson's – the Ulster Unionists – which stood unyieldingly on partition. The other powerful element did not even put in an appearance, for Sinn Féin refused to send any representatives.

And Sinn Féin, changing shape and colour in order to comprehend an even wider range of opinions, was gaining power. From the gallimaufry of pre-war ideas and theories a simple and authoritative programme had been extracted: 'Sinn Féin aims at securing the international recognition of Ireland as an independent republic.'

It was, however, the progress of the war that defined the future of Ireland. America had joined the Allies in April 1917, but it was not until September 1918, eight weeks before the German capitulation, that American troops launched their first offensive. The crisis had come in March of that year when the last great German attack penetrated deep into France. Only by the end of July had it finally been halted, and in the first days of fearful apprehension the demand for more troops was pressed, often almost hysterically. The government found itself obliged to take powers to extend conscription to Ireland. Resisting this, the Irish parliamentarians, led by John Dillon after Redmond's death in March, were impelled into the arms of Sinn Féin. Although conscription was never enforced in Ireland, the episode marked the end of the Irish constitutional reformers, the heirs of Parnell. Whatever transpired after the war, it would be something decisively different from Gladstonian Home Rule.

After November 1918 Ireland was in a state of nervous apprehension and suspicion, and weary of war. Protestant Ulster was unanimously determined to have nothing to do with Home Rule in any form, whilst the rest of Ireland was either eagerly awaiting it, or was at least tolerably resigned to the prospect. An immediate chance for the people to register their opinions was given by the December general election, in which the electorate, now including women over thirty, was more democratic than ever. In the voting the Irish Nationalist parliamentarians were nearly obliterated, hanging on to only six seats. Ulster Unionists obtained a solid twenty-three, with only another three Unionists in the South, where Sinn Féin captured seventy-three seats for an independent Irish republic. A claim could well be made with so massive a majority that Sinn Féin could therefore speak for the majority of the Irish nation, were it not for the fact that a majority of the votes cast were for parties which opposed Sinn Féin. That party won 485,105 votes, but the total 'anti-republican' vote was 557,435.[19]

In fact, and in spite of assertions to the contrary, it was painfully clear that a united Irish nation did not exist: Ireland was sharply divided into two opposed and inimical cultures – three, if the Southern Unionists, the heirs of the old Ascendancy, nearly half a million strong, are included. There was no indication that any were given to compromise. The new government in Westminster was not in a strong position, composed as it was of a coalition between 335 Conservative and 144 Liberal and Labour supporters, with Lloyd George continuing as Prime Minister. Sinn Féin demonstrated its authority in Ireland by boycotting Westminster and establishing its own legislation, the Dáil Éireann, in Dublin on 22 January 1919. Those Sinn Féin Members who had been elected to the Westminster Parliament chose instead to constitute themselves as the successors to the phantom republic proclaimed at Easter 1916. At a stroke some substance was given to the vision, and an institution created which could speak with some authority, but only for a minority of the Irish electorate – a fact which many Nationalist writers prefer to ignore.

A new generation of leaders emerged from this, the 'First Dáil', the most prominent of whom were Eamon de Valera and Michael Collins, both veterans of the Easter Rising. Sharply contrasted and later sharply opposed characters, the Hispano-Irish de Valera coldly intransigent, pursuing his own puritan ideals, and Collins, gregarious and ebullient, with an impressive aptitude for administration coupled with complete ruthlessness, were to become the founders of independent Ireland.

Almost contemporaneously a much less constitutional Nationalism was expressed. On 21 January 1919 nine gunmen ambushed a convoy of gelignite and killed the two police guards (it was not untypical that the raiders omitted to take the detonators). Dan Breen, the leader of the Soloheadbeg ambush, explained that his action was prompted by his friends having gone into politics; the idea that political points are best made by killing one's fellow citizens has remained a consistent and peculiar feature in Irish affairs. Those thirty-four deputies who attended the Dublin Dáil agreed no policies apart from an appeal to the Paris Peace Conference, and, as usual, entirely neglected the fact of Ulster opposition. No leader able to speak with unanimous authority had yet emerged: the only likely candidate, de Valera, prudently took himself off to the United States on 1 June 1919, where he stayed until December the following year.

After March 1919, when those Members who had been imprisoned during the war had either escaped or been released, the Dáil settled down in Dublin's Mansion House, where O'Connell had ruled as Lord Mayor, to constitute an alternative government. Loans were raised, a Land Bank founded, local government reorganised and an entirely new system of courts established, ranging from parish tribunals to a Supreme Court in Dublin.

Irish events were, however, only one of the problems facing the post-war British coalition government. Foreign affairs – the peace negotiations at Versailles (in which the Dáil, unavailingly, attempted to be included), the continuing war in Russia, the establishment of the League of Nations, a crisis with Turkey – occupied much of Lloyd George's energies. At home reconstruction, industrial discontent, endemic on 'Red Clydeside' and flaring into the bitter miners' strike of April 1921, and, above all, the threatening economic climate, with rampant price inflation – 323 per cent between 1914 and 1920 – and the enormous overhang of public debt incurred during the war, were more urgent than the troubles in Ireland.

The 'War of Independence'

An entire gallery of the National Museum in Dublin commemorates the 'War of Independence'. The title is hardly appropriate. If the campaign of discriminatory murder currently carried out in Spain by the Basque separatists is a war, then the 'series of murderous attacks, cowardly, brutalising and productive only of a vicious circle of savagery' that harassed Ireland was a 'war', but not by any other standards. Nor could the struggle be for 'independence' pure and simple, which had been largely conceded in the 1914 Home Rule Bill and its successor the 1920 Government of Ireland Act; what was at issue is what form independence should take. On that subject there was much dissension, eventually culminating in a vicious civil war, with the end result being just another compromise. Nor was it an 'Anglo–Irish War', another description sometimes accorded, since no such entity as 'Ireland' was a combatant, the island being deeply divided between Crown forces and insurgents.[20] The bloodiest engagements were such brutal skirmishes as the ambush at Kilmichael where seventeen auxiliary police were massacred, the sole survivor left 'crippled and comatose', or 'Bloody Sunday', 21 November 1920, which left twenty-eight people dead, fourteen of them in midnight raids on suspected British spies and twelve in a revenge attack on a football crowd. Until the guns were silent, no constitutional settlement was possible. It took two years of squalid irregular fighting, terrorist attacks being answered by fierce retaliation, both often untargeted, before any negotiations could be started in July 1921. The gunmen, few in number, now generally known as the Irish Republican Army (IRA), could often rely upon a populace which, if not co-operative, was willing to turn a blind eye. Assassinating policemen rather than engaging in battles with soldiers was the IRA's preferred tactic – some four hundred of the Royal Ulster Constabulary had been killed by the time a truce was called. When armed police reinforcements were called in – the infamous 'Black and Tans' – their brutal adoption of IRA tactics only alienated the civilian population.

Westminster could do little but press ahead with attempting to restore order and fulfilling their commitments to Home Rule. A Bill was introduced on 25 February 1920, accepting the partition of the island between North and South. The IRA showed its opinion by murdering the Dublin Magistrate, Alan Bell. Over much of Ireland central authority disintegrated, as local authorities distanced themselves from the Crown government; Dáil courts replaced, not unsuccessfully, the now-disregarded operation of justice. In December the Better Government of Ireland Act – a deceptive title – received royal assent. Separate parliaments for North and South were to be instituted, but it was made clear (Article 2.(1)) that this was 'with a view to the eventual establishment of a Parliament for the whole of Ireland', to implement which a 'Council of Ireland' would be constituted. Ulster, or at least the six most Protestant counties of it, the exact boundaries being left for later agreement, was now, and against its own wishes, given Home Rule, in a form that was intended to apply to an Ireland well on the way to independence. If the Ulster constitution had been designed only for the six counties it would have been a much more modest measure of devolution, probably much like that which in 1999 was accorded to Scotland. As it was the Northern Ireland Parliament was vested with extensive powers, including those to alter its own constitution. Partition was a done deal, but many in the other twenty-six counties of Ireland cherished the hope for unification expressed in the Act itself, whilst others maintained the fiction of an indivisible republic proclaimed in 1916.

The new Parliament of Northern Ireland, in which forty Unionists faced twelve Nationalists, was opened by King George V on 22 June 1921. Much concerned about the future of Ireland, North and South, the King had given serious thought to what he could do to help, and consulted, among others, Smuts, now Field Marshal, and a greatly trusted counsellor. The King's speech in Belfast was a notable royal intervention in the cause of conciliation.

> I speak from a full heart when I pray that my coming to Ireland today may prove to be the first step towards an end of strife amongst her people, whatever their race or creed.
>
> In that hope, I appeal to all Irishmen to pause, to stretch out the hand of forbearance and conciliation, to forgive and forget, and to join in making for the land which they love a new era of peace, contentment, and goodwill.

The IRA responded the next day in what was becoming its usual fashion, by blowing up the train carrying the royal cavalry escort back to Dublin, killing eighty horses and four men; in other quarters, however, the King's appeal was not without effect.

By that time nearly two thousand IRA men had been interned – Michael Collins put the total actively in arms at only three thousand – and intelligence, which had largely dried up, whether through fear of the IRA or support for it, began once more to flow. The British government, although committed to a settlement, was preparing plans to enforce one if absolutely necessary. Lord French, the military commander, outlined his plans in October 1921.

> He would enclose a large area round each of the seaport towns of Ireland with forts and barbed wire entanglements. Within these areas he would have large concentration camps and

> intern all except loyalists, then gradually extend these fortified
> areas till they met cleansing the country all the time. He thinks
> that three weeks would practically suffice to prepare the areas
> and that the conquest of the country would not take long.[21]

Churchill was not necessarily bluffing when he told the Irish
negotiators that the alternative to agreement was 'a long and terrible
war'.

In Britain public opinion, shocked by the savage methods employed,
ostensibly on their behalf, by the Black and Tans and auxiliary police,
and apprehensive about the continued cost of the Irish garrison,
encouraged reluctant members of the government to accept negotiation. Smuts, more experienced than anyone else in such matters, was
unequivocal. Writing to the Prime Minister on 14 June, he had
described the situation as 'an unmitigated calamity . . . a negation of
all the principles of government which we have professed . . . Besides,
the present methods are frightfully expensive in a financial no less
than a moral sense; and what is worse they have failed.'[22] Discussions
with de Valera had tentatively begun in April 1921. The elections in
Southern Ireland, scheduled under the Better Government Act, were
held in May, and resulted in a clean sweep for Sinn Féin, all but four
of their candidates being returned unopposed – it would, in most
constituencies, have been literally suicidal to attempt to stand in opposition. It was at that stage that the King's speech of 22 June, and its
reception, gave Lloyd George the support to offer discussion to de
Valera; a truce was agreed, to come into operation from 11 July 1921.

New nations

The First World War shattered the old Europe; the subsequent treaties
reassembled the Continent, and a good deal of the rest of the world,
in a new shape. Poland, Lithuania and Hungary regained independence
after centuries of subordination; Finland, Estonia, Latvia, Czechoslo-
vakia and Yugoslavia had no history of independence; other such new
states as Ingria, Belorussia, the Ukraine, Georgia and Armenia had
only a brief existence before being snuffed out.[23] Since the 1920s all
these polities have suffered violent changes. Only in Ireland have the

two new political entities survived unchanged, albeit with a terrible amount of internal bleeding.

Changes of attitude within Ireland were rapid, but have proved permanent. In 1914 most Irish people acknowledged twin identities, of Irishness in a British context – not necessarily within a British state, for Home Rule was still a majority demand, and had indeed been conceded, but within an Empire that included such very distinctively individualist nations as South Africa and Canada. After 1921, when the emerging Free State of Ireland and the province of Northern Ireland were created, attitudes had become both clearer and more antagonistic.

The immediate difficulty after the ceasefire was the equivocal position of the Irish negotiators, of whom the two most influential were Arthur Griffith and Michael Collins. In theory they were 'plenipotentiaries' authorised by the Southern Ireland Parliament, or the Second Dáil, elected under the Government of Ireland Act. Since all the Members of the Dáil were Sinn Féin members, elected without opposition, Southern Unionists were unrepresented; and of course, the North already had its own elected Parliament. Sinn Féin itself was divided. There were those, including Griffith, who were willing to accept, at least as a first instalment, the 'dominion status' previously offered by Lloyd George. Others held out, some violently so, for nothing but an independent republic, and that immediately.

It took another six months before finality was reached. De Valera, President of the Dáil, distanced himself from the negotiations. After having appointed a delegation so mixed as to arouse the suspicion that he did not want to have to ratify a decision in which he had played no part, unanimity was only painfully achieved. Even though four of the six Members eventually refused to accept the implementation of their own agreement, Griffith and Collins argued their way through to a conclusion. After some tense cliff-hangings, culminating in Lloyd George presenting an ultimatum, articles of agreement were signed. Churchill was particularly struck by the effect of the concentrated pressure on Michael Collins: 'In all my life I have never seen so much passion and suffering invested.'

The agreement that the plenipotentiaries brought back to Dublin was that Southern Ireland was to become completely independent in domestic matters, and given 'dominion status' within what was becoming the British Commonwealth, rather than the Empire. Since it was clear that two major dominions were committed to ending any but formal acknowledgment of British hegemony, Collins appreciated that dominion status could finally lead to complete independence. Others wanted to demand more, and in Dublin the split was immediate. De Valera publicly announced that he would not support the plenipotentaries' agreement. After a long debate in the Dáil, the agreement was ratified on 7 January 1922 by sixty-four votes to fifty-seven. Rather than accept the majority decision and participate in a democratic constitution de Valera withdrew his supporters, leaving the field clear for Arthur Griffith as Chairman of the new provisional government. Events then moved quickly: on 16 January Dublin Castle was handed over to what has been called the 'first native Irish government for seven hundred years' (forgetting, as usual, the prior existence of the Belfast government). But outside there were the dissidents, those who would not accept the constraints of democracy, who included violent extremists, 'wild men screaming through the keyhole', as Kevin O'Higgins described them, insisting on a republic now.[24]

Efforts were made to patch up an agreement between the provisional government and de Valera's followers, but the 'wild men' made the running by occupying some strategic Dublin buildings on 3 April. There they remained through the election, which was eventually held, under the treaty arrangements, on 16 June 1922. The results confirmed that the Dáil's acceptance of the Anglo–Irish agreement was supported by the overwhelming majority, over 78 per cent of whom voted for the anti-Republicans and the treaty; the IRA countered by assassinating Field Marshal Sir Henry Wilson, a rigid Unionist. The new country was to be known as the Irish Free State, reflecting the 'Orange Free State' created by the British South African administration in the 1850s, which later became the Boer republic of the same name – a precedent which was certainly present in many Irish minds. There was now a democratically elected legal government in Dublin, with ninety-four of the 128 Members supporting Griffith's treaty; but democracy did not appeal to the stubborn and committed followers of de Valera.

The civil war that followed between the government forces and the IRA 'Irregulars' was essentially a conflict between those who accepted the parliamentary tradition and the minority determined to impose their will by violence.[25] It was, unlike the previous fighting, a real war, with artillery and tanks being deployed to defeat the Irregulars. Neither Griffith, perhaps fortunately, nor Collins survived to see the end of it, Collins being killed by an IRA ambush in August 1922, within days of Griffith's death from a heart attack. Casualties in the civil war were proportional to the scale of the fighting: some eight hundred Free State soldiers and many more IRA. So too were the swingeing punishments. Seventy-seven IRA men were quite arbitrarily and officially shot as reprisals, an act which the British had, although tempted, never allowed. Many others were executed – Liam Lynch, Rory O'Connor, Liam Mellows and Erskine Childers were only some of the prominent opponents, first of British and then of democratic Irish government, to be shot by their compatriots for their rebellion. Prisoners were routinely shot, or worse. In one incident outside Tralee, on 7 March 1923, nine IRA prisoners were tied together over a mine, which was then exploded; one survived. It was 122 years since Ireland had experienced so much bloodshed – in the famous year of 1798.

On 24 May 1923 de Valera formally called upon the IRA, not to surrender, but simply to stop fighting. His supporters refused to take their seats in the Dáil, so leaving the field open to Griffith's successor, Wiliam Cosgrave, another survivor of the Easter Rising, a reliably honest figure with a safe pair of hands. There was at first little unanimity within the government. After the death of Collins, Griffith and Childers, Gavan Duffy alone remained of those who had negotiated the treaty (Robert Barton and Edmond Duggan both having retired in the sulks).

After 1922 the Irish Free State was no longer part of the United Kingdom; but it was not until 1949, when Ireland formally declared itself a republic, that all political ties with Britain were severed. Indeed, even then, there was no clean break. The special relationship that continues has given Ireland a unique status as a semi-detached part of Britain. No passports are needed for travel, and Irish people living in Britain have always enjoyed the same rights to welfare, and the same access to the vote, as have British subjects (the reciprocal courtesy was only extended by Ireland in 1970). Britain remains an accessible safe haven for hundreds of thousands of Irish citizens.

Less formal links also continued. Well before the ceasefire the British government had begun preparations for the handover which, in one form or another, was implicit in the Government of Ireland Act. Behind-the-scenes co-operation between civil servants is certainly less exciting a topic than ambushes, assassinations, arson and destruction, but a strong argument must be made that the successful foundation of the new Ireland owes more to such practical efforts than to the flowery romanticism of such as Pearse, or the savagery of psychopathic killers. Nevertheless it is surprising that, for example, neither Professor R.F. Foster's *Modern Ireland*, nor Professor Lyons' *Ireland Since the Famine* so much as mentions Sir Warren Fisher, who was personally responsible for much of the eventual smooth transfer of power.[26]

Head of the British Civil Service for twenty years between 1919 and 1939, Fisher was sent to Dublin in May 1920 in order to prepare for the eventual handover of power. That, it is worth emphasising, was during the first stages of the 'War of Independence'. Fisher was scathing on the conditions of the Irish administration:

> The prevailing conception of the post of Under Secretary – who should be the principal permanent adviser of the Irish Government in civil affairs – appears to be that he is a routine clerk . . . The Chief Secretary, for his part appears to be under the illusion that a Civil Servant – even though he has the position and emoluments of permanent head of the Irish administration – is entirely unconcerned with the exploration or settlement of problems which the Irish administration exists to solve.[27]

Fisher recommended that Sir John Anderson, later Lord Waverley, probably the finest administrator the British Civil Service has ever seen, be despatched to reorganise, indeed revolutionise, the Irish Civil Service. British civil servants were therefore seconded to Dublin and competent Irish officers selected to head the new state's administration; Dr Ronan Fanning, the historian of the Irish Department of Finance, described the continuing relationship between British and Irish officials: 'Both, simply, wanted the Free State to be a success, and financial stability was one of the prerequisites of that success.' The success of the first major Irish loan, issued in December 1923 after the civil war had spluttered to an end, and a fresh election given solid support to the new state (102 adherents and forty-four dissident Sinn Féiners), was not only a vote of confidence, but the result of collaboration between the Irish Department of Finance and the British Treasury.[28]

The Irish Free State inherited – thanks in part to Warren Fisher and John Anderson – a fully functioning modern state: the lawyers did not need new books, nor even to change their wigs and gowns; the continued Dáil and Senate functioned according to Westminster practice. Speeches, in spite of the polite fiction that Irish was the first language, continued to be in English. Dáil Members, now distinguished as 'Teachta Dala' – TD – had their names cast in Irish for the division list, Thomas Johnson becoming Tomas MacEoin and John Butler Sean Boitleir, but they remained firmly English in the official reports. Pillarboxes retained the royal initials, but were painted green. At least seventeen prominent Irish institutions still (in 2001) retain the prefix 'Royal', ranging from the Royal Irish Academy to the Royal National Lifeboat Institution. Where new departures were contemplated, they usually either became dead letters, as has the attempted Gaelicisation of society, or were soon cancelled, as was done with the original constitutional provisions for popular participation in government through referenda or initiatives (proposals for new laws).[29]

Irish politicians in both parts of the country were obliged, either by prejudice or political necessity, to use very different language from the constrained and precise terms employed by civil servants. The failure either to improve living conditions, perhaps an inevitable result of the financial orthodoxy adopted by the Cumann na nGaedheal– Fine Gael governments between 1922 and 1932, or to fulfil any of the blowsy ideals advanced with such passion before 1922, ensured that disappointments would provoke extremist rhetoric, and more than merely verbal challenges.

George Orwell, in the concluding lines of *Animal Farm*, described how revolutions tended to end in governments very like those they replaced. In Ireland of the 1920s Cosgrave's government of 'tough but talented gunmen' was forced into following exactly the same policies that their Dublin Castle predecessors had adopted; but, having a democratic mandate and after an often violent personal past, their coercion laws were more drastic than anything a Westminster government had dared impose. Neither military defeat nor democratic rejection had persuaded the rejectionists to accept the majority will. To de Valera and his followers the fictions of the Toy Theatre had become reality. His 'metaphysical' position was that he remained President of that republic proclaimed in 1916, with a parallel government, a Minister of Defence (Sean Lemass) and a regularly constituted army – the IRA. The democratically elected government of the Free State were, they considered, nothing but impostors, tools of a foreign government. Reality eventually forced de Valera to abandon his pretence, but the illusion has persisted. In 1925 some survivors of the civil war Irregulars split off from their 'President' to begin their own campaign of terror, which over three-quarters of a century later has not ended. As Balfour and his British predecessors had done, Cosgrave was forced into pushing through successive Coercion Acts. On 10 July 1927 the IRA responded, as the Fenians had done with Lord Frederick Cavendish forty years earlier, by shooting Kevin O'Higgins, the Minister for Home Affairs and Michael Collins' old colleague; they had killed his father four years previously. Cosgrave's government replied with harsher emergency legislation, with special courts empowered to inflict the death penalty on anyone carrying illegal arms; but imprisonment and executions did not end the succession of assassinations. Deserted by his gunmen de Valera was forced into accepting modified legality. As Fianna Fáil – 'the Warriors of Destiny' – de Valera's 'slightly constitutional party' became the official opposition, and eventually, in 1932, the government.[30]

Cosgrave could then look back upon some solid achievements. Membership of the United Kingdom had been replaced by that of the British Commonwealth of Nations (the term was first officially used in the Anglo–Irish Treaty), and the period between 1921 and 1931 had been one where the nature of this 'immature League of Nations', as O'Higgins described it, had evolved into its definitive shape. Alongside South Africa, Canada, Australia and New Zealand, Ireland played an important and distinctive part in the regular conferences of Commonwealth leaders, held in 1926 and 1931. By one of those delectable ironies that litter Irish history it was old Lord Balfour, 'Bloody Balfour' himself, 'with a smile like moonlight on a tombstone' – Kevin O'Higgins again –

who produced the initial formulation at the 1926 Imperial Conference: 'Great Britain and the Dominions are autonomous communities within the British Empire, equal in status, in no way subordinate one to another ... although united by a common allegiance to the Crown, and freely associated as members of the British Commonwealth of Nations.' When this was enshrined in the Statute of Westminster in September 1931 Ireland was to all intents and purposes as much an independent country as France or Spain.

Free State to Republic

It was an independence that de Valera, coming to power after a general election in March 1932, was quick to exploit. It is tempting to look for parallels. Finland had undergone an even bloodier civil war between the constitutional Whites and totalitarian communist Reds, in which, as with Ireland, the democratic will prevailed. Portugal was about to become, from 1932, a theocratic corporatist state under Dr Antonio Salazar. De Valera, once having given up his guns, designed a constitution in which the Roman Catholic Church was given as privileged a place as that accorded by Salazar, and more so than it would be in Franco's Spain. Comparisons with authoritarian European states should not be pressed too far: de Valera was no such totalitarian leader as Franco or Mussolini – his speeches were bloody enough, talking of having to 'wade through the blood' of the lawful government to achieve his aims, but Irish governments continued to assume or relinquish power according to the results of democratic elections. Nevertheless de Valera made it clear that his democratic principles were flimsy, a reluctant recognition of what was possible: 'if he had at his disposal the forces of Hitler', de Valera told the American minister John Cudahy, as emphatically as he could, 'he would move on the north and settle partition conclusively'.

De Valera was still the implacable ascetic revolutionary of 1916, determined to make the metaphysical republic a practical actuality. Having also developed into a very skilful politician with an acute sensitivity for public opinion, his policies were eventually accepted, but their very success carried with them the penalty of an increasingly alienated Northern Ireland. The more distinctively 'Irish' the Free State became, the more strongly Ulster Protestants detested it. Dominion status carried with it the power to amend the constitution, and therefore the treaty (a power denied by the Irish courts, but confirmed – irony again – by the London Privy Council). Accordingly in July 1937 a new constitution, Republican in everything but name, was promulgated.

Nothing could have been more calculated to infuriate the Protestant Ulstermen. The very preamble, in which God was enlisted on the side of Nationalism, was to them an almost blasphemous affront: 'In the Name of the Most Holy Trinity ... We, the people of Eire, humbly acknowledging all our obligations to our Divine Lord, Jesus Christ, Who sustained our fathers through centuries of trial, Gratefully remembering their heroic and unremitting struggle to regain the rightful independence of our Nation ...'; but the second article, claiming that 'the national territory consists of the whole island of Ireland', was a flat denial of Northern Ireland's right to exist. A cool observer might have dismissed this as a piece of Irish extravagance, like Article 8, which claimed that Irish was the national language, only 'recognising English as *a* second official language' – an obvious fiction that could hardly be taken seriously – but cool observers were uncommon in Ulster.

The Irish people did not evince overmuch enthusiasm for their new constitution, approving it only by 685,105 votes to 526,945, an unconvincingly small majority for so fundamental an innovation. Civil servants tended to take a sceptical view of politicians' antics. J.J. McElligott, the long-serving Secretary to the Department of Finance, himself a veteran of the 1916 Rising, mercilessly exposed the contradictions embodied in the constitution, and accurately forecast their eventual outcome. The claim to sovereignty over the North

> will be described, and with some justice, as a fiction. Having been at such pains to expel fictions from the existing Constitution it seems inconsistent now to import an even greater fiction ... From the practical point of view, apart from the fear of consequences, these articles will not contribute anything to effecting the unity of Ireland, but rather the reverse.

In another episode that has been as far as possible deleted from Irish history (*The Military History of Ireland* makes no mention of it in its 458 pages), another 'Irish Brigade' left for Spain 'to strike a blow for Christ the King' and General Franco. It was a remarkably ineffective blow. Faced with a real war rather than a campaign of ambush and assassination, and opposed by Spanish government troops, who included a number of Irishmen of opposing political opinions in the International Brigade, the Irish Falangists disintegrated. After the first few casualties – seven in all – the nearly seven hundred volunteers were packed off home as a danger to Franco's campaign. Nevertheless, they were given a heroes' welcome and a civic reception in Dublin; their leader, General Eoin O'Duffy, in due course was also accorded a state funeral.[31]

It was inevitable that, watching from behind their parapets, the Northerners wanted nothing to do with this new state. Unsympathetic though they might also be to the Spanish left, and as attached to family life as any devout Catholic, Ulster Unionists found themselves faced with a theocratic sectarian state which denied the worth of their own traditions.

Ulster Protestants felt that they had vindicated their reputation for loyalty during the war; the fact that at least half of the total Irish casualties of the conflict were Catholics was usually ignored. James Craig, a man of great tenacity and stamina but little imagination, appointed Ulster Unionist leader in March 1921 was thereafter unquestioned controller of Northern Ireland governments for nearly twenty years. The violence of 1920 and 1921, as bloody in Ulster as in the South, had only settled prejudices more rigidly. Just as the IRA attempted, not without success (Protestant numbers in the Free State fell from 327,000 before the war to 221,000 in 1926), what would later be miscalled 'ethnic cleansing', so brutal attacks on Northern Catholics were launched with exactly the same intention. In the two years after July 1920 557 died – 303 Catholics, 172 Protestants and eighty-two members of the police; in Belfast alone some twenty-three thousand Catholics had been driven from their homes. It was not until August 1922 that the provisional Irish government decided on a peace policy that should govern 'future dealings with North East Ulster'.[32]

Craig's grasp of power had been cemented in the May 1921 elections to the Northern Ireland Parliament. Eighty-nine per cent of the electorate, now substantially enlarged, especially by the admission of women to the franchise, turned out to vote. The results demonstrated how well the boundaries had succeeded in providing for a Unionist majority: forty Unionists, six Sinn Féiners and six Nationalists gained seats. With such a mandate Craig was able to sit tight during the Anglo–Irish treaty negotiations and refuse to contemplate any relaxation of Northern independence. Since the Better Government of Ireland Act had given Northern Ireland powers similar to those of the Free State its government was endowed with near-independent status. Had the constitution been designed merely for a region of the United Kingdom the devolved powers would have been significantly fewer, and the permanent majority less able continuously to frustrate and victimise the Catholic Nationalist minority.

It would have taken leaders of considerable generosity and breadth of vision to have taken forward 'a society which was, from its start, bitterly divided, intrinsically unstable, and prone to periodic outbreaks of rebellion and violence', and such men did not come forward. Proportional representation in local government elections, which gave minorities a fair chance of sharing in at least some restricted power, was immediately abolished by the Unionist government. Michael Collins told Winston Churchill that the proposal to do so was designed 'to oust the Catholic and Nationalist people of the six counties from their rightful share in local administration'. Churchill, who had formed considerable respect for Collins, agreed, and ordered the Bill to be blocked, whereupon Craig threatened resignation. Given the strength of Unionism, even under proportional representation, the only alternative would have been the suspension of the new Northern government and the resumption of direct rule by Westminster. In all probability this would have been the better choice, but it was one which a debilitated coalition government in London – which collapsed a few weeks later – could not accept.[33]

The Act removing that important safeguard for minorities was duly passed on 11 September 1922. The stage was set to entrench Unionist power, an achievement rendered easier by the refusal of the Nationalist and Sinn Féin Members to take their seats in the Ulster Parliament and make their presence felt. This abdication of responsibility did much to bolster Unionist hegemony, already well established. Another blow against possible reconciliation was struck by the Unionist government's Education Acts. Protestant bigots succeeded in overturning an Education Bill which would have ensured that the state paid all teachers' salaries in schools 'where children of different faiths might study and play together', with no religious education allowed during school hours. Catholic bigots, on the other hand, refused to accept 'simple bible teaching', which implied an alien freedom of thought, 'the fundamental principle of Protestantism [being] the interpretation of sacred scriptures by private judgment'. As a result, the insistence on total Church control meant second-rate education for Catholic children. As it later turned out, the Unionist legislation was in fact illegal: had Nationalists taken any action the Acts would have almost certainly been cancelled; the policy of abstention was singularly damaging to its own cause.[34]

In November 1925 the existing boundaries of Ulster were confirmed, the recommendations of the Joint Boundary Commission, which had been established under the treaty to define the frontier, having had to be abandoned after a leaked report (the report itself was only released in 1967). But the three governments declared themselves 'united in amity' and agreed to mutual aid 'in a spirit of neighbourly comradeship'; and the elected Nationalists, who included the admirable Joe Devlin, decided, after all, to take their seats in the Ulster Commons.

It was a short-lived participation, since Craig decided to complete the Unionist hold on power by abolishing proportional representation in parliamentary as well as local elections. Again an Act was passed, this time without any interference by Westminster, which had the effect, within a few years, of ensuring that in single-Member constituencies there was little point in voting, a Unionist victory being inevitable. By 1933, 70 per cent of such seats went to Unionists by default. Devlin's Nationalists once again absented themselves, with their leader bitterly reproaching the Unionists: 'You had opponents willing to co-operate. We did not seek office. We sought service. We were willing to help. But you rejected all friendly offers . . . You went on on the old political lines, fostering hatreds, keeping one-third of the population as if they were pariahs in the community.'[35] It was a just accusation of a policy which continued little changed for the next forty years. The splendid new government building at Stormont, designed on an imperial scale, was to house a solidly Unionist Parliament. Lord Craigavon, as Craig had become in 1927, was left free, behind secure boundaries, to disregard the interests of any inhabitants of Northern Ireland who did not support him.

Until de Valera's accession Ulster had been relatively quiet, but King George V's Jubilee in 1935 combined with de Valera's legislation to provoke a violent reaction. Belfast was again ravaged by savage sectarian riots in which eight Protestants and five Catholics were killed and much physical damage inflicted. The more extreme Protestant opinion welcomed the provocation afforded by the Irish constitution: Lord Craigavon did not object to the Catholic Church's 'special position', since 'while the Government of the South is carried on along lines which I presume are very suitable to the majority of Roman Catholics ... surely the Government of the North, with a majority of Protestants, should carry on the administration according to Protestant ideas and Protestant desires'.

In the Free State the dafter aspirations that Irish independence would create a prosperous nation of contented Gaelic-speaking smallholders practising traditional crafts – as many as thirty million of them in the more optimistic estimates – were very rapidly proved totally illusory. Ten years of prudent and conservative Cosgrave government had at least kept the Free State on an even keel, but de Valera's politically inspired economics rocked the boat. In 1914 Irish GDP per capita has been estimated as between 57 per cent and 62 per cent of that of Great Britain; by 1938 it had fallen to 51 per cent. Part of this decline must be attributed to de Valera's 'Economic War', declared in 1932 by a refusal to continue payments guaranteed under the treaty, thereby provoking British retaliatory tariffs, and in turn the raising of import duties in Ireland. Inevitably, the results were much more damaging to the smaller economy. Only by 1939 did real agricultural wages in Ireland regain 1923 levels, their nadir being during the Economic War. Famine was once again regarded as a real possibility.[36]

The first thaw in unfriendly relations began with an approach by the Irish High Commissioner in London, J.W. Duranty, for a specific reciprocal agreement on Irish cattle and Welsh coal. Once more Warren Fisher, still in office at the British Treasury, threw his very considerable weight in favour of agreement on generous terms, only to be refused by his political master, Prime Minister Neville Chamberlain. Fisher persisted: 'if the age-old tension between Ireland and England could be effectively and permanently ended the importance to us of these particular money claims is in my view negligible'. His efforts were assisted by the appointment in November 1935 as Secretary of State for the Dominions of Malcolm MacDonald, son of the former Labour premier Ramsay MacDonald, and a conciliatory liberal.

Once de Valera's new constitution had been accepted, the political benefits of challenging Britain were minimised, and the warnings of his civil servants became increasingly agitated, 'stressing the absolute necessity of finally settling all our economic and financial differences with Great Britain'. In large part due to MacDonald's flexibility, reinforced by the essential Treasury support offered by Fisher (ministers find great difficulty in facing down Treasury opposition, usually firmly against anything more than minimal expenditure), an Anglo–Irish agreement was finalised in 1938. It not only ended the 'Economic War' but provided for the return to Ireland of the three naval ports – Queenstown, Berehaven and Lough Swilly – still in British control under the terms of the 1921 treaty. A chain of results ensued. At the outbreak of hostilities in September 1939 both Ireland and South Africa faced the question of whether to join with the rest of the Commonwealth in declaring war on Nazi Germany. Smuts, at that time in precarious power, was able to persuade the South African Parliament to do so. For de Valera there was no question. Ireland was to remain neutral, in spite of the later American pressure (the American Ambassador, David Gray, pressed Roosevelt to seize the ex-treaty ports).[37] Popular feeling was divided. The poet John Betjeman, press officer to the British High Commission in Dublin during the war, gloomily commented:

> . . . people . . . are either anti-British, anti-German and pro-Irish (faintly a majority) . . . pro-Irish and pro-German (about 48 per cent) . . . the Irish papers are all anti-British . . . and the best-selling writers are pro-German. I am beginning to hate the Irish. God bless England! God save the King! Up the British Empire!

Neutrality did not entirely spare Ireland, since some presumably poorly-navigated German planes bombed Dublin in a night raid, killing thirty-four people; but once again differences between North and South were exacerbated when Belfast was shattered by a series of raids in April and May 1941, in which over a thousand died and more than half the city's homes were destroyed or badly damaged.[38]

For the rest, Irish official conduct during the war was, in many respects, disgraceful. Anti-Semitism had always been prevalent in Ireland (as indeed elsewhere), and was not discouraged by the Catholic hierarchy. When, in the Dáil, Oliver Flanagan praised Hitler for ridding Germany of Jews, claiming, 'I doubt very much if they are human,' his attacks were not challenged by any other Member. Indeed J.J. Walsh, a former Cosgrave minister, described Irish Jews as 'a gang of parasites'. It was hardly surprising that during the war only about sixty European Jews were admitted into Ireland.[39]

When in May 1945 de Valera visited the German Legation in Dublin to commiserate with the officials on the death of their beloved Führer, indignation in Britain and America was incandescent. If it was, as claimed, nothing more than a diplomatic gesture demanded by protocol, it was one that not even Franco felt obliged to make.[40] Since de Valera's visit to the Legation took place on 2 May, two weeks after the concentration camp at Bergen-Belsen had been liberated by British troops (accompanied by an Irish doctor), the pro-Axis nature of Irish government sentiment seemed – inaccurately as it happened – to have been made manifest; but the British Union of Fascists sent a message of support, and the Dublin mob smashed the windows of the British High Commission and the American Embassy.[41]

Attitudes hardly changed after the war. In December 1945 de Valera declared, 'our policy [towards admitting displaced persons] should be liberal and generous'. In practice the liberality and generosity resulted only in an agreement that 'five Jewish families might be allowed in for up to two years'. The offer came so tardily and reluctantly that it was never taken up. A decade later, after the Hungarian uprising, the Minister for External Affairs proudly announced that the government would accept over five hundred Hungarian refugees as permanent immigrants. Subsequent ill-treatment in the reception camps and the insistence that all refugees should be Catholics so alienated the refugees that most left for other countries, some even returning to Hungary.[42]

Given such a record Ireland's treatment by the Allies resembled that accorded to Spain. Although hardly a pariah state, Ireland did not qualify for Marshall Aid, was scornfully rebuffed by the USA, and was not admitted to the United Nations until 1957.[43] The effects were two-fold: although Northern attitudes were, *pari passu*, not a great deal more liberal – it took spirited Quaker efforts to get Jews housed in Northern Ireland – the sense of moral superiority bolstered Unionist self-satisfaction, already high enough at their consciousness of having fought the good fight against so great an evil while others held back. Louis MacNeice expressed some of the bitterness at the thousands of deaths which might have been saved by Allied bases in Ireland; asking the 'neutral island' to

> Look into your heart, you will find fermenting rivers,
> Intricacies of gloom and glint,
> You will find such ducats of dream and great doubloons of
>   ceremony
> As nobody to-day would mint.
>
> But then look eastward from your heart, there bulks
> A continent, close, dark, as archetypal sin,
> While to the west off your own shores the mackerel
> Are fat – on the flesh of your kin.

Again, by refusing admission to refugees Ireland was deprived of that influx of European talent that made so great a contribution to British post-war life. The Republic, as it was to become in 1949, remained a narrow, moralistic, dull and unattractive community. Emigration, naturally, continued high.

'Lay the lash upon their backs'

The record of the first two parts of the United Kingdom under independent administrations was hardly encouraging. Any ability a British government had to push Stormont towards a more equitable distribution of advantages was considerably diminished by the actions of

President John Costello, head of a coalition government that displaced de Valera's Fianna Fáil in February 1948. Without warning, or proper consultation, during a press conference in Canada, Costello announced that Ireland was leaving the Commonwealth and would become a republic. By so doing, the President sealed in partition, probably without realising what he had done. After some dissension Westminster accepted the *fait accompli*. The Republic of Eire was permitted to retain all Commonwealth preferences and rights to British citizenship, but the British government was obliged to placate Northern Unionists by guaranteeing that 'in no event will Northern Ireland or any part thereof cease to be a part of His Majesty's dominions or of the United Kingdom without the consent of the Parliament of Northern Ireland'. Even without the new Republic such protection had been rendered inevitable by de Valera's wild efforts to end partition, which included seriously suggesting to the appalled United States minister, David Gray, that Northern Unionists should all be deported to Britain, and Ulster repopulated by the Irish living in Britain. It was now clear that, even by less drastic means than forcible ethnic cleansing, any hopes of ending partition were dissolved.[44]

There was not much to attract Northerners towards closer ties with the South, struggling under a pall of national depression, a morose community under the influence of a reactionary hierarchy. Symbolised by John Charles McQuaid, Archbishop of Dublin, a caricature of reactionary clericism, the absolute ban on divorce, contraception and abortion was commonly accepted. A flavour of the Church's heavy hand, unmatched in Western Europe outside Spain and Portugal, is conveyed by the range of forbidden works, an eclectic list, almost a guide to the best of twentieth-century literature, which included Leon Blum, Simone de Beauvoir, Christopher Isherwood, Sean O'Faolain, Sean O'Casey, Margaret Mead, Alberto Moravia, John Steinbeck, George Orwell, Jean Paul Sartre, Daphne du Maurier, Malcom Muggeridge and Stella Gibbons. Foreign dances, 'importations from the vilest dens of London, Paris and New York – direct incitements to evil thoughts, evil desires and the grossest acts of impurity', together with jazz – 'Nigger music' – were anathematised. Yet the counsel given by the most reverend clerics was hardly in close accordance with the teaching of their Master. Bishop O'Doherty of Galway advised fathers that 'If your girls do not obey you, if they are not in at the hours appointed, lay the lash upon their backs.' The Christian Brothers needed no such exhortations to inflict savage beatings on the boys in their care.[45]

Extensive and expensive efforts had been made to ensure that the new Ireland would be Gaelic as well as Catholic. All children were taught the language, essential for any official job, and attempts were made to extend the educational scope, all without effect. Once out of school, or the post secured, the Irish resumed the near-universal use of English; only occasionally would some enthusiast essay the ancient language in the Dáil, and almost all official publications were, as they still are, in what was claimed to be only the 'second language'.

It was hardly surprising that young Irish people voted with their feet, taking up what still remained the alternative, residence in Britain. No passports were needed, and full access to the franchise and social services was available straight off the boat. Between 1951 and 1961 some 375,000 Irish people, mostly young, emigrated, 90 per cent of them to Britain, for so long the object of official disdain, but now the promised land (the quota for Irish immigration to the United States was never filled during that period). It was a terrible indictment of Republican rule.

One consistent voice of sanity and good humour was raised in the general gloom. The brilliantly eccentric editor of the *Irish Times*, R.M. Smyllie, enlisted Brian O'Nolan, alias Flann O'Brien and Myles na gCopaleen, as a columnist. From 1940 onwards his devastating comments on censors and censored, and on affairs far and wide, in an inimitable blend of Joyce and Beachcomber, had readers both giggling and reflecting. This is Myles on a visit to the National Museum in 1943:

> I am certain that under the Statute of Westminster H.M. Government are bound to hand over to us the chains with which Ireland was bound . . . Ha-ho, those wretched jacobins. Twenty years of serf-government (stet, by jove!) and not an attendant in the 'National' Museum can show me the true badge of nationhood![46]

No voice like Myles enlivened the North. Most Northern Irish voters would have agreed with the restrictive notions of the South. Sexual mores in Ulster were at least as strict and artistic life a good deal more limited. Belfast had nothing to compare with Dublin's theatres or galleries; Archbishop McQuaid's worries about masturbation were paralleled by the hysteria of the Reverend Dr Ian Paisley, who accused the Queen of 'spiritual fornication' after she paid a visit to the irreproachable Pope John XXIII.[47]

By 1965, however, both Irelands seemed to be experiencing something of a revival. The IRA campaign in the North was called off in February 1962. In the South Sean Lemass had taken over from de Valera in 1959 and Craigavon's successor, Lord Brookeborough, had been politely ejected to make way for Terence O'Neill. Both new leaders were prepared to abandon some of the fixed positions of their predecessors. The nervous ('I shall get into terrible trouble for this') visit by Lemass to O'Neill on 14 January 1965 paid dividends in improved relationships.[48] It was the first meeting of two heads of government since Craig had met Cosgrave forty years before, and aroused deep passions in the North, almost incomprehensible to outsiders. The emergence of Ian Paisley as a leader of one faction was matched by that of John Hume, a Derry activist, and Gerry Fitt, the Republican Member for West Belfast, elected to Westminster in 1966, committed to revitalising the moribund Nationalist Party, accepting that any change in the status of Northern Ireland could only come about with the consent of the majority.

It is easier to understand the grievances of the Catholic minority than to sympathise with the extreme Protestants. Blatant discrimination against Catholics had been widespread, especially in that part of the Province west of the River Bann and in Armagh. In Dungannon, evenly divided between Catholics and Protestants, only thirty-four Catholic families had been allocated council houses, as against 264 Protestant ones: in nearby Portadown the Mayor replied to a question on the number of Catholics given council houses: 'One – and that's too bloody many.'[49]

Such a discriminatory policy was not universal. Housing in Belfast was usually allocated fairly, with Catholics in fact receiving rather more than their proportionate share, but the whole ethos of the administration was at least as strongly tilted towards Protestantism as that in the South was to the Roman Church – and with much less excuse, in view of the dwindling Protestant population of the Republic. Senior official posts were actually monopolised by Protestants in 1943; even by 1969 fewer than 8 per cent of such posts were held by Catholics. Applicants for jobs in business had to state their religion – although in Dublin the *Irish Times* still carried advertisements stating 'Protestants preferred'. A British engineer in charge of recruitment was reprimanded for defining himself as 'Christian'.[50]

Protests against discrimination originated in England, when journalists began to take an interest in the unpopular subject of Britain's piece of Ireland, and were taken up especially by the younger generation of post-war Ulster university graduates who had been brought up to expect better things. The Northern Irish Civil Rights Association was formed to agitate for the same standards that were observed in Britain. Uncomfortable comparisons could be made with civil rights protests in the United States and Europe. In Prague Communist restrictions of freedom were being dismantled; on 4 April 1968 Martin Luther King was assassinated; student riots blazed out in Paris the following month, and were transmitted all over the world by the television cameras. Ivan Cooper, later an independent Stormont MP, called for people to fight for their rights 'as the Blacks in America are fighting'. Protests crystallised in October 1968: a march, which included Hume, Fitt and three Labour Westminster MPs, was brutally dispersed by police batons; and also, for the first time, captured on television. Reluctantly, as British governments always had been, Harold Wilson's administration was forced to pay attention.

CHAPTER 12

⟨◦⟩

1950–2001

Not just yet

WESTMINSTER POLITICS changed drastically with the departure of the Southern Irish MPs, who had previously formed a reliable supplement to the Liberal Party. With Irish representation confined to a dozen or so Ulster Unionists, siding consistently with the Conservatives, the balance of power had shifted. Until the Labour Party had grown strong enough to form a viable alternative Conservatives would remain the natural party of government. Unionism as a cause was now dead, obliging Conservatives to refocus their programme on social and economic issues, but Scottish and Welsh nationalism was also moribund. Sufficient Scottish interest was rekindled by a revived Scottish Home Rule Association to provoke the emergence of a Scottish Home Rule Bill, which became a regular event, occurring in 1919, 1920, 1921, 1924 and 1927. All proposals were examined with polite interest, and all allowed to die, but the electoral statistics highlighted the essential anomaly: in 1923 the Conservative-Unionist vote controlled Britain by a majority of 347 to 268, whereas Scotland had chosen fifty-nine Liberal and Labour MPs and only fifteen Conservatives. The two countries clearly wanted very different governments.[1]

After 1927 the regular Home Rule Bills petered out, and the Labour Party made a formal disclaimer of any present intentions to promote Home Rule. That mantle passed to an odd collection of enthusiasts, including such romantic Celticists as the Catholic novelist Compton Mackenzie, aspiring to 'an intuitive, female Scotland [which would] find her identity with her sisters, Ireland, Wales and Brittany and from there with the Federation of Celtic States', and the journalist and poet Christopher Grieve (Hugh MacDiarmid), who, finding a national language lacking, invented one from etymological dictionaries and

370

the extant Border dialects. Grieve tended to an absolutist stance, a contradictory mixture of Leninism, anarchy and eccentric economic theories:

> Any refusal to give Scotland free choice to remain or go out of the Empire . . . is to subject Scotland to a species of slavery . . .

and, on the other hand, an adulation of totalitarianism:

> Here lies your secret, O Lenin, yours and oors
> No' in the majority will that accepts the result
> But in the real will that bides its time . . . [2]

But far from anyone refusing Scottish liberties, there was no sign of any demand there for 'free choice'. The National Party of Scotland, formed in 1928, put up a candidate in a Midlothian by-election in January 1929, attracting 4.5 per cent of the vote. In the subsequent general elections, of that year and of 1931, the party's share was 0.1 per cent and 1 per cent. A merger of the NPS with the more moderate Scottish Party, masterminded by the dedicated young nationalist John MacCormick in 1934, produced the present Scottish National Party (SNP), which won 1.3 per cent of the 1935 general election vote. None of these minuscule minorities indicated a general interest in nationalist politics; more serious issues preoccupied the electorate.[3]

Some at least of the earlier objections to Westminster rule, that Scotland was not receiving its fair share of parliamentary and government attention or of national expenditure, seemed well-founded. The Depression of the thirties was especially damaging in Scotland, dependent as that country was on heavy industry. Unemployment was running at over 20 per cent, and production in 1934 was lower than it had been in 1913. During a period (1924–37) when the UK economy as a whole was growing at an annual rate of 2.2 per cent Scotland managed only 0.4 per cent, and experienced an absolute decline of 20 per cent between 1928 and 1932. It was true that conditions just south of the border, in the north-east of England, were as bad, or even worse – the abiding symbol of the waste years is still the 1936 'hunger march' from Jarrow – but to some Scots the blame could conveniently be put on the 'English' government.[4]

An important step had been taken in 1926 when the post of Scottish

Secretary was upgraded to that of a Secretary of State. Much depended on the personal weight of metal that any Scottish Secretary could bring to bear on his cabinet colleagues, which was often not very much, for the post was generally regarded both as a dead end from which further promotion could rarely be expected, and as a specialised post to which only Scots representing Scottish constituencies could be appointed. Among the first appointments, however, three exceptionally talented Secretaries were numbered. Sir John Gilmour, an experienced public servant who held the post between 1924 and 1929, not only reorganised the existing department, but later headed a commission which recast the Office, installed in Edinburgh in impressive new headquarters, as what was almost a Scottish government. The move was carried out by the universally popular Walter Elliot, Secretary between 1936 and 1938, from which time the new St Andrew's House, magnificently sited on Calton Hill, rather than the Palace of Westminster became the centre of Scottish political gravity.[5]

Gilmour and Elliot had both been Conservatives, although markedly non-partisan. Tom Johnston, a Labour MP, Scottish Secretary between 1941 and 1945 in Churchill's coalition government, carried on the same tradition of putting Scottish interests before party requirements. Endowed with special wartime powers, Johnston was able to effect what was practically a revolution in Scottish affairs. By creating the Scottish Council (Development and Industry) he added a new arm to the Scottish administration, one that enabled Scotland to get its fair share – disgruntled English regions would protest more than a fair share – of new industries and government funding. Another Johnston initiative, the North of Scotland Hydro-Electric Board, became in due course the most efficient of British energy industries, accepting social responsibilities, acting almost as a smaller Tennessee Valley Authority by initiating regional development. Other new bodies – a Tourist Board, and all the local National Health Service Boards, administered by an ever-increasing number of civil servants – swelled the Scottish Secretary's fief. Johnston was himself a supporter of devolution – he had insisted on the need for a legislative assembly in 1936 – but his very success within the Westminster system damaged the nationalist case. A Scottish Secretary may not have been a major player in the power games of Westminster – few of the post-war appointees rose much above the worthy level until Willie Ross was appointed in 1964 – but the post carried clearly-defined and extensive responsibilities. Ross, an authoritative figure in the mould of Tom Johnston, had a National Plan for Scotland developed, which served the whole issue of future development better than the subject has ever been addressed in England. Even a feeble Scottish Secretary of State exercised very considerable power in the country, and deployed great patronage – some five thousand public posts, to say nothing of potentially generous grants and rewarding contracts, lay within his gift.

With the war drawing to an end and the election of Clement Attlee's new Labour government in July 1945, the first such with real power and a vigorous will to reform, attention was diverted from devolution towards what was proving to be a transformation of British society. Prominent Scottish and Welsh cabinet ministers, notably Emmanuel Shinwell and Aneurin Bevan, played a leading part in the new centralising government, and radical Scottish opinion was caught up in what looked like the beginning of a socialist Britain. Catering for any local whims was not on the Labour Party's agenda. What might have been a nationalist triumph, the election of Dr Robert McIntyre in a Motherwell by-election in April 1945, proved a false dawn after the seat was lost in July's general election, and the SNP found itself again with a negligible 1.2 per cent of the total vote.[6]

British society was indeed transformed by Attlee's governments, if not quite as socialists had expected. Post-war reconstruction and the impetus of the Korean War gave a temporary boost to employment, and Scotland benefited from the influx of new industries, tempted not only by generous grants but by new housing – more than half a million homes between 1945 and 1964 – constructed, again, with massive injections of public money. The prosperity was real enough, but Scotland remained a place to get away from. The beginning of the Edinburgh International Festival in 1947 only highlighted the cultural poverty of the city during the other eleven months – south of the border Newcastle had five theatres in 1951; Edinburgh, with twice the population, only two[7] – and ambitious Scots still headed for England. Heavy industry, still the motor of the Scottish economy, did nothing to improve its unprofessional managements and dreadful industrial relations. Home Rule for Scotland was a popular notion, but as little relevant as it had been after the previous war. A cross-party endeavour to promote devolution attracted two million signatures in 1950 for a pledge 'to do everything in our power to secure for Scotland a Parliament with adequate legislative authority in Scottish affairs', but this new Covenant's signatories did not follow through with their votes.

Neither of the large parties took much interest in Scottish affairs. From 1951 to 1964 Conservative governments were in power, brushing regional discontents aside as matters of minor importance, to be dealt with by the now-flourishing Scottish bureaucracy. Any remaining nationalist hopes of Labour support were ditched when in 1956 Hugh Gaitskell, the party's leader, committed it once more to opposing Scottish Home Rule.

By 1964, when a Labour government under Harold Wilson gained tenuous power, the British electorate distrusted both the main parties. Voters in Scotland had, at least, a further element of choice than that provided elsewhere by the Liberals, who never remotely approached being able to form a government, although attracting a respectable percentage of the vote – 11.2 per cent in Britain and 7.6 per cent in Scotland. Nationalists were beginning to emerge from obscurity, gaining the support of more than 1 per cent of the Scottish electorate for the first time. What had hitherto been a straightforward tussle between Labour and Conservative was transformed in March 1967 when SNP intervention lost Labour the Glasgow Pollok seat to the Conservatives, and more dramatically that November when the SNP candidate, Winnie Ewing, actually won what had been one of the safest Labour seats, at Hamilton.

Admittedly both Pollok and Hamilton were by-elections, occasions on which voters are notoriously fickle, but the threat to Labour was clear. Much less clear was the confused reaction of both parties. Edward Heath, the opposition leader, pledged the Conservatives in his 1968 'Declaration of Perth' to a policy of an elected Scottish Assembly. The more cautious Harold Wilson kicked for touch in appointing a Royal Commission, the Crowther/Kilbrandon Commission, which reported only in 1973. By that time the Conservatives were back in power, Wilson's tergiversation and weakness in the face of arrogant trades unions having brought Edward Heath into office in June 1970. Only Heath's mishandling of the same problem, which brought the economy almost to a standstill, gave Wilson a second chance. The two general elections in the single year of 1974 not only brought the return of a Labour government, but upset all previously received electoral wisdom.

Neither Tories nor Labour yet commanded much confidence. In the February 1974 election the Conservative vote fell from 46.4 per cent to 37.9 per cent; that of Labour from 43 per cent to 36.2 per cent, in spite of which Labour won two more seats. Hanging precariously on to power Wilson's government was obliged to rely on the other parties, including fourteen Liberals, seven Scottish Nationalists and two members of the Welsh nationalist party Plaid Cymru. In Scotland the contrast between the elections of 1959 and November 1974 was stark. The only SNP candidate in the Labour heartland of Glasgow polled 3549 votes in 1959; in 1974 the SNP was the runner-up in nine of the Labour-held Glasgow constituencies, and Scotland as a whole returned twelve SNP Members. Since Labour's overall majority nationally was only three, the threat to the party was grimly clear. Self-preservation demanded that the Labour government make some progress towards devolution, and it was certainly limited devolution rather than anything more radical that was considered. The Northern Ireland experiment had proved that granting too much power to a regional authority could lead to uncontrollable strife.

'Ye Happie Ilands set within the British Seas' (Michael Drayton)

Other instances of devolution, of great antiquity, were present for comparison and example in the offshore islands, the Isle of Man and the Channel Islands. Geographically, Man, twenty to thirty miles from Scotland, England and Ireland, is as much part of the British Isles as Jersey, Guernsey, Alderney and Sark are of France. Yet all have retained a notable degree of independence – quite remarkably, so far as the Channel Islands are concerned, given the strained relations over the centuries between Britain and France. Jersey and Guernsey are both still governed by their own Assemblies of the States, presided over by Bailiffs; Guernsey still has its Procureur, Conseillers, Jures-Justiciers and Douzainiers; Sark has its Seigneur and Seneschal. 'Griefs' in the courts are introduced by the 'Clameur de Haro', as they were in the days of William the Conqueror's forebears. Only after the accession of George III was the Duke of Normandy not represented at coronations, given precedence even before the Archbishop of Canterbury.[8]

The last remnants of the Duchy left hanging in the air after the battle of Bouvines in 1214 had finally restored mainland Normandy to the French, the Channel Islands – 'les Îles Anglo-Normandes' – remained ecclesiastically part of the diocese of Coutances, and at the same time a possession of the English Crown. To the islanders there was little difference between a French administration in Paris and a very similar one in London. Very sensibly, they preferred the more inaccessible as being likely to interfere less in their own affairs. As long, that was, as the indignant French could be repelled. Being islands, this depended on sea-power; the distances between the coast of France and those of England were of less importance than the relative naval strengths, and the will of the islanders to defend themselves.

French attacks were persistent throughout the Middle Ages, but England could always exercise decisive naval strength, deployed from the concentration of harbours around the Cinque Ports and Southampton. The unproductive stalemate was ended only in 1481 when Pope Sixtus IV issued an edict, to be fixed to church doors from Salisbury to Nantes, proclaiming that the islands and their waters should be neutral; almost incredibly this command was usually observed for the next two centuries. Since that time the history of the Channel Islands paralleled that of Britain. The Reformation was accepted quickly enough, with more ease on Jersey than on Guernsey; Mary's heretic-burnings took place on Guernsey, and were executed by Jerseymen, but both islands thereafter remained very much Protestant. During the Civil Wars Guernsey supported Parliament, while Philip de Carteret and his nephew George held out for the Crown on Jersey; the issue was only settled after nine years with the arrival of the Cromwellian fleet in 1651. George Carteret was later rewarded for his loyalty by having part of the newly-acquired territory of New Amsterdam named in honour of Jersey.

Thereafter, with the exception of one French descent in 1781, immortalised in the splendid painting of Major Peirson's death by John

Singleton Copley, and the German occupation of the islands between 1940 and 1945, the Channel Islands have remained peaceably independent, not only of the United Kingdom government, but of each other.

Political reality dictates limits to such independence. A confrontation took place in 1852 when, after a number of Royal Commissions had reported, three Orders in Council pertaining to legal matters on Jersey were issued from London. These were energetically resisted, the Queen was petitioned, and six Acts passed by the States of Jersey setting out what they themselves wanted. Submitted to the Judicial Committee of the Privy Council, the Jersey Acts were approved, and the original British orders revoked. This was to be the pattern of subsequent legislation. Jersey, and Guernsey also representing Alderney, would advance their own recommendations, not to the UK Parliament, but to Her Majesty's Privy Council (not, of course, in any way exempt from parliamentary influence by the government of the day), and have their Acts, after due discussion, authorised.

The islands were valued for their exceptional seamen – Hardy, Saumarez and D'Auvergne being only some of the names famous in naval history – and for their utility as anchorages. In other fields the Jerseyman John Lemprière of the dictionary and Thomas de la Rue of Guernsey, whose firm has printed banknotes for the world, are not likely to be forgotten. Today the islands have not lost their reputation for gaining an honest livelihood from the sea and from their limited hinterland, but have found rather more comfortable ways of doing it, by becoming a tax haven and a reliable centre for international banking.

The Isle of Man forms the central point of the Irish Sea province. Its highest ground, Snaefell, is over two thousand feet, looming into sight from the coasts of Ireland, England and Scotland. Accessible harbours on the east coast provide an inviting prospect for any sailors coming from Britain, and were taken advantage of by successive waves of emigrants.[9]

The first Celtic-speakers – the just-surviving language is akin to Irish and Scots Gaelic, but its spelling makes it simpler to follow – formed societies similar to those in Ireland. The geological formation divides the island into north and south divisions, each centred around a massif of higher land, shadows of which continue in the present administrative system of the island, which remains separate from that of the UK.

What chiefly distinguishes the island today is the survival of the Norse constitution, first brought by the Viking raiders, who appreciated the facilities of the island as a wintering base, and later as a permanent colony. Whether this was to be subordinate to the Ostmen of Dublin, or the Earls of the Northern Isles, or to be annexed by the English or Scottish kingdoms, remained an open question, and ensured a turbulent existence for the Manx. The first ruler of a united island was a refugee from the defeat of the Norwegian army at Stamford Bridge by Harold Godwinson in 1066. Godred Crovan, 'King Orry', put together a small force which subdued the islanders, and established a dynasty which ruled for nearly two centuries. Prudent kings subsequently contrived to combine acknowledging the feudal superiority of Norwegian monarchs with maintaining friendly relations with England. Olaf I (1113–53) had been brought up at Henry I's court, and continued to benefit from English protection. His rule extended as far north as the Isles of Skye and Lewis, justifying the family's title of King of Man and of the Isles – thirty-two of them altogether. So extended an area almost ensured that the Manx rulers were perpetually embroiled with feuds and local wars, as well as conflicts with England and Norway.

King John, tidying up his realm, sent an expedition to recall King Reginald (1187–1228) to his duties; Harald I (1237–48) managed to remain on friendly terms with both England and Norway, but it was the Scottish King, Alexander, who eventually succeeded, after the battle of Largs in 1263, in obtaining Man and the Western Isles (confusingly, in Manx law, these were the Southern Islands, the Sudreys; the diocese is still Ecclesia Sodorensis, and the episcopal title is that of 'Sodor and Man'). Since this concession was unacceptable to the English Crown, the following years of Anglo–Scottish wars caught the Manx in the crossfire. Only after the decisive battle of Neville's Cross in 1346 was the island's future settled as a dependency of the English Crown.

Throughout all these tumults the original form of local government had been preserved. All Norse communities met together annually at the 'Thing' to settle disputes, return straying beasts to their rightful owners, and pass laws. The Manx Thing, the Tynwald, continues to meet on 5 July. The seat of Odin's priest is today taken by his successor, the Bishop, and that of the King of Man by the President. Two judges, the 'deemsters' who pronounce the 'dooms', according to the Laws and Customs and Ordinances of the Isles, represent the two divisions of the island. The House of Keys – the Keys being twenty-four selected freeholders, the Claves Legis – forms the legislative assembly.

Both civil and religious lords attempted from time to time to reduce the Tynwald's powers. From 1405 the Lancashire family of Stanley, now the Earls of Derby, were granted the island by Henry IV, and continued to hold it as a feudal possession for well over three hundred years, first as Kings, and then, after Henry VII began to reduce the pretensions of his magnates, as Lords of Man. At the beginning of the nineteenth century the British government decided to buy back the island (from the Duke of Atholl, who had succeeded to the Stanleys' title), and by 1860 got round to doing something about their expensive new acquisition. The passage of time had entrenched the Manx in their affection for the ancient system, and the Governor at the time was Sir Henry Loch, who later proved himself an adept Imperial official in Hong Kong, Victoria, and eventually in South Africa, and who devised an acceptable solution for the islanders. This was to allow what was essentially a lease-back from the Crown, by which the island retained its venerable political structure, and was entitled to full control of its own finances, after payment of an annual sum to cover the reserved services, essentially defence. Amended and confirmed in the 1960s, Loch's arrangement remains the foundation of Man's current status.

The value of the offshore islands as patterns for devolution was limited. Their geographical situation and small populations – about 150,000 in the Channel Islands and half that in Man – made devolution a simpler proposition. Very small states, like Monaco and Andorra, contrive to exist harmoniously in the shadow of large nations; their ambitions are limited to being allowed to conduct their domestic affairs without too much interference. Historically the offshore islands had accepted for centuries some similar dependent status, while retaining their traditional forms of government. Scotland was both too large, and with too established a unitary national history, for such a solution; Wales, whose subordination had been implicit, if often resisted, since the days of Hwyl Dda's sub-kingdom, had never possessed national institutions, but did have a lively, if divided, sense of nationality.

Oil and vinegar

The recommendations of the Crowther/Kilbrandon Commission, although not unanimous, were clear. There was, they found, nothing resembling a general vote for independence, but 'Devolution could do much to reduce discontent with the system of government. It would counter over-centralisation and, to a lesser extent, strengthen democracy, in Scotland and Wales it would be a response to national feeling.' Scottish and Welsh 'Assemblies' should therefore be established. In the subsequent White Paper of August 1976 (Cmd.6585) it was proposed that the Scottish Assembly should be returned by proportional representation, and would elect its own executive, with responsibility for all the work previously carried out by the Scottish Office. The Bill intended to effect this perished in the House of Commons as a result of Labour dissent, particularly from northern English MPs, resentful at what they saw as a diversion of resources from their own region.

The government tried again in November 1977, with a Bill which experienced a difficult passage, but succeeded in reaching the Statute Book in July 1978. One of the amendments it had sustained was a proposal put by the Scottish Labour MP, George Cunningham, that the Act would only become effective if 40 per cent of the electorate voted in favour in a referendum. Reasonable arguments could be advanced that a constitutional measure of such importance should be assented to by at least a substantial minority of those affected. What was perhaps weightier was the fact that such a qualification suited government policy, retaining as it did the vital support of the Nationalists but carrying with it the welcome possibility that the electorate might turn the measure down.

In the event Scottish voters showed themselves unconvinced. The total turnout in the March 1979 referendum was only 63.7 per cent, and of these 51.6 per cent voted in favour of the Bill, thereby falling into the Cunningham 40 per cent trap. The Scottish Bill fell to the ground, and the parallel Welsh Bill was rejected by a substantial majority. Within a month of the referendum the SNP had their revenge, assisting to bring down Jim Callaghan's Labour government by a single

Westminster vote. The subsequent general election produced a convincing Conservative victory; the Thatcher revolution had begun.

Two factors had already appeared to complicate the debate. The major achievement of Edward Heath's premiership had been to negotiate terms for joining the European Economic Community, an agreement effected in January 1973. British membership of the EEC marked the formal end of whatever remained of the British Empire. Whereas previously Commonwealth citizens were privileged by free entry into the UK and their products guaranteed preferential access to British markets, they were henceforth undifferentiated foreigners, compelled to apply for visas, and to take second place to citizens of other EEC countries. Ironically, only Ireland, which joined the EEC at the same time as Britain, escaped this fate. Since the end of the war Britain had been, sometimes reluctantly but usually with great relief, abandoning former colonies to self-government. In spite of clinging on to a disproportionate number of senior officers the armed forces and colonial services shrank, and with them Britain's position as a great power. Whatever attractions the British Empire had for Scots as a source of influence and prestige had evaporated; the Union had to be justified on different grounds.

By joining the EEC Britain had boarded a moving train. The EEC was more, and promised to be very much more, than a simple free market. Whatever autarky the United Kingdom possessed in Lord Salisbury's day, it has since 1973 been continuously eroded. In such a context, where both devolved and retained powers are circumscribed by a series of international restraints, any nation-state is forced into constitutional flexibility.

It took the SNP, which had opposed Britain's entry, some time to adjust to the situation; they did not perhaps appreciate that a new possibility had opened, that of independence within Europe, rather as had Ireland (or part of it) accepted in 1923 the concept of independence within the Commonwealth. As boundaries between nation-states became blurred in a wider union, and as Irish citizens had retained British rights, Scottish independence would seem a less dramatic event. The possibility was rendered more attractive by a second new factor, the development of the North Sea oil and gas fields. Had Scotland been independent, it was asserted that the country would have garnered a large part of the proceeds of these, and avoided the charge of relying on English-generated handouts. There was some truth in this last accusation, since between 1974 and 1978 Scots had received £175 per capita more each year in public expenditure than they paid in taxation, a difference by some way the highest of any British region. Relative deprivation was one explanation of this, but does not explain why Scotland should do proportionately so much better than Wales (£120 per capita) or the north of England (£114), both areas of similar poverty; but neither presented so great a threat to the Labour government, and in democratic politics votes count more than equity.

Exploring the oil question further, the Scottish Nationalist argument looks less convincing. The division between those areas of the North Sea in which Scots and English law is taken to apply totals 62,500 and 32,800 square miles respectively. If the government revenue arising from oil had been credited to Scotland in the proportion 625:328 it would still have left Scotland in deficit, relying on subsidies from the English regions even at the height of the oil extraction. An unknown factor, however, and one that might well have tipped the balance, is the way in which an independent Scotland ought to have spent the oil income. It is entirely possible, even likely, that a Scottish government might have invested much more wisely than did Britain in the boom years of the 1980s.[10]

Europe and oil, however, were outweighed in their effects on Scottish opinion by the eleven years of Conservative government under Margaret Thatcher. No twentieth-century Prime Minister since Winston Churchill received so much applause; none since Lloyd George earned so much indignant abuse, amounting sometimes to hatred.

Many unwelcome birds came home to roost during the Thatcher years, and Scotland was badly affected. An integrated steel plant at Ravenscraig near Motherwell, launched and kept afloat by streams of taxpayers' money, failed to perform properly and was eventually closed. Companies previously attracted to Scotland by government gifts discovered the disadvantages of their location, exacerbated since the development of the EEC into the more powerful European Community. London and the south-east were integrated into an axis with Brussels, Frankfurt and Paris which excluded Scotland. Traditional industries there were shattered: famous Border textile mills closed, shipbuilding was destroyed by the application of *laissez-faire* economics, and the Dundee jute industry extinguished by the development of new products.

Between 1979 and 1994 jobs in Scottish manufacturing fell from 604,000 to 402,000, in spite of the prosperity brought by construction and servicing of the new oil and gas rigs. In Scotland resistance to unpopular Conservative policies culminated in the extraordinarily inept imposition of a new system of local taxation, immediately christened the 'Poll Tax' and resisted by refusals to pay and even riots. Local government found itself robbed of much of its income and, by the accompanying ideologically-motivated alterations to local authority structures, of substantial powers. Nemesis was delayed by the ignominious dismissal of the Prime Minister by her own frightened colleagues in November 1990. Her successor, John Major, was able to enjoy the enormous advantage of not being Mrs Thatcher for a further unexpected seven years.

However angry Scots were about Thatcherism they were not attracted by the Labour Party, still in the middle of self-destructive turmoil during which many Scottish Labour local authorities had degenerated into corrupt oligarchies immune to criticism. From 36.2 per cent in 1974 the Labour vote dropped even further, to 35.1 per cent in 1983, not to the advantage of the desperately unpopular Tories (28.4 per cent) but to the new Liberal Democratic Party (24.5 per cent). 'The Third Claim of Right', issued in 1988, outlined a more hopeful way forward. Echoing the Claim of Right made three hundred years before, and its forgotten successor in 1841, it was the work of a Constitutional Convention, shared by Labour and Liberal Democrats, with the SNP looking on suspiciously from the outside. Shorn of a doubtfully accurate excursus into British history the Claim boiled down to the undeniable fact that Scotland was being governed by a party in Westminster which it had rejected – 28.4 per cent of Scottish votes went to the Conservatives in 1983, and only 24 per cent in 1987. If Scotland was a historic nation, and of that there was no doubt, such a situation was intolerable. The fact that the Scottish Labour Party had endorsed the Claim, and that the new national leader, John Smith, was an active proponent, ensured that the alternative party of government was now committed to devolution.[11]

During the long period of Conservative rule frustration bubbled away, producing a stream of Declarations and Claims, none definitive, but all encouraging debate about what shape the future should take. For all practical purposes this was an issue between Labour and the Liberal Democrats, who had participated in the Constitutional Convention from its inception, and the SNP, now pushed into participation by its new leader, Alex Salmond. The violently hostile reception to the Poll Tax in Scotland had left the Conservatives wary of alienating Scottish voters any further. A sensible Secretary, Ian Lang, appointed able opponents to some positions of influence, and began a 'hearts and minds' assault, encouraging Scottish cultural institutions. Continued by Lang's successor Michael Forsyth, who 'appeared as a new man, a benign manager cum cultural nationalist' who 'strutted his stuff in a kilt' (the only Secretary of State ever to wear one), the old Balfour policy of 'killing Home Rule by kindness' was resurrected. This included returning the ancient Stone of Destiny, appropriated by Edward I to Westminster in 1296, to Edinburgh Castle, which piece of philolithopy did not save the Tories from obliteration in the 1997 general election.

Its period in the wilderness had given the Labour Party time to overhaul its incoherent structure and irrelevant doctrines, and to acquire in the person of John Smith a leader who looked like a potential Prime Minister. The unexpected success of the SNP's Jim Sillars at the Govan by-election in 1988 had acted as a grim warning, and before Smith's premature and unexpected death in 1994 the Scottish Labour Party had been recreated, with young MPs such as Gordon Brown, Robin Cook and George Robertson coming into prominence, while Tony Blair, part-educated in Scotland, succeeded Smith as national leader and proceeded to create the 'New Labour' Party. Donald Dewar, a veteran by comparison, who had been Shadow Scottish Secretary since 1980, and had pushed forward the Constitutional Convention, was acknowledged as Labour's senior Scot, and one who would take the leading role in any devolved assembly.[12] The scale of Labour's eventual victory in May 1997 came as a shock. The party was triumphantly resurgent, gaining fifty-six Scottish seats, with Liberal Democrats at ten and the SNP reduced to six. Conservatives were banished, not a single Scottish Tory being elected. With a majority at Westminster of 241 over all other parties Tony Blair's new government could well have afforded to ignore devolutionary demands, but, like Campbell-Bannerman's Liberal administration in 1906, New Labour kept its word, and very much more quickly: it was after all the most Scottish Parliament Britain had ever had, with Scots as Lord Chancellor, at the Foreign Office and the Ministry of Defence, and the duo of Blair and Brown as Prime Minister and Chancellor of the Exchequer.

Once again a referendum was required, and this time elicited a more positive response, with 74 per cent voting for devolution, on a higher turnout. The SNP was faced with the problem previously encountered by Irish Nationalists: to co-operate in a devolved government or to stand aside, holding out for their policy of an independent republic? The fact that the Scottish Parliament was to be elected by a complex system of proportional representation ensured that Labour, the Liberal Democrats, and the SNP would each have a sizeable bloc of seats. Both Labour and the SNP had their fundamentalists, and Labour was still harassed by an ossified and widely corrupt local government, but the SNP leader, Alex Salmond, combined political realism with personal magnetism, and Donald Dewar, who later emerged as the First Minister of the Scottish Parliament, commanded support from both old and New Labour.

One ambiguity had perplexed politicians since the first discussions on Irish Home Rule. If Irish – or Scottish or Welsh – issues were to be removed from Westminster, was it fair that English questions should remain to be decided by a House of Commons containing Irish, Scottish or Welsh MPs? There had, after all, been times when a minority of English MPs could force through measures with the help of Members from the other countries, as had indeed happened in the 1970s. Tam Dalyell, the ruggedly independent Labour Member for West Lothian, had made this paradox his own, and had received no satisfactory answer. In the event the size of the Labour majority at Westminster reduced the 'West Lothian question' to at least temporary irrelevance. Whatever Scottish Members might choose to do about English issues would be unlikely to affect any vote, given the majority of English Labour Members alone. The division in the Labour Party remained one between modernists and traditionalists, not between English and Scots.

Independence too remained in the realms of theory. Alex Salmond had debated the issue of independence v. devolution with Labour's George Robertson in February 1995, and had put his party's case succinctly:

> The present-day reality is of a borderless continent with free trade, free movement and freedom of employment. There is a stark contrast between the SNP's open vision of the new Europe and Labour's narrow view of regional Scotland cowering behind the walls of fortress Britain. Scotland has the right to regain our sovereignty – indeed, this is the only choice we can make for ourselves. Devolution would require the votes of England to bring it about, but independence requires only the votes of Scotland.[13]

Setting aside the constitutional complexity involved, and avoided by Mr Salmond's assumption that 'independence requires only the votes of Scotland' – the financial negotiations alone would be massively difficult – the question of who would be negotiating with whom would once more arise. The Scottish Parliament, with its strictly limited powers, would be the only candidate, and one quite unable to speak with any authority on that subject, even if fortified by a referendum, which would have in turn to be authorised by a British government. Even given such agreement, an independent Scotland would only be possible within the European Community. The sort of deal that had been done with Ireland, of passport-free travel and voting rights, would be impossible if England were an EC member and Scotland not, and Scotland would be placed at a crippling disadvantage.

Yet acceptance within the EC would be, under present conditions, inconceivable. Too many separatist movements are already agitating for independence, some violently, as in the Basque country and in Corsica. EC members would find it near impossible to condone any breach in the dam which might encourage fragmentation, not only in Spain and France, but in Belgium and Italy, where angry divisions are also deepening. Six years later, at a time when 'globalisation' and the dominance of international companies is becoming a great issue, Mr Salmond's other assumption that the 'commanding heights' of the Scottish economy would be transferred to an independent Scotland looks invalid. Scottish financial institutions have indeed flourished, and cut great swathes in the London market, famously demonstrated by the Royal Bank of Scotland's takeover of the National Westminster Bank in 1999, but no country can confidently rely upon any other than indirect influence on the movements of international investment.

'Languages are the pedigree of nations'
(Samuel Johnson)

Welsh language and culture had survived into the twentieth century better than that of Ireland, and Welsh issues could be pursued with indignant determination, but little desire for Welsh independence was manifested. Welsh aspirations were concentrated on such issues as Church disestablishment, licensing laws, educational advances and the status of the Welsh language. Dragging its heels for over a decade behind the Irish Home Rule Bill, Welsh disestablishment finally became law in 1920. Its passage had been a long haul, forced on by 'an extremist mentality' in an 'atmosphere of distrust, suspicions and pious malice'.[14] It proved in fact to be a successful adjustment. The funds of the now-independent Church being wisely invested (Bush House in Aldwych being one of the better purchases) helped to bring about something of a revival in the Welsh Church. Nonconformity, so strong a force in the previous century, was declining. Even the largest, the Welsh Methodists, now revealing their true colours as the Presbyterian Church of Wales, saw their younger members fall away during the bitter twenties and thirties. As religious fervour subsided, survival, in common with the rest of the UK, was the prime concern of the Welsh population. After a brief post-war spurt of prosperity industrial troubles beset Wales' primary industries. Welsh coalfields, although they had their individual characteristics, were definably Welsh, and quite different from the older industry in the north-east of England. Wales had inherited a tradition of ready violence, exemplified in the Tonypandy riots of 1910, the anti-Semitic violence in Tredegar the following year and the Llanelli railwaymen's strike, in which six were killed. Such violence was not paralleled in the English coalfields.

Welsh miners' intransigence had, in 1916, forced the government to take direct control of the South Wales pits. When a Royal Commission report recommending permanent nationalisation was rejected in 1920 a national miners' strike was called. In spite of the advice of fellow unionists and their own leaders – Herbert Smith, the miners' president, accused the militants of 'unequalled cant and hypocrisy' – the strikers persisted until being obliged to accept worse terms than had been offered at the beginning.[15] The ensuing distress among the families was grim, and encouraged the extreme left; communism in Wales was stronger than anywhere in England. It was the class war, and not nationalism, that distinguished Welsh politics, and the Labour Party that was its ultimate beneficiary. Nationalism focused on an old issue, that of language.

Irish Gaelic had required much constitutional effort and expense in order to ensure even a precarious survival. Its use today is confined to those wishing to make a political point, even if only by spelling their names differently, and that handful of country folk and intellectuals to whom it is still a precious cultural heritage. Welsh has, by contrast, not only survived but even flourished. The nineteenth-century English hostility to the language had diminished, replaced by an amused toler-ance, and Welsh had found some influential advocates.

Plaid Cymru – the Welsh Party – founded in 1925, took its inspi-ration from the work of J. Saunders Lewis. Most Scottish writers between the wars had been politically left of centre – some, like Grieve, often very far in that direction. Saunders Lewis and his colleagues moved decisively to the right, specifically adopting positions close to that of the pro-fascist and anti-Semitic Action Français, whose most prominent member, Charles Maurras, was eventually sentenced to life imprisonment for his support of the abominable Vichy government:

> Its [Plaid Cymru's] journal, rejecting any and every English political position, refused to resist Hitler and Mussolini, ignored or tolerated anti-semitism and, in effect, came out in support of Franco and Salazar, despite agonisings from its left wing, despite the fate of Basques and Catalans, despite the deaths of Welsh men in arms for the Spanish Republic.

Such rhetoric was combined with a shrill insistence that only Welsh-speaking persons of similar views were truly 'Cymru'; the other seven-

Right Daniel O'Connell, the 'Liberator'.

Below 'Miss Kennedy distributes clothing to the needy at Kilrush' (1849). After Lord Russell's government callously and prematurely declared the Irish famine over, relief depended mainly on private charity. Miss Kennedy's father, Sir Arthur, was one of the many Irish colonial governors.

'Varieties of Races in England and Wales'. A nineteenth-century ethnologist's view:
1. Gaelic; 2. Cymbrian; 3. Jutish; 4. Saxon; 5. Scandinavian

'The Irish Bobadil'. Few of William Smith O'Brien's contemporaries could take his pretensions seriously.

'*Plus ça change*'. The American cartoonist Thomas Nast satirises Irish-American enthusiasm for giving cash, ostensibly for 'England's Destruction'.

'Waking the Home Rule Bill'. Gladstone, at the head of the coffin, accompanied by his cabinet and the mournful Parnell.

After Parnell's divorce, the Irish party disintegrated. Parnell (left) is restrained by William O'Brien and John Dillon; his opponent, Tom Healy, by Justin McCarthy.

Erskine Childers' yacht, with Mrs Childers and Mary Spring Rice as crew, bravely managed to bring 1500 obsolete rifles to arm Irish nationalists.

The Protestant Ulster Volunteers chartered a steamer to import over twenty-four thousand modern rifles, with the encouragement of British Conservatives.

Above Bloody Sunday, 30 January 1972, when British troops opened fire on a Londonderry civil rights demonstration, killing thirteen people.

Opposite above Punch's cartoon of 12 April 1922 was prophetic. Four months later Michael Collins was killed by the IRA.

Below Punch's view of Collins' death in August 1922; it seemed to many that Ireland had lost its one great man.

Right In the foreground, the new Scottish Parliament arises, much delayed and over budget. The earlier suggested home, the old Royal High School, on Calton Hill, is in mid-scene.

Below Although the Welsh Assembly made a workmanlike beginning its future home is still the subject of acrimonious debate. The Assembly site, 2001.

eighths were merely 'Welsh'. Not surprisingly these attitudes won minimal support, which, after a brief revival in 1935, when Lewis and some helpers set fire to an RAF station, disappeared on the outbreak of war. Under a less unbalanced leader, Gwynfor Evans, Plaid Cymru made a slow post-war recovery. Saunders Lewis' extravagant attacks demanding the 'annihilation' of English, which 'must be deleted from the land called Wales', were replaced by more moderate politics.[16]

It was the use of Welsh in the courts that stimulated, in 1938, the organisation of a Petition to Parliament to restore Welsh to parity with English. Only a modest success, aiming for a million signatures, the petition took some years to achieve a third of that number, and a financial contribution amounting to £1250. It did however succeed in ensuring, in 1942, that the use of Welsh in law courts was permitted, and that the first day of parliamentary debate (17 October 1944) be set aside for consideration of Welsh affairs. The post-war Labour government, idealistically dedicated to constructing a new Britain, was almost contemptuously dismissive of Welsh aspiration. Few Welsh MPs were any more enthusiastic than was Aneurin Bevan, then beginning his historic involvement in the creation of the National Health Service, who accepted that 'there may be an argument – I think there is an argument – for considerable devolution of government', but that it was hardly a priority.[17] He seemed to be proved correct when the greatest Welsh indignation was reserved for the last stand of the Non-conformist conscience, the question of allowing public houses to open on Sundays. Heated debates led to an Act of 1960 permitting local options, based on a poll to be held every seven years. That of 1968 showed once more the fissure that had appeared in the 1890s between the English- and Welsh-speaking areas: only Caernarvonshire, Cardiganshire, Merioneth and Anglesey decided to stay 'dry'. This, Plaid Cymru's heartland, 'Y Fro Gymraeg', was the nursery of the Welsh Language Society, a project of a now older and more prudent Saunders Lewis, whose campaign for increased status for Welsh began in 1963 in Aberystwyth, on the slightly odd issue of having summonses issued in Welsh. Nationalist aspirations of self-government were subordinated to the single issue of language, sometimes to the embarrassment of Lewis' own party of Plaid Cymru.[18]

One painless method of devolution was the foundation by Harold

Wilson's Labour government in 1964 of a Welsh Office, headed by a Secretary of State, on the model of the Scottish Office. The new Office was given a general oversight of all matters concerning Wales and specific responsibilities for local government, planning, housing, roads, transport, education and agriculture, together with some aspects of health. With Cledwyn Hughes, a nationally-minded Welsh-speaker, as Under-Secretary of State proposals for an elected Welsh Assembly were prepared, only to be watered down to the point of extinction by committed Labour centralists. After the Office was moved to Cardiff in 1971 it developed more influence, but much always depended on the character and political weight of the Secretary of State, which in Conservative governments was usually slight. Viewed as a political reinforcement for Labour hegemony in Wales, the innovation was not a great success. Plaid Cymru had remained in the doldrums, but after 1966 a revival began. Wilson's Labour government was as unpopular in Wales as elsewhere, and by-election results have to be accepted with caution, but Gwynfor Evans' success for Plaid Cymru at Carmarthen in July 1966 came as a thunderbolt. When the SNP won the Hamilton by-election the following year the message from both countries was the same: the government were 'mired in . . . a bog of Celtic devolution', whence they must contrive to flounder.[19]

The Welsh-language issue had become more prominent, and more ill-tempered, as students made vocal and sometimes violent protests. Compared with student activity elsewhere it was comparatively low-key, yet it succeeded in alienating a number of supporters (one child had its hands blown off by a home-made bomb, which shocked public opinion). Popular use of Welsh declined: in 1951 715,000 people, mostly over forty-four, claimed to speak the language; by 1961 this was 656,000; ten years later it was down to 542,000. A mere handful claimed to speak Welsh only. Naturally, indeed inevitably, such internationally acclaimed Welsh writers as Dylan Thomas and R.S. Thomas wrote in English.

On the other hand, Plaid Cymru votes were growing even in the Labour redoubts of South Wales. In Caerphilly, in 1968, the Labour majority collapsed from twenty-one thousand two years previously to only 1874, a swing to Plaid Cymru of nearly 40 per cent. Some gestures were made on the language issue, including the signposting of towns with their Welsh names (confusing for tourists looking for Brecon and finding Aberhonddhu). The decision made in 1976 to have a fourth television channel with Welsh programmes was something more than gesture politics, and eventually proved influential. Labelling a taxi a '*tacsi*' and a bank a '*banc*', or stretching the language of Dafydd ap Gwilym to accommodate signs for 'service station', are more than faintly silly, but encouraging Welsh-language television programmes was a genuinely creative advance.

Language apart, the progress of events in Wales followed a similar path to that in Scotland. Kilbrandon's recommendations, more uncertain concerning Wales than Scotland, were distilled into a devolutionary Act which was submitted on St David's Day (1 March) 1979 to a Welsh electorate. Their verdict was a massive negation of nationalism. Even in the Plaid Cymru heartland majorities voted against: Gwynedd, with two Plaid Cymru MPs, produced the highest affirmative vote, but that was only 21.8 per cent of the electorate. In the country as a whole only 11.8 per cent of the electors voted for devolution, with four times as many voting against. The requirement that devolution be accepted by 40 per cent of the electorate, which had doomed the Scottish Bill, was not needed in Wales, where nationalism appeared 'in full retreat, devolution in the shadows'.

Welsh Conservatives did well in 1979, finishing with their highest score of seats for half a century, but Mrs Thatcher's subsequent government had little patience for devolution. The first Secretary of State, Nick Edwards, a decent City of London figure with impeccable Welsh antecedents, was succeeded by three Secretaries who had no connection with Wales and did not even sit for a Welsh constituency. Labour, torn with internal dissensions, was no challenger, and Peter Walker, in charge at the Welsh Office between 1987 and 1990, followed the Balfour precedent in quelling opposition with kindness. Walker was what was derisively known as a 'wet', i.e. one who dissented to some extent from the Thatcherite obsession with extinguishing local democracy and public initiative. He was eventually replaced by a figure from the opposite extreme of Conservatism, John Redwood, the best hope of the stern unbending Thatcherites, who had earned an exaggerated reputation for intellectual ability and administrative competence. Mr Redwood does, however, deserve credit, perhaps more than any other individual, for the eventual establishment of the Welsh Assembly by his complete misunderstanding of Wales, Welsh tradition and the Welsh themselves: 'Redwood often gave the impression of being an exotic specimen in an alien habitat, an impression reinforced by his tragi-comic rendition of the Welsh national anthem. All these things conspired to give Redwood the look of a governor-general who had been imposed on a people against their will.' The final blow to his political credibility was given when he diverted some £100 million from Welsh resources back to the Treasury 'in an effort to champion public expenditure cuts'.[20]

In Labour's electoral triumph in 1997 it was made apparent that the mood in Wales had changed. Eighteen years of Conservative rule had been more than enough. For the first time in history there was as in Scotland a complete electoral wipe-out, the Tories securing not a single seat, with thirty-four going to Labour, four to Plaid Cymru and two to Liberal Democrats. The parliamentary path of a Devolution Bill was relatively easy.

Ireland North and South

Manifestations of nationalism in Wales and Scotland had been some-times exuberant and unruly, but perhaps within the limits of acceptable expressions of opinion. Events in Ulster were tragically different. Ever since the original divisions in 1922, the weaknesses of both North and South had been exposed. Both had inherited the same concepts and mechanism of law, the same civil service, and the same infrastructure. Both had become unpleasant, restricted and opinionated societies, with little tolerance for other opinions. To Britain Northern Ireland was something of a Frankenstein's monster. Unlike Scotland – and Wales since 1964 – Northern Ireland had no Secretary of State, its affairs being the concern merely of a division within the Home Office. At the time of the Londonderry riots in 1969, more violent than in the previous year, the Home Secretary was James Callaghan, later Labour Prime Minister and the first British minister to concern himself constructively with Irish affairs since Balfour. Straightforward, decent and receptive to all views, himself of Irish descent, Callaghan took charge, initiating a series of measures that made it appear for the first time that the two Northern Ireland communities might be able to co-exist peaceably.

This prospect dissolved when Labour lost the 1970 election and Callaghan was succeeded as Home Secretary by the idle, incompetent and corrupt Reggie Maudling. It was under Maudling's ineffective administration that the events of Sunday, 30 January 1972 changed the whole course of subsequent events.

Protestant terrorists, with excuses provided by such irresponsible Nationalist agitators as Bernadette Devlin, who encouraged violence at the same time that John Hume was attempting to suppress it, revived the fortunes of the IRA wild men, in the form of the Provisional IRA – the Provos, Provies or PIRA. Terrorism of the most horrifying type, including indiscriminate bombings, was met with internment of suspects without trial, consequently giving rise to even more terrorism. The Light Infantry, who had dealt with really dangerous situations with disciplined restraint – thirty soldiers had been killed in the previous three months – were replaced by the 1st Battalion of the Parachute Regiment. Paratroops in any army are trained for assault, expected to have quick and aggressive reactions, and generally to make life very disagreeable for anyone opposed to them. Their use in support of the civil power was therefore either a grave mistake, or a deliberate provocation. Whether it was poor training for this special situation, simple inbuilt automatic reaction, or incompetent leadership (the officer commanding later appeared as a caricature of hoary imperialism), the paratroops opened fire on a Londonderry civil rights demonstration, killing thirteen people with 108 rounds of aimed fire. The army second-in-command, Major General Robert Ford, had written to his superior, Sir Harry Tuzo, that the DYH (the Derry Young Hooligans) could only be controlled by 'shooting selected ringleaders', thus 'reverting to the methods of internal security found successful on many occasions overseas', and suggesting using small-calibre rounds 'to minimise lethal effects'.[21] To direct aimed fire with standard 7.62mm rounds on an unarmed crowd (none of those killed were carrying weapons, although it may have been true that the first shots were fired on, rather than by, the troops) in a UK city centre was at best grossly irresponsible. Thirty years afterwards legal investigations were still attempting to establish the course of events, and the effects of what can only be called a massacre were long-lasting. Britain stood condemned by international opinion, and only the subsequent atrocities of the PIRA and the 'Loyalist' paramilitaries, combined with the generally restrained actions of army and police, retrieved the country's credit – and, it should be noted, within a month Republican bombers killed more civilians than did the army on 'Bloody Sunday'.

It was then clear to Whitehall that the Northern Ireland government was no longer in effective charge of events. On 25 March the Ulster Parliament was prorogued, ending half a century of devolved government. Power was transferred to a Secretary of State, and for the next twenty-seven years Northern Ireland was ruled from London. Logically enough, the PIRA extended its bombing attacks to England (although, perhaps significantly, not to Scotland or to Wales).

As Republican terror was answered by equally violent and even more indiscriminate Unionist attacks, and countered when possible by hard-pressed security forces, British politicians – Conservatives and Labour both – agreed not to differ on the 'Irish question', accepting that if any ordered life was to continue in Northern Ireland very different constitutional arrangements would have to be devised. These must include 'power-sharing', the representation of all major political parties on the executive, and some formal arrangements that would include the Dublin government were essential. Dogged Unionist opposition to such proposals would be inevitable.

Since Sean Lemass' retirement in 1966 the Republic had not presented an encouraging picture. Traditional 'pork-barrelling' and sheer incompetence had led to economic near-collapse; Northern violence had spilled over as the IRA and Protestant terrorists raided banks, shot policemen and planted bombs.[22] Emergency legislation of the old 'coercion' type was introduced on both sides of the border. Unyielding British policies, in particular those leading to the death of hunger-strikers among IRA prisoners, made co-operation between Dublin and Westminster difficult, although Jack Lynch's Fianna Fáil governments were, in spite of provocations, steadfast against violence. The Catholic hierarchy continued to oppose contraception, divorce and abortion, and turned a deaf ear to the ecumenical movement begun by Pope John XXIII's Second Vatican Council in 1962. They were more comfortable with the reactionary policies of Pope John Paul II after 1979, and were able to persuade the government to spend a great deal of money on ecclesiastically approved but wasteful projects. Under the corrupt and partial rule of Charles Haughey, whose administration granted £100,000 to the Irish Red Cross, a large portion of which was used to buy arms for the IRA, little could be expected, but when a serious effort began in 1985 it was fortunate that the Taoiseach was Garret FitzGerald, another descendant of the Norman invaders, and an internationalist of unusual sophistication. His interlocutor, Margaret Thatcher, was at her best in a crisis, and FitzGerald was able to forgive the Prime Minister's masterly offensiveness. Together with John Hume of the SDLP, FitzGerald had established the New Ireland Forum which explored, in public and to modest applause, potential solutions. In spite of some particularly savage IRA atrocities (in separate incidents bombs killed Lord Louis Mountbatten with two children and his mother-in-law, and the Conservative MP and war hero Airey Neave in the Palace of Westminster itself, while the attack on the Grand Hotel in Brighton during the Conservative Party Conference in 1984 was specifically targeted at the cabinet), Mrs Thatcher was able to override Unionist objections.

The Anglo–Irish Agreement of November 1985 accepted the need for a formal North–South body, the 'Intergovernmental Conference', to be held at ministerial level and with a permanent secretariat, meeting 'To promote cross border co-operation and deal with security, legal and political matters – political concerns were to be of particular interest to the Catholic minority and included discrimination, electoral arrangements, the status of the Irish language and the use of flags and emblems.'[23]

Loyalists objected furiously, one *enragé*, Peter Robinson, 'cold, ruthless and intransigent', who called Mrs Thatcher 'a political prostitute' and prescribed electrocution, attempted an 'invasion' of the Republic.[24] Official détente did not progress after FitzGerald was replaced by Charles Haughey, but secret contacts – strenuously denied – began between the British Secret Intelligence Service and Republican leaders. In spite of the succession of terrorist acts, the discussions carried out between Michael Oakley of the SIS, with what must have been great courage and discretion, and Gerry Adams, the most prominent of the

Sinn Féin-IRA leadership, were eventually successful in establishing at least a basis of trust. As Sinn Féin, without distancing itself from violence, began to show electoral successes, the Nationalist/Republican front began to draw closer together. Although many constitutional Nationalists found Sinn Féin's connection with terrorism distasteful, the Catholic minority had been near-totally alienated by what was seen as state acquiescence in Unionist-sponsored violence. Unionists, on the other hand, were starting to fragment, the deepest division being between the Democratic Unionists, Dr Paisley's followers, and their paramilitary allies, every bit as capable of terrorism as the IRA, and the original Unionist Party, more middle-class and less vehemently intransigent. It would need great political skill to establish a constitutional system in which all these passionately diverse strands could co-operate.

Intergovernmental co-operation became easier as the Republic began that transformation which made it, at the end of the decade, the prosperous, tolerant and honourable country that it always should have been. The election in 1990 of Mary Robinson as President, the first woman to achieve political eminence in Ireland, North or South, the final collapse of Charles Haughey and his replacement in 1992 by the 'neutral-tinted' pragmatist Albert Reynolds all marked the start of a new era. So too did the appointment of an Englishman, Jack Charlton, as manager of the Republic's national football team. Charlton's wry Geordie humour, and the astonishing success of the Irish team in the 1994 World Cup, made him probably the most popular man in Ireland, the first Englishman to enjoy that distinction since Gladstone.

With John Major replacing Mrs Thatcher in November 1990, the new participants were able to work in a much improved climate. The most astonishing indication of the changing circumstances was the new attitude of Sinn Féin-IRA (although always protesting their independence of each other, the leaders of the organisations were frequently the same). Until 1994 the IRA had continued their campaign of indiscriminate murder (the bombing of Enniskillen on Remembrance Day 1987, killing eleven civilians, especially shocked Irish opinion). The 'Downing Street Declaration' of November 1993, negotiated between Taoiseach Albert Reynolds and Prime Minister John Major, led to a change of policy.[25] Together with its successor, the 'Framework Document' of February 1995, the Downing Street Declaration promised that some sort of constitutional body would be established on which both Northern and Southern interests would be represented. To Republicans and Nationalists this was the potential initial step towards a reunited Ireland, and in August 1995 Sinn Féin-IRA declared the first serious ceasefire. For their leaders Gerry Adams and Martin McGuinness, remembering the fate of Kevin O'Higgins and many like him, this was an act of considerable courage, the first hesitant move towards a possible future solution, which led in turn to the 'Good Friday Agreement' of 1998 and the establishment of the latest, but certainly not the last, constitutional experiment, the Northern Ireland Assembly.

The end of the United Kingdom?

1998 was the most important year for British constitutional history since 1707. In their previous year's manifesto the Labour Party had specified their intention to introduce devolutionary measures. Their unprecedented success at the ensuing general election, with 418 parliamentary seats won, indicated wide support for this. Approval might have been expected in Scotland and Wales, but English voters also backed the manifesto's proposals: Labour won 328 of the 529 English seats as well as fifty-six of the seventy-two Scottish and thirty-four of the forty Welsh constituencies. A single year's legislation subsequently saw assemblies authorised for Scotland and Wales, an Act establishing an entirely new political system in Northern Ireland, an agreement to establish a new Greater London Assembly and a gesture towards the English regions. Each separate Act acknowledged the peculiar shape into which history had forced the current problems. As in 1979 each had to be put to a referendum, although without the previous requirement of a minimum electoral vote. Opposition was muted, centring on growls from a demoralised Conservative Party about the 'break-up of the United Kingdom', ignoring the fact that the unitary state had been disintegrating for over a century.

Whereas devolution in Scotland and Wales was a domestic British issue, the constitution of Northern Ireland had an international dimension. British and Irish involvement was essential, a fact recognised by all but the most intransigent Unionists, and two generations of experiments had at least provided numerous examples of what would not work. A potential solution was provided by the Good Friday Agreement, validated by a later referendum. The phased release of 'paramilitary' prisoners was to be accompanied by 'demilitarisation' and 'decommissioning' of illegal weapons; Nationalist parties recognised that the North would remain part of the UK until a majority no longer wished it, and that an administration would be formed, elected by proportional representation, in which all major parties would have a formulated share. Both Britain and Ireland endorsed the agreement, as did the representatives of the largest Northern Ireland parties, and valuable support was given by the United States, led by President Clinton in person.

Within months of the agreement the worst atrocity seen in Ireland since the terrible year of 1798 was perpetrated when a bomb in the small town of Omagh killed twenty-eight people and maimed dozens more. It was the work of the successors of Kevin O'Higgins' wild men screaming through the keyhole, the 'Real IRA', financed from America,[26] protesting at the possibility of a peaceful settlement which did not immediately satisfy all their ancient and absurd ambitions. The Sinn Féin leaders, Adams and McGuinness, had been outflanked in the same way that Cosgrave and O'Higgins had been in the 1920s, but just as the IRA violence then had driven de Valera into 'slightly constitutional' policies, so the popular revulsion after Omagh reinforced a general demand for a peaceful outcome.

Whereas in Wales and Scotland new departures were initiated, the Northern Ireland Act was primarily the reform of an existing institution. John Major had advanced the constitutional debate patiently and with some skill; Tony Blair inherited a not-unpromising situation, and was able to stake out a new constitutional position. The previous Ireland Act of 1949 had required the 'consent of the parliament of Northern Ireland' before any part of the existing state ceased 'to be a part of the United Kingdom'. The new Act (Part 1, Sections 1 and 2) was more specific:

> Northern Ireland in its entirety remains part of the United Kingdom and shall not cease to be so without the consent of the majority of the people of Northern Ireland voting in a poll held for the purpose.

> But if a majority wishes to form part of a United Ireland, the Secretary of State shall lay before Parliament such proposals to give effect to that wish as may be agreed between Her Majesty's Government in the United Kingdom and the Government of Ireland.

This was glossed in Schedule I to provide that: 'If at any time it seems likely to [the Secretary of State] that a majority of those voting would express a wish' for such an alternative, he might order a referendum to be held. A limitation that this could only be done at a minimum interval of seven years was inserted to ensure that the subject would not be a perpetual irritation, but it would not be unduly difficult for a Secretary of State sympathetic to Nationalist aspirations to judge the moment when a referendum might produce a majority for re-union with the South. Were that so, it is unlikely that any British Parliament would offer much objection. Both the opportunity to Nationalists and the threat to Unionists was now much clearer, it being well understood that the nature of referenda is such that timing and the wording of the questions posed can do a great deal to provoke the desired response.[27]

Misty dissimulation was a necessary part of the Northern Ireland constitution, based as it was on the previous agreements, which had stipulated that paramilitary disarmament had to be completed by May 2000. It was understood by all concerned that the IRA at least had no intention of so doing. The only effect of compliance would have been that the wild men would merely re-form under another title and carry on their campaign. All that the Sinn Féin party could do was to ensure that their IRA supporters targeted only the socially undesirable members of their own community, and to obfuscate the issue by talking of 'demilitarisation', thus equating the forces of law with the illegal paramilitaries. Clarifications in these matters would not have been helpful.

It is difficult to avoid the conclusion that, just like the 1920 Act, that of 1998 was designed as a temporary measure. If it lasted for long enough for the new Assembly, with its compulsory representation of Unionists and Nationalists on all committees, and their joint consent to all legislation, to settle into a general acceptance, then it would have served its purpose, and the next stage could be tackled. The fact that generous salaries and expenses were given to Assembly Members (ministers received salaries of £74,000), together with the satisfaction that some would find from being once more able to serve their community, were incentives encouraging everyone to persevere in the hope that something would turn up. So far it has not, but the efforts continue.

The Government of Wales Act 1998 C.38, establishing a National Assembly for Wales, limited its powers by prescribing in some detail what its responsibilities would be. The Act was particularly concerned with regulation of quangos, that useful acronym (quasi-autonomous non-governmental organisations) for a number of different bodies which had flourished in the eighteen years of Conservative government. It had been made clear from the first days of the 1979 Conservative administration that all public organisations must be staffed by reliable Tories. Previous governments had paid at least some attention to the principle of non-partisanship, but Mrs Thatcher was firm. The more active sympathisers who could be placed in positions of power, the better. 'Is he one of us?' was the watchword.

Where Conservative parliamentary representation was weak, as in Wales and Scotland, quangos were particularly helpful in shifting power from civil servants, open to parliamentary scrutiny, to non-accountable agencies comfortably insulated from popular examination. The explosive growth of quangos in Wales during Conservative rule resulted in the formation of somewhere between eighty and 340 such bodies, with no fewer than 1400 appointments lying in the Welsh Secretary's gift. These government appointees controlled a budget of some £2,300,000,000, employing over sixty thousand people. In an attempt to ensure that this extraordinary proliferation was brought under better control the new Act contained two sections (27 and 28) dealing specifically with quangos. These were analysed under four headings:

1. Those over which the new Assembly would have full powers to add, or to remove, functions: there were thirteen of these, including the most important, the Welsh Development Agency.
2. Those, predominantly health authorities, where this could only be done with government consent.

3. Those, three in all, whose functions could only be increased.

4. Five whose functions could only be increased with government approval.

In addition forty-five other reporting bodies were listed, including a number of national authorities, such as the Environment Agency, members of which could be required to give evidence, in person if necessary, and upon oath, thus endowing the Assembly with powers similar to those of a Royal Commission on a wide range of subjects. That, however, was to be that, since the Assembly was given no power to raise funds, and no opportunity to extend its remit by initiating legislation.[28]

When the proposals were put to the Welsh people in a referendum in September 1997 their response, fuelled by a general resentment of the Conservatives, was a good deal more positive than it had been in 1979, although still not enthusiastic. Only half the voters came to the poll, but of those a bare majority, 50.3 per cent, gave a positive vote. It was a swing of 30 per cent, but with only a quarter of the population actively wanting a Welsh Assembly the project could hardly be said to have received enthusiastic popular backing. Old divisions, apparent over a century earlier, were reflected in the results both of the referendum and of the preceding 1997 election. Welsh Nationalists had performed poorly in the 1997 general election throughout the industrial south, with proportions of the vote between only 2.5 and 6.6 per cent. Plaid Cymru's four parliamentary seats were all in the west, in Welsh Wales: Caernarvon, Anglesey (now to be known again as Yns Mon), Ceridigian and Merioneth. Referendum results showed a similar but less pronounced trend, but with the old Marcher counties returning a negative vote. It did seem, however, that just as local authority votes were traditionally cast in a different pattern from those at general elections, so referendum voting differed. Such a theory was to be reinforced when the complex election system designed in the White Paper was eventually deployed. That the results were disappointing to Labour was largely the party's own fault.

New Labour had come to power on 2 May 1997 flushed with triumph. Tony Blair and his supporters had succeeded in dragging the Labour Party out of its introspective impotence and launching it almost

immediately into government. Self-confidence and a certain triumphalism carried the new government through a series of radical innovations, including the delegation of monetary control to the Bank of
England, restriction of the hereditary principle in legislation, acceptance of European social norms and, perhaps most important, the
implementation of devolved government. In the cold light of day,
apprehension settled on the Labour cabinet. Party unity had demanded
the firm imposition of leadership, which devolution might threaten.
Feelings of disappointment at the failure immediately to improve
public services and Social Security were soon stirring among the rank
and file, and the possibility of a strong 'Old Labour' challenge from a
devolved power base was unsettling. The New Labour cabinet was
suspicious of the Principality, which had provided two of the party's
recent national leaders, Michael Foot and Neil Kinnock, who stood
accused – largely unfairly as far as Kinnock was concerned – of causing
Labour's previous problems. It was deemed essential to put a reliable
Labour loyalist in charge, but the inevitable choice to lead the Welsh
Assembly was that of Ron Davies, Secretary of State in Mr Blair's
cabinet. Davies, who had been as much responsible for the successful
advocacy of Welsh devolution as Donald Dewar had been for Scotland,
was not entirely trusted by Downing Street, but he was too popular,
and too well-entrenched, not to be given the job. When he was forced,
by an altogether unrelated indiscretion, to resign both his cabinet post
and leadership of the Welsh Labour group, a contest developed. His
successor as Secretary of State, Alun Michael, was pushed into the gap,
against the wishes of many in Welsh Labour, who would have preferred
the more personable and outgoing Rhodri Morgan. Just as Stuart
Rendel had feared a century before, it seemed that, in spite of devolved
powers, Wales was still going to be harassed by Whitehall. Following
a leadership election in which the whole Labour Party machine was
mobilised, the result the government wanted was achieved, but only
at the cost of upsetting Morgan's supporters, who formed a majority
of the Welsh party members. A price was paid for Whitehall's arm-
twisting. Popular support diminished, and the following elections to
the Welsh Assembly gave Labour only twenty-eight seats of the sixty.
Plaid Cymru mopped up the Labour votes, almost exactly, to gain
seventeen seats. Either a coalition or a minority administration was

therefore necessary. Since a coalition could hardly be effected with either Plaid Cymru or the Conservatives, Labour was obliged to form Wales' first parliamentary government relying on Liberal Democrat votes, with decisions being delegated to cross-party committees and a Presiding Officer – essentially the Speaker – from Plaid Cymru.

Alun Michael duly became First Secretary of the Welsh Assembly (the odd title reflecting the different status of the Welsh government to that of the Scottish, able to boast a First Minister), but not for long. Chancellor Gordon Brown's hold on the purse strings was too tight, and led to a successful no-confidence vote against Mr Michael in February 2000. The Labour members were then able to have their way, and elected Rhodri Morgan in his place. It was a notable victory for Welsh democracy, and since the new First Secretary was generally popular with all parties the devolved Assembly got off to a good start, marred only by a very expensive altercation over the new Assembly building. Accusations and counter-accusations were exchanged between Edwina Hunt, the responsible Assembly Member, and the architect, Lord Rogers, but the incontrovertible issue was that the building was delayed and the costs quite unnecessarily increased.

The concentration of population around the new Assembly – two-thirds of the Welsh people live within an hour's drive – and its relatively restricted powers made its task easier. Political sentiment was strongly behind the coalition administration: after the 2001 general election the Conservatives still held no seats in Wales and Plaid Cymru was confined to the four western coastal counties, with the Liberal Democrats successful in the old Marcher counties. Rhodri Morgan's administration was popular, and performed the valuable – from London's point of view – function of keeping unreconstructed Welsh Labour Party members, yearning for purer socialism, occupied with Welsh issues. After three years' experience the more modest intentions of Welsh devolution looked like being successfully realised.

Scottish devolution was not accompanied by the political upsets that had occurred in Wales. Many senior ministers were Scots themselves, representing Scottish constituencies. As Shadow Scottish Secretary in the Thatcher days, Donald Dewar had cajoled an unenthusiastic Scottish Labour Party into accepting the principle of devolution and participating in launching the Constitutional Convention. Scotland, it was acknowledged, was to be Dewar's own personal responsibility. The relationship he had created with the Liberal Democrats and their leader, Jim Wallace, would enable him to function effectively in the role of First Minister.

Devolution of powers from Westminster to Edinburgh was effected by the Scotland Act, which involved the amendment of two articles (4 and 6) of the 1707 Act of Union with England. If the Scottish National Party had had its way the amendment would have been more fundamental. During the debate an able speech from Alex Salmond argued for a Scottish constitutional court rather than the Judicial Committee of the Privy Council to act as the arbiter on constitutional questions. The issue directly addressed one of the key factors in devolution – how far could the Scottish Parliament extend its original power?

The Better Government of Ireland Act of 1920 had been drafted to allow for change, since it was commonly acknowledged that Ireland's constitutional status was bound to develop, as it subsequently did in the South under the terms of the Anglo–Irish Treaty. If the Act had been concerned only with the northern six counties it would, or at any rate should, have been drafted more restrictively. As it was the Unionist government had entrenched their position by altering the Act (both legally and illegally) in order to abolish the protective device of proportional representation, the barrier to perpetuating Unionist hegemony. The Scots were not going to be accorded the same opportunity. Any alterations to the 1998 Act would have to come before the Westminster Parliament.

Whereas the Welsh Assembly had been allocated specified powers, those given to Scotland were wider-ranging. Following the example of the Irish Home Rule Bills some subjects were reserved to Westminster – foreign policy, defence, social security, transport and energy. Fundamental economic planning was also excluded, but the Scottish Parliament was allowed to raise funds by varying the basic rate of income tax by 3p in the pound, or some £450 million, a significant sum. Such powers left it open to a Scottish executive to develop Scottish interests in new ways, some of which might prove inconvenient to Westminster. The other old question, that of continued representation at Westminster, was ignored. It was a delicate matter for a Labour government to address, since it had been proved twenty years before in the Kilbrandon Report that Scotland had more MPs than its population warranted. In 1997 seventy-two Scots MPs were elected by 2,817,482 voters. In the nearest English region, the north, it took 1,637,906 votes to elect thirty-six MPs. Each Scottish MP therefore represented 39,150 voters, and each northern MP 45,440. Nationally the disproportion was even greater, with 30,505,440 votes cast for 659 MPs, or some 46,306 to each. On purely demographic grounds a good case could be made for reducing Scottish seats from seventy-two to, say, sixty-two, but given the fact that this would mean a permanent reduction in the future Labour share of seats, any redistribution is extremely unlikely until such time as a Conservative government came to power.

The fact that proportional representation was specified, added to the complexity of the electoral system, made it possible that no party would emerge as a clear victor, and so it transpired. In the 120-seat Scottish Parliament Labour gained only fifty-six seats, but as the largest party was able to appoint Donald Dewar as First Minister. He was therefore obliged to share power with the Liberal Democrats, who had seventeen seats, and face the SNP as the official opposition, with thirty-five seats and their leader, Jim Wallace, as Deputy First Minister. Labour could no longer regard Scotland as secure, but neither could the SNP claim a triumph for their advocacy of an independent Scotland: 71 per cent of the votes went to parties opposing Scottish independence. Some relief must have been felt at Westminster when the Scottish Parliament was promptly faced with some unpopular decisions, on homosexuality and university fees, and with the revelation of chaos in the schools' examination system: the unpopularity generated by these was absorbed in Edinburgh, rather than London.[29] Devolution, it was clear, had its benefits as well as its dangers.

As with Wales, the major advantage of Scottish devolved government was its accessibility. Thanks to the evolved electoral system each voter could claim the attention of up to eight Members, most of whom were anxious to make themselves felt, and very ready to pursue any constituent's cause. Three-quarters of the Scottish population live within a couple of hours of Edinburgh, and the Parliament has gone out of its way to facilitate access by publicising MSPs' telephone numbers and email addresses, and by the system of public petitions.

Looming large on the debit side was another, less comfortable parallel to the Welsh experience, the spectacular muddle of the MSPs' new home. Originally intended to be the old Royal High School on Calton Hill, near the original St Andrew's House, it was switched to a much less convenient site adjacent to Holyroodhouse, the old royal residence magnificently extended by the first great Scottish architect, William Bruce. A famous and fashionable Catalan architect, Enric Miralles, was engaged, and a complex series of disasters ensued. Completion dates slipped, and costs inexorably rose, from an original £10 million for the redevelopment on Calton Hill to something near £400 million.[30] Indignant accusations were levelled – was it the fault of the Downing Street Scots' intervention, or the Edinburgh Scots' incompetence? Or sheer bad luck: both Miralles (in July 2000) and Dewar (in October of the same year) died unexpectedly. What was certain is that the Scottish administration's reputation was badly dented, to the extent that by 2001, with completion still two years distant, a majority of Scots were recording dissatisfaction with the Parliament.

More unfinished business

The break-up of the United Kingdom, that Conservative bugbear of the 1990s, has been an evolving process since 1922, and has yet some distance to go. The 1997 Labour government had originally premised, if not promised, a radical constitutional reform of which Scottish and Welsh devolution were only a part. Taken together, Scotland and Wales accounted for only one-eighth of the UK's total population. What of the fifty million who lived in England? The population of what used to be Yorkshire alone was as great as, if not greater than, that of Scotland. Manchester was nearly as populous as the whole of Wales.

The only important move towards devolving power within England was the creation of an elected Mayor, with extensive responsibility, for Greater London – and this got off to a poor start. As with Wales, the government was anxious to ensure that the new post would be held by a reliable supporter, in a Blairite image, who would not make life uncomfortable for the administration in the nation's capital. The ignominious result of Downing Street's attempt to impose Frank

Dobson, a reliably obedient supporter, as the Labour candidate was to see Ken Livingstone successful instead – and 'Red Ken', the last Chairman of the Greater London Council abolished by Mrs Thatcher, was the worst of all possible candidates from 10 Downing Street's point of view, a populist and popular left-winger.

The other English regions had some reason to complain of undue advantages gained by the newly-devolved administrations, but either could not – the politics were touchy – or did not – having no united voice – press the issue hard. Had they wished to, good arguments were at hand. If comparisons are made not with the whole of England, distorted as that is by the greater wealth of London and the south-east, but with comparable regions, the differential is striking. Scotland has twice the population of northern England (5,120,000:2,550,000). This proportion is reflected equitably in European Union funding (£1234 million:£662 million) and rather less so in national lottery grants (£709 million:£338 million). But when it comes to UK government expenditure on regional preferential assistance to industry, the disproportion is exaggerated – £125.5 million to Scotland, and less than one-fifth of that sum (£22.3 million) to northern England.

The justification is sometimes advanced that Scottish conditions are so much worse that extra help is needed. The facts contradict this. People are poorer in the north of England: per capita GDP in 1998 was £9819; in Scotland it was £11,902. Unemployment is higher: 10 per cent to 7.4 per cent; the north has the lowest rate of employment in the UK, and the second-lowest rate of personal savings (Northern Ireland comes at the bottom of that list). Both regions have worse than average health, to some extent self-inflicted. Scots drink rather more and smoke rather less than northerners, but both are above the national average. Scotland has however considerably better access to health care, with waiting lists at only half the UK average.[31] On education the *Financial Times* reported in April 2001: 'The evidence is clearly visible in the decaying fabric of Northumberland schools against their Scottish counterparts, complete with new roofs and humming with computers.'[32] In some respects Wales does even better than Scotland: with a population very similar to that of the north of England, and lower levels of unemployment, Wales receives six times the amount of Regional Preferential Assistance as does the north.

The formula for allocating funds between the constituent parts of the United Kingdom was first determined by Lord Barnett as a temporary expedient in the very different circumstances of 1978. Since that time its unfairness has been acknowledged, not least by Lord Barnett himself. 'The levels of spending per head between Scotland and the other parts of the UK are now very different,' he acknowledged in 1997, and the Treasury committee appointed to report on the subject agreed (the Scottish members predictably dissenting).[33] It is not only the disproportionately low funding that annoys the northerners, but the fact that they have much less freedom than the devolved assemblies to choose how to spend it. Flexibility to meet local needs would make the relatively miserly sums go further. Resentment has been expressed for many years. Back in the 1960s, when the Newcastle City fathers wanted a royal representative to inaugurate their new city hall, they went not to London but to Oslo, and invited the King of Norway to do the honours. Forty years later the Governor of the Bank of England, Eddie George, was given a hard time by Novocastrians, angry that monetary policies which might well be best for the prosperous south were damaging the north's economy.

The remedies offered by New Labour were unconvincing. The English regions were tossed the placebo of 'Regional Chambers', grafted on to the existing Regional Development Agencies 'to provide regional accountability', and composed of nominees from local authorities and 'strategic partners'. Retitling themselves as Regional Assemblies invited comparisons with the elected Welsh Assembly, of which they were little more than a shadow, meeting only three times a year, and with almost total invisibility outside their immediate circle. Some indignation was expressed by such champions as the respected elder statesman of local government Sir Jeremy Beecham, but politely brushed aside until, with the prospect of a general election looming, ministers began to make encouraging noises. The Regional Assemblies had at least started to make their own cases to central government and to the European authorities, and protests against the more obvious lack of equity began to make themselves felt as cabinet ministers began to promise better things to come. Their promises appeared empty after Labour's successful 2001 election, when once again regional devolution seemed to have been thrust back into the recesses of the deepest

Whitehall cupboards. Whether they are to be dragged forth will depend on the level of discontent engendered among backbench English MPs, seeing Scots and Welsh apparently always doing better than their own constituents.

There are good arguments to be advanced. The alarmingly low level of participation in the 2001 general election – fewer than four in ten voters turned out in the constituency of Manchester Central, and nationally just over 60 per cent of those entitled to the franchise exercised their right – indicated a loss of faith in the democratic process, emphasised by violence later in the summer in other Lancashire and Yorkshire towns. Elections to local authorities have long been affected by similar apathy, following a justified suspicion that little improvement would be effected whatever party held the reins of office. The very existence of the Scottish Parliament has focused attention on issues which would otherwise have been shrugged off as a Westminster concern impervious to Scottish pressures. Once an electorate is convinced that an administration can be responsive, then voting becomes not an irrelevant chore but a valuable privilege, a more effective weapon than violence in the streets; and devolved administrations may well become the only alternative to rioting and arson in twenty-first-century Britain.

Other options are limited. A fully federated system, along the lines of Germany or Australia, is rendered impossible by the preponderant strength of England. Not all states of national federations are by any means equal – Vermont is a fraction of the size of Texas, and Tasmania of New South Wales – but England is out of all proportion so much bigger than all the other constituent parts of the United Kingdom. Nor are English regions in any way so clearly defined – unlike Scotland, Northern Ireland or Wales – as to justify the creation of regional assemblies with as much power as a Scottish Parliament.

A more feasible possibility is an approximation to the Spanish example of 'Rolling Devolution'. With two centres of similar size and importance, Barcelona and Madrid (provincial populations of 4.7 and five million respectively), and a distrust of over-centralisation generated by the period of authoritarian government between 1939 and 1975, democratic regional government has flourished. The devolution policies agreed after 1975 accord different levels of autonomy to different regions, although all have parliaments, a supreme court and a civil service. The Basque country and Navarre have, like Scotland, been given tax-raising powers; Catalonia has extensive educational and cultural independence, reflecting the strong traditions of Catalan society (as many books are published in Catalan as in Castilian). Both the Basque region and Catalonia have their own languages, and both straddle the border with France, whilst other Spanish regions have characters no more distinct than those of England (quite distinct enough, one might say, thinking perhaps of Yorkshire, Devon or Essex). Considering the violent background of recent Spanish history, the indications that devolution is working and that 'the new regional state has reached a point of equilibrium and stability' make it an instructive example for the decreasingly United Kingdom to follow.[34]

Some peculiarities of the British system militate, however, against easy solutions. In Spain, and in other older federal countries, a written constitution secures the powers of the individual states or provinces. In Britain Westminster remains sovereign; what has been given can be – and is, as in Northern Ireland – taken away. It would therefore be theoretically possible for a British government to dissolve the Scottish Parliament, to remove its executive and to resume London rule. In practice it would take an extremely unlikely chain of events to translate this to the realms of the practical; Mr Blair's government has found itself in the position of a labrador stuck in a cat flap – progress is impossible and an alternative strategy has to be devised.

Such a strategy would have to include a radical revision of the concept of parliamentary sovereignty, which has resulted in something resembling an elective dictatorship. Nothing less than a written constitution, with a supreme court to interpret and enforce it, will suffice. Whilst it is true that most other countries have developed such institutions, and that the task is made simpler by the restrictions on parliamentary sovereignty already in place, it would constitute a momentous step for any British government to take. Cherished traditions and assumptions, including the place of the monarchy and the composition of the House of Lords, would be brought into question.

What is more, the English people would have to be consulted. Few English voters can have cast their votes for the Labour Party in 1997 or 2001 with much thought of thereby allowing devolution to Scotland and Wales. Although not a few Conservatives, fretting about the 'break-up' of the United Kingdom, might well have voted against devolution, it was not a question that engaged much English attention. A revision of the British constitution, which would guarantee such rights, would certainly attract much discussion, in the course of which it is more than likely that English regional autonomy and a fairer share, or what so appeared to English voters, would be required. But there are few votes in such a painful exercise.

NOTES

INTRODUCTION

1. Entertaining and original though it is, *The Isles* needs a second edition to remove the worst inaccuracies. Professor Hugh Kearney's *British Isles* is altogether more successful, but allows the twentieth century only a score or so pages. The multi-volume *Oxford History of England* (in fact of the British Isles), in course of revision, remains the one essential, if often outdated, source.

2. The best – or worst – examples are to be found in American publications, such as D.J. Casey and R.E. Rhodes, *Views of the Irish Peasantry*, but even quite respectable writers fall into this common trap.

3. Strictly speaking Caerphilly (Caerffili) is not Edwardian, having been built by the Marcher Lord Gilbert de Clare, but it is the largest and most formidable of all Welsh castles.

4. See pp. 364–5. Although England is not guiltless in this matter, one has only to imagine music, the theatre, hospitals, restaurants or academic life without the contribution of recent immigrants.

5. Or Latin or even Dutch, the great exception being Chaucer.

6. The phrase is G.R. Elton's; see *England Under the Tudors*, Chapter 7.

7. When those responsible for the worst Irish atrocity in two centuries, the Omagh bombing of 1998, were exposed, it was revealed that their American supporters had raised over $1 million to finance their activities.

8. These points are discussed in the text; for Ussher see DNB.

CHAPTER 1 : 54 BC–AD 500

The best history of Roman Britain is still that of Peter Salway. I have used the revised 1982 edition, published in paperback in 1984. Sheppard Frere, *Britannia*, another excellent book, is now somewhat out of date, as is Collingwood and Myres' *Roman Britain*. For pre-Roman Britain John Collis, *The Iron Age in Britain* is unfortunately also out of date, but remains a brisk and informative account. There is an excellent essay by R.R. Davies in *Transactions of the Royal Historical Society*, presidential address 22 September 1996, 'Peoples of Britain and Ireland'. For Celts see H.D. Rankin, *Celts and the Classical World* and N. Chadwick, *The Celts*. All historians of the first century AD rely on the remarkable works of Tacitus. Since history *is* about maps the Ordnance Survey Historical Series – Roman, Dark Age and Monastic Britain – are valuable aids to following developments.

1. *Studia Celtica*, vol. xxx, 1996, J. Collis, 'The Origin and Spread of the Celts'; M. Green, *Celts in Italy*; *Études Celtiques*, vol. xxxii, 1996, P.M. Freeman, 'Earliest Greek Sources on the Celts'; *Cambrian Mediaeval Celtic Studies*, no. 36, P.

Sims-Williams, 'Celtomania and Celtoscepticism'.

2. *Nichomachean Ethics*, iii, 7.7.

3. A sometimes querulous debate has persisted on whether the British tattooed themselves. The most authoritative judgment – that they did – is found in *Études Celtiques*, vol. xxxiii, 1999, C.W. Macquarie, 'Insular Celtic Tattooing', and in the same author's Chapter 3 in J. Caplan, *Written on the Body*.

4. The quotation is from *Diodorus Siculus*, v.31. For druids see Chadwick, op. cit., Chapter 6; Salway, op. cit., pp.677–81.

5. By Rankin, op. cit., p.215.

6. Quoted in Frere, op. cit., p.50.

7. *Annals*, xiv, 33, quoted in Salway, op. cit., p.119.

8. Whatever the racial origins of the Picts, they were clearly understood by the Romans as a Celtic society very much like those in Britannia. See A.P. Smyth's exhaustive examination in Chapter 2 of his authoritative *Warlords and Holy Men*. For a more popular, well-illustrated approach see L. and J. Laing, *Picts and Scots*.

9. *Agricola*, xxi, quoted in Salway, op. cit., p.142.

10. A. Birley, *People of Roman Britain*, p.159. Ausonius (*c.*310–95) was himself a distinguished poet, whose most memorable work is an ode to the Moselle fish.

11. The best works are K.H. Jackson, *Language and History*, P. Trudgill, *Language . . .* and G. Price, *Languages of Britain*, Parts 1 and 2. See also S.R. Fischer, *A History of Language*.

12. K.H. Jackson, op. cit., p.170.

13. This is the contemporary poet Claudian, quoted in Salway, op. cit., p.423.

14. This is the historian Zosimus, writing at the end of the fifth century, and quoted in Salway, op. cit., p.434.

15. Ibid., p.451.

16. For the saints see E.A. Thompson, *St Germanus*.

17. Gildas' brief mention of a conflict at 'Mons Badonicus' is investigated in G. Ashe, *The Quest for Arthur's Britain* and in John Morris' excellent *The Age of Arthur*, which surveys the whole period from 350 to 650. More recently N.J. Higham's *Rome, Britain and the Anglo-Saxons* presents (Chapter 8) a convincing reconstruction of the period. Gildas is explored in some detail in M. Lapidge and D. Dumville, *Gildas*. K.R. Dark, *Civitas to Kingdom* is convincingly detailed.

18. The metre is trochaic tetrameter catalectic. Its origins in Greek verse, it became popular in Latin: Caesar's troops marched to it: '*Caesar Gallias subegit, Nicomedes Caesarem*' etc. – all indelicate; one of its more recent appearances is in 'Clementine'. For Fortunatus (*c.*530–*c.*609) see F. Brittain, *Latin Verse*.

19. E.P. Hamp, in *Studia Celtica*, vol. 30, 1996, p.293 suggests this may be a misreading – not a title, but a translation.

CHAPTER 2 : AD 500–1066

1. For Anglo-Saxon verse generally, see K. Sisam, *Studies*.

2. Smyth, op. cit. is authoritative: p.18.

3. D. Johnston, *Literature of Wales*, is a good introduction, and *The Mabinogion*, trans. G. and T. Jones, a work of elegant scholarship.

4. Bede is the prime source of all English history before 740. I have used the Oxford paperback (ed. McClure and Collins). P. Hunter Blair, *The World of Bede* and *Northumbria in the Days of Bede* and N.J. Higham, *Northumbria* are the most recent works, all informative and sympathetic. For a focused view see Corfe, *Before Wilfred*. Bede was fervently,

'patriotically' – an unhistorical expression – English, with much more sympathy for the Irish, from whom his teachers had come, than for the Welsh, with whom the English shared their part of the island. For an illuminating discussion see J. Hines, *Anglo-Saxons* and M. Richter, *Ireland and her Neighbours*, Chapter 4. S. Foot, in *Transactions of the Royal Historical Society*, vol. v, 1996, claims that 'the force of this sense of a common identity is striking . . . at least from Bede's time onwards, coupled with the fact that it was clearly recognisable to outsiders . . . Bede invented the English as a people in the sight of God' (p.49).

5. *'Brittanos'* were transferred together with lands, as by King Ecgfrith's grant of Cartmel to St Cuthbert, *'omnes Britannos cum eo'* (Jackson, op. cit., p.217). For thanely or thegnly status see N.J. Higham, *An English Empire* – an excellent book – p.239. Dr Higham suggests that by *c.*731 Anglo-Saxons were being 'incorporated in the ranks of the vulgar while the Britons were being themselves increasingly exposed to anglicisation' (p.240). His book also contains a good account of the Tribal Hideage, attributing it to Edwin in *c.*626.

6. M. Magnusson, *Scotland*, p.30, suggests that the fine Pictish stone at Aberlemno is a memorial of the battle.

7. See D. Brooke, *Wild Men and Holy Places*, for St Ninian and medieval Galloway; W.G. Collingwood, *Early Christian Crosses*.

8. See P. Herbison, *Pre-Christian Ireland*. The 'Trading Station' is at Lambey Island, Dublin.

9. The dates here are confused. Patrick's death has recently been advanced from 463: see Smyth, op. cit., p.18.

10. *The Oxford History of Ireland*, ed.

R.F. Foster, a useful work itself, has an excellent bibliography. The standard work is the multi-volume Oxford New History of Ireland. S. McMahon, *A Short History of Ireland*, is a good, cool summary.

11. The geographical spread of missions is illustrated in S. Duffy, *Atlas of Irish History*, pp.20–3. The book is helpful to understanding all Irish history.

12. D. Moran, 'Expounding Eriugena', in *Irish History Studies*, vol. xxi, no. 122, November 1995.

13. *Studia Hibernica*, no. 28, 1994, 'Bishops in the Early Irish Church: A Reassessment' by C. Etchingham, who suggests that bishops were not quite as common as thought.

14. This is the sympathetic Bede, himself one of the barbarians (Chapter 23).

15. The best work is still H. Mayr-Harting, *The Coming of Christianity*.

16. Whitby is dealt with by N.J. Higham in *Convert Kings*, pp.256ff. He suggests that it was Agilbert's inability to speak English that caused the young Wilfred to act as spokesman for the Roman party, which raises interesting questions as to how far English had already become a common tongue in Britain. See also Mayr-Harting, op. cit., Chapter 7.

17. P.B. Ellis makes a gallant effort in *Celtic Women* but is forced to rely on hagiography and the singular figure of Grainne Ni Maille – Grace O'Malley – the interesting widow of Richard Bourke of Connacht: but it is precisely Grainne's singularity that proves the point. See also A. Chambers, *Granuaile*.

18. For the continuing influence of Irish traditions in England see C.D. Wright, *Irish Tradition* and *Studia Celtica*, vol. xxii, 1991, C. Ireland, 'Aldfrith of Northumbria'. Wilfred epitomises in his own person the

contrast between Celtic and Roman-Anglican practices. A younger contemporary of Saints Colman and Cuthbert, monk/bishops of ascetic and claustral life, the princely Wilfred travelled over Europe with a retinue of masons, glaziers and armed followers, amassing wealth and influence at Rome, in the style of a Renaissance prelate such as Wolsey.

19. For the artistic contrasts see D.M. Wilson, *Anglo-Saxon Art*. Northumbrian sophistication spread as far north as Lothian, but never reached Irish stonecarvers. Biscop also brought with him the Benedictine rule, another contrast with the Irish monasteries.

20. The word 'probably' may need to be understood when referring to the origin of the Book of Durrow. I have followed the general opinion expressed by Wilson, op. cit., p.33. Although much smaller, the Stonyhurst St John's Gospel is equally remarkable, possibly Bede's own copy, still in its original binding. The magnificent Book of Kells probably found its way to Ireland from Iona. For Bede himself see the works of P.H. Blair, M. Lapidge, *Bede and his World* and M. Richter, *Ireland . . .* , Chapter 4.

21. J. Earle, *Hand Book*, pp.4–5, 102–5; the earliest charter in English is perhaps that of the Mercian King Aethelbald giving land in 'lundentunes hythe' about 743.

22. Smyth, op. cit., is the best source for this period, especially Chapters 5 and 6.

23. Canterbury was the first, followed by Oxford, Winchester and Wallingford. Apart from London, the largest towns – York, Lincoln, Norwich and Thetford – were in the east.

24. Some idea of the relative size of even early Saxon churches can be gained at Hexham, where the nave of the abbey, from the south wall to the north arcade, dates from Wilfred's time.

25. There is a single-volume history of Wales, that of J. Davies, a commendable work but confusing in its lack of notes. Remarkably, the book was first published, and enjoyed considerable success, in Welsh, a measure of how far Welsh, unlike Irish, has flourished as a living language. The best history by far, and the best of any part of the British Isles, is the Oxford History of Wales, which covers the period from 1063–1980. Taken with the work of Wendy Davies, the five volumes admirably cover the whole of Welsh history.

26. Writers grinding nationalist axes often refuse to concede the point, but the OED is clear.

27. See *Welsh History Review*, vol. viii, no. 1, 1976, D.P. Kirby 'Hywell Dda: Anglophil?'.

28. Ibid., vol. x, no. 3, 1981, H. Loyn, 'Wales and England in the Tenth Century'; W. Davies, *Wales in the Early Middle Ages*, pp.113ff; *Welsh History Review*, vol. xvi, no. 2, 1992, N.J. Higham, 'Medieval Overkingship in Wales', which also makes some useful observations on Gildas.

29. For 'Armes Prydein' see *Études Celtiques*, vol. xxii, 1999, A.C. Breeze.

30. *Collected Verse*, pp.712–13.

31. See *Scottish History Review*, vol. lxxii, no. 194, 1993, R.O. Oram, 'A Family Business?'.

32. See *Welsh History Review*, vol. xviii, no. 1, K. Mann, 'The March of Wales'.

33. The interaction between England/Britain and the papacy was often of considerable importance. Following it has been made much easier by R.P. McBrien's *Lives of Popes*, from which all later references are taken.

CHAPTER 3 : 1066–1300

1. A good single-volume history of Scotland, which has been well-used here, is M. Lynch, *Scotland*, but R. Mitchison's book has great charm and apt judgment. J. Prebble, *The Lion in the North* is passionately argued and very well illustrated, and, like all this writer's work, eminently readable. From 1700 T.M. Devine is the last, authoritative word. A good overview of Scottish historiography is found in *Scottish History Review*, 'Whither Scottish History?'.

2. Scotland developed the machinery of central government very much later than did England. The first English charters date from the early seventh century, those of Scotland from the end of the eleventh, based on English practice, usually that of Durham: see *Scottish History Review*, vol. lxviii, April 1989, J. Donnelly, 'Earliest Scottish Charters'. The first Scots currency is that of David I in 1136 – and that came from the English north – many centuries later than that of Offa (see *Scottish History Review*, vol. lviii, no. 2, 1979, W.W. Scott, 'The Use of Money in Scotland'). The Northumbrian styca was commonly used in Scotland.

3. For David I see G.W.S. Barrow, *Scotland and its Neighbours*.

4. G.W.S. Barrow, *Kingship in Mediaeval Scotland*; *Scottish History Review*, vol. lxviii, no. 2, 1989, J. Bannerman, 'The King's Poet', and Chapters 6 and 7 of A.A.M. Duncan, *Scotland*.

5. W.L. Warren is still the authority on Henry II, and his book one of the great royal biographies: the short section on Ireland (pp.187–206) puts the expedition in the context of European history.

6. *Welsh History Review*, vol. xiv, no. 4, P. Latimer, 'Henry II's Campaign'.

7. R. Roche, *The Norman Invasion* has lasted well and has good illustrations. A. Cosgrove, *Medieval Ireland* and R. Frame, *Colonial Ireland* are excellent. A.J. Otway-Ruthven, *Medieval Ireland* remains the most comprehensive.

8. J. Watt, *The Church in Medieval Ireland* is good and compact; see also his *The Church and Two Nations*.

9. *Eriu*, vol. xlii, 1991, Colman Etchingham, 'The Early Irish Church', p.118. This view is modified by D. Ó Croinin, *Early Medieval Ireland*.

10. Giraldus is one of the great medieval personalities: all his works are full of interest, and his prickly character shines clearly through. For a critical assessment see R. Kearney, *The Irish Mind*, p.311, n3; to follow Giraldus through Wales, see C. Kightly, *Mirror of Medieval Wales*.

11. Giraldus, ed. A.B. Scott and F.X. Martin, para. 37. Gerald uses the word '*familia*' for 'races'.

12. Ibid., para. 34.

13. Law books exist: see e.g. Etchingham, 'The Early Irish Church', op. cit.; but given the absence of a network of literate and organised clergy the oral tradition must have been considerably more influential.

14. Giraldus, op. cit.

15. King Richard and King John both have good new biographies – J. Gillingham, *Richard I* and W.L. Warren, *King John*.

16. William actually suggested a part-fusion of the two kingdoms: his daughter Margaret was to marry Richard's nephew Otto, with Lothian as dowry. Richard would make Northumbria over to Otto, who would become heir to the Scottish throne (Gillingham, op. cit., p.279).

17. See *Scottish History Review*, vol. lviii, 1979, R.I. Lustig, 'The Treaty of Perth'.

18. For the period in Wales see R.R. Davies, *The Age of Conquest* in the Oxford History of Wales; a remarkable book.

19. For the Suliens see *Studia Celtica*, vols viii/ix, 1973–74, M. Lapidge, 'The Welsh-Latin Poetry of Sulien's Family'.

20. For Owain see *Welsh History Review*, vol. xix, no. 1, H. Pryce, 'Owain Gwynedd and Louis VII', which details Owain's attempt to enlist the French King's help for '*Owinus Waliarum princeps, suus homo et amicus fidelis*' – the first claim made to the title.

21. For Llywellyn ap Gruffudd, and much of what follows, see J.B. Smith, *Llywelyn*, an excellent new work.

22. R.R. Davies, op. cit., p. 323.

23. Ibid., p.385.

24. Quite extraordinarily G.A. Williams, a Professor of History at Cardiff, who should have known better, has Edward born in 1301 in 'the most overcrowded delivery room in history'; the prince was then seventeen years old! *When was Wales?*, p.97.

25. *Bulletin of the Board of Celtic Studies*, 1974, N.M. Fryde, 'Welsh Troops in the Scottish Campaign of 1322'; ibid., 1993, A. Welsh, 'The English Mercenary Force in Ireland'; *Welsh History Review*, vol. iv, A.D. Carr, 'Welshmen and the Hundred Years War'.

26. R. Bromwich, *Dafydd* has parallel texts: this is 'The Skylark'; see also 'Trouble at the Inn' and 'The Goose-Shed'.

CHAPTER 4 : 1300–1540

1. For King Edward's changing policies in Scotland see M. Prestwich,

'Colonial Scotland', in R.A. Mason, *Scotland and England*.

2. Devorguilla might be claimed as an example of a (partly) Celtic woman exercising real power, were it not that she was operating in a distinctively Anglo-Norman elite. See Oram, 'A Family Business?', op. cit.

3. Although the battle was truly decisive, the end of that struggle that had continued since Bouvines, over two centuries before, it has been entirely forgotten by the English. Castillon is replayed entirely every year near the site of the battle; the Earl, represented by one of the Talbot family, is the hero.

4. Piccolomini, *Secret Diaries*, pp.29–31.

5. Americans often distinguish between Scots and Scots-Irish, surely largely meaningless. Culturally speaking Lowland Scots shared a very similar identity whether they lived in Antrim or Lothian; the real distinction was between Lowlands and Highlands, so clearly defined in Sir Walter Scott's novels.

6. See R.R. Davies, op. cit., Chapter 16.

7. For Owain Lawgoch see Carr, 'Welshmen and the Hundred Years War', op. cit., p.31. The author also discusses the confusion between '*gallois*' – Welshman or boon companion – and '*Galloise*' – a prostitute; see also *Welsh History Review*, vol. vii, 1994–95, A. Trotter, 'Merry, Welsh or Both'.

8. Owain has a considerable literature, mostly inaccurate. The authoritative work is R.R. Davies, *The Revolt of Owain Glyn Dwr*, from which much of what follows is drawn. For a vivid contemporary account see Adam of Usk.

9. As late as December 1402 Sir Edmund Mortimer stated that the rebels' intention was 'if King

Richard be alive to restore him to his crown'.

10. J. Abse, *Letters*, pp.33–4; see also p.33 for a letter from Owain to an innominate Irish chieftain referring to 'our beloved cousins in Ireland' and 'our deadly enemies the Saxons'. Such appeals to Celtic solidarity were rarely fruitful. R.R. Davies, *The Revolt of Owain Glyn Dwr* suggests that some of Owain's frustration sprang from the fact that to the Welsh he was a 'baron', an 'archaic hangover in terminology', which gave rise to the 'illusion' that this was a rank equal to that of the English baron; outside Wales Owain was, at best, a respectable esquire (p.134).

11. 'Magnanimity was the keynote' is R.R. Davies' judgment; *The Revolt of Owain Glyn Dwr*, p.455.

12. K. Simms, *From Kings to Warlords*, p.25.

13. See *Irish Historical Studies*, vol. vi, 1948–49, J. Otway-Ruthven, 'The Request of the Irish for English Law', and vol. xxix, no. 115, 1995, J. Lydon, 'Ireland and the English Crown'.

14. For the indignant Arnold Power, and more, see Lydon, op. cit.

15. Quoted in R.F. Foster, *Ireland*, p.76.

16. For Richard's visit see *Irish Historical Studies*, vol. xxii, no. 85, 1980, D. Johnston, 'Richard II and the Submissions of Gaelic Ireland'. The writer concludes: 'what is remarkable is the extent of his success in authenticating the Crown's position in Gaelic Ireland, providing Henry VIII with a convincing title for his claim to be called king throughout all Ireland'. An overview is given in B. Bradshaw, *Irish Constitutional Revolution*, pp.14–29. And William II's appearance in 1690 was for a very specific purpose!

17. For Prior Butler see A. Cosgrove,

'*Hiberniores ipsis Hibernis*', in Cosgrove and McCartney, *Studies in Irish History*. Galls and Gaels together were described as '*Erenchaig*'.

18. See Lydon, op. cit.

19. S.G. Ellis, *Tudor Ireland*, p.187, and the chapter 'The Impact of Religious Reform' generally.

20. By Philip Bocht Ó Huiginn, quoted in J. Watt, *The Church in Medieval Ireland*, pp.213–14.

21. B. Bradshaw, in Cosgrove and McCartney, op. cit., p.23.

22. J. Guy, *Tudor England*, p.169.

23. J.D. Mackie, *The Earlier Tudors*, p.141. For Henry VIII in Scotland see *Scottish History Review*, vol. lxi, no. 171, 1982, D.M. Head, 'Henry VIII's Scottish Policy'.

24. G. Price, *The Complaynt of Scotland*; and see P.H. Scott, *Scotland*, pp.10–11.

CHAPTER 5 : 1540–1603

The works of G.R. Elton, although modified by later writers, still form the bedrock of Tudor revolution studies. John Guy and J.J. Scarisbrick are more accessible but equally authoritative. Works on Elizabeth I are legion, but D. Starkey's is noteworthy.

1. In a letter to Peter Martyr, 16 November 1559 (H. Robinson, *The Zurich Letters*, p.55). Jewel's letters are still eminently readable; we think of Elizabethan bishops as dignified ancients, but Jewel was only thirty-seven at the time of his appointment.

2. Ibid., vol. ii, Jewel to Peter Martyr, 1 August 1559.

3. R. Lemprière, *The History of the Channel Islands*, pp.51ff.

4. J.B. Black, *The Reign of Elizabeth*, p.139.

5. A papal communication was commonly known as a 'bull', from the Latin *bullus*, a lead seal, a fact

which delighted English satirists for three centuries.

6. For the immediate Catholic reaction see J. Bossy, *The English Catholic Community*, Chapter 2. From the opposite camp Richard Hilles' reaction was typical: an 'impudent popish bull' had been 'vomited forth against our most serene Queen' by 'the Roman anti-Christ' – Robinson, op. cit., p.242; see also J. Lock, 'How Many Tercios has the Pope?', in *Studia Hibernica*, no. 28, for Elizabethan anti-popery.

7. For Penry see DNB. Penry was accused of sedition, Catholic priests of treason; the only men to die solely for their religious beliefs were Henry Barrow and John Greenwood, sentenced under a draconian 1581 Act which made any 'writing with malicious intent' punishable by death.

8. Glanmor Williams (not to be confused with G.A. Williams) has made this subject his own, and what follows relies largely on his books and articles.

9. In the Court of Great Sessions the use of the Welsh language was prohibited. Although later amended, the inferior status of Welsh in legal affairs was a subject of just resentment until well on in the twentieth century. See T. Skyrme, *Justices of the Peace*, Chapter 20.

10. See G. Williams, op. cit., *Welsh History Review*, vol. iv; Carr, 'Welshmen and the Hundred Years War', op. cit., especially p.38, for Sir Lewis John, MP, Master of the London and Calais Mints; *Bulletin of the Board of Celtic Studies*, 1993, W.B.R. Robinson, 'Some Welsh Members of Henry VIII's Household'. For the Inns of Court see W.P. Griffith, *Learning*: Welshmen were 'neither better nor worse behaved than the rest'; but one Leyson Price was 'fined for wearing a beard' (p.173). One Welsh

official, Rees ap Davyd, found a post in Ireland as Controller of the Drogheda Customes (*Irish Fiants of Tudor Sovereigns*, 1522). For the universities see *Cymmrodorion*, 1996; W.T.R. Price, *Wales as a Culture Region* (Oxford); and P. Cunich et al., *A History of Magdalene College* (Cambridge).

11. W.B.R. Robinson, 'Some Welsh Members of Henry VIII's Household', op. cit.

12. But G. Williams in *The Welsh Church* notes the influence of Catholic humanists, which strengthened intellectual allegiance to the Church, and the career of William Thomas, author of *The Pilgrim* and clerk to Edward VI's Privy Council, burnt by Queen Mary (pp.532ff).

13. G. Williams, *Wales and the Reformation*, p.389.

14. See *Welsh History Review*, vol. x, no. 3, 1981, G. Williams, 'Wales and the Reign of Queen Mary'.

15. S.G. Ellis, op. cit. (on which I have relied for much of what follows), pp.136–41, 144. The Earl of Surrey specifically wanted Northumbrian lancers, but had to make do with mounted archers; his total force was only 550 men (p.109). The same author's *Reform and Revival* marshals convincing arguments that late-medieval Irish government functioned much better than Nationalist historians have been willing to acknowledge (pp.207–13), and as part of similar policies in Wales and on the Scottish Borders.

16. Lydon, op. cit., p.287 & n36.

17. For the decline of the pre-Reformation Irish Church see Watt, op. cit., Chapter 6 and pp.265–6, where he quotes M. Haren, 'Vatican Archives', in AH, vol. xxix, 1984.

18. S.G. Ellis, op. cit., p.192.

19. 'Libelle of Englyshe polycye' – an anonymous political poem of c.1436.

'The first to emphasise the importance of sea power in English foreign policy', Lydon, op. cit., p.284.

20. *Irish Fiants of Tudor Sovereigns*, 1556.

21. J.B. Black, op. cit., p.471.

22. B. Bradshaw is, quite rightly, virulent about the Elizabethan atrocities. The killings at Smerwick were 'surpassed in sheer villainy, by the ambush and extermination of the O'More rebels ... in 1577 ... deeper depths of inhumanity [were] plumbed by Essex's massacre on Ruthlin island' (in C. Brady, *Interpreting Irish History*). Well, yes, but most European countries could provide similar examples. J.G. Crawford, in *Anglicizing ...* , finds Bradshaw 'shrill and unsympathetic'.

23. One interesting facet of the rebellion was the influence of Finola O'Donnell, the 'Dark Daughter' of James and Lady Agnes Campbell, the Earl of Argyll's sister, whose dowry was a large force of Scottish Redshanks. This was a dangerous development, since English intelligence judged '300 Skottes are harder to be vanquished than 600 Yryshmen', and considered mother and daughter to be the source of 'all mischief against the inglishe Pale'. When Finola, who hated the English, married Hugh O'Donnell, the two great Ulster families were united, and with a formidable military force. See J.E.A. Dawson in 'Two Kingdoms or Three?', in Mason, op. cit.

24. J.B. Black, op. cit., p.479.

25. For the episode see J.J. Silke, *Kinsale*.

26. J. Bardon, *A History of Ulster*, p.113.

27. For the period see M.K. Walsh, *Destruction by Peace*; on the so-called 'Flight of the Earls', Walsh convincingly claims (p.143) that 'Spanish sources provide clear evidence' that their action 'was neither a panic decision nor a journey into voluntary exile, but a planned and tactical retreat' in order to gain Spanish support for an Ireland free to develop under Spanish protection. See also IHR, vol. xxxi, no. 123, J. McCavitt, 'The Flight of the Earls'.

28. 'The First Blast of the Trumpet against the Monstrous Regiment of Women' was the title of Knox's pamphlet attacking Queen Mary; he had some difficulty in explaining it away when Queen Elizabeth came to the English throne, but Calvin himself helped (*Zurich Letters*, vol. 2, pp.34–6) by conveying his personal disapproval of Knox to the English Queen.

29. I.B. Cowan, *Scottish Reformation*, p.60. Another reformer, Archbishop Hamilton, attempted to ban clerics dressing in 'top boots and double-breasted or oddly cut coats' (p.79).

30. One particularly Scottish contribution to Reformation literature was the popular *Gude and Godlie Ballatis*, written about 1550, which included songs on 'The Paip, that Pagane full of Pryde'; F.D. Bardgett, *Scotland Reformed*, p.45.

31. For Mylne's martyrdom see J. Wormald, *Mary*, in which he records the Earl of Argyll's warning to the Archbishop of St Andrews against listening to those who would urge him to burn 'poor men' in order 'to serve their wicked appetites'.

32. E. Bonner in 'Auld Alliance', *History*, vol. lxxxiv, no. 273, 1999, calls the subject 'more than usually endowed with fable', but notes that contemporary Scots and French both were 'firmly convinced' that it 'stretched back over eight centuries to the time of Charlemagne'.

33. For James see R. Lockyer, *James VI & I*, a good, clear book.

CHAPTER 6 : 1603–1660

1. For the background to the Union see R.A. Mason, *Scots and Britons*; M. Lee, *Great Britain's Solomon* and B. Galloway, *The Union* are authoritative.

2. In addition to the income granted by Queen Elizabeth to King James after 1596 – £58,000 over seventeen years – some individuals benefited and English intelligence services exerted themselves to encourage support for English policies: see K.M. Brown, 'The Price of Friendship', in R.A. Mason, op. cit. The actual form which the Union would assume had been discussed for many years; see M. Merriman, 'James Henrisoun', and Brown, 'The Price of Friendship', both in Mason, op. cit.

3. See W.B. Patterson, *King James and the Reunion of Christendom*. M. Lee, op. cit., p.208, points out that the King attempted also 'to create a Church that would appeal to the native Irish'. For James' intentions, and much more, see J. Wormald's definitive article in *Transactions of the Royal Historical Society*, September 1992, pp.175–94, 'The Creation of Britain'.

4. Lockyer, op. cit., p.57 and Chapter 3, 'The Union', *passim*.

5. Quoted in Galloway, op. cit., p.164.

6. Quoted in Mitchison, op. cit., p.155.

7. The literature on seventeenth-century Britain is enormous and constantly developing. There are good bibliographies in C. Durston, *Cromwell's Major Generals* (Manchester 2001) and M. Bennett, *Civil War Experienced* (London 2000). Some original sources should not be neglected, those of Lord Clarendon, *History of the Rebellion* and Bishop Burnet, *History of his own Times* written by participants.

8. Quoted in G. Davies, *The Early Stuarts*, p.87.

9. The 'Thirty Years War' formed a training ground for many of the soldiers in the British civil combats.

10. For the Covenant see particularly J. Morrill, *Scottish National Covenant* and D. Stevenson, *Union, Revolution and Religion in Seventeenth-Century Scotland*.

11. For Irish history since 1600, and especially for the short biographies, R.F. Foster's *Modern Ireland* is essential.

12. Bardon's *A History of Ulster* is unsurpassed; this is p.123.

13. Referring to the city as 'Derry' or 'Londonderry' is today taken as an indication of one's politics. I have made no attempt at consistency.

14. Henderson, DNB. C.V. Wedgwood, *The King's War*, p.552 and n76 has an account of the debate.

15. See J.R. Tanner, *Constitutional Conflicts*, pp.146–9.

16. From the diary of John Nicoll, quoted in Mitchison, op. cit., pp.227–8.

17. For King Charles in Scotland see Burnet's introductory summary, from which the following extracts – the information being given by the King himself to Burnet – are taken.

18. The 1641 rising takes a central part in Irish myth, some writers dismissing it as English propaganda; but see M. Perceval-Maxwell, *Irish Rebellion*, who clarifies the truth, and K.M. Noonan in *Historical Journal*, vol. xli, no.1, 1998, 'Cruell Pressure'. N. Canny in 'Religion, Politics and the Irish Rising', in J. Devlin and R. Fanning, *Religion and Rebellion*, gives a wider, European, view.

19. In a letter to Sir Robert Knight; see *Irish Historical Studies*, vol. xxi, no. 82, 1978, M. Perceval-Maxwell, 'The Ulster Rising', p.158.

20. For Milton's activities see D.

Norbrook, *Writing the English Republic*.

21. '*Disputatio Apologetica*', see Norbrook, op. cit., p.248 n12.

22. A staunch resistance was offered by Alice, Lady Colclough of Tintern Abbey, Wexford, who sustained a five-month siege; see R. Sawyer, *We are but Women*.

23. See A. Fraser, *Cromwell*, pp.350–1 – like all Lady Antonia's biographies, informed and entertaining.

24. P.B. Ellis, *Hell or Connaught*, p.176.

25. Richard Power, DNB.

26. For Commonwealth adminstration see G.E. Aylmer, *The State's Servants*.

27. For these see C. Webster, *Great Instauration*, Part 2, v and Part 3, x.

28. M. MacCurtain, 'Rural Society', in Cosgrove and McCartney, op. cit., p.135. For Trinity College see T.C. Barnard, *Cromwellian Ireland*. The Book of Kells was secured for the library by Dr Henry Jones, whose committee for the new university comprised Anglicans, Presbyterians and Independents, a remarkable convocation (pp.206–12).

29. The best account is F.D. Dow, *Cromwellian Scotland*, but see also W. Ferguson, *Scotland's Relations*. Ferguson sees the Cromwellian Union, in at least some aspects, as 'remarkable for its vision and its idealism', and the regime as 'an admirable system of executive government and of firm and impartial administration' (p.138).

30. Quoted in Dow, op. cit., p.57. Dr Dow remarks however that 'behind the velvet glove of the negotiator [Broghill] lay the cold calculation of an "English" politician' (p.138).

31. Quoted in ibid., p.57.

CHAPTER 7 : 1660–1750

1. John Evelyn has a wonderful account of a meeting at Lambeth Palace on 15 January 1689, when he found 'no accord among the distinguished assembly, some wanting Mary to be queen, others calling for a regency, Tories for recalling James and even some republicans'.

2. Mitchison, op. cit., p.270.

3. His Irish supporters deserved a better leader than the condescending, indecisive James. The French King's representative, the Comte D'Avaux, groaned (12 May 1689) that '*Il faut ... donner ordre à toutes choses, et on ne donne ordre à rien.*'

4. There are many books and articles on the Darien project. P.W.J. Riley, *King William* and J. Robertson (ed.), *Union for Empire* include accounts; among the chapters in the latter that of D. Armitage, 'The Intellectual Origins of the Darien Venture', is authoritative. See also I.M. Cullen, 'Scottish Exchange', in S.J. Connolly et al., *Conflict . . . .* J. Prebble, *The Darien Disaster* tells the whole story.

5. See Prebble, *The Darien Disaster*, p.58. The King was otherwise engaged at the time, fighting against France from May to October, then organising a general election.

6. Burnet, vol. 2, p.126.

7. For Scottish banking see A. Cameron, *The Bank of Scotland*.

8. See Armitage, op. cit., p.101. By that time investors had already paid their first call: in effect the Company had issued a false prospectus – they had been 'warned comprehensively' against accepting Paterson's scheme, but, sensibly in the circumstances, committed little to writing.

9. *Scottish History Review*, vol. lxii, 1992, E.G. Graham, 'Scottish Maritime Interest'. The Scottish Secretary of State James Ogilvy, later Lord Seafield, realistically commented: 'I think it will do little hurt to the English seeing that we want a fleet.' The three ships bought

took no part in the adventure.

10. Armitage, op. cit., p.111.

11. Riley, op. cit., p.132: 'It was easier to have a scapegoat, particularly one so satisfying as the ancient enemy, than to look for the causes of the disaster nearer home.'

12. The Act of Union, being a critical point in Scottish history, and of less significance in that of England, has become a favourite subject of Scots historians. J. Robertson, op. cit., is essential. C.A. Whately has a stimulating chapter, 'The Union of 1707', in A. Cooke et al., *Modern Scottish History*.

13. See T.C. Smout, *Scottish Trade*, p.255, which is also informative on Darien. E.G. Graham, op. cit., comments that at the end of the seventeenth century 'the ailing Scottish economy was suffering from a decade of trade deficits, failing exports, and a haemorrhage of scarce bullion'. By 1684 Newcastle was exporting £77,000-worth of coal to Scotland. The total trade of Tyne and Wear was over £600,000. See J. Nef, *The Rise and Fall of the British Coal Industry*.

14. Prebble, op. cit., p.337.

15. Robertson, op. cit., justly claims that 'the quality of the Scottish Union debate was due almost entirely to the inspiration of one man, Andrew Fletcher'. But it was essentially a debate not on whether, but in what manner.

16. By one of life's little ironies the Commissioners included John Clerk, composer of '*Leo Scotiae*'.

17. C. Petrie's *The Jacobite Movement* (two vols) remains a classic. Many Jacobites were imprisoned and fined in 1708, but there were no executions.

18. Defoe's own analysis is extracted in R. West, *Daniel Defoe*, p.142.

19. B. Harison, 'Jacobitism', in Cooke et al., op. cit., vol. 1, p.28, comments on the 'singular insensitivity and clumsiness with which the English political establishment treated Scotland after 1707', a situation which endured for half a century, and which has still not entirely disappeared.

20. The debate about the advantages or otherwise of the Union has been sometimes acrimonious, some Scottish nationalists colouring the picture in the darkest hues. The view presented here is that the settlement was generally fair, but that given the gross inequality between the two economies the adjustment was painful. The Scottish achievement was to overcome the initial obstacles and to make an astonishing success of the opportunities offered.

21. Prebble, once more, has the best account of the battle, in *Culloden*; but see also G. Menary, *Duncan Forbes*, for a contemporary participant.

22. For an overview of eighteenth-century Scottish society see J. Dwyer and R. Sher, *Sociability and Society* and J. Dwyer, *Virtuous Discourse*. Hugh Blair, the best of the fashionable Scottish preachers, very clearly defined his 'native country' as 'that happy island, to which we have the honour and blessing to belong'. *Sermons*, vol. 5, n6.

23. Gibbon proudly reproduced Hume's letter in full in his *Autobiography*, pp.145–7. It should be noted, however, that even the superior Hume was worried about 'Scotticisms' which he endeavoured to eradicate – see J.G. Baker in Dwyer and Sher, op. cit. – complaining that Scots 'are unhappy, in our Accent and Pronunciation, speak a very corrupt dialect of the Tongue which we make use of' (letter of 1757, quoted in J.Y.T. Greig, *Letters*). Scotticisms, according to Baker, included such

now-respectable words as 'placate', 'hopeful' and 'giggle'.

24. J.G. Simms, *William Molyneux*, p.103.

25. In his *Drapier's Letters*.

26. John Carteret, DNB; Swift confessed that Carteret 'has a genteeler manner of binding the chains of the kingdom than most of his predecessors'.

27. In his 'Letter to the Whole People of Ireland'.

28. Some chose less honourable methods. Lord Altham had his servants overpower his wife's lover while the Baron removed the man's ears. F.G. James' excellent *Lords of the Ascendancy*, pp.155–6.

29. Quoted in G.H. Jenkins, *Foundations of Modern Wales* (p.34), one of the admirable volumes in the Oxford History of Wales.

30. Richard Davies, a feltmaker, received a more homely punishment, being violently beaten by his mistress for using the Quaker 'pure language'. Jenkins, op. cit., p.79.

CHAPTER 8 : 1750–1830

1. Op. cit., p.205 – but the real damage had been done in the previous two centuries. The O'Connells were beaglers rather than fox-hunters, but some famous Irish packs, including the Black and Tans, had Catholic followers and masters. On a more intellectual plane the career of the Catholic antiquarian and landowner Charles O'Conor is interesting (see C. O'Halloran, 'Ownership of the Past', in S.J. Connolly, *Ireland and Scotland*). That writer's assessment of Catholic land losses is more drastic – from 14 per cent in 1702 to 5 per cent in 1776 – but suggests that these figures were exaggerated. On the Butler estate of Cahir ninety-seven of the 141 leases

granted between 1720 and 1750 were to Catholics (K. Whelan, *Tree of Liberty* – a rewarding book – p.7).

2. This is J.F. Hering, in A. O'Day and J. Stevenson, *Irish Historical Documents*, pp.17–19.

3. As for the Aylwards see Whelan, op. cit., p.28. They could produce more than £2500 in gold as premium for a single thirty-one-year lease.

4. M. Wall, *Catholic Ireland* is a good account on which the following relies.

5. As early as 1730 a scandalised Protestant found the Mullingar Mass house with three galleries and 'a spacious altar, painted and set off with images'; W.A. Maguire, *Up in Arms* – the best source book – p.38.

6. BL.Add.Mss. 29252.

7. R.F. Foster, *Modern Ireland*, p.178. The 'Modest Proposal' suggests that surplus Irish babies should be fattened to provide nutritious table dishes. Gullible Americans have been known to accept this as yet one more instance of English savagery.

8. William Petty, DNB. Ulster in particular was sending hopeful settlers from Belfast and Londonderry, often literate and corresponding with the homeland: 'the young men of Ireland who wish to be free and happy should leave it and come here as quick as possible' was the advice of John Dunlop of Strabane, printer of the Declaration of Independence. W.H. Crawford and B. Trainor, *Aspects of Irish Social History*, p.55.

9. Resolution of 12 October, passed nem. con. and printed in N. Kissane, *Grattan's Parliament*, Document 5; the refusal to grant taxes was on 24 November. Both the National Library of Ireland and the Public Records Office of Northern Ireland have similar excellent facsimile collections.

10. Quoted in Foster, *Modern Ireland*, p.249; and see Kissane, op. cit., Document 8, Declaration of Right: 'I will never be satisfied as long as the meanest cottager in Ireland has a link of the British chain clanking to his rags.'

11. Although almost all the initiatives for reform in Ireland came from Britain, Dundas being a prime mover, and were accepted more or less reluctantly in Ireland. F.G. James, op. cit., reviews the 'more or less' on pp.164–6. Considering that the very modest Catholic Relief Act of 1778 led directly to the disastrous Gordon riots in London, continuing with this policy was a political act of some courage. There is a good description of the Relief Acts in T. Bartlett, *Fall and Rise*. The writer concludes that the English Act of 1791 'marked the end of the penal laws strictly so called' (p.126). The Act was indeed sweeping: no Catholic 'shall . . . be liable or subject to any penalties, forfeitures, disabilities, or incapacities, or to any laws . . . save such as his Majesty's subjects of the Protestant religion are liable and subject to'. It is extraordinary that so many later writers still assume that the Penal Laws continued in existence. Presbyterian opposition in Scotland prevented the 1778 English Act being passed there.

12. From an appendix to 'The History of the Proceedings of the Volunteer Delegates' of 1784, published as Document 12 in Kissane, op. cit.

13. Orders of chivalry were, and remain, an economic way of rewarding loyal supporters. The 'most ancient' Order of the Thistle only dates to 1687, and the quite spurious 'revived' Order of the Bath to 1725.

14. Given that in the Quebec Act of 1774 French Canadians had already been given not only the ability to hold civil office by means of an amended oath, but the Catholic Church established, in receipt of tithes, it would have been illogical to deny these benefits to British and Irish Catholics; but consistency is not a good argument in politics. See R.B. Sher, *Church and University* for the Scottish parallel.

15. Napper Tandy is one of the most unlikely heroes, only remembered by his inclusion in the song 'The Wearing of the Green'. Many accounts of the 1798 rebellion are propagandist on one side or another. Tom Pakenham's *Year of Liberty* is essential, and O. Knox, *Rebels and Informers* perhaps the best on the previous events. M. Elliott, *Partners* remains the classic work on the United Irishmen. R. Kee, *The Most Distressful Country* is the first volume in his three-volume popular history. Among the best more specialised works are N.J. Curtin, *United Irishmen* and D. Dickson, *United Irishmen*. For the coalition with the Defenders see J. Quinn, 'United Irishmen and Social Reform', in *Irish Historical Studies*, vol. xxxi, no. 22, and J. Gray, *Sans Culottes*.

16. The standard biography is that of M. Elliott, but Tone's own writings (ed. T.W. Moody et al.) are essential. O. MacDonagh, *States of Mind* has some perceptive comments noting Tone's contempt for the Irish and his fascination for uniforms, flags, weapons and battles (pp.73–4).

17. See F. Campbell, *Dissenting Voice* for Protestant Ulster.

18. This is the inimitable Tone. Two years previously the first anniversary of Bastille Day was celebrated by the Northern Whig Club, at which toasts were drunk to George III as King of Ireland, the National Assembly of France, George Washington ('the ornament of

mankind') and Tom Paine. Among the guests were Lord Charlemont and Robert Stewart, the future Lord Castlereagh (F.G. James, op. cit., p.163). Support for the French Revolution soon began to fade.

19. Crawford and Trainor, op. cit., pp.181–2.

20. For contemporary accounts see D.W. Miller, *Peep O' Day Boys*, pp.103–7.

21. K. Whelan, op. cit., p 156; attention is drawn to the contrast between such realists as Thomas Emmett, who wanted an 'essentially "paper" army whose principal purpose would be to assist the French', and the radicals who dreamed of 'a successful revolution using wholly indigenous sources'; given a divided Ireland, an impossibility.

22. For the disturbances see Miller, op. cit., *passim*; for the attitude of the Catholic hierarchy see W.D. Griffin, 'Green and Black', in *Consortium on Revolutionary Europe*, vol. xiii, 1984.

23. See A. Blackstock, 'An Ascendancy Army', and T. Bartlett, 'End to Moral Economy', in C.H.E. Philpin, *Nationalism*.

24. Tone did not think much to the land of the free – 'a cultural desert' inhabited by 'a selfish, churlish, unsocial race, totally absorbed in making money' (UMC, p.113).

25. See e.g. Pakenham, op. cit., Chapter 4, *passim*.

26. See ibid. for examples of the 'unpardonable acts'. The Welsh Fencible Squadron of 'Ancient Britons' had one of the worst reputations.

27. For Tandy see Castlereagh, *Correspondence*, vol. 1, p.406; despatch of the Secret Service chief William Wickham, 25 October 1798. Wickham obtained his information from an agent on the French ship, whose officers despised Tandy as '*infame, imbecile*', a '*scelerat*' who

also pissed in one of their number's boots. Tandy's 'Northern Army of Avengers' was a joke – in poor taste.

28. See G.M. Trevelyan, *Lord Grey*, pp.113–15.

29. Edward Cooke, the Irish Under-Secretary, likened Ireland to 'a ship on fire [which] must be extinguished or cut adrift'. Quoted in O. MacDonagh, *Union and Aftermath*.

30. Quoted in M. Fry, *The Dundas Despotism*, pp.63–4.

31. See *History*, 1997, D. Wilkinson, 'How did they pass the Union?'.

32. For Emmett, in addition to the standard histories see documents edited by G. Hume and A. Malcomson; and E. Sparrow in *Secret Service*, p.307, for an interesting sidelight.

33. C. Ó Gráda, *Ireland: A New Economic History* is essential: see pp.45–6.

34. For early-nineteenth-century viceroys see E. Brynn, *Crown and Castle*.

35. O'Day and Stevenson, op. cit., pp.21–2.

36. See F.M.L. Thompson, *English Landed Society*, pp.281–2.

37. See J. Prebble, *The Highland Clearances* for Macdonnell and Sutherland.

38. For Ribbonmen see Foster, *Modern Ireland*, pp.292–4.

39. Muir was an unlikely martyr, his sentence clearly unjust – Dundas demanded it stand – but his exile a comfortable one. His great mistake was escaping, thus beginning some extraordinary adventures which brought him to an early grave. For the 1820 rebels see P.B. Ellis and S. Mac A'Ghobhainn, *Scottish Insurrection*.

40. Fry, op. cit.; see also *History*, 1998, D.J. Brown, 'The Government of Scotland'. Harry the Ninth, as Boswell called him, did well for

himself and his friends, but during his period of office Scottish interests were well attended to: 'Scots felt a measure of pride, but a greater sense of relief, that Scottish institutions were becoming attuned to the rhythm of English prosperity and civil liberty'; C. Kidd in *Historical Journal*, vol. lxix, no.2, 1996.

41. Mountstuart Elphinstone and Dalhousie are two of the great Indian names, but Allan Octavian Hume should not be forgotten: he founded the Indian National Congress in 1885 – Gandhi's party, which for many years formed Indian governments; see C. Harvie, *Scotland and Nationalism*, pp.61ff, and DNB. See also *Transactions of the Royal Historical Society*, vol. viii, 1998, J.M. McKenzie, 'Empire and National Identities'.

42. D.H. Akenson, *Small Differences*, a valuable corrective view; see Appendix J.

43. P.H. Scott, *Scotland*, pp.91ff.

44. J.G. Lockhart, *Life*, pp.482ff.

45. Quoted in *Irish Historical Documents*, vol. ix, p.118.

46. The best source for the whole topic is W. Hinde, *Catholic Emancipation*. The word emancipation is thoroughly misleading, especially in view of the 1793 Act, and is used here with a strong health warning.

47. For Lawless as 'a miserable maniac' see Hinde, op. cit., p.102. For the rest, and Wyse's reaction, see MacDonagh, op. cit., p.19. The same author's elegant two-volume O'Connell biography is published as *Hereditary Bondsman* and *The Emancipist*.

48. Such disturbances brought 'the terrible and unuttered threat of mass disorder' to force action on Tory governments. MacDonagh, op. cit., p.48. For the faction fights themselves see *Irish Historical Studies*, vol. xxx, no. 117, 1996, 'A Moral Insurrection'.

49. For Blake see D.A. Kerr, *Peel, Priests and Politics*, p.136; for the duties of Assistant Barristers see T. Skyrme, op. cit., pp.286ff; for Wellesley see I. Butler, *Eldest Brother*.

50. Royal Archives GEO 24176/96, 'A Sketch of the Measures of Lord Wellesley's Administration'. Colonel Meyrick Shaw, the Under-Secretary, wrote to Sir William Knighton on 18 September 1827 that 'a party ... jealous of the monopoly they had long enjoyed' had frustrated the Viceroy's plans and ensured that all available posts were filled by 'their friends and adherents'. In the circumstances Wellesley did well to get three out of ten legal appointments given to Catholics.

51. The progress of the discussion is recorded at length in the first volume of Peel's *Memoirs*. The Tory government's success in forcing through the measure against the sustained opposition of King and Lords proved that the Constitution was not sacrosanct, thus clearing the deck for the subsequent Whig reforms. 'This question has stood like a Michael Angelo in a gallery, blinding us to everything else,' *Edinburgh Review*, March 1829.

52. The letter is in O'Connell, *Correspondence*, vol. 7, p.157; see also E.D. Steele, 'Gladstone and Irish Violence', in Cosgrove and McCartney, op. cit., and MacDonagh, *Emancipist*, p.210.

53. Trevelyan, op. cit., p.292.

54. In the same letter Palmerston states that 'I have pretty much made up my own mind' that the Catholic question 'must be a sine qua non to my own return to office'. Lord Palmerston (ed. K. Bourne), *Letters to Laurence and Elizabeth Sulivan*.

55. '1st and 2nd Reports of His Majesty's Commissioners on Exchequer Revenue & Patronage:

Ireland', respectively 1833 and 1834.

56. For objections to tithes see Crawford and Trainor, op. cit., items 10–13.

57. For Nicholls see G. O'Brien, 'A Question of Attitudes', in R. Mitchison and P. Roebuck, *Economy and Society*, p.162, quoting William Voules of Cork. See also O. MacDonagh, *The Union*, pp.38ff. I. Anstruther's *Scandal* is a fine study of English conditions.

58. For Resident Magistrates see T. Skyrme, op. cit., pp.268–94.

59. W.M. Thackeray, *Irish Sketch Book*, Chapter 32. The inmates were of course free to leave, as many had for the harvest.

60. Ó Gráda, op. cit., p.98.

CHAPTER 9 : 1830–1860

1. Lord John's own account was *Six Weeks in Ireland*, published in 1833. See also D.A. Kerr, *Nation of Beggars?*.

2. Thomas Drummond, DNB.

3. See MacDonagh, *Emancipist*, Chapter 8.

4. The experienced Peel – who had collected an extensive library of works on Ireland – was well aware of Ireland's need for administrative justice, and continued to urge Dublin to 'look out' for suitable Catholics, since 'considerations of policy and justice demand a liberal and indulgent' approach (letter to Lord de Grey, 24 July 1843, quoted in Kerr, *Peel, Priests and Politics*, p.111).

5. *Irish Historical Studies*, vol. xxx, no. 117, 1996, R. Sloan, 'O'Donnell's Liberal Rivals'.

6. The effect of C. Woodham-Smith's *The Great Hunger* has been to spread the 'populist–nationalist paradigm. In this oversimplified view, the excess mortality in the

1840s was entirely, or almost entirely due to a negligent government and cruel landlords.' This is the opinion of one the best books on Irish history, C. Ó Gráda's *Ireland: A New Economic History*. Professor Ó Gráda could have carried the characterisation further: 'genocide' is a term still liberally applied. A brisk corrective is also applied by Joel Mokyr, *Why Ireland Starved*. The evidence in the following paragraphs is from Ó Gráda. See also Kerr, *A Nation of Beggars?* and Ó Gráda, *Irish Famine* – surely the definitive work – and Black *'47 and Beyond*.

7. Ó Gráda, *Ireland: A New Economic History*, pp.14, 17; for public health see p.97. The writer makes the qualification, 'formally, at least, public health provision in Ireland rivalled the best in Europe in the 1820s and 1830s'.

8. Bardon, op. cit., pp.280–1.

9. On 17 August 1846. See *Irish Historical Studies*, vol. xxix, no. 116, G.L. Bernstein, 'Liberals . . .', an excellent arrticle which also reviews some of the current interpretations of Famine history. The previous quotation is Spring Rice in March 1839 on Irish railway construction. Ó Gráda, *Irish Famine*, p.49, aptly characterises 'A dogmatic obsession with the moral hazard and "pauperization" arising from gratuitous or over generous relief'. For workhouse mortality see ibid., p.51.

10. The views are those of, *seriatim*: i. Russell himself; ii. R. Vernon Smith MP, 1 June 1847; iii. J.A. 'Tear 'em' Roebuck, a hotheaded Radical MP, 19 January 1847 – all in the House of Commons debates.

11. Hunt's reports from Parliamentary Papers, 'Irish Famine, 1st Report of the Relief Commissioners'.

12. Ibid.

13. Most Commissioners – two of the seven were Catholics – were

dedicated public servants. One, Sir Randolph Routh, former Commissary General, was 'convinced that potato cultivation was morally debilitating' and led to indolence and all kinds of vices. It was such attitudes, rather than incompetence or malevolence, that earned British governments a bad reputation; see P. Gray, *Famine, Land . . .* , pp.119, 128.

14. See Bernstein, op. cit., p.535. The editor, James Wilson, believed that 'It is no man's business to provide for another.' For this, and other such comments, see Ó Gráda, *Black '47 and Beyond*.

15. Ibid., p.535.

16. J. Mokyr, *Why Ireland Starved* considers that 'The only area in which British rule in Ireland failed was, significantly, poor relief', which makes his assessment that 'in the frightful summer of 1847, the British simply abandoned the Irish and let them perish' the more damning. For accusations of genocide and 'shocking colonial mindlessness' see e.g. D.J. Casey and R.E. Rhodes, *Views of the Irish Peasantry*.

17. P.H. Scott, op. cit., pp.114ff.

18. Young Ireland 'loathed what they saw as O'Connell's lack of sensibility, vulgar oratory, coarse populism, financial chicanery' and more; but when the split occurred, O'Connell's subscriptions trebled – MacDonagh, *Emancipist*, pp.292–6. Thomas Davis particularly attempted to convince Protestants that Young Ireland shared their distaste for the identification 'Irish = Catholic'. See *Two Lands*, pp.141ff. This was not an attitude likely to commend itself to the mass of O'Connell's followers.

19. For a documentary account of the bathetic rising see R. Kee, *The Most Distressful Country*, Chapter 13.

20. Denis Mack Smith is the authority on modern Italy.

21. Wiseman trailed his coat aggressively, claiming that 'We shall continue to administer with ordinary jurisdiction the counties of Middlesex, Hertford & etc.', words calculated to alarm a public suspicious of Rome. L. Woodward, *Age of Reform*, p.522.

22. See G. Rude and E. Hobsbawm, *Captain Swing*.

23. For Welsh unrest see D. Jones, *Before Rebecca*. The Saesen gave good grounds for Welsh resentment. George Cornewall Lewis, later a Liberal Chancellor, and himself a Welshman who ought to have known better, compared the south Wales coalfield to a 'penal colony' inhabited by 'bad characters' and 'runaway vagrants'. When his friend Edmund Head suggested that the Welsh might be civilised 'in about three centuries', Lewis questioned this 'while they retained their villainous Celtic language'. See K. Robbins, *Nineteenth Century Britain*, pp.31–2.

24. For Welsh industry see Jenkins, op. cit., pp.283–99.

25. For Iolo see DNB. For Welsh newspapers see K.O. Morgan, *Rebirth of a Nation*, pp.49–51, and *History*, vol. lvi, no. 186, 1971, G. Williams, 'Language, Literacy and Nationality'.

26. See Ellis and Mac A'Ghobhainn, op. cit.

27. M. Fry, 'Politics', in A. Cooke, *Modern Scottish History* makes the point (p.47) that 'The preserved national institutions were so distinctive that they could only be manned by Scots: it would be no use trying to put Anglican vicars into the Kirk, or English barristers into the courts, or dons from Oxford and Cambridge into the Universities.' He might have added that it would have taken a remarkable Englishman to be successful in Scottish business.

28. For Scottish banking see A. Cameron, op. cit.

29. James Mill left Scotland for London, and neither he nor his super-talented son John Stuart showed any desire to return. Among later Scottish writers who opted for the south were Arthur Conan Doyle, Robert Louis Stevenson and James Barrie.

30. M.R.G. Fry, 'Disruption and the Union', in Brown and Fry, *Scotland* . . . , pp.43, 51–2.

31. P.H. Scott, op. cit., pp.111ff.

CHAPTER 10 : 1860–1893

1. Bardon, op. cit., pp.334–6.

2. Ibid., pp.302–4.

3. For education see Lyons, *Ireland* . . ., pp.83–98. For modern Irish history Lyons is indispensable.

4. For farming in the period see Ó Gráda, *Ireland: A New Economic History*, Part 1, Chapter 2 and Part 2, Chapter 5. On tenure etc. Paul Bew, *Land and the National Question* is authoritative.

5. For outrages see S.J. Connolly, *Ireland and Scotland*, p.176.

6. A careful examination of Fenianism, theoretical and otherwise, is found in R.V. Comerford, *Fenians in Context*.

7. The Royal Irish Constabulary were themselves overwhelmingly Catholic and equally strongly anti-Fenian: see *Church and State* . . . , pp.116ff. It is typical of the hyperbole that surrounds such scenes that even R. Kee in *Bold Fenian Men* (p.42) describes Thomas Bourke, the fugitive American, as being sentenced to be hanged, beheaded etc., but did not point out that in cold fact no one was executed as a result of these risings, the most severe penalties exacted being quite short terms of imprisonment.

8. Gladstone's commitment to Ireland is recorded in one authoritative volume – J.L. Hammond, *Gladstone and the Irish Nation*, which has been supplemented and extended by A. O'Day, *Irish Home Rule*. In *The Irish Question and British Politics* D.G. Boyce offers a perceptive commentary. R. Shannon's two volumes are the best biography, and with M.R.D. Foot's edition of the *Diaries* form an unmatched picture of that extraordinary statesman; but J. Morley's *Life* remains useful. Andrew Roberts's biography of Lord Salisbury is excellent.

9. Somewhat surprisingly, the Queen helped to ensure the passage of the contentious Church Bill.

10. For the Land Act see Bew, op. cit., Appendix 2. Boyce, op. cit., summarises the period in Chapter 1, and H.W. Luce, *Diary of Two Parliaments*, vol. 2, gives a blow-by-blow account of the debates.

11. The debate on the University Bill is recorded in Morley, vol. 2, Chapter 16.

12. The standard work on Parnell is now P. Bew, *Parnell*, but see also R. Kee, *The Laurel and the Ivy* and two excellent essays, 'Interpretations of Parnell' and 'Parnell and his People', in R.F. Foster, *Paddy and Mr Punch*.

13. Registrar General's report from *Field*, 20 March 1880.

14. For the Land League see A. Mitchell and P. Ó Snodaigh, *Irish Political Documents*, nos 14–18. Davitt's own works, especially his *Prison Diary*, remain interesting.

15. Rather quaintly, Professor Lyons (p.165) refers to 'attempts' on landords' lives. There were in fact many successful murders, including that of the well-hated Lord Leitrim, together with his agent and driver, in 1878. For the overall statistics and examples see S.J. Connolly, *Ireland and Scotland*, pp.176–9.

16. Royal Archives VIC/D32/10.

17. The incident is recorded in Kee, *The Laurel and the Ivy*, p.439. For Gladstone's reaction see Morley, vol. 3, Chapter 5 – Morley himself being closely involved in the whole episode.

18. Gladstone mishandled Chamberlain; the generation and culture gap between the two made mutual understanding near-impossible. For Chamberlain see P.T. Marsh, *Joseph Chamberlain*.

19. R.C.K. Ensor, *England*, p.87.

20. Before 1884 only some 18 per cent of adult Irishmen had the parliamentary vote; after that year the proportion rose to 64 per cent.

21. Queen Victoria, ed. G.E. Buckle, *Letters*, vol. 3, pp.712–16.

22. Gladstone was standing for Midlothian; see Hammond, op. cit., pp.421–5.

23. Ibid., pp.515–17. Gladstone temporised in his answer to Mrs O'Shea, but noted one item which was later to be of prime importance – money: 'finance is only touched on at one single point'.

24. For the Colonel see O'Day, op. cit., p.113; for Gladstone see R. Shannon, op. cit., p.417.

25. See A. Roberts, op. cit., p.384. Salisbury's daughter Gwendolen attempted to explain her father's gaffe in her biography, vol. 2, p.302, quoted in Hammond, op. cit., pp.468–9. Salisbury was not the only guilty party. Sidney and Beatrice Webb, the Fabian socialist pioneers, visited Ireland in 1887 and 1892: 'The people are charming, but we detest them – as we should the Hottentots – for their very virtues. Home Rule is an absolute necessity in order to depopulate the country of this detestable race' (July 1892, quoted in R.J. Harrison, *Sidney and Beatrice Webb*, p.213). 'Hottentots' as well as Irish are libelled: Adam Kok's South African state had been managing its own affairs competently enough.

26. Bardon, op. cit., pp.376–7; Churchill despised the 'foul Ulster Tories'.

27. Ibid., pp.380–2.

28. For Chamberlain and Ireland see *History*, vol. lxxvii, no. 250, J. Loughlin, 'Joseph Chamberlain and the Ulster Question'.

29. For the forgeries see L. Ó Broin, *Prime Informer*, and A. Roberts, op. cit., pp.446ff.

30. Hammond, op. cit., pp.635–6.

31. McCarthy wrote a lively *History of his own Times*; the retrospective chapters on Irish affairs (57–8) in vol. 2 are particularly interesting.

32. Bardon, op. cit., p.410.

33. R. Shannon, *Gladstone: Heroic Minister*, p.237.

34. R.R. James, *Rosebery*, p.113. During his period of office the young Rosebery 'immersed himself in the subject of Scottish administration', which he found 'a ridiculous state of affairs . . . a patchwork affair' (p.122).

35. This in a letter to Gladstone's secretary, Eddie Hamilton; James, op. cit., p.134.

36. H.J. Hanham's *Scottish Nationalism* is indispensable for the subject.

37. For such examples of English neglect see R.J. Finlay, *Partnership for Good?*, Chapter 2.

38. There were exceptions, such as that of Stuart Ruadri Erskine, author of *The Kilt and how to Wear it*, who wanted to 'Celticize the whole of Scotland' and form a Gaelic federation with Ireland. He survived to be disillusioned. See Hanham, op. cit., 'The Beginnings of Modern Nationalism', *passim*.

39. See Finlay, op. cit., pp.52–60.

40. Queen Victoria visited Ireland on four occasions, and spent every autumn after 1848 at Balmoral; but Wales, only four hours by train from Windsor, she saw only once.

41. See Morgan, op. cit., Chapter 2, and

Shannon, op. cit., p.527.

42. *Welsh History Review*, vol. xii, no. 2, A. Jones, 'Trades Unions and the Press'.

43. Morgan, op. cit., pp.117–19.

44. For education see *Welsh History Review*, vol. xix, no.2, H.G. Williams, 'Arthur Acland, Thomas Ellis', and Morgan, op. cit., *passim*.

45. An investigation in 1863 found that the average Welsh farmhand was better fed than his English counterpart; but the diet in south Wales, where wages were lower, was 'inferior in all respects': I.G. Jones, *Mid-Victorian Wales*, p.43, and E.P. Thompson and E. Yeo, *The Unknown Mayhew*. For the Tithe War see *Welsh History Review*, vol. xii, 1988, no. 1, D. Richter, 'The Welsh Tithe War'.

46. Morgan, op. cit., p.175.

CHAPTER 11 : 1893–1950

1. Asquith's position was easier than had been Gladstone's, in that he had no powerful Whig right wing to placate, and the parliamentary Labour Party could be relied upon to support Home Rule measures.

2. Winston Churchill was in the cabinet from 1908 to 1915, and in the later period was increasingly in charge of Irish affairs. Vol. 2 of Randolph Churchill's *Life*, together with the companion papers, is therefore relevant; see especially Chapters 12 and 13.

3. Churchill referred to the 'fatuous and arrogant mind of the Hotel Cecil'. R. Churchill, op. cit., companion volume 2, Part 2, p.1089.

4. F. Welsh, *A History of South Africa*, pp.464–74.

5. O'Day, op. cit., pp.250–4.

6. Ibid., p.240.

7. Bardon, op. cit., pp.437–9.

8. The speech is printed in Mitchell and Snodaigh, op. cit., pp.81–6.

Michael Balfe might also be mentioned in the irish musical world.

9. See F.S.L. Lyons, *Culture and Anarchy*, pp.163–9. Patrick Pearse ranted that 'Synge blasphemes against a nation'. D. Kiberd, *Synge*, p.253.

10. C. Petrie, *Chamberlain*, p.313.

11. The 'British Covenant' supporting Ulster was signed by many prominent individuals, including the Catholic composer Edward Elgar. J.N. Moore, *Elgar*, p.664.

12. Petrie, op. cit., p.367.

13. Revd J.B. Armour, a sensible Presbyterian, commented ironically (*Letters*, 7 May 1916): 'Sir Edward Carson came to Ireland and proclaimed that he had come to break every law of the land . . . the guns were not to shoot crows with, but were intended to shoot his own army's soldiers . . . where is the moral difference between Carson's gun-runners and the Sinn Feiners?'

14. Perhaps surprisingly, this Irish Brigade has its own display in the National Museum.

15. Michael Laffan, perhaps the best writer of recent Irish history, comments: 'Few people remembered that until the Easter Rising British rule in Ireland had been characterised by moderation and forbearance: the republicans' policy of radicalising the nationalists by goading the crown forces into repressive measures had succeeded beyond all possible expectations'; *Resurrection*, p.4.

16. The literature on Pearse is copious and disputatious. See e.g. S.F. Moran, *Pearse*; K. Toolis, *Rebel Hearts*, p.53. For a parallel between the Nazi attitude to 'decadent' art and the Gaelicists see *Journal of Contemporary History*, vol. ii, no 60, G. Gerson, 'Cultural Subversion'; for Pearse's attacks on Sinn Fein see

Pearse (ed. Ó Buachalla), *Letters*, pp.266–7.

17. See M. Kenny, *Goodbye to Catholic Ireland*.

18. By early 1916, 78,852 Irishmen had volunteered to join the British forces; the numbers who may have been willing to join the rebels were between two and three thousand. See P. Bew, *Ideology*, p.160. The date follows the Gregorian alteration to the calendar; for the action see Bardon, op. cit., pp.454–6.

19. P. Bew, 'Moderate Nationalism', in *Historical Journal*, vol. xlii, 1999. One interesting proposal that emerged from Irish concerns in 1918 was that for a federal United Kingdom; it foundered on the assessment of English antipathy: see *History*, vol. lxxxvi, no. 187, 1971, J. Kendle, 'Federation and the Irish Problem'.

20. K. Jeffrey, 'British Security Policy', in P. Collins, *Nationalism and Unionism*: the term 'implies that it was a war between "the English" and "the Irish" which it certainly was not'. J.M. Regan, *Irish Counter-Revolution* stresses its aspect as a civil war 'fought between Irishmen in the Irish Republican Army and the Royal Irish Constabulary, or for that matter between Irish Catholics and Protestants in the streets of Belfast and Derry'.

21. To Lord Oranmore, *Diaries*.

22. For Smuts see Royal Archives PS/GV/K1702/3; for British public opinion see D.G. Boyce, *Englishmen and the Irish Troubles*. Trades unions, the Labour Party and many Conservatives in the Peace with Ireland Council, headed by Lord Henry Cavendish Bentinck, joined in the plea for negotiation.

23. See J. Jorstad, 'Nations Once Again', in D. Fitzpatrick, *Revolution?*.

24. O'Higgins described the new government as 'simply eight young men ... standing amid the ruins of one administration ... with wild men screaming through the keyhole'. Quoted Bardon, op. cit., p.494.

25. Wilson's murder was the final straw for the British government: if the Irish government did not act against the wild men, Britain would do it for them – Blake, *The Unknown Prime Minister*, p.441. According to the Dublin National Museum, the civil war did not take place. There is a good short account (pp.511–15) in Foster, *Modern Ireland*. M. Hopkinson, *Green Against Green* is authoritative – for the Tralee massacre see p.241; see also D. Fitzpatrick, *Two Irelands* and P. Hart, *The IRA and its Enemies*.

26. The necessary and centrally important book is R. Fanning, *Irish Department of Finance*.

27. Ibid., p.10.

28. Ibid., pp.80–98.

29. Brian Farrell in *Creation of the Dáil*, p.4, draws attention to the continuity of Irish history, describing the 1916 Rising as 'more of a hiccough in Ireland's uneven yet remarkable emergence into statehood'.

30. Had O'Higgins lived – he was only thirty-seven when murdered – the future of Ireland would have been different, and probably brighter. He was the only politician to match de Valera's strategic ability with the added gifts of humour and freedom from the foggy mysticism that often enveloped de Valera – and of which a good example is his choice for his new party's name. Only clothed in the decent obscurity of Irish could the 'Warriors of Destiny' avoid being ludicrous.

31. F. McGarry, *Irish Politics*, pp.35–50. Fourteen men remained to fight in Franco's Foreign Legion.

32. The extent of the psychic shocks which had conditioned (warped?)

Ulster Protestants shold not be underestimated. They remained vividly conscious of their own Irish identity and history, but were 'confronted by an alien definition of Irishness' which drove them to seek refuge in a 'British' identity few other Britons would recognise: see T. Hennessey, *Dividing Ireland*, pp.235–9.

33. Bardon, op. cit., pp.499–501.

34. Ibid., pp.501–5.

35. Ibid., p.511.

36. M. Craig, 'The Blueshirt Movement', in *Irish Historical Studies*, vol. xxix, no. 114, 1994, considers that 'apart from Sadam Hussein's treatment of the people of Iraq, no government ever inflicted such a punishment as did the economic war on us'.

37. Fanning, op. cit., p.293.

38. John Betjeman (ed. C.L. Green), *Letters*, vol. 1, p.269; Bardon, op. cit., Chapter 12 *passim*.

39. E. O'Halpin, *Defending Ireland*, pp.222–3.

40. Ibid., p.256.

41. For IRA–Nazi links see B.P. Murphy, *John Chartres* and D. O'Donoghue, *Hitler's Irish Voices*, Francis Stuart being by some way the most interesting of these. Dan Breen, the hero of Soloheadbeg, was particularly pro-Nazi. O'Halpin, op. cit., pp.225ff, describes the 'highly secret' close collaboration between the British and Irish security services, MI5 and G2.

42. '. . . the immigration of Jews is generally discouraged', noted the Justice Department in November 1945, and for 'liberal and generous', the five families and the Hungarians see O'Halpin, op. cit., pp.293–7.

43. 'Almost total isolation from the rest of mankind' was Professor Lyons' view of the Irish wartime experience; post-war, Franco did much better (P. Preston, *Franco*, p.785).

44. D.G. Boyce, *The Irish Question . . .* , pp.100–3. R. Hanlon, in *Twentieth Century British History*, vol. x, no. 1, 1999 describes the British government's 'willingness, even enthusiasm, for granting privileges to the Irish regardless of their repudiation of the crown'. Officially, the Irish government granted reciprocal privileges only in 1975, but in practice many resident Britons continued to vote in Ireland.

45. These aspects of Irish life are considerably sanitised in both Lyons' and Foster's histories. For a balanced view see M. Kenny, op. cit.

46. *Flann O'Brien at War*, p.112. Myles is addictive: writing of 'autochthonous chauvinism', he brags, 'Today I am cured. I am no longer Irish. I am merely a person. I cured myself after years of suffering' (pp.104–5). The *Irish Times* also employed that other ornament of Irish humour, Patrick Campbell.

47. Bardon, op. cit., p.631: for the 'Archbigot' of Dublin see the *Independent*, 15 November 1999. The biographer of Sean Lemass, R. Savage, concludes (p.77) that McQuaid's pronouncements meant that 'Northern Irish Protestants had good reason to fear that their religious liberties would not be respected in a united Ireland'.

48. *Partition and the Limits of Irish Nationalism*, pp.185–8.

49. Bardon, op. cit., pp.637, 642.

50. For religious proportions in the workforce see S. Wichert, *Northern Ireland*, tables 1.3–1.7. 'Discrimination under the Unionist Regime' concludes that 'the most serious charge' was not that the Northern Irish government was directly responsible for widespread discrimination, but that it 'allowed discrimination on such a scale over a substantial segment of Northern Ireland' (p.31).

CHAPTER 12 : 1950–2001

1. T.M. Devine and R.J. Finlay, *Scotland in the Twentieth Century* is essential.
2. Admiring MacDiarmid's verse must put a severe strain on the sense of humour: what can be made of such works as his 'Hymns to Lenin'?
3. There is a lively account of Nationalist politics in Eric Linklater's *Magnus Merriman*.
4. See C.H. Lee, *Scotland and the United Kingdom*, Chapter 3, and Finlay, op. cit.
5. G. Pottinger, *Secretaries of State* has a series of useful biographies.
6. A. Thorpe, *History of the British Labour Party* is a useful guide.
7. Things have not changed much since: Edinburgh's only theatre has a thin diet, occupied a few days each month by some travelling company.
8. For the Channel Islands see R. Lempriere, *History of the Channel Islands*.
9. For Man see R.H. Kinvig, *The Isle of Man*, R.A. McDonald, *The Kingdom of the Isles* and D.G. Kermode, *Devolution*.
10. C.H. Lee, op. cit., pp.148–52.
11. The full text of the Third Claim of Right is given in P.H. Scott, op. cit., Chapter 11.
12. There is a good account of the 're-invention' of the Labour Party in D. Black, *All the First Minister's Men*, Chapters 3 and 4.
13. Quoted in P.H. Scott, op. cit., p.194.
14. This is Sir Henry Jones, quoted (p.136) in Morgan, *Rebirth of a Nation*, likely to remain the classic text.
15. F. Welsh, *The Profit of the State*, p.38.
16. The quotations in this paragraph are from G.A. Williams, *When was Wales?*, Chapter 11; and see Morgan, *Rebirth*, pp.206–7, 253–7.
17. J.G. Jones, 'Parliament for Wales Campaign', *Welsh History Review*, vol. xvi, no. 2, 1992.
18. For the licensing laws see Morgan, *Rebirth*, pp.353ff.
19. K.O. Morgan, *Callaghan*, p.540.
20. K. Morgan and G. Mungham, *Redesigning Democracy* is relied on here (pp.63–6).
21. *Guardian*, 23 November 2000.
22. See T.P. Coogan, *The IRA*, Chapter 22.
23. See D.G. Boyce, *The Irish Question* . . . , Chapters 4 and 5. This essential book also has a useful appendix which summarises all Anglo–Irish agreements between 1868 and 1995.
24. Bardon, op. cit., p.767.
25. See A. Seldon, *Major: A Political Life*, pp.263–81, 412–30.
26. When the leaders of the Real IRA were exposed and charged in June 2001, their American fundraisers vehemently objected to their 'betrayal'. The Irish Toy Theatre still has its admirers, who delight in real blood.
27. D. Ó Ceallaigh, *Britain and Ireland* has a careful analysis of possible outcomes.
28. Again, Morgan and Mungham, op. cit., have the whole story.
29. For the first weeks of the new Parliament see M. Watson, *Year Zero*.
30. The story is unravelled in D. Black, *All the First Minister's Men*.
31. The figures are from the latest available *Regional Trends*, HMSO.
32. Kevin Brown, *Financial Times*, 20 April 2001.
33. 17 December 1997, quoted in R. Hazell, *Constitutional Futures*, pp.199ff.
34. M. Newton, quoted in ibid., p.26.

BIBLIOGRAPHY

Abse, J. (ed.), *Letters from Wales* (Bridgend 2000)

Abura, N., *Anglo-Saxons in England* (Upsala 1926)

Adamson, I., *The Identity of Ulster* (1982)

Anderson, M.S., *War and Society in Europe* (London 1998)

Anstruther, I., *The Scandal of the Andover Workhouse* (London 1973)

Arber, E., *Dunbar and his Times* (London, n.d.)

Armour, J.B., *Letters* (Belfast 1981)

Ashe, G. (ed.), *The Quest for Arthur's Britain* (London 1971)

Aspinall, A. (ed.), *The Letters of King George IV* (3 vols, London 1938)

Aylmer, G.E., *The State's Servants: The Civil Service of the English Republic 1649–1660* (London 1973)

Bardgett, F.D., *Scotland Reformed* (Edinburgh 1989)

Bardon, J., *A History of Ulster* (Belfast 1992)

Barnard, T.C., *Cromwellian Ireland* (Oxford 1975)

Barnard, T.C. et al. (eds), *A Miracle of Learning* (Aldershot 1998)

Barrow, G.W.S., *Scotland and its Neighbours in the Middle Ages* (London 1992)

Barry, T. (ed.), *The History of Settlement in Ireland* (London 2000)

Bartlett, T., *The Fall and Rise of the Irish Nation* (Dublin 1992)

Bartlett, T. and Jeffery, K., *A Military History of Ireland* (Cambridge 1996)

Barzun, J., *From Dawn to Decadence* (London 2001)

Bede (ed. Collins, R. and McClure, J.), *The Ecclesiastical History of the English People* (Oxford 1994)

Bell, J.B., *The Gun in Politics* (New Brunswick 1987)

Best, G., *Mid-Victorian Britain 1851–1875* (London 1985)

Betjeman, J. (ed. Green, C.L.), *Letters* (London 1994)

Beveridge, C. and Turnbull, R., *The Eclipse of Scottish Culture* (Edinburgh 1989)

Beveridge, C. and Turnbull, R., *Scotland after Enlightenment* (Edinburgh 1997)

Bew, P., *Land and the National Question in Ireland* (Dublin 1978)

Bew, P., *C.S. Parnell* (Dublin 1980)

Bew, P., *Conflict and Conciliation in Ireland 1890–1910* (Oxford 1987)

Bew, P., *Ideology and the Irish Question* (Oxford 1994)

Birley, A., *The People of Roman Britain* (London 1979)

Black, D., *All the First Minister's Men* (Edinburgh 2001)

Black, J., *A History of the British Isles* (London 1998)

Black, J.B., *The Reign of Elizabeth* (Oxford 1959)

Blackburn, M.A.S. and Dumville, D. (eds), *Kings, Currency and Alliances* (Woodbridge 1998)

Blackstock, A., *An Ascendancy Army: The Irish Yeomanry* (Dublin 1998)

Blair, H., *Sermons* (5 vols, London 1808)

Blair, P.H., *Northumbria in the Days of Bede* (London 1976)

Blair, P.H., *The World of Bede* (Cambridge 1996)

Blake, R., *The Unknown Prime Minister* (A. Bonar Law) (London 1955)

Blake, R., *Disraeli* (London 1966)

Bossy, J., *The English Catholic Community* 1570–1850 (London 1975)

Bowen, D., *Protestant Crusade* (Dublin 1978)

Boyce, D.G., *The Irish Question and British Politics 1868–1996* (London 1996)

Boyce, D.G. and O'Day, A., *Nationalism in Ireland* (London 1982)

Boyce, D.G. and O'Day, A. (eds), *The Making of Irish History* (London 1996)

Boyce, D.G. and O'Day, A. (eds), *Defenders of the Union* (London 2001)

Bradshaw, B., *The Irish Constitutional Revolution of the Sixteenth Century* (Cambridge 1979)

Brady, C. (ed.), *Ideology and the Historians* (Dublin 1991)

Brady, C. (ed.), *Interpreting Irish History* (Dublin 1994)

Brander, M., *Scottish and Border Battles and Ballads* (London 1975)

Branson, R., *Britain in the 1920s* (London 1977)

Breen, C.W., Buckland, P. and Kelly, S., *Steps to Partition* (Dublin 1997)

Breeze, D.J., *Northern Frontiers* (London 1982)

Brittain, F., *The Penguin Book of Latin Verse* (London 1962)

Bromwich, R., *Dafydd ap Gwilym* (Cardiff 1974)

Bromwich, R., *Dafydd ap Gwilym* (a selection of poems) (Cardiff 1982)

Brooke, D., *Wild Men and Holy Places* (Edinburgh 1998)

Brown, A. et al., *The Scottish Electorate* (Basingstoke 1999)

Brown, S.J., *Thomas Chalmers* (Oxford 1982)

Brown, S.J. and Fry, M.R.G. (eds), *Scotland in the Age of Disruption* (Edinburgh 1993)

Brynn, E., *Crown and Castle: British Rule in Ireland 1800–1830* (Dublin 1978)

Butler, I., *The Eldest Brother* (London 1973)

Butler, J., *Lord Oranmore's Journal*

Cameron, A., *The Bank of Scotland* (Edinburgh 1995)

Campbell, F., *The Dissenting Voice* (Belfast 1991)

Caplan, J. (ed.), *Written on the Body* (Princeton 2000)

Carradice, P., *The Last Invasion* (Pontypool 1992)

Casey, D.J. and Rhodes, R.E., *Views of the Irish Peasantry* (Hamden 1977)

Cecil, Lord, *All the Way* (London 1949)

Chadwick, N., *The Celts* (London 1991)

Chambers, A., *Granuaile* (Grace O'Malley) (Dublin 1988)

Chathain, P.N. and Richter, M., *Ireland and Europe in the Early Middle Ages* (Stuttgart 1996)

Chenevix-Trench, C., *George II* (London 1973)

Clapham, J., *A Concise Economic History of Britain* (Cambridge 1949)

Clark, J., *Saxon and Norman* (London 1989)

Clark, J.C.D., *Revolution and Rebellion* (Cambridge 1986)

Clark, J.C.D., *The Language of Liberty* (Cambridge 1993)

Colley, L., *Britons: Forging the Nation 1707–1837* (London 1994)

Collingwood, R.G. and Myres, J.N.L., *Roman Britain* (Oxford 1987)

Collingwood, W.G., *The Early Christian Crosses of Galloway* (Whithorn 1984)

Collini, S., *English Pasts* (Oxford 1999)

Collins, P. (ed.), *Nationalism and Unionism in Ireland 1885–1921* (Belfast 1994)

Collis, J., *The Iron Age in Britain: A Review* (Sheffield 1977)

Comerford, R.V., *The Fenians in Context* (Dublin 1985)

Condrot, R. et al. (eds), *Old Tales of Fingal* (Dublin 1984)

Connolly, S.J., *Political Ideas in Eighteenth-Century Ireland* (Dublin 2000)

Connolly, S.J. et al. (eds), *Conflict, Identity and Economic Development: Ireland and Scotland 1600–1939* (Preston 1995)

Coogan, T.P., *The IRA* (London 1995)

Coogan, T.P., *Wherever Green is Worn* (London 2000)

Cooke, A. et al. (eds), *Modern Scottish History: 1707 to the Present* (East Linton 1998)

Cooke, A.B. and Malcomson, A.P.W. (eds), *The Ashbourne Papers* (Belfast 1994)

Corfe, T. (ed.), *Before Wilfred* (Hexham 1997)

Cosgrove, A. and McCartney, D. (eds), *Studies in Irish History* (Dublin 1979)

Cowan, I.B., *The Scottish Reformation* (London 1982)

Crawford, J.G., *Anglicizing the Government of Ireland* (Dublin 1993)

Crawford, W.H. and Trainor, B., *Aspects of Irish Social History, 1750–1800* (Belfast 1969)

Crossman, V., *Politics, Law and Order in Nineteenth-Century Ireland* (Dublin 1996)

Cullen, L.M. (ed.), *Comparative Aspects of Scotland and Ireland* (Edinburgh 1977)

Cunich, P., Hoyle, D., Duffy, E. and Hyam, R., *A History of Magdalene College* (Cambridge 1994)

Curren, J.M., *The Birth of the Irish Free State* (Alabama 1980)

Curtin, N.J. *The United Irishmen* (Oxford 1994)

Curtis, E., *Irish Historic Documents* (1943)

Curtis, E., *The History of Medieval Ireland* (London 1988)

Daiches, D., *Charles Edward Stuart* (London 1973)

Daiches, D., *Scotland and the Union* (London 1977)

Dark, K.R., *Civitas to Kingdom: British Political Continuity 300–800* (London 1994)

Davies, G., *The Early Stuarts*

Davies, J., *A History of Wales* (London 1994)

Davies, N., *The Isles* (London 1999)

Davies, R.R., *The Age of Conquest* (Oxford 1993)

Davies, R.R., *The Revolt of Owain Glyn Dwr* (Oxford 1997)

Davies, W.E., *Early Medieval Wales* (Leicester 1978)

Davies, W.E., *Wales in the Early Middle Ages* (Leicester 1982)

Derry, J.W., *Castlereagh* (London 1976)

Devine, T.M., *Ireland and Scotland* (Edinburgh 1983)

Devine, T.M., *Scotland Since 1700* (Edinburgh 2000)

Devine, T.M. and Finlay, R.J., *Scotland in the Twentieth Century* (Edinburgh 1996)

Devine, T.M. and Mitchison, R. (eds), *People and Society in Scotland 1760–1830* (Edinburgh 1988)

Devlin, J. and Fanning, R. (eds), *Religion and Rebellion* (Dublin 1997)

Dickson, C., *Revolt in the North* (London 1997)

Dickson, C., *The Wexford Rising in 1798* (London 1998)

Dickson, D. et al. (eds), *The United Irishmen* (Dublin 1993)

Dillon, M: and Chadwick, N.R., *The Celtic Realms* (London 1967)

Doerries, R.R., *Prelude to the Easter Rising* (London 2000)

Donaldson, G., *The Scottish Reformation* (Cambridge 1960)

Donaldson, G., *Scottish Church History* (Edinburgh 1985)

Donoghue, D., *The Parnell Lecture 1997–98* (Cambridge 1998)

Dow, F.D., *Cromwellian Scotland* (Edinburgh 1979)

Duffy, S. (ed.), *Atlas of Irish History* (Dublin 1997)

Dumville, D., *Britons and Anglo-Saxons in the Early Middle Ages* (Aldershot 1993)

Duncan, A.A.M., *The Nation of Scots and the Declaration of Arbroath (1520)* (London 1970)

Duncan, A.A.M., *Scotland* (Edinburgh 1975)

Dunleary, J.E. and Dunleary, G.W., *Douglas Hyde* (Berkeley 1991)

Dwyer, J., *Virtuous Discourse: Sensibility and Community in Late Eighteenth-Century Scotland* (Edinburgh 1987)

Dwyer, J. and Sher, R. (eds), *Sociability and Society in Eighteenth-Century Scotland* (Edinburgh 1993)

Dyrrik, S. et al. (eds), *The Satellite State* (Bergen 1979)

Earle, J., *A Hand Book to the Land Charters and Other Saxonic Documents* (Oxford 1888)

Edwards, O.D. (ed.), *Conor Cruise O'Brien Introduces Ireland* (London and Dublin 1969)

Edwards, O.D., *Eamon de Valera* (Cardiff 1988)

Edwards, R.D., *The Age of Reason* (London 1994)

Edwards, R.D., *Patrick Pearse* (London 1997)

Elliott, M., *Partners in Revolution* (Yale 1982)

Ellis, P.B., *Hell or Connaught* (London 1975)

Ellis, P.B., *Celtic Women* (London 1995)

Ellis, P.B. and Mac A'Ghobhainn, S., *The Scottish Insurrection of 1820* (London 1970)

Ellis, S.G., *Reform and Revival* (Woodbridge 1980)

Ellis, S.G., *Tudor Ireland* (London 1985)

Ellis, S.G., *Nationalist Historiography* (Dublin 1997)

Elton, G.R., *England Under the Tudors* (London 1962)

Eluere, C., *The Celts: First Masters of Europe* (London 1997)

English, R., *Ernie O'Malley: IRA Intellectual* (Oxford 1998)

Ensor, R.C.K., *England 1870–1914* (Oxford)

Ervine, St J., *Craigavon* (London 1949)

Evelyn, J. (ed. Bray, W.), *Diary and Correspondence* (London 1902)

Falls, C., *The Birth of Ulster* (London 1998)

Fanning, R., *Irish Department of Finance 1922–58* (Dublin 1978)

Farrell, B. (ed.), *The Creation of the Dáil* (Dublin 1994)

Ferguson, W., *Scotland: 1689 to the Present* (Edinburgh 1968)

Ferguson, W., *Scotland's Relations with England* (Edinburgh 1997)

Ferguson, W., *The Identity of the Scottish Nation: An Historic Quest* (Edinburgh 1999)

Finberg, H.P.R., *The Formation of England 550–1042* (London 1976)

Finlay, R.J., *A Partnership for Good?* (Edinburgh 1997)

Finn, M.C., *After Chartism* (Cambridge 1993)

Fischer, S.R., *A History of Language* (London 1999)

Fisk, P., *In Time of War* (London 1983)

Fitzpatrick, D. (ed.), *Revolution?* (Dublin 1990)

Fitzpatrick, D., *The Two Irelands* (Oxford 1998)

Fletcher, A. (ed. Daiches, D.), *Selected Political Writings* (Edinburgh 1979)

Flinn, M. (ed.), *The Scottish Population* (Cambridge 1977)

Foster, R.F., *Modern Ireland 1600–1972* (London 1989)

Foster, R.F. (ed.), *The Oxford History of Ireland* (Oxford 1989)

Foster, R.F., *Paddy and Mr Punch* (London 1995)

Francis, M. and Morrow, J., *A History of English Political Thought in the Early Nineteenth Century* (London 1994)

Fraser, A., *Cromwell: Our Chief of Men* (London 1973)

Fraser, G.M., *The Steel Bonnets* (London 1971)

Fraser, W.H. and Morris, R.J., *People and Society in Scotland* (Edinburgh 1990)

Fry, M., *The Dundas Despotism* (Edinburgh 1992)

Fuller, J., *The History of Berwick upon Tweed* (Newcastle 1799/1973)

Gaber, L.C. and Gragg, F.A. (eds), *Piccolomini, Aeneas Sylvius* (London 1960, 1988)

Galloway, B., *The Union of England and Scotland 1603–8* (Edinburgh 1986)

Garvin, T., *The Evolution of Irish Nationalist Politics* (Dublin 1987)

Gash, N., *Mr Secretary Peel* (London 1961)

Gash, N., *Aristocracy and People: Britain 1815–1865* (London 1985)

Gibbon, E., *Autobiography* (London 1796 and 1911)

Gillingham, J., *Richard I* (London 1999)

Giraldus Cambrensis (ed. Scott, A.B. and Martin, F.X), *Expugnatio Hibernica* (Dublin 1978)

Gladstone, W.E. (ed. Foot, M.R.D.), *Diaries* (Oxford 1968)

Goffart, W., *Barbarians and Romans* (Princeton 1980)

Gogarty, O. St J., *It isn't this Time of Year at All!* (London 1954)

Grainger, J.D., *Cromwell Against the Scots* (East Linton 1997)

Gray, J., *The Sans Culottes of Belfast* (Belfast 1998)

Gray, P., *Famine, Land and Politics* (Dublin 1999)

Griffith, W.P., *Learning, Law and Religion* (Cardiff 1996)

Guinnane, T.W., *The Vanishing Irish* (Princeton 1998)

Guy, J., *Tudor England* (London 1988)

Hamilton, H., *An Economic History of Scotland in the Eighteenth Century* (Oxford 1963)

Hammond, J.L., *Gladstone and the Irish Nation* (London 1938)

Handley, J.E., *The Irish in Modern Scotland* (Oxford 1947)

Hanham, H.J., *Scottish Nationalism* (London 1969)

Hardinge, Lord (ed. Singh, B.W.), *Letters* (London 1986)

Harris, W.J.A, *Spender* (London 1946)

Harrison, R.J., *The Life and Times of Sidney and Beatrice Webb* (Basingstoke 2000)

Hart, P., *The IRA and its Enemies* (Oxford 1998)

Harvie, C., *Scotland and Nationalism* (London 1977)

Haseler, S., *The English Tribe* (Basingstoke 1996)

Hazell, R., *Constitutional Futures* (Oxford 1999)

Hennessey, T., *Dividing Ireland: World War I and Partition* (London 1998)

Herbison, P., *Pre-Christian Ireland* (London 1988)

Higham, N.J., *Rome, Britain and the Anglo-Saxons* (London 1992)

Higham, N.J., *The Kingdom of Northumbria 350–1100* (Stroud 1993)

Higham, N.J., *The English Conquest: Gildas and Britain in the Fifth Century* (Manchester 1994)

Higham, N.J., *An English Empire: Bede and the Early Anglo-Saxon Kings* (Manchester 1995)

Higham, N.J., *The Convert Kings* (Manchester 1997)

Higham, N.J., *The Death of Anglo-Saxon England* (Stroud 1997)

Higham, N.J. and Jones, B., *The Carvetti* (Stroud 1985)

Hinde, W., *Catholic Emancipation* (Oxford 1992)

Hines, J. (ed.), *The Anglo-Saxons from the Migration Period to the Eighth Century: An Ethnographic Perspective* (Woodbridge 1997)

Hobhouse, H., *Seeds of Change* (London 1985)

Hobman, D.L., *Cromwell's Master Spy* (London 1961)

Hodgkin, R.H., *The History of the Anglo-Saxons* (Oxford 1952)

Hogan, J. (ed.), *D'Avaux: Negotiations in Ireland* (Dublin 1934)

Holder, P.A., *The Roman Army in Britain* (London 1982)

Holmes, R., *Shelley: The Pursuit* (London 1976)

Hopkinson, M., *Green Against Green* (Dublin 1988)

Horston, R.A., *Scottish Literacy and the Scottish Identity* (Cambridge 1985)

Howe, S., *Ireland and Empire* (Oxford 2000)

Hughes, E., *North Country Life in the Eighteenth Century* (London 1965)

Hume, D. (ed. Greig, J.Y.T.), *Letters* (Edinburgh 1932)

Hume, G. and Malcomson, A., *Robert Emmett* (Belfast, n.d.)

Irish Fiants of Tudor Sovereigns (Dublin 1994)

Jackson, J.W. (ed.), *Flann O'Brien at War* (London 2000)

Jackson, K.H., *Language and History in Early Britain* (Edinburgh 1953)

James, F.G., *Lords of the Ascendancy* (Dublin 1995)

James, R.R., *Rosebery* (London 1963)

Jeffries, K., *Ireland and the Great War* (London 2000)

Jenkins, B., *The Era of Emancipation* (Montreal 1988)

Johnston, D., *The Literature of Wales* (Cardiff 1994)

Jondolf, G. and Dumville, D. (eds), *France and the British Isles* (Woodbridge 1991)

Jones, D., *Before Rebecca: Popular Protests in Wales 1793–1835* (London 1973)

Jones, G. and Jones, T. (trans.), *The Mabinogion* (London 1993)

Jones, I.G., *Mid-Victorian Wales* (Cardiff 1992)

Kautt, W.H., *The Anglo–Irish War* (Westport/London 1979)

Kearney, R. (ed.), *The Irish Mind* (Dublin 1985)

Kearney, R., *States of Mind* (Manchester 1995)

Kearney, R., *Post-Nationalist Ireland* (London 1997)

Kee, R., *The Green Flag*, vol. I: *The Most Distressful Country* (London 1972)

Kee, R., *The Green Flag*, vol. II: *The Bold Fenian Men* (London 1972)

Kee, R., *The Green Flag*, vol. III: *Ourselves Alone* (London 1972)

Kee, R., *The Laurel and the Ivy: The Story of Charles Stewart Parnell and Irish Nationalism* (London 1994)

Kelly, J., *Henry Flood* (Dublin 1998)

Kemp, D.W., *Bishop Pockocke's Tours in Scotland* (Edinburgh 1997)

Kenny, M., *Goodbye to Catholic Ireland* (Dublin 2000)

Kenyon, J.R., *The Popish Plot* (London 1974)

Keogh, D., *Twentieth-Century Ireland* (Dublin 1994)

Keogh, D., *Jews in Twentieth-Century Ireland* (Cork 1998)

Ker, N. and Ker, M., *A Guide to Anglo-Saxon Sites* (London 1982)

Kermode, D.G., *Devolution at Work: A Case Study of the Isle of Man* (Farnborough 1979)

Kerr, D.A., *Peel, Priests and Politics* (Oxford 1982)

Kerr, D.A., *A Nation of Beggars?* (Oxford 1994)

Kiberd, D., *Inventing Ireland* (London 1995)

Kiberd, D., *Synge and the Irish Language* (London 1999)

Kidd, C., *Subverting Scotland's Past* (Cambridge 1993)

Kightly, C., *Mirror of Medieval Wales* (Cardiff 1988)

Kinvig, R.H., *The Isle of Man* (Liverpool 1975)

Kipling, R., *Definitive Edition of Verse* (London 1941)

Kishlansky, M., *A Monarchy Transformed: Britain 1603–1714* (London 1997)

Kissane, N., *The Dungannon Convention and Grattan's Parliament* (Dublin 1982)

Knox, J. (ed. Mason, R.A.), *On Rebellion* (Cambridge 1994)

Knox, O., *Rebels and Informers: Stirrings of Irish Independence* (London 1997)

Kynaston, D., *The City of London*, vol. II: *Golden Years, 1890–1914* (London 1996)

Laffan, M., *The Resurrection of Ireland* (Cambridge 1999)

Laing, J. and Laing, L., *The Picts and the Scots* (Stroud 1997)

Laing, L.J., *Celtic Britain and Ireland AD 200–800* (Dublin 1990)

Langford, P., *Englishness* (London 2000)

Lapidge, M. (ed.), *Bede and his World* (Aldershot 1994)

Lapidge, M. and Dumville, D., *Gildas: New Approaches* (Woodbridge 1984)

Lee, C.H., *Scotland and the United Kingdom* (Manchester 1995)

Lee, J.J. (ed.), *Ireland 1945–70* (Dublin 1979)

Lee, J.J., *Ireland 1912–1985* (Cambridge 1989)

Leith, D., *The Act of Union* (Stanford 1998)

Lemprière, R., *The History of the Channel Islands* (London 1980)

Lenman, B., *An Economic History of Modern Scotland* (London 1977)

Levack, B., *The Formation of the British State: England, Scotland and the Union* (Oxford 1987)

Linklater, A., *Compton Mackenzie* (London 1987)

Lockhart, G. (ed. Szechi, D.), *Scotland's Ruine* (Aberdeen 1995)

Lockhart, J.G., *The Life of Sir Walter Scott* (London 1896)

Lockyer, R., *James VI & I* (Harlow 1998)

Longford, E., *Wellington: Pillar of Stone* (London 1972)

Longford, E., *A Pilgrimage of Passion: The Life of W.S. Blunt* (London 1979)

Luce, H.W., *Diary of Two Parliaments* (2 vols, London 1885, 1886)

Lynch, M., *Scotland: A New History* (London 1992)

Lyons, F.S.L., *Ireland Since the Famine* (London 1973)

Lyons, F.S.L., *Culture and Anarchy in Ireland* (Oxford 1982)

McBride, L.W., *The Greening of Dublin Castle* (Washington 1991)

McBrien, R.P., *Lives of the Popes* (San Francisco 2000)

McCartney, D., *W.E.H. Lecky* (Dublin 1994)

McCash, C., *Writing the Irish Famine* (Oxford 1995)

MacDiarmid, H. (ed. Craig, D. and Manson, J.), *Selected Poems* (London 1976)

MacDonagh, O., *States of Mind* (London 1983)

MacDonagh, O., *Hereditary Bondsman* (London 1988)

MacDonagh, O., *The Emancipist* (London 1989)

MacDonagh, O., *O'Connell and Parnell* (Cambridge 1993)

MacDonagh, O., Mandle, C.S.F. and Travers, R., *Irish Culture and Nationalism* (London 1983)

McDonald, R.A., *The Kingdom of the Isles* (East Linton 1997)

Macdougall, N., *Church, Politics and Society: Scotland 1408–1929* (Edinburgh 1983)

McDowell, R.B., *Ireland in the Age of Imperialism and Revolution* (Oxford 1979)

McDowell, R.B., *Crises and Decline* (Dublin 1997)

McGarry, F., *Irish Politics and the Spanish Civil War* (Cork 1999)

Mack Smith, D., *Mazzini* (London 1994)

Mackay, J., *Michael Collins* (Edinburgh 1996)

Mackay, T., *The History of the Poor Law* (3 vols, London 1899)

Mackie, J.D., *The Earlier Tudors* (Oxford 1972)

Mackie, J.D., *A History of Scotland* (London 1991)

McKitterick, D., *Endgame* (Belfast 1994)

McMahon, S., *A Short History of Ireland* (Cork 1996)

McNeill, P. and Nicholson, R. (eds), *An Historical Atlas of Scotland* (St Andrews 1975)

Madgwick, P.J., *The Politics of Rural Wales* (London 1973)

Magnusson, M., *Scotland: The Story of a Nation* (London 2000)

Mansergh, N., *Documents and Speeches in British Commonwealth Affairs* (Oxford 1953)

Mansergh, N., *Nationalism and Independence* (Cork 1997)

Margary, I.D., *Roman Roads in Britain* (London 1973)

Marsh, P.T., *Joseph Chamberlain: Entrepreneur in Politics* (New Haven and London 1994)

Mason, R.A. (ed.), *Scotland and England 1286–1815* (Edinburgh 1987)

Mason, R.A., *Scots and Britons: Scottish Political Thought and the Union of 1603* (Cambridge 1994)

Maxwell, C., *Dublin Under the Georges* (London 1936)

Maxwell, W.H., *The Irish Rebellion* (London 1881)

Mayr-Harting, H., *The Coming of Christianity to Anglo-Saxon England* (London 1977)

Menary, G., *Life and Letters of Duncan Forbes* (London 1936)

Metress, S.P., *The American Irish and Irish Nationalism* (Lanham 1995)

Middlebrook, S., *Newcastle upon Tyne* (Newcastle 1950)

Miller, D.W., *Peep O' Day Boys and Defenders: Selected Documents on the County Armagh Disturbances 1784–96* (Belfast 1990)

Mitchell, A. and Ó Snodaigh, P. (eds), *Irish Political Documents 1869–1916* (Dublin 1989)

Mitchison, R., *Economy and Society in Scotland and Ireland* (Edinburgh 1988)

Mitchison, R. and Roebuck, P. (eds), *A History of Scotland* (London 1970)

Mokyr, J., *Why Ireland Starved* (London 1983)

Molony, J.N., *A Soul Came into Ireland: Thomas Davis 1814–1845* (Dublin 1995)

Moore, D., *The Irish Sea Province in Archaeology and History* (Cardiff 1976)

Moore, J.W., *Edward Elgar* (Oxford 1984)

Moran, S.F., *Patrick Pearse and the Politics of Redemption* (Washington 1994)

Morgan, K. and Mungham, G., *Redesigning Democracy* (Bridgend 2000)

Morgan, K.O., *Wales in British Politics 1868–1992* (Cardiff 1980)

Morgan, K.O. (ed.), *The Oxford History of Britain* (Oxford 1984, 1999)

Morgan, K.O., *Modern Wales* (Cambridge 1995)

Morgan, K.O., *Callaghan* (Oxford 1997)

Morgan, K.O., *Rebirth of a Nation: The History of Modern Wales* (Oxford 1998)

Morley, J., *Life of W.E. Gladstone* (London 1903)

Morrill, J. (ed.), *The Scottish National Covenant in its British Context* (Edinburgh 1990)

Morris, J., *The Age of Arthur* (London 1973)

Mowat, R.B., *The Victorian Age* (London 1995)

Murphy, B.P., *Patrick Pearse and the Lost Republican Ideal* (Dublin 1991)

Murphy, B.P., *John Chartres* (Dublin 1995)

Nairn, T., *After Britain* (London 2000)

Nef, J., *The Rise and Fall of the British Coal Industry* (London 1966)

Norbrook, D., *Writing the English Republic* (Cambridge 2000)

O'Brien, C.C., *The Shaping of Modern Ireland* (London 1960)

Ó Broin, L., *The Prime Informer* (London 1971)

Ó Ceallaigh, D., *Britain and Ireland, Sovereignty and Nationality: The Peace Process in Context* (Dublin 1996)

O'Connell, D. (ed. O'Connell, M.R.), *The Correspondence of Daniel O'Connell* (Dublin 1972–80)

Ó Croinin, D., *Early Medieval Ireland* (London 1995)

O'Day, A., *Irish Home Rule 1867–1921* (Manchester 1998)

O'Day, A. and Stevenson, J., *Irish Historical Documents* (Dublin 1991)

Ó Gráda, C., *Ireland: A New Economic History* (Oxford 1994)

Ó Gráda, C., *The Great Irish Famine* (Cambridge 1995)

Ó Gráda, C., *Black '47 and Beyond* (Princeton 1999)

O'Haloran, C., *Partition* (Dublin 1987)

O'Halpin, E., *Defending Ireland* (Oxford 1999)

O'Leary, O. and Burke, H., *Mary Robinson* (London 1998)

O'Sullivan, P. (ed.), *Religion and Identity* (London 1996)

Otway-Ruthven, A.J., *A History of Medieval Ireland* (London 1968)

Palmerston, Lord (ed. Bourne, K.), *Letters to Laurence and Elizabeth Sulivan* (London 1979)

Pašeta, S., *Before the Revolution* (Cork 1999)

Pashley, R., *Pauperism and Poor Laws* (London 1882)

Paterson, L., *A Diverse Assembly* (Edinburgh 1998)

Paton, H.J., *The Claim of Scotland* (1968)

Patterson, W.B., *King James VI & I and the Reunion of Christendom*

Pearse, E., *Lines of Most Resistance* (London 1979)

Pearse, P.H. (ed. Ó Buachalla, S.), *Letters* (Gerrards Cross 1980)

Peel, R., *Memoirs* (2 vols, London 1857)

Pelteret, D.A.E., *Slavery in Early Medieval England* (Woodbridge 1995)

Perceval-Maxwell, M., *The Scottish Migration to Ulster in the Reign of James I* (London 1990)

Perceval-Maxwell, M., *The Outbreak of the Irish Rebellion* (McGill 1994)

Petrie, C., *Life and Letters of the Rt Hon. Sir Austen Chamberlain* (London 1929)

Petrie, C., *The Jacobite Movement 1688–1716* (London 1948)

Petrie, C., *The Jacobite Movement 1716–1807* (London 1950)

Phillips, G.R., *Brigantia* (London 1976)

Philpin, C.H.E. (ed.), *Nationalism and Popular Protest in Ireland* (Cambridge 1987)

Piccolomini, A.E. (ed. Gragg, F.), *Secret Diaries of a Renaissance Pope* (London 1988)

Poole, R.L., *Chronicles and Annals: A Brief Outline of their Origin and Growth* (Oxford 1926)

Pottinger, G., *Secretaries of State for Scotland* (Edinburgh 1972)

Poynter, J.R., *Society and Pauperism* (Melbourne 1969)

Prebble, J., *The Highland Clearances* (London 1963)

Prebble, J., *The Darien Disaster* (London 1968)

Prebble, J., *The Lion in the North* (London 1971)

Prebble, J., *Culloden* (London 1973)

Preston, P., *Franco* (London 1993)

Price, G., *The Languages of Britain* (London 1984)

Rankin, H.D., *The Celts and the Classical World* (London and Sydney 1987)

Regan, J.M., *Irish Counter-Revolution* (Dublin 1999)

Richardson, H.G., *The Irish Parliament in the Middle Ages* (1952)

Richmond, I.A., *Roman Britain* (London 1955)

Richter, M., *Ireland and her Neighbours in the Seventh Century* (Dublin 1999)

Riley, P.W.J., *The Union of England and Scotland* (London 1974)

Riley, P.W.J., *King William and the Scottish Politicians* (Edinburgh 1979)

Robbins, K., *Nineteenth Century Britain* (Oxford 1988)

Roberts, C., *Schemes and Undertakings* (Columbus 1985)

Robertson, J. (ed.), *A Union for Empire* (Cambridge 1995)

Robinson, H. (ed.), *The Zurich Letters* (2 vols, Cambridge 1842, 1845)

Roche, P.J. and Barton, B., *The Northern Ireland Question* (Aldershot 1991)

Roche, R., *The Norman Invasion of Ireland* (Dublin 1979)

Rose, K., *King George V* (London 1983)

Rude, G. and Hobsbawm, E., *Captain Swing* (London 1965)

Salway, P., *Roman Britain* (Oxford 1984)

Sawyer, R., *We are but Women* (London 1993)

Schwoerer, L.G., *The Declaration of Rights* (London 1981)

Scott, P.H., *Scotland: An Unwon Cause* (Edinburgh 1995)

Seldon, A., *Major: A Political Life* (London 1997)

Senior, H., *Orangeism in Ireland and Britain* (London 1966)

Shannon, R., *The Crisis of Imperialism* (London 1976)

Shannon, R., *Gladstone: Peel's Inheritor 1809–1865* (London 1982)

Shannon, R., *Gladstone: Heroic Minister 1865–1898* (London 1999)

Sher, R.B., *Church and University in the Scottish Enlightenment* (Princeton 1985)

Silke, J.J., *Kinsale: The Spanish Intervention in Ireland* (Liverpool 1970)

Simms, J.G., *William Molyneux of Dublin* (Blackrock 1982)

Simms, K., *From Kings to Warlords* (Woodbridge 1987)

Simpson, G.G., *Scotland and the Low Countries 1124–1994* (East Linton 1996)

Simpson, W.D., *St Ninian and the Origins of Christianity in Scotland* (Edinburgh 1942)

Skyrme, T., *History of the Justices of the Peace* (London 1994)

Smith, G., *Something to Declare* (London 1980)

Smith, J.B., *Llywelyn ap Gruffudd, Prince of Wales* (Cardiff 1998)

Smout, T.C., *Scottish Trade on the Eve of Union* (Edinburgh and London 1967)

Smout, T.C., *A History of the Scottish People, 1566–1830* (London 1985)

Smout, T.C. and Wood, S., *Scottish Voices* (London 1991)

Smyth, A.P., *Warlords and Holy Men: Scotland AD 80–1000* (Edinburgh 1984)

Spalding, R., *The Improbable Puritan* (London 1975)

Sparrow, E., *Secret Service: British Agents in France* (Woodbridge 1999)

Speck, W.A., *The Birth of Britain: A New Nation 1700–1710* (Oxford 1994)

Spender, J.A., *Great Britain: Empire and Commonwealth, 1886–1935* (London 1935)

Stacey, F., *The Government of Modern Britain* (Oxford 1969)

Stenton, F., *Anglo-Saxon England* (Oxford 1971)

Stephens, M., *Selection: A Book of Wales* (London 1987)

Stevens, W.M., *Bede's Scientific Achievement* (Newcastle 1985)

Stevenson, D., *King or Covenant* (East Linton 1996)

Stevenson, D., *Union, Revolution and Religion in Seventeenth-Century Scotland* (Edinburgh 1997)

Stevenson, J., *We Wrecked the Place* (New York 1996)

Stewart, R., *Henry Brougham 1778–1868* (London 1986)

Sutherland, E., *Five Euphemias: Women in Medieval Scotland* (London 1999)

Sutherland, G., *Elementary Education in the Nineteenth Century* (London 1971)

Terry, C.S., *The Cromwellian Union* (Edinburgh 1902)

Thackeray, W.M., *Irish Sketch Book etc.* (London 1879)

Thompson, E.A., *St Germanus of Auxerre and the End of Roman Britain* (Woodbridge 1984)

Thompson, E.M., *Chronicon Adae de Usk* (London 1904)

Thompson, E.P. and Yeo, E., *The Unknown Mayhew* (London)

Thompson, F.M.L., *English Landed Society in the Nineteenth Century* (London 1963)

Thorpe, A., *History of the British Labour Party* (London 1997)

Tone, T.W. (ed. Moody, T.W., McDowell, R.B. and Woods, C.T.), *Writings* (Oxford 1998)

Toolis, K., *Rebel Hearts* (London 1995)

Trevelyan, G.M., *England Under Queen Anne* (London 1930)

Trevelyan, G.M., *Lord Grey of the Reform Bill* (London 1952)

Trudgill, P. (ed.), *Language in the British Isles* (Cambridge 1981)

Vane, C., *Memoirs and Correspondence of Viscount Castlereagh* (4 vols, London 1849–53)

Venning, T., *Cromwellian Foreign Policy* (London 1996)

Vincent, J., *The Formation of the British Liberal Party* (London 1972)

Wade, J.F., *Customs of Newcastle upon Tyne 1454–1500* (Durham 1995)

Walker, B.M., *Ulster Politics* (Belfast 1989)

Walker, I.W., *Harold: The Last Anglo-Saxon King* (Stroud 1997)

Wall, M., *Catholic Ireland in the Eighteenth Century* (Dublin 1989)

Walsh, M.K., *Destruction by Peace* (Armagh 1986)

Warner, G. (ed.), *Libelle of Englyshe Polycye* (Oxford 1926)

Warren, W.L., *Henry II* (London 1971)

Warren, W.L., *King John* (Newhaven and London 1997)

Watson, M., *Year Zero* (Edinburgh 2001)

Watt, J., *The Church and Two Nations in Medieval Ireland* (Cambridge 1970)

Watt, J., *The Church in Medieval Ireland* (Dublin 1998)

Wedgwood, C.V., *The Thirty Years War* (London 1964)

Wedgwood, C.V., *The King's Peace* (London 1966)

Wedgwood, C.V., *The King's War* (London 1966)

Welsh, F., *The Profit of the State* (London 1982)

Welsh, F., *A History of South Africa* (London 1998)

West, R., *Daniel Defoe* (London 1997)

Whately, C.A., *Bought and Sold for English Gold* (1994)

Whelan, K., *The Tree of Liberty* (Cork 1996)

Whittington, G. and Whyte, I.D., *An Historical Geography of Scotland* (London 1983)

Whyte, I.D. and Black, J. (eds), *Scotland's Society and Economy in Transition 1500–1760* (London 1997)

Wilkinson, L.P., *The Roman Experience* (London 1975)

Williams, E.N., *The Eighteenth Century Constitution* (Cambridge 1960)

Williams, G., *The Welsh Church from Conquest to Reformation* (Cardiff 1962)

Williams, G., *The Welsh Church* (Cardiff 1976)

Williams, G., *Religion, Language and Nationality in Wales* (Cardiff 1979)

Williams, G., *Recovery, Reorientation and Reformation in Wales 1415–1642* (Oxford 1987)

Williams, G., *Wales and the Reformation* (Cardiff 1997)

Williams, G., *Renewal and Reformation: Wales* (Oxford 1998)

Wilson, D.M., *Anglo-Saxon Art* (London 1984)

Woodham-Smith, C., *The Great Hunger* (London 1962)

Woodward, L., *The Age of Reform* (Oxford 1962)

Wooley, B., *The Queen's Conjurer* (London 2001)

Wormald, J., *Court, Kirk and Community: Scotland 1470–1625* (London 1981)

Wormald, J., *Mary Queen of Scots: A Study in Failure* (London 1988)

Wrench, J.E., *Alfred Lord Milner: The Man of no Illusions 1854–1925* (London 1958)

Wright, C.D., *The Irish Tradition in Old English Literature* (Cambridge 1996)

Wright, F., *Two Lands on one Soil* (Dublin 1996)

Wright, K., *The People Say Yes* (Argyll 1997)

Young, P. and Holmes, R., *The English Civil War, 1642–1651* (London 1974)

PERIODICALS

Bulletin of the Board of Celtic Studies
Cambrian Mediaeval Celtic Studies
Celtica
Consortium on Revolutionary Europe
Contemporary Irish Studies
Cymmrodorion
Edinburgh Review
English History Review
Eriu
Études Celtiques
Historical Journal
History
Irish Historical Studies
Irish Sword
Journal of British Studies
Journal of Contemporary History
Mediaeval Celtic Studies
National Review
New Welsh Review
Regional Trends
Scottish History Review

Seventeenth Century
Studia Celtica
Studia Hibernica
Transactions of the Royal Historical Society
Twentieth Century British History
Welsh History Review

The items from the Royal Archives are reproduced by permission of Her Majesty Queen Elizabeth II.

INDEX

The Five Giants

A Biography of the Welfare State

Nicholas Timmins

'Giant Want. Giant Disease. Giant Ignorance. Giant Squalor. And the insidious Giant Idleness, "which destroys wealth and corrupts men". These were evils to be vanquished by the post-war reconstruction of Britain. Nicholas Timmins' book recaptures brilliantly the high hopes of the period in which the welfare state began to be created, and conveys the cranky zeal of its inventor, William Beveridge. The onslaught of the five Giants was the work of five gargantuan programmes that made up the core of Beveridge's welfare state. These were social security, health, education, housing and a policy of full employment . . . It is impossible not to respond in personal terms to a book that is a part of so many of our histories, woven into the day-to-day texture of our lives.' FIONA MACCARTHY, *Observer*

'The welfare state deserves a biography on a grand scale. Nicholas Timmins provides just that.' JOHN REDWOOD, *The Times*

'*The Five Giants* is an extraordinarily comprehensible account of half a century's welfare policies and programmes. It will be used for years as a quarry from which to mine historical gems. It succeeds in being comprehensive without ever being incomprehensible.'

ROY HATTERSLEY, *Independent*

The tale is a remarkable one, and it is remarkably told. Timmins' fine history . . . is beautifully written. The story speeds along and there are some wonderfully funny jokes.' FRANK FIELD, *Literary Review*

ISBN 0 00 686318 3

FontanaPress
An Imprint of HarperCollins*Publishers*

The English

A Social History
1066-1945

Christopher Hibbert

'An eminently readable book; erudite, amusing and superbly illustrated.' RAYMOND CARR, *The Spectator*

'Christopher Hibbert writes so well, and presents a huge amount of material with such skill, that this 900-page volume can be read more quickly and enjoyably than many novels . . . an admirable evocation of the past and a lasting analysis of the English character.' JOHN MORTIMER, *Sunday Times*

'From tournaments, pilgrims and kings through to bus conductors and summer holidays, he isolates the changing habits of successive generations. His greatest – and extraordinary – success is to have extracted from this mass of material the exact character of each century he touches.' *The Independent*

'Enthralling . . . Barons and peasants, contemporaries of Pepys and Boswell, a people revolutionised by technology – all leap from his page like figures on a canvas by Lowry . . . How anyone can write as much and as well as Hibbert is a mystery. His big, rich book deserves a place on the shelves of anyone remotely interested in our history.' *Mail on Sunday*

'A glorious cavalcade of 900 years of life and death, work and play, sex and sensibility amongst the English . . . Christopher Hibbert blends erudition, energy and elegance to perfection . . . Get beyond the myths of history; treat yourself to this feast of a book.' ROY PORTER, *The Standard*

'Compiled with flair and skill and with that flair for particularity and even oddity which no historian, "popular" or otherwise, can afford to dispense with.' *Times Literary Supplement*

0 586 08471 1

India: A History

John Keay

'In an environment where every fact is infinitely malleable, every interpretation politicised, the need for clear, accessible and unbiased popular history is all the greater. It is hard to imagine anyone succeeding more gracefully in producing a balanced overview than John Keay has done in *India: A History* . . . a book that is as fluent and readable as it is up-to-date and impartial. Hardly a page passes without some fascinating nugget or surprising fact . . . one can only hope that John Keay's *India* will be widely read, and its lessons taken to heart.'

WILLIAM DALRYMPLE, *Guardian*

'[John Keay's] astute commentary on the development of Indian history is a delight . . . one of the best general studies of the subcontinent.' ANDREW LYCETT, *Sunday Times*

'Certainly the most balanced and the most lucid [one-volume history of the subcontinent] . . . his passion for India shines through and illuminates every page . . . puts Keay in the front rank of Indian historiographers.' CHARLES ALLEN, *Spectator*

0-00-638784-5

The Rise and Fall of the Great Powers

Economic Change and Military Conflict
from 1500 to 2000

Paul Kennedy

'One of the masterpieces of modern historical writing.'
CHRISTOPHER ANDREW, *Daily Telegraph*

'I doubt whether the story of the rise and fall of the great powers has ever been told so professionally, with such a command of sources, or with such close attention to the connections between economics, geography and politics.' ROBERT SKIDELSKY, *Independent*

'Paul Kennedy has written a brilliantly original book which has become a best-seller in the US and made its author a pundit to be seen and heard. It is intended for the intelligent layman as well as the academic historian, combining in Toynbee-esque manner the sweeping conception with careful attention to historical detail.'

ZARA STEINER, *Financial Times*

'Despite the irresistible fascination of the subject, Paul Kennedy's outstanding new book is the first to tackle it with any real historical rigour. He ranges across five centuries and around the whole world. He seems to have read every relevant book in every possible language. And he has produced a general argument so deceptively simple that no politician, however busy, should ignore or misunderstand it.'

DAVID CANNADINE, *Observer*

'A masterpiece of exposition. It is erudite and elegantly written.'
LAWRENCE FREEDMAN, *New Society*

'A remarkable book, reported to be compulsory reading in exalted circles in Washington and Moscow. It is long, clever, often funny, and crammed with remarkable insights; it is tinged with the genius that unravels complexity.' ANDREW WHEATCROFT, *Evening Standard*

ISBN 0 00 686052-4

FontanaPress
An Imprint of HarperCollins*Publishers*

May the Lord in His Mercy be Kind to Belfast

Tony Parker

'A remarkable record of conversation by ordinary – occasionally extraordinary – Belfast people . . . Tony Parker's editing of the conversations produces brilliant, funny, tragic, and often infuriating talk . . . a compulsively readable book.'

JOHN COLE, *Sunday Times*

'This is Tony Parker at his best . . . a precious work. Through the uncanny integrity of these dramatic monologues the spirit of the North moves with soft, haunted steps.'

ROBERT WINDER, *The Independent*

'One of the most original and telling books to come out of the Northern conflict' *Irish Times*

'An amazing achievement . . . scrupulous, thorough, detached and yet utterly compassionate . . . the best book that I have read about Northern Ireland.'

EDNA O'BRIEN

No solution to Northern Ireland's long-drawn-out agony will be found without a proper and widespread understanding by all parties of the hopes and fears, the passions and prejudices, the suffering and grief of the people who live there. As a contribution to this understanding, Tony Parker's book is a landmark achievement. By earning the trust of priests, politicians, prisoners, terrorists (both Loyalist and Republican), doctors, nurses, lawyers, bus-drivers, bomb-disposal experts, shop assistants, single mothers, teachers and schoolchildren, he has crossed every sectarian and social divide and, in these extraordinary encounters, exposed the core of the problem in the hearts and minds of individuals. The result makes quietly devastating reading – by turns moving, inspirational, disturbing, chilling but consistently illuminating.